N. G. CHERNYSHEVSKY

SELECTED PHILOSOPHICAL ESSAYS

FOREIGN LANGUAGES PUBLISHING HOUSE

Moscow 1953

PUBLISHER'S NOTE

The works of N. G. Chernyshevsky given in this
volume have been translated from the latest Russian three-volume edition of N. G. Chernyshevsky's *Selected Philosophical Essays* prepared by
the Institute of Philosophy of the Academy of
Sciences of the U.S.S.R. and published by the
State Publishers of Political Literature in Moscow,
in 1950-1951.

CONTENTS

N. G. CHERNYSHEVSKY'S WORLD OUTLOOK

Nikolai Gavrilovich Chernyshevsky, the great revolutionary democrat and forerunner of Russian Social-Democracy, was an outstanding scientist and a profound and original thinker. His materialist philosophy marked the peak of pre-Marxian philosophy. He stood very high in the estimation of V. I. Lenin, who wrote that he was "the only really great Russian writer who, from the fifties until 1888, was able to keep on the level of an integral philosophical materialism and who spurned the wretched nonsense of the Neo-Kantians, positivists, Machians and other muddleheads." * Marx carefully studied the works of Chernyshevsky and called him the "great Russian scholar and critic." ** Comrade Stalin has mentioned him among the most distinguished representatives of the great Russian nation.

Being a revolutionist, Chernyshevsky never studied philosophical problems in the abstract. Science and philosophy served him as weapons in the struggle for revolutionary-democratic changes, in the struggle against tsarism and serfdom. He brought up and elaborated philosophical problems in the light of the concrete needs of revolutionary-democratic practice. His was a new attitude towards philosophy.

Chernyshevsky understood perfectly well that the victory of the people and the ideals of emancipation could be achieved only by revolutionary struggle, by revolutionary political activity. To this political struggle he devoted all his life; it was the starting point of all his theoretical work. For him, theoretical work was one of the forms of the revolutionary struggle, and it always had a definite practical aim.

Thus, Chernyshevsky's philosophy was a philosophy of life, a philosophy of revolutionary action and struggle.

---

* V. I. Lenin, *Materialism and Empirio-Criticism*, Moscow 1952, p. 377.
** K. Marx, *Capital*, Vol. I, p. 19.

It was not expounded in textbooks on the history of philosophy and logic, or taught in universities and academies;
it was disseminated through newspaper and magazine articles, and in these essays, reviews and comments on the most
diverse questions, which were always of lively and topical
interest, Chernyshevsky gave what for his time was a profound scientific explanation of reality.

The name of N. G. Chernyshevsky is closely associated
with the social-political movement of the "sixties" in Russia. As Chernyshevsky himself stated, the "sixties" was
the period when the peasant question, i.e., the question of
emancipating the serfs, had become "the sole subject of all
thoughts and of all conversation." * The fact that the peasant question was the central question in that period was
an indication of the deep social changes that were taking
place in Russia at that time. Economic development was
pushing Russia on to the path of capitalism. This found
expression in the fairly rapid development of industry in
the towns, the growth of the elements of capitalism in feu-
dal-landlord farming and of commodity relationships in
peasant farming. The development of capitalist relationships in Russia was hindered by age-old feudal relationships,
and particularly by serfdom. The further untrammelled
development of capitalism called primarily for a mass of
free workers. The necessity of expanding the home market,
of developing trade and the money system, of introducing
new techniques and machines in production, and in agriculture in particular, in short, the needs of developing
capitalism, came into direct conflict with the prevailing
feudal relationships. Russia's defeat in the Crimean War
(1853-56) glaringly revealed the utter wretchedness and
backwardness of the Russian serf system. The tsarist autocracy was compelled to take the path of "reform" from above,
the more so that revolutionary unrest in the country, primarily the spontaneous peasant "revolts," threatened the
autocracy and the serf system with more radical changes
from below.

Thus, "the force of economic development, which was
drawing Russia on the path of capitalism," ** brought the

---

* N. G. Chernyshevsky, *Collected Works*, Russ. ed., Vol. I,
1906, p. 87.
** V. I. Lenin, *Collected Works*, 4th Russ. ed., Vol. 17, p. 95.

peasant question into the forefront, and the way this question was settled was to determine the character and path of development of capitalism in Russia. It was quite natural, therefore, that this fundamental question should have become the point of collision of the principal classes in Russian society at that time.

The ruling landlord class was unable to withstand the rising tide of peasant revolt; the serf-owners "could no longer retain the old, tottering forms of economy";* on the other hand they realized that if they themselves took measures to change the forms of serfdom, they could make the incipient development of capitalism serve their own interests.

The "divergent" interests of the various groups among the nobility in connection with the reform did not concern the principle of "emancipation," but only the method of carrying it out. As Lenin observed: "The notorious struggle between the serf-owners and the liberals, which was so exaggerated and embellished by our liberal and liberal-Narodnik historians, was an *internal* struggle among the ruling classes, chiefly an *internal struggle among the landlords, exclusively* over the extent and form of the *concessions*." ** There was agreement between the reactionary landlords and the liberals on the main point, namely, the land: landlordism was to remain, the peasants were to have no right to land, and all the measures for the "emancipation" of the serfs were to be carried out in the name of the tsar. Both the diehards and the liberals stood for the "emancipation" of the serfs "from above." This meant the gradual reform of the serf system, its adaptation to the new conditions of capitalism; such was the path the landlord and liberal sections of Russian society of that time stood for.

This determined the class content of the so-called "peasant reform." As Lenin wrote: "The 'peasant reform' was a bourgeois reform carried out by the serf-owners. It was a step in the direction of transforming Russia into a bourgeois monarchy. The content of the peasant reform was bourgeois...." *** Chernyshevsky fully appreciated the bourgeois character of this reform; in his celebrated article "Unad-

---

* *Ibid.*
** *Ibid.*, p. 96.
*** *Ibid.*, p. 95.

dressed Letters," he wrote: "... The powers that be [i.e., the serf-owning landlords—*M. G.*] undertook to carry out a program that was not their own [i.e., it was the program of the bourgeoisie—*M.G.*], a program based on principles out of harmony with the character of these powers." The inevitable result of this was "a change in the forms of relationship between the landlords and the peasants, with only a slight, almost imperceptible, change in the content of this relationship.... The intention was to preserve the content of serfdom and to abolish only its forms." *

Lenin wrote: "It required the genius of a Chernyshevsky to understand so clearly at that time, when the peasant reform was only being introduced (when it had not yet been properly elucidated even in Western Europe), that its character was fundamentally bourgeois, that even at that time Russian 'society' and the Russian 'state' were ruled and governed by social classes which were irreconcilably hostile to the toilers and which undoubtedly made the ruin and expropriation of the peasantry a foregone conclusion." **

Lenin noted that in the period when the "peasant reform" was carried out a revolutionary situation existed in Russia. During the years immediately preceding the reform there had been a steady increase in the revolutionary activity of the serf-peasant masses, and after the promulgation of the Manifesto of February 19, 1861, proclaiming the abolition of serfdom, these activities, far from subsiding, grew in intensity. The peasantry's profound disappointment with the character of the "reform" carried out by the ruling class stirred up a new revolutionary wave in the country. In many places the peasants reacted to their "emancipation" by open unrest, disorders and revolts. For example, when the Manifesto was proclaimed, an insurrection broke out in the village of Bezdna, in the Kazan Gubernia, which was cruelly suppressed by the armed forces of the tsar.

Unrest also broke out in the principal centres of the country. The underground revolutionary forces widely extended their activities. Large quantities of secretly printed leaflets and manifestoes appeared, calling for a deter-

---

* N. G. Chernyshevsky, *Collected Works*, Russ. ed., Vol. X, Part 2, 1906, pp. 301-302.

** V. I. Lenin, *What the "Friends of the People" Are and How They Fight the Social-Democrats*, Moscow 1951, p. 258.

mined struggle to overthrow tsarism. For example, a clergy-man named Belyustin wrote to Pogodin: "Seditious manifestoes are pouring down like hail.... These manifestoes are being distributed chiefly by the hungry youth among the civil service people. Among them there are *hosts* of proletarians. They are all future sansculottes." "The *pocket printing presses* are working tirelessly...."

Underground revolutionary literature also spread to the provincial towns and to the rural districts. In the Chernigov Gubernia, copies of Herzen's *Baptised Property* and other of his works were found among peasants. Belinsky's "Letter to Gogol," and copies of the *Sovremennik* * containing essays by Chernyshevsky and Dobrolyubov passed from hand to hand. The dissemination of revolutionary-democratic ideas by means of political manifestoes, essays and literature had a stimulating effect upon the minds of the advanced section of Russian society and roused it for the struggle against the conditions that oppressed and degraded human individuality.

One of the important manifestations of the rising revolutionary tide in the period we are discussing was the student movement. Despite the repressive measures taken by the authorities and the efforts of the reactionary section of the professors to foster among the mass of the students the spirit of submission and loyalty to the tsar, the minds of the young people were dominated by the ideas propounded by Belinsky, Herzen and Chernyshevsky. Things reached such a pitch that the tsar issued an order that the universities be temporarily closed.

The crisis in the "upper circles" expressed itself in the attempts of the ruling landlord class to "renovate" the country by means of what were in essence bourgeois reforms. We have already spoken of these reforms. It must be emphasized once again that the ruling upper circles were compelled to take this step by their fear of the revolutionary initiative of the "lower classes." Political and moral confusion reigned in the ruling circles. But the temporal and spiritual agents of tsarism were not the only ones to be filled with fear and alarm; the liberal critics, professors and writers also hastened to the side of "law and order." From the moment it arose, Russian liberalism, to its eter-

---

* See Note 5 to "Polemical Gems."—*Ed.*

nal disgrace, displayed abject loyalty to tsarism. Unite
at all cost—everybody, from the most reactionary serf-
owners to bourgeois liberals, rally in one camp—this
became their most urgent slogan of the day. Shevyryov wrote
from his deathbed in Paris: "It is a pity that Aksakov and
Katkov are quarrelling. This is not the time for quarrelling.
Pride must be thrust aside." Katkov, displeased with Turgenev's *Fathers and Sons*, and regarding Bazarov, the hero
in this novel, as an apologist of the *Sovremennik*, wrote:
"... Remember that in addition to art there is also the
political question. Who can tell what this fellow can
turn into?"

The united camp of counterrevolution was fully aware
of the direction from which the chief danger threatened
it, and who was the ideological inspirer of the ever-spread-
ing revolutionary movement. It was Chernyshevsky, the
finest representative of the revolutionary commoners who
had taken the place of the revolutionaries of the nobility.

Chernyshevsky was, indeed, the generally recognized
leader of the revolutionary-democratic trend. His activities reflected the fundamental interests of the vast masses
of the Russian peasantry and their struggle against serfdom
and tsarism. Chernyshevsky consistently and resolutely
fought autocracy and serfdom, ruthlessly exposed the Russian liberals, and strove to formulate from the point of
view of advanced science of his time the conduct, the
tactics and strategy of the democratic revolutionaries who
were at the head of the peasant revolution. Chernyshevsky
was the central figure who most fully and comprehensively
reflected that revolutionary epoch.

That is why he earned the bitter hatred of the Russian
feudal landlords and of the Russian liberals who followed in their wake. That is why they resorted to every despicable means to attack him: open persecution, denuncia-
tion, blackmail and provocation. So eager were Chernyshevsky's class enemies to bring about his destruction that
they even accused the tsarist police authorities of being
tardy and irresolute. In an anonymous letter to Potapov
of the Third Department, i.e., the Secret Service, somebody wrote: "Rid us of Chernyshevsky for the sake of
public peace."

But right to the end Chernyshevsky remained at his
fighting post, the post of great leader of the peasant

revolution. He fought his enemies not only in the political field, but also in the ideological, the theoretical field. His superiority over them as a theoretician was undisputed. He was always the victor in the ideological battles he fought against them: the aesthetes among the critics Dudyshkin and Druzhinin; the economist Vernadsky, the ideologist of the Russian bourgeoisie; the bourgeois professor and "guardian" Chicherin; the philosophizing obscurantist Yurkevich, and their ilk, for in his duels with them he was guided by the materialist and revolutionary-democratic world outlook.

The historical importance of Chernyshevsky's literary activities lies in that they most correctly generalized from the point of view of science of that time the revolutionary experience in Russia in the epoch of the profound crisis of the serf system. By this Chernyshevsky undoubtedly made an immense contribution to the development of revolutionary thought not only in his own country, but in all the advanced countries in the world. Marx studied Chernyshevsky's works on the "peasant reform" with special attention and expressed the opinion that they did "real honour to Russia." * For the importance of the services he rendered, Chernyshevsky has no equal in the history of the revolutionary movement before Marx, for his theoretical system reflected one of the most important and acute periods of human history and its direct purpose was to serve as a weapon of the broad masses of the people who were striving to abolish the feudal form of exploitation in a vast country like Russia. By his work in the field of theory, Chernyshevsky ideologically prepared the political revolution that was maturing in Russia in the sixties.

In his famous manifesto "To the Gentry's Peasants" he called upon the people to take up the axe as the only reliable means of achieving real emancipation, of abolishing serf dependence and oppression.

Thus, the object of Chernyshevsky's public and literary activities was to transform the peasant revolution from a possibility, as it was then, into reality. He tried to give the sporadic, spontaneous revolts of the peasants an organized character, and to take into account and utilize in the

---

* The Correspondence of K. Marx and F. Engels with Russian Political Leaders, Russ. ed., 1947, p. 29.

struggle against tsarism the revolutionary experience accumulated by the Russian people and also by the toiling masses in the West. His idea was that the victorious peasant revolution in Russia would deprive the landlords of all the land, abolish tsarism, and open the road for the socialist transformation of the country. His aim was to rouse the peasantry for a socialist revolution. This was the epoch when, as Lenin said, "democracy and socialism were merged in one inseparable and indissoluble whole...."

The revolution that Chernyshevsky envisaged, however, could only result in the thorough eradication of serfdom, in the organization of Russian society on the most consistent democratic basis, and in the opening of the road of development in Russia not for socialism, but for capitalism. Objectively, Chernyshevsky was the advocate of the revolutionary-democratic path of development as against the path of liberal compromise. His peasant revolutionary socialism was a form of utopian socialism. He linked socialism with the backward Russian village community.

As is known, the revolutionary situation of 1859-61 did not develop into revolution. At that time Russia still lacked that social class that is capable of bringing about a successful social revolution. The sporadic peasant revolts did not smash the tsarist regime. Reaction increased in the country. Chernyshevsky, the leader of the Russian revolutionary democrats, was arrested and sentenced to a long term of exile in Siberia.

Chernyshevsky is a landmark in the history of our people's liberation movement. "At first—nobles and landlords, the Decembrists and Herzen. This was a narrow circle of revolutionaries, very far removed from the people. But they did not work in vain. The Decembrists awakened Herzen. Herzen launched revolutionary agitation.

"This agitation was taken up, extended, strengthened, and tempered by the revolutionary commoners, beginning with Chernyshevsky and ending with the heroes of the 'Narodnaya Volya.' The circle of fighters widened, they established closer contacts with the people. 'The young helmsmen of the impending storm,' Herzen called them. But as yet it was not the storm itself.

"The storm is the movement of the masses themselves. The proletariat, the only class that is revolutionary to the end, rose at the head of the masses and for the first time aroused millions of peasants to open revolutionary struggle." *

The Russian proletariat came out at the head of the liberation movement in Russia and raised the Russian revolution to a new and higher level. Under the guidance of the Communist Party, of its great leaders Lenin and Stalin, the Russian proletariat overthrew the rule of the landlords and the bourgeoisie and, in a stern struggle against all the enemies of the people, led our country to the victory of socialism.

* * *

The name of Nikolai Gavrilovich Chernyshevsky is closely associated with the social revolutionary movement of the "sixties." True, he lived beyond that period, but he spent those later years in prison, penal servitude and exile. In this respect, the glorious life of this great Russian revolutionist was profoundly tragic. During his childhood and youth (1828-46) he lived in Saratov. After that, for five years (1846-50) he was a student of the History and Philological Faculty of the St. Petersburg University, and after graduating he, for two and a half years (1851-53), taught literature at a gymnasium in Saratov. He returned to St. Petersburg in 1853 and became a contributor to the magazine *Otechestvenniye Zapiski*. Later he began to contribute to the *Sovremennik* and soon became chief editor of this magazine, which at that time practically represented the radical-democratic movement.

In the *Sovremennik* he published his famous literary reviews: "Essays on the Gogol Period of Russian Literature," "Lessing and His Times," and "Pushkin"; his essays on history: "The July Monarchy," "The Conflict of Parties in France in the Reign of Louis XVIII and Charles X," and "Cavaignac"; his essays on philosophy: "The Anthropological Principle in Philosophy," and "A Criticism of the Philosophical Prejudices Against Common Ownership"; and his essays on political economy: "Comments on Mill's *Principles of Political Economy*" and "Outlines of Political Economy According to Mill." The "Comments" and "Outlines" are important in themselves, for in them

---

* V. I. Lenin, *Selected Works*, Two-Volume ed., Moscow 1952, Vol. I, Part 2, p. 280.

Chernyshevsky stands forth as a brilliant critic of bourgeois political economy. This was noted at the time by Marx, who wrote:

"... It is a declaration of bankruptcy by bourgeois economy, an event on which the great Russian scholar and critic, N. Tschernyschewsky, has thrown the light of a master mind in his 'Outlines of Political Economy According to Mill.'" *

In 1862, Chernyshevsky was arrested for his revolutionary activities and confined in the Fortress of St. Peter and Paul. There he wrote his famous novel *What Is To Be Done?*, which served as a textbook for generations of revolutionists. In 1864 the tsarist authorities sentenced Chernyshevsky to "civil execution," (i.e., mock execution) followed by penal servitude (1864-72) and by exile to Vilyuisk (1872-83).

From Siberia he went to live in Astrakhan and a few months before he died he went to Saratov, but in both places the conditions for him were as stringent as they had been in Siberia. Chernyshevsky died on October 17, 1889, at the age of 61.

Thus, he spent more than half of his independent active life as a prisoner of the tsar. Heroically he bore his long isolation and the refined moral torture and physical privation to which he was subjected, and remained to the last moment an indomitable revolutionary and materialist thinker.

* * *

Of course, Chernyshevsky was brought up, and his mind was moulded, primarily under the influence of his Russian environment. The opinion, formerly widespread, and still held in some quarters, that his social-political and philosophical views were influenced entirely by the West totally contradicts the Marxist-Leninist view of the matter. There can be no doubt that the West, which was revolutionary at that time, did help to mould his mind to some extent; but it is perfectly obvious that in tracing Chernyshevsky's development as a revolutionist and thinker, we must

* K. Marx, *Capital*, Vol. I, p. 19: Author's Preface to the Second Edition.

start from the social and ideological conditions in Russia in his time.

From his childhood Chernyshevsky had before him the gloomy picture of tyranny, cruelty and human suffering. The majority of unhappy and suffering people he saw in his childhood were serf peasants. Everyday life confronted him with the problem of the cause of the people's suffering and with the necessity of finding a way out of these unbearable conditions. An enormous factor in his mental development were the advanced Russian thinkers, particularly Herzen and Belinsky, with whose works he was already acquainted when he was in Saratov.

Chernyshevsky entered the St. Petersburg University with the firm intention of devoting himself to the noble and patriotic task of helping to develop science in Russia. He soon realized, however, that the chief obstacles to this were tsarism and serfdom. His attitude towards the autocracy and the serf system that prevailed in Russia took definite shape in his student years, and it was in this period that his revolutionary-democratic convictions took shape.

The struggle against serfdom and autocracy had been started by progressive Russian people long before that; in fact, it had never ceased in spite of the cruelties perpetrated by the tsarist authorities. This struggle found reflection in the works of the Russian poets and fiction writers which Chernyshevsky had eagerly read since his youth, and through which he became acquainted with the advanced democratic ideology that had developed in Russian society. This struggle found reflection particularly in journalism, which, owing to the conditions prevailing in the country was, perhaps, the only sphere where, resorting to every device to overcome the obstacles raised by the censorship, it was still possible to discuss urgent social problems. Shevyryov, one of the ideological servitors of tsarism, aptly described the role played by journalism in Russia when he wrote: "Is not a magazine a pulpit, but one that towers over the whole of vast Russia and influences all its parts?..."

It was from this pulpit that for fifteen years the voice of Belinsky was heard, inspiring and rousing the people for a self-sacrificing struggle against serfdom and tsarism. Belinsky's influence was enormous in St. Petersburg, where Chernyshevsky went to take up his studies. Shortly afterwards, having found his bearings in the course of events, he established contact with the underground revolutionary movement and came into close relations with Khanykov, a prominent member of Petrashevsky's circle. As is known, one of the chief reasons for the cruel punishment meted out to the members of this circle was the discovery among its members of copies of Belinsky's "Letter to Gogol." It is interesting to note also that it was with Khanykov that Chernyshevsky first discussed the possibility of revolution in Russia, the classes that were capable of and interested in taking part in it, the emancipation of the serfs, and other urgent questions. Belinsky was still alive when Chernyshevsky arrived in St. Petersburg. He died in the year when that decisive change took place in Chernyshevsky's life, which finally determined the great role he was to play in the revolutionary movement in Russia. It may be said that Chernyshevsky took over the banner of the struggle against tsarism directly out of the hands of Belinsky.

Another person who exercised strong influence in the moulding of Chernyshevsky's opinions was Herzen. In St. Petersburg, Chernyshevsky was closely connected with the circle conducted by I. I. Vvedensky; he joined that circle and was one of its active members. The following is what Chernyshevsky himself says about a visit he paid to Vvedensky: we talked about "a revolution in our country," about "the cruelty and coarseness of the tsar," and about "how good it would be if a man could be found brave enough to sacrifice his life to put him out of the way," and "towards the end we read Iskander." * Further evidence of the profound respect young Chernyshevsky entertained for Herzen is provided by his conversation with A. G. Klientova, who was personally acquainted with Herzen's wife and received letters from her. "Again we talked about Iskander, about Russian literature...," writes Chernyshevsky. We repeat, in addition to Belinsky and Herzen, the best traditions of Russian literature and poetry influenced Chernyshevsky's development; Pushkin, Gogol and Lermontov were objects of his admiration and pride.

Chernyshevsky himself later fully described his social-political and ideological genealogy in his "Essays on the Gogol Period of Russian Literature."

---

* Herzen.—*Ed.*

Chernyshevsky's period at the university coincided not only with the crisis in the serf system in Russia and with the rising tide of the struggle against it, but also with the period of revolutionary upheavals in the West. As is known, the lessons of the revolutions of 1848 were colossal for the whole of subsequent revolutionary development. Young Chernyshevsky followed the development of the 1848 revolutions with close attention, and this also helped him to devise more effective means of fighting serfdom and the tsarist autocracy than those possessed by his predecessors.

The Soviet reader has at his disposal extremely valuable documentary evidence of Chernyshevsky's mental evolution. We have in mind the diary he began to keep in the middle of 1848. Nearly every day he made a detailed record of his thoughts and ideas, defined his attitude towards the social events that were taking place at the time, expressed his opinion, favourable or unfavourable, of the writer whose work he was studying. When reading this diary one feels the pulsation of his passionate heart and can trace the development of the militant, revolutionary, materialist thinker.

The diary shows that Chernyshevsky reacted primarily to urgent political events. Grasping more and more thoroughly the meaning and significance of the revolutionary events that were unfolding, he could soon say of himself with complete justification that in his convictions he belonged to the "extreme party," to the advocates of a "red republic." But already at that time he was aware that the bourgeois republic for which the struggle was raging in the West would not create real equality between the haves and the have-nots. He, therefore, stood for the principle that "the majority must always prevail and the minority must exist for the majority and not the majority for the minority...." He detested the bourgeois liberals who were fond of talking about liberty and equality, but left untouched the social system that was based on the enslavement and oppression of the people. Addressing the liberals, he wrote: "Oh, gentlemen, gentlemen, you think it is a matter of having a republic in name and of you being in power. But it is not so. It is a matter of freeing the lower class from slavery not only in law, but in fact ... so that they may eat, drink, marry, bring up their children, maintain their parents and receive education, that men should not become corpses or desperadoes and that women should not have to sell their bodies."*

Somewhat later Chernyshevsky exposed the nature of the monarchist state. A monarch, and still more so an absolute monarch, he said, is the apex of the aristocratic hierarchy and belongs body and soul to it. "It is like the apex of the aristocratic cone."** It is not a matter of the individual monarch, but of the class on which his power rests and whose interests he serves. It was impossible, in his opinion, to abolish the colossal machine of exploitation of the toilers by peaceful means; the people could achieve their freedom only by fighting. He wrote: "Let the oppression of one class by another begin, then there will be a struggle; then the oppressed will realize that they are such under the present order of things, but that there can be a different order of things under which they will not be oppressed; they will realize that they are not oppressed by god, but by men, that they have no hope of justice or of anything else, and that there are no people among the oppressors who stand up for them."*** These thoughts that ran through the mind of young Chernyshevsky subsequently led him to the firm conviction that the whole of human history is the history of uncompromising and fierce struggle between classes, that a genuine revolutionist cannot ignore this fact, but must take it as his starting point, for the class which does not fight for power and exercise political power cannot save itself from oppression, poverty and ignorance. It is this aspect of Chernyshevsky's activities that marks the fundamental difference between him and the utopian Socialists of the West.

* * *

The moulding of Chernyshevsky's revolutionary democratic convictions proceeded hand in hand with the moulding of his philosophical views. In his student days in St. Petersburg he studied the works of the outstanding scientists and thinkers of his time: historians, sociologists, economists and philosophers. When he graduated from the

---

* N. G. Chernyshevsky, *Collected Works*, Russ. ed., Vol. I, 1939, p. 110.
** *Ibid.*, p. 356.
*** *Ibid.*

university he was already a convinced revolutionist and materialist. As has already been stated, this was due primarily to the whole course of social life and of advanced public thought in Russia. In the last of his works Belinsky had firmly taken the stand of materialism. Herzen, in his "Letters on the Study of Nature," as Lenin said, "stood on the threshold of dialectical materialism." It was from them that Chernyshevsky first learned philosophy. It was they who fired him with the passion for freedom and filled his heart with burning hatred for autocracy and serfdom and for all forms of human exploitation and oppression. Chernyshevsky was undoubtedly influenced by Feuerbach's materialism.

Continuing the materialist line in Russian philosophy that was independently developed by Belinsky and Herzen in the forties, Chernyshevsky raised it to a new and higher stage—to the level of "an integral philosophical materialism" (Lenin).

As Belinsky and Herzen had done, Chernyshevsky concentrated his attention on the criticism of German idealist philosophy. Under the conditions then prevailing the latter constituted a grave danger, and Chernyshevsky regarded its exposure as a most urgent task. It must also be observed that he was broadly aware of the class nature of German idealism as the ideology which justified the political conservatism of the German bourgeoisie and the feudal backwardness of Germany; he realized that it was the reaction to materialism.

The object of Kant's philosophy, said Chernyshevsky, was "to defend free will, the immortality of the soul, the existence of god ... these convictions so dear to his heart...," to defend them "from Diderot and his friends."* He pointed out that Schelling was a representative of that party in Germany, which, terrified by the revolution, "sought tranquility in medieval institutions" and in the restoration of the feudal state.** He wrote that Hegel's system was imbued with the spirit that "dominated public opinion at the time of the Restoration...." ***Slavish submission to the abominable conditions then prevailing in Germany, the desire always to be reconciled to these conditions and to reconcile

---

* See p. 534 of this book.—*Ed.*
** *Ibid.*, p. 51.
*** *Ibid.*, p. 67.

2*

science to them the constant striving to show that the political measures of their dull and despotic feudal rulers were adequate forms of expression of reason and truth—this, in Chernyshevsky's opinion, was what was behind the abstract constructions of the German idealists.

In addition to his social-class characterization of German philosophy, Chernyshevsky gave a brilliant critique of its theoretical principles, particularly of those of Hegel's philosophy. As is known, in many ways, this critique coincides with that given by Engels of Hegel's philosophy. Chernyshevsky pointed to its inherent "contradictoriness," its "duality," to the contradiction between Hegel's "deductions," i.e., his system, and his "principles," i.e., his method. He described the principles (method) of Hegel's philosophy as "broad," "profound," and "fruitful," and its deductions (system) as "narrow," "paltry" and "false," i. e., conservative and reactionary. He said that the dialectical principle had presented itself to Hegel in a "nebulous," i. e., distorted form, and that he had not adhered to it consistently. The great Russian thinker set himself the task of freeing the "sound part"* of Hegel's philosophy, i. e., the idea of development, from its idealism and mysticism, to rework it thoroughly and to use it.

This alone shows how much higher Chernyshevsky stood than Feuerbach. The intellectual development of this brilliant Russian materialist thinker proceeded along the same path as that of Marx and Engels. In Russia the same path had been taken before Chernyshevsky by Belinsky and Herzen, who, as Chernyshevsky said, independently undertook critically to overcome Hegel by their own efforts. In the persons of its outstanding representatives Belinsky, Herzen and Chernyshevsky, Russian advanced philosophy developed in the direction of Marxism.

Subjecting Hegel's idealism to thorough criticism, Chernyshevsky shows that Hegel was unable to eliminate the contradiction between the abstract and the concrete, between the general and the individual. He points out that for Hegel, the concrete was the form of the realization of the idea and, therefore, he shifted the "centre of interest" to the logical and abstract, in this sharing the grave mistake of all idealists who believed that this was the foundation

---

* See p. 468 of this book.—*Ed.*

and essence of all the phenomena of the world. In Chernyshevsky's opinion, this metaphysical rupture between the
general and the individual, which is the logical corollary
of the very essence of the idealist system, made Hegel's
philosophy totally unsatisfactory.

Chernyshevsky severely castigated Hegel also for his
idealist conception of the relation between life and knowledge, between theory and practice. Hegel the idealist
transformed theoretical knowledge into an end in itself.
Naturally, Chernyshevsky could not accept such a conception of theory elevated to a deified mystical absolute.
The revolutionarydemocrat Chernyshevsky strove to create
a theory that grew out of life and would become a powerful
weapon in the struggle for the revolutionary transformation of society. In his opinion, life does not exist for theory,
as Hegel and the other idealists proclaimed, but theory
exists for life, for its transformation and improvement.

Chernyshevsky, however, did not limit himself to criticizing the reactionary ideology propounded in Germany
by the German philosophers, and by Hegel in particular.
He gave an exceptionally apt and scathing characterization
of many of the French thinkers in the period of the Restoration who paraded in the garb of bourgeois liberalism—
Guizot, Thiers, Cousin and others. He pointed out that in
French science "conceptions had become frightfully shallow," that the scientists in that country had lost their former "resolute principles" and "strict consistency in their
mode of thought," and were concerned "with reconciling
the irreconcilable," with justifying prejudices, with "combining scientific truth with arbitrary fantasies," and so
forth. He said that the liberalism of these gentlemen was
utterly false, putrid, sheer affectation. He rightly observed
that they "were concerned only with abstract rights and not
with the welfare of the people," the very conception of
which was alien to them. Their liberalism was only "a
bait with which to catch the nation on their hook," in order
to capture power, which they needed only "in order to fill
their pockets."* These were people filled with narrow and
smug egoism and, of course, nothing else could be expected
"from these degenerates who survived the great internal
struggle which had absorbed all the noblest forces of the

* *Ibid.*, p. 472 .—*Ed.*

French people."* These observations of Chernyshevsky's are a correct appraisal of the despicable and bloody role played by Thiers, Guizot and others who at that time were the leaders of bourgeois reaction.

* * *

Studying the history of philosophical doctrines (he was not acquainted with Marx's theory), Chernyshevsky realized that in none of the philosophical systems of the past was it possible to find a ready-made theoretical weapon that the toilers could use in their struggle for the revolutionary transformation of society. He showed that every philosophical system grew on a definite social-political basis and therefore corresponded to the interests of one or other ruling class. He emphasized the class character of philosophy and science. He showed the connection between the various idealist trends that were widely current in the beginning of the latter half of the nineteenth century and the mood of the bourgeoisie at that time. He wrote that the ruling classes of Western Europe were terrified by the inevitable changes in society, i.e., revolution, that were threatening them. "Grief over their impending fate creates confusion in their minds." They lose all ability objectively to cognize the historical process and in the sphere of ideology create various anti-scientific theories and systems.

Chernyshevsky was profoundly convinced that a progressive science and philosophy could be created only by a thinker who firmly adhered to the point of view of the toilers. He plainly said that the toiler, "thanks to his robust nature and to his stern experience of life ... understands the essence of things much better, more correctly, and more deeply than people of the more fortunate classes."

The conclusions Chernyshevsky drew from all this were the following: First, the working classes cannot and must not be guided in their struggle by the old philosophical theories, which are the ideological weapons of the exploiting classes. Second, the working classes must elaborate their own philosophical world outlook, which will be different from that of the exploiting classes. Third, only materialist philosophy can serve as the scientific world

* See p. 473 of this book.— *Ed.*

outlook of the working classes. Chernyshevsky was convinced that the creation of a working-class materialist world outlook would be the forerunner and inevitable condition of the victorious struggle for the revolutionary transformation of society.

These were extremely profound postulates. A successful struggle for socialism cannot be waged without a materialist philosophy, a materialist science, to light up the path of struggle. Lenin wrote: "... *the role of vanguard fighter can be fulfilled only by a party that is guided by the most advanced theory.* In order to get some concrete understanding of what this means, let the reader recall such predecessors of Russian Social-Democracy as Herzen, Belinsky, Chernyshevsky...."*

Chernyshevsky counted himself among the ideologists of the toiling masses. In his works he developed a system of philosophical materialism in the conviction that such a system would serve as the spiritual weapon of the people who were fighting against the reign of violence and oppression and for socialism.

To be able properly to understand and appraise the character of Chernyshevsky's materialism we must first of all elucidate the fundamental principle of his philosophy, what he himself called the anthropological principle in philosophy. It must be borne in mind that Chernyshevsky ardently championed this principle under the peculiar conditions that prevailed in Russia in the sixties of the nineteenth century, when various fashionable idealist and eclectical theories were very widespread. Naturally, in these theories special attention was devoted to man, who, as a rule, was regarded from the subjective and dualist point of view. It was in combating these views that Chernyshevsky propounded his anthropological principle.

What, then, was the essence of this principle?

Explaining the essence of the anthropological principle, Chernyshevsky wrote: "... a man must be regarded as a single being having only one nature; ... a human life must not be cut into two halves, each belonging to a different nature...."** The anthropological conception of man is an integral conception of man, a conception of the unity of the human organism. According to Chernyshevsky's an-

---

* V. I. Lenin, *What Is To Be Done?*, Moscow 1952, p. 43.
** See pp. 132-33 of this book.—*Ed.*

thropological principle, the unity of human nature is based
on man's bodily organism. The body, i.e., matter, is primary. Chernyshevsky said that natural science had reached
the stage of development where it was possible to show that
man's sensations and psychology were conditioned by
inner physiological processes without resorting to the "aid"
of other, outside forces. For Chernyshevsky, the mind, thinking, was only a special property of highly-developed matter. He denied that the mind had independent, substantial
existence as the idealists claim, and asserted that it is the
product of the development of matter. Chernyshevsky's
anthropological principle was a principle for the materialist solution of the fundamental problem of philosophy, namely, the relation of mind to matter, since it took the bodily organism as the basis and regarded psychic phenomena
as the result of the work of the brain.

But what is man himself, his organism, from the standpoint of Chernyshevsky's anthropological principle? He
wrote: "Physiology and medicine find that the human organism is an extremely complex chemical combination that
goes through an extremely complex chemical process that
we call life."* Man is a link in the general chain of the
development of matter. Rocks, plants and animals, including
man, are different combinations of matter. Thus, the anthropological principle developed by Chernyshevsky leads to the
materialist-monistic conception of man and, regarding man
as a part of nature, to the materialist-monistic conception
of the entire objective material world, and of its laws, that
exist outside of the mind.

Thinking on these lines, Chernyshevsky sometimes
slips into mechanicism, but for all that he remains a consistent
materialist in his understanding of the phenomena of nature.
In his hands, the anthropological principle in philosophy
was an important means of upsetting the ideological props
of the old world of exploitation, namely, religion and idealism. This was the fundamental progressive significance of
Chernyshevsky's anthropological principle under the conditions prevailing in Russia in his time.

In propounding the anthropological principle when combating idealism and religion, Chernyshevsky mentioned
Feuerbach as a thinker who advocated this principle in his

---

* See p. 104 of this book.—*Ed.*

philosophy; but this must not be urged as a reason for identifying Chernyshevsky's position with that of Feuerbach's, for there was a big difference between their respective philosophies.

Feuerbach specialized in the study of religion, and of Christianity in particular. He asserted that the conception of god is based on the essence of man and argued that the supernatural, religious world consists of man's mystically disturbed feelings, desires and thoughts. The chief conclusion he drew from this was that the secret of religion is anthropology. Feuerbach's anthropology was clothed in theological garb and was proclaimed a new religion.

Chernyshevsky's materialism was entirely free from the idealist and religio-ethical coating that was characteristic of Feuerbach's philosophy; and he made no attempt whatever to give his philosophy a religious hue. He clearly saw the fundamental antithesis between the materialist and the religious world outlooks, and he consistently opposed his materialist principle to religion and clericalism.

Further, criticizing idealism, and Hegel's idealism in particular, from the standpoint of his anthropologism, Feuerbach argued that the Absolute Idea in Hegel's philosophy was nothing but human reason released from its sensual restrictions. According to Feuerbach, anthropology was also the secret of idealism. From this he arrived at the conclusion that true philosophy is neither idealism nor materialism, but anthropology. One cannot help perceiving in this a striving to place anthropological philosophy above materialism and idealism, to find a new, "third" path for philosophy. It is known that Feuerbach objected to the term "materialism."

Chernyshevsky, however, while propounding the anthropological principle in philosophy, had no thought of placing his philosophy somewhere in between idealism and materialism. On the contrary, he unreservedly and emphatically regarded himself as belonging to the materialist camp, and was of the opinion that the fundamental division in philosophy was precisely between materialism and idealism. He was the thinker in the pre-Marx period who waged the most resolute and consistent struggle against idealism in all its forms.

Feuerbach made anthropology his universal philosophical principle, and on it he based his sociology; but all his attempts to explain the phenomena of social life on the basis of abstract and immutable physical or spiritual human qualities invariably led to idealistic speculation and metaphysics. Clothing social relationships in a religious garb, he misinterpreted the actual process of historical development.

Chernyshevsky, however, took the anthropological principle in philosophy as a methodological basis and set out, with its aid, also to study as deeply as possible the phenomena of social life. He strove to apply this principle to aesthetics, ethics, political economy and sociology. But whereas the anthropological principle made it possible to find materialist solutions for the initial problems of philosophy concerning the relation of thinking to matter, to nature, it proved incapable of explaining the transition from the abstract to the concrete, historical man, i.e., of providing a materialist solution of the problems concerning the theory of society. Chernyshevsky's anthropological principle is materialism when it is applied to nature, but it is idealism when it is used to explain the transition to history. That is why in his *Philosophical Notebooks* V. I. Lenin wrote: "...Feuerbach's and Chernyshevsky's term 'anthropological principle' in philosophy is *n a r r o w.*"*

Chernyshevsky was not a philosopher in the narrow sense of the term; he was a man of revolutionary action, of revolutionary practice. Unlike Feuerbach, who was extremely indifferent to political activity, Chernyshevsky fully appreciated the powerful role played by revolutionary politics, and he closely linked the philosophy of revolutionary democracy with its practice.

Already in those days, Chernyshevsky ruthlessly criticized the race theory and exposed the class interests that fostered it. He saw a direct connection between this race theory and the slave system that then existed in the United States. "The slaveholders," he wrote, "belonged to the white race, the slaves were Negroes; therefore, in scientific treatises, the defence of slavery assumed the form of a theory that there are radical differences between the different races of mankind." The theory was created that "the bulk of the slaves were people of a different breed" and that there were people who "by nature's decree had to be slaves."

---

* V. I. Lenin, *Philosophical Notebooks*, Russ. ed., 1947, p. 58.

Chernyshevsky strongly opposed such theories. "Those who are seeking in anthropology solutions for important historical problems," he wrote, can have no doubt that "all races have sprung from the same ancestors." According to Chernyshevsky, all the differences between races, and even between nations of the same race, are purely "historical" and are due to the different conditions of their social life. He noted that the conditions of life, not only of different races and nations, but also of the members of a given nation, were different. Nations are divided into classes and occupational groups, which differ sharply from one another. By way of example he pointed to the Portuguese grandees who, he said, in their way of life and conceptions resembled the Swedish aristocrats more than they did the peasants of their own country. Similarly, the Portuguese peasants resembled the Scottish and Norwegian peasants more than they did the wealthy Lisbon merchants. Economic inequality created oppressed and ruling classes within each nation and gave rise to a struggle between them. Chernyshevsky rose to the level of understanding the class division of society and the role of the class struggle in the process of historical development.

Thus, when examining the concrete problems of social life, Chernyshevsky rose high above the narrow horizon of the abstract anthropological conception of man. "Man," he wrote, "is not an abstract legal entity, but a living being in whose life and happiness the material side (economic conditions) is of extreme importance." Thus, the active revolutionary struggle gave him a more concrete historical and materialist conception of man, and this led him beyond the abstract anthropological principle. Chernyshevsky was a great economist of the pre-Marx period. Insisting on a concrete historical approach to social phenomena, he rose ever so much higher than Feuerbach, whose sociology was based on the abstract principles of "love." But, although constantly turning to "economic position," "forms of social life" and "material conditions" as the source of social development, Chernyshevsky was not yet able to show that the real basis of society were the total definite relations of production in the given historical period. He was not able to create the theory of the materialist conception of history.

* * *

As regards the theory of knowledge, Chernyshevsky firmly adhered to the standpoint of materialism and strongly combated scepticism, agnosticism, Kantianism, neo-Kantianism and other varieties of idealism.

. Take a man whose arms are both sound, has he arms? Chernyshevsky ironically asks the naturalists who adhere to the standpoint of subjective idealism. After showing that this standpoint leads to denial of the existence of our own organism, he continues: "... if we possess knowledge of our organism, then we possess knowledge of the clothes we wear, of the food we eat, of the water we drink, of the wheat from which we make bread, of the utensil in which we make it; of our houses, of the fields in which we grow wheat, of forests, brickyards, quarries from which we obtain the materials for building our houses, etc., etc. In short: if we are people, then we possess knowledge of an incalculable number of things; straight, direct knowledge of them; of the things themselves; we obtain this knowledge from our real life."

In Chernyshevsky's opinion, thinking is objective, i.e., there can be no thinking divorced from objects existing independently of us. "By its very nature, sensation necessarily presupposes the existence of two elements of thought, merged into one thought: firstly, there is the external object which creates the sensation; secondly, the being that is conscious of the sensation." A man's perceptions "depend not on himself, but on the objects he meets with ... The idea is created by the objects or phenomena which produce the impression."

This is a purely materialist conception of the source of cognition. The starting point is objects that exist independently of our minds, objects that influence us, create our perceptions and ideas. Truth is not engendered by reason, but is created by life, by reality, and we acquire it through our sense organs.

From the fact that human knowledge is determined by the external world, by its influence upon our sense organs, Chernyshevsky unhesitatingly drew the further materialist conclusion that our sensations must be an adequate reflection of the objects that caused them. He strongly attacked Kant and his supporters who argued that man is not endowed with the gift of knowing things as they really are. "This is utter nonsense,

when we are of sound mind and our eyes are sound," he
wrote. "A man of sound mind with sound eyes sees the
objects that he sees." "We see things exactly as they actually exist."

He did not deny that our knowledge is relative, but
he rightly observed that in the language of the subjective
idealists and agnostics the term relative knowledge has
quite a different meaning. "It is used," he said, "as a respectable term, not likely to shock simpletons, to mask the idea
that all our knowledge about external objects is not knowledge, but illusion." Here he quite rightly pointed to the
chief vice of the subjectivists, agnostics and relativists, in
whose opinion relative knowledge precludes objective
knowledge.

Chernyshevsky emphatically rejected such an interpretation of relative knowledge. Take man's knowledge
about water, he said. The savage, perhaps, knows water
only in one state—the liquid. Later, men learned that
when water is boiled it is converted into vapour, and when
frozen it is converted into ice. Still later the chemical composition of water was discovered. But does the fact that man
gradually enriched his knowledge about water contradict
what the savage knows about it? No, it does not. "Water,
when it is not ice, or snow, or vapour, but water in the
narrow sense of the term, is the same water that they know of.
Their knowledge of water is true knowledge; very scanty,
but true."

Thus, according to Chernyshevsky, the expansion of
knowledge only supplements, deepens, enriches our former
conceptions and brings us nearer to objective truth. He
refused to recognize the insurmountable barriers the agnostics erected between human knowledge and the material
world. He believed in the power of reason, science and
practice, regarding the latter as the decisive criterion of
truth. Noting the enormous role practice plays in the process
of cognition, he wrote: "Practice is the great exposer of
deception and self-deception not only in practical matters,
but also in matters of feeling and thought. And that is why
science accepts it today as an essential criterion of all
controversial points." "What is a matter of controversy in
theory is fully settled by the practice of real life." Chernyshevsky drew quite close to the problem, solved for the
first time by dialectical materialism, of the relation

between absolute and relative truth. He expressed the profoundly correct idea that "without a history of a subject there can be no theory of the subject."

* * *

The principles of Chernyshevsky's philosophical materialism are most fully expressed in his famous essay "The Anthropological Principle in Philosophy," published in 1860. This was the theoretical manifesto of Russian revolutionary democracy, and around it raged one of the fiercest ideological battles ever fought until then in the history of the struggle between materialism and idealism, a battle that was an element of the general revolutionary situation of that epoch.

The first to reply to this essay was Professor Yurkevich of the Kiev Theological Academy. In an article entitled "From the Science of the Human Spirit," this obscurantist attacked Chernyshevsky primarily for his materialist solution of the fundamental problem of philosophy. In opposition to Chernyshevsky, he asserted that the unity of human nature has a spiritual basis, the eternal spirit; he erected an insurmountable barrier of dualism between "external" and "internal" experience. Striking at Chernyshevsky's materialism, he asserted that the idea that it is possible to pass from external influence to sensation is absurd; sensation is a barrier, a wall, which separates the mind from the external world. In opposition to Chernyshevsky's call for an alliance between philosophy and natural science, psychology and physiology, Yurkevich denied in principle that it is possible to explain human mentality by the physiological processes upon which it is based; he argued that the "science of the spirit" is quite autonomous of the natural sciences. Later, in the *Russky Vestnik** of February 1861, an article in reply to Chernyshevsky appeared, entitled "Old Gods and New Gods," written by Katkov, the editor, who accused the trend of which Chernyshevsky was the head of being unable to approach philosophical views critically and independently. At the end of this article Katkov strongly recommends the article of Yurkevich. In the third issue of *Russky Vestnik* another article by Katkov appeared

---

* See Note 2 to "Polemical Gems."—*Ed.*

entitled "Our Language and What Scoffers Are," written in
opposition to Chernyshevsky and Dobrolyubov. In the April
and May issues of *Russky Vestnik*, Katkov published long
excerpts from Yurkevich's article, preceded by a rapturous
comment on that author.

Raising Yurkevich's article as the banner of the struggle against Chernyshevsky's materialism, the Katkov camp
set out on a wide front to give battle to Chernyshevsky's
party also in other spheres, primarily in the sphere of politics, in the endeavour to discredit Chernyshevsky as the
distinguished ideologist of the peasant revolution.

Thus, the struggle that flared up around "The Anthropological Principle in Philosophy" least of all resembled
a controversy between academic schools and trends. The opposing camps disagreed all along the line of theoretical,
social and political activity. It was a struggle between
two world outlooks—materialism and idealism—and
reflected the collision between the two chief social and political trends in Russia in the sixties of the last century—
revolutionary democracy and the united reaction. The
spiritual weapons of all those who stood for the old order—
from its avowed defenders to its liberal "critics"—were
religion and idealism; against them was the revolutionary-
democratic camp in Russia, under the banner of atheism,
the natural sciences and materialism. It was this that lent
the controversy over "The Anthropological Principle in
Philosophy" its exceptional acrimony.

Chernyshevsky replied to his critics in his celebrated
essays "Polemical Gems." After the appearance of the first
series of the "Polemical Gems" the liberal *Otechestvenniye
Zapiski** joined in the fray against Chernyshevsky. The
July issue of that magazine contained a special review of
the first of the "Polemical Gems" by Dudyshkin, the editor
of the "Literary Criticism" section, who also waxed enthu-
siastic over Yurkevich.

Chernyshevsky was perfectly aware of the social and
political significance of the campaign that had been raised
against him and he was, therefore, quite justified in calling
his opponents reactionaries and in describing the idealist
philosophical systems they defended as old junk utilized
by reactionaries.

---

* See Note 14 to "Polemical Gems."—*Ed.*

The cool and contemptuous tone in which the "Polemical Gems" were written roused Chernyshevsky's enemies to fury. They attacked him more fiercely than ever and sometimes denounced him in terms that undoubtedly prepared the ground for the harsh measures the tsar's government took against the great Russian revolutionist a year later.

Chernyshevsky was incarcerated in a fortress and prevented from speaking just at the time when freedom-loving Russia sorely needed his voice. The cruel rite of "civil (i.e., mock) execution" was performed over him, after which he was sent to penal servitude.

The progressive section of the Russian public, however, was fully aware that the victor in this ideological struggle was Chernyshevsky. His advocacy of materialist philosophy left indelible traces on the Russian public mind. In his fierce struggle against religion and idealism Chernyshevsky further developed the materialist traditions of Russian philosophy and made it a harder and sharper weapon. Speaking of the splendid materialist traditions in Russian philosophy, V. I. Lenin placed Chernyshevsky on a par with Plekhanov. Chernyshevsky rendered a great service by spreading these traditions and imbuing generations of progressive people in Russia with them.

After getting Chernyshevsky out of the way, the tsar's government tried to eradicate the enormous revolutionary influence he exercised upon the progressive section of the Russian public. But far from falling into oblivion, Chernyshevsky became for revolutionary Russia a symbol of devotion to people and country. The tsar's government believed that the cruel and inhuman conditions of life in penal servitude and in exile would break Chernyshevsky's spirit as a revolutionist and thinker, but in this it was also mistaken. Chernyshevsky was a man of iron will, character and convictions.

Although in complete isolation, Chernyshevsky learned from the fragmentary information that reached him of the growing danger of neo-Kantian and subjective-idealist philosophy that was coming into vogue at that time and began to seek means of combating it. His only means of communication with the outside world were the letters he sent to his relations and friends; but he turned these means into a pulpit from which, in the most detailed manner, he expounded his ideas about the necessity of having an ad-

vanced materialist world outlook and about the hostility
between idealism and science, and called for an uncompromising struggle against idealism. He ridiculed those naturalists who in their quest for a general philosophical theory
were caught on the hook of the bourgeois philosophers who
preached subjectivism and agnosticism. He fiercely attacked
those scientists who regarded Kant as their "companion."
In one of his letters he, ridiculing Helmholtz, wrote: "My
dear fellow, a mathematician, or a naturalist in general,
has no right to look upon anything 'together with Kant.'
Kant repudiates all natural science, and he denies the reality of pure mathematics. My dear fellow, Kant doesn't care
a hang about what you do, or about you. Kant is no companion for you."*

In his letters from Siberia Chernyshevsky again stands
before us as an uncompromising fighter against all devia-
tions from the scientific world outlook, as a militant materialist. The struggle he waged against the Kantians and subjective idealists in the seventies and eighties of the nineteenth century undoubtedly constitutes one of the brilliant
pages in the history of materialist philosophy in Russia.

As is known, for its ideological level and adherence
to principle, Lenin placed this struggle that Chernyshevsky waged on a par with Engels' criticism of this same
bourgeois philosophy in that very same period. While
noting certain flaws in Chernyshevsky's materialism due
to historical conditions, Lenin emphasized that in his criticism of idealism "Chernyshevsky is entirely on Engels'
level in so far as he takes Kant to task not for realism, but
for agnosticism and subjectivism, not for recognition of
the 'thing-in-itself,' but for inability to derive our knowledge from this objective source...."**

* * *

Chernyshevsky was not only a great materialist, but
also an outstanding dialectician. He consistently adhered
to the idea of the unity of the world, seeing this unity in
the world's materiality; but his conception of unity included differences, contradictions. Thus, he says, the unity of
human nature reveals itself in two, qualitatively different,

_____
* See p. 533—534 of this book.— *Ed.*
** V. I. Lenin, *Materialism and Empirio-Criticism*, Moscow
1952, p. 376.

kinds of phenomena: physical and moral. He advocated the idea that "the combination of heterogeneous properties in one object is the general law of things." He argued that highly complex combinations of matter reveal properties that are absent in the simple elements that comprise the complex bodies. For example, a compound in certain proportions of hydrogen and oxygen forms water, which possesses many properties that are not observed in either oxygen or hydrogen. Chernyshevsky uses this example to show that "quantitative difference passes into qualitative difference." In his commentary on Carpenter's book *Energy in Nature* he speaks of the different forms of motion and says that the conversion of heat into mechanical motion and vice versa is a law of nature.

This conception of matter and motion relieves Chernyshevsky's materialism of the crude, mechanistic one-sidedness of the old materialism. He saw reality as it is, in its dialectical movement and development. In contrast to the idealist Hegel, and following in the footsteps of Belinsky and Herzen, he elaborated dialectics on a materialist basis.

He did not, however, interest himself in dialectics in the abstract. For him, dialectics was a methodological instrument for unerringly determining the way, the approach, to the achievement of the aims of the revolutionary-democratic movement. He was one of the first men in Russia consciously to apply certain aspects of the dialectical method for the purpose of substantiating revolutionary-democratic practice.

Chernyshevsky taught that no success can be achieved in any historically important cause without a struggle; but he was fully aware that the struggle that has most chance of success is one that is properly directed and organized. But what is needed to make a man cease to be a passive onlooker and become an active participant in oncoming events? He must base his practice not on an abstract ideal but on reality. "Only those desires that are based on reality," he wrote, "are of real importance; only those hopes that are roused by reality can be realized, and only in such matters as are accomplished with the aid of the forces and circumstances provided by reality."* Hence the paramount

---

* See p. 491 of this book.—*Ed.*

importance of taking into account the conditions upon which the given action directly or indirectly depends, for this enables us to know to what the events are leading, and to decide what conduct would be to our advantage. Thus, successful revolutionary action is inconceivable without the science of tactics; and a genuine revolutionist cannot but be a tactician. In Chernyshevsky's opinion, a concrete approach to phenomena, concrete thinking, are most essential conditions for correct conduct, or tactics; and this, he urged, was the primary characteristic of the dialectical method.

He contrasted his concrete dialectical method to abstract, metaphysical thinking. Abstract thinking is guided by eternal, absolute principles, whereas, said Chernyshevsky, "everything depends upon circumstances, upon the conditions of place and time." For example, is war disastrous or beneficial? This question cannot be answered in the abstract. There are wars that are disastrous for a nation; such are aggressive, predatory wars. But there are wars of another kind, beneficial, just wars, such as the war of 1812, "which was the salvation of the Russian nation."

There is nothing stationary or immutable in nature or in human society. Chernyshevsky knew that this is due to inherent contradictions. "... All life," he wrote, "is polarization, magnetism, electricity—everywhere you see divaricated forces striving in opposite directions...." * A revolutionist must not ignore these opposite sides, these mutually excluding tendencies. He must be able to determine his conduct in conformity with the circumstances of place and time.

Chernyshevsky subjected to scathing criticism those who see only gradual evolution in history and rely on reforms. He sharply attacked the American economist Carey who preached the harmony of class interests. Chernyshevsky pointed out that the process of development is not a conflict between equivalent and equilibrate forces; in the process of development, one side gains preponderance over the other. "... The fundamental unity breaks up in numerous directions, of which the one that is most favoured by historical circumstances gains predominance and pushes

---

* N. G. Chernyshevsky, *Unpublished Works*, Russ. ed., 1939, p. 60.

3*

the others into the background."* The conflict of irreconcilable contradictions leads to a revolutionary solution,
to upheavals, to the destruction of the old and the rise of
the new. "... Motion takes leap after leap...."** In Chernyshevsky's opinion, not a single historically important problem can be solved otherwise than by revolution. Revolution is the greatest creative force in history. Thus, the dialectical method served Chernyshevsky as a means of theo-
retically substantiating the inevitability of a peasant
revolution.

In his well-known essay "A Criticism of the Philosophical Prejudices Against Common Ownership," Chernyshevsky
set out to prove on the basis of the dialectical law of the
negation of the negation that it was possible for Russia to
go over to socialism without passing through the capitalist phase of development. He was perfectly well aware
that capitalism changed only the form of exploitation
of man by man, and that it caused the ruin of the vast masses
of the working population. This brilliant ideologist of
the revolutionary peasantry did not want his own beloved
Russian people to share this fate. In his works he gave a
profound critique of capitalism. While paying high tribute
to the technical and scientific progress that capitalism promoted in the initial period of its development, and admitting that it was necessary to utilize it, he strongly opposed
capitalism as a social and economic system for Russia.

Deeming it possible for Russia to avoid the capitalist stage of development, he advanced important theoretical arguments in support of his thesis. In doing so he came
out not as an armchair theorist, but as the political opponent of the scientific apologists of capitalism. A convinced
socialist and enemy of private ownership, he mustered all
his arguments to refute what the bourgeois economists
preached about the "beneficial nature" and "eternity" of
capitalism. He proved convincingly that private ownership
must inevitably give way to the collective ownership of
the means of production. Thus, the highest stage, coincid-
ing in form with the initial stage, i.e., the stage of primitive common ownership, is, as it were, a reversion to the

---

* N. G. Chernyshevsky, *Collected Works*, Russ. ed., 1906,
Vol. III, p. 742.
    ** *Ibid.*, Vol. V, p. 491.

latter, but on a new basis. Chernyshevsky regarded this as a manifestation of the universally predominating dialectical law of the negation of the negation.

He was profoundly convinced that capitalism must give way to socialism and that the transition to socialism could be made without passing through capitalism. And he regarded Russia as a country in which such a transition could be made with the aid of the still existing peasant communities. It must be stated that Chernyshevsky's arguments on this score are abstract and contradict the very principle of concrete thinking that he himself advanced. It is beyond dispute, however, that here too he tried to keep to the dialectical method; he was convinced that the application of dialectics to the history of society armed us with the consciousness that the fall of tsarism and the triumph of socialism were necessary and inevitable.

Chernyshevsky's assertion that it was possible for Russia to pass on to socialism through the peasant communities without going through capitalism was utterly utopian, although, in itself, the presentation of the question of non-capitalist development was extremely interesting. Thus, Chernyshevsky's socialism, to be brought about by a peasant revolution, was utopian socialism, and the dialectical method that served as the theoretical basis of this peasant revolution and utopian socialism was still abstract and limited. The combination of scientific socialism with materialist dialectics could be brought about only in Marxism, only on the basis of the class struggle of the proletariat, which is conscious of its world-historical role of builder of the new society.

Chernyshevsky did not create an integral doctrine of dialectics. We find in his works a profound understanding and application of a number of the elements of dialectics, but these do not yet form a harmonious and systematic theory of dialectics; his anthropological principle was a grave hindrance to this. Chernyshevsky is on firm ground when he speaks of the unity of man, of the universe, of the laws of nature, and of the possibility of our knowing the world through our sense organs. But he is on much weaker ground when he tries to perceive in this unity a multiplicity of quality, the specific nature of every phenomenon, form of transition, and the specific nature of cognition. Basing himself on the practice of the revolutionary peasantry in Russia, he went further than any other thinker of the pre-Marx period; he represents the peak of pre-Marx materialist philosophy. Leninism—the most revolutionary doctrine in modern times—absorbed the progressive traditions of the Russian revolutionary democrats, of whom Chernyshevsky was the greatest representative.

* * *

The field in which Chernyshevsky engaged in his first battle with idealism was aesthetics. It was in this field that the outstanding Russian materialist and revolutionary-democrat received his baptism of fire.

His interest in aesthetics was not fortuitous. Progressive Russian art, and primarily our great Russian literature— the literature of Pushkin, Griboyedov, Lermontov, Gogol and others—played an immense role in developing progressive public opinion. Aesthetics had long been in Russia the arena of a fierce struggle between diverse social forces, a field of battle for influence in the intellectual and social life of the country. Continuing the line pursued by the revolutionary democrat Belinsky, Chernyshevsky strove to place art entirely at the service of the great struggle for emancipation.

The chief obstacle to this was the idealist aesthetics that predominated in the West at that time, and which, after Belinsky's death, had raised its head again in Russia and tried to divert art from the path of realism by championing so-called "pure art." The class significance of the "pure art" theory lay in that it tried to divert public opinion from the burning questions of the day to the world of "lofty emotions," remote from the reality of serfdom, from the struggle against serfdom. That is why the exposure of this theory was not only of enormous theoretical, but also of urgent practical political importance.

As is known, idealist aesthetics obtained its chief arguments from the arsenal of German philosophy. Hence, by striking at Hegel and his school, Chernyshevsky also struck at the Russian idealists in the camp of the nobility and the liberals.

Chernyshevsky was profoundly convinced that aesthetics is determined by the general world outlook, that it is a part of the world outlook. He said that the character of the general scientific conceptions with which aesthetics had to be brought into line was determined by "respect for real life, distrust of a priori hypotheses, even though they tickle one's fancy...." In his opinion, objectless flights of fancy are harmful not only "in scientific matters," but "even in the field of art," which must also take its stand on firm, realistic ground. In his dissertation, "The Aesthetic Relation of Art to Reality," he set out to bring the problems of aesthetics in line with his materialist philosophy. Under the conditions prevailing in Russia in his time, when idealism predominated in the theories of aesthetics, the elaboration of the general principles of aesthetics, was, perhaps, more important and urgent than the investigation of any other problem. It was necessary to strike at the foundations of the idealist theories of aesthetics and thus bring down the whole edifice; for Chernyshevsky this task was also a process of building the edifice of a new, materialist theory of art. Therefore, those who asserted that his aim was to destroy all aesthetics were utterly wrong. While combating the old, idealist aesthetics, he continuously championed materialist aesthetics, scientific and effective aesthetics that fully corresponded to the interests of revolutionary democracy.

Chernyshevsky deemed his first task to be to employ the principles of materialist philosophy for the purpose of finding a realistic solution for the problem of the relation of art to reality.

The prevailing theory of art approached this problem from the standpoint of idealist philosophy. According to this theory, there was no true beauty in nature or in the real life of man; beauty is created by our imagination, by art. Art springs from man's desire to make up for the absence of beauty in objective reality. Chernyshevsky proved that this point of view of idealism was unsound.

Naturally, to solve the problem of the relation of art to reality, the materialist Chernyshevsky had to approach the subject from a standpoint that is the very opposite of idealist aesthetics. He took reality as the starting point of the theory of art in general, and of the theory of beauty in particular. "Beauty is life"—such was the basic formula he advanced for his theory of aesthetics. "Beautiful is that being in which we see life as it should be according to our conceptions; beautiful is the object which expresses life, or reminds us of life."

Further, he established that the different classes of society have different conceptions of life. For example, the peasant's conception of life always includes the concept of work, a good house, plenty of food, and so forth. A fresh complexion, rosy cheeks and a buxom figure expressing sound health, are the signs of beauty according to the conceptions of the common people. The ruling classes who do not perform physical work and lead an idle life have different conceptions of beauty. In their eyes a pale face, frail figure, etc., which express a definite mode of life, acquire the virtue of beauty. Thus, Chernyshevsky made a brilliant sociological analysis of the conception of beauty. He reached a conception of the economic and class basis of aesthetic norms. In the sphere of aesthetics, as in the sphere of philosophy, Chernyshevsky also came near to Marxism.

Demolishing all the arguments of the idealist aestheticists, Chernyshevsky arrived at his chief materialist conclusion, namely, that reality is higher than art, that art is a reflection of reality, that art is not as vivid or as complete as the objects, phenomena and events of real life it depicts. He strongly emphasized that, in relation to works of art, material reality is primary. He advanced the idea that material reality is primary in "The Aesthetic Relation of Art to Reality," long before he wrote "The Anthropological Principle in Philosophy," but both these works equally reveal his uncompromising hostility to the principles of idealism in all its forms and manifestations, and the ardent struggle he waged against it. The revolutionary-democratic movement in Russian society needed an effective philosophical, ethical and aesthetic theory, and for his time it was created by the great leader of that movement, Chernyshevsky.

Idealist aesthetics limited the sphere of art to the beautiful. Chernyshevsky emphatically opposed this. He said that the sphere of art is wider than the sphere of the beautiful. The subject of art is nature, life, but, he explained, "by real life we, of course, mean not only man's relation to the objects and beings of the objective world, but also his inner life. Sometimes a man lives in a dream—in that case the dream has for him (to a certain degree and for a certain time) the significance of something objective. Still more often a man lives in the world of his emotions; these states, if they become interesting, are also reproduced by art." Art, like science, takes for its subject everything that can interest man. The difference between them is that science speaks with the aid of logical conceptions, of reasoning, whereas art speaks with the aid of artistic images. Following Belinsky, Chernyshevsky developed the view that the role of art, like that of science, is to help man to know the world.

While arguing that art is the reproduction of reality in artistic images, Chernyshevsky did not in the least imply that this can be achieved merely by copying. In his opinion, artistic creation is a process that calls for a vivid imagination, a penetrating mind and fine taste. He regarded the qualities of a writer as good when he combines "talent with thought, which gives strength and meaning to his talent, which gives life and beauty to its productions." Chernyshevsky was an ardent champion of lofty ideology in art and literature, which, he urged, can be achieved when the writer is in the front ranks of society, when he not only reflects but also explains reality in his works, and pronounces his judgment on it; when he acts as a herald of the progressive ideas of his time.

Plekhanov strongly objected to Chernyshevsky's demand that art must be active. He was convinced that to put demands to art from the standpoint of what it ought to be means transcending the borders of scientific analysis. Art and literature must be taken as they are, he said, and we must be content with explaining their meaning. This point of view clearly expresses Plekhanov's Menshevism.

Notwithstanding the flaws in it due to the anthropological principle in philosophy, Chernyshevsky's aesthetics, like Belinsky's, is very close to ours. As Comrade Zhdanov said: "Militant art, which fights for the finest ideals of the people—that is how the great representatives of Russian literature pictured art and literature to themselves. Chernyshevsky, who of all the utopian socialists came nearest to scientific socialism, and whose works, as Lenin said, 'breathed the spirit of the class struggle,' taught that, in addition to helping us to know life, the purpose of art is to teach the people how to correctly appraise social phenomena." *

* * *

* Comrade Zhdanov's *Address on the Magazines "Zvezda" and "Leningrad,"* Gospolitizdat, Moscow 1946, p. 24.

In attacking the foundations of the serf system, Chernyshevsky waged a consistent struggle on all fronts, and, consequently, in the field of ethics. In opposition to the prevailing ethics of the oppressors, he advanced his own doctrine, which, in complete harmony with his general philosophical conceptions, had in view man, his natural requirements, his happiness. This was his celebrated theory of rational egoism, which was a form of expression of his revolutionary-democratic ethics.

Chernyshevsky was of the opinion that a man who is prompted in his actions not by abstract ideas that are alien to him, but by his own interests, is an egoist. Here, the egoist is contrasted to the individual whose human dignity is suppressed, a passive, submissive, obedient individual. "Egoism," properly understood, is only complete freedom of the individual, said Pisarev. On the lips of the radical thinkers of the sixties of the last century who lived under the conditions of stern regimentation of social and individual life, this term did, indeed, possess a profound liberating meaning.

Chernyshevsky sharply opposed his ethics not only to religious-feudal ethics, which doped the people with all sorts of fables about a life hereafter, but also to the bourgeois-philistine ethics of crude, narrow, self-interest. His ethics does not divorce individual interest from public interest, but strives to combine them in a rational way. Moreover, the ethics of rational egoism demands that the individual should become conscious of the common good. This is characteristic of the chief personages in Chernyshevsky's novel *What Is To Be Done?* Imbued with great love for the toilers, they, like Chernyshevsky, feel burning hatred for those classes and individuals who subject the masses of the people to cruel exploitation, privation and degradation, for those who encroach upon the happiness of the majority. In this novel Chernyshevsky depicts the positive ideal of a man of moral strength and integrity who is capable, at the risk of his life, of fighting against serfdom and for the happiness of the people. The aim of Chernyshevsky's ethics was to train devoted revolutionists, to arm the fighters in the peasant revolution. The generation of proletarian revolutionists, in their battles against the tsarist autocracy and the bourgeoisie, retained and further developed the fine ethical precepts preached by Chernyshevsky.

Chernyshevsky repudiated free will and held that all our actions are, at bottom, prompted by the desire to satisfy human requirements and to achieve happiness. But if that is the case, why are some of our actions regarded as ethical and some not? Chernyshevsky says that it is not because they are in themselves bad or good; they become one or the other owing to the conditions of life. The organization of society is to blame for the fact that private and public interests do not harmonize, and that a man who strives for his own happiness comes into conflict with the interests of other people. Create normal conditions of life for man, remove the circumstances that degrade and corrupt him, and then, not only a broad and enlightened mind, but also noble moral qualities will become qualities that can be acquired by all. They will be the inalienable qualities of man living under conditions favourable for the development of his powers and capabilities. Although prompted by the desire to satisfy their individual requirements, people's actions will, at the same time, be altruistic. Thus, in his ethics also, Chernyshevsky arrives at the necessity of a revolution and of the reorganization of society on socialist lines.

In Chernyshevsky's opinion, the firm basis of human action is rational motive. Truth and good are the same thing, he said. But there are different kinds of reason, and there are different conceptions of what is rational; what, then, is the basis of common morality? The reason of "man in general." "Science recognizes as truth only that which constitutes human nature; only that which is useful to man in general is regarded as true good; all digressions from this norm in the conceptions of a given nation, or class, are a mistake...." This statement shows that although it contained a number of profound ideas concerning the difference in the character of "good" and "evil" in different epochs, and among different nations, Chernyshevsky's ethics as a whole was based on anthropology and therefore suffered from abstractness.

Plekhanov sharply attacked Chernyshevsky for attributing in his ethics too big a role to motive, to consciousness; but while pointing to the idealist aspects of Chernyshevsky's views on ethics, he himself fell into the opposite error of underrating the role of consciousness, the role of the subjective factor in history. This was due to his Menshevik errors. In developing the theory of historical materialism, Lenin and Stalin always emphasized the accelerating, organizing and transformatory role of revolutionary ideas, parties and classes. On this question Chernyshevsky stands near to us. In attacking the foundations of serfdom he strove to create an effective morality, and emphasized the active, creative, revolutionary role played by people. But in the period in which he lived he could not rise to a genuinely scientific conception of the social activities and, therefore, of the ethics of the people.

* * *

The decisive factor in Chernyshevsky's great and many-sided life was his boundless love for the Russian people, his constant readiness to fight for the happiness of his country. Patriotism was the guiding idea of all his sentiments and moods. Lenin wrote that Chernyshevsky was filled "with genuine love for his country...."*

Chernyshevsky wrote: "... The historical importance of every great Russian is measured by the services he rendered his country, and his human dignity is measured by the strength of his patriotism."** Having Belinsky in mind, he wrote: "Numerous are the merits of the critics of the Gogol period, but they all acquired life, meaning and strength from the passion that inspired them—ardent patriotism."

Chernyshevsky waged a fierce struggle against the bourgeois cosmopolites Babst, Chicherin, Katkov and others. He said that among the Russian people "the sense of national pride is more strongly developed than among any other civilized nation." He was fully convinced that Russia had a great future before her. "We are ensured for many centuries ahead of the happy lot of improving ourselves and of arranging our lives ever better and better." At the same time, however, he fought against nationalism; he stood for the solidarity of the toilers of all nationalities.

Chernyshevsky's love for his country was organically linked with his revolutionary democratism. In his opinion,

---

* V. I. Lenin, *Selected Works*, Two-Volume ed., Moscow 1952, Vol. I, Part 2, p. 409.
** N. G. Chernyshevsky, *Collected Works*, Russ. ed., 1906, Vol. II, p. 121.

to be a patriot meant fighting with all one's might those who were enslaving the people, those who were preventing Russia from becoming strong and happy. When still a young man he mused: "To work not for the transient but for the eternal glory of one's country and for the good of mankind —what can be loftier and more desirable than this?"

All Chernyshevsky's subsequent life was one of honest and devoted service to his country. By his activities as a revolutionist and thinker he added to the glory of Russia and left deep traces on her social and intellectual life. He played a very big part in the spiritual development of Dobrolyubov, Antonovich, Pisarev, Shelgunov, Serno-Solovyevich and of many other distinguished figures in the Russian revolutionary-democratic movement. His influence on Russian literature and art was great and fruitful. In Russian natural science his ideas were brilliantly confirmed by the work of Sechenov, whose *Reflexes of the Brain*, published in 1863, marked a real triumph for materialism. The finest men of many other nations: Shevchenko and Franko in the Ukraine; Nikoladze and Chavchavadze in Georgia; Nalbandyan in Armenia; Akhundov in Azerbaijan, Svetozar Markovich in Serbia; Karavelov and Botev in Bulgaria, and many others, were under Chernyshevsky's benign influence.

In the diary he kept when he was a student Chernyshevsky wrote: "... I will not hesitate to sacrifice my life for the triumph of my convictions ..." and indeed, the interests of his country were always more important to him than everything else; nothing could shake his determination in the struggle for the interests of the people.

Chernyshevsky warned that nothing can be more fatal for the revolutionary cause than irresolution in the struggle against enemies. The genuine revolutionist must know that the interests of the opposing sides are irreconcilable, that it is a life and death struggle, that if you do not destroy the enemy, he will destroy you. Therefore, the supreme law in the revolutionary struggle is: rout the enemy. Honest service to one's country and the revolution entails privation and sacrifice. And by his works Chernyshevsky constantly trained people who were not daunted by difficulties, who went boldly out to meet them, and fought to overcome them. He declared that the revolutionist and ardent patriot is a man of special mould, strong, energetic, devoted to his people and to his country.

Chernyshevsky had deep faith in the Russian people's bright socialist future, and he therefore issued the call: "Love it, strive for it, work for it, bring it nearer, carry as much as you can of it into the present."

Chernyshevsky, and the revolutionary commoners he headed, regarded it as their historic mission to bring socialist society nearer by means of their revolutionary activities. They regarded it as a great honour to be destined, as they believed, to carry out this difficult, but glorious and noble task. But socialism could, and did, triumph in our country only as proletarian socialism, based on the great teachings of Marxism-Leninism. The Great October Socialist Revolution was triumphant because its victory was organized by the party of the working class, the Communist Party.

The great merit of Chernyshevsky, the forerunner of Russian Social-Democracy, lay in that he was one of the geniuses who, as he himself expressed it, "running ahead of their epoch, enjoyed the glory of foreseeing the dawn of the coming day and had the courage to welcome it."

Russia succeeded in throwing off the long-borne yoke of tsarism, landlordism and capitalism, in abolishing exploitation and in building socialism, and she is now boldly and confidently proceeding towards communism. Russia has become the most advanced country in the world and is pointing out the road for other nations. And we, the Soviet people, cherish the name of the great revolutionary-democrat, fighter and thinker, Chernyshevsky.

* * *

The literary work of N. G. Chernyshevsky was extraordinarily diverse. Brilliant philosopher, political economist, sociologist, historian, literary critic, philologist, novelist, journalist and organizer of revolutionary democracy—such is the by no means complete list of his encyclopedic learning and fields of activity. His activities covered all the branches of learning in his time.

M. Grigoryan

N. G. CHERNYSHEVSKY

SELECTED PHILOSOPHICAL ESSAYS

THE ANTHROPOLOGICAL PRINCIPLE
IN PHILOSOPHY

("ESSAYS ON PROBLEMS OF PRACTICAL PHILOSOPHY,"
BY P. L. LAVROV. "1. INDIVIDUALITY."
ST. PETERSBURG, 1860)[1]

I

IF MR. LAVROV'S pamphlet could serve only as a subject for a critical review, and had we begun to read it with
the idea of analyzing the conceptions he expounds in it,
we would have stopped reading it after the very first pages,
because—we shall be quite candid—we have not read
most of the numerous books the author has taken into consideration, and we even think that we shall never read them;
and without being acquainted with these books, it is impossible to give an accurate appraisal of the special merits
of Mr. Lavrov's pamphlet. But not only have we read it,
it has served as the reason for our writing a rather lengthy
essay that is most closely related to it.

Mr. Lavrov's research begins straight off with a reference
to a writer, not one of whose books have we read—with
a quotation from Jules Simon, a very well-known French
theoretician. If we did not know the trend to which this
writer belongs, the two lines of his that are quoted at the
very beginning of the pamphlet would have been sufficient
to rob us of all desire to make his acquaintance: "a book
on political theory unrelated to current politics is almost
a novelty today," says Jules Simon, according to Mr. Lavrov, at the opening of his book *La Liberté*. This dozen or
so words quoted from his book are sufficient to show that
the author totally fails to understand the manner in which
everything in the world takes place, including the writing
of theoretical works. Nowadays, political theories arise
under the influence of current events, and scientific treatises
serve as echoes of the historical struggle; their aim is to
retard or to accelerate the course of events. In Jules Simon's
opinion, this was not the case in the past; otherwise, he

4 — 3857

would not have employed the word "today." But this is
not all: Jules Simon also thinks that all the people of our
epoch, including scientists, are not behaving quite properly
in being not merely representatives, or followers, of abstract doctrines that have no relation to the passions that
stir their country at the given time, but also the interpret-
ers and advocates of the strivings of their particular parties. If he did not censure them for this, he would not have
said that his book is "unrelated to current politics." Lastly,
he imagines that he can induce his readers to believe, or
perhaps he himself honestly believes, that he is speaking
the truth when he says that his book is "unrelated to current politics." The words of Jules Simon that Mr. Lavrov
quotes were written under the influence of these three views,
and all three are so obviously mistaken that they testify
either to Jules Simon's extraordinary simplicity and short-
sightedness, or to his total inability to speak the truth.
We are inclined to accept the first assumption, because a
cunning person is artful, whereas Jules Simon talks such
obvious nonsense that it can be prompted only by extreme
simplicity.

Political theories, and all philosophical doctrines in
general, have always been created under the powerful influence of the social situation to which they belonged, and
every philosopher has always been a representative of one
of the political parties which in his time contended for
predominance in the society to which the philosopher belonged. We shall not speak of the thinkers who have made
a special study of the political aspect of life. Their affiliation to political parties is only too obvious to everybody.
Hobbes was an absolutist, Locke was a Whig, Milton was
a republican, Montesquieu was a Liberal after the English
taste, Rousseau was a revolutionary-democrat, Bentham
was simply a democrat, revolutionary or nonrevolutionary
as circumstances demanded. It is needless to speak of writers like these. Let us turn to those thinkers who have engaged in building more general theories, the builders of
metaphysical systems, to the so-called philosophers proper.
Kant belonged to the party that wanted to enthrone liberty
in Germany in a revolutionary way, but abhorred terroristic methods. Fichte went a few steps farther; he was not
afraid even of terroristic methods. Schelling was a representative of the party that was terrified by the revolution

and sought tranquility in medieval institutions, that wanted to restore in Germany the feudal state that had been destroyed by Napoleon I and the Prussian patriots, whose spokesman Fichte had been. Hegel was a moderate Liberal, he was extremely conservative in his deductions; but he adopted revolutionary principles for the struggle against extreme reaction in the hope of preventing the develcpment of the revolutionary spirit, which served him as a weapon for the purpose of overthrowing that which was old and too antiquated. Our point is not that these people held such convictions as private individuals, that would not be so very important, but that their philosophical systems were thoroughly permeated with the spirit of those political parties to which the authors of these systems belonged. To say that what is the case today was not always the case in the past, to say that only now have philosophers begun to build their systems under the influence of political convictions, is extremely naive, and it is still more naive to express such an opinion about those thinkers who made a special study of the political department of philosophical science.

Whether present-day thinkers do or do not resemble those of the past in that they serve as representatives of political parties makes no difference; whatever may have been the case in the past, the fact is that at the present time we see that every man of intelligence is very greatly interested in political events. Newspapers are read even by people who are unable to read books that are at all serious. Are the thinkers of our epoch to blame for not being inferior in intellectual development to army officers and government officials, landlords and factory owners, shop assistants and artisans? Must a thinker be more stupid and blinder than the ordinary literate person? Everybody who has reached intellectual independence has political convictions and judges everything from the standpoint of those convictions. Is a philosopher, or a political theorist, to blame if his trend of thought is the same as that of the people he sets out to enlighten? Must a teacher be more ignorant than his pupils? Must a man who writes on a given subject be less interested in it than those who do not claim to be able to write books on the theory of this subject? One must be as naive as a lamb to censure a scientist for not being more foolish and stupid than uneducated people.

4*

But most amusing of all is the simplicity with which
Jules Simon wants to convince the public, or has managed
to convince himself, that his work is unrelated to current
politics. We have heard about the character of the theoretical works Jules Simon has written in different years.
Under the July monarchy, his doctrine was distinguished
for its moderate spirit of freedom and for its supercilious,
half-approving and half-censorious attitude towards really
progressive people. Under the Republic the element of freedom was overshadowed by a fierce reaction against the
resolute progressives who nearly succeeded in capturing
power. When the Empire was consolidated, when the resolute progressives began to seem impotent and reaction
was completely triumphant, Jules Simon began to write
as a very ardent lover of freedom. From this we see that his
theories not only reflected the convictions of his party, but
even yielded to every transient state of feeling in that party. We would certainly have known that this was the case
even if we had not read about it. It would have been sufficient
for us to know that Jules Simon enjoys some reputation in
France and, therefore, is not quite bereft of intelligence.
An intelligent man cannot fail to note the events that take
place around him and to take them into consideration—
consequently, his system too, cannot but reflect the course
of events. Everybody, except a few naive people, understands this. Mr. Lavrov frankly states that the author he
quotes failed to keep his unrealizable promise. That being
the case, what was the use of Jules Simon telling this improbable fable about his system being isolated from the
influence of current politics?

A man who says such a naive, foolish thing may be a
good paterfamilias, a good citizen and a pleasant gossip,
but he cannot be a thinker, because there is no logic in his
head. If he becomes a writer, his works may have fictional,
archeological and every other merit, but they cannot have
any philosophical significance whatsoever. For this reason,
we abandon all hope of reading Jules Simon's philosophical works. If we wanted feuilleton merit we would go straight
to the feuilletons written by Madame Emile Girardin,
Louis Dunoyer and Theophile Gautier. If we wanted to
enjoy poetry we would read the novels of George Sand and
the songs of Béranger. If, finally, we wanted to read empty
chatter, we would take up the novels of Alexandre Dumas

the Elder, or, perhaps the Younger, or even of Marquis
de Foudras. But what can induce us to read the philosophical works of Jules Simon, which may contain much pleasant gossip and feuilleton spice, or even poetry, but which,
after all, by the very nature of their subject, are far
inferior in these respects to decent feuilletons, good novels, and even bad ones, and lack the merit that makes
a philosophical work interesting—lack logic?

Similarly, we do not think that we shall be able to
read the works of the present-day Fichte, who, we know,
is always referred to as "the son of the celebrated Fichte."
This testimonial reminds us of a funny incident that occurred in St. Petersburg five or six years ago. Two gentlemen,
strangers to each other, met at an evening party, and after
conversing for a while they felt they would like to become
more closely acquainted. "With whom have I the pleasure
of speaking?" one of them asked the other. The other mentioned his name and in his turn asked: "And with whom have I
the pleasure of speaking?" "I am the husband of Madame
Tedesco," came the answer. We have never had any desire
to hear the husband of Madame Tedesco sing.

For the same reasons that deprive us of the opportunity
of acquainting ourselves with the works of Jules Simon and
Fichte junior, we have not read the philosophical works of
Schopenhauer or Frauenstädt, nor shall we do so. In all
probability these authors are excellent men, but in philosophy they are what Madame K. Pavlova is in poetry.
Mr. Lavrov also quotes one of her productions, viz., *A Conversation in the Kremlin.*

Not being sufficiently acquainted with many of the
sources that Mr. Lavrov utilized, we are, of course, unable
to make an exact appraisal of the merits of his work. We
can only assume that if he possessed no more philosophical
talent than Jules Simon or Fichte junior, his pamphlet
would have been as totally lacking in philosophical spirit
as their works are, and his "Theory of Individuality" would
have been as bad as their theories. But his pamphlet must
be positively regarded as a good one. From this it must
be concluded that Mr. Lavrov noted many of the blunders
committed by the mediocre philosophers he has studied,
and understands many things much better than they do.
In short, it must be concluded that the flaws in his pamphlet
were carried over from other books, such as those of Jules

Simon and Fichte junior, whereas the merits of the pamphlet
are largely due to the author himself. We think that this
assumption is correct, and we would therefore like Mr.
Lavrov to continue writing essays on philosophy.

Similarly, he must be given considerable credit for
studying philosophy not only from thinkers of the category
of Schopenhauer and Jules Simon. In our society, which is
so little acquainted with the truly great thinkers of present-
day Western Europe and which regards as the best guides for
the study of philosophy either the works of people of the
present generation who lag far behind the present development of thought, or the works of great thinkers, but of the
too distant past, who are no longer satisfactory in view
of the present development of science and social relations—
in our society, it must be regarded as a great merit when
a man, in addition to the poor and obsolete guides he is
advised to read by everybody he meets, and particularly
by specialists, seeks better ones, manages to find them, and
is able to understand them. Mr. Lavrov leads his readers
most of the way along the good, straight road forward.
This does him great honour, because nobody in our society
has pointed this road out to him. On the contrary, all those
who at any time have acted as his advisers probably pushed
him on to all sorts of crooked paths leading across a bog,
and mostly backward, but not forward.

We highly appreciate both these merits, i.e., the fact
that Mr. Lavrov possessed the intellectual strength to achieve
much better results than those obtained by the Fichte
juniors and the Jules Simons, and the fact that he was able
to find for his philosophical researches guides that are
much better than mediocre and obsolete books. But the
combination of excellent ideas borrowed from the really
great thinkers of the present day, or suggested to the author
by his own mind, with conceptions that are either not
quite up-to-date or do not belong to the trend of thought
to which Mr. Lavrov in the main adheres, or, lastly, that
are characteristic of the special position of thinkers among
a public that differs from ours, and therefore acquire a
false colour when repeated among us—this combination
of his own merits and other people's defects, lends, if we
are not mistaken, Mr. Lavrov's system the character of
eclecticism, which creates an unfavourable impression upon
readers who are familiar with the requirements of philosoph-

ical thinking. In Mr. Lavrov's pamphlet we find ideas that are hardly compatible with one another. We shall quote one example of this.

Mr. Lavrov is a progressive thinker, there is no doubt about that. Everything goes to show that he is imbued with the sincere desire to help the society to which he belongs to acquire those moral and social benefits which we still lack owing to our ignorance, which prevents us from knowing the goal of our strivings and the means by which this goal can be reached. And yet, on the very first page of his pamphlet we meet with the phrase "public despotism in the United States" and to it in confirmation is added a quotation from Mill's book *On Liberty*:[2] "It is affirmed that in the United States, the feeling of the majority, to whom any appearance of a more showy or costly style of living than they can hope to rival is disagreeable, operates as a tolerably effectual sumptuary law, and that in many parts of the Union it is really difficult for a person possessing a very large income, to find any mode of spending it, which will not incur popular disapprobation." It is all very well for Mill to say this: the English public understands the meaning of these words, but God knows what our public will think when they hear them without explanation. Mr. Lavrov quotes this passage from Mill not for any important purpose, but merely in order to lengthen by the six words "public despotism in the United States" a long list of different political or social forms mankind in the West has gone through, or is going through now. For the unimportant purpose of presenting twenty-seven instead of twenty-six references, it was not worth touching upon a fact that calls for very lengthy argument. Mr. Lavrov was unwise in quoting it; but what is worse, in our opinion, is that he pointed to a fact without explaining to our public what it meant. We must fill this gap. Firstly, the fact which Mr. Lavrov calls public despotism does not exist in the whole of the United States, but almost exclusively in one part of the country, the so-called New England states, and chiefly in the city of Boston. Secondly, this fact, which is not universal as we see, is not a consequence of the character of the North-American institutions, as superficial observers think, but is simply a survival of puritanism, which is waning year after year. It is well known that the New England states were founded by the Puritans, who regarded luxury as a sin. Thirdly, even among the descendants of the Puritans restriction does not by any means exist to the degree assumed by credulous people who take the words uttered by rich misers at their face value. Misers everywhere look for pretexts to excuse their miserliness; usually they complain about being short of money, about the hard times, and in the New England states they have found another excuse—the alleged restriction imposed by some sort of a tradition, which has already practically ceased to exist.

If it was necessary to speak of public despotism in the United States, reference should have been made not to this insignificant feature of the moribund past, but to another fact which at the present time is creating such great turmoil in the United States. In those parts where slavery still exists, public opinion, which is dominated by the planters, does not permit the utterance of a single word that even hints at abolition. People who speak against slavery are robbed, outcast and treated as criminals. But it is sufficient to say that in that half of the Union, in the Southern, or slave, states, the aristocracy dominates. All power is practically in the hands of several tens of thousands of rich planters who keep not only their Negroes, but also the mass of the white population of these states in ignorance and poverty. It is well known that all the land in Virginia and in the other old slave states, belongs to the descendants of the old nobility who received it as grants in the reign of the Stuarts. They gradually extended their possessions to those parts of the country where new slave states were founded. They maintain gangs of ruffians like the notorious Walker. In general, the difference between the southern and northern halves of the United States is greater than the difference between Naples and Switzerland. It is only recently that the Northern (free) states have begun to realize that it is the aristocrats of the Southern (slave) states who have been up till now dominating the Union; and the fundamental idea underlying the struggle between the abolitionists and the planters is that the democracy that prevails in the Northern states wants to wrest political power in the Union out of the hands of the aristocratic planters.*

---

* In North America, many words pertaining to political life are used in a sense different from that in which they are used in Europe. This gives rise to the extremely numerous mistakes Europeans make in their judgment of North-American affairs. The abolitionists,

Western Europe is very rich in political experiments, in political theories, says Mr. Lavrov; but what has she come to after paying so dearly for experiments and exerting so much mental effort in appraising them? Only to a feeling of discontent with her present and of fear for her future. "Everywhere there is nothing but criticism; hopes, which only recently bubbled with such force, have waned; the future frightens everybody." Mr. Lavrov supports this deduction with passages from Jules Simon, Mill, and from the author of the book entitled *De la Justice*.[3] We shall not discuss Jules Simon's opinion, but we draw attention to the views of the two other authors Mr. Lavrov quotes, because these men are really very wise, and absolutely honest.

We have great respect for Mill; he is one of the most powerful thinkers of the present epoch, and the most powerful thinker among the economists who have remained faithful to the teachings of Adam Smith. Incidentally, this last recommendation would not in itself be a true measure of the man's intellectual faculties, because this trend of political economy has no other men at all strong in logic. But speaking, not in comparison with the other economists of the Smithonian school, with whom it is indecent to compare great minds, but in comparison with scholars in general in all sciences, it may be said that Mill belongs to the category of those second-rank, but, for all that, very remarkable thinkers, whose intellectual faculties we shall most clearly define by saying that they are as great as, for example, the poetical talent of the best of our modern fiction writers. Mr. Pisemsky, for example, is by no means a Gogol, but for all that, his talent is out of the ordinary. Similarly, Mill does not by a long way come up to the level of Adam Smith, or Hegel, or Lavoisier—men who have introduced new

who, according to European conceptions, ought to be called democrats, are now simply called republicans in North America. Their opponents, the aristocrats, have usurped the name democrats. This is not the place to explain how this conversion of names took place; we mention it only in order that the reader may see that in ascribing an aristocratic character to the defenders of slavery in the United States we have not forgotten the name democrats, which they have falsely usurped. Such a conversion of the meaning of political terms is very often met with also in European history. For example, in France, at the end of the last century, the republicans called themselves patriots, and in Germany, at the beginning of the present century, this very name was adopted by the defenders of feudal institutions.

fundamental ideas in science; but fairly independently
to develop ideas that are already prevalent, to take several
steps forward in the direction indicated by others—is
the work of men like Mill. They are deserving of great respect. Let us, then, see what Mill says, and why he says it.

He can be characterized by means of a certain event that
occurred recently. The reader knows that in England, today,
they are discussing the question of widening the franchise.
Even the most conservative people agree that this is inevitable. They are doing all in their power to stave it off, to
restrict it; they talk about the risks incurred by big changes,
about the dangers that threaten the Constitution; but they
admit that some concession must be made. At the beginning
of last year, when people's minds, not yet greatly distracted by foreign affairs, were very much engaged with Franchise reform, Mill published a pamphlet, and also a letter, in
which he explained that before rights are granted to people
of a particular class, an exact scientific investigation ought
to be made of the mental, moral and political qualities of
the people of that class. We do not know, he said, what the
political convictions are of the various categories of artisans,
small shopkeepers and other people who do not now enjoy
the franchise: whom they will elect as their representatives,
to what path their representatives will lead the House of
Commons. But the principal subject of his remarks was
the question of substituting secret for open ballot. The conservatives say that open ballot develops civic courage,
frankness and all sorts of other virtues, whereas secret ballot
is needed only by cowards who had better keep out of public affairs until they have acquired civic courage, or by
dishonest people who will promise to vote for one candidate
and actually vote for another. All the progressives, on the
contrary, are demanding secret ballot and argue that this
alone can safeguard the independence of the voter. Mill,
although a great progressive himself in theory, did not hesitate to say that he did not share the opinions of his political friends on this point. This does him all the more honour
as a man, because he had held a different opinion before
and now, with noble frankness, he openly says that he feels
obliged to abandon his former opinion because of its unsoundness. Did the publication of this pamphlet, over which all
the conservatives went into raptures, mean that Mill had
ceased to be a progressive? No, in theory he still stands for

granting the suffrage to all adult persons; in this he goes even further than the Chartists and argues that the suffrage should also be granted to women, whereas even the Chartists advocate only manhood suffrage. But the point is that Mill approaches this vital question with the ideal desire to proceed along what is indeed the best path from the scientific point of view: before introducing a reform it is, of course, necessary to collect the best and fullest data concerning the quality of the object to be affected by the reform in order to be able to forecast its results with mathematical precision. This is what is done, for example, in tariff reform: it is calculated to the last kopek how much customs revenue will drop in the first year as a result of the reduction of tariffs, and how quickly they will begin to grow later, how many years it will take to reach a certain figure, etc. Mill wanted parliamentary reform to be carried out in the same wise and circumspect way. No statistics have been collected showing how many honest and by no means cowardly people have been placed by their material circumstances in such dependence that with open ballot, they either do not go to the polls at all, or, if they do go, they do not vote for the candidate whom in their hearts they prefer. Such data have not been collected, and so, after pondering over the matter for many years, Mill at last decided that there were insufficient grounds for preferring secret to open ballot. If, however, proof were collected, sufficient to convert the progressives' preference for secret ballot into a scientific truth, Mill would be very glad to share the wishes of his political friends. In short, in his pamphlet he appeared as a very honest man and as much a progressive as he had been before, only he advanced impractical demands. Why did he do so? Simply because of his excessively strong desire that the development of social life should proceed on absolutely rational lines. This does not happen in important affairs either in the life of an individual or in the life of a nation. Only minor things are done quite coolly, calmly, deliberately and rationally. See how deliberately and thoughtfully a man chooses the young lady who is to be his partner in a quadrille or mazurka, how keenly he weighs up her beauty, her attire, pleasantness in conversation and lightfootedness in dancing before he goes up to her to invite her to dance with him. But that is because this is not an important matter to him. Will he behave in the same way in choosing a wife? It is a well-known fact that nearly all decent people become engaged without knowing how it happened: the swain loses his head, he blurts out the words—and the thing is done. True, very many men choose their wives deliberately and thoughtfully, but that happens only in those cases when marriage is simply a matter of convenience for the person who decides to marry, i.e., something just a little more important than choosing a comfortable apartment, or a good cook. Even people who marry for purely selfish motives only too often make an unwise choice, i.e., those whose desire to get rich reaches the point of passion. Where passion enters, deliberation and coolness are impossible—this is a truth well known from copybook maxims. It is also well known that every important public question rouses passion. If a reform affects only a small section of society, or, though affecting all interests it involves only a small gain or loss for each, in short, if a reform is not very important, it can be carried through calmly. For example, the duty on tea, or sugar, was reduced in England without any fuss or excitement. Who would want to get excited over a reduction of a few pence in the price of a pound of tea, or of a few shillings in the price of a hundredweight of sugar? Everybody was pleased to be able to save fifteen or twenty shillings a year as a result of it; but nobody felt it necessary to get excited over such a trifle. The reform caused no loss to anybody. But another reform, also a useful one, caused great loss to the English shipowners. This was the repeal of the Navigation Act, under which goods carried in English ships enjoyed preferential duties in English ports, compared with those carried in foreign ships. The shipowners were furious at the time, and they are still burning with resentment and demanding the reintroduction of the Navigation Act. But shipowners constitute only an insignificant part of the merchant class, which, except for the former, gained a great deal by the reform. The people who were angry about it were powerless, and therefore, the public was quite calm about it. But was this the case with the repeal of the Corn Laws, when people who were strong in English society lost a privilege? The reader knows that those who wanted this useful reform succeeded in vanquishing the powerful opposition only when passion was roused among the majority in society, who gained a great deal from this valuable re-

form; and when society is disturbed by passion, the cool
passing of a reform is impossible. Did Robert Peel have
time to indulge in long years of statistical investigation
when the reform became inevitable? No, he made use of
whatever data were available, the situation brooked no
delay. But this was not quite rational. Who can tell? Perhaps, if the matter had been gone into more deeply, some
of the details of the law might have been drafted better
Perhaps it would have been possible fully to achieve the
aim without damaging the interests of the numerous opponents of the reform, who really suffered loss by it. Of course,
that may have been the case, but things that are very
important for society are never done that way. See how
feudalism was abolished, or how the Inquisition was destroyed, or how the middle class won its rights, or, in general,
how any great evil was abolished, or how any important
beneficial reform was introduced. Mill understands this
very well as a scientific truth, as a general principle of
historical development; but when he saw this principle
being put into practice he caught fright and began to talk
God knows what. Why was a man who clearly understood
a principle, and bravely advocated it, frightened by a fact
begotten of this principle? Because the impression created
by an abstract idea is different from that created by a fact
which affects the senses. A tangible object has a much
stronger effect than the abstract conception of that object.
A man who calmly considers what he will do under given
circumstances rarely retains all his coolness when those
circumstances actually arise, if the matter is at all important. If it is a pleasant matter, then at the first symptoms
of its approach we are overcome by pleasurable excitement. If it is unpleasant, we are filled with foreboding.
These feelings are roused so easily that often they are
due simply to the fact that our senses deceive us: no real
signs are apparent yet, but we already rejoice or grieve
owing to our inclination to perceive in everything traces
of the matter that interests us, and we take as signs of the
approaching fact things that actually have no relation to
it. That is why every political party constantly sees the approach of its ideal, each interpreting in its own way the
same phenomena as signs of changes that are the direct
opposite of each other. Be that as it may, whether expec-
tations of great changes are justified or not, whether the

people interested in them look forward to them with joy or with sorrow, the fact remains that their judgment of them, right or wrong, cannot possibly be a cool one. We have seen with what feelings Mill met the actual signs of the approach of parliamentary reform, the necessity of which he himself had admitted in theory. In the abstract, he is in favour of it, but the fact filled him with some apprehension. This shows that, in essence, the change is unpleasant to him personally, that although he had the moral courage to fight down this feeling in theory, he did not find the strength to vanquish the stronger impression created by the fact.

We can now turn to the general appraisal of the state of affairs in Western Europe, which Mr. Lavrov takes from Mill. "The modern *régime* of public opinion is, in an unorganized form, what the Chinese educational and political systems are in an organized; and unless individuality shall be able successfully to assert itself against this yoke, Europe, notwithstanding its noble antecedents and its professed Christianity, will tend to become another China." Many people in our country, taking these words at their face value, gladly clutched at them; others were grieved by them. Western Europe is slipping into the condition of China, it is no longer able to work out new forms of life, it will only complete the systematic construction of the old forms, which are already unsatisfactory; the needs of the present day that are incompatible with those forms will be suppressed by tradition, and all over the West there will be enthroned the uniform and methodical compulsory routine such as we see in China. This is what is said by even the best of our people, and they point to Mill's gloomy verdict as very strong confirmation of this.[4] But it is easy to see what confidence can be placed in matters like these in the judgment of a man who was frightened even by such a partial change as parliamentary reform, and, moreover, a change of such moderate dimensions as that demanded by even the radical party in Parliament represented by Bright, who, by the by, has no hope of realizing his proposals even in the most modified and moderate form. Since Mill was frightened by parliamentary reform, can he be expected to judge calmly the signs of the change that is striving to encompass the whole of public and private life in Western Europe, to change all institutions and customs, beginning with the form of the state down to family relationships

and economic conditions? What is there surprising in the
fact that the signs of such a tremendous change obscure the
cold clarity of judgment of a man who can without trembling
analyze abstract concepts, but who dislikes the facts that
correspond to these concepts? In the words of Mill that
Mr. Lavrov quotes we see not an analysis of the essence of the
matter, but only the impression created by this matter
on a man who, although of noble trend of mind, personally
belongs to the classes which anticipate loss to themselves
from a change that is beneficial for society as a whole.
When he says: Western Europe is in a state of crisis, the
outcome of which is doubtful; that to avert this crisis,
to stop development, to go back to the past is impossible,
but nobody can tell how the crisis will end: whether it will
lead Western Europe to the development of higher forms
of life or to the condition of China, to despotism in the guise
of freedom, to stagnation in the guise of progress, to barbar-
ism in the guise of civilization—when he says this, it
reminds us of the feelings and statements of the honest
section of the English landlords at the time of the repeal
of the Corn Laws. Those landlords who were of a noble trend
of mind also said at the time: Yes, we see that it is necessary to repeal the Corn Laws; all resistance will be useless
and can only enhance the victory of Cobden and his friends;
but what will this inevitable change lead to? Will it not
kill English agriculture? Will it not ruin our class? That
would not be the worst; we would bear our misfortune un-
complainingly. But will it not also ruin the farmers and
reduce the millions of rural labourers who plough the farmers' fields to pauperism and starvation? These people
spoke in earnest, but facts proved that their gloomy doubts
were unwarranted, and it was evident to the outsider from
the very beginning that these fears for the future were suggested to these people by the fact that the change was to
the disadvantage of the class to which they belonged. Mill's
fears for the future of Western Europe are of exactly the
same origin: his doubt concerning the future fate of the
civilized countries is no more than the elevation to a formula of his personal foreboding that the further development of civilization will reduce the privileges appropriated
by the class to which he himself belongs. The outsider can
very clearly see the unsoundness of the syllogism that converts the loss of privileges into a danger to society as a whole.

In Mill we see a reflection of the feelings with which noble-minded people of the wealthy classes in Western Europe are meeting the forthcoming changes in social relations. No less interesting are the views of the other thinker, who represents the mental state of the common people of Western Europe. The author of *De la Justice* was the son of a village cooper—not the master of a big yard—no, an ordinary peasant, working alone, without any hired workers, knocking hoops on peasants' barrels, and living as poorly as all the peasants in his village. In his boyhood, the thinker partly worked as a shepherd, and partly helped his father to knock hoops on barrels. Some kind people belonging to the wealthy class perceived the boy's intelligence and helped his father to send him to school in Besançon. But the pupil had no money with which to buy books, so he borrowed his schoolmates' books and hurried through his lessons in the classroom a few minutes before the lessons began. His family's poverty soon forced him to leave school and go back to work. At the age of eighteen he managed to get a place as a compositor at a printing office in Besançon; after several years he became a proofreader and later reached the position of manager. And so fifteen years passed; the young compositor read books, thought, tried to write something himself, and for one of his compositions received a three-years' scholarship of 1,500 francs from the Besançon Academy (a Literary Society). This helped him in his studies. He continued to write while remaining a printer; but the Besançon Academy now rejected his compositions, for it perceived the disloyal trend of thought revealed by the pupil who had at first seemed to hold the most conservative opinions. Later, the author, who had proved to be very capable in handling commercial affairs, obtained a situation as commissioner (manager) in the office of Gautier Brothers, land and water transport agents in Lyons. He served in this office until the year 1848, which provided him with the opportunity to obtain a livelihood by his writing alone. As manager of Gautiers' office he proved to be an efficient and practical businessman and raised the firm he served to a flourishing state. This external side of the life of the author of *De la Justice* is a true reflection of the general relations of the common people in the West in their working careers. The common people must extricate themselves from the most wretched conditions. The wealthy classes are at first moved to pity at the sight of intelligent, honest and industrious people living in hopeless poverty and degradation. Out of pure human kindness the great help their less fortunate brothers. Thanks to the charitable concern of well-to-do people, the son of a poor artisan, shepherd and cooper's apprentice goes to school and enters the road that leads him to honour and out of poverty. But, praiseworthy though it is, this assistance is inadequate; humane though it is, this concern is not sufficiently close. The boy is left without a crust of bread before reaching manhood, he must leave the road to a good position in society and go back to drudgery in order to provide food for himself and his family. Much strength and time is wasted in toiling as a day labourer, living from hand to mouth, working fourteen hours a day in order to obtain irregular and scanty food. The youth's natural talents are great, however; he has not yet learned anything, but he knows, at all events, that only learning can save him. He will not abandon intellectual work no matter how straitened his circumstances may be. Besides, he wants to know the truth. In addition to the material need of knowledge, his sense of inquiry is already developed. And so, sacrificing sleep, pleasure and even rest, he sits up reading for an hour, or half an hour, every night, no matter how hard he had been working at his drudgery during the day. In this way he learns much, but he thinks much more. Even while his hands are engaged in drudgery, his mind is taken up with general human problems and with the problems of the conditions of the whole class to which he belongs. This is a long and painful road. It takes him fifteen years to acquire knowledge which under better conditions he could have acquired in two or three years. But this gives him time to ponder deeply over all he learns and his mind acquires great penetration. At last he knows all that learned people know, but his judgment is clearer than theirs. He can tell them things worthy of their attention. There is something new in his ideas, because they were engendered by a life of which the classes to which learned people belong have no experience. At first these new thoughts please the learned men in respectable society in the same way as they had been pleased by the gifted village lad. They encourage his labours, he continues his intellectual occupations, he develops his ideas. But at last his patrons awaken to the fact that there is a pernicious

side to his thoughts, which at first had seemed so innocuous
to them. Their former rather proud sympathy for him
gives way to suspicion, which grows, is confirmed, develops
into positive dislike and then into hatred because of his pernicious trend of thought, of his dangerous strivings. He is
cast out by all who occupy a good position in society, he
is subjected to persecution. But too late: he no longer needs
patronage, he is already stronger than his persecutors, he
is a celebrity, and everybody fears him, for he crushes everybody against whom he is compelled to raise his hand. This
biography of a single individual is the history of the class
to which he belongs.

This individual is interesting as a complete illustration
of the intellectual position that is reached by a plebeian in
the West. Passing to his theories, we find that all their
aspects, including their defects, reflect the history of his
development. He is self-taught; what books did he learn
from? Did he know what books to choose, did he know to
which doctrines he should turn his attention as really modern doctrines? No, he learned from the books that chanced
to come his way, and chance books are mostly books written in the spirit of theories that are already predominant in
society, that is to say, theories that are rather old and to
a large degree obsolete. Such is the lot of every self-educated
man. If anyone of us who has not studied chemistry, for
example, took it into his head to take up the study of this
science now without the assistance of good guides, he would
in all probability take either the school textbooks that are
merely receptacles for all sorts of rubbish, or the books
written by celebrities in chemistry whose fame is already
widespread in society: Liebig, perhaps, or even old Berzelius. But people who are familiar with chemistry at its
present level say that the conceptions not only of Berzelius,
but also of Liebig, are already obsolete and are of no use
as a guide for a man who wants to study modern chemistry,
that this science must now be studied from other writers,
and that Liebig's books can serve now only for reference,
and only for a man who has already assimilated other views
on the subject.

Mr. Lavrov is interested in the philosophical aspect of
the system propounded by the author of *De la Justice*,
and we too will here devote attention to this aspect, although
his books are much more important for economic science

than for philosophy. The author of *De la Justice* has a great advantage over his rival French philosophers in that he is familiar with German philosophy. It cannot be said that any other French philosopher possesses this knowledge. It is said that Cousin had studied Schelling and Hegel, but both were of the opinion that he had totally failed to grasp the spirit of their doctrines and that in the guise of their systems he conjured up a lot of nonsense which in his head constituted a jumble of unintelligible German terms and principles that contradicted not only German philosophy, but the spirit of scientific research in general. The French celebrities in philosophy who followed Cousin remained, like him, alien to the spirit of the great German thinkers, or were even totally unacquainted with them. This cannot be said about the author of *De la Justice*. He is deeply imbued with the principles of German philosophy. We have read that he did not know German. Even if this is true, it is of no importance. Belinsky did not know German, but his knowledge of German philosophy was such that even in Germany you could not find ten men who understand it as deeply and as clearly as he did. We have heard that the chief source from which the author of *De la Justice* obtained his knowledge of this science was similar to that from which Belinsky had acquired his knowledge of it, namely, conversations with people who had studied German philosophy. It is even said that the people concerned were the same. [5] It may be supposed that this information is correct. Be that as it may, Proudhon is imbued with the spirit of German philosophy. This is one of his strong sides. It must be added that his knowledge of this philosophy is also one of the reasons for the unsatisfactory nature, or at all events, the vagueness of his concepts, namely, the fact that he learned German philosophy in the form of Hegel's system and halted at this system as the final deduction, whereas science in Germany has developed further. Hegel's system, which is imbued with the spirit that dominated public opinion at the time of the Restoration and had come into being during the First Empire, in itself no longer corresponds to the present state of knowledge. And it must also be added that Hegel, either because of his nature, or, perhaps, deliberately, clothed his principles in very conservative habiliments when he discussed political or theological subjects. The brave French plebeian, having assimilated Hegel's method, could not remain satisfied with his deductions and began to seek a development for his principles that would be more in keeping with their spirit and with his own trend of thought than Hegel's had been. Had he been familiar with the later development of science in Germany he would have found what he sought; but he lacked this aid and was left to his own resources. The history of his intellectual development, however, prevented him from preserving, or acquiring, those mental qualities that are needed for building an integral and homogeneous philosophical system. He had read too many of the new French philosophers before he became a pupil of Hegel's. While altering his system, he too often came under the influence of the ideas to which he had become habituated from the French books. Thus, his own system consisted of a combination of Hegel's philosophy and the concepts of the French philosophers, which often lacked scientific spirit. All through it one sees evidence of an extremely powerful mind, but one also too often sees that this mind was shackled by views that lacked scientific foundation. The result of these unfavourable conditions was obscurity. He himself was conscious of this and tried to escape from it by passionate outbursts of hatred for tradition, which had shackled him against his will, or by efforts to give that tradition a rational meaning.

In all this we see again the common features of the intellectual position in which the West-European plebeian finds himself. Thanks to his robust nature and to his stern experience of life, the West-European plebeian understands the essence of things much better, more correctly, and more deeply than people of the more fortunate classes. But he has not yet grasped the scientific concepts which correspond most to his position, inclinations and needs, and, we think, that correspond most to the truth, but at all events to the present state of knowledge. Being unacquainted with these concepts, he was obliged to learn from books that were positively bad, or else obsolete, and remain under the influence of the mistaken opinions that prevailed among so-called educated people, among whom only that which is already obsolete in science gains predominance. He was obliged to exhaust his strength combating prejudices that had already been exposed by truly modern science with which he was not yet acquainted, or else to yield to these prejudices, to pass from anger against them to submission to them, instead of coolly brushing them aside as exposed lies no longer dangerous to him once he realized that they were utter nonsense.

That is why we think that neither the author of *De la Justice* nor Mill can serve as authorities in philosophy. Both are extremely important for a man who wants to ascertain the trend of thought among certain classes in West-European society; from Mill he will learn that the noble-minded section of the privileged classes in Western Europe is greatly disturbed when it sees the realization of the very ideas, the theoretical correctness of which it defends, regards as logically irresistible and as being beneficial for society as a whole, but disadvantageous for these classes. The author of *De la Justice* shows that plebeians thirsting for change are hindered in achieving it by the fact that they were educated in the spirit of obsolete concepts and had not yet become acquainted with the views that corre-spond to their needs. But neither Mill nor Proudhon can be regarded as representatives of these views which modern science has developed.* Now, as in the past, its true rep-resentatives must be sought in Germany. We may be mis-taken, but it seems to us that Mr. Lavrov was obliged to seek by his own efforts solutions which had already been found by present-day German philosophy. It seems to us that before becoming acquainted with the latest German thinkers he studied the obsolete forms of German philosophy and books written by English and French thinkers, and that, had it been otherwise, had he read the books he read first several years later, and had he read several years earlier those books he read when his mental work in building his trend of thought was already finished, he would have writ-ten somewhat differently. We do not say that he would

---

* Of course, when we say that Mill is not a representative of modern philosophy, we mean in particular that section of science which among us is called philosophy—the theory of the solution of the most general problems of science that are usually called meta-physics, for example, problems of the relation between spirit and mat-ter, free will, immortality of the soul, etc. Mill has not even directly studied this part of science. He deliberately refrains from expressing any opinion on these subjects, as if he regarded them as being beyond the limits of exact investigation. Properly speaking, he is not a phi-losopher in the sense that we call Kant or Hegel philosophers, but do not call Cuvier or Liebig such (in English, Cuvier and Liebig are also called philosophers).

have arrived at different views—we think that, in essence, his views are correct—but they would have presented themselves to him in a simpler form. Perhaps we have not put it correctly and should have said: he would more certainly have found that the lie he rejects is absolutely hollow, capable only of calling forth a pitiful smile, but not serious reflection about whether it can be rejected absolutely. It is quite possible that the conviction that truth is simple and that the rupture that has taken place between modern views and the empty sophistry in which the crude ancient lies were clothed is absolutely justified, would have found reflection in his mode of exposition, which would have been more intelligible to the majority of the public. Perhaps his essays, which everybody now respects, would be read more by that section of the public which is too prone to leave unread books and essays which inspire it with too much awe. Without entering into a criticism of Mr. Lavrov's views, we shall attempt to expound our own views on these same subjects. We think that, in essence, they are in keeping with Mr. Lavrov's line of thought; the difference will lie almost exclusively in the mode of exposition and presentation of the problem.

That part of philosophy which deals with the problems of man, just like the other part which deals with the problems of external nature, is based on the natural sciences. The principle underlying the philosophical view of human life and all its phenomena is the idea, worked out by the natural sciences, of the unity of the human organism; the observations of physiologists, zoologists and medical men have driven away all thought of dualism in man. Philosophy sees him as medicine, physiology and chemistry see him. These sciences prove that no dualism is evident in man, and philosophy adds that if man possessed another nature, in addition to his real nature, this other nature would reveal itself in some way, but since it does not reveal itself in any way, since everything that takes place and manifests itself in man originates solely from his real nature, he cannot have another nature. This proof is beyond doubt. It is as convincing as the grounds on which you, dear reader, are convinced, for example, that at the moment you are reading this book there is no lion in the room in which you are sitting. You think that this is so because you do not see the lion with your eyes, you do not hear

it growl; but is this alone a sufficient guarantee that there
is no lion in your room? No, you have a second guarantee:
this guarantee is the fact that you are alive. Had there
been a lion in your room it would have sprung upon you
and would have torn you to pieces. The inevitable consequences of the presence of a lion in your room are absent,
and therefore you know that there is no lion there. Tell us,
also: why are you convinced that a dog cannot speak? You
have never heard it speak; but that in itself would not be
sufficient. You have seen many people who did not speak
at the time you saw them. It was not that they could not
speak, but that they did not wish to do so. Perhaps a dog
too does not speak because it does not wish to and not because it cannot do so? That is what is actually believed by
people of low mental development who believe the fables
in which animals are made to speak. They explain their
assumption in the following way: the dog is a very clever
and cunning animal, it knows that speech often leads to
trouble and so it keeps quiet, calculating that silence is
safer than speech. You laugh at this ingenious explanation
and have a simpler one: you have had occasion to see dogs
when they could not have refrained from speaking had they
been able to do so. For example, when a dog is beaten, it
howls with all its might; it is obvious that it cannot restrain
itself from expressing the thought that it is in pain, that
it is being treated cruelly. It seeks every means to express
this, but finds only one—to howl, but it cannot utter
any words. That shows that it lacks the gift of speech. Had
it possessed that gift, it would have behaved differently.
We are given the circumstances in which the presence of
a certain element would inevitably have led to a certain
result; that result is absent, hence, the element is absent.
Let us take another case. How do you know that Mr. Hume,
whose conjuring tricks created such a furore in St. Petersburg a couple of years ago, is really only a conjurer and
cannot foretell the future, cannot know secrets that have
not been divulged to him, cannot read books and papers
that are not in front of his eyes? You know it because, were
it possible for him to foretell the future, he would have
been appointed diplomatic adviser at some court and would
have told the ministry of that court in advance everything
that would happen in given circumstances. For example, he
would have told Rechberg last March that if the Austrians

went to war they would be defeated at Palestro, Magenta and Solferino, and would lose Lombardy.[6] The Austrians would then not have gone to war, and all the things that happened in Italy, France and Austria last year would not have occurred, and something entirely different would have happened. If he could read books that are not in front of his eyes, governments and scientific societies would not send their scientists to the Orient to search for ancient manuscripts, but would turn to him, and he, from Paris, would read and dictate to them the work of some still unknown ancient Greek writer whose manuscript has survived in some remote part of Syria. But it is not so. Mr. Hume and his fellows in the art have revealed nothing either to the diplomats or to the scientists. They certainly would have communicated important things to them had they been able to do so, because this would have been ever so much more profitable and honourable than conjuring. Hence, they do not possess the abilities credulous people ascribe to them. Concerning all these cases, it is not enough to say: we do not know whether a certain element exists. No, reason compels us to say outright: we know that this element does not exist, for, if it existed, something would have happened different from what is happening now.

But while there is unity in man's nature, we see in man two categories of phenomena: phenomena of what is called a material order (a man eats, walks), and phenomena of what is called a moral order (a man thinks, feels, wishes). In what relation do these two orders of phenomena stand to one another? Does not the difference between them contradict the unity of man's nature that is demonstrated by the natural sciences? The natural sciences answer that there are no grounds for such a hypothesis, for there is no object that possesses only one quality. On the contrary, every object displays an incalculable number of different phenomena which, for convenience, we place in different categories, calling each category a quality, so that every object has numerous qualities of different kinds. For example, wood grows, and it burns; we say that it possesses two qualities: vegetative power, and combustibility. Is there any resemblance between these two qualities? They are entirely different; there is no concept that can cover both these qualities except the general concept—quality. There is no concept to cover both categories of phenomena except the concept—

phenomenon. Or, for example, ice is hard and bright. What is there in common between hardness and brightness? The logical distance between these two qualities is immeasurable, or it would be more correct to say that there is no logical distance between them, short or long, because there is no logical relation between them. This shows that the combination of heterogeneous properties in one object is the general law of things. But in this diversity the natural sciences also discover connection—not in the forms of manifestation, not in the phenomena, which are totally unlike each other, but in the way the diverse phenomena originate from the same element during the strain and relaxation of the energy of its action. For example, water has the property of having temperature—a property common to all bodies. No matter what the property of bodies that we call heat may consist in, under different circumstances it reveals itself in extremely diverse degrees. Sometimes a given object is cold, that is to say, it reveals very little heat. Sometimes it is very hot, that is to say, it reveals very much more heat. When water, no matter under what circumstances, reveals very little heat, it is a solid—ice. When it reveals slightly more heat it is liquid. And when there is very much heat in it, it becomes vapour. In these three states, the same quality reveals itself in three categories of totally different phenomena, so that one quality assumes the forms of three different qualities, it branches off into three qualities simply according to the different quantities in which it is revealed: quantitative difference passes into qualitative difference.

But different objects differ from one another by their ability to exhibit a quality common to them all in very different quantities. For example, iron, silver, and gold exhibit a very considerable quantity of the quality that is called gravity, which here, on earth, is measured by weight. Air exhibits this quality in such a small quantity that it was discovered only by special scientific research, and whoever is unacquainted with science necessarily supposes that air has no weight. The same was thought about all gaseous bodies. Let us take another quality—the ability to contract under pressure. Without the special means of analysis provided only by science, nobody will notice that liquids contract under any pressure. Indeed, it seems as though water completely retains its former volume under the strongest pressure. But science has discovered facts which show that even water contracts to some degree under pressure. From this it must be concluded that when a body seems to us to be devoid of a particular quality, scientific analysis must be employed to test this impression, and if this analysis shows that the body does possess this quality, then we must not stubbornly reiterate: our senses, not equipped with the weapons of science, tell us the opposite. We must simply say: the result obtained by an investigation of the object with the proper scientific means shows the unsatisfactory nature of the impression obtained by the senses which lack the necessary aids for this purpose.

On the other hand, when it seems to us that a certain object possesses some special quality which is totally absent in other objects, it is also necessary to make a scientific investigation. For example, it seems to us that wood possesses a very distinct property not possessed by the majority of other bodies: it burns, whereas stone, clay and iron do not burn. But when we investigate the process known as combustion by scientific means we find that it consists in the combination of several of the elements of certain bodies with oxygen. At the same time science shows that exactly the same process of combination of all or some of the components with oxygen is constantly taking place in the majority of the so-called noncombustible bodies. For example, iron is constantly being oxidized —in ordinary language this form of the process is referred to by the special term "rust"; but science reveals that rusting and combustion are exactly the same process, and that we get the impression that these two cases of it are different because in one case the process is far more rapid and intense than in the other.

Why, then, do different objects exhibit a certain quality with different degrees of intensity under equal conditions? Why does a stone under ordinary, everyday conditions exhibit to a very strong degree the quality known as weight, whereas in air, this quality can be discovered only with the aid of special scientific means which magnify the power of our senses? Why does the oxidation of iron in an ordinary atmosphere take place much slower than the oxidation of wood when both objects are placed in the same hot furnace? Science tells us that it has not yet managed to investigate the laws that govern this difference in the few bodies that remain in chemistry under the name of simple bodies, but that in all the other bodies that it has been able to decompose, this difference is due to the different composition or different states of the component parts of the compound bodies. For example, the difference between water and oil, or between vapour and stone, corresponds to the difference in the composition of these bodies. The difference between coal and diamond is that the component parts of coal are in an uncrystallized state, whereas the component parts of diamond are in a crystallized state. The natural sciences also point out that simple bodies, or compound bodies composed of them, on chemically combining, form a body which exhibits qualities not revealed by its component parts before they were combined. For example, the combination in certain proportions of hydrogen and oxygen forms water, which possesses many qualities that were not observed in the oxygen or in the hydrogen. Concerning these compounds, chemistry tells us that the more complicated ones are, in general, distinguished for their greater mutability, mobility, so to speak. For example, iron rust, which consists only of a combination of iron and oxygen in a very simple proportion, is very constant, so that extremely high temperature, or extremely strong reagents, must be used to cause a change in that body. But a blood corpuscle, of which iron oxide is only one of the elements in a complicated chemical compound containing admixtures of different other bodies, water, for example, cannot preserve its composition long: it may be said that it does not exist in a constant form like the particles of rust, but is always changing, acquiring new particles and losing old ones. The same must be said about all complicated chemical compounds: they show a very strong tendency to exist by constant birth, growth and renewal, and they finally perish under ordinary circumstances, so that the existence of an object consisting of such compounds is a ceaseless renewal of parts and represents a continuous chemical process.

Complicated chemical compounds possessing this character reveal it equally, irrespective of whether they are in so-called organic bodies or arise and exist outside of them in so-called inorganic nature. Not so very long ago it seemed that the so-called organic substances (for example, acetic acid) existed only in organic bodies. It is now known, however, that under certain circumstances they arise also outside of organic bodies, so that the difference between an organic and an inorganic combination of elements is insignificant. The so-called organic compounds arise and exist in conformity with the same laws, and all equally arise out of inorganic substances. For example, wood differs from an inorganic acid in that this acid is not a complicated compound, whereas wood is a combination of numerous complex compounds. It is, as it were, the difference between 2 and 200—a quantitative difference, not more.

Thus, the natural sciences regard the life of an organic body, such as a plant or an insect, as a chemical process. Concerning this phenomenon in general, the natural sciences observe that during a chemical process bodies reveal qualities that are totally unobserved when they are in the state of an immobile compound. For example, wood by itself does not burn; tinder and flint also do not burn of themselves. If, however, a particle of steel made red-hot by friction (a blow) with flint falls on the tinder and greatly raises the temperature of some part of this tinder, it creates the conditions necessary for the beginning of the process that is called combustion in this particle of tinder. The latter, drawn into this chemical process, will begin to burn, which it did not do when it was not going through this chemical process. If brought in contact with wood while undergoing this process, it will draw the latter into its process of combustion, and during this process the wood will also burn, radiate light and reveal other qualities that it did not display before the process began. If we take any other process we shall see the same: the bodies going through it will reveal qualities they did not display before the process began. Take, for example, the process of fermentation. The brew in the vat is still; the yeast in the cup is also still. Put the yeast into the vat; a chemical process called fermentation will commence; the brew bubbles, froths, and seethes in the vat. It goes without saying that when we speak of the different states of bodies when going through a chemical process and when they are not going through such a process, we speak only of the quantitative difference between an intense and rapid course of the process and a very slow and feeble course. Properly speaking, every body is constantly in a state of chemical process. For example: if a log is not cut up for firewood and burnt in a stove, but lies quietly, seemingly without change, in

the wall of a house, it will in time reach the same end it
would have reached had it been burnt. It will gradually
decay, and nothing will be left of it but ashes (the dust of
decay, which will in the end leave nothing but the mineral
particles of ash). When this process, for example, the decay
of a log in a wall, is very slow and feeble, the qualities inherent in the body that is going through the process will
be microscopically feeble and quite imperceptible in ordinary life. For example, during the slow decay of the wood
in the wall heat is also engendered, but the quantity that
in the course of combustion would be concentrated within
several hours is here rarefied (if one may so express it)
over several score of years, so that it achieves no result
perceptible in practice. The existence of this heat is too
insignificant for practical consideration. It is the same as
the winy taste of the water in a pond into which a single
drop of wine has been dropped: from the scientific point
of view, that pond contains a mixture of water and wine,
but for practical purposes it must be taken that there is
no wine in the water.

The reader will probably say that all our arguments
are as correct as those to the effect that the earth revolves
round the sun, that it is cold at the poles and hot in the
tropics, and that these arguments have as little to do with
the case as the latter have. The reader will, without a doubt,
be right if he says that we are now indulging in idle talk.
But it is much easier to note a defect in oneself, or agree
with those who point to it, than to rectify it. People, in
general, are prone to flaunt their knowledge of things about
which they really know little; and they are fond of flaunting their fictitious knowledge in and out of season. Why
should we be free from this defect? And if we are afflicted
with it, why should it not reveal itself? Let it, then, reveal
itself while we continue to discuss the natural sciences, which
have little to do with the case, and with which we are little
acquainted, until we get tired of flaunting our ignorance—
and then we shall take up something else, of which, perhaps,
we are also ignorant, say, for example, moral philosophy.
The reader will think to himself: it will not be so easy to
pass from chemistry to social institutions. But is it so difficult to find a phrase that will connect totally unconnect-
able parts of a discussion? When we are prompted by the de
sire to discuss philosophy instead of chemistry, we shall

simply say: "and so, up till now we have been discussing
this ... now we shall discuss this," and that's all; we shall
have passed from one to the other. Do not very celebrated
authorities constantly pass from one subject to another in
this way? They write two sentences that simply will not
hang together, stick "and so," or "consequently," between
them—and the syllogism is ready, and everything is
proved.

We, however, feel that our desire to talk about the
natural sciences, which, as the reader justly observes, have
nothing to do with the case, rather than about philosophy
can last for several more pages, but one difficulty disturbs
us: we have already exhausted our meagre stock of knowledge
about chemical compounds and processes; we have nothing
more to say. Nevertheless, we feel an awful urge to speak,
and this gets us out of our difficulty: it whispers into our
ear: "you have said all you know about one thing, pass on
to the next, whatever subject comes to your mind." We
take this good advice. Let us, then, speak about the kingdoms of nature. Everybody knows something about them,
although some know rather little. We too know something
about them, even though it is rather little, but still, enough
to fill a few pages. But here, the desire to keep away from
the actual subject of discussion for as long as possible, to
go on talking as much as possible about what has nothing
to do with the case, whispers other advice in the other ear:
"of the three kingdoms of nature, mineral, vegetable and
animal, don't for the time being say anything about the
one which alone could provide examples of at least some
analogy with human life, about the life of ants, bees and
beavers. Don't say anything about the animal kingdom."
We take this advice too, although it is obviously absurd;
but one does so many absurd things in one's life that one
more or one less will make absolutely no difference, no more
than the presence of a decaying chip of wood has any effect
on temperature. Let us, then, speak about inorganic nature
and the vegetable kingdom.

We like this new subject, particularly because, apart
from the fact that we know little about it, nothing practical can be said about it, for it itself lacks reality, having
introduced a division in nature that does not exist. It is
only to the uninitiated that rock seems to be one thing
and a plant a totally different kind of thing. Actually, it

is found that both objects, so dissimilar, consist of the same
parts, combined in conformity with the same laws, only
combined in different proportions. When rock is analyzed
it is found that it consists of gases and metals. When a
plant is analyzed, gases and metals are also found in it.
In rocks, the metals are not found in the pure form, but
in various combinations with oxygen. The same applies
to plants. In rocks, each gas is not found separately, but
in various combinations with other gases and metals. The
same applies to plants. Plants consist most of all of parts
that are just bare rock: in living plants this rock accounts
for two thirds or three fourths of their total mass, if not
more. This rock is —water. It differs from the things that are
usually called rock only in that it melts at a very low temperature, whereas ordinary rocks melt only at an exceedingly high temperature. But if melted quartz does not cease
to be quartz, rock, then the mineral which in a melted
state is water (ice), does not cease to be a mineral when
melted. Thus, plants differ from ordinary ores, rocks and
other inorganic bodies only in that they constitute a much
more complex combination of elements and therefore go
through a chemical process in an ordinary atmosphere much
faster than inorganic bodies, and, because of their complexity, go through a much more complicated process. For example,
in inorganic bodies, oxidation of only one kind takes place,
but in plants, oxidation takes place in several degrees simultaneously. Furthermore, in an inorganic body, one or
two elements of its uniform combination are oxidized, whereas in a plant several chemical compounds, each fairly
complex, are oxidized simultaneously. It goes without
saying that, when going through such a rapid and complex
chemical process, a body exhibits qualities that are not
revealed in slower and less complex processes. In short,
the difference between the inorganic kingdom of nature
and the vegetable kingdom is like the difference between
a tiny blade of grass and a huge tree; it is a difference in
quantity, in intensity, in complexity, but not in the fundamental character of the phenomena. A blade of grass
consists of the same parts, and its life is governed by the
same laws, as an oak, except that the oak is much more
complex than the blade of grass. The oak has tens of thousands of leaves, whereas grass has only two or three. Again
it goes without saying that here the similarity exists for

a theoretical knowledge of the odject and not for practical purposes: houses cannot be built with blades of grass, but they can be built from oak trees. In ordinary life we are quite right in regarding ore and plants as belonging to totally different categories of things; but we are also quite right when in ordinary life we regard timber as a thing that belongs to a category different from that of grass. A theoretical analysis brings us to a different result: we find that these things, so different in practical respects, must be regarded only as different states of the same elements which enter into different chemical combinations in conformity with the same laws. To discover the identity between a blade of grass and an oak tree a mental analysis was sufficient without a great stock of observations or precise means of investigation. To discover the similarity between an inorganic thing and a plant, much more mental effort, assisted by much more powerful means of investigation, was required. Chemistry is, perhaps, the greatest glory of our age.

Incidentally, an immense stock of observations and exceptionally precise means of analysis are needed not so much to enable a genius to see a truth, the discovery of which calls for profound thought—it most often happens, at all events in general philosophical problems, that a man with an inquiring and logical mind sees the truth at the first glance. Extensive research and powerful scientific instruments are useful in such cáses because, without them, a truth discovered by a genius remains his own private opinion for which he is unable to bring exact scientific proof and, therefore, it either remains unaccepted by people who cling to their erroneous opinions, or, still worse, perhaps, is accepted by other people not on the basis of reason, but out of blind faith in the words of an authority. The principles that have now been explained and proved by the natural sciences were found and accepted as true by the Greek philosophers, and even much before them by the Indian thinkers. In all probability, they were discovered by men with powerful logical minds in all ages, and among all peoples. But these geniuses of ancient times were unable logically to develop and prove the truth. It was always known everywhere, but it became a science only during the past decades. Nature is compared with a book which contains the whole truth, but in a language which has to be learnt if one is to understand the book. Using this simile, we shall say that it is quite easy to learn any language sufficiently to be able to understand the books that are written in it. Hard and long study, however, is needed to be able to remove all doubts about the correctness of the meaning we ascribe to the words in the book, to be able to explain every expression in it, and to write a good grammar of this language.

The unity of the laws of nature was understood by geniuses long ago; but only during the last decades has our knowledge reached such dimensions as to prove scientifically the correctness of this interpretation of the phenomena of nature.

It is said that the natural sciences have not reached such a degree of development as to provide a satisfactory explanation of all the important phenomena of nature. This is quite true; but the opponents of the scientific trend in philosophy draw from this truth a totally illogical deduction when they say that the gaps left in the scientific explanation of natural phenomena justify the preservation of certain remnants of the fantastic world outlook. The fact is that the results achieved by analysis of the parts and phenomena that have been explained by science are sufficient evidence of the character of the elements, forces and laws that operate in the other parts and phenomena which have not yet been fully explained. If there were anything in the unexplained parts and phenomena different from what has been found in the explained parts, then the explained parts would not bear the character they bear now. Let us take any branch of the natural sciences, say geography, or geology, and see what character the knowledge we have not yet acquired about various parts of the subject investigated by these sciences *can* have, and what character it cannot have. At the present stage of development of geography we still lack satisfactory information about the countries near the poles, about the interior of Africa, about the interior of Australia. Undoubtedly, these gaps in geographical knowledge are very deplorable for science and, no doubt, it is necessary to fill them even for the purposes of practical life, because it is quite possible that something new and useful for life will be found in these countries. It is quite possible that in the interior of Australia new gold and ore deposits will be found richer than those found on the coast. It is quite possible that in the interior of Africa all kinds of new

minerals, new plants, new meteorological phenomena will
be found. All this is quite possible, and until these countries
are thoroughly explored we cannot say exactly what things
and phenomena will be found there. But we can already say
for certain what things and what phenomena will not be
found there. Near the poles, for example, a hot climate and
luxuriant vegetation will not be found. This negative deduction is beyond doubt, because if the mean temperature
at the poles were high, or even moderate, the northern part
of Siberia, the northern part of the British possessions in
America and the seas adjacent to the poles would not be
in the state they are in now. In Central Africa arctic cold
will not be found, because, if the climate in the central
part of the African continent were cold, climatic conditions
in the southern zone of Algeria, Upper Egypt and of other
countries bordering on Central Africa would not be what
they are now. We do not know exactly what rivers will
be found in Central Africa or Central Australia, but we
can say for certain that if rivers are found there, they will
flow down and not up. The same must be said about those
parts of the globe which geology has not yet explored. We
have explored only a very thin stratum of the earth's crust,
amounting to less than one-thousandth part of the globe.
In the immeasurable mass of matter that lies beneath this
crust there must, of course, be bodies and phenomena not
met with in that insignificant part that is accessible to us.
But from this one part we know for certain what character
the objects and phenomena in the inaccessible parts of the
globe can have and what character they cannot have. We
know that the temperature there is terrific—if it were not
so high, the things that are found and take place on the
earth's surface would not be what they are now. We know
that in such a temperature the chemical compounds that
constitute the so-called organic kingdom could not exist;
therefore we know that the plant and animal life that exists
on the earth's surface cannot exist in the bowels of the earth.
There are no organisms there in any way like our plants
and animals. If we say that at the poles, or in Central
Africa, or in the bowels of the earth, there are bodies of
such-and-such a category, that phenomena of such-and-such
a kind take place there, it will be only a hypothesis, perhaps
an erroneous one. We cannot guess whether there is water
or land at the poles. If there is sea there, we cannot say

whether it is always covered with ice or sometimes clear of it. If there is land there, we cannot say whether it is covered with eternal ice or at times has any kind of vegetation. Positive conclusions on this score would only be guesses lacking scientific validity. But negative conclusions, such as, for example, that grapes, or oak trees, cannot grow at the poles, that neither monkeys nor parrots can live there, such negative conclusions have complete scientific validity. They are not hypotheses, or surmises, they are definite knowledge, based on the relation of the phenomena that take place in countries on the earth's surface that we know of to the uninvestigated phenomena in the unknown parts. Can there be any doubt that parrots do not live at the poles? Parrots need a mean annual temperature of not less than 15° or 18° above freezing point, and if this were the temperature at the North Pole, Greenland would have a climate at least as warm as that of Italy. Or, is it possible to doubt that there are no vegetable organisms in those strata of the earth that are close to the centre? For them to exist there the temperature would have to be no higher than the boiling point of water, because there is no vegetation without water; and if the temperature there were below the boiling point of water, we would not find that the deeper we go, the higher is the temperature of the strata of the earth's crust that are being investigated.

Why are we dealing at such length with phenomena and deductions that are known to everybody? Simply because, being unaccustomed to systematic thinking, too many people are too apt to fail to grasp the meaning of the general laws which have the same meaning as the individual phenomena they do understand. We wanted to bring out as strongly as possible one of these general laws although, in the present state of scientific induction (inductive logic) we are in most cases as yet unable with certainty to determine from the part of an object we have investigated the character of the uninvestigated part, we are always able to determine with certainty the character it cannot have. At the present stage of science, the positive conclusions regarding the character of the unknown that we draw from the character of the known are still at the guessing stage, are open to dispute, and may be mistaken. The negative conclusions, however, are quite valid. We cannot say what the unknown may turn out to be, but we already know what it is not.

6 *

The fantastic hypotheses destroyed by these negative conclusions in chemistry, in geography and in geology, are already not worth combating, because everybody with the least education admits that they are nonsense. The geographer does not have to prove that there are no monkeys at the poles, that headless people are not to be found in Central Africa, that there are no upward flowing rivers in the interior of Australia, or that in the bowels of the earth there are no wonderful gardens, or Cyclops forging weapons for Achilles under the supervision of Vulcan. But a man with a logical mind also regards the fantastic hypotheses in the other sciences in the same way. Here too he sees that all this nonsense is incompatible with the present state of knowledge. It is said that the discoveries made by Copernicus in astronomy changed man's conception of things that are apparently very remote from astronomy.[7] Exactly the same change, in exactly the same direction, but on a far more extensive scale, is now being brought about by discoveries in chemistry and physiology. They are changing man's conception of things that are apparently very remote from chemistry. In our next essay we shall endeavour to explain the present views of thinkers who are faithful to the scientific spirit concerning those philosophical problems which serve as the subject of Mr. Lavrov's pamphlet. At present, in order to some degree to link the end of this essay with its beginning, we shall again turn our thoughts to the future of Western Europe, which we were compelled to discuss in connection with the passages from Mill and Proudhon that Mr. Lavrov quoted concerning the allegedly dire prospect that threatens mankind in the West. Chemistry, geology —and suddenly a discussion about political parties in England or in France, about West-European customs, and the hopes and fears of different classes and different publicists—what an arbitrary transition, what an absence of logic! But what can one do, reader? We can give you only what we've got, and you ought not to have expected anything else from our essay. Let us attempt to apply to its character the method of drawing negative conclusions concerning the character of the unknown from the character of the known and see what you could not possibly have expected from this essay had you taken the trouble to employ this method before you began to read it. The essay is written in Russian for the Russian public. You knew this even from the cover of this magazine. The essay set out to deal with philosophical problems. This was also evident from the title on the magazine cover. Now judge for yourself: is there any logic in these two facts that were known to you? A certain gentleman wrote an essay for the Russian public; but does the Russian public need magazine essays? Judging by all things, they certainly do not, for if they did, those essays would not be of the kind that appear now. Thus, this gentleman unknown to you, the author of this essay, acted quite illogically, he did something that the public does not need—he wrote an essay. But you, because of your generous nature, allowed this absurd action to pass without censure. You thought to yourself: he took it into his head to do something the public does not need, well, let it go—it's written now, what does it matter? But now another question: what did he write about? About philosophy. Oh, philosophy! Good heavens, who in Russian society thinks about philosophical problems? Nobody, except Mr. Lavrov, and even that is doubtful. Perhaps Mr. Lavrov himself is far more interested in our mundane social affairs than in all sorts of philosophical problems. The choice of an object for an illogical action like writing a magazine article is even more illogical than the action. What could you have expected of an essay at the very beginning of which there are such two big stamps with the inscription: "No logic"? In the present state of science in Russia one cannot say with certainty what you might have expected to find in this essay, judging by its title. But it can be said with certainty that you could not have expected logic. And where there is no logic, there is incoherence. Thus you have a little experiment in applying the theory of drawing negative conclusions about the character of the unknown from the character of the known. The validity of this method has been brilliantly confirmed by this article, has it not? We say, not with an author's conceit, but with sincere and true conviction, that the incoherence and fatuity of this essay exceeds that of all the other essays you have read at least to the same degree that the intensity of the chemical process in plant life exceeds the intensity of that process in inorganic nature. Tell us now: should we not, in order to avoid changing the character of this essay, leap from the discussion of chemistry to the discussion of the future of Western Europe?

We have seen the character of the trend of thought of the noble-minded section of those classes in Western Europe which anticipate loss from changes which they themselves admit are inevitable and just. Grief over their impending fate creates confusion in their minds. They lack the will to apply to a fact that closely concerns them the principle which they accept in its general abstract form. We have seen what stage of development has been reached by the trend of thought of a plebeian in Western Europe. He has not yet grasped the general idea of present-day science, the deductions from which correspond to his needs. He still clings to the obsolete principles, although he sees the inconsistency of the deductions drawn from them by his teachers, the people who advanced the old systems, and constantly passes from jaundiced repudiation of them to submission to them. He cannot remain in this state of submission long and again bursts out in caustic tirades only to submit to routine once again. This jaundiced indecision, this vacillation, is totally alien to the spirit of the new ideas. On the contrary, instability of views, expressed by a mixture of scepticism and excessive credulity, is due to insufficient acquaintance with the ideas that have been elaborated by present-day science. The reader sees the character of its principles and deductions. Its theories are based on the truth discovered by the natural sciences by means of a most exact analysis of facts, truths as authentic as that the earth revolves round the sun, the law of gravity, the operation of chemical affinity. From these principles, which are beyond all dispute or doubt, modern science draws its deductions with the same circumspection as that with which it arrived at the principles themselves. It accepts nothing without the strictest and all-sided test, and draws no conclusions from what it accepts except such as irresistibly follow of themselves from facts and laws which cannot possibly be logically refuted. Since the new ideas bear this character, a man who once accepts them has no road of retreat or compromise with the fantastic errors of the olden days. He regards the prejudices of the olden days in exactly the same way as we regard the Greek fables about nymphs and nectar, about Elysian fields, and about the punishments inflicted upon Tantalus and Sisyphus. You will agree that it is not enough to say: "we cannot prove that these legends are true." No, we know positively that they are not true. The new science says nothing except that which is absolutely authentic; but among the concepts which are so much beyond doubt is the deduction that fantastic prejudices are totally unfounded.

Thus, the essential character of present-day philosophical views is their unshakeable validity, which precludes all wavering of opinion. From this it is easy to conclude what fate awaits mankind in Western Europe. It is in the nature of every new doctrine to require rather a long time to spread among the masses, to become the prevailing conviction. In ideas, as in life, the new spreads rather slowly, but there cannot be any doubt that it spreads, gradually penetrating deeper and deeper among different strata of the population, beginning with the more developed, of course. There can be no doubt that the common people of Western Europe will become acquainted with the philosophical views that correspond to their needs and, in our opinion, correspond to the truth. Then, representatives quite different from Proudhon will come forward from among them, writers whose ideas will not, like those of Proudhon, be shackled by tradition, and who will not cling to obsolete scientific forms in analyzing social conditions and reforms beneficial for society. When that time comes, when the representatives of the elements which are now striving to remould life in Western Europe will already be unshakeable in their philosophical views, it will be a sign of the speedy triumph of the new principles in the social life of Western Europe. It is quite possible that we are mistaken in thinking that that time already commenced in the years that followed the first period when thought was dumbstruck by reaction after the events of 1848. It is quite possible that we are mistaken in thinking that the generation that has been trained by the events in Western Europe during the past twelve years is already acquiring the clarity and firmness of mind that is needed for the transformation of West-European life. But if we are mistaken, it is only in respect to time. If the result that lies in the very nature of things, and is therefore inevitable, does not come in our generation, it will come in the next; and if our generation does not succeed in bringing it about, it will, at all events, do much to facilitate this task for its children.

It now strikes us—too late, unfortunately—that this essay, in spite of its incoherence, can serve as a preface to an exposition of the conceptions of present-day science concerning man as an individual. Had we noticed this before, we would have tried to shorten our winding digressions from philosophy to the natural sciences. The preface would then not have been so long and we would have had enough pages left for an outline of the theory of individuality as understood by present-day science. It is too late, however, to rectify the matter now, and we can only hope that this essay which, as we see, might have served as a preface to an outline of the philosophical conceptions of man, will actually serve as such.[8]

II

The word "science" in English does not by any means cover all the branches of knowledge that this term covers among us, and among the other continental nations. By science the English mean: mathematics, astronomy, physics, chemistry, botany, zoology, geography—those branches of knowledge that we call the "exact" sciences, and those closely related to them in character. But they do not apply this term to history, psychology, moral philosophy, or to metaphysics. It must be said that there is, indeed, a tremendous difference between these two halves of learning as regards the quality of the concepts that prevail in each of them. From one half, every man who is in the least enlightened has already expelled all groundless prejudices, and all rationally-minded people already adhere to the same fundamental conceptions in these subjects. Our knowledge about these branches of life is very incomplete, but, at all events, everybody knows what we know definitely in these branches, what we do not yet know, and lastly, what has been definitely refuted by exact research. For example, if you say that the human organism needs food, or needs air, nobody will dispute it. If you say that we do not yet know whether the substances that now serve as man's food are the only substances that can serve this purpose, and that other substances may, perhaps, be found that will be useful for this purpose, no enlightened person will dispute it, he will only add that although new food substances may be found, and in all probability will be found, they have not been found yet, and for the time being man can use as food only the known substances, such as cereals,

meat, milk or fish. You, in your turn, will fully agree with
this observation, and no dispute can possibly arise. The
only point of dispute you can raise is whether the probability of the speedy discovery of new nutritive substances is
great or small, and to what category of things these new,
as yet undiscovered, substances are likely to belong. But
in this dispute, you and your opponent will both know and
admit that you are merely expressing assumptions which
lack full validity, which may be more or less useful to
science in the future (for assumptions, hypotheses, give
direction to scientific research and lead to the discovery of
truths which confirm or refute them), but are not yet scientific truths. If, finally, you say that man cannot live without
food, here again everybody will agree with you and understand that this negative statement has inseverable logical
connection with the positive statement: "the human organism needs food." Everybody will understand that if one
of these two statements is accepted, the other must also
be accepted. It is entirely different in moral philosophy,
for example. No matter what you say, some clever and educated people will always come forward and say the opposite.
If, for example, you say that poverty has a bad effect upon
a man's mind and heart, many clever people will object
and say: "No, poverty sharpens the mind, it compels it to
seek means to avert it; it ennobles the heart by turning our
thoughts away from the vanities of pleasure to the virtues of patience, self-sacrifice, sympathy for the needs and
misfortunes of others." But if, on the contrary, you say that
poverty has a beneficial effect upon a man, there will also
be lots of clever people, perhaps even more than in the
first case, who will object and say: "No, poverty deprives
a man of the means for intellectual development, hinders
the development of an independent character, leads to
unscrupulousness in the choice of means for averting poverty,
or simply of sustaining life; it is the chief source of ignorance, vice and crime." In short, no matter what conclusion
you might think of drawing in the moral sciences, you will
find that it, and the opposite one, and many others, which
do not hang together either with your conclusion or with
the opposite one, or with one another, have earnest cham-
pions among clever and enlightened people. The same
applies to metaphysics, and to history, with which neither
the moral sciences nor metaphysics can dispense.

This situation in the sphere of history, the moral sciences and metaphysics, causes many people to think that these branches of science do not and even cannot ever give us anything as valid as we get from mathematics, astronomy and chemistry. It is a good thing that we happened to use the word "poverty"; it reminds us of a mundane fact that occurs every day. As soon as any gentleman, or lady, in a large family achieves a good position in society, he or she at once begins to drag his or her relatives out of poverty and obscurity. Around an important or wealthy person appear brothers and sisters, nephews and nieces, all attach themselves to him and, clinging to him, rise to the top. Even gentlemen and ladies who had not deigned to recognize this important or wealthy person when he was poor and obscure now boast of their kinship with him. In his heart of hearts, this person may dislike some of them, but he helps them—after all, they are his relatives—and so, either loving his kinsmen or vexed with them, he improves their conditions. Exactly the same thing is happening in the sphere of knowledge now that some of the sciences have succeeded in emerging from their lowly position and in reaching high perfection, in reaching scientific wealth and intellectual importance. The rich ones who are now helping their obscure relations are mathematics and the natural sciences. Mathematics has long held a good position, but an extraordinary amount of its time was taken up with caring for its closest relative, astronomy. This period of nursing lasted for about four thousand years, if not more. At last, in Copernicus' time, mathematics put astronomy on its feet, and with Newton it attained a brilliant position in the intellectual world. Barely having ceased to grieve day and night over the poverty-stricken condition of its sister astronomy, barely having received some opportunity, after making her position secure, to devote attention to its other relatives, mathematics began to help other members of the family, which up till now had retained undivided ownership of the family property under the name of physics. Acoustics, optics, and several other sisters who bore the family name of physics, particularly enjoyed the favours of mathematics; and many other members of this numerous family attained decent positions. Here, the process was much quicker than that of dragging astronomy out of obscurity. The experience it had gained in nursing its

closest relative enabled mathematics to help the others.
Furthermore, it did not now have to bear the burden alone;
astronomy became an efficient adjutant. After they had,
by their joint efforts, raised to respectability the numerous
members of the physics family who hitherto had cringed
in abject poverty and had been addicted to the basest scientific vices, mathematics already had a whole tribe at its
command, became the president of a fairly large and prosperous state. At the end of the last century that intellectual state was in a position equal to that occupied by the
United States in the political world at about that time.
Since then, both states have been growing with equal rapidity. Nearly every year some new region joins the young
North American Union, is converted from a wilderness into
a prosperous state. This enlightened and vigorous nation
is steadily pushing aside the wretched tribes which refuse
to accept civilization, and is annexing to its Union other
tribes which are seeking civilization, but are unable to
find it without its aid. The French in Louisiana and the
Spaniards of North Mexico have already joined, and within
a few years have become so imbued with the spirit of the
new society that they cannot be distinguished from the
descendants of Washington and Jefferson. Millions of drink-
sodden Irishmen and no less wretched Germans have become
respectable and prosperous citizens of the Union.⁹ In the
same way, the union of the exact sciences, under the government of mathematics, that is, counting, weighing and measuring, is year after year spreading to new spheres of knowledge, is growing by the inclusion of newcomers. Chemistry
was gradually followed by all the sciences concerned with
plant and animal organisms: physiology, comparative anatomy, various branches of botany and zoology. Now the
moral sciences are joining it. The same is happening to
them as what we see in the case of proud but poverty-strick-
en people when a distant relative, not, like themselves,
proud and boastful of their ancient lineage and incomparable
virtues, but a plain, honest man, acquires wealth. For a
long time these proud hidalgos look down upon him with
disdain, but poverty compels them to accept his alms.
For a long time they live on his charity, considering it
beneath their dignity to turn, with his aid, to honest work,
by means of which he got on in the world. But gradually,
feeding better and wearing better clothes, they become more

reasonable, their empty boastfulness subsides, they become respectable and at last understand that not work but pride is shameful, and finally they adopt the habits that enabled their relative to get on in the world. Then, with his assistance, they quickly attain a good position and begin to enjoy the respect of rational people not for the imaginary virtues they had boasted of in the past, but for their new and real qualities that are useful for society—for the work they do.

It is not so long ago that the moral sciences could not have possessed the content that could justify the title of science that they bore, and the English were quite right then in depriving them of the title they did not deserve. The situation today has changed considerably. The natural sciences have already developed to such an extent that they provide material for the exact solution of moral problems too. All the progressive thinkers among those who are studying the moral sciences have begun to work out these problems with the aid of precise methods similar to those by which the problems of the natural sciences are being worked out. When we spoke about the controversies between different people on every moral problem, we were referring to the old, most widespread, but now already obsolete conceptions and methods of investigation and not to the character the moral sciences are now acquiring among progressive thinkers. We were referring to the former routine character of these branches of science and not to their present form. In their present form, the moral sciences differ from the so-called natural sciences only in that they began to be worked out in a truly scientific way later, and, therefore, have not yet been developed to the same degree of perfection as the latter. Here, the difference is only one of degree: chemistry is younger than astronomy and has not yet attained the same degree of perfection; physiology is still younger than chemistry and is still further removed from perfection; psychology, as an exact science, is still younger than physiology and has been worked out even less. But, while differing from each other in the amount of exact knowledge acquired, chemistry and astronomy do not differ either as regards the authenticity of what has been learned, or in the methods employed to arrive at exact knowledge in the particular subjects. The facts and laws discovered by chemistry are as authentic as the facts and laws discovered

by astronomy. The same must be said about the results
achieved by present-day exact research in the moral sciences. An outline of the subjects provided by astronomy,
physiology and psychology would resemble maps of Great
Britain, European Russia and Asiatic Russia respectively.
Great Britain has been covered by an excellent trigonometrical survey. Only half of European Russia has been covered
by a trigonometrical survey, the other half has been surveyed
by less perfect methods. In Asiatic Russia there are areas
in which the positions of a few chief points have been determined in passing, while all that lies between them is plot-
ted on the map "by eye," which is a very unsatisfactory
method. But larger and larger areas are coming under the
trigonometrical survey every year, and the time is not far
distant when this will also be the case in Asiatic Russia.
But we already know many parts of this country fairly well,
some parts even very well, and the whole of it well enough
to be able easily to point to the cruder mistakes in the
ancient maps; and if anybody wanted to assure us that the
Irtysh flows southwards and not northwards, or that Irkutsk
is near the tropics, we would only shrug our shoulders.
Whoever cares to can go on repeating the stories told by
our ancient cosmographers about the peoples of the Land
of Shem and the "dumb tongues" living across the Pechora,
imprisoned in the mountains by Alexander of Macedon
behind gates which yield not to fire or iron; we, however,
know what to think about these stories, which are based
only on fantasy.

The first result of the entry of the moral sciences into
the sphere of the exact sciences was that a strict distinction
has been drawn between what we know and what we do not
know. The astronomer knows that he knows the dimensions
of Mars, and he knows just as positively that he does not
know the geological composition of that planet, the character of the plant and animal life on it, or whether there is
any plant or animal life on it at all. If anybody took it
into his head to claim that there was clay, granite, birds or
molluscs, on Mars, the astronomer would answer: you are
asserting what you do not know. If the fantast were to go
even further in his assumptions and assert, for example,
that the birds that inhabit Mars are not subject to disease
and that the molluscs do not need food, the astronomer,
assisted by the chemist and physiologist, would prove to

him that this is impossible. Similarly, in the moral sciences, a strict distinction has been drawn between what is known and what is not known, and on the basis of what is known the unsoundness of some of the previous assumptions concerning what still remains unknown has been proved. It is definitely known, for example, that all the phenomena of the moral world originate from one another and from external circumstance in conformity with the law of causality, and on this basis all assumptions that there can be any phenomena that do not arise from preceding phenomena and from external circumstances are regarded as false. Hence, present-day psychology does not accept, for example, the following assumptions: "in one case a man performs a bad action because he wanted to perform a bad action; and in another case he performs a good action because he wanted to perform a good action." It says that the bad action, or the good action, was certainly prompted by some moral or material fact, or combination of facts, and that the "wanting" was only the subjective impression which accompanies in our minds the rise of thoughts or actions from preceding thoughts, actions or external facts. The following is a very simple example of an action prompted by nothing except our will: I get out of bed. What foot do I put out first? If I want to, I put out my left foot; or if I want to, I put out the right. But this only appears to be so at a superficial glance. Actually, facts and impressions determine which foot a man puts out of bed first. If there are no special circumstances or motives, he will put out the foot that is most convenient for the anatomical position of his body in the bed. If there are special motives that outweigh this physiological convenience, the result will change in conformity with the alteration of the circumstances. If, for example, the thought occurs to the man: "I won't put out my right foot, but the left one," he will do that. Here, however, one cause (physiological convenience) was simply displaced by another (the thought of displaying independence), or it would be more correct to say, the second cause, being the stronger, triumphed over the first. But how did the second cause arise? Whence came the thought of displaying independence of external conditions? It could not have arisen without a cause. It was created either by something said in conversation with someone, or by the recollection of a previous dispute, or something like that. Thus, the fact that a man can, if he wants to, put out a foot that is not convenient for the anatomical position of his body in the bed does not prove that he can put out this foot, or that foot, without any cause. It only proves that the manner of getting out of bed can be determined by causes that are stronger than the anatomical position of the body before the act of getting out of bed. The phenomenon that we call will is itself a link in a series of phenomena and facts joined together by causal connection. Very often, the immediate cause of the manifestation of our will to perform a certain action is thought. But the definite inclination of the will is also due only to a definite thought: whatever the thought is, so is the will. If the thought were different the will would be different. But why did a particular thought arise and not a different one? Because it too arose from some thought, some fact, in short, from some cause. In this case, psychology says the same thing that physics and chemistry say in similar cases: if a certain phenomenon occurs, we must seek the cause of it and not be satisfied with the vapid statement: it occurred of its own accord without any special cause—"I did this because I wanted to." That's all very well, but why did you want to? If you answer: "simply because I wanted to," it will be the same as saying: "the plate broke because it broke; the house was burned down because it was burned down." These are not answers at all; they are only a cloak to cover up laziness to seek the real cause, lack of desire to know the truth.

If, in the present state of chemistry, somebody were to ask why gold is yellow and silver white, chemists would answer frankly that they do not yet know the reason for this, that is, they do not yet know what connection there is between the yellowness of gold, or whiteness of silver, with the other qualities of these metals; that they do not know by what law, owing to which circumstances, the substance that took the form of gold, or silver, acquired in that form the quality of producing on our eyes the impression of yellowness or whiteness. That is a straightforward and honest answer; but, as we see, it is simply a confession of ignorance. It is easy for a rich man to confess that at the particular moment he is short of money; but it is easy to make such a confession only when everybody is convinced that he is really rich. On the other hand, it is not easy for a poor man who wants to have the reputation of being rich, or for a man whose credit is shaken, to say that he is short of money at the particular moment. On the contrary, he does his utmost to conceal the truth. Such, until recently, was the state of the moral sciences. They were ashamed to say: we have not sufficient knowledge about this or that. Happily, things are different now: psychology and moral philosophy are emerging from their scientific poverty; they now possess a considerable amount of wealth, and if they do not know something or other they can afford to say frankly: "we do not know."

But if the moral sciences are still obliged to say "we do not know" in answer to very many questions, we shall be mistaken in assuming that among the problems they have not yet solved are those which, according to one of the prevailing opinions, are insoluble. No, the ignorance of these sciences is not of this kind. What, for example, does chemistry not know? It does not at present know what hydrogen will be when it passes from the gaseous to the solid state—a metal or nonmetal. There are strong grounds for assuming that it will be a metal, but we do not yet know whether this assumption is correct. Chemistry also does not know whether phosphorus or sulphur are simple substances or whether they will in time be resolved into the simplest elements. These are cases of theoretical ignorance. Another category of problems that chemistry cannot solve at present are the numerous cases of inability to satisfy practical demands. Chemistry can make prussic acid, acetic acid, but it cannot yet make fibrin. As we see, these, and other problems it cannot at present solve, are of a very special character, a character so special that they occur to the minds only of people who are fairly well acquainted with chemistry. The problems the moral sciences have not yet solved are exactly of the same kind. Psychology, for example, discovers the following fact: a man of low mental development is unable to understand life that is different from his own; the more his mind develops, the easier is it for him to picture life that is different from his own. How is this fact to be explained? In the present state of science, a strictly scientific answer to this question has not yet been found; all we have are various surmises. Now tell us, would this question arise in the mind of anyone not familiar with the present state of psychology? Scarcely anybody except scientists, has even noticed the fact to which this question applies. It is like the question as to whether hydrogen is a metal or not a metal. People unacquainted with chemistry are not only unaware of the question concerning hydrogen, they are even unaware of the existence of hydrogen itself. For chemistry, however, this hydrogen, the existence of which would not have been noticed had it not been for chemistry, is extremely important. Similarly, the fact that a man of low mental development is unable to understand life that is different from his own, whereas a mentally developed man is able to do so, is extremely important for psychology. Just as the discovery of hydrogen led to an improvement in the theory of chemistry, so the discovery of this psychological fact led to the building of the theory of anthropomorphism, without which not a step can now be taken in metaphysics. Here is another psychological problem, which also cannot be definitely solved in the present state of science: children have a propensity for breaking their toys; why is this? Must it be regarded only as a clumsy form of the desire to adapt things to one's requirements, a clumsy form of what is called man's creative activity, or is it here a trace of the pure inclination to destroy, which some writers ascribe to man? Nearly all the theoretical problems which science cannot as yet definitely solve are of this kind. The reader sees that they belong to the category of problems, the need and importance of which are revealed only by science, and are intelligible only to scientists. They belong to the category of so-called technical or special problems, which are not in the least interesting to laymen and often seem to them to be of no importance. They are all problems of the same kind as: from what old Slavonic sound did the letter y in the word "рука" arise; from the simple y or from ю, and in conformity with what law is the noun "воз" formed from the verb "везу": why was the letter o substituted for the letter e? For the philologist, these questions are very important, but for us who are not philologists, they can be said to be nonexistent. But let us not rashly laugh at the scientists who are engaged in research on things which to us seem so petty; the discovery of the truth in these seemingly unimportant facts had important results for us ordinary people. Conceptions of a whole series of important facts were made clear, important everyday relationships were changed. The fact that some

people cleared up our phonetics by discovering the significance of юс, made the teaching of grammar more rational,
and our children will be tormented by it less than we were,
and will learn it better than we did.

Thus, the theoretical problems that are still unsolved
in the present state of the moral sciences are, in general,
of such a character that they arise in hardly anybody's
mind except that of specialists. The layman even finds
it hard to understand how learned people can spend their
time investigating such petty things. On the other hand,
the theoretical problems that usually seem to be important
and difficult to the layman have, in general, ceased to be
problems for present-day thinkers, because they are solved
beyond doubt with extreme ease at the very first application of the powerful means of scientific analysis. It is found
that half of these problems arise simply from the fact that
people are unaccustomed to think, and the other half find
answers in phenomena with which everybody is familiar.
What becomes of the flame of a burning candle when we
extinguish the candle? Would a chemist agree to call this
question a problem? He would say that it is simply a jumble
of words arising from ignorance of the most fundamental,
the simplest facts of science. He would say: the burning of
a candle is a chemical process; flame is one of the phenomena
of this process, one of its aspects, one of its qualities, to
express it in ordinary language. When we extinguish the
candle we put a stop to the chemical process; naturally,
with its cessation its qualities vanish. To ask what becomes
of the flame when we extinguish a candle is the same
as asking what becomes of the figure 2 in the figure 25 when
we strike out the whole figure—nothing is left of either
the figure 2 or of the figure 5; both have been struck out.
Such a question can be asked only by one who does not understand what writing a figure and then striking it out
means. To all the questions put by people of this type there
is one answer: friend, you are totally ignorant of arithmetic and you will do well if you begin to learn it. For
example, the following baffling question is asked: is man a
good or an evil being? Lots of people rack their brains in
the endeavour to solve this problem. Nearly half of them
decide that man by nature is good; others, also constituting
nearly half of the brain-rackers, decide otherwise: they
say that man is by nature bad. Outside of these two oppo-

site dogmatic parties there are several sceptics who jeer
at the two sides and say that the problem is insoluble. But
at the very first application of scientific analysis the whole
thing turns out to be as clear as clear can be. A man likes
what is pleasant and dislikes what is unpleasant—this,
one would think, is beyond doubt, because the predicate
simply repeats the subject: A is A, what is pleasant to a
man is pleasant to a man; what is unpleasant to a man is
unpleasant to a man. Good is he who does good to others,
bad is he who is bad to others—this, too, is clear and simple one would think. Let us now combine the simple truths;
we will get the following deduction: a man is good when,
in order to obtain pleasure for himself, he must give pleasure
to others. A man is bad when in order to obtain pleasure
for himself he is obliged to cause unpleasantness for others.
Here, human nature cannot be blamed for one thing or
praised for the other; everything depends on circumstances,
relationships [institutions]. If certain relations are constant,
the man whose character is moulded by them is found to
have acquired the habit of acting in conformity with them.
Therefore, we may think that Ivan is good, while Pyotr
is bad; but these opinions apply only to individual men,
not to man in general, in the same way as we apply to individual men and not to man in general the conception of
the habit to saw planks, to forge iron, etc. Ivan is a carpenter, but we cannot say that man in general is a carpenter
or not a carpenter. Pyotr can forge iron, but we cannot say
that man in general is a blacksmith or not a blacksmith.
The fact that Ivan became a carpenter and Pyotr a blacksmith
merely shows that under certain circumstances, which existed in Ivan's life, a man becomes a carpenter; and under
other circumstances, which existed in Pyotr's life, a man becomes a blacksmith. In exactly the same way, under certain circumstances a man becomes good, under others,
he becomes bad.

Thus, from the theoretical aspect, the problem of the
good and bad qualities of human nature is solved so easily
that it cannot even be called a problem: it contains within
itself a complete solution. It is quite another matter, however, when you take the practical aspect, for example,
when it seems to you that it is much better for a man himself, and for all those around him, to be good rather than
bad; and when you want to make everybody good. From

7*

this aspect the matter presents many difficulties. As the reader will observe, however, these difficulties do not relate to science, but to the practical application of the means indicated by science. In this respect, psychology and moral philosophy are in exactly the same position as the natural sciences. The climate in North Siberia is too cold. If you were to ask how it could be made warmer, the natural sciences would have no difficulty in finding an answer: Siberia is closed to the warm atmosphere of the South by mountains, and its northern slope is open to the cold atmosphere of the North. If there were mountains on the northern border and none on the southern, that part of the country would be much warmer than it is now. But we, as yet, lack the means with which to put this theoretical solution of the problem into practice. Similarly, the moral sciences already have theoretical answers to nearly all the problems that are important for life, but in many cases man lacks the means to put into practice what is indicated by theory. Incidentally, in this respect, the moral sciences have an advantage over the natural sciences. In the natural sciences, all the means belong to the sphere of so-called external nature; in the moral sciences, only half the means belong to this category, while the other half are contained in man himself. Consequently, half the matter depends entirely upon man feeling strongly enough the need for a certain improvement. This feeling in itself provides him with a very considerable part of the conditions necessary for the improvement. We have seen, however, that the conditions that depend upon the state of man's own impressions are not enough: material means are also needed. In respect to this half of the conditions, in respect to material means, the practical problems of the moral sciences are in a much more favourable position than they are in respect to the conditions which lie within man himself. Formerly, when the natural sciences were still undeveloped, insurmountable difficulties could be met with in external nature that prevented the satisfaction of man's moral requirements. This is not the case now: the natural sciences already offer man such powerful means of command over external nature that no difficulties arise in this respect. Let us return, for an example, to the practical question of how people could become good, so that bad people should become an extreme rarity in the world, and that bad qualities should lose all

perceptible importance in life because of the extremely
few cases in which they would be displayed by people.
Psychology tells us that the most abundant source of the
display of bad qualities is inadequacy of means for satisfying requirements; that a man commits a bad action, that
is, harms others, almost only when he is obliged to deprive
them of things in order not to remain himself without the
things he needs. For example, in time of famine, when there
is not enough food for everybody, there is a great increase
in crime and of all sorts of evil deeds; people rob and cheat
one another for the sake of a crust of bread. Psychology
also adds that human requirements are divided into extremely different degrees of intensity. The most urgent need of
every human organism is to breathe; but sufficient means
for satisfying this need are available to people in practically
all situations, so that evil deeds due to the want of air
are hardly ever committed. But if an extraordinary situation arises, when there is not sufficient air for everybody,
then such quarrels and wrongdoing do arise. For example,
if a large number of people are locked in a stifling room with
one window, quarrels and strife nearly always arise, and
even murder may be committed for a place near that window. Next to the need to breathe (continues psychology),
a man's most urgent requirement is food and drink. Very
often, very many people suffer from a shortage of the articles
needed to satisfy these requirements properly, and this is
the cause of the largest number of bad actions of all kinds,
of nearly all the situations and institutions that are the
constant causes of bad actions. If this one cause of evil
were abolished, at least nine tenths of all that is bad in
human society would quickly disappear. Crime would be
reduced to one tenth. In the course of one generation coarse
manners and conceptions would yield to humane manners
and conceptions. The restrictive institutions that are based
on coarseness and ignorance would be robbed of their
foundation, and soon, nearly all restriction would be abolished. We are told that this indication of theory could
not be put into practice before because of the imperfection
of the technical arts. We are not sure whether this is true
in respect to the past, but it is beyond dispute that in the
present state of mechanics and chemistry, with the means
with which these sciences provide agriculture, the land in
every country in the temperate zone could provide ever so

much more food than is needed for an abundant supply of provisions for populations ten and twenty times larger than the present populations of these countries.* Thus, external nature creates no obstacles to supplying the entire population of every civilized country with an abundance of food; the only task that remains is to make people conscious of the possibility and necessity of energetically striving towards this goal. Rhetorically, it may be said that they are already concerning themselves with this matter sufficiently, but exact and cold scientific analysis reveals the hollowness of the pompous phrases we so often hear on this subject. Actually, not a single human society has as yet adopted on any extensive scale the means indicated by the natural sciences and the science of public welfare for the promotion of agriculture. Why this is so, why such unconcern for the application of scientific advice in the matter of satisfying such an urgent need as the need for food prevails in human societies, what circumstances and relations give rise to and foster this bad state of economy, and how circumstances and relations must be changed in order that the state of economy may be improved—are again new problems, the theoretical solution of which is easy; and again, the practical application of the scientific solutions depends upon man becoming imbued with certain impressions. We shall not, however, deal here with the theoretical solution, or with the practical difficulties in the way of these problems; this would lead us too far away, and we think that our foregoing remarks are already sufficient to explain the present position of the moral sciences. We wanted to say that the working out of the moral sciences on precise scientific lines is only just beginning and that, therefore, exact theoretical solutions for very many extremely important moral problems have not yet been found. But these problems for which theoretical solutions have not yet been found are of a purely technical character and are of interest only to

---

* In England, the land could feed at least 150,000,000 people. The panegyrics sung in praise of the astonishing perfection of English agriculture are justified insofar as rapid improvements are taking place there, but it would be a mistake to think that the resources of science are already being employed on a sufficiently wide scale. This is only just beginning, and nine tenths of the cultivated land in England is still tilled by routine methods that in no way correspond to the present state of agricultural knowledge.[10]

specialists, while, on the other hand, the psychological and moral problems that are extremely interesting, and seem to be extremely difficult to the layman have already been precisely solved, and, moreover, have been solved very easily and simply with the very first application of exact scientific analysis, so that the theoretical answers to them have already been found. We added that from these indubitable theoretical solutions arise very important and useful scientific indications as to what means must be employed to improve the conditions of human life; that some of these means must be taken from external nature, and in the present state of development of the natural sciences external nature no longer creates any obstacles to this, whereas others must be provided by the reasoning faculty of man himself, and the only obstacles that may be met with today are obstacles to its awakening arising from the apathy and ignorance of some people and the deliberate opposition of others and, in general, from the power that prejudice exercises over the vast majority of people in every society.

The object of all these observations has been to explain how the present high development of the natural sciences facilitates the rise of exact sciences in branches of life and departments of theoretical problems which formerly were only subjects of surmise, sometimes well-founded, sometimes groundless, but never providing exact knowledge. We have in mind moral and metaphysical problems. The next subject to be dealt with in our essays is man as an individual, and we shall endeavour to explain what solutions of the problems concerning this subject have been found by an exact scientific elaboration of psychology and moral philosophy. If the reader remembers the character of our first essay he will, of course, expect us to make a promise and immediately break it and go into a long dissertation on a matter that has nothing to do with the subject. The reader will not be mistaken. We shall put aside for a time the psychological and moral-philosophical problems concerning man and deal with the physiological, medical, or any other problems you please, but not with man as a moral being, and try first of all to say what we know about him as a being that possesses a stomach, a head, bones, veins, muscles and nerves. We shall examine him only from the aspect that the natural sciences see him; the other aspects of his life we shall examine later, if time allows.

Physiology and medicine find that the human organism is an extremely complex chemical combination that goes through an extremely complex chemical process that we call life. This process is so complex, and its subject is so important for us that, because of its importance, the branch of chemistry that is engaged in research in it has been awarded the title of a special science and is called physiology. The relation of physiology to chemistry may be compared with the relation of Russian history to world history. Of course, the history of Russia is only a part of world history, but the subject of this part concerns us particularly closely, and is therefore treated as if it were a special science. In educational establishments the history of Russia is dealt with as a special subject apart from world history, and at examinations students receive separate marks for it; but it must not be forgotten that this superficial division is made only for the sake of practical convenience and is not based on any theoretical difference between the character of this branch of science and all the other parts of this science. The history of Russia is intelligible only in connection with world history, it is explained by it and represents only a variety of the same forces and phenomena as are dealt with in world history. In the same way, physiology is only a variety of chemistry, and its subject is only a variety of the subjects dealt with in chemistry. Physiology itself has not kept all its departments in strict unity under a common name; some of the aspects of the subjects it investigates, i.e., the chemical processes that take place in the human organism, are of such special interest for man that researches in them, which are part of physiology, have been awarded the name of separate sciences. Of these aspects we shall mention one: investigation of the phenomena that cause and accompany the various digressions of this chemical process from its normal form. This part of physiology bears the special name of medicine. Medicine, in its turn, branches out into numerous sciences with special names. Thus, the part that separated from chemistry split up into a number of parts, which, in their turn, also split up into parts. But this phenomenon is of exactly the same order as the division of a city into districts and the districts into streets. This is done merely for practical convenience, and it must not be forgotten that all the streets and districts of a city constitute one whole. When we say: Vasilyevsky

Ostrov, or Nevsky Prospect, we certainly do not mean that the buildings on Vasilyevsky Ostrov or Nevsky Prospect are not part of St. Petersburg. Similarly, phenomena in medicine are part of the system of physiological phenomena, and the entire system of physiological phenomena is part of the still more extensive system of chemical phenomena.

When a subject under investigation is very complex, it is useful, for the sake of convenience, to divide it into parts. Hence, physiology divides the complex process that goes on in the living human organism into several parts, the most marked of which are: respiration, nutrition, circulation of the blood, motion, sensation. Like every other chemical process, this entire system of phenomena has birth, growth, decline and an end. Therefore, physiology regards the processes of respiration, nutrition, blood circulation, motion, sensation, and so forth, and conception or fertilization, growth, senility and death, as if they were special subjects. But here again it must be borne in mind that these different periods and aspects of the process are divided only in theory, to facilitate theoretical analysis; actually, they constitute one indivisible whole. In the same way geometry divides a circle into circumference, radius and centre, but actually, there is no radius without a centre and circumference, no centre without a circumference and radius, and no circumference without a radius and centre—these three concepts, these three parts of the geometrical investigation of the circle, together constitute one whole. Some parts of physiology have already been elaborated very well. Such, for example, are the researches into the processes of respiration, nutrition, blood circulation, conception, growth and senility. The process of motion has not been explained in such detail, and the process of sensation still less. Strange as it may sound, as little progress has been made in the investigation of the process of normal death, i.e., that which takes place not as a result of extraordinary circumstances, or disturbance (disease), but simply as a result of the exhaustion of the organism in the course of life. But this is because, firstly, not very many cases of such death present themselves to the observation of medical men and physiologists: one in a thousand persons dies that way; the organism of the rest is prematurely destroyed by disease or by fatal external circumstances. Secondly, scientists

have up till now not had the time to devote even to these
few cases of normal death the attention they have paid to
disease and cases of violent death. Up till now the forces of
the science that deals with the problem of the destruction
of the organism have been absorbed in the quest for means
of averting premature death.

We have said that some parts of the process of life have
not been explained in as great a detail as others; but this
does not mean that we have not already positively learned
a great deal about those parts, the investigation of which
is at present in a very imperfect state. Firstly, even supposing that some special aspect of the vital process were
still totally inaccessible to exact analysis on the lines of
mathematics and the natural sciences, its character would be
approximately known to us from the character of other
parts that have already been fairly well investigated. This
would be a case like that of determining the shape of the
head of a mammal from the bones of its leg. We know
that merely from an animal's shoulder blade or collar
bone, science can fairly precisely reproduce its entire
figure, including its head, so much so, that when, later on,
a whole skeleton is found, it confirms the view of the whole
arrived at from one of its parts. We know, for example,
what nutrition is. From this we already know approximately
what, for example, sensation is: nutrition and sensation are
so closely interconnected that the character of one determines the character of the other. In our previous essay we
said that such deductions concerning unknown parts drawn
from known parts are particularly valid and particularly
important when they are presented in a negative form:
A is closely connected with X; A is B; from this it follows
that X cannot be either C or D, or E. For example, supposing the shoulder blade of some antediluvian animal is
found; perhaps we shall not be able unerringly to determine
to what particular category of mammals it belonged, or
perhaps we shall mistakenly put it into the cat or into the
horse category. But from this shoulder blade alone we shall
know without error that it was neither a bird, a fish, nor a
testacean. We have said that these negative deductions are
important in all sciences, but they are of exceptional
importance in the moral sciences and in metaphysics,
because the errors which they have removed were exceptionally harmful for these sciences. In the olden days, when the

natural sciences were still undeveloped, the whale was mistakenly regarded as a fish and the bat was regarded as a bird; but, in all probability, not a single person suffered as a result of this. Owing to the same cause, however, i.e., inability to subject a thing to exact analysis, mistaken opinions arose in metaphysics and in the moral sciences which caused people much more harm than cholera, plague and all infectious diseases. Let us suppose, for example, that idleness is pleasant and that work is unpleasant. If this hypothesis becomes the prevailing opinion, every man will take every opportunity to ensure for himself a life of idleness and compel others to work for him. This will give rise to every kind of enslavement and robbery: from so-called slavery proper and wars of conquest to the present more refined forms of these phenomena. This supposition was actually made by people, it actually became the pre-vailing opinion and prevails to this day and has actually caused so much suffering that it cannot be calculated. Let us now try to apply to the concept pleasure, or enjoy-ment, the deduction drawn from an exact analysis of the vital process. The phenomenon pleasure, or enjoyment, belongs to that part of the vital process which is called sensation. Let us suppose for the moment that this separate part of the vital process has not yet been sufficiently inves-tigated. Let us see whether anything about it can be de-duced from the exact information that science has acquired about nutrition, respiration, blood circulation. We see that each of these phenomena constitutes the activity of certain parts of our organism. We know what parts operate in the phenomena of respiration, nutrition and blood circu-lation, and we know how they operate. Perhaps we would err if from this information we drew any conclusion about what particular parts of the organism operate in the phe-nomenon of pleasant sensation, and about how they operate; but we have clearly seen that only the action of some part of the organism gives rise to what are called the phenomena of life. We see that when there is action there is a phenom-enon, and that when there is no action there is no phenom-enon. From this we see that in order to obtain a pleasant sensation there must be some kind of action on the part of the organism. Let us now analyze the concept action. Action calls for the existence of two things—the thing that acts, and the thing that is acted upon, and action consists in

that the acting thing exerts its efforts to alter the thing upon
which it is acting. For example, the chest and lungs trans-
pose and decompose air in the process of respiration; the
stomach digests food in the process of nutrition. Thus, a
pleasant sensation must also consist in the alteration of
some external object by the human organism. We do not yet
know what object is altered, or how it is altered, but we
already see that the source of pleasure must be some kind of
action on the part of the human organism upon external
objects. Let us now try to draw a negative deduction from
this result. Idleness is the absence of action; obviously, it
cannot produce the phenomenon that is called pleasant
sensation. It now becomes perfectly clear to us why the
well-to-do classes of society in all civilized countries complain of constant ennui, complain that life is unpleasant.
This complaint is quite justified. For the rich, life is as
unpleasant as it is for the poor, because owing to the custom
introduced in society by a mistaken hypothesis, wealth
is associated with idleness, that is, the thing that should
have served as a source of pleasure is deprived by this hypothesis of the possibility of affording pleasure. Whoever
is accustomed to abstract thinking will be convinced in advance that observation of everyday relationships will not
contradict the results of scientific analysis. But even those
who are unaccustomed to abstract thinking will be led to
the same conclusion by pondering over the meaning of the
facts that constitute so-called high society life. In it there
is no normal activity, i.e., activity, the objective side of
which corresponds to its subjective role; there is no activity
that deserves the name of serious activity. To avoid a subjective disturbance in the organism, to avoid sicknesses
that are the result of inaction, to avoid ennui, the society
man must create fictitious activity in place of normal
activity. He lacks motion that has an objective rational
purpose, so he "takes a constitutional," i.e., spends as much
time putting one foot in front of the other as he ought to do
in walking to work. He has no physical work to do, so he
spends as much time "doing gymnastics for the benefit
of his health," i.e., waves his arms and bends his body
(if not in the gymnasium, then at the billiard table, or at a
turning lathe for a hobby) as he ought to spend on physical
work. He has no practical cares concerning himself or his
family, so he engages in scandal and intrigue, i.e., spends

as much mental effort on nonsense as he ought to spend on practical affairs. But none of these artificial means can afford the human organism the satisfaction that is required for good health. The life of the rich man of the present day is like that of the Chinese opium eater: unnatural excitement is followed by lethargy, intense satiety by purposeless activity, which leaves him in the same state of ennui as that from which he tried to escape by indulging in it.

We see that even if we assume complete absence of exact research in some part of the vital process as a special part, the present state of exact knowledge about other parts of this same vital process already gives us an approximate idea of the general character of the unknown part, gives us a firm basis for important positive and even more important negative deductions concerning it. Of course, we have assumed the complete absence of exact research in certain parts of the vital process only for the purpose of explanation, argumenti causa. Actually, there is not a single part of the vital process on which science has not acquired more or less extensive and exact knowledge, especially concerning the particular part. For example, we know that sensation belongs to certain nerves, motion to others. The results of these special researches confirm the deductions drawn from general observations of the vital process as a whole, and of the more investigated parts of it.

Up till now we have spoken of physiology as a science that investigates the vital process in the human organism. But the reader knows that the physiology of the human organism is only a part of physiology, or to put it more exactly, a part of one of its departments—zoological physiology. Having noted this, we shall rectify the mistake we have made in the preceding pages: we should not have said that the phenomena of respiration, nutrition and the other parts of the vital process in man constitute the subject of physiology; physiology deals with the phenomena of this process in all living beings. The physiology of man exists in the same sense as the geography of Great Britain, as a chapter of a book—a chapter which may grow to the size of a whole book.

When we superficially survey two countries very remote from each other in development, a country inhabited by savages and one inhabited by a highly civilized nation, it seems to us as though in one of them there is not even a trace of the phenomena which in the other country astonish us by their colossal dimensions. In England we see London and Manchester, docks filled with ships, and railways. Among the Yakuts, say, there does not seem to be anything corresponding to this. But read a good description of the life of the Yakuts; its chapter headings alone will suggest to you that your superficial view was mistaken. The chapter headings in a book on the Yakuts, exactly like those in a book on the English, are: soil and climate; mode of procuring food; habitations; mode of dress; means of communication; commerce, etc. You will ask yourself: What, have the Yakuts too means of communication and commerce? Yes, of course. Just as the English have. The only difference is that among the English, these phenomena of social life are highly developed, whereas among the Yakuts they are slightly developed. The English have London, but among the Yakuts there are phenomena that arise from the same principle upon which London arose. In the winter the Yakuts suspend their nomadic life and live in pit dwellings. These are dug near to one another, so that they form a group —here you have the embryo of a city. In England it began in the same way; the embryo of London was also a group of the same kind of pit dwellings. The English have Manchester with its gigantic machines which are called cotton mills. But the Yakuts too are not content with animal skins in their natural form, they sew them together. They make felt out of the hair, and making felt already comes near to weaving cloth. The needle is not far removed from the spindle, and Manchester is simply a conglomeration of tens of millions of spindles with their necessary appurtenances. The work of a Yakut family making clothing contains the embryo of a Manchester, just as the Yakut pit dwelling contains the embryo of a London. To what degree a certain phenomenon is developed in a certain place is another matter. The fact is that phenomena of all categories in various degrees of development exist among all nations. The embryo is the same among them all, it develops everywhere according to the same laws, but its environment is different in different places, and this explains the difference in development. The sour grapes that grow in Berlin are the same as the grapes that grow in Champagne and in Hungary, but the climate is different, and so, from the practical point of view, it may be said that the Berlin grapes, which are

fit for nothing, are things of a kind totally different from
the grapes of Tokay or Épernay, from which splendid
wines are made. Thus, the difference is enormous, obvious
to everybody; but you must admit that the scientists are
right in asserting that there are no elements in the Tokay
grapes that will not be found in the Berlin grapes.

We must survey the whole sphere of nature in order to
get to man, but up till now we have spoken only about
what is called inorganic nature and the vegetable kingdom;
we have not yet said anything about the animal kingdom.
In its most developed forms, the animal organism differs
very much from plants, but the reader knows that mammals
and birds are connected with the vegetable kingdom by
numerous transitional forms by which we can trace all the
stages of development of so-called animal life from plant
life. There are plants and animals that scarcely differ from
one another, so that it is difficult to say in which kingdom
each should be classed. Some animals scarcely differ from
plants in the epoch of the full development of their organism;
but all animals, in the first period of existence, are almost
like plants in the first period of their growth. In both animals and plants the cell serves as the embryo. The cell
that serves as the embryo of the animal so closely resembles the cell that serves as the embryo of the plant that it is
difficult to distinguish one from the other. Thus, we see
that all animal organisms begin from the same thing that
plants begin from, and only later do some animal organisms
assume forms very different from those of plants and reveal
to a very high degree qualities which in plants are so feeble
that they can be discovered only with the aid of scientific
instruments. For example, a tree contains the embryo of
locomotion; its sap moves within it as in animals; its roots
and branches stretch in all directions. True, this locomotion
affects only its parts, the plant organism as a whole does
not change its location; but nor does the polyp do so; its
power of locomotion does not exceed that of a tree. But
there are plants which do change their location: among
these are several species of the Mimosa family.

We must not offend anybody, and we would offend the
animals if, having observed that they must not regard themselves as beings of a nature different from that of plants,
reducing them to the degree of only a special form of the
same life that is seen in plants, we did not say a few words

in their honour. Indeed, scientific analysis reveals the fallacy of bare statements to the effect that animals totally lack different honourable qualities, such as, for example, some capacity for progress. Usually it is said: an animal remains all its life what it was when it was born; it learns nothing and makes no progress in mental development. This opinion is demolished by facts known to everybody: bears learn to dance and to perform all sorts of tricks; dogs learn to fetch and carry and to dance; elephants are even taught to walk the tightrope, and even fish are trained to assemble at the sound of a bell—all this is done by trained animals, they would not be able to do it if they were not trained; training gives them qualities they would not have otherwise. Animals are not only taught by man, they teach one another. It is known that beasts of prey teach their young to hunt; birds teach their young to fly. But, we are told, this training, this development, has a certain limit beyond which the animal does not go, so that every species remains stationary, development affects only individual members of it. The individual animal may have its history, but the species remains without a history, meaning progress. This is also wrong; whole species of animals improve under our very eyes. The breeds of horses, or cattle, are improving in a certain country. Man benefits only from the development of an animal's economic qualities: the increased strength of horses, the heavier fleece of sheep, the larger yield of milk and meat from cattle. That is why we improve whole species of animals only in their external qualities. But after all, this shows that animals can improve not only as individuals but in whole species. This one fact alone would be sufficient to enable us to draw the indubitable conclusion that even the mental faculties of animals in every species do not remain stationary at one point, but also change. The natural sciences tell us that the cause of change in the muscles, i.e., change in the quality of the blood, necessarily causes some change in the nervous system too. If a change in the composition of the blood which feeds the muscles and the nerves changes the nutrition of the muscles, then the nutrition of the nervous system must also change; and a change in nutrition must necessarily change the quality and the action of the parts of the organism that receive this nutrition. A horse of an improved breed must necessarily receive impressions somewhat different from those received by a common horse; you see that its eyes shine with a more vivacious light. This shows that its visual nerve is more perceptive, more sensitive. If the visual nerve has changed in this way, then some change must have taken place in the entire nervous system. This is not merely a hypothesis, it is a positive fact, known, for example, from the fact that the foal of a domesticated horse, of a well-brought-up horse, if one may so express it, gets accustomed to harness more quickly and easily than the foal of a wild, untrained horse. This shows that the mental faculties of one are more developed in a certain direction than those of the other. But this is a matter that serves the purposes of man and not the needs of the animal itself; this development affects only the lower aspects of mental life, like all development imposed for purposes alien to those who are being developed. Animals display still greater capability of progress when their development is prompted by their own needs. Our domesticated animals, which have become accustomed to their slavery, which have developed in respects needed by their masters, have, in general, become stupefied by their slavery. They have become timid and unresourceful in unforeseen circumstances. When, however, they recover their freedom, they recover the resourcefulness and daring of the free state. A horse that has run wild learns to defend itself from wolves, to get at the grass under the snow in winter. Wild animals in general are able to adapt themselves to new circumstances. Books on the habits of animals are replete with stories about how wasps, spiders and other insects that are put in glass cases are able to adapt their lives to the new circumstances. At first the insect tries to go on living in its customary way; gradually, failure teaches it that the old way is unsatisfactory and it tries new ways, and if the circumstances do not kill it, it, at last, arranges its life in a new way. A bear that has found a keg of wine at last finds out how to knock the bottom out. We shall not quote the innumerable stories that are told about the resourcefulness of animals but will mention only one general fact relating to whole species. When men appear in an uninhabited place, the birds do not know how to safeguard themselves against them; but gradually experience teaches them to be cautious, to be wary of this new enemy, and all species of game learn to behave more cleverly towards the hunter than before, learn to evade and to outwit him.

8 — 3857

We have used the term "mental faculties" in relation to animals. Indeed, it cannot be denied that they possess memory, imagination and power to think. It is needless to speak of memory; everybody knows that there is not a single mammal or bird that does not possess this faculty, and in some species it is very strongly developed. In dogs it is very great. A dog recognizes a man it has not seen for a very long time; it is able to find its way to its master's house from very remote places. If memory exists, there must also be imagination, for imagination only regroups different scenes retained by the memory. If there is nervous activity, i.e., if there is a continuous change of sensations and impressions, the old conceptions must necessarily continuously present themselves in combination with the new ones, and this phenomenon is exactly what we call imagination. That animals possess imagination is positively proved by the fact that cats dream. Often a sleeping cat behaves like a somnambulist, now expressing anger and now joy. But there is no need to attach too much importance to the particular fact that cats dream; that animals possess imagination is revealed by a much more general fact—the inclination of the young of all animals to amuse themselves by playing with external objects which could not serve as the objects of such games if the young animals did not regard them as something in the nature of dolls. A kitten plays with a chip of wood, or a scrap of wool, as if it were a mouse. It throws the piece of wool, pretending that it has run away, crouches and then jumps and catches the imaginary mouse. This is positively like playing with a doll, only this doll is not in the role of a baby to a mother, or of a maid to a young mistress, but in the role of a mouse. That cannot be helped, every being ascribes to objects the role that interests it.

Thinking consists in choosing with the aid of memory from the different combinations of sensations and conceptions prepared by the imagination those that correspond to the needs of the thinking organism at the given moment; it consists in choosing the means for action, in choosing the conceptions by means of which it is possible to achieve a certain result. This applies not only to thinking about mundane objects, but also to so-called abstract thinking. Take, for example, the most abstract thing: the solution of a mathematical problem. Newton, interested in the prob-

lem of the law governing the quality, or force, manifested
in the motion of the celestial bodies, accumulated in his
memory very many mathematical formulae and astronomical
data. His senses (chiefly one sense—sight), continuously
acquired new formulae and astronomical data from reading
and from his own observations. The combination of these
new impressions with the preceding ones gave rise in his
head to diverse combinations, formulae of figures. He
devoted his attention to those which seemed to suit his
object, to suit his need to find the formula of the given
phenomenon. As a result of the attention devoted to these
combinations, i.e., of the intensification of energy in the
nervous process when they appeared, they developed and
grew until, at last, by different arrangements and rear-
rangements, the aim of the nervous process was achieved,
i.e., the formula sought was found. This phenomenon, i.e.,
the concentration of the nervous process on the combinations of sensations and conceptions that satisfy its desire
at the given moment must necessarily take place once the
combinations of sensations and conceptions exist, or in
other words, once there is a nervous process which is itself
a series of different combinations of sensations and conceptions. Every being, every phenomenon, grows and gains
strength on the appearance of data which satisfy its needs,
attaches itself to them, feeds on them—and this, properly
speaking, is what we call choosing conceptions and sensations
in thinking, and this choice, this attachment, is the essence
of thinking.

It goes without saying that when we find that a theoretical formula expresses both the process that takes place
in Newton's nervous system in discovering the law of
gravity and the process that takes place in the nervous
system of the fowl that finds an oat grain in a dung heap,
it must not be forgotten that the formula expresses only
the same essence of the process. It does not mean that the
dimensions of the process are the same, that the impressions
the phenomena produce on people are the same, or that
both forms could produce the same external result. For
example, in our previous essay we said that although grass
and oak trees grow in conformity with the same law, out
of the same elements, grass cannot possibly produce the same
activity, produce the same results as an oak tree. From oak
trees man can build huge houses and ships, whereas from

grass, tiny birds can build only nests. Or, for example, the same process takes place in a heap of decaying wood as takes place in the furnace of a huge steam engine, but the decaying heap cannot carry people from Moscow to St. Petersburg, whereas a steam engine with its furnace carries thousands of people and tens of thousands of poods of merchandise. A fly flies thanks to the same force and in conformity with the same law as does the eagle, but this does not mean, of course, that it can fly as high as the eagle.

It is said that animals do not reason—this is utter nonsense. You raise a stick at a dog; the dog runs away with its tail between its legs. Why? Because the following syllogism took shape in its head: when I am beaten with a stick I feel pain; that man wants to beat me with a stick: I shall run away from him to avoid the painful sensation his stick can cause. It is ridiculous to hear people say that in such a case the dog runs away by instinct, mechanically, and not from reason, not consciously. It did indeed act by instinct and mechanically, but not entirely; by instinct, from habit, it mechanically put its tail between its legs when it ran away from you, but conscious thought induced it to run. In the actions of every living being there is a side of unconscious habit, or the unconscious action of organs; but this does not preclude the participation of conscious thought in an action which is accompanied by some unconcious movements. When a man is frightened, his facial muscles unconsciously, instinctively, assume the expression of fright; nevertheless, there takes place in that man's mind another part of this phenomenon which belongs to the sphere of consciousness. He is conscious of being frightened, he is conscious of having done something that expresses fright; this conscious side of the fact gives rise to new consequences. Perhaps the man will be ashamed of having been frightened, perhaps he will take measures to protect himself from the thing that frightened him, or perhaps he will run away from it.

But we have forgotten: some people say that animals have no consciousness, that they are not conscious of their sensations, of their thoughts, their syllogisms, they only have them. How this is to be understood, and how the people who utter these words can understand this themselves, has always been a riddle to us. Not to be conscious of one's sensations—tell me, is there any sense in these words? How can one obtain a distinct picture of the combination of conceptions they are supposed to rouse? Sensation is precisely the term that is applied to a phenomenon that one feels; to have an unconscious sensation would mean the same as having an unfelt feeling, seeing an invisible object, or, to use a celebrated expression, "hearing silence." There are very many senseless expressions consisting of a combination of words that correspond to concepts that do not hang together; anybody can utter them, but everybody who utters them thereby shows that either he himself does not understand what he is saying, or that he is acting the charlatan. For example, some people say: "imponderable liquid"; but what is a liquid, not matter of what kind? After all, it is a body; after all, it is something material. All matter possesses the property that is called attraction, or gravitation, which is, that every particle of matter attracts to itself other particles and is itself attracted by them. On earth, this property is revealed by weight. i.e., gravitation to the centre of the earth. And so, all liquids necessarily have weight, and the term "imponderable liquid" is a nonsensical combination of sounds such as the expressions: a blue sound, sugar saltpetre, etc. Considering that the nonsensical expression "imponderable liquid" was employed for so long in physics, it is not surprising that there should be an abundance of such expressions in psychology, which has been elaborated less than physics. Scientific analysis reveals their absurdity, and one of the aspects of the development of science is their expulsion.

The hypothesis that animals lack consciousness becomes still more amusing when it assumes a sort of absurdly lofty tone and divides the phenomenon of consciousness into two categories: simple consciousness and self-consciousness, and claims that animals possess simple consciousness, but not self-consciousness. This is such an absurdity that it can be compared only to the following distinction: a violin gives forth only a blue sound, it cannot give forth a self-blue sound; that kind of sound is made by the violoncello. Whoever understands this subtle conclusion concerning the sounds of the violin and of the violoncello will also quite clearly understand that in animals sensation is accompanied by consciousness, but not by self-consciousness; in other words, that animals sense external objects, but do not feel that they sense them; in other words, they have feelings which they do not feel. From this one ought to conclude that in all probability animals eat with teeth with which they do not eat, that they walk on legs on which they do not walk. The existence of pigeon's milk is obvious to us now. Pigeons have milk which they do not have. Since they have it, it exists; but since they do not have it, the common saying rightly assumes that it cannot be obtained anywhere. Whoever believes these so well-founded opinions only has to sit over a fern on St. John's eve and he will receive the flower of invisibility.

If we apply precise analysis to the fact of sensation, the whole phantasmagoria will vanish at the very first touch. By its very nature, sensation necessarily presupposes the existence of two elements of thought, merged into one thought. Firstly, there is the external object, which creates the sensation. Secondly, the being that is conscious of the sensation. Conscious of the sensation, it is conscious of being in a certain state. Consciousness of the state of a certain object means, of course, being conscious of the object itself. For example, I feel a pain in my left hand; at the same time I also feel that I have a right hand; at the same time I feel that I, of whom this left hand is a part, exist, and, in all probability, I also feel that the pain is in *my* hand. Or perhaps it is not I who feels the pain? Or, if I feel the pain, I feel it not in *my* hand, but in the hand of some Chinese in Canton? Is it not ridiculous to argue about such things, to argue whether the sun is a sun, a hand a hand, and about similar intricate problems?

In what way does Rothschild differ from a poor man? Is it in that the twenty kopek piece in the poor man's pocket is an ordinary silver coin, whereas the heaps of silver coins in Rothschild's vaults are minted from some sort of a self-silver, which is much better than ordinary silver? If Rothschild were not rich, but merely vain, he might have invented such nonsense in order to prove that he was superior to the poor man. But as the man is really rich, there is no need for him to conjure up such absurd fantasies. He plainly says to the poor man: my silver is exactly the same as yours, but you have less than one-hundredth part of a pound of it, whereas I have tens of thousands of pounds of it. Therefore, measuring the right to respect by wealth, I think that I deserve far more respect than you do.

It is also said that animals lack the feelings that are called exalted, altruistic and ideal. Is it necessary to prove the utter absurdity of this opinion by adducing universally known facts? A dog's devotion to its master is proverbial. The horse is so filled with ambition that when racing with another horse it needs not the whip and spur, but the curb; it is ready to go all out, to run until it drops dead, only to outpace its rival. We are told that animals are conscious of consanguinity, but are not conscious of kinship based on the exalted feeling of affection. But a hen which has hatched chicks from the eggs of another hen has no consanguine relations with those chicks; their organisms do not contain a particle of hers. We see, however, that the fact that the chicks she hatched came from another hen's eggs does not in the least diminish the care she devotes to them. What is the care she devotes to the chicks from another hen's eggs based on? On the fact that she has hatched them, on the fact that she is helping them to become hens and cocks, sound and healthy cocks and hens. She loves them as their nurse, governess, teacher and benefactress. She loves them because they are a part of her moral being—not material being, no, they do not possess a particle of her blood—in them she loves the results of her care, of her kindness, of her prudence, of her experience in poultry affairs. This is purely a moral relationship.

It is generally observed that children, on reaching adult age, are much less devoted to their parents than their parents are to them. The principal basis of this fact can be very easily discovered: a man primarily loves himself. Parents see in their children the result of the care they had bestowed upon them; but children take no part in bringing up their parents and, therefore, cannot regard them as the result of their activity. Under the present arrangement of society, the moral relation of adult children to their parents consists almost exclusively in that they keep them in their old age, and even this duty is performed voluntarily by very few children. The rest would not perform it if they were not compelled to do so by that sense of subordination to public opinion which, in general, compels them to refrain from behaving indecently, to avoid rousing public indignation by their behaviour. Of course, species of animals which do not live in societies have no social relationships which compel them to perform such a duty. We do not know how aged larks, swallows, moles and foxes spend the period of their decrepitude. Their lives are so insecure that, in all probability, very few of them live to old age; they probably fall a prey to other animals when the strength to fly, run away, or defend themselves wanes. It is said that hardly a single fish dies a natural death, is not devoured by other fish. The same must be presumed about most wild birds and mammals. The few who do live to old age probably die of hunger a few hours or days earlier than they would have done had they had food near them. But the fact that these aged mothers and fathers are neglected by their children must not cause us to be too severe in our judgment about the absence of filial affection among animals. Here we must be lenient, for our judgment on the subject is almost fully applicable to human beings.

When one speaks without a plan, one never knows where one's speech will lead to. We see now that we have got to the point of speaking about moral or exalted feelings. On the question of these feelings, practical deductions from ordinary, everyday experience have absolutely contradicted the old hypotheses which ascribed to man a multitude of diverse altruistic strivings. People learned from experience that every man thinks only about himself, is more concerned about his own interests than he is about the interests of others, that he nearly always sacrifices the interests, honour and life of others to his own. In short, everybody learned that all people are egoists. In practical affairs, all prudent people have always been guided by the conviction that egoism is the only motive that governs the actions of everybody they have dealings with. If this opinion, daily confirmed by the experience of every one of us, were not countered by a fairly large number of other facts of everyday life, it would, of course, in theory too, soon gain the upper hand over the hypotheses that egoism is only a corrupted heart, and that a man who is not corrupted is guided by motives that are the opposite of egoism: that he thinks of the interests of others and not of his own, that he is prepared to sacrifice himself for others, and so forth. But the difficulty arose precisely from the fact that the hypothesis that man is prompted in his strivings by the interests of others, a hypothesis refuted by hundreds of experiences in everyone's daily life, seemed to be confirmed by fairly numerous cases of altruism, self-sacrifice, and so forth.

For example, Curtius throws himself into the abyss to save his native city; Empedocles jumps into a crater to make a scientific discovery; Damon offers to die in order to save Pythias; Lucretia stabs herself in order to vindicate her honour. Until recent times there were no scientific means of precisely deducing these two categories of phenomena from one principle, of bringing opposite facts under one law. A stone falls to the ground, vapour rises. In the olden days people thought that the law of gravity which operates in a stone does not operate in vapour. It is now known that both these opposite movements, the falling of the stone and the rising of vapour, are due to the same cause, are governed by the same law. It is now known that under certain circumstances, the force of gravity, which generally tends to make things fall, manifests itself by compelling some bodies to rise. We have repeated many times that the moral sciences have not yet been elaborated as fully as the natural sciences, but even in their present by no means brilliant state the problem of bringing all, often contradictory, human actions and feelings under one principle has already been solved, as have been nearly all the moral and metaphysical problems which had puzzled people before the moral sciences and metaphysics began to be elaborated according to strictly scientific method. As in all aspects of his life, human strivings are not prompted by two natures, two fundamental laws, differing from or contradicting one another. As in human life as a whole, all the diverse phenomena in the sphere of human motives and conduct spring from one nature, they are governed by one law.

We shall not discuss those actions and feelings which everybody recognizes as being egoistic, selfish, prompted by selfish interest. We shall turn our attention only to those feelings and actions which seem to bear a character opposite to this. In general, it is only necessary to examine more closely an action or a feeling that seems to be altruistic to see that all are based on the thought of personal interest, personal gratification, personal benefit; they are based on the feeling that is called egoism. There will be very few cases where this basis will not be apparent even to a man who is not accustomed to make psychological analyses. If a husband and wife have lived in harmony together, the wife will quite sincerely and very deeply grieve over the death of her husband; but listen to the words in which she expresses her grief: "Who will care for me now? What shall I do without you? Life will be impossible for me without you!" Underscore the words "me, I, for me": they express the meaning of her lamentation, they are the basis of her grief. Let us take a feeling that is far loftier, purer than the greatest connubial love: a mother's love for her child. Her lamentation over its death is exactly the same: "My angel! How I loved you! What a joy you were to me! How I nursed you! How much suffering, how many sleepless nights you cost me! I have been robbed of all my hopes in you, I have been robbed of all my joy!" Here again we have the same "My, I, to me." The egoistic basis is just as easily discovered in the most sincere and tenderest friendship. Not much more difficulty is presented by those cases in which a man makes sacrifices for the object of his love. Even though he sacrifices his life, the basis of the sacrifice is personal interest, or a paroxysm of egoism. Most cases of self-sacrifice cannot be called self-sacrifice; they do not deserve that name. The inhabitants of Saguntum committed suicide to avoid falling alive into the hands of Hannibal. Such heroism may rouse wonder, but it was entirely prompted by egoistic interest. These people had been accustomed to live as free citizens, to suffer no wrong, to respect themselves and to be respected by others; the Carthaginian general would have sold them into slavery and their lives would have been a constant torment. They acted in the same way as a man with a toothache who goes to have the bad tooth drawn. They preferred an instant of mortal pain to endless years of torment. In the Middle Ages, heretics burnt at the stake at a slow fire of raw logs would try to break their chains in order to throw themselves into the flames: better to suffocate in an instant than to choke for several hours. Such indeed was the position of the inhabitants of Saguntum. We were wrong in assuming that Hannibal would have merely sold them into slavery. Had they not exterminated themselves, the Carthaginians would have exterminated them, but they would have first subjected them to barbarous torture, and common sense prompted them to prefer a quick death to a slow and painful one. Lucretia stabbed herself after Tarquinius Sextus had raped her, but she too was prompted by self-interest. What awaited her in the future? Her husband might have spoken words of consolation and endearment to her, but such words would have been sheer nonsense, testifying to the nobility of the one who uttered them, but by no means averting the inevitable consequences of the incident. Collation might have said to his wife: " I regard you as pure and love you as before." With the conceptions prevailing at that time, however, and prevailing with but little alteration today, he could not have proved his words by deeds; willy-nilly, he had already lost considerable respect and love for his wife. He might have attempted to conceal this loss by deliberately exaggerated tenderness towards her, but such tenderness is more offensive than coldness, more bitter than beating and abuse. Lucretia was right in thinking that suicide was preferable to living in a state that was degrading compared to the life she had been accustomed to. A fastidious man would prefer to go hungry rather than touch food that had been in any way polluted. A self-respecting person would prefer death to degradation.

The reader will understand that we are not saying all this with the object of belittling the great praise of which the inhabitants of Saguntum and Lucretia are worthy. To argue that a heroic action was at the same time a wise one, that a noble deed was not a reckless one, does not, in our opinion, mean belittling heroism and nobility. From these heroic deeds, let us pass to a more ordinary kind of action, although still only too rare. Let us examine cases like the devotion of a man who gives up all pleasure and all freedom to dispose of his time in order to look after another man who needs his care. A man who spends whole weeks at the bedside of a sick friend makes a far greater sacrifice than if he were to give him all his money. But why does he make this sacrifice; what feeling prompts him to do it? He sacrifices his time, his freedom, to his feeling of friendship—we emphasize, *his* feeling. This feeling is so strong in him that gratifying it gives him greater pleasure than he would obtain from any other occupation, even from his freedom. Were he to ignore it, refrain from gratifying it, he would feel greater discomfort than he would from failing to satisfy all other needs. Of exactly the same kind are the cases when a man forgoes all pleasure and gain for the sake of science or some conviction. Newton and Leibnitz, who denied themselves all love for women in order to devote all their time and all their thoughts to scientific research, were, of course,

heroes all their lives. The same must be said about those
active in the political field who are usually called fanatics.
Here again we see that a certain need becomes so strong in a
man that it gives him pleasure to satisfy it even at the expense
of other very strong needs. By their nature, these cases
differ very sharply from the motive that prompts a man to
sacrifice a very large sum of money in order to gratify some
base passion, but in their theoretical formula they all come
under the same law: the strongest passion gains the upper
hand over those that are less strong, which are sacrificed to
the former.

A careful examination of the motives that prompt
people's actions shows that all deeds, good and bad, noble
and base, heroic and craven, are prompted by one cause:
a man acts in the way that gives him most pleasure. He is
guided by self-interest, which causes him to abstain from a
smaller gain, or a lesser pleasure, in order to obtain a larger
gain or a greater pleasure. The fact that good and bad actions
are prompted by the same cause does not, of course, diminish
the difference between them. We know that diamond and
coal are both pure carbon, nevertheless, a diamond is a
diamond, a very costly article, while coal is coal, a very
cheap article. The great difference between good and evil
fully deserves our attention. We shall begin with an analysis
of these concepts in order to ascertain what circumstances
develop or weaken good in human life.

It has long been noted that different people in the same
society regard as good, things that are quite different, and
even opposites. For example, if a man bequeaths his property to people outside his family, those people regard it as
a good action, but the relatives who lose the legacy regard it
as a very bad one. The same difference in the conception of
good is observed in different societies, and in different epochs
of the same society. For a long time, the conclusion drawn
from this was that there is nothing constant, nothing
independent in the concept good that could be subject to a
common definition, that it is a purely conventional concept,
dependent upon the arbitrary opinion of people. But when we
examine more closely the relation of the actions that are
called good to the people who call them that, we find that
this relation always has one common, invariable feature,
which causes an action to be placed in the category of good.
Why do the people outside the testator's family who receive

the legacy regard the action by which they came into possession of the property as good? Because that action was beneficial for them. On the other hand, it was detrimental to the testator's relatives who lost the legacy, and that is why they regard it as a bad action. War against infidels for the spread of Mohammedanism seemed to the Mohammedans to be a good cause because it benefited them, it brought them booty. This opinion was fostered among them particularly by the higher clergy, whose power grew with new conquests. Individuals regard as good the actions of other people that are beneficial for them; society holds as good what is good for the whole of society, or for the majority of its members. Lastly, people in general, irrespective of nation or class, describe as good that which is beneficial for mankind in general. There are frequent cases when the interests of different nations and classes clash either with one another or with the interests of mankind in general. Equally frequent are cases when the interests of a given class clash with the interests of the nation. In all these cases a controversy arises over the character of the action, institution or relation that is beneficial for some and detrimental to other interests. The adherents of the side to which it is detrimental say that it is bad; the advocates of the side that benefits from it say that it is good. In such cases it is very easy to decide on which side theoretical truth lies. The interests of mankind as a whole stand higher than the interests of an individual nation; the common interests of a whole nation are higher than the interests of an individual class; the interests of a large class are higher than the interests of a small one. In theory, this gradation is beyond doubt; it is merely the application to social problems of the geometrical axioms: "the whole is greater than the part," "the larger quantity is bigger than the smaller quantity." Theoretical fallacy inevitably leads to practical harm. In those cases when, for its own advantage, an individual nation tramples upon the interests of mankind, or when an individual class tramples upon the interests of the nation, the result is always detrimental not only to the side whose interest had been encroached upon, but also to the side that had hoped to gain by this. It always turns out that a nation which enslaves mankind ruins itself; an individual class that sacrifices the whole nation to its own interest comes to a bad end itself. From this we see that when the national interests clash with class interests, the class which thinks of turning a national misfortune to its own advantage is mistaken from the very outset; it is dazzled by false calculations. The illusion that entices it sometimes bears the form of very sound calculation, but we shall quote two or three cases of this kind to show how fallacious such calculations can be. Manufacturers think that prohibitive tariffs are to their advantage; but in the end it is found that with prohibitive tariffs the nation remains poor and, because of its poverty, it cannot maintain an extensive manufacturing industry. Thus, the manufacturing class itself remains not nearly as rich as that class is under free trade. All the millowners in all the countries that have prohibitive tariffs taken together do not, of course, possess half the wealth that has been acquired by the millowners of Manchester. Landowners in general hope to gain from slavery (serfdom) and from other forms of forced labour; but in the end it is found that the landowning class in all countries where forced labour exists is ruined. Bureaucracy sometimes deems it necessary for its own good to hinder the intellectual and social development of the nation, but here too the result is always that it finds its own affairs disturbed and it becomes impotent. We have cited cases in which the calculations of a class which acts to the detriment of the interests of the nation in pursuit of its own appear to be extremely well-grounded; but here too the result shows that this was only apparent, that the calculations were wrong, that the class which had acted to the detriment of the nation had deceived itself with respect to its own interests. Nor can it be otherwise: the French or Austrian manufacturer is, after all, a Frenchman or inhabitant of Austria, and everything that is detrimental to the country to which he belongs, the strength of which is the basis of his own strength, the wealth of which is the basis of his own wealth, is detrimental to him too, for it dries up the source of his own strength and wealth. Exactly the same must be said about the cases where the interests of an individual nation clash with the interests of mankind in general. Here too it is always found that the calculations of the nation which set out to further its interests by damaging those of mankind were totally mistaken. Conquering nations have always ended by being exterminated or enslaved themselves. The Mongols led by Genghis Khan had lived in their plains in such a state of wretched savagery

that one would think it would have been difficult for it
to have become worse. But bad as had been the conditions
of the savage hordes that set out to conquer the agrarian
countries in Southern and Western Asia and Eastern Europe,
when these conquests were completed, the lives of these
unhappy people who had caused so much harm in pursuit
of their own enrichment soon became even more deplorable
than the wretched lives continued to be led by their fellow
countrymen who had remained in their native plains. We
know what end befell the Tatars of the Golden Horde.
Half of them, of course, perished during the conquest of
Russia and the unsuccessful incursions into Lithuania and
Moravia. The other half, which had seized an immense
amount of booty, was exterminated by the Russians after
the latter had recovered. Scientists claim that of the present-day Crimean, Kazan and Orenburg Tatars, there is
scarcely one who is a descendant of Batu's warriors, that
the present-day Tatars are the descendants of tribes which
had inhabited these places before Batu came, which had
been conquered by Batu in the same way as he had conquered
the Russians, and that the conquerors had vanished, had
been utterly exterminated by the fury of the vanquished.
The conditions of life of the Germans in the time of Tacitus
were only a little better than those of the Mongols before
Genghis Khan; but they gained little from the conquest of
the Roman Empire. The East Goths, the Langobardi, the
Heruli and Vandals, all perished to the last man. Of the
West Goths the name has remained, but only the name.
The Franks were not slaughtered by the tribes they had
conquered only because they slaughtered one another under
the Merovings. The Spaniards who devastated Europe
under Charles V and Philip II were ruined themselves;
they fell into slavery, and half of them died of starvation.
The French who devastated Europe under Napoleon I
were themselves conquered and ruined in 1814 and 1815.
It is not for nothing that the members of the class that enriches itself to the detriment of the nation are compared
to leeches; but remember what fate awaits the leeches who
enjoy sucking human blood. Only rare ones among them do
not encompass their own ruin by this pleasure; nearly all
of them perish, and if some do survive, they are subject
to severe illness, and they remain alive only thanks to
the care of those whose blood they sucked.

We have said all this in order to *show* that the concept good is not shattered, but, on the contrary, is strengthened, is most sharply and precisely defined when we discover its real nature, when we find that good means utility. Only if we interpret it in this way are we able to eliminate all the difficulties that arise out of the contradictory conceptions of good and evil prevailing in different epochs and civilizations, among different classes and nations. Science deals with nations, not with an individual man; with man, but not with a Frenchman or Englishman, not with the merchant or the bureaucrat. Science recognizes as truth only that which constitutes human nature. Only that which is useful to man in general is regarded as true good. All digressions from this norm in the conceptions of a given nation, or class, are a mistake, a hallucination, which may cause much harm to many people, but most of all to that nation, or class, which falls into this error by adopting, through its own fault, or that of others, a position among other nations, or classes, that makes it think that what is detrimental to mankind in general is beneficial for itself. "Perished like the Avers"—history repeats these words over every nation and every class that is overcome by the fatal hallucination that its interests clash with the interests of mankind in general.

If there is any difference between good and utility, it is only that the concept good very strongly brings out the feature of constancy, durability, fertility, an abundance of lasting and beneficial results, which, by-the-by, is also possessed by the concept utility. It is precisely this feature that distinguishes it from the concepts pleasure, enjoyment. The object of all human striving is pleasure, but there are two kinds of sources from which we derive pleasure. One kind is associated with transient circumstances over which we have no control, or if we have, they pass off without durable result. The other kind is associated with facts and circumstances firmly embedded within us, or if they are outside of us, they are there constantly for a long time. A sunny day in St. Petersburg is the source of much relief in life, of innumerable pleasant sensations for the inhabitants of that city. But this sunny day is a transient phenomenon, entirely lacking a basis, and leaving no durable result in the lives of the inhabitants of St. Petersburg. It cannot be said that that day provided utility, it provided only

pleasure. Good weather in St. Petersburg is a useful phenomenon only in those few cases, and only for a few people,
when it is fairly prolonged and, as a consequence, manages
to create a lasting improvement in the health of a few in-
valids. But whoever leaves St. Petersburg to live under a
good climate acquires something useful with respect to
his health and the enjoyment of nature, because, by going
there, he acquires a durable source of lasting pleasure. When
a man receives an invitation to a good dinner he receives
only pleasure, not something useful (and, of course, he receives even pleasure only if he is a *gourmet*). But if this man
with gourmet proclivities comes into a large sum of money,
he receives something useful, that is to say, the opportunity to enjoy good dinners for a long time to come. Thus,
by useful things we mean, so to speak, the durable principles
of enjoyment. If this fundamental feature of the concept
"utility" were always borne in mind when that term is used,
there would be absolutely no difference between utility
and good. But, firstly, the term "utility" is sometimes friv-
olously, so to speak, applied to principles of pleasure not
quite transient, it is true, but not very durable either. And
secondly, these durable principles of enjoyment can be
divided into two categories according to degree of durability: not very durable and very durable. It is this latter
category that is designated by the term good. Good is, as
it were, the superlative of utility, very useful utility, as
it were. A doctor has restored to health a man who had
suffered from a chronic illness—what did the doctor bring
his patient, good or utility? Here it would be equally convenient to use both terms, because the doctor brought his
patient the most durable principle of enjoyment. Our mind
is in the mood constantly to recall external nature, which
is supposed to be the only thing that comes within the pur-
view of the natural sciences, which are supposed to embrace
only one part of our knowledge and not the whole of it.
Moreover, we have observed that these essays of ours indicate that we have a very cold heart, and a vulgar and low
mind, which seeks in all things only utility, which pol-
lutes everything with the quest for material grounds, which
understands nothing lofty and lacks all poetic feeling. We
want to mask this shameful lack of poetry in our heart. We
shall look for something poetical with which to ornament our
essays. Influenced by the thought of the importance of the

natural sciences, we set out in search of poetry in the sphere of material nature, and there we find flowers. Let us then decorate one of our dry pages with a poetical comparison. Flowers, these enchanting sources of fragrance, these exquisite but fleeting sources of delight to our eyes, are pleasure, enjoyment. The plant on which they grow is utility. On one plant there are many flowers, some fade, others bud in their place. Hence, that from which many flowers grow is called a useful thing. But there are numerous annual flowering plants, and there are also rose trees and oleanders, which live many years, and every year bring forth many flowers. Similarly, it is by its lasting nature that good excels the other sources of pleasure that are simply called useful things and are not vouchsafed the name good, in the same way as a violet is not vouchsafed the name tree. They belong to the same category of things, but they are not all of the same magnitude and durability.

The fact that the term good is applied to very durable sources of lasting, constant and very numerous pleasures, of itself explains the importance that all thinking people ascribe to good when discussing human affairs. If we think that "good is higher than utility" we only say "very big utility is higher than not very big utility," we only express a mathematical truism, such as, 100 is more than 2; an oleander bears more flowers than a violet. The reader sees that the method of analyzing moral concepts on the lines of the natural sciences, divesting the object of all pomposity and transferring it to the sphere of very simple and natural phenomena, places moral concepts on an unshakeable foundation. If by useful we mean that which serves as a source of numerous pleasures, and by good, simply that which is very useful, no doubt whatever remains concerning the aim that is ascribed to man—not by extraneous motives or promptings, not by problematical assumptions, or by mysterious and fallacious beliefs—but simply by reason, by common sense, the need of pleasure. That aim is—good. Only good actions are prudent; only he who is good is rational, and he is rational only to the degree that he is good. When a man is not good he is merely an imprudent wastrel who pays thousands of rubles for things that are worth kopeks, spends as much material and moral strength in acquiring little pleasure as could have enabled him to acquire ever so much more pleasure.

But in this same conception of good as very durable utility we find yet another important feature, which helps us to discover precisely what phenomena and actions chiefly constitute good. External objects, no matter how closely they may be attached to man, nevertheless, only too often part from him: sometimes the man abandons them, sometimes they desert the man. Country, kinsmen, wealth— all these things can be abandoned by man, or they can abandon him; but there is one thing he cannot possibly part from as long as he lives, there is one being that is inseparable from him—himself. If a man can be useful to people because of his wealth, he can cease to be useful if he loses his wealth. If, however, he is useful to other people because of his own virtues, because of his own spiritual qualities, as the saying goes, all he can do is commit suicide; but as long as he refrains from doing that he cannot cease to be useful to other people—not to be so is beyond his strength, beyond his power. He may say to himself: I will be wicked, I will do people harm; but he will not be able to do that, any more than a clever man can be a fool even if he wanted to be one. Not only is the good done by the qualities of the man himself much more constant and lasting than the good done merely because he owns certain external objects, but the results are far greater. The good or bad use to which external objects are put is casual; all material means are as easily, and as often, used to people's detriment as to their benefit. The rich man who uses his wealth to benefit some people in some cases, harms others, or even the same people, in other cases. For example, a rich man can give his children a good upbringing, develop their health and their minds, and impart much knowledge to them. All this is useful for the children; but whether this will be done is uncertain, often it is not. In fact, the children of the rich receive an upbringing that makes them weakly, sickly, feeble-minded, vacuous and pitiful. In general, the children of the rich acquire habits and ideas that are harmful to them. If such is the influence of wealth upon those whom the rich man cherishes most, then, of course, still more perceptible is the harm it does to other people who are not so dear to the rich man's heart, so that it must be supposed that the wealth of an individual does more harm than good to the people who have direct relations with the rich man. But while it is possible to harbour some doubt about whether the harmful influence wealth exercises upon these individuals is equal to the benefit they derive from it or, as in all probability is the case, it greatly exceeds it, it is a totally indisputable fact[11] that the effect the wealth of individuals has upon society as a whole is far more harmful than good. This is revealed with mathematical precision by that section of the moral sciences which earlier than the others began to be elaborated in conformity with an exact scientific system, and some of the departments of which have already been fairly well elaborated by the science of social material welfare that is usually called political economy. What we find in relation to the superiority that material wealth gives some people over others applies to an even greater degree to the concentration in the hands of individuals of another means of influencing the fate of other people, a means outside of the human organism, namely, power. It too, in all probability, does much more harm than good even to the people who come into direct contact with it, and the influence it exercises upon society as a whole is incomparably more harmful than beneficial. Thus, the only real source of perfectly durable benefit for people from the actions of other people that remains are the useful qualities that lie within the human organism itself. That is why it is these qualities that are designated as good, and that is why the term "good" properly applies only to man. His actions are based on feeling, on the heart, and they are directly prompted by that side of organic activity which is called will. Therefore, when discussing good, a special study must be made of the laws that govern the action of the heart and will. But the will is given means of gratifying the feelings of the heart by the conceptions formed by the mind, and therefore, it is also necessary to pay attention to that aspect of thinking that relates to means of influencing the fate of other people. We make no definite promise, we shall merely say that we would like to elucidate the exact conceptions of present-day science of these subjects. It is quite possible that we shall succeed in doing so.

But we have almost forgotten that the term "anthropological" in the heading of our essays has still remained unexplained. What is this "anthropological principle in the moral sciences"? The reader has seen what this principle is from the very character of the essays. It is that a man must be regarded as a single being having only one nature;

that a human life must not be cut into two halves, each belonging to a different nature; that every aspect of a man's activity must be regarded as the activity of his whole organism, from head to foot inclusively, or if it is the special function of some particular organ of the human organism we are dealing with, that organ must be regarded in its natural connection with the entire organism. This is a very simple demand, one would think, and yet it is only recently that the thinkers engaged in the moral sciences have begun to understand its importance and to conform to it, and then not all by a long way, but only some of them, very few, whereas the majority in the scientist caste, which, like the majority in every caste, always sticks to routine, continues to work according to the old fantastic method of unnaturally cutting man into halves, each purported to spring from different natures. As a consequence, all the works of this routine majority now turn out to be the same kind of old junk as the works of Emin and Yelagin on Russian history, Chulkov's collections of folk songs, or the works of Mr. Pogodin and Mr. Shevyryov in our days. Here and there something resembling the truth can be found in them,— after all, Mr. Pogodin does quite rightly say that Yaroslav was Prince of Kiev and not of Cracow, that in Constantinople, Olga accepted the Greek Orthodox and not the Lutheran faith, that Alexei Petrovich was the son of Peter the Great. After all, Mr. Shevyryov does rightly observe that the food of the Russian common people is scanty and indigestible, that handsome lads are to be found among coach drivers, and in the Paisi Collection[12] he found rather interesting evidence of Russian paganism. But in the books of the learned couple from the late lamented *Moskvityanin*[13] these excellent truths are covered up by such a heap of absurd opinions that to separate the truth from nonsense is as difficult a task as finding rags fit for papermaking in places that have been explored by the keen eye and deft hook of the ragpicker. Therefore, ordinary people will do much better to refrain from undertaking this unpleasant task and leave it to the toilers who are accustomed to it. But these toilers, the specialists who keep in line with the conceptions of present-day science, tell us that the quantity even of scientific rags found in books like the works of the gentlemen we have mentioned and of their predecessors is so small that reading them is a positive waste of time, the only result of which can be a muddled head. The same thing must be said about all the old theories of the moral sciences. Their neglect of the anthropological principle deprives them of all merit. The only exceptions are the works of a very few of the old thinkers who followed the anthropological principle, although they did not yet employ this term to characterize their conceptions of man. Such, for example, were Aristotle and Spinoza.

As for the word "anthropology," it comes from the word "anthropos," which means "man"—but the reader knows this without our telling him. Anthropology is a science which, no matter what part of the human vital process it may deal with, always remembers that the process as a whole, and every part of it, takes place in a human organism, that this organism is the material which produces the phenomena under examination, that the quality of the phenomena is conditioned by the properties of the material, and that the laws by which the phenomena arise are only special cases of the operation of the laws of nature. The natural sciences have not yet reached the point of bringing all these laws under one general law, of uniting all the particular formulae into one, all-embracing formula. But that cannot be helped, we are told that even mathematics has not yet succeeded in bringing some of its parts up to this point of perfection. We have heard that a common formula has not yet been found for integration, as there is for multiplication and for raising to a certain power. This, of course, hinders scientific research. We have heard that the mathematician does all the parts of his calculations very quickly until he comes to integration, and then he has to spend whole weeks and months on a matter that could be done in two hours if a general formula for integration were already found. This is still more the case in the natural sciences. Up till now only separate laws have been discovered for individual categories of phenomena: the law of gravity, the law of chemical affinity, the law of disintegration and integration of colours, the law of the operation of heat, of electricity; but we have not yet brought them under an exact general law, although there are very strong grounds for thinking that all the other laws are somewhat particular variations of the law of gravity. Our inability to bring all the separate laws under one general law greatly hinders and delays all research in the natural sciences. The researcher gropes his way along haphazard, he has no compass, he is compelled to use less reliable methods of finding the right road, he wastes much time in useless wandering along round-about roads, only to go back to his starting point when he finds that they lead nowhere and begin to explore another road. And he wastes still more time in the endeavour to convince others that the wrong roads are really wrong, and that the good roads are really good and convenient. In the moral sciences it is exactly the same as in the natural sciences. But in both the natural sciences and the moral sciences, these difficulties merely delay the discovery of the truth and the spread of belief in it when it is discovered. When it is discovered its validity is, after all, obvious. The acquisition of this validity, however, cost far more effort than similar discoveries will cost our descendants when the sciences are more developed. And however slowly belief in truths may spread among people owing to their present lack of training to love truth, i.e., to appreciate its benefits and the inevitable harmfulness of all falsehood, truth will spread among them, because, no matter what they may think about it, however much they may fear it, however much they may love falsehood, after all, truth corresponds to their needs, while falsehood proves to be unsatisfactory. What the people need the people will accept, however mistaken they may be in trying to ward off what is imposed upon them by the necessity of things. Will the Russian husbandman who, up till now, has been a bad husbandman, ever become a good one? Of course he will. This conviction is not based on any transcendental hypotheses concerning the qualities of the Russian, not on a lofty conception of his national qualities, of his superiority to others in intellect, industry or skill, but simply on the fact that the necessity is arising for the Russian husbandman to conduct his husbandry more wisely and prudently than before. One cannot escape from, or evade, necessity. In the same way, man will not escape truth, because in the present state of human affairs it is, year after year, becoming an ever greater and more imperative necessity.

POLEMICAL GEMS [1]

GEMS COLLECTED FROM
RUSSKY VESTNIK [2]

> *Of Achilles' wrath, to Creece*
> *The direful spring*
> *O f woes unnumbered,*
> *Heavenly goddess sing.*
>
> *The Iliad.*

I

IN No. I, *RUSSKY VESTNIK* just frolicked a little
(and how prettily it did so), but in the February issue
it published a fundamental essay against us under the heading "Old Gods and New Gods." This heading implies that,
because of our inborn obsequiousness, we cannot refrain
from grovelling on our knees before some idol and, therefore, having overthrown our old ones, we are setting up
others, worse, perhaps, than the old ones, and are proclaiming blind worship of them. Well, this is a very cunning manoeuvre—we are always glad to give *Russky Vestnik* its due; it has decided to pose as the champion of the
right of human reason to freedom, in opposition to us, the
enslaver of reason to a new superstition in place of the
old prejudices. It has failed, however, to adhere to one
of the conditions of wit—it must be plausible, otherwise it is not wit, however subtle it may be. That section
of the public which disagrees with us, while perceiving
numerous shortcomings in us, never thought that we set up
idols. As for that section of the public which sympathizes
with us, the essay in *Russky Vestnik* can only cause amusement—it indicts us on the wrong count. We set up idols!—
please, do us a favour and accuse us of this more often, and
more strongly. We like it.

But let us examine this essay, in which the subject
of indictment is so skilfully chosen that we are sincerely
delighted with it. It begins by censuring us for some-

times speaking in a roundabout way about various subjects which can be discussed openly.

Why those sly winks, cunning hints, mantles of allegory, profuse irony, and heaps of parables, when the matter is very plain, and there is not the slightest necessity for all these military stratagems?

Good. But why is the entire essay, which starts with this reproach, written in the very style which is censured as superfluous? Why is it so completely enveloped in a "mantle" of stratagems that many readers believe that *Russky Vestnik* is defending materialism against us in the literal and not in the ironic sense? Why these stratagems? Because you could not explain the matter "plainly." We fully understand this, and we praise *Russky Vestnik* for the generosity with which it refrained in this article from using weapons which cannot yet be used in our country. This is indeed good. But if you yourself feel that it is impossible to speak plainly, why censure others for resorting to methods that they and you are forced to employ by the disgusting conditions under which we are all living?

Then follows a pretty "parable" about Ivan Yakovlevich, which, by the by, looks very much like an imitation of an article in the *Sovremennik* on Mr. Pryzhov's book. Why imitate those you jeer at? But perhaps it is not imitation, but only irony?[3]

The point of this parable is that for the nonsense we write we can be compared with Ivan Yakovlevich—very pretty and graceful; but why borrow your wit from nonsensical people like us? If proof that we are nonsensical is needed, here it is:

"Is X getting married?" somebody asked Ivan Yakovlevich. "No work no kololatsi," came the reply. *Kololatsi* is a mysterious word, but, evidently, the questioner was satisfied with it without delving into its meaning. *Kololatsi* is a meaningless word. But if you listen carefully you will hear this *kololatsi* so often that you will not blame this poor inmate of a lunatic asylum.

Kololatsi! Kololatsi! But is not much of that which is taught and printed *kololatsi*? Are not the philosophical articles that are sometimes published in our magazines *kololatsi*?

It is not a matter of what you say or write, of what you believe or do not believe in, of what you accept, or what you deny, it is not a matter of what truths you want to preach, harsh or tender, but whether you yourself understand what you are saying, whether you are capable of thinking, or only of weaving words which may seem to be very striking to unthinking people, but which. in essence, are nothing more than Ivan Yakovlevich's *kololatsi*.

Pretty, very pretty. "The kololatsi of a poor inmate of a lunatic asylum"—what genteel polemics! Then follow, all applied to us: "Madhouse," "nonsense," "obsequiousness," "fanatical worship of idols created by our ignorance," "pollution of thought at its source," "outrageous"—all this on one page, 894. Count up how many such gems you will find in the twelve pages of the article. This implies that other magazines cannot behave decently, but *Russky Vestnik* can.

After this comes a review of Mr. Antonovich's article on the *Philosophical Dictionary*.⁴ Mr. Antonovich is quite able to defend himself, and so, leaving this part of the article to his generosity, I shall quote an excerpt from the end of it that is addressed to me.

After reading Mr. Antonovich a long lecture, *Russky Vestnik* advises him to read "an article published in the *Papers of the Kiev Theological Academy*."

This article, entitled "From the Science of the Human Spirit," is a rather comprehensive work. Its author is Mr. Yurkevich, a professor at the Kiev Academy. He was prompted to write it by several articles on philosophical subjects that appeared in the *Sovremennik*.⁵ Mr. Yurkevich exposes the insolent charlatanry that is given out as the highest modern philosophy, and exposes it with a thoroughness that ought to satisfy even a man so exacting as Mr. Antonovich. It is an ill wind that blows nobody any good. We are grateful to charlatanry at least for having been the cause of the appearance of this excellent philosophical work. Mr. Yurkevich's article is not merely a denial, or an exposure; it possesses positive interest, and we have rarely had occasion to read in Russian anything so mature on philosophical subjects. But we do not wish to discuss Mr. Yurkevich's article merely in passing. In the next issue of *Russky Vestnik* we shall publish a lengthy excerpt from this treatise, which bears all the marks of mature, independent and fully self-controlled thinking.

Let us hope that the philosophical conceptions of the gentlemen who write for the *Sovremennik* will gradually clear up, and that they will, at last, find it possible to dispense with charlatanry. We already see considerable progress in some parts. Mr. Chernyshevsky, who is evidently the chief leader of this group, is already beginning to speak in human language on subjects of political economy. Il s'humanise, ce monsieur.* We enjoyed reading the articles over his signature in the last issues of that magazine. These no longer contain the nonsense that he on previous occasions gave out as profound wisdom obtained from the bottom of a mysterious well. His reasoning is sound, and in conformity with the principles of political economy, so that he need not now dissociate himself from the economists whom in the past he had called *poor numskulls*. He is one of them now in the arti-

---

* This gentleman is becoming human.—*Ed.*

cles signed [by him. We must give him his due: he learns his lessons well, and he is not wasting his time in preparatory school.

But while the former nonsense is not to be found in Mr. Chernyshevsky's articles that are signed by him, it is still to be found in others that do not bear his signature. In those, the *great* Russian economists Messrs Vernadsky, Bunge, Rzhevsky and Bezobrazov with whom are classed M. de Molinari, and, lastly, Carey and Bastiat, are still spoken of in a tone of mountebank irony. The litte screed we are referring to is a very curious one, it is a review of Carey's recent book *Letters to the President of the United States*. It contains a remarkable passage (a paraphrase of a passage in this article dealing with the drama *Judith* and ending with the words: "The path of history is not the pavement of the Nevsky Prospect; it runs entirely through dusty or muddy fields, through marshes and through dense forests. Whoever is afraid of being covered with dust and of soiling his boots with mud, let him not engage in public activities.").

After this charming episode, in which one can positively hear the mournful sigh uttered by "Judith" who had defiled herself to save her motherland, the reviewer returns to the subject of tariffs and free trade. This charming poetry could not have invaded this dry and prosaic subject if it had not been invited into it by the writer's own heart. It could have burst out only from the depth of his soul, impelled only by the irresistible force of involuntary confession. What tears and tenderness there are in this story, an unexpected oasis in the desert of protective duties, where a different wind, dry and harsh, blows!

Indeed, is not charlatanry a sort of defilement? Is it not a great sacrifice that is made by those brave people who engage in public activities, and who by the unthinking rabble are called charlatans? But, O new Judiths, tell us, for the sake of what great gain are you defiling your immaculate purity "the like of which men have never seen"?

Oh, gentlemen, do not defile yourselves in vain! Do not make unnecessary sacrifice! Do not try to justify yourselves by heroism: there is no heroism here. You are deluding yourselves and deceiving others. You yourselves do not know, you do not feel what a pernicious hindrance you are in the midst of this society, whose strength and life are not yet firmly established. If you are capable people, so much the worse. In time, perhaps, you will abandon charlatanry; your conceptions will become clearer (after all, little by little, Mr. Chernyshevsky's economic conceptions are becoming clearer, and this is a good sign); you will realize it afterwards, but it will be too late. You will look back on your past with disgust and, perhaps, you will deeply regret the clownish part you are playing now.

The "Judith" episode indeed deserves ridicule, and its application to my "charlatanry" is pretty—we can say without joking that this excerpt from the article is very playful and clever. With all my heart I join with *Russky Vestnik* in laughing at the idea of putting me on a par with Judith in the sacrifices I make to save my country.

It is indeed very amusing; here *Russky Vestnik*'s ridicule
hits the mark. And the melodramatic tone of the Judith
episode is indeed very amusing, coming, not quite appropriately, in an article on such a dry subject as tariffs
and Carey. This is excellent banter. And, of course, I wrote
that article; that goes without saying. This is what
Russky Vestnik hints at. It is not mistaken. But I am
afraid that *Russky Vestnik* is mistaken in assuming that my
economic opinions are becoming rectified. I take this
merely as a kindness towards myself, no more; but I decline it with thanks. There is a different explanation. Until
last year I wrote articles on separate problems of political economy that interested me most; these, of course, were
problems which seemed to me to have been exceptionally badly elucidated by the writers of the prevailing school
of economics.[6] Therefore, these articles were almost entirely in the nature of polemics against the prevailing theory, explanations of ideas which it has not yet accepted
because of their novelty, or has rejected because of their
trend. At the beginning of last year it occurred to me that
it would be useful to give the Russian public a systematic
treatise on economic science in its entire scope. I began to
translate Mill and to supplement him. Mill mostly explains
undisputed problems; many of my supplementary remarks
were also necessarily related to these problems. This is the
reason for the different impressions created by my previous articles and my edition of Mill. When writing the
articles I said in effect: I will deal only with those things
on which I disagree with you. In my translation of Mill,
my object was to explain everything that concerns the
subject, whether on points of agreement or disagreement
with you. The fact that *Russky Vestnik* failed to guess that
this was the principal reason for the difference in its impressions does no credit to its power of penetration. Shall
I give the other reasons? It is a rather delicate matter for
me to mention them myself, but I will not stand on ceremony, because I am not very much afraid of ridicule when
I know that I am speaking the truth. So here is another
reason why *Russky Vestnik* began to find that the articles
signed by me are less "nonsensical." My reputation is
growing—I am saying this without false modesty, for I am
not overproud of my literary activities.[7] Why? *Russky
Vestnik* itself says:

Pitiful literature! We are in the schoolroom stage. Our mind has
no self-respect, and it is difficult for it to have any. It burrows in the
ground and hides; it is developing slavish propensities (*Russky
Vestnik*, March, "Literary Reviews," p. 210).

After this explanation there is no need for me to stand
on ceremony either with myself or with others. In many
people this feeling is mitigated by a certain amount of
self-satisfaction, which to some extent is justified.
Whatever situation they may be in,[8] they remain honest
men. This is some consolation for them. As a writer I am
as honest as they are; but this is no consolation for me
whatever, and my feeling towards literature, including
the part I contribute to it, is one of unmitigated harshness.
Whoever wishes to can make fun of this explanation;
I am quite aware that it can very easily be turned into
ridicule against me. But laugh at and berate me as much
as you please, you know that I am right, and I know that
you agree with me in this to a very considerable extent.

Consequently, I am dead to praise and to censure of
what I write. I am my own judge, pronouncing verdicts
on myself and others that cannot be corrected or vitiated
by anything. And my attitude towards what the public
thinks about me is the same as that towards what may be
said about some Mlle Rigolboche. Whether she is clever
or foolish, good-looking or ugly, makes no difference;
the life she is leading is such that no compliments can
modify opinion about her.

There are people of a different type; they are timid
in the presence of celebrities. Of such a type is *Russky
Vestnik*. Formerly it was bold enough to say that there was
nothing but nonsense in my articles; now it is too timid
to say that. That is all. Are you satisfied with this explanation, *Russky Vestnik*? If not, I will give a fuller one.
I have not over much pity for myself, and for others, you,
for example, I have, of course, no more pity than I have
for myself. Consequently you stand no chance in a controversy with me, not because I am cleverer than you are,
or because I wield the pen more skilfully than you do, but
because, at least in this matter, my tongue is free, whereas yours, even in this matter, is tied.

But when I said that I was indifferent towards my literary reputation I did not say all. I cannot be indifferent
towards myself as a man. I know that better times will

come for literary activity, when it will be of real benefit to society, and when the one who possesses talent will
really earn a good name.[9] And so I am wondering whether
I will still be able to serve society properly when that
time comes. Fresh strength and fresh convictions are
needed for this. But I see that I am beginning to enter
the company of "respected"* writers, that is to say, of
the writers who are played out, who lag behind the movement of social requirements. That rouses a bitter feeling. But what can be done? Age tells. One cannot be young
twice. I can only envy the people who are younger and
fresher than I am. Mr. Antonovich, for example. What?
Shall I deny that I do indeed envy them, that I envy them
with a shade of vanity wounded by their freshness, with
the resentment of one who has been outstripped?

Would you also like me to tell you what contribution
Russky Vestnik has made to my reformation? Permit me.
Here, too, I will tell the truth. I read *Russky Vestnik*
when it first began to appear, up to No. 17, or No. 18,
I do not quite remember, of the first year of issue. After that, until the end of the first year, I had occasion
to read two or three articles in the subsequent numbers,
because that year the bookseller sent the *Russky Vestnik*
to my home. In the following year I requested that this
be stopped. From that time until the beginning of this
month I literally read nothing in *Russky Vestnik* except
four articles, which I will enumerate. A biography of
Radishchev was sent to the *Sovremennik* containing, according to the person who sent it, many important additions
to what had been published in *Russky Vestnik*.[10] It so
happened that there was nobody in the office to compare
the two versions except myself. I took a copy of *Russky
Vestnik* and compared it with the manuscript and found
that the additions were unimportant and not worth publishing. Last summer I read some polemical articles about Mme.

---

* All this will afford *Russky Vestnik* the opportunity to utter
jeering remarks about me: "Mr. Chernyshevsky thinks that his reputation is growing—what a pleasant delusion." "Mr. Chernyshevsky is
transformed from Judith into Mlle Rigolboche" (develop parallel
between him and Mlle Rigolboche). "He grieves over the fact that
he is a respected writer—let him not grieve, nobody respects him,"
and so on and so forth. Such jeers may be caustic and amusing if
they are written with skill and vivacity.

Svechina, because, being short of material for the magazine, I had thought of writing a short article about this affair.[11] The issue of *Russky Vestnik* in which the pot shots at Mme. Tours were taken contained an article by Mr. Malinovsky (if I am not mistaken) on, I think, gunpowder explosions.[12] The magazine happened to open at this place and I read several pages. Lastly, sitting at a sick man's bedside one day, I read a few pages to him of a story by Mme. Kokhanovskaya; I do not remember the title; all I know is that it is told in the first person by a woman who frequently quotes fragments of folk songs.[13]

Does this satisfy you, *Russky Vestnik*? Or perhaps you would like to know why I did not read you? I will tell you: because of utter indifference. If you want to know more, I will tell you that too, it makes no difference to me.

But now I have begun to read. These are dull, stupid times, I thought to myself; let me try to find some amusement in polemics which, as I hear, *Russky Vestnik* is craving for. And so I am amusing myself. Not much of an amusement, but better than taking to drink from ennui. When I get tired of it I will drop it, no matter what they write about me, or about the *Sovremennik*. But I am not tired of it yet, and so I am amusing myself, as you see.

II

Well, here is a most fundamental essay in the polemical section in No. IV of *Russky Vestnik*: "From the Science of the Human Spirit" by P. Yurkevich. Papers of the Kiev Theological Academy, 1860. In "Old Gods and New Gods" *Russky Vestnik* promised to publish a lengthy excerpt from the exemplary article by that profound and excellent thinker, Mr. Yurkevich. It is now redeeming its promise. No. IV contains the beginning of the excerpt and the end is to be published in No. V. The excerpt is preceded by a preface by *Russky Vestnik*. I read the preface and was content with that. The matter became clear to me from the preface alone.

It appears that Mr. Yurkevich's essay was written for the purpose of refuting my article on "the anthropological principle." This refutation is published in a magazine issued by the Kiev Theological Academy, and Mr. Yurkevich is a professor at that Academy.

I myself am an old seminary student. I know from my own experience the position of people who were educated as Mr. Yurkevich was educated. I have seen people who occupy the same position that he occupies. It is, therefore, hard for me to laugh at him; it would mean laughing at a man who is unable to get hold of decent books, who is utterly unable to control his own development, who is in a position that is inconceivably restricted in every possible respect.

I do not know how old Mr. Yurkevich is; if he is no longer a young man it is too late to bother with him. But if he is still young, I gladly offer him the small stock of books that I possess.

That is all I have to say about Mr. Yurkevich, but I have not yet finished with *Russky Vestnik*, for I must tell it that it (unintentionally, of course) has played Mr. Yurkevich a scurvy trick. We seminary students all wrote exactly what Mr. Yurkevich has written. If *Russky Vestnik* wishes, I can send it what in seminary language is called the "tasks," that is, compositions, short dissertations, that I wrote when I was in the philosophical class at the Saratov Seminary. The editors will be able to see for themselves that these "tasks" contain exactly what is no doubt contained in Mr. Yurkevich's article. I am sure it contains exactly the same stuff, although I have not read it, and will not read it, as I will not read the whole of the excerpt published in *Russky Vestnik*, but will read in the proofs only that part which I have marked off for inclusion in this article. I know beforehand what I would find in it if I read it, all, down to the last word. I remember very much of it by heart. How these things are written, and what is written in them is known, that is, we seminary students know. Others may think they are new, they may, perhaps, think they are good; that is as they please, but we know what these things are.

If Mr. Yurkevich's position changes, he will very soon find it unpleasant to recall his article. If it had remained only in the "Papers," it would have remained unknown to the public. By publishing this excerpt from it, *Russky Vestnik* has discredited Mr. Yurkevich in the eyes of the public.

I would like to refrain from quoting the passage from this unfortunate excerpt, but my duty to *Russky Vestnik* compels me to do so. It thinks that I am refuted by Mr. Yurkevich's article; I have no right to conceal from my readers this article which, as *Russky Vestnik* assures us, refutes me....*

SECOND COLLECTION

GEMS COLLECTED FROM
OTECHESTVENNIYE ZAPISKI[14]

I

I have just received for the adornment of my collection No. 7 of *Otechestvenniye Zapiski* containing a big polemical diamond, which I shall conscientiously endeavour to polish into an excellent gem. This diamond is in that abundant mine of rarities, the literary criticism section. It is just the thing I want. Up till now I have quoted little from this section, and Mr. Dudyshkin, who is the editor of this section, is probably annoyed about it. He may think that I have deliberately ignored him. Well, I can now make up for my omission and avert this reproach.

Oh, Mr. Dudyshkin! In a matter on which even a layman would dare to have his own opinion, you fear to exercise your intelligence; but in a matter that requires expert knowledge you rely on your own judgment. Take, for example, Mr. Yurkevich's refutation of my essays on the anthropological principle in philosophy —now, can a layman judge whether Mr. Yurkevich is talking sense or nonsense? The whole subject is full of methodological, psychological and metaphysical subtleties; it is a subject for profound reflection even for that great sage Kuno Fischer, a translation of whose work is published in this very July issue of *Otechestvenniye Zapiski*. To understand these subtle divisions and subdivisions one must be an expert. Take Mr. Katkov, for example; he understands these things. He understands what Mr. Yurkevich says in his article; he saw that Mr. Yurkevich's views run close to the trend of thought that he himself regards as correct, and he made no

---

* Further follows a long excerpt from Yurkevich's acticle.—*Ed.*

mistake in publishing in his magazine an excerpt from Mr.
Yurkevich's article, accompanied by words of great praise.
I disagree with this trend and, therefore, express myself
harshly about all its followers, but it is quite natural
that they should mutually admire one another. But why do
you and *Otechestvenniye Zapiski* express admiration for Mr.
Yurkevich's article? Do you think that you belong to the
same trend? Just imagine! To your ill luck, I happened
to glance at the upper part of the inner side of the cover
of that same No. 7 of *Otechestvenniye Zapiski* in which
you go into raptures over Mr. Yurkevich. What did I see
on that page? The following announcement in big type:

"By the editors"

"As many of our readers have expressed the wish to
read the whole of Buckle's *History of Civilization in England* in a Russian translation, the editors of *Otechestvenniye Zapiski*, having already published six chapters of
this work, intend, if they meet with no special obstacles,
to have the whole work translated and to publish it in
this magazine in the order in which it will appear in the
English original."

Do you realize how comical this is? Well, listen. Except for a very few pages in the section dealing with the
Encyclopedists, of which you will not approve when
you read them, and of which I do not approve, the whole of
the first volume of Buckle's work is the very opposite
of the trend followed by Mr. Yurkevich, and which you
took it into your head to admire. What a joke! Verily
it may be called "The History of Civilization in *Otechestvenniye Zapiski*."

But do not let the comical result of your announcement about the translation of Buckle's work grieve you;
you are doing an excellent thing in having it translated,
and I hope from the bottom of my heart that you will meet
with no obstacles in this useful undertaking. The Russian
public will be grateful to you for it.

Would you like me to describe the psychological process that took place in your mind when, publishing Buckle,
you expressed admiration for Mr. Yurkevich? If you find
that my explanation of this astonishing occurrence is not
mistaken, it will prove to you that I am a past master in
the art of psychological observation, and that I know the

laws of psychology as well as I know the five fingers on my hand. You will agree that I am putting myself to a very severe test, for the psychological act that I am about to analyze is an unusually intricate one, and appears to violate all the laws of thinking. To praise a thing which you are helping to destroy by publishing an excellent work is surely a psychological phenomenon that even Kant could not unravel. But I will unravel it and bring it under the general laws of psychology.

First law. An ignorant person tries to copy one who knows. *Russky Vestnik* praised Mr. Yurkevich, so you praised him.

Second law. It is pleasant to hear abuse hurled at a man whom you yourself berate. Mr. Yurkevich takes up the cudgels against me; you do the same; that is why it gives you pleasure to listen to Mr. Yurkevich.

Ponder deeply over yourself, watch your own psychological process with your mind's eye; you will see that my explanation is flawlessly correct.

But confess that this observation of your own psychclogical process was a difficult matter for you. Confess that you were continuously distracted from this difficult task of self-observation by the flicker of all sorts of extraneous thoughts such as the following: "No, I did not follow the example of *Russky Vestnik* in finding that Mr. Yurkevich was right; I thought of it myself; I am impartial; I understand the essence of the controversy; Mr. Yurkevich's trend is my trend; I did not express admiration for Mr. Yurkevich because he opposed Chernyshevsky," and so on, and so forth. Confess that these illusions forced themselves into your mind, and you found it very difficult to repulse them. But your love of truth triumphed over these seductions. The concentrated attention you paid to the actual course of your psychological process drove these dreams away and you, at last, grasped the two psychological laws quoted above and fearlessly applied them to the strange fact that a magazine which publishes a translation of Buckle's excellent book praises Mr. Yurkevich. You deserve all honour and praise. Your feat was a difficult cne, but you performed it.

Do you realize now how difficult is the self-analysis of one's mind, what special methods it requires? Do you see that a man who has not made a special study of a

subject cannot judge of the merits or demerits of an
article written about it? But the fruits of this learning
are very sweet for vanity, are they not?

If they are, I hope that in gratitude to me for this
lesson you will not refuse to join me in reviewing the contents of the article written against me and published in
the July issue of *Otechestvenniye Zapiski*, in the section
of which you are the editor (Mr. Krayevsky will probably
not take offence at my addressing myself entirely to you).

II

After a few preludes concerning language, the article
in which Mr. Yurkevich is admired mentions a review of
Mr. Lavrov's book on philosophy made by Mr. Antonovich in
No. IV of *Sovremennik* of this year.[15] This review is mentioned
in connection with a statement that its trend is similar to
that of my essays on the anthropological principle. Supposing it is, but should you have mentioned this article,
which had such ludicrous results for your magazine, showing
that as soon as you read it you changed your mind about
the merits of Mr. Lavrov's works. You would have done
better had you remained silent; but since you felt an
irresistible urge to speak, you should have admitted
that Mr. Antonovich's article had opened your eyes.

But you want to berate it. It would be interesting
to know what for. Here is the only flaw you find in it:
"no mental strain is required to understand all that Mr.
Antonovich says. The lucidity" (of this article) "has
amazed everybody." Judge for yourself: should lucidity be
regarded as a merit or a demerit? It goes without saying
that everybody but a fool would think that in pointing
to this feature of Mr. Antonovich's article you were praising it. You, however, think that you discredited it by
doing so. Let me tell you how this second "history of your
civilization" happened.

You had heard a lot about philosophy being a brain-
racking subject. You had tried to read philosophical
articles like those written by Mr. Lavrov and utterly
failed to understand anything. But in your opinion, Mr.
Lavrov was a good philosopher, and so the following syllogism formed itself in your mind: "I don't understand

philosophy; hence, what I do understand is not philosophy."
This is actually what you say: Mr. Antonovich writes lu-
cidly; hence, there is no philosophy in his article. It was
proper for you to think that way when you formed your
judgment of philosophy from Mr. Lavrov's articles. But
now you are of the opinion that Mr. Lavrov's philosophical
articles were bad (confess that this is so: we have evidence to prove it). That being the case, should you not
have reasoned in this way: "No matter what subject a man
with a confused trend of thought may discuss, his speech
will be confused, puzzling. As for philosophy, perhaps
it is not such an unintelligible subject after all." Had
you reasoned in this way, you would not have been mistaken.

But all that is said about Mr. Antonovich's article,
in passing, as it were, is that it is just like Chernyshevsky's
articles on the anthropological principle—there cannot
be any philosophy in these articles because they are lucid.
Then it goes on to speak of me alone.

"Mr. Chernyshevsky's article called forth a reply
by Mr. Yurkevich in the *Papers of the Kiev Theological
Academy*, a reply which at once placed Mr. Yurkevich in
front of all those in our country who have ever written
about philosophy" (hence, in front of Belinsky, who wrote
a great deal about philosophy, in front of the author of
"Letters on the Study of Nature"?[16] So be it. But surely
not in front of Mr. Gogotsky and Mr. Orest Novitsky? Why
offend these great thinkers of the same school as that to
which Mr. Yurkevich belongs?). "We can only recall the
articles by I. V. Kireyevsky" (excellent! So, in your opinion, good and esteemed I. V. Kireyevsky was really a
philosopher and not merely a naive dreamer? But if that
is the case, you ought to regard the late Khomyakov as your
chief authority, and it would be quite appropriate for you
to change the name of your magazine from *Otechestvenniye
Zapiski* to *Russkaya Beseda*,[17] or *Vozobnovlyonni Moskvityanin*), "which were distinguished for the same simplicity
and lucidity of philosophical exposition as that which we
have found in Mr. Yurkevich's article. Knowledge of philosophical systems, complete mastery of the subject and
an independent attitude towards it—such are Mr. Yurkevich's merits" (God send him every perfection!). "In trend,
he is an idealist, and the fulcrum of his doctrine is so deeply
investigated and so finely brought out that we have never

read anything like it in Russian" (but Mr. Gogotsky has also investigated all this just as deeply and finely) "and in this we entirely agree with *Russky Vestnik*" (just as I entirely agree with the *Mining Journal*—I don't know the subject, I don't understand the articles, but I presume they are written by people who do know and, therefore, I take all they say on trust), "which published this article. We shall not reprint this article, we shall only quote two passages from it: one on 'the transformation of nerve stimulation into sensation,' and the other, on the 'transformation of "quantity" into "quality."' All the other theses rest on these two" (*Otech, Zap.* "Russ. Lit.," pp. 41, 42). But before that the end of Mr. Yurkevich's article is quoted, and I, being an ignoramus, was greatly astonished by it. Supposing I am an ignoramus, but did it not occur to you that you should not have mentioned this. I have never written for *Russky Vestnik*; so it does not discredit itself by talking about my ignorance. For *Otechestvenniye Zapiski*, however, I wrote a good deal at the beginning of my literary career; it follows, therefore, that ignoramuses can be contributors to your magazine, and even be thought a lot of by the editors.

You are wrong in repeating what other people say about my ignorance, Mr. Dudyshkin. Other magazines may say that I am an ignoramus, but it is unbecoming for your magazine to say so. Quoting Mr. Yurkevich's remarks about my ignorance, *Otechestvenniye Zapiski* also quotes his statement that "spatial movement of the nerve is not in itself nonspatial sensation," and that "the transition from quantity into quality is clear only to *Sovremennik*, but for everybody else it is an insoluble problem." You see, Mr. Dudyshkin, what technical subtleties Mr. Yurkevich discusses, but you undertake to pass judgment on his article and decide that he is right, when you are not even able to tell in what spirit he is writing, and whether he does not disagree as much with your Buckle, for example, as he disagrees with me. *Otechestvenniye Zapiski* goes on to say:

"The reader sees from the passages quoted, which can give one an idea of Mr. Yurkevich's splendid article containing an entire treatise on philosophy, that he is dealing with a man who well understands the subject" (the reader may or may not see this; the point is, do you see it yourself, or are you merely repeating what others have said?). "Mr. Yurkevich does not resort to clownish antics to put his readers in a good humour, he is not afraid to approach a subject and say: this has not yet been proved by anyone, it is unknown to us, although he had much more grounds for speaking with assurance than Mr. Chernyshevsky had. At least one thing is clear, namely, that such a reply deserves a detailed rejoinder." (I assure you that it does not deserve one, from my point of view. If any scientist were to argue that you are wrong in rejecting alchemy or cabalistics, would you deem anything in his article worthy of refutation? I regard the school to which Mr. Yurkevich belongs in exactly the same way as you regard scientists who adhere to the doctrines of alchemy or cabalistics. Everyone is at liberty to think as he pleases about whether the theory I hold is good or bad, but it is a fact known to every specialist that a man who holds such a theory must regard as ridiculous and hollow the arguments raised against it by the theoreticians of the school to which Mr. Yurkevich belongs. This surprises you only because you are little acquainted with the mutual relations of the different philosophical trends.) "But what does Mr. Chernyshevsky do? What he always does when a serious reply is demanded of him: he brushes it aside with unpardonable levity" (why "always"? I have not engaged in polemics for several years and have not answered any challenges or arguments, so there could be no levity or gravity in my answers, for the simple reason that no answers were given. But before that, when I did engage in polemics, I wrote extremely lengthy and extremely comprehensive answers to the observations made against me), "which, at last, grew into insolence towards Mr. Yurkevich." (That cannot be helped. If you respect a certain trend and I do not, my attitude towards it will seem to you to be unpardonably insolent. This is exactly what people who respect Mr. Askochensky's trend think about your attitude towards him). "We are sure that Mr. Chernyshevsky's followers will think that such a reply is extremely witty. This is what Mr. Chernyshevsky says" (*Otech. Zap.* "Russ. Lit." p. 55). Here follows the first half of my review of Mr. Yurkevich's article. Then comes the following:

"How do you like this answer? In other words, Mr. Chernyshevsky says: you are an unfortunate man, Mr. Yurkevich, because you were educated at a seminary and had unsatisfactory textbooks" (but isn't that true?). "But I, later on, got hold of splendid books, and they contain everything I say. Believe me, if you are not too old, I can help you in your misfortune, I will send you my books. And in them you will see that I am right!" (I think that here I expressed good will. Tell me, would you give a different answer to a man who criticized your articles on history and literature by quoting Mr. Zelenetsky's textbook?)

"These words remind us of Baron Brambeus of blessed memory, who always answered in this way when Belinsky demanded a categorical answer from him. The only difference is that Baron Brambeus' answers were often much more witty than Mr. Chernyshevsky's. For example, sometimes he answered as follows: 'Some time, when I have the leisure, I will write an answer in Latin.' At the present time even Baron Brambeus would not write such replies because times have changed, and it is possible" (Yes? How fortunate you are!) "to answer the questions that are put to you. In those dreadful times when our philosophy hid under the wing of aesthetic reviews of Gogol, George Sand and Sue, Belinsky's opponents, of whom Senkovsky was one, for the purpose of debating in a roundabout way, changed Mme Dudevant's name to Mme 'Infront' and played on this in intricate reviews.[18] But even in those days such reviews roused disgust; what can one say when Mr. Chernyshevsky resorts to the same trick against Mr. Yurkevich in a controversy of first-class importance on a clearly-put question? If Baron Brambeus fell in general esteem in the dreadful times in which he lived and the public turned away from him for playing such tricks, what does Mr. Chernyshevsky expect in our times?"

So you compare me with Baron Brambeus, do you? Very well, but an examination of this comparison will show that you made it without thinking what would come of it.

The point at issue is the extent of my knowledge. I am like Baron Brambeus, that is, like the late Senkovsky. But who has any doubt that Senkovsky was a man of amazingly wide knowledge? So what can be said of my knowledge if I am like him? This is what comes of being unskilled in debate. You wanted to show that I am an ignoramus, but from what you said it follows that you regard me as a man of very extensive knowledge. Are you not unwise in rushing into polemics?

But according to what you say, I am like Senkovsky in that I like to brush arguments against me aside with a joke. Very well, but why was Senkovsky fond of jesting? Because he was a man of powerful intellect and considered that he could afford to treat his opponents with disdain. Is that what you wanted to say about me? Obviously not, but that is what follows from what you said. I thank you: you are suggesting to your readers that I am a man of powerful intellect, conscious of my superiority to my opponents. I do indeed feel (and you too must feel) that I am superior to you. What is to be done? I cannot help feeling that. You are such a poor debater.

But Senkovsky fell in public esteem, and you prophesy the same fate for me. In firing your abuse at me, however, you overshot the mark. You said things that show that I am quite safe from this danger. You mentioned that Senkovsky took up the cudgels against Belinsky, Gogol and George Sand, that is, against those whom I defend. Hence, if Senkovsky fell in public esteem because of his trend, then my fate must be the very opposite to his. I will rise in public esteem. Is that what you wanted to say? You did not? But that is what follows from what you said. You are a poor, very poor debater. Let us see what else you have to say.

"Really, Mr. Chernyshevsky, one cannot know everything in our times—the natural sciences, philosophy, political economy, world history, Russian history and literature. He who knows everything knows nothing. Our literature has taught us at least this axiom and we can bring it against you. You know everything. There is something suspicious about that." (*Otechestvenniye Zapiski*, July, "Russian Literature," pp. 56, 57.)

But who told you that I know everything? Nobody knows everything—neither Montaigne, Voltaire, Heine, nor even Bayle knew everything. Do I have to explain to you the difference between a well-read man and a specialist, between a scientist specialist who promotes the progress of a particular science, or a particular branch of science, and a journalist, for whom it is sufficient to be educated, whose function is only to popularize the conclusions drawn by the scientists, only to ridicule crude prejudice and backwardness? Do you not realize what a ridiculous position you, a journalist, have put yourself into by pretending that you do not know what a journalist is? I cannot understand what pleasure there can be in posing as an ignoramus who does not even know the functions of his own profession. Do you really think that a journalist should write only on subjects in which he is a specialist? If that were so, a magazine would resemble the *Comptes rendus* of the Institut de Paris.

But you are interested in me personally: you would like to know whether I am a learned man. Well, here you are. For a long time already I have not been studying any special subject except political economy. Formerly, I studied certain other subjects rather diligently, so that, although I have forgotten many of their minor details, I am quite able to form an opinion about what others write on these subjects. What is there surprising in this? But above all, by profession I am a journalist, like yourself, that is, a man who tries to keep abreast of the progress made in intellectual life in all questions of interest to educated people. Is that what you understand the profession of a journalist to be, or is it not?

Or, perhaps, it is not this that you want to know, but the extent of my knowledge? The only answer I can give to this is: my knowledge is incomparably wider than yours. You know that yourself. Then why did you strive to get this answer in print? You acted unwisely, very unwisely in leading up to it.

But please, do not think I am proud; there is nothing to be proud of in knowing much more than you do. And also, do not think that I want to say that you possess very little knowledge. No, you do know some things, and, in general, you are an educated man. The only pity is that you are such a poor debater. Well, have I given a straight answer, or have I brushed the question aside with a jest?

Then follows a passage from Lewes' book on physiology, dealing with the difference between physiological and chemical processes. Imagining that Mr. Yurkevich sees things in the same light as Lewes, Mr. Yurkevich's advocate in *Otechestvenniye Zapiski* says:

"Compare this excerpt from Lewes with what Mr. Yurkevich says; you will find that our Kiev professor is just as familiar with the latest researches as Mr. Chernyshevsky. Hence, his knowledge is not confined to seminary exercise books and textbooks, as Mr. Chernyshevsky asserts.

We are saying this only for the benefit of those who think that every rash sweeping statement" (whose? Mine?) "must always be true. Unfortunately, there are very many people like that among us" (well, are you a skilled debater when you admit that there are very many people who approve of my articles. Oh, what stupidity! And yet you rush into debate!). "People would think that Mr. Yurkevich is a scholastic and that Mr. Chernyshevsky is a progressive."

It seemed to you that there was a resemblance between the words of Mr. Yurkevich and those of Lewes. There is a resemblance in the words, but there is none in their meaning. Do you realize where Mr. Yurkevich is tending? Towards support of ideas that are the very opposite of— how can I express it?—well, say, the very opposite of the ideas of Buckle, whose work you are having translated. But that is not where Lewes is tending. All he says is that every separate science examines partial variations of the general laws of nature under special conditions. Read the whole chapter of Lewes' book from which you have taken the excerpt; it will convince you that Mr. Yurkevich's ideas are as remote from his as they are from mine. I fully agree with Lewes, but ask Mr. Yurkevich what he thinks of the school to which Lewes belongs; he will express himself with a bluntness that will make you sorry you had anything to do with Lewes, that is, if you value Mr. Yurkevich's opinion. But in speaking to you, one must be more explicit. The subject about which Mr. Yurkevich entered into controversy with me is still vague to you. Let me explain it to you as far as that is possible.

Do you at least see what I am doing with you? I miss hardly a word you have said, I take your speech in its entirety. But why do I do that? To agree with you? No, I make interpolations between your words, I rearrange them, turn them the other way round, and they acquire a meaning opposite to what you gave them. For example, you say that I am an ignoramus; I reset your words and it follows from them that I am a man of extraordinary learning. You say that I find it difficult to reply to arguments levelled against me; again I reset your words and it follows that you yourself admit that I am a far better debater than the people who argue against me. Do you see now how, and why, I use your words? And I have used them, haven't I?

This is exactly the way the school to which Mr. Yur-kevich belongs uses the works of the natural scientists. It scours the works of honest specialists in order to turn the facts in favour of a theory that is the very opposite of the views held by these natural scientists.

In all probability, you think that I am distorting the meaning of your words, don't you? But I think that you yourself did not understand what you were saying, and that I am imparting to your words their true meaning, which you failed to see.

In exactly the same way Mr. Yurkevich's school thinks that the natural scientists do not know what they are talk-ing about, and that it alone imparts the true meaning to the facts it borrows from them, a meaning that is the very opposite of the view held by the erring natural scientists. And the natural scientists think that this school is dis-torting the facts it borrows from them.

Perhaps you still fail to understand what this is all about. I will explain it by means of an example—I have a passion for examples (now here is something you might have jeered at, for this passion sometimes makes my articles too long drawn out—you would be quite able to denounce me for this defect, but you clutch at aspects of the matter with which you cannot cope). Well, here is the example.

You smoke cigars, don't you? You know very well that raw cigars are bad; dry ones are much better. Very well. How do we get dry cigars? You know that too. After mak-ing a stock of cigars, the manufacturer who is concerned about the reputation of his factory lets them lie for a very long time, two or three years, perhaps, at ordinary room temperature. In the course of this time the cigars dry. Good. But the cigars could be brought to the same degree of dryness in a matter of two hours by putting them in a hot temperature, say, 60°. Why is this not good? For this reason, as you yourself know. When a cigar dries quickly, the ingredients upon which its flavour depends enter into a chemical combination which spoils the flavour; when, however, it dries very slowly, these ingredients combine in a way that gives the cigar a good flavour. You know that this is so? Good. Then what follows from it? This. The process of evaporation of the moisture in the raw cigar leads to one result when it takes place slowly, and to an entirely different result when it takes place quickly.

It is exactly on these lines that Lewes reasons on the difference between the chemical process that takes place in the retort and the digestion that takes place under circumstances entirely different from those in a chemical retort. He says something like this: boil a piece of beef on a quick fire and you will get broth of a certain kind. Boil a piece of beef on a slow fire and you will get broth of an entirely different kind. If, however, you boil the beef not in ordinary water, but in some acid solution (such as the liquid from sauerkraut), you will get broth of a third kind. In short, the result of a process changes with every change in the conditions in which the process takes place. And so Lewes says that every case must be examined separately and not be mixed up with the others. Well, I think he is right.

But what does the school to which Mr. Yurkevich belongs deduce from facts of this kind? That the natural sciences explain to us only one aspect of life, while we become cognizant of the other, higher side, and so on, and so forth, and that the naturalists are doomed to perdition. Do you agree with this trend?

Is the matter clear to you at last?

Perhaps it is not clear to you even now? If not, we shall continue our talk a little longer. What do you think, is the celebrated Hume assisted by some wonderful inner power, or is he merely a clever trickster? From what I know about you, I am sure that you think he is merely a trickster. But in conformity with the method adhered to by the school of which Mr. Yurkevich is the spokesman, this question must be answered as follows: "Pause, don't be rash. Can chemistry or physiology explain the fact that from St. Petersburg Mr. Hume can see a man in Pennsylvania, in America, can give us precise information about his health, can see that he is suffering from a gumboil and that he is putting a leech to his gum? Permit me to ask you, my dear sir, how this fact can be explained by your chemistry or your physiology, by your catoptrics or your dioptrics. Confess, my dear sir, that Mr. Hume is assisted by some special inner power!" From what I know about you I am sure that you will very coldly retort to such an interrogator: "My dear sir, what you say is sheer fiction; the truth, which you do not wish to see, is that Mr. Hume saw nothing in America from St. Petersburg, he simply fooled you."

This is exactly the kind of controversy that is going on between the theory of the natural scientists, which I think is right, and which I as a professional journalist am trying to popularize, and the school to which Mr. Yurkevich belongs. On whose side are you in this controversy? From what I know about you I am sure that you would be on my side, only you don't know what the controversy is about.

But my example is not ended. I halted at the point where you say to your opponent, i.e., Hume's supporter: "I deny that Hume is assisted by a special inner power, because I do not look upon the fact that deluded you with the same eyes that you do." But your opponent will not leave your remark unanswered. He will tell you that "the people who watched Hume were convinced that it was not a trick"; and he will add: "make the acquaintance of these people, they will tell you much that you don't know. As for your rejection of my opinion about Hume, it is only insolence begotten of your ignorance." What will you do with a man like that? That depends upon your mood. If you are not in the mood to laugh, you will walk away from him; but if you are in the mood to laugh, you will laugh at him. In either case you will be right. Such a man is either not worth talking to at all, or if you do talk to him you cannot refrain from ridicule. I shall now ask you to read the following passage from the article in which you berate me for my attitude towards Mr. Yurkevich. After quoting the second half of my review of Mr. Yurkevich's article, where I said that there was no need for me to read that article because, judging by what *Russky Vestnik* itself said, it was exactly the same sort of stuff that I had once been compelled to learn by rote, *Otechestvenniye Zapiski* goes on to say:

"Do you understand what this means? Do you see what we are driving at?" (I don't know whether you can see what I am driving at even now; but you certainly did not see what Mr. Yurkevich was driving at, at the time you wrote these lines.) "All this is nonsense, which we do not want to read. This is what we understand Mr. Chernyshevsky's words to mean.

"My dear sir, Mr. Yurkevich argues: 1) that you know nothing about the philosophy you are talking about; 2) that you confuse the method of the natural sciences applied to

psychic phenomena with the actual elucidation of psychic
phenomena; 3) that you fail to understand the importance
of self-observation as a special source of psychological cognition; 4) that you mix up the metaphysical theory of the
unity of existence and the physical theory of the unity
of matter; 5) that you concede the possibility of the
conversion of quantitative into qualitative differences;
6) lastly, that you concede that every view is already a
scientific fact and thereby lose sight of the difference between human and animal life. You destroy the moral individuality of man and concede only the egoistic promptings
of the animal.

"Clear, one would think. This concerns no other person but yourself, not philosophy and physiology in general,
but your ignorance of these sciences. What has seminary
philosophy to do with it? It is only a red herring. Why
mix up totally different things and say that you knew all
this before, when at the seminary, and that you still know
it by heart now?"

The only thing I would like to say to all this is: how
can I refrain from saying what I think is absolutely correct? But to please you I shall explain the matter to you,
but again, by referring to those very same exercise books
that you were unacquainted with, and which prevented
you from understanding the matter.

Had you taken the trouble to peruse these exercise
books, you would have found that they ascribe to Aristotle,
Bacon, Gassendi, Locke, etc., etc., to all the philosophers
who were not idealists, all the shortcomings that Mr. Yurkevich ascribes to me. Hence, these reproaches do not
apply to me as an individual writer; properly speaking,
they apply to the theory which I deem useful to popularize.
If you do not believe me, take a look at the *Philosophical
Dictionary*, published by Mr. S. G., which belongs to the
very same trend that Mr. Yurkevich belongs to; there you
will find that the same is said about every nonidealist:
that he is ignorant of psychology, that he is unacquainted
with the natural sciences, that he rejects inner experience,
that he is smashed to atoms by the facts, that he confuses
metaphysics with the natural sciences, that he degrades
man, and so on and so forth. Tell me, why should I take
seriously the author of a certain article and the people
who praise him, when I see that they bring against me

personally what has been for ages said about every thinker of the school to which I belong? I must reason in the
following way: either they do not know or pretend not
to know that these are not reproaches against me personally, but against a whole school, and, consequently, are
people little acquainted with the history of philosophy,
or they are resorting to tactics which they know are
dishonest. In either case, it is not worth while entering
into serious debate with opponents of such a kind.

Tell me, if anyone were to reproach you for being ignorant because, for example, you think that popularity is
an important element for literature, would that reproach
apply to you personally? No. It would apply to a whole
school. Would you deem it necessary to argue: "the fact
that I call popularity an important element of literature
is not evidence of my ignorance?" Of course not; you would
deem it beneath your dignity to do so.

But perhaps, since you fail to understand the issue in
this controversy, what I say is not yet quite clear to you?
I shall, therefore, add a few explanations for your benefit.

Do you know that it is not only I who has been called
an ignoramus, but also, for example, Hegel? Do you know
why he was called an ignoramus? Because his trend of
thought was displeasing to certain scholars. What do you
think, was Hegel an ignoramus, or not? And who do you
think called him an ignoramus? People from the very same
school to which Mr. Yurkevich belongs.

Do you know that Kant was called an ignoramus? Why
was he called that? Was it right to call him that? Who
called him that? The answers are the same as in the preceding example.

Do you know that Descartes was called an ignoramus?
Why? Was it right? Who called him that—see the preceding example.

Take any other thinker you please who has promoted
the progress of science—every one of them was accused of
the same thing, for the very same reason, and by the
very same kind of people.

Are you capable of drawing some conclusion from these
facts? If you were, there would have been no need for me
to enter into these explanations; but everything goes to
show that you are not capable of doing so, and that being
the case, I must suggest the conclusion to you. Here it is:

People bound by routine accuse every pioneer of being ignorant simply because he is a pioneer.

Please remember this. This will help you to avoid numerous blunders.

But you are aware of this conclusion only as a fact. It is evident, however, that you are inclined to interest yourself in philosophical matters. For your benefit I will show that this fact is an inevitable deduction from the laws of psychology.

Let us suppose that a certain man is quite satisfied with a certain proposition concerning intellectual or material affairs. Another man comes along and says to him: "it is unsatisfactory." In the mind of the man who is satisfied there inevitably arises the thought: "he is dissatisfied with it because he is not familiar with it." And this is how the thought arises: what is quite satisfactory is good. He to whom good seems not good fails to see that it is good. He who speaks about good without seeing good, does not know what good is. That is how people who are satisfied with something that is not satisfactory arrive at the idea that the one who is dissatisfied with the unsatisfactory thing is not acquainted with it. This invariably happens in all spheres of life and thought. If, for example, you say to a drunkard that drink is harmful, he will certainly answer: "take a drink yourself, you will see how good it is." If you suggest to a merchant accustomed to our ways of trading to sell his wares at fixed prices, prix fixe, without haggling, without bargaining, he will certainly answer: "You say that because you know nothing about our business." „You no doubt remember that when the stethoscope was first recommended for detecting chest and other internal complaints, experienced practitioners objected and said: "You are talking about the stethoscope because you are incompetent healers. We don't need a stethoscope." So it is in all things, including philosophy. Do you understand now?

Or is it all still unclear to you? If it is, then I must say that I am tired of explaining. It will have to remain unclear to you. Evidently, it has not fallen to your lot to understand anything about philosophy. But in order not to grieve you, I will assume that you have, at last, understood, and will tell you what the deduction is from all you have read as if you have understood what you have read. Here it is:

The theory which I think is right is the latest link in a series of philosophical systems. If you do not know this, and do not want to take my word for it, I advise you to take up any history of modern philosophy you please, and in every book you will find confirmation of what I say. One historian will say that the theory is right, another will say that it is wrong, but all will unanimously tell you that this theory is really the latest, that it emerged from Hegel's theory, just as the latter emerged from Schelling's. You may censure me for perceiving progress in science and for thinking that its last word is the fullest and most correct. That is as you please. Perhaps you think that the old is better than the new. But concede that it is possible to think otherwise.

Now recall the psychological law that people who are bound by routine call every pioneer an ignoramus. You will understand that the founder of the theory[19] to which I adhere is called an ignoramus by the adherents of the preceding theories.

But now, I hope, you will understand without explanation on my part, that when certain people hurl a certain reproach at a teacher, that reproach also falls upon the pupils who are faithful to the spirit of his teachings; consequently, it must fall upon me, among others.

But perhaps the matter is still unclear to you, and probably you would like to know who this teacher is that I am talking about? To help you in your inquiries I will tell you that he is not a Russian, not a Frenchman or an Englishman, not Büchner, not Max Stirner, not Bruno Bauer, not Moleschott, not Vogt. Who is it then? You begin to guess: "It must be Schopenhauer!" you exclaim, after reading Mr. Lavrov's essays. The very man; you have guessed right.

But tell me, am I to blame for speaking superciliously to you? Am I to blame for this, when you put yourself in a position in relation to me where I have to explain such things to you? If, for example, you were to say that Emperor Peter the Great defeated Charles XII at Poltava, and some gentleman bawled at you: "Ignoramus, you don't know Russian history!" would you be to blame if you answered that gentleman in the same tone in which I answer you?

Now admire the moral that I will draw for you from the concluding part of the article in *Otechestvenniye Zapiski*. Addressing me, it asks:

"You say that you have not read this article" (that is, Mr. Yurkevich's article). "But is this true? Is not the hidden, deliberate purpose of this, too, to impress the public with your profundity, which had been so discredited? As much as to say: we don't read such stuff.... But it turns out that you did read the article, and you know what it contains. You yourself start your answer with the following words: 'Here is a most fundamental essay in the polemical section of No.IV of *Russky Vestnik.*' How did you know that this was a most fundamental answer to your philosophizing?" (*Otech. Zap.*, July, "Russ. Lit.," pp. 60, 31).

It seems to you incredible that I was not curious enough to read Mr. Yurkevich's article. I can quite believe this. Every man judges others by himself. If there is anything inferior or equal to him in other people, he understands it and believes it is possible; but if there is anything in them that is superior to his capabilities, or his development, he does not understand it, and does not believe it is possible. Shall I prove this to you? Here you are. A man who has not been prompted by the desire to learn to read cannot understand what pleasure other people find in reading books. You and I, who have managed to rise above such a man, understand him. But we have not studied higher mathematics. Now confess that you do not quite understand what pleasure people find in sitting whole days over formulae of integrals; to you and me it seems strange. So much for degree of development of capabilities. Now about natural capabilities. A man of strong character who is capable of self-sacrifice understands acts of self-sacrifice; but a man with a hard heart cannot understand how people can sacrifice themselves for others, or for ideas—it seems to him to be madness, or hypocrisy. A man who is naturally clumsy positively cannot understand how people can be graceful; and if he tries to be graceful, he will only be clumsier than ever. This shows that he really does not know what gracefulness is. This is exactly the case with us.

You may regard what I am about to say as self-praise or whatever else you please, but I feel that I am so superior to the thinkers of Mr. Yurkevich's school that I

11*

am not in the least curious to know what they think about
me, in exactly the same way as you are not in the least
curious to know what merits or demerits are found in your
literary reviews by some admirer of Mr. Rafail Zotov's
novels.[20]

Now imagine that this admirer of Mr. Rafail Zotov's
novels has published a review of your reviews. If you have
a lot of work to do and have other plans for amusement, or
some favourite occupation for your leisure hours, will it be
surprising if you don't read this review? This precisely
illustrates my attitude towards Mr. Yurkevich's article.

You think that this is improbable? That cannot be
helped; you only compel me to assume that much that is
petty to me is big to you.

What is the use of your rushing into debate when you
lay yourself open to answers like these?

Yes, you still have a very strong argument left: if
I have not read Mr. Yurkevich's article, how do I know
that it is "a most fundamental polemical essay in No.4
of *Russky Vestnik*?" But *Russky Vestnik* announced this itself in the article "Old Gods and New Gods," promising to
publish an excerpt from an excellent article by Mr. Yurkevich, to which is attached extraordinary importance. In
the preface to this excerpt, which I read, it repeated this
again—and so, in jest, I called it a most fundamental
essay. But you failed to understand that I used the word
"fundamental" here ironically. How naive you are! Fancy
not knowing that when terms of praise or solemnity are
used in polemics they must be understood as irony! To
make this clearer to you I will quote an example: "When
reading the admirable article in *Otechestvenniye Zapiski*
about Mr. Yurkevich, I was filled with awe at the author's
great philosophical learning"—now try to make out in
what sense I say this, in the literal or the ironic? Or can't
you make it out?

Your power of penetration surprises me. How is it
that you failed to understand the following fact? I took
nine whole pages of Mr. Yurkevich's article in which he
exposes my ignorance and quoted them in my article without
any comment. Do you suppose that I would have done this
were I not convinced that the pages I quoted were really
very bad? If you were able to think, this one fact alone
should have shown you how weak must be the arguments

that can be advanced against me by a philosopher of such a trend as Mr. Yurkevich's.

I have addressed myself to you, Mr. Dudyshkin, only because you are the editor of the section in which the article I have discussed was published. Perhaps you did not write it. If you did not, I shall be very glad for your sake.

I like to say surprising things. You, Mr. Dudyshkin, of course, expect me to advise you not to publish any more articles like the one I have discussed—but how can I do so? Am I an enemy to myself? Do me a favour and publish more and more articles like this one, I shall be extremely obliged to you.

* * *

What can I amuse myself with next time? I am thinking of taking *Russky Vestnik* and *Otechestvenniye Zapiski* together and, perhaps, of adding a few gems from *Russkaya Rech*, and from anything else that comes to hand.[21]

THE CHARACTER
OF HUMAN KNOWLEDGE[1]

"TAKE A MAN whose both arms are sound—has he arms?"

"He has."

"Is it so?"

"It is."

"Is that your opinion too?"

"Yes."

And we continue.

"How many arms has the man both of whose arms are sound?"

"Two."

"Good evening, gentlemen."—A scientist I know, enters.— "What are you discussing?"

"Whether a man both of whose arms are sound has two arms."

"In your opinion he has?"

"Yes, that is our opinion."

"You are mistaken, gentlemen, it is not so."

"Not so? How's that?"

"Like this: A man who thinks that both his arms are sound thinks that he has two arms. If he knew that he had arms, he would have two arms. But he does not know whether he has arms or not, nor can he or anybody else know. We know only our perceptions of things, but we do not, and cannot, know the things themselves. Not knowing the things, we cannot compare our perceptions of them with them. Therefore, we cannot know whether our perceptions correspond to the things. Perhaps they do, but they may not. If they do, then they are perceptions of actually existing things. If they do not, then they are perceptions not of existing, but of nonexistent things. We do not, and cannot, know which of these two cases corresponds to the facts. We have a perception of an arm. Hence, something exists that rouses in us the perception of an arm. But we do not, and cannot, know whether our perception of an arm corresponds to that 'something' which roused it. Perhaps it does: in that case, what we perceive as an arm is really an arm, and we really have arms. But our perception of the arm may not correspond to the actually existing something to which we relate it. In that case, that which we perceive as an arm does not exist, and we have no arms. Instead of arms we have some sort of groups of something or other unlike arms, some sort of groups of things unknown to us, but we have no arms. And we know nothing for certain about these groups except that there are two. We know for certain that there are two because each of our two perceptions—each of which is a separate perception of a separate arm—must have a separate basis. Hence, the existence of two groups of things leaves no room for doubt. Thus, the question as to whether we have arms or not is unanswerable. All we know is that if we have arms, then we actually have two arms, but if we have no arms, then the number of groups of things that we have instead of arms is also not any number, but two. Such is the theory of the relativity of human knowledge. It is a fundamental truth of science. You see now, gentlemen, that scientific truth is as remote from your ignorant prejudice in assuming that we can know that we have two arms as it is from the fantastic ideas of those scientists who assert that we have no arms, and cannot have any. These scientists also call their scholastic hairsplitting the theory of the relativity of human knowledge, but they are philosophers, that is to say, fantasts, but not naturalists. Their theory is nonsense, and contradicts natural science. Can we know that our perceptions of things do not correspond to the things when we know only the perceptions of the things, but do not know the things themselves, that is to say, when we cannot compare our perceptions with the things? That we know only our perceptions of things and do not, and cannot, know the things ⟨themselves⟩ is a fundamental truth of science, that is, of natural science."

As you see, my acquaintance is a naturalist.

Is he the only naturalist who thinks that way? Probably. At all events, it would be very strange if even one other naturalist could be found who holds that the question as to whether a man has arms is unanswerable.

I do not know why the other naturalists of this type—if there are others—think the same on this question as my acquaintance does, but he thinks so only because he does not know what he is thinking about, or what he is thinking. He is fond of philosophizing, but he has no time to study philosophy seriously, and so he philosophizes like a dilettante. He is unaware that, in conformity with logic, to philosophize as he does means accepting the deductions of those very philosophers whom he so severely censures. The logical deduction from his fundamental idea that we know only our perceptions of things, but not the things themselves, is that our perceptions of things cannot correspond to the things. It leads to this deduction because it is itself only a deduction from the negation of the reality of the human organism. As long as the negation of the existence of the human organism is not accepted as a truth, logic does not permit the question as to whether we know things even to be raised. Only when it is accepted as a truth that we are not people, that we are mistaken in imagining that we are people, does the question as to whether we can know things arise—and the logical answer will be: we cannot.

My acquaintance is unaware that these ideas are logically interconnected; and he is unaware of this only because he is a simpleton, fooled by the "fantasts," about whom he talks so superciliously.

We have laughed enough at my—and your?—scientist acquaintance who does not, and cannot, know whether people have arms or not. Let us leave him and turn to the question as to how the misunderstanding arose that caused rather a large number of naturalists to imagine that the idea that man has no knowledge of things, but has knowledge only of his perceptions of things, that is, the idea that denies the existence of the subjects of natural science, is in harmony with natural science.

* * *

People know very little compared with what they would like to know, and with what would be useful for them to know. Their scanty knowledge is very imperfect; it includes much that is doubtful and, in all probability, much that is erroneous. Why is this? Because the perceptibility of our senses is limited, and our mental faculties are not boundless. In other words, because we humans have our limitations.

The naturalists call this dependence of human knowledge upon human nature the relativity of human knowledge.

In the language of the philosophy which we shall call illusionism, the term "relativity of human knowledge" has an entirely different meaning. It is used as a respectable term, not likely to shock simpletons, to mask the idea that all our knowledge about external objects is not knowledge, but illusion.

Mixing up these two meanings of the term, illusionism gets the careless simpleton into the habit of confusing them; and although he had been for a long time convinced of the truth of one of these meanings, he, in the end, imagines that he has long been thinking—not as clearly as he thinks so now, but fairly clearly — that our perceptions of external objects are illusions.

The naturalist who reads an illusionist treatise, believing that the subject is honestly expounded, is all the more likely to yield to this temptation for the reason that he knows from his special studies that, in general, our sense perceptions contain a fairly large admixture of cogitation. The sophistic argument leads the trustful reader to exaggerate more and more the role of the subjective element in the sense perceptions, to forget more and more that not all sense perceptions come into the class of those that have admixtures of cogitation; and he is all the more likely to forget this because he has had no occasion in his special studies to inquire whether they have admixtures of the subjective element.

And the naturalist is all the more likely to trust the honesty of the exposition because all the authors in his special science express their thoughts without subterfuge. A man who is accustomed to deal only with honest people can very easily fall a victim to deception when dealing with crafty people, even if he is not a simpleton.

Is it surprising, therefore, that the naturalist is inveigled into a theory that appertains to illusionism? Those who yield to the influence of this system of philosophy, be they naturalists or not, may be pardoned for doing so, because the majority of professional philosophers are followers of illusionism. Most educated people are, in general, prone to regard as coming nearest to the scientific truth those solutions of problems which are accepted as true by the majority of the specialists in the science to which these problems appertain. And like all educated people, naturalists, too, find it difficult to resist the influence of the philosophical systems that prevail among the specialists in philosophy.

Should the majority of specialists in philosophy be blamed for clinging to illusions? Of course not; it would be unjust to blame them. The character of the philosophy that predominates at the given time is determined by the general character of the intellectual and moral life of the advanced nations.

Thus, the majority of the philosophers of our times cannot be blamed for being illusionists; nor can those naturalists who yield to the influence of illusionism be blamed for doing so.

But although the illusionist philosophers are not to blame for being illusionists, it must be said that their philosophy runs counter to common sense. And about the naturalists who yield to the influence of this philosophy it must be said that the ideas they borrow from it are appropriate only for it, and totally inappropriate for natural science.

Do we know that we are people? If we do, then our knowledge of the existence of the human organism is straight knowledge, knowledge that we possess without any admixture of any kind of cogitation; it is the being's knowledge of itself. And if we possess knowledge of our organism, then we possess knowledge of the clothes we wear, of the food we eat, of the water we drink, of the wheat from which we make bread, of the utensil in which we make it; of our houses, of the fields in which we grow wheat, of forests, brickyards, quarries from which we obtain the materials for building our houses, etc., etc. In short: if we are people, then we possess knowledge of an incalculable number of things; straight, direct knowledge of them; of the things themselves. We obtain this knowledge from our real life. Not all our knowledge is of this kind. We possess information that we have obtained by thinking; we possess information that we have obtained from what other people have told us, or from books. When that information is authentic, it is also knowledge; but it is not direct, straight knowledge, but indirect, not actual but mental knowledge. It may be said that it is not knowledge of things themselves, but merely conceptions of them. The difference between straight, actual knowledge and indirect, mental knowledge runs parallel with the difference between our real life and our mental life.

To say that we possess only conceptions of things but no direct knowledge of the things themselves, means denying our real life, denying the existence of our organism. This is exactly what illusionism does. It argues that we do not, and cannot, possess an organism.

Its mode of argument is very simple. It employs the methods of the medieval scholastics. Real life is cast aside. Instead of investigating facts, it analyzes arbitrarily formulated definitions of abstract concepts. These definitions are falsely formulated, and, of course, analysis shows that they are false; and everything that should be refuted is refuted. An arbitrary interpretation of the meaning of the deductions of the natural sciences provides a heap of quotations that confirm the deductions from the analysis of the false definitions.

This is scholastics. A new form of medieval scholastics. It is a fantastic story, but a coherent one, replete with learning.

It runs as follows:

The being of which we know nothing except that it has perceptions which comprise the content of our mental life, we call our "self."

You see: man's real life is cast aside. For the concept man there is substituted the concept of a being; and whether this being possesses real life or not, we do not know.

You will say: but if the content of this being's mental life is identical with that of man's, then we cannot help knowing whether that being possesses real life, for that being is man.

Yes, and no; it is man, and it is not man. It is man because its mental life is identical with man's mental life; but it is not man, because we do not know whether it possesses real life. It goes without saying that this ambiguous definition is employed only for the purpose of preventing you from seeing at the very outset where this argument is going to lead. It would be unwise to say straight off, without preparing the ground: "we have no organism"; too many people would recoil from it. Therefore, it is necessary, at first, to give an ambiguous definition, through which looms vaguely, as through a mist, the possibility of casting doubt on the existence of the human organism. Everything that follows is of the same kind: subterfuges, the presentation of different concepts under one term, all sorts of ruses of scholastic syllogistics. This one sample of dialectical jugglery is enough for us for the time being, however. In order to explain briefly the theory of illusionism we shall set it forth in a simple manner.

When analyzing our perceptions of objects that seem to us to exist outside of our minds, we find that every one of these conceptions contains the conception of space, time and matter. When analyzing our conception of space, we find that it contradicts itself. We find the same thing when we analyze our perception of time and of matter: each of them contradicts itself. Nothing can contradict itself. Hence, nothing can correspond to our perceptions of external objects. That which we perceive as the external world is a hallucination. Nothing corresponding to this phantom exists, nor can exist, outside of our minds. We think that we have an organism; we are mistaken, as we now see. Our perception of the existence of our organism is a hallucination; it does not, and cannot, actually exist.

As you see, this is a fantastic story, and nothing more: a story about the unreal mental life of a nonexistent being. We wanted to relate this story as briefly as possible because we thought that long fantastic stories are dull unless they tell of the adventures of beautiful maidens and youths who are persecuted by wicked magicians, protected by kind magicians, and similar entertaining things; but this is a yarn about a being that has no life in it, and it is spun entirely out of abstract concepts. Such stories are dull, and the more briefly they are told, the better. That is why we deemed it sufficient to enumerate only the most important of the concepts that are analyzed in it. But all other abstract concepts, any kind you like, as long as they are very broad, for example: motion, force, cause, are analyzed in exactly the same way as are the concepts of space, time and matter. We shall quote those that are analyzed in nearly all illusionist treatises. There is nothing to prevent other concepts, whichever you please, from the concept "change" to the concept "quantity," from being analyzed in exactly the same way. Analysis by this method will always produce the same result: "the concept," no matter which, as long as it is a broad one, will "contradict itself."

For amusement, we will try to ascertain what fate this method of investigating truth holds out for the multiplication tables.

You remember that arithmetic says that "the product of a fraction multiplied by itself is a fraction."

Let us find the square root of 2. The result is an irrational number. It is a fraction.

Arithmetic says: the product of the square root of a number multiplied by itself is the number of which it is the square root.

Thus, the product of the square root of 2 multiplied by itself is 2. That is to say: the product of a fraction multiplied by itself is a whole number.

What follows from this? That the concept of multiplication is one that contradicts itself, that is to say, it is an illusion, and nothing corresponding to it exists, or can exist. There is not, nor can there be, any relation whatever between numbers that in any way correspond to the concept of multiplication.

Note what we are discussing. Not only that there are not, and cannot be, two pair of gloves in a glove shop; you have reconciled yourself to that since you were convinced that there are no glove shops and no gloves in the world, and that there cannot be. But you are still of the opinion that when you have a conception of two pair of gloves, you have a conception of four gloves. You see now that you were mistaken. Your idea that twice two is four is absurd.

A splendid analysis, is it not? You will say: excellent; and it would be a pity if we had to add that it contradicts mathematics, for in that case we would have to regard it as nonsense.

But have no fear, we shall not do that. Surely we would not say that it contradicts mathematics! We took mathematical truths for its basis and deduced a mathematical truth from it. We have ascertained the true significance of multiplication: multiplication is an illusion. This is a mathematical truth.

Such are all the analyses made by the scholastics called illusionism. And such is the harmony of its results with mathematics. It has its own special mathematical truths; therefore, it is in harmony with mathematics in all things. Contradict mathematics? Is that possible?

Never! Mathematics confirms everything in it; it is based on mathematics!

It arrives at its mathematical truths in the same way as that in which we succeeded in proving to you that the multiplication tables are nonsense, to which no relation between numbers can correspond. How did we arrive at this deduction, which is in complete harmony with mathematics? Very simply: we twisted the concept of a square root by stating that that fraction was the square root of 2. Arithmetic says that we cannot obtain the square root of 2; that we cannot obtain a number which, if multiplied by itself, would result in 2; that we can only write a series of numbers, each of which, beginning from the second, if multiplied by itself, would result in a number nearer to 2 than that obtained from the preceding number in the same series when multiplied by itself. And if arithmetic, in any given case, calls any one of the numbers in this series "the square root of 2," it explains that it uses this term only for the sake of brevity instead of saying: "This number, when multiplied by itself, results in a fraction so close to 2 that for the given case the degree of approximation is sufficient for practical purposes." We cast aside this explanation of the true meaning of the term "square root of 2," gave the term a meaning that is the opposite to the true one, and in this way acquired a "mathematical truth" which gave us the deduction that there can be no relation between numbers in any way corresponding to the concept of multiplication—a deduction that also constitutes a mathematical truth.

Deny mathematics! In our times! No, that is impossible in our times. Medieval scholastics could do that. Neither the analysis of the concept of multiplication that we made according to the rules of analysis laid down by illusionism, nor any analysis made on these lines, can refute mathematics. On the contrary, illusionism bases itself on mathematical truths, and its deductions harmonize with mathematics in the same way as our analysis of the concept of multiplication and the deduction from this analysis harmonize with it.

Mathematics! Oh, it is the basic science of sciences; illusionism cannot help basing itself on it, and it loves to do so. Although its analyses are confirmed by the truths of all the other sciences, it bases itself chiefly on mathematical truths. Although many mathematical truths are useful to it, it is particularly fond of the following two. All the other mathematical truths are also of use to it, but these two, which it is particularly fond of, are especially useful. On them are based the most important analyses— the analyses of the concepts of space, time and matter.

The first of these is: "the concept of infinite division is a concept of which we cannot conceive."

This is a mathematical truth. How is it that in mathematics we constantly meet with ideas based on the concept of the infinite divisibility of numbers? And, for example, what is a progression with an invariable numerator and constantly increasing denominator? Mathematics not only speaks of them as progressions which can and must be understood; it is also able to add up many types of them.

The second mathematical truth most beloved by illusionism is: "to understand infinite series is beyond the power of our mental faculties."

But what, for example, are those "converging" geometrical progressions which one can easily learn to add up, however infinite the series? If we can add them up, then surely we can understand them, is that not so? But very many of the infinite series, the sum of which exceeds any definite quantities, are quite understandable even when one possesses only a modest knowledge of mathematics. For example: the infinite series

$$1, 2, 3, 4...$$

is understandable to everybody who has learnt to count. It is still easier to understand the infinite series

$$1+1+1+1+1....$$

To understand it, it is sufficient to ascertain the significance of the figure 1 and of the sign $+$; so it can easily be understood even by a man who is not yet familiar with any figure except the figure one. But the sum of either one of these series exceeds any given quantity.

It would not be so bad if the series, the understanding of which illusionism proclaims as being beyond the power of man's mental faculties, were such as could not be understood without understanding formulae unintelligible to people who have not studied higher mathematics. But we are dealing with series which can be understood by every liter-

ate person. The mathematical truth that the human mind
is incapable of understanding infinite division is proclaimed
in relation to the question as to whether a man can understand the simplest of converging geometrical progressions,
which arithmetic teaches anybody who wishes to do so to
understand and add up. We are referring to the progression

$$1, \ \tfrac{1}{2}, \ \tfrac{1}{4}, \ \tfrac{1}{8} \dots$$

The human mind is incapable of conceiving of this
series of numbers. And the second mathematical truth to
the effect that to understand infinite series is beyond
the power of man's mental faculties asserts this in relation to the simplest series of numbers formed by addition,
in relation to the series of numbers, the unintelligibility
of which we have already discussed:

$$1+1+1+1+1 \dots$$

Yes, concerning these two series of numbers, precisely
these two, mathematical truth says that to understand them
is beyond the power of man's mental faculties.

Why should mathematical truth want to say this?
Well, please read this:

"The conception of space demands that we should conceive space as infinitely divisible and boundless. Our
mind cannot conceive infinite division; this is beyond
the power of man's mental faculties. And to conceive of
the boundless means conceiving of an infinite series
formed by adding up finite quantities; this is also beyond
the power of man's mental faculties. Thus, the concept
space demands that we should conceive that which we cannot conceive. Every attempt on our part to conceive space
is an attempt to conceive the inconceivable. It is evident
from this that the concept of space is one that contradicts
itself, that is to say, it is an illusion, and that there is not,
nor can there be, anything corresponding to this illusion."

This analysis, as you see, is a very good one; it is in
no way inferior to our analysis of the concept of multiplication. Mathematical truth is very fond of analyses of
this kind, and it is very fond of this one. But if we could
conceive of the series of fractions we mentioned above, and
if we could conceive of a series of added units, we would
find that this excellent analysis of the concept of space is
a falsehood that contradicts arithmetic. That is precisely

why mathematical truth says that our mind can neither form any converging geometrical progression nor conceive of addition. As you see, it is compelled to say this; but you thought it was caprice! It was unkind of you to think that, very unkind!

Illusionism analyzes the concept of time by literally repeating its analysis of the concept of space, except for the alteration of the corresponding terms; put the word "time" in place of the word "space" and the word "eternal" in place of the word "boundless," and there you are: the concept of time is an illusion; there is nothing corresponding to it, nor can there be.

The concepts of motion and matter automatically vanish from our minds when the concepts of space and time vanish, so that there should be no need for special analyses to expel them. But illusionism is generous; it gives us a separate analysis of the concept of motion, a separate one for the concept of matter, and analyses of the concepts of force and cause—all on the basis of mathematical truth, on the basis of the very same assertions that destroyed our concepts of space and time, or of similar assertions, just any kind it pleases. Mathematical truth is so fond of its analyses that it gladly says everything that is needed for them.

In doing this, mathematical truth behaves in a praiseworthy manner. But where does it obtain the strength to do so? It goes without saying that mathematical truth cannot possess enough talent of its own to cope with a matter like that of denying arithmetic. Obviously, it must obtain resources for this from some other truth that penetrates the mysteries of scholastic wisdom more deeply than it does itself. It is easy to guess the source from which it obtains the strength to say everything that illusionism needs. Mathematics is merely the application of the laws of thinking to the concepts of quantity, a geometrical body, and so forth. It is merely one of the forms of applied logic. Thus its assertions are governed by logical truth. As for logical truth, illusionism freely invents any kind it wants. Scholastics is chiefly dialectics. Illusionism regards itself as complete master of logic: it is able to stick the words "the laws of our thinking" to every thought that it wants to give out as logical truth. And it creates an impression that way. Its strength lies in its ability to split up and combine abstract concepts, to weave and weave syllogistic nets which ensnare those who are unaccustomed to unravelling dialectical word weaving.

"The human mind is the mind of a finite being; hence, it cannot conceive of the infinite. So says logic. From this it is evident that to conceive of the infinite is beyond the power of the human mind."

Mathematical truth cannot contradict logical truth.

This trap, set by illusionism by confusing the concept of ontological infinity, unknown to mathematics, with the mathematical concept of the infinite, ensnares people who are familiar with mathematics and even first-class specialists in this subject. And having fallen into the trap, they try to imagine that there is some truth in the assertion of illusionism that mathematical truth, like logical truth—which says nothing about this—demands the admission that the human mind is incapable of conceiving of mathematical infinity.

Illusionism is fond of mathematics. But it is also fond of natural science.

Its analyses of the basic concepts of natural science, analyses that convert all that natural science deals with into a mirage, are based on the truths of logic and mathematics; but the deductions from its analyses are confirmed by the truths of natural science. It has great respect for the truths of natural science, just as it has for the truths of logic and mathematics. That is why all the natural sciences confirm its deductions. In gratitude for the respect it entertains for their truths, physics, chemistry, zoology and physiology certify that they do not know the objects they investigate, that they know only our concepts of reality, which cannot correspond to reality, that they do not study reality, but our hallucinations, which in no way correspond to it.

But what is this system of transforming our knowledge of nature into a mirage with the aid of the mirages of scholastic syllogistics? Do the adherents of illusionism really regard it as a system of serious thought? There are some such cranks among them; but the overwhelming majority admit that their system has no serious significance whatever. They do not say this in so many words, but they say it clearly enough:

Philosophical truth is philosophical truth and not any other kind. From the mundane point of view it is not truth; nor is it from the scientific point of view.

That is to say, they love to indulge in fantasy. And they know that they are indulging in fantasy.

And so we will leave them.

* * *

Our knowledge is human knowledge. Man's cognitive powers are limited, as are all his powers. In this sense of the term, the character of our knowledge is determined by the character of our cognitive powers. If our sense organs were more perceptive, and if our mind were stronger, we would know more than we know now; and, of course, some of our present knowledge would be different if our knowledge were wider than it is now. In general, the widening of knowledge is accompanied by a change in some of our former stock of knowledge. The history of science tells us that very much of our previous knowledge has changed because we know more now than we did before.

This is so. But we must not confine ourselves to borrowing from the history of science the indefinite statement that "the widening of knowledge is accompanied by a change in this knowledge." Let us examine this history more closely and see what features of knowledge change as a result of the widening of knowledge. We will see that the essential character of factual knowledge remains unchanged, no matter how much it may have widened. Take, for example, the history of the widening of our knowledge of water.

The thermometer gave us knowledge of the exact temperature at which water boils and the exact temperature at which it freezes. This we did not know before. What change did this new knowledge bring about in our former knowledge? All we knew formerly was that when water gets very hot it boils, and when it gets very cold it freezes. Has the indefinite concept "water boils when it is heated very much and freezes when it cools very much" ceased to be true? No, it remains true. The new knowledge changed it only in that it made it more definite than it was before. Chemistry gave us entirely new knowledge, viz., that water is a compound of oxygen and hydrogen. We had no knowledge of this before, even the most indefinite. But has water ceased to be such because we have learned its origin, of which we knew nothing before? No. Water is the same now as it was before this discovery was made. And all that we knew about water before remains true now. The only change the new knowledge brought about in the old was that it added the definition of the composition of water.

There are savages who have no knowledge of ice and snow. And, perhaps, there are still savages who are unable to boil water and, perhaps, have no idea that mist is water vapour. If that is the case, there are people who have knowledge of only one of the three states of water, viz., the liquid state, and do not know that water can be in the solid and also in the gaseous state. But is this one thing they know about water in the state they are familiar with erroneous knowledge? Water, when it is not ice, or snow, or vapour, but water in the narrow sense of the term, is the same water that they know of. Their knowledge of water is true knowledge; very scanty, but true.

What widening of our knowledge of water, or of anything else, would cause a change in the properties of water that we know of? Will water remain a liquid at ordinary temperature as it does now, however much our knowledge about it widens? Or will the widening of our knowledge alter this fact? Will the specific gravity of water at a given temperature change as a result of our knowledge about it, or about anything else? It was the same as it is now when we were unable to determine it; now we are able to determine it with a fair degree of accuracy, but not with complete accuracy; what will our wider knowledge about it give us? Only a more accurate determination of what we already know with a fair degree of accuracy.

It is in the nature of human beings to err; and every one of us errs often in everyday life. Therefore, every prudent person knows that one must be very careful and circumspect in everyday affairs to avoid making too many crude blunders. It is the same in scientific matters. Therefore, every special science has worked out the particular rules of precaution it needs. Furthermore, there is a special science, logic, which deals with the rules of precaution that must be observed in all scientific matters. But however good these rules may be, and however diligently we strive to observe them, we still remain beings whose faculties are all limited, including the faculty to avoid error. Therefore, notwithstanding all the possible care taken by conscientious investigators of truth to distinguish between the authentic and the unauthentic, there has always remained in human knowledge, and there now undoubtedly remains, an admixture of the unauthentic and erroneous which has escaped the attention of investigators.

It remains, and in order to reduce it, scientists must test all knowledge concerning the complete authenticity of which there is the slightest possible reasonable doubt.

This is what reason demands. Let us examine this demand more closely, as closely as possible.

Let us suppose that an adult person with an inquiring mind who, however, has not had the opportunity to learn arithmetic, at last gains this opportunity and gradually arrives at the multiplication tables. What ought to be said about him if he decides that he cannot accept them as true unless he tests them? That his decision is reasonable. If you watch him just when he is engaged in ascertaining with the aid of pebbles, or peas, whether the figures in the multiplication tables are correct, you will say that he is a wise man for doing so. Well, when he has tested the tables and has found all the figures in them to be correct, what will you advise him to do next? Test the tables all over again? He will laugh at you if you do that, and he will be right. Reason demands of one who is learning arithmetic that he should test the multiplication tables. But after he has done that, reason will say to him: "They are now beyond doubt for you for the rest of your life."

But does reason demand that the person who is learning arithmetic should test every one of the multiplication tables? Had you asked the sensible adult person whom you found testing the multiplication tables whether he had started the test from the very first line, he would have answered: "the first line says that one multiplied by one is one; there is nothing to test here; and there is nothing to test in the whole table where the figures are multiplied by one. It is different with the next tables; these must be tested. But I did not test the line where it says that twice two is four; there was no need for me to test that, I learnt that figure long ago without a book, and I tested it long, long ago, so it would be silly of me to test it again now." Had you said: "You are wrong to trust your memory," would you have been right?

Caution is necessary, but there is a reasonable limit to it. This is what reason says about everyday affairs. Reasonable doubt has its limits in science as well as in everyday life.

You write a letter, rather a long one. When you have finished you go over it to see whether you have not made any mistakes, and you correct those that you catch. Would it not be wise to read it over again? Since it is a long one, that would certainly be useful. But perhaps you have left some mistakes after the second reading, and even after the third? This is quite possible. Even if you read the letter twenty or thirty times, some mistakes may still have escaped your eye; the letter is a long one. But you will not read it ten times, let alone thirty. So what do you do? The letter is a long one, and perhaps every word is important. That does not matter; after all, only a few words are of vital importance. All the rest, important though they may be, are of no importance compared with these few. And so, reading the letter over once, at most twice, you pay special attention to these few words. They are not numerous, and it is not very difficult to go over them carefully. And if you are in the habit of exercising ordinary concentration, just ordinary concentration, you can confidently say to yourself, "that's enough," and put the letter in the envelope. You know very well that there are no mistakes in the essential parts, and if some mistakes in this long letter have escaped your attention, they are in the less important part, even if it is big counting by the number of lines, and no great harm will be done. Is not this what reason prompts you to do in everyday affairs? And is not this what it prompts you to think about the various degrees of doubtfulness in various parts of these affairs? Does it not say that even in everyday affairs, in which, owing to their multiplicity, we cannot vouch for the absolute accuracy of all the parts, there are some parts that are absolutely accurate?

But supposing the letter consists of only a few words, or of only one brief word? Supposing, for example, you wrote a letter consisting only of the words "are you well?" Will it be difficult for you to examine it well enough so that your reason will tell you that there are no mistakes in it, that the absence of mistakes can be fully vouched for—will it be difficult to verify such a short letter with such thoroughness? And if you yourself receive a letter containing just the one question: "are you well?" and answer it in a letter containing the one word "yes," will it be difficult for you to study what you wrote thoroughly enough to leave no possibility of reasonable doubt about the absence of mistakes?

This is about everyday affairs. In relation to them, reason prompts us to be careful, but it sets a limit to our caution, and beyond this limit reasonable caution becomes folly. But does reason lose in scientific matters the rights it enjoys in everyday affairs?

We leave aside the point as to whether reason concedes the possibility of doubting the mathematical knowledge that we have acquired. That is abstract knowledge. We shall deal only with concrete knowledge, which alone rational scientists have in mind when they discuss the question of the authenticity of our knowledge.

As long as a scientist is disposed to admire the power of human reason to pronounce judgment on everything, or, on the contrary, is disposed to deplore the weakness of our cognitive faculties, and, carried away by ardent sentiment, forgets about modest truth, it is very easy for him to write sweeping tirades about all our knowledge being subject to doubt. This, however, will be the play of heated fantasy, but not anything rational. But as soon as we begin coolly to examine the content of some branch of scientific knowledge, no matter which, we shall constantly find knowledge of a kind concerning which the reason of every educated man will say: "you cannot doubt the absolute authenticity of this information without renouncing the name of a rational being."

Take, for example, one of the sciences in which the admixture of the unauthentic is largest, viz., history.

"The Athenians defeated the Persians at Marathon," is this authentic or doubtful? "The Greeks defeated the Persians at Salamis," "the Greeks defeated the Persians at Plataea," and so on, and so forth. Can an educated man have the slightest doubt about the authenticity of this knowledge formulated in these simple, brief words? The details of our information about, say, the battle of Marathon, can and should be verified, and many of them which seem to be quite authentic may prove to be doubtful or untrue. But the essence of our knowledge about the battle of Marathon has long ago been verified by every educated man, verified by his reading not only of stories relating directly to this battle, but by all his reading, by all his conversations, by all his knowledge about the civilized world, not only of the past, but also, and mainly, of the present life of the civilized world, the life in which he himself is taking part. If the battle of Marathon had not been fought, and if the Athenians had not been victorious in it, the whole history of Greece would have been different, the entire course of the subsequent history of the civilized world would have been different, and our present-day life would be different. For an educated man, the result of the battle of Marathon is one of the obvious factors of our civilization.

With these important facts are associated others, the authenticity of which rests unshakeably upon the authenticity of the former. But what do we find in relation of our knowledge of history? That it undoubtedly contains very much unauthentic information, and very many wrong opinions; but it contains knowledge, the authenticity of which is so unshakeable for an educated man that he cannot subject it to doubt without renouncing reason.

It goes without saying that what reason says about historical knowledge, it also says about all other concrete knowledge.

Has every educated man verified by his own life in educated society the knowledge that he possesses that in England there is the city of London, in France the city of Paris, in the United States of America the city of New York, etc., etc., of hundreds and hundreds of cities? In some of them he has been himself and is now living in or visiting one of them, in most of them he has never been; but does his reason permit the slightest doubt about the authenticity of his knowledge that these hundreds of cities do exist, even though he knows this only from pictures, books, and conversation?

We shall conclude with the questions: has a horse four legs? Do lions and tigers exist? Are eagles birds, or not? Can nightingales sing? A little child may not be able to answer these questions with certainty; in educated society it must be a very little child, for a ten-year-old child not only acquired this knowledge at a much earlier age, but is already too old to subject this authenticity to the slightest doubt without renouncing reason.

Reason tests everything. But every educated man possesses considerable knowledge already tested by his reason, and it has proved to be such as he cannot subject to the slightest doubt while he remains a man of sound mind.

THE GRADUAL DEVELOPMENT OF ANCIENT PHILOSOPHICAL DOCTRINES IN CONNECTION WITH THE DEVELOPMENT OF PAGAN RELIGIONS

BY OR. NOVITSKY, PART 1.
"THE RELIGION AND PHILOSOPHY OF THE ANCIENT ORIENT."
KIEV. UNIVERSITY PRESS. 1860 [1]

ONE OF THE inevitable features of military campaigns are the crowds of stragglers whose numbers increase as the army and the General Staff push further and further forward. When the advance is rapid, a point is reached where the bulk of the troops are left far behind. These crowds of stragglers far outnumber the troops that are marching with the colours, but they take no part in the battles. They are only a hindrance to their former comrades who bear the entire brunt of the struggle, and who, for that reason, win all the glory. The same thing happens in mankind's intellectual advance towards the conquest of truth. At first all nations march in step. Aristotle's forefathers, at one time, lived in the same state as the Hottentots, and held the same conceptions as the latter. But the intellectual advance among some tribes became more rapid, and the vast majority of mankind lagged behind them. The Greeks described by Homer were already far in advance of the Troglodytes, the Laestrygones and other tribes described in the *Iliad* and *Odyssey* as wretched savages, fierce because of their very intellectual and material poverty. After a few more advances the majority of the Greeks, in their turn, dropped behind the advanced tribes. At the time of Solon, the Athenians had progressed far beyond the state in which they had been in Homer's time, whereas the Spartans had barely taken one step forward, and other tribes had made no progress at all. After a few more advances, the same thing was repeated within the Athenian tribe.

The wisdom of Solon was intelligible to every Athenian citizen, whereas Socrates was regarded as a freethinker by the majority of his fellow countrymen. Only a few understood him; the rest calmly condemned him to death as an atheist. We find the same in later history. At first, the entire mass of the people who inhabited the provinces of the former West Roman Empire, a mixture of the Germanic conquerors and the former subjects of Rome, held the same view of things. All were Catholics, and all, from the highest to the lowest, understood Catholicism in the same way. In the seventh or eighth century, the Popes differed from the least educated French or Irish peasants only in that they could remember more scriptural texts and prayers, but not in that they interpreted them differently. Learning existed in the shape of proverbs and folklore, which were equally known to the people of all classes. Poetry consisted of folk songs, which were known and cherished by all. After some time the difference in the material conditions of the classes created a difference in their intellectual life. The wealth of the church enabled the theologians to arise. The majority of the theologians were supposed to be faithful to Catholic tradition, but for all that, they gave it an interpretation that differed from the conceptions still held by the common people. A few of the more gifted theologians carried this revision to the point where their conceptions were rejected by the majority of the clergy, but were accepted by the laity of the middle and lower classes in those places where circumstances had been exceptionally favourable for the development of the masses. And so, from Catholic society there sprang up the Albigenses and other heretics. Learning also gradually assumed a form that was unknown to the masses and developed a content that was unintelligible to the layman. From the commonly-held conceptions of the constellations there developed something resembling astronomy, and astrology itself became a branch of knowledge much wider than the common people's superstitions from which it had arisen. These successes were based on the material resources at the command of the clergy and the middle class. The burghers also participated in the production of the new poetry, which the common people, clinging to their old folklore and folk songs, did not understand. In the city guilds companies of meistersinger, masters of poetry, were formed. But this change was facilitated even more by the wealth of the feudal barons who had their court poets, the troubadours. A little more time passed and the gap between the masses and the advanced people grew still wider. What had been heresy became advantageous for certain temporal rulers, and in some countries doctrines differing from the Catholic tradition were proclaimed the ruling doctrines. At the beginning of the Middle Ages, all the princes had helped the Catholic clergy to persecute heretics. At the beginning of the latter half of the Middle Ages the Counts of Toulouse were already patronizing the Albigenses, but they dared not yet proclaim themselves their adherents, nor were they able to protect the heretics, and themselves, from the persecution raised against them by the people who adhered to the old conceptions. At the end of the Middle Ages the Hussites were already able successfully to resist Catholic persecution; and a hundred years later, the new conceptions officially took the place of Catholicism. Many rulers preferred Luther to the Pope. But this only widened the gap between the advanced people and the masses not only in the countries which remained subject to Catholicism, but also in the Protestant part of Europe. The enthusiasm of the common people which gave the temporal powers the strength to secede from the Pope was succeeded by the former lethargy, and nearly the entire people in the Protestant countries again fell into an intellectual routine that strongly resembled Catholicism. On the other hand, however, small sections of the people went on very far ahead. From Lutherism there quickly developed Anabaptism and other Protestant heresies. The majority of the Protestant theologians displayed the same spirit of immobility as that displayed by their Catholic rivals, but a few of the exceptionally gifted ones, Sozzini, for example, lent learned development to the conceptions corresponding to the needs of the progressive minority of the common people. Secular learning also developed among the specialists with remarkable rapidity, but the overwhelming majority of the people everywhere remained in a state of ignorance very similar to that in, say, the ninth or tenth century. Poetry developed among the educated classes with equal rapidity, but the masses everywhere still had nothing more than garbled scraps of the popular poetry of the Middle Ages.

A similar relation exists between the bulk of the specialists and the educated classes, on the one hand, and the small number of advanced scholars and the few people ready to accept their views, on the other. We see that only a few English poets of the last century understood Shakespeare, and very few people among the educated public were able to appreciate these poets, and Shakespeare himself; whereas the majority of the English public, and of the English poets, continued for a very long time to adhere to the pompous rhetoric or cold primness which belonged to a degree of poetical development far below that of Shakespeare's realism. The same took place, and is taking place today, everywhere, in all departments of intellectual life. In our country, for example, the overwhelming majority of poets and of the public continue to regard Pushkin as the best representative of Russian poetry, whereas Pushkin's time has long passed away. In Germany, in Kant's time, Wolffian scholastics still prevailed, and Kantian philosophy became predominant when learning in the transcendental school of philosophy had already gone far beyond the Kantian phase of its development. And today, the majority of scholars and of the educated public in Germany adhere to the views of transcendental philosophy, whereas science has long ago abandoned this former stage of its development. To lag behind has always been the lot of the majority.

So it has been up till now, and it continues to be so now; but it must not be inferred from this that it will always remain so. Let us return to our first comparison. Only a small part of the original army has the strength to remain with the colours in a rapid advance; it alone fights the battles and makes the conquests. The other former comrades of these warriors are either in hospital or are wearily straggling far in the rear. But at some time this gap closes. The small section of the originally vast army decides the issue of the struggle, the conquests are made, the enemy has been subjugated, the victors are resting. Every day crowds of stragglers join them in order to share with them the spoils of victory. At the end of the campaign the entire army is again mustered around the colours as it was at the beginning. The intellectual movement must end in the same way. The truth that has been won turns out to be so simple and intelligible to everyone, so suitable for the requirements of the masses, that it is far easier to accept it than to

strive to discover it. Transitional stages are extremely
difficult, one-sided manifestations of truth are extremely
obscure, but this is not the case with the whole truth.
The weakest possess enough strength to embrace it when it
has, at last, been discovered. We see that the theory of
every science becomes simpler as it becomes more perfect.
Something takes place here that is similar to what takes
place when the poetry of the educated classes has reached
high development. In the end, this poetry assumes forms
that are intelligible to the common people. Corneille and
Racine were understood and known by only a small class
of people who had received a very careful education.
Even Rousseau, who was understood by a far larger circle,
was still incomprehensible to the majority of the people
who could read. When educated people were reading the
New Héloise and *The Social Contract*, the common people
who could read were still reading the cheap editions of
the garbled remnants of medieval literature. But today,
the songs of Béranger and Pierre Dupont are sung by the
common people in the French cities, and all read George
Sand. True, fully two thirds of the literate people in
France, those among the peasantry, have not yet been drawn
into this rapidly expanding circle in which the conceptions of the most advanced people are akin to those of
the very common people. It is also true that quite a half
of the French people have not yet learned to read; but
we already see the direction in which things are going.
We can already count on our fingers how many years remain
until the time when every Frenchman and Frenchwoman will
be able to read, and when all those able to read will educate themselves not with the aid of the trashy literature
that the majority of the French rural population is content
with today, but with the aid of the works of first-class
people in science and poetry. The prospect is still rather
remote, but the goal is already in sight. Even in our country,
small as our success may be compared with advanced countries, there are signs that the higher results of our intellectual development are beginning to penetrate the masses to
whom the lower phases of this development have been unintelligible. Lomonosov was understood only by people who
had received a good school education. Derzhavin's poems
could not be known or appreciated by the people, and, to
tell the truth, they were of a nature that was undeserving

of any appreciation. But the young people of the middle
class could already admire Zhukovsky's ballads. For the
common people, these ballads were too subtle and sentimental, but Pushkin's *The Black Shawl* was sung by the
young women of the common people in the provinces. The
other day, passing the stalls on which the cheap woodcuts
are sold, we saw prints of the principal scenes in Lermontov's
song about Kalashnikov, and under each picture there was
a corresponding excerpt from the song.

At the beginning, people of high intellectual development spring up from the ranks of the masses and, owing
to their rapid advance, leave the masses farther and farther behind. But, on reaching very high degrees of development, the intellectual life of the advanced people assumes
a character that becomes more and more intelligible to the
common people, that corresponds more and more to the simple requirements of the masses. And in its relation to the
intellectual life of the common people, the second, higher,
half of historical intellectual life consists in a gradual reversion to that unity of national life which had existed at
the very beginning, and had been destroyed during the
first half of the movement.

The advanced people whose activities develop science
cause its results to permeate the life of the whole people. The backward people, who are only a hindrance to
the development of science, are also of no use in spreading it among the masses; they are useless in all respects,
and in many they are positively harmful. Whoever agrees
with this has no reason whatever for being lenient with
them. He would have no excuse if he concealed his opinion
about them, if he were to say that their works were of some
value when he himself sees that they are of no value whatever either for science, or for the dissemination of knowledge
even about that unsatisfactory phase of its development
to which those works belong. For example, even if he thought
that it is better for a man to be acquainted with obsolete philosophical views rather than remain ignorant of all
philosophy, we could not say that Mr. Or. Novitsky's
book was of any use for Russian literature. Indeed, who will
read it? One can foresee with certainty that it will not even
be a bookseller's success. Nobody will buy it, except students who will have to prepare for their examinations with
its aid. And the fact that these young people will buy it

will by no means be a sign of the spread of knowledge of philosophy among the young university generation. On the contrary, it will only show that the young people who now want to obtain knowledge of philosophy are compelled by their backward teachers to acquaint themselves with it in a form that will not satisfy them, that will bore and disgust them, and in the case of many, will kill that desire to study philosophy which had already arisen in them without this book, and would not have had such a deplorable end had the book not appeared. But let not anybody think that in saying this we deny all historical merit in the system we find reflected in Mr. Or. Novitsky's book. In itself, it was at one time very good, only it seems to us that it is unsatisfactorily explained in his book. It also seems to us that even in its original form it is no longer suitable for our times, for it is the fruit of circumstances that have now changed.

The character of Mr. Or. Novitsky's book is as follows: when knowledge of Kant's philosophy spread in Germany, most of the specialists, who always cling to routine, still clung to their routine scholasticism, to their medieval conceptions. For the sake of decency, however, they began to clothe these concepts in words borrowed from Kantian terminology. When transcendental philosophy spread, this mixture of the old scholastic concepts and the new Kantian terms was supplemented in routine books with a further admixture of terms taken from the Schelling and Hegelian systems. Of the new spirit there is not a trace in these routine books, just as there is no trace of the new social ideas in the reactionary newspapers which flaunt the terminology that came into fashion after Rousseau. Mr. Or. Novitsky borrowed the main ideas in his book from these obsolete German philosophers who expound medieval ideas in the language of Kant, Schelling and Hegel. To what extent he himself laboured to paint these medieval ideas in Kantian and Hegelian colours we do not know, and it is not particularly necessary for anybody to know, for if anyone today were to publish an ode in the Derzhavin style, the opinions of the critics and the public concerning it would be just the same, irrespective of whether it was an original work, merely a revised version of another author's ode, or simply a translation from the German. It would certainly not be worth while to inquire into the matter.

It must be said in praise of Mr. Or. Novitsky that he writes in conformity with the rules of grammar, puts conjunctions and prepositions in their proper places, and possesses a thorough knowledge of the theory of punctuation. But this is not the chief merit of his book. He has a habit of employing numerous philosophical terms, some of which are not bad at all when they are employed, not by Mr. Or. Novitsky, but by Hegel. Moreover, one of his sources for the exposition of Chinese philosophy was Joachinf's *China, Its Inhabitants, Manners, Customs and Education,* published in St. Petersburg in 1840. The reader knows that this book is written in the form of questions and answers, and looks like this: "What do the Chinese call gubernia administration? How many assessors are there in a Chinese gubernia administration? To what posts are collegiate clerks appointed in China?" All this is very precisely explained in the answers.

But it is time we presented at least one example of Mr. Or. Novitsky's philosophizing. For this purpose we shall choose that part of the introduction which explains the relation of philosophy to religion. The essential content of religion and philosophy is the same, says Mr. Or. Novitsky, but they "differ from each other in the manner in which they assimilate this content, in the form in which they conceive of the same truth.

"In religion, the absolute reveals itself as its direct presence in the human mind, whereas in philosophy it does so as the idea of the absolute. Religion lives mainly in the convictions of the heart, whereas philosophy does so in concepts of reason. This difference between philosophy and religion (continues Mr. Or. Novitsky in a footnote) is expressed in a few but profoundly true words in our Orthodox catechism (p. 2): "Knowledge belongs properly to the mind, although it can also affect the heart; faith belongs properly to the heart, although it begins in thoughts."... Although the same in content (he continues in the text), philosophy and religion differ from each other not only in form, but also in their *significance and merits.* Whatever the significance of philosophical knowledge and the merit of philosophy itself may be, faith is always higher than this knowledge.... Philosophy (Or. Novitsky goes on to say) boasts of the distinctness of its concepts in its own sphere, but these concepts lack the depth and virility that belong only to religion. Religion springs from the innermost and deepest foundation of the life of mankind, and is therefore the expression of its innermost secrets. On the other hand, the human spirit reveals itself by different manifestations—the sciences, art, the interests of political life, but all these manifestations and the further concatenation of human relations, all that has significance and merit for man, finds its final focal point in religion, in our thoughts, consciousness, sensibility of God. The separate rays of all the relations of human life converge in religion, as its focus, everything finds affirmation in it and is vivified by it. Thus, it may be said that philosophy and art are the flower of the people's mind, but their living root, like that of all popular education, is religion and only religion. Torn from this root and enclosed in purely abstract concepts, philosophical thinking is numbed and brings forth unripe and bitter fruit. Only in religious sentiment has philosophy always found an inexhaustible source of lofty, vivifying thought. True, philosophy can, in its turn, render religion some service—it can purge religious sentiment of, not its own, perhaps, but alien admixtures of false conceptions, superstitions, fanaticism, and so forth. But philosophy can do this only when it heeds the voice of this sentiment; it is real knowledge only when it expresses this sentiment in its purity. Lastly, philosophy develops amidst endless contradictions and conflict of concepts, and therefore, while it may more or less satisfy the inquisitiveness of the mind, it cannot bestow peace and serenity, it cannot satisfy the heart. It thinks about the absolute, but only thinks about it, it does not lead to unity with this absolute, for which the human spirit is constantly yearning. Religion, however, is a sphere of consciousness in which all the riddles of the universe are solved, in which all contradictory thoughts are reconciled, where all the grief and anxiety of the heart is assuaged—it is the sphere of eternal truth, of eternal rest, of eternal peace. Religion alone, and not thinking about it, bestows bliss on man; and that is why, we repeat, faith is higher than knowledge, religion is higher than philosophy (pp. 12, 13, 14 and 15).

"In their different forms (continues Mr. Or. Novitsky), philosophy and religion stand in different relations to each other. He sees in religion two essential varieties: religion of natural revelation, or natural religion; and religion of the higher, supernatural revelation.

"The religious and moral sense (says Mr. Or. Novitsky), notwithstanding its original grandeur and holiness, can, like everything human, become tarnished and corrupted by passions; and it is, indeed, tarnished and corrupted by sin, of which everybody can easily be convinced, not only by the history of the natural religions and by the history of pagan deeds, but also by dispassionate inner experience, which even the pagan thinkers did not deny. Therefore, the *higher, supernatural* revelation, the possibility of which is understood by the mind, became a necessity for the human race and, by divine grace, was indeed given to men. The Lord repeatedly announced His will to men through His chosen ones until, at last, the incarnate Son of God brought to Earth the divine revelation in all its fullness and perfection, and thereby bestowed on mankind the *Christian, supernaturally revealed religion* (pp. 16 and 17).

"Natural religion (continues Mr. Or. Novitsky) could not give man a true and soul-saving consciousness of God, whereas divine religion "little by little purged and elevated the conceptions of the people, subdued passions, strengthened the will to do good, transformed man's domestic and social life, and exercised a new, beneficial influence on art and science, and hence, on philosophy. It revealed to man the mysteries about God, the world and man such as the human mind in the pagan world never grasped either in religion or in philosophy, and which the human mind could never grasp by its own efforts. In view of this significance of divinely revealed religion, philosophy can no longer set itself up against it without harm to itself, and still less can it overpower it and stimulate further development, as was the case in the pagan world. The human cannot rise higher than the divine; but, on the contrary, this divine religion, by the very grandeur of its truths, their loftiness and depth, can stimulate philosophical thought to further development ever so much more than natural religion, so that it may, in its own way, the way of pure thinking, little by little draw near to the inexhaustible wealth of content given by divine revelation, become permeated with it and rise to its level...."

A still greater change in the relation between religion and philosophy was brought about by the development of philosophy. At first, philosophy 1) kept within the borders of religion, and later, according to Mr. Or. Novitsky, "2) it separated from religion, developed independently of it, assumed an entirely different form, the form of distinct and independent reasoning, and often adopted a hostile attitude towards religion, refused to recognize its knowledge in the latter's faith. Finally, 3) philosophy again turned to religion, strove for reconciliation with it, to recognize by reason what religion recognizes by the heart, to unite its faith with confidence in reason, and again appeared in the form of unity, but distinct and clear."

Before the appearance of supernatural religion, philosophy, according to Mr. Or. Novitsky, had its first period in the East and its second period in Greece, where "it set itself up against the public religion." The third period was the Alexandrian philosophy, which "collected religious traditions and melted them all down to speculative contemplation." After the appearance of supernatural religion the same three periods must repeat themselves, according to Mr. Or. Novitsky.

We find the same changes in philosophy also in the Christian world. Here too philosophy first kept within the borders of the Christian religion, developed under its influence and expressed its content in its general form. Such was *the philosophy of the Fathers of the Church and the Scholastics*; such also was the philosophy of the *Arabians* in its relation to Islam. Later, philosophy renounced religion, took the path of independent research and in its zeal for independent development sometimes openly took a stand against religious ideas. Such is the *new philosophy* of the English, the French and the Germans. Finally, we must expect a third period—the return of philosophy to the Christian religion. This expectation is not a forecast of the future, which we cannot foresee. Since the Christian world has had two periods corresponding to the first two of the three periods in the pagan world, sound analogy leads us to expect a third, like the deduction from two premises. We already feel the need of a rapprochement between philosophy and religion, and the time is approaching when religious conviction and philosophical contemplation will merge in harmonious unity, in conformity with the highest demands of reason and faith. For the time being, however, this is still a matter of desire and hope.

Not being a theologian, we shall not go into the question as to whether the merging of philosophy with religion that Mr. Orest Novitsky desires was ever useful for religion. We think that every man should stick to his own trade (assuming, of course, that this trade is not harmful). But if, while doing one thing he thinks he is doing something else, he will be working under the influence of error, and all his work will be erroneous. According to Mr. Orest Novitsky, religion differs from philosophy and all other science in its source, and in the faculty that serves as its organ: it springs from revelation, and it consists in sentiment. Philosophy, like the other sciences, is based on observation, it is created by the mind. Religion consists in faith; science in knowledge. But is this the chief difference between them? No. If we turn for an explanation of the question to the teachers who understood revealed religion in the most thorough fashion, to the great Fathers of the Church, we shall learn from them that revealed religion differs from secular science in the very nature of the truths it teaches. Revealed religion reveals to man a spiritual world inaccessible to external perceptions; it tells us about the mysteries of a holy trinity, about an eternal divine counsel for the redemption of men by the death of God the Son, about a hierarchy of angels, about the fall of wicked angels, about the resurrection of the dead, about a last judgment, about the mysteries of a future life. Mundane science does not deal with these great truths, which belong to a sphere that is inaccessible to it because of its loftiness; it can provide us with information only about external and material nature, and about man as an earthly and material being. Divine revelation introduces men to a knowledge of "divine wisdom and hidden secrets," tells men truths that "eyes have not seen and ears have not heard," and which "never entered man's mind" until they had been revealed to him from above. This is what is taught by the Fathers of the Church, who understood revealed religion with perfect clarity. According to their doctrine—their true doctrine, confirmed by the present-day philosophers who have renounced the errors of the scholastics and the self-delusion of the transcendental a priori-ness of Schelling and Hegel—the difference between revealed religion and mundane science is not that religion gives only faith but no knowledge, whereas science gives knowledge. No, according to the doctrine of the Great Fathers of the Church, revealed religion, like science, also gives man knowledge, not, however, of the subjects that are accessible to mundane science, but of entirely different, incomparably loftier ones. Repeating the error of the scholastics who confused Aristotle's philosophy with the doctrines of the Christian religion, and following the example of the transcendental philosophers who fused revealed religion with science, Mr. Orest Novitsky, like them, obscured for himself the true conceptions of both. He understands neither the doctrines of the Fathers of the Church, nor the spirit of mundane science. This was due to his desire to be a specialist in two subjects, each of which is so big that it cannot be fully embraced even if a man spent all his efforts studying it all his life. Mr. Orest Novitsky had neither the time nor the energy to make a thorough study either of religion or of mundane science.

Mr. Or. Novitsky imagines that he is a philosopher; that being the case, he should be a philosopher and not a theologian. What is accessible to one is inaccessible to the other. But everything goes to show that he thinks that science is unsatisfactory, that he regards religion as being higher than philosophy in validity and in the merits of its ideas. That being the case, he ought to drop science, cease to regard himself as a philosopher and become a teacher of religious doctrine. He himself says that the latter is more useful than philosophy; why, then, does he waste time on a matter that is of little use and not engage in something that is incomparably more useful? He is not just to himself.

We shall leave him to censure himself and turn to his book. Had he written it from the standpoint that he himself regards as correct, his book might have satisfied those people who share his point of view. From the theological point of view, the pagan doctrines were the sinful creations of the Father of Lies, into whose power men fell after they had fallen away from the true god. The Fathers of the Church found particles of truth even in the teachings of the ancient philosophers, but they attributed these flashes of revealed truth to the revelation of the divine word. In conformity with his understanding of the relation between religion and philosophy, which is not quite in harmony with the truth that we find at the purest source, Mr. Or. Novitsky should have spoken about the pagan religions and systems of philosophy in a tone denouncing their incompatibility with Christian doctrine, showing that all of them without exception taught men licentiousness and crime, or to put it more precisely, sinful, diabolical deeds. From this point of view he would also have exposed the wicked side of Buddhism, which seduces man with its humility and apparent moral purity, and of the teachings of Socrates, and even of Plato's philosophy. He would then have seen that all these systems were the result of the wicked machinations of Satan who dressed his children in sheep's clothing in order the more easily to devour the deluded pagan souls with his wolf's fangs. Mr. Or. Novitsky could have pursued this line of argument very consistently, and then there would have been logic in his book. He, however, took it into his head to act otherwise, to speak about pagan doctrines in a tone that refutes his own point of view, and his book became a totally useless jumble of sinful philosophical ideas and ideas approved by theology. Half of the lines in it contradict the other half.

Nay, more, had Mr. Or. Novitsky acted in accordance with his convictions, he would not have chosen the ancient pagan religious and philosophical doctrines as the subject for his book. A man who finds absolute truth in supernaturally revealed religion cannot write on the pagan doctrines with a dispassionate scientific object. For him, they are all the fruit of falsehood and sin. Only one of two attitudes can be taken towards falsehood and sin: either yield to and serve them, or combat and refute them. But Mr. Orest Novitsky is already aware of the vanity of falsehood and the deadliness of sin, consequently, he cannot serve them. Thus, the only course left open to him was to denounce them, to polemize against them, to uproot them. But he cannot fail to see that this is totally unnecessary in our times in civilized Europe, to which the readers of Russian books belong. Russians may have certain intellectual and moral defects, but nobody will say that the pagan doctrines of the ancient East, Greece and Rome are a danger to them. None of our fellow countrymen worships Zeus, or Shiva, or Ariman, or Osiris; it is totally unnecessary to warn us against these errors. It would be just like warning Russians against cannibalism, or against eating poisonous mushrooms, or loam, against the vicious habits that prevail among the savages of Java, the Chukchis and the Bushmen. Happily, we are already very much above such habits, and we would not slip into them even if we were not warned against them. It is necessary to speak about paganism from the theological point of view not to Russians, but to the Chuvashes, Buryats and Samoyeds. They do stand in need of having the falsehood and sinfulness of paganism exposed to them. But it is of no use writing Russian books for them, for these unfortunate people are unable to read books in Russian, or even in their own language. There is only one way to expose paganism to them, and that is to learn their language, become a missionary and go among them from tent to tent and talk to them. If Mr. Or. Novitsky were to do that, if he were to go as a missionary among the Buryats and Tunguses, he would do something useful and praiseworthy, provided, of course, he preached in a spirit of humility. But holding conceptions which enable one to talk about paganism only to Samoyeds, and in the language of a humble missionary, Mr. Or. Novitsky took it into his head to write about paganism for the Russian public in the tone of a scientist. We are afraid that all his work has been in vain.

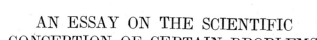

AN ESSAY ON THE SCIENTIFIC
CONCEPTION OF CERTAIN PROBLEMS
OF WORLD HISTORY[1]

1

RACES

THE DISTINCTIONS by which mankind is divided into races have existed since very ancient times. Several decades ago the majority of specialists in anthropology even asserted that the appearance of racial distinctions coincides with the appearance of man; that every race is a separate species, having its own separate origin. In scientific treatises this opinion was clothed in scientific garb and given out as a deduction from scientific facts. Actually, it was prompted by a motive that had nothing in common with scientific truth. The planters in the slaveholding states of the North American Union began to fear that the Union legislature would abolish slavery throughout the Union, as it had already been abolished by the legislatures in the Northern states. The slaveholders in the British colonies, and in some other colonies and states, also passed through such a period of apprehension, but this was a minor thing compared with the abolition of slavery in the slaveholding states of the North American Union. Who, except philanthropists, or a few very progressive-minded people, was interested in the question of slavery in states or colonies which were of no importance for anybody outside of these thinly populated countries or small islands? The controversies between the supporters and opponents of slavery in the states that were formed out of the former Spanish possessions in America attracted little attention outside of these weak countries. And what scientific forces did the advocates of slavery in these countries have at their command? Naturally, they exercised little influence on the thoughts of the majority of anthropologists. France possessed slaveholding colonies, but they exercised little influence on political life even in France. Moreover, their slaveholders were confident that as long as lawful government existed in France their interests would not be threatened. They may have been displeased with the fact that there were people in France who were opposing slavery; they may have answered these opponents; but they knew that the latter were powerless, and they were probably little interested in the controversy. They engaged in it merely in conformity with the rule that every attack must be answered rather than out of any real necessity to reply. The slaveholders in the British colonies were not of sufficient importance for their voice to be heeded even in England. The question of slavery assumed an entirely different character when the abolitionists in the North American Union gained such influence upon public opinion in the free states that the planters in the Southern states began to fear that the Union legislature would abolish slavery. The planters in the Southern states were the strongest political party in a country which had already become one of the most powerful in the world, and which in the opinion not only of its own citizens, but of the majority of serious people in Europe, would soon become the most powerful in the world. The slaveholders had long governed that country almost continuously, and they governed it continuously from the time the opponents of slavery began to acquire an influence that threatened their interests. When they became seriously alarmed about the fate of their plantations and deemed it necessary to repel the attacks of the abolitionists, they found among themselves tremendous forces for the oratorical, journalistic and scientific struggle, just as they subsequently found the forces for the military struggle. Just as at the beginning of the military conflict[2] the majority of the military specialists took the side of the slaveholders, so in the scientific conflict the planters had at their command the services of people who were more authoritative than the abolitionist anthropologists. It is sufficient to recall that the voice of Agassiz was raised in defence of slavery.

The slaveholders belonged to the white race, the slaves were Negroes. Therefore, in scientific treatises, the defence of slavery assumed the form of a theory that there are radical differences between the different races of mankind. The argument ran as follows. The white race fully possesses those qualities of mind and character that are needed for the wise management of state affairs and of extensive private enterprises such as large factories and farms. Negroes, by

their nature, not only lack the qualities needed for political life, but also the ability wisely and diligently to engage
in economic affairs. Therefore, they are not to be citizens of
a well-ordered state, but must work under the supervision
of white masters. Their slave status is not only profitable for
their masters, but is the only means by which they themselves can be protected from poverty. They are so shiftless
and lazy that they cannot procure for themselves sufficient
food and even the minor comforts of life unless they are
compelled to do so. This we see in Africa; there, they live
in distress. Under their white masters in America they live
in abundance. Slavery is a beneficial institution for them.

The Southern states of North America were not the first
powerful societies to be based on slavery. The theory expounded by the learned advocates of slavery in the Southern
states was not essentially new. The ancient Greeks justified their rule over slaves on the ground that the bulk of the
slaves were people of a different breed. This is what Aristotle,
for example, said. He divided people into categories, one
appointed by nature to rule over the other, whom nature
had destined to be slaves.

Slaveholding interests were not the only source of the
opinion that prevailed among the Greeks (and the Romans)
that nature had appointed some peoples to be slaves, just
as they themselves had been appointed to be free. Vanity
can be unselfish; the advocates of slavery in the world of
antiquity held this opinion not only because it was profitable, but also out of vanity. Influenced by the respect it entertained for the social system and ideas of the Greeks and
Romans, educated society in modern Europe was inclined
to praise slavery even after it had disappeared in Europe.
Specialists in anthropology shared this inclination of the society to which they belonged. But when it became evident
that slavery in Europe had gone never to return, European
society, and its specialists, ceased to feel any lively interest in arguments of this kind. The learned advocates of slavery repeated the old, customary ideas, but had no inclination to study them much. The problem remained at approximately the stage of elaboration that had been reached by
Aristotle and the other Greek advocates of slavery. The
listless repetition of the ancient ideas to which praise of
slavery was restricted in the eighteenth century corresponded little to the state of knowledge at that time about the

physical nature of man, knowledge that was much greater than in Aristotle's time.

But when the planters in the Southern states became alarmed about their right to own slaves, the scientific arguments in defence of slavery were quickly elaborated in the form required to refute the arguments advanced by the party which had become dangerous to the slaveholders of the Southern states. This was in the first half of the present century. The theory of the relations between groups of living beings was then based on the idea that beings having a common origin produce offspring capable of bearing offspring, which in their turn are capable of bearing offspring equally fecund. The theory that Negro slavery was in conformity with nature was a deduction from this theory. It assumed the following form:

The cohabitation of white men and Negro women, or of Negroes and white women, does not result in as many children as cohabitation between white men and white women, or Negro men and Negro women. Children born from the cohabitation of white and black people are much less capable of bearing children than people of the white race, or of the black race. Thus, the intermediate race (Mulattoes) very quickly dies out if it is not replenished with new births from cohabitation between white and black people. Mulatto males and females are unable to maintain the existence of their race by cohabitation with each other. What follows from this? The deduction is as follows:

Comparing this fact with the results of mating between the males of one species of mammals with the females of another, we find that the difference between white and black people is smaller than the difference between the horse and the ass, but greater than the difference between the wolf and the dog. The offspring of a stallion and a she-ass, or of an ass and a mare, are quite sterile. The offspring of a wolf and a bitch, or of a dog and a she-wolf are perfectly fecund. Mulatto males and females are not sterile, like mules, but are far less fecund than the crossbreeds from wolves and dogs.

Obviously, just as our conception of wolves differs from our conception of dogs and our attitude towards each of these kinds of animals is different, and just as we cannot demand or expect from the ass the qualities which earn horses our sympathy and respect, so we cannot judge Negroes in conformity with our conceptions of white people, and there fore, the social status of Negroes must be different from that of white people.

Let us suppose that we find it necessary to keep a wolf in our yard; can we allow it to run loose as we do a dog? No. If we did, we would only cause harm to ourselves and cause the death of the wolf. The wolf would probably maul us; most likely it would devour the domestic animals in our own and in our neighbours' yards. In either case, it would be killed. It would be best to keep it chained up. That would be a blessing for it too. With us it would get enough food, whereas in the forest it always suffered the torments of hunger.

The planters were so powerful that cautious people in the Northern states thought it dangerous to quarrel with them. They declared that if the Union legislature encroached on their slaveholder rights their states would secede from the Union and form a separate Confederation. Intimidated by this threat, the majority of the inhabitants of the free states yielded to the planters and allowed them to govern the Union. In books, this compliance found reflection in that scientists of the Northern states went over to the side of the advocates of the planters' race theory. Thus, Agassiz himself, one of its strongest advocates, was a professor in the Northern states, but he yielded entirely to the influence of the planters. It goes without saying that when people accept other people's opinions in order to avoid quarrelling with them, the majority of these yielding proselytes imagine that they are not prompted by any blameworthy motives, by timidity, or by selfish interest, but by sincere conviction. This is the excuse for people like Agassiz. He probably imagined that he was being guided by his conscience and not by servility.

Just as scientists in the Northern states yielded to the authority of the Southern advocates of slavery, so the majority of the European scientists yielded to the authority of the North American scientists on the race question. Indeed, how could they refuse to accept the theory that there is a radical difference between races? Mulattoes, male and female, are even less fecund than the crossbreeds of the wolf and dog; the North American scientists said this; they had studied the subject on the spot. How could one not believe them?

But the European scientists should also have asked themselves whether the North American scientists had really and impartially studied the facts about which they spoke with such conviction, whether they had honestly communicated at least those facts which are obvious and strike the eye without special study. The European scientists did not deem this necessary. They were whites; the planters' race theory flattered the white race; why should they doubt its soundness?

The Northern states were intimidated by the planters. Europe heard that the planters were threatening to break up the Union; she knew that secession would lead to civil war; civil war would hinder work on the cotton plantations, and Europe would suffer from a cotton shortage. And what would happen if the war resulted in the victory of the Northern states? Slavery would be abolished; the liberated Negroes would not work because they were lazy brutes who had no desire to acquire the comforts of life by work, because they preferred to live like brutes rather than work. White people cannot work on cotton plantations, only Negroes are fit for that. That is what the planters said, and Europe believed them. If the Northern states were victorious, Europe would be left without cotton and this would lead to a grave economic disaster; therefore it was in Europe's interest that the Northern states should continue to submit to the Southern states and that slavery should continue in those states. That is what the majority of the influential people in Europe thought at that time.

But the disaster which the complying people in the Northern states had feared, and which Europe also had been afraid of, occurred. The planters seceded from the Union, civil war broke out and lasted nearly four years. The export of cotton from the Southern states to Europe ceased; those parts of Europe where the cotton industry was developed suffered prolonged distress. The war resulted in the abolition of slavery in the Southern states. The reckless section of the planters' party dreamed of reintroducing it. Soon, the majority of the planters became convinced that this was impossible. The slavery question ceased to have any political importance and became exclusively the subject of scientific investigation. What transpired? That facts proved the opposite of what the learned advocates of slavery had said about the sterility of the Mulatto race: in respect to fecundity, Mulatto males and females do not differ in the least from whites or blacks.

What provided the pretext for speaking of their sterility was the fact that very many Mulatto women did indeed
remain childless, although they cohabited with men. or,
if they bore children, a large proportion of them died before
reaching puberty. But it was found that the conditions of
life of these Mulatto women were the same as those which
produced the same results among women of all races, white,
yellow or black. Those Mulatto women whose conditions of
life were such as are favourable for childbearing and for the
upbringing of healthy children by women of all races, had as
many children as Aryan, Mongolian and Negro women
living under the same conditions, and brought them up as
healthy as those brought up by the women of these races.

People who did not know what influence false public
opinion exercises upon the minds of scientists were surprised
at the carelessness for truth with which it had been asserted that Mulatto women were incapable of bringing up
large healthy families. A stranger thing than this happened.
It was observed that at the degree of fecundity of half-
breeds at which their offspring could continue for an indefinite number of generations without diminishing and even
increasing, it very often happened that the type of this
offspring was inconstant; the children did not preserve the
type of their half-breed parents, but reverted to the type
of one or the other race from which the half-breed parents
had originated. It was noted, for example, that if the crossing of a white with a black breed of animal results in piebald offspring, only a few of the offspring of these piebalds
will be of this type; the majority of them will be either white or
black. It is doubtful whether facts of this kind have been analyzed with sufficient accuracy; but let us assume that they are
quite accurate. The learned advocates of slavery applied to
male and female Mulattoes the observation that was deemed
accurate for the piebald offspring of different coloured
sheep and dogs. They said: the Mulatto type is inconstant;
the children of Mulattoes do not resemble their parents,
they deviate either to the white or to the Negro type; the
children of those who approximate to the Negro type, for
example, will be still nearer to it than their parents, so that
in the course of a few generations the offspring of Mulattoes
will become fully Negro.

To be able to judge whether the people of any given
type are fecund or sterile, statistics are needed. In this

matter ordinary people can, of course, be deceived by the self-confident tone of the specialists; and, of course, specialists, having no statistics at hand, may be led into error by trusting their fellow specialists who speak with confidence. But the question as to whether children resemble their parents can be settled by simple observation without any scientific means. Every person who has lived in a slaveholding country knows perfectly well that the children of Mulattoes resemble their parents in exactly the same way as the children of white people and Negroes resemble theirs, and that, therefore, the Mulatto type is quite constant. But it was convenient for society in slaveholding countries to ignore this knowledge and to repeat the pleasing statement of the learned advocates of slavery that the children of Mulattoes do not preserve their parents' type.

How is this departure from the obvious truth to be explained? The forgery was committed in a very unceremonious way, but one quite suitable for the purpose of obtaining the pleasant lie. In the United States the Mulattoes did not live in separate communities, they did not live in compact groups. Usually they lived in the houses or cabins of white or black families. Mulattoes were the lovers, or husbands, of Negro women more often than they were of Mulatto women. Mulatto women were the lovers of white men or the wives of Negroes more often than lovers or wives of Mulattoes. In the majority of cases, of course, the children of a Mulatto woman and a Negro were of a type between that of the father and mother, that is to say, were nearer to the Negro type than their mother was. The daughters of these daughters, becoming the wives of Negroes, had children who were still nearer to the Negro type. The same thing, only in the reverse direction, occurred as a result of the cohabitation of Mulatto women with white men, and of their daughters with white men. The steps of the genealogical ladder which brought the offspring of Mulatto women nearer to the white type were defined with the fullest accuracy and, on the first steps at any rate, the features were so obvious that everybody in the slaveholding country was able at a glance to tell definitely the genealogical degree of a person of the type between that of the Mulatto and the white. The daughter of a Mulatto woman and a white man was a tierceroon; the daughter of a tierceroon and a white man was a quadroon; the features of the tierceroon were so well-marked that nobody could take her either for a Mulatto or for a quadroon; everybody saw that she was a tierceroon. The daughter of a quadroon and a white man could only with difficulty be distinguished from a white by anybody who had not lived in a slaveholding country. When her offspring for another two or three generations had children with white men, these children could scarcely be distinguished from whites even by an experienced observer. In the tenth or twelfth generation they were already indistinguishable from whites even for the experienced observer. In short, this proceeded in conformity with the same laws as those that operate in the cohabitation of all people of a particular type with people of another type, for example, the cohabitation of the offspring of a Spaniard and a Frenchwoman with people of French nationality, or the cohabitation of the offspring of a Catalonian male and an Andalusian female with Catalonians. When, however, people of the Mulatto type cohabited with one another, their type remained constant in their offspring. Everybody in the slaveholding states was aware of this, but it suited all the supporters of slaveownership to repeat the lie that favoured slavery, namely, that the Mulatto type was inconstant.

Serious anthropologists have now cast aside all the arguments about the sterility of Mulatto women, or about the inconstancy of the Mulatto type, as pure inventions of the scientists who were in the service of the slaveholders.

To this day the classification of races is uncertain as regards details. Specialists who are rightly regarded as the most competent judges in questions of this kind disagree with one another in respect to the number of races that should be counted as such. And the followers of a given mode of classification disagree with one another as to whether this or that tribe belongs to this or that race. The characteristics according to which people ought to be divided into races are also still a matter of dispute.

The most popular characteristic of race is colour of skin. But some very authoritative specialists are of the opinion that this is of very little scientific importance. Some think that difference in the shape of the hair on the head is of far greater importance. They divide people into three main races: the cross section of the hair of one race is round and does not curl; that of another race is slightly elliptical and curls slightly; that of the third race is sharply elliptical so that it is like ribbon with rounded edges; such hair is as curly

as a sheep's fleece. In general, this classification rather closely coincides with the division of people into the yellow,
white and black races. It is remarkable for the fact that its
order is not the same as in the classification according to colour of skin, in which the white race is at one end, the black
race at the other, and the yellow race in between. In the
classification according to shape of hair, the bulk of the nations that constitute the white race stand between the yellow
and black races. Of far greater importance is, undoubtedly,
difference in the shape of the head. These shapes can be
classified from two points of view: from one, the shape of
the skull is taken as the basic principle of division, from the
other, the profile is taken. The deduction regarding the division of people into races is approximately the same from
both points of view. There are exceptions, but, in general,
the division is: oval skull combined with the so-called Cau-
casian (or Greek, European) profile; angular skull with
flat (Chinese, Mongolian) profile; long and flattened skull
with Negro profile. Everybody admits that shape of
skull and profile are far more important than colour of
skin and shape of hair, but some specialists think it is inconvenient to make this the basis of race classification because
it is less constant than colour of skin or shape of hair. It
was observed, for example, that the children of American
Negroes who had been bought in Africa have, in general,
profiles that are less remote from the Aryan than their fathers', and this change increases with every generation.
True, even today, the facial features of Negroes in the United
States are still very much unlike those of Aryans, but, in
general, these Negroes are only fourth, at most fifth, generation descendants of African Negroes. In Africa there is
a great difference in profile among tribes of the same colour of
skin and shape of hair. Some of them have profiles very
similar to the Aryan. Perhaps the reason for this difference
is the difference in the history of the tribes. Those who for
a very long time had lived under less distressful conditions
than the others and are somewhat more developed mentally
and morally acquired a shape of head that resembles more
the shape of those peoples who have long emerged from savagery. Later their material and moral conditions of life deteriorated, but the slow changes in facial features brought about
by this deterioration have not had time to develop fully
and so, although these tribes have lapsed into their former

state of savagery, they have retained the features of their former higher development. This explanation, however, appears to be based only on analogy; it is doubtful whether any facts have been discovered that directly confirm it. Analogy is an argument unworthy of much confidence.

According to present-day conceptions, the question of the origin of races presents itself as follows:

Not only groups of living beings like the wolf, the dog and species related to them, or the horse, the ass and species very closely resembling them, but all mammals undoubtedly have a common origin. Hence, the sterile mating between mammals of different groups has nothing to do with the case when we are discussing the question as to whether they have a common origin. They all have a common origin. Sterility is not proof of difference in origin, but only of the fact that the difference in the structure of the organisms of the mating beings is greater than that which permits of their having offspring. The origin of this difference is purely historical. If beings from two groups have offspring from their mating, but sterile offspring, it shows that the difference in their organisms is greater than that which permits them to have fecund offspring.

To the lay observer, the people of different races look very different because of colour of skin, character of hair and shape of skull and profile; but he also sees that they all resemble one another to the same degree that, say, different breeds of the ordinary domestic (European, or properly speaking, Egyptian) cat or of the European bear resemble one another. This common opinion is now fully confirmed by science. In no breed of mammals is it possible to find two beings exactly alike. There are mammals which give birth to whole litters, but the young in each litter differ somewhat from one another. Hence, when speaking of the identity of the organisms of two mammals of the same breed, the scientific meaning of the words "their organisms are identical" is not that there is no difference whatever between them, but only that the difference is infinitesimal compared with the elements of similarity.

Are we, entitled, then, to say that all races of people are identical not only in their physical structure, but also in their mental and moral qualities? In the eighteenth century the opinion was very widespread among progressive people that we can say so. They spoke of the unity of human nature in very broad and strong terms. Some of the celebrated thinkers who had received their education at the end of that period held to this opinion all their lives. For example, Pestalozzi and Hegel continued in the twenties of our century to speak of the identity of people in the categorical tone of Rousseau: all men who are born healthy are born with the same inclinations; the natural difference in the mental and moral faculties of people who are born not diseased, but healthy, is very small. But ten or twenty years later there were very few scientists left who did not scoff at this opinion as being too naive. Contempt for it was one of the specific results of the hatred that was entertained for the theories of the eighteenth century. But the period of hatred passed away, and the new generations inclined to the opinion that the thinkers of the eighteenth century had not been as naive as they had seemed to be to the generations that had hated it. One of the results of this change was the rise of that trend which is now predominant in natural science. As regards the particular question of human races, it may be characterized as follows: the differences between races run through the entire physical structure; not only has each race its own special shape of skull and profile, or foot, but every bone, every muscle, every gland is peculiar to the given race. Not only the frontal lobes of the hemispheres of the brain, but every nerve of the stomach or leg has some feature peculiar to the given race. But all these differences are fairly insignificant compared with the elements of similarity in the physical structure of all races.

Natural science adopted the now prevailing trend only very recently. The naturalists not yet of elderly age obtained their knowledge from books of the opposite trend. The present trend is only in its initial stage, and one cannot say definitely how far it will go in its development. At all events, the significance of differences between races is rapidly waning in science. Specialists are not people of a special breed. The vast majority of them, like the vast majority of all other people, yield to public opinion, which is moulded by the overwhelming influence of events. Hence, the further course of this scientific trend, as of every other, depends very much upon the course of events. It is sometimes said that the naturalists' thoughts have a perfectly firm basis, so that they cannot yield to the demands of public opinion. Of course, not only astronomy but physiology too must be regarded as systems of concepts which are very firm compared with the theories of the political and social sciences; but let us recall facts from the history not of physiology, but actually of astronomy. Tycho de Brahe may have had a very good excuse for inventing his own system in order to avoid the scientific necessity of accepting Copernicus' system, to adhere to which was for him if not as dangerous as it was for Galileo, then at all events inconvenient. But what grave consequences threatened the French astronomers of the end of the seventeenth and the beginning of the eighteenth century had they accepted Newton's theory? None whatever; but they were Frenchmen; they lived in French society; the latter preferred the astronomical system of their fellow countryman Descartes to that of the Englishman Newton; and so, for several decades, the majority of French astronomers rejected Newton's theory and defended Descartes'.

There is much controversy among anthropologists about which differences must be taken as the basis for classifying people according to race, about how many basic races should be recognized, and in which race, or mixture of races, this or that tribe should be included. But there are facts of the utmost authenticity which apply to the overwhelming majority of the human race. For those who are seeking in anthropology solutions for important historical problems, these indisputable facts are sufficient.

The question as to the number of races into which people are divided is not of very great importance for the history of mankind. Only three races are important: the white, the yellow and the black; or the races with wavy hair, straight hair and hair like a sheep's fleece; or the race with oval skull, marked profile and not prominent lower jaw; that with angular skull, flat face and not prominent lower jaw; and that with flattened skull, flat face and very prominent lower jaw. These three races probably comprise more than nine tenths of the total population of the globe. Even if we regard any other races as basic, their numbers, taken as a whole, are very small, and they are of relatively little historical importance. There is not a single nation or tribe that occupies an important place in the present composition of mankind, about which any doubt exists concerning the race it belongs to. Nor is there any doubt concerning this about any nation that has played an important part in the history of mankind provided more or less exact information has come

14*

down to us about their appearance. This is sufficient for the investigator, or for the writer on world history. If we have no exact information about some nation that has played a fairly important part in the history of mankind as regards the race to which it belonged, that information is unsatisfactory not because it tells us little about the outward appearance of its people, but because it tells us little about them in general.

All races have sprung from the same ancestors. All the specific features which distinguish one from the other are of historical origin. But what is their degree of permanence? It differs. The skin colour of Negroes is very permanent. It can hardly be supposed that if Negroes lived for twenty generations in a country whose people are fair-haired and white-skinned, they would acquire skins of a much lighter hue than that of the first generation. Yellow skin and white skin much more quickly attain shades that bring them closer together in colour. Strictly speaking, the skin of a Mongolian which has become lighter in shade retains its own peculiar colour, which is different from the colour of the skin of a very dark man of pure Aryan race. Many people of the Mongolian race have a very light skin, but close examination shows that it is not white, but sallow. On the other hand it can be seen that the skin of a very dark Aryan is not yellow, but dull white. This, at all events, is what the specialists say. And it will scarcely be credulity to regard it as the truth. As regards shape of skull, it is definitely known that with the development of intellectual life among the people of any given tribe, their foreheads grow higher. This goes hand in hand with the shortening of the lower jaw, which alters the profile; there is an increase in what is called the facial angle. The rapidity with which this change can take place and the degree it can attain have not yet been definitely investigated; but individual, casual observation has revealed many cases where the foreheads of great-grandsons are much higher than those of the great-grandfathers. It is observed among many tribes and nations that the upper classes have more developed foreheads than the mass of the people. In some cases this is due to difference in origin. There are many cases where it is known for certain that the upper and lower classes are of the same origin; the difference in profile here is obviously due to the difference in material and intellectual life.

White people have always regarded their race as being superior to the yellow race and have been prone to despise the black race. The opinion of the people of these races about themselves seems to vary considerably. Much information is available showing that Mongolians regarded the features of their race as being more beautiful than those of the white race; but much information is also available to the effect that they have regarded the people of the white race as being more beautiful than their own. Among the Negroes, some also prefer their own race to the white, others prefer the white. The fact that many people of the yellow and black races think that the white race is more beautiful than their own would seem to confirm the high opinion white people hold concerning the beauty of their race. But if the overwhelming majority of the yellow and black people seem uncomely to the white, we must inquire to what degree this impression is created by circumstances extraneous to the essence of the question, such as, for example, the fact that the material conditions of the yellow and black people are inferior to those of the white, and that their intellectual life is less developed. Can yellow and black people, under circumstances favourable to the acquisition of beauty, become very beautiful from the point of view of white people? We have the abundant testimony of white travellers that there are tribes of the Negro race which have very beautiful features. These tribes are met with in places remote from the sea, where life for Negroes is less arduous than it is in the coastal districts of Africa. All the white people who have been to Japan say that many Japanese women have very beautiful faces. Colour of skin and facial beauty are not features that have direct relation to mind and character. As regards colour of skin, it goes without saying that it has no direct relation to the functioning of the brain. There is no physiological reason whatever for thinking that a white, yellow or black skin should be regarded as being favourable or otherwise for a high development of intellectual life, or as being the result of any degree of such development. We have a strong inclination, however, to assume that goodlooking people possess good intellectual and moral qualities. One is prompted to think that there is some connection between the two; a beautiful face is the result of the good organization of the whole body, and we cannot help regarding a well-organized body as a basis for the good functioning of the brain. But although these conditions must be regarded as fundamental, the development of man's moral and intellectual life is subjected to such strong outside influences that very often the result is not in accord with physical structure. Good-looking people ought to be wise and kind. Nobody has collected data showing what proportion of good-looking people are wise and kind, or whether there are more of this type among good-looking people than among plain people (of the same social status); but every one of us knows from our personal everyday experience that among good-looking people there are very many who are dull-witted and whose characters do not rouse sympathy. Ugly people ought to be much inferior in mind and character to good-looking people; but every one of us knows that very many ugly people are very kind and wise. The fact of the matter is that a person's appearance may be marred by influences that do not penetrate deeply into the organism; the face may suffer, but the brain will not. On the other hand, there may be influences that will damage the brain, but not mar the face. In general, we cannot to this day obtain exact information about a man's mind or character by any reasoning on any general grounds. Such information is obtained only by studying that man's behaviour.

The foregoing was said strictly in relation to the connection between facial beauty and mental and moral qualities. The depression of the front part of the skull is a different matter; it is direct evidence of a low development of the person's forebrain. Hence, among those Negro tribes in which the people's foreheads are very much depressed, their forebrains are underdeveloped, of course. But the point is not whether their present state of intellectual life is low, but whether they are fit for a higher civilization, whether their forebrains can develop, whether their foreheads can grow higher. The facts show that they can.

As long as slavery existed in the United States, the controversy necessarily revolved around the question as to whether Negroes were fit or unfit to be citizens of a well-ordered state. This controversy has now become superfluous. Negroes have received civic rights and are using them in the same way as those sections of the white population of the United States who, owing to the unfortunate circumstances of their history, are still at a low degree of development. There is no difference between the way the ballot is used by most of the Irish who came to America when they were no longer young and the way it is used by the majority of the Negroes; both yield to the wiles of intriguers to an equal degree. We cannot tell how Negroes in the United States will vote several decades from now, but impartial people say that today, twenty years after they obtained the right to vote, they are already using it much more wisely than they did at first.

But the Negro question has lost its former significance since the Negroes were liberated in the United States. Where they have been liberated they lawfully enjoy all, or nearly all, the rights of free citizens,[3] and if they are subjected to certain restrictions in social life due to the habits the whites acquired in the days of slavery, these restrictions are gradually diminishing to the degree that the whites are abandoning their slaveholding habits. The abolition of slavery in Cuba and Brazil is a matter of the near future; even the slaveholders themselves have no doubt about this. It is highly probable that, after a time, relations will arise in Africa which will bring the Negro question there very much to the forefront: the whites from the South, and particularly from the West, are pushing into those parts of Africa that are inhabited by Negroes. One can be greatly interested in these future relations even today, but we lack sufficient data to enable us to judge in advance what the lot of the Negroes in Africa will be when the rule of the whites, or their very powerful influence, spreads to their lands.

The most important of the race problems at the present time are those relating to the yellow race.The latter is far more numerous than the black and, moreover, nobody doubts the fitness of the yellow people to have big, well-ordered states with the present-day attribute of big powers, a numerous, well-disciplined army. We often hear it asked whether the European countries will not be gravely menaced by China, whose population is so numerous. In proportion to the armies in France, Germany and Russia, China could raise an army of fifteen to twenty million men, and if she could acquire sufficient financial resources, she could send to Europe seven or even ten million men. Considering the present relations between the European states, it is not at all probable that they could unite for joint defence; on the contrary, they would behave like the states in ancient Greece during the Macedonian invasion. Quite a number of people in Europe believe that Europe will be crushed by the Chinese. These apprehensions are fantastic. By the time the Chinese learn the European arts well enough to build, we will not say a good army, but at least one not inferior to the present Turkish army, China will no longer be a single state. The diverse tribes of the Chinese people remain united in a single state only because they are not yet able to protect their independence from the foreign yoke.

But there is another aspect of the yellow race problem that is of real and not of fantastic interest, namely, whether the race to which half of mankind belongs is capable or not of attaining high intellectual and moral development. Until recently, the attitude towards the yellow race that predominated among European scientists was one of disdain. Negroes were not regarded as human, but as brutes. It was impossible, however, to speak about a race that had had great thinkers and had made great technical discoveries in the same terms as Negroes were spoken about; it could not be denied that the Chinese were human. But, it was argued, they were humans of a lower breed; their mental and moral organization bore features that were substantially different from the qualities that constitute the truly human merits of the white race. In those times it was believed that imagination was a purely human quality; animals had no imagination then; now they have. We know that imagination is one of the inevitable functions of thinking, and that every being that has conceptions of any kind, necessarily has some that correspond not to real impressions, but to combinations of impressions, that is to say, conceptions that belong to the sphere of imagination. At that time this was strongly denied. Scientists, forgetting that on one page of a treatise they had written about dogs and cats who had dreams, coolly wrote on the next page that animals had no imagination. Incidentally, at that time animals were even unable to think. It could not be said that the Chinese were unable to think, but, it was argued, their imagination was extremely feeble. They were capable only of concerning themselves with material gain and that was all they thought about. When one thinks only about mundane affairs, there is, of course, little scope for imagination. That was precisely the state the Chinese were in. True to the character of their race, they thought only about mundane affairs and therefore did not need imagination; and they did not in the least resent the fact that nature had denied them this highest of human faculties.

True, nature's niggardliness in endowing the Chinese with human qualities had very important material results. Lacking imagination, the Chinese could not, of course, create any ideals, still less could they strive to realize any. Lacking ideals, they could not conceive of anything better than the environment in which they lived, and of nothing better than the customs to which they adhered. From this follows the fatal law of their life: stagnation. China's history fully confirms this. When a European wrote only ten lines having any relation to Chinese history, he always found space in those ten lines for the observation that the Chinese are now living in exactly the same way as they lived two thousand years before the present era, that since then no change has taken place in Chinese customs, no change in the Chinese conception of things. In general, those Chinese were very queer people.

This, of course, was quite natural, for the origin of the yellow race was different from that of the white race, and people having different origins must necessarily differ very much from each other.

But now, alas, we whites must abandon the idea that the white and the yellow races are two groups of beings of different origin. The Chinese have descended from the same ancestors that we had. They are not people of a separate breed, they are of the same breed as we are. Hence, the same laws of life and thought must apply to them as apply to us, and, therefore, they must have imagination. Speaking seriously, it is difficult in the present state of anthropology to conceive of anybody holding the queer ideas about the Chinese which only recently seemed reasonable to the majority of scientists. The careful observer cannot help seeing that the yellow people think and feel exactly as white people having the same degree of development think and feel. The specific qualities that we observe among the Chinese are not specifically Chinese, but the common qualities of all people living under the same historical conditions and of the same social position. It is said, for example, that the Chinese are very industrious and are content with very little. This is the common characteristic of all people whose ancestors, since ancient times, have lived a settled life, have lived by their labour and not by pillage, have lived under oppression and in poverty. Those sections of the European nations to whom these conditions apply are just as industrious as the Chinese, [and are equally content with scanty reward. And exactly the same is found to be the case with the other so-called specific qualities of the Chinese. They are not specifically Chinese, but the common qualities of all people, of all races, including whites, living under the same conditions.

It remains for us to deal in particular with one of the features claimed to be specifically Chinese, namely, the so-called stagnation of Chinese social life and Chinese conceptions. Chinese history bears the same features as the history of every nation under the same circumstances. It is now known that with certain combinations of circumstances, the life of every civilized nation fell into decline. The most usual of these factors that degraded civilization was the devastation of the country by alien invaders. In its extreme form this disaster assumed a permanent character in the shape of foreign rule. In the history of Western Europe such disasters were, for example, the invasion of the Huns, later the Hungarian raids, and lastly the Turkish invasion. Let us open any treatise on the history of Western Europe that comes to hand; in every one of them we shall find the same true remark that these disasters caused a prolonged degradation of the welfare and culture of the nations that were afflicted by them. To make the point clear, let us compare the history of China with the history of England. England has not been subjected to foreign invasion since the latter half of the eleventh century. The people of England had time to recuperate and, on recovering their previous degree of welfare and culture, they achieved new successes. Open a history of China and count up how many times she was conquered by barbarians during this period. Chinese history shows not stagnation, but a series of declines of civilization due to the oppression of barbarian invasion and conquest. After every decline the Chinese recovered, sometimes succeeded in rising to the previous level and sometimes even above it, only to sink again under the blows of barbarians. Why barbarians were able to vanquish a civilized nation more numerous than themselves is a question that calls for special elucidation, but it does not relate exclusively to Chinese history. Other civilized nations have been conquered by relatively small barbarian tribes, and this has happened both in Western Asia and in Europe.

There can be no doubt that the people of the yellow race possess some natural qualities that distinguish their mental and moral organization from that of the people of the white race, because, for every external difference there must be a corresponding difference in the structure of the brain. The connection between these differences, however, has not yet been investigated and, therefore, to make this the principle for an explanation of any definite facts of intellectual or moral life means talking nonsense at random without a scientific basis. To show how unsound such explanations are, let us examine the kinship of those mammals with which we are all particularly familiar.

The horse is a fairly obedient servant of man. The ass, which is closely related to it, also serves us. But there are several species of mammals that are even more closely related to the horse, but they are not obedient to man. Of the animals closely related to the bull, some are more or less obedient to man, for example, the yak and the buffalo, but the American bison remains untamed to this day. We have domesticated the cat. The dog has long been man's most faithful friend. The cheetah, which partly resembles a cat and partly a dog, also serves man in some ways. But the wolf, which is much more closely related to the dog than the cheetah, remains untamed. In short, no matter which of the mammals that have become our servants we take, they have very close kin who refuse to serve us, or, owing to their character, are found to be unfit for our service. The few mammals which serve us are representatives of families that are very remote from each other in organization. The dog and the cat belong to different families of the beasts of prey. The horse and the ass belong to the solid-hoofed family. The bull, sheep and goat belong to different families of ruminants. The elephant and pig belong to different families of the pachydermata.

We are able to see how elusive the connection between a mammal's mental faculties and its external appearance is still for us when we recall which mammals (apart from the monkeys) are regarded as being intelligent. They are the elephant, the horse and the dog. There are many animals which occupy places very close to these in the zoological classification, but they have not earned the reputation of being particularly intelligent. One of two things: either we are unjust to the animals which we do not regard as being particularly intelligent, or classification according to external characters does not provide sufficient data for judging mental faculties. In many cases we are probably unjust. For example, in all probability, the ass deserves to be regarded as a very intelligent animal. But in many cases, small external differences probably correspond to very big differences in mental faculties, while, conversely, very big differences in externals cause no big differences in mental faculties.

In view of this state of our knowledge of the connection between external characters and mental faculties, scientific caution prevents us from making the differences between the white and yellow races a principle in explaining any facts of history. The old habit of explaining historical differences by racial differences is still very strong; but this mode of explanation is obsolete and produces two bad results: first, the explanation based on it is usually wrong in itself; second, content with this false explanation, we stop looking for the true one.

In many cases the truth would be obvious to us were it not obscured by the fantastic explanation of facts by racial differences. For example, we could easily see the alleged stagnation of Chinese social life and conceptions in its true light as a series of declines of civilization due to barbarian oppression were our attention not distracted from these disasters by arbitrary talk about the inability of the yellow race to rise above a certain level of civilization.

Let us halt here for the time being.

3

DIFFERENCES IN NATIONAL CHARACTER

The mode of life and the events in the lives of people are determined partly by external factors that have no relation to their qualities, and partly by their own qualities. The groups of people that history speaks of are nations, parts of nations, federations of nations or of parts of nations.

From these indisputably correct ideas it automatically follows that our knowledge of the qualities of nations can serve as a means of explaining the mode of life and the events in the life of historical groups of people.

The qualities of any group of people are the sum total of the qualities of the individuals comprising that group.

Hence, our knowledge of the qualities of this group is only the sum total of our knowledge of the individual qualities of the people comprising the group. Thus, our knowledge of the qualities of a nation cannot be anything else than a compound of our knowledge of the qualities of the individuals comprising that nation.

In the case of individuals, we can often obtain a fairly good knowledge of their qualities without knowing their mode of life, or any important facts in their lives. Everybody who attends large assemblies has acquaintances about whom he knows nothing except the impressions they create upon him and his friends in company. These meetings may be quite unimportant and may be confined to an exchange of greetings and conversation about casual subjects. Nevertheless, they can provide sufficient material to enable us to form a fairly correct opinion about some of our acquaintance's mental and moral qualities. For example, if we have talked to him about the news of the day, or about the anecdotes going round the town, we have very likely gained a good knowledge of his opinions on public and moral questions, and these opinions give us a clue to his moral qualities.

When we have thus learned the moral qualities of a man about whom we know nothing except his appearance, his clothes and these qualities, we can draw conclusions concerning his mode of life; and if we hear about some important action on his part, or about some event in his life, we can, in some cases, satisfactorily explain this fact by his moral qualities. Let us suppose, for example, that our conversations with him convinced us that he is a man of common sense and strong will. From this we may surmise that he has arranged his household affairs very well, that, for example, he has regular meals every day of a quality commensurate with his means and does not spend so much money on one dinner as to compel him to go hungry for several days after. Let us suppose that we heard that he had been in some danger and had got through unscathed. From what we know about him we have a right to conclude that in this danger he had acted with prudence and courage. Will these surmises be authentic knowledge? Of course not; but until we receive information that refutes them, we have a reasonable right to regard them as credible, and in some cases even highly probable.

Thus, in relation to individuals, we can often know much more about their qualities than about their mode of life, or important facts in their lives. In such cases our knowledge of these qualities can help us to explain the little and unsatisfactory information we possess about their mode of life and about the important events in their lives.

Does this relation between our knowledge of the qualities of individuals and our knowledge of their mode of life and of the important facts in their lives also apply to nations? Usually, in the case of nations, the relation between these two categories of knowledge is the very reverse. We have much more, and more exact information about their mode of life and about the important facts in their history than we have about their qualities, and our conceptions of their qualities are usually only deductions from what we know about their life and history. Take, for example, our knowledge of one of the qualities of the ancient Greek people: whether the Greeks were a cowardly or a brave people.

We all say: the Greeks were a brave people. If we ask ourselves: how do we know? we will recall Marathon, Salamis, Plataea[4] and numerous other battles in which the Greeks vanquished foes more numerous than themselves. True, we know that they excelled these foes in discipline and were better armed; but no arms will bring a small army victory over a big one if it does not consist of brave men; and discipline can be maintained in the midst of a battle only by brave men. The same applies to all the other references to the superiority of the Greeks, apart from bravery. While making the utmost concession that reason permits to these references, we are nevertheless forced to admit that the victories the Greeks achieved are evidence of their bravery.

What is our knowledge about this quality of the Greeks? It is a deduction from our knowledge about the battles they fought. Similarly, it is not the events in Greek history in general that are explained by our knowledge of the qualities of the Greeks, but on the contrary, their qualities are known to us from the facts in their lives. We know that they were brave from the facts about the battles they fought. We know about other qualities of theirs from the results of other activities of theirs; for example, we know about the mental qualities of the Greeks from their works of art and from their literature.

Thus, all our knowledge about the mental and moral qualities of past nations and of past generations of present nations is not direct knowledge, but deductions from our knowledge of the important facts in their history, of their mode of life, and of the results of their physical, mental and moral activities.

Can such derivative knowledge serve to explain facts of a category that is based on other facts in the same category? Undoubtedly. Let us suppose, for example, that the Greek historians relate something like the following: When the Greek forces drew near to a certain river, the Persian forces on the other side retreated without defending the crossing. Let us suppose that we have no more information about this incident, that we have no information about the numerical strength of the Greek and Persian forces, or why the Persian forces retreated without attempting to hold up the enemy. On the basis of our knowledge that the Greeks were brave and that the Persians acknowledged their superiority in this respect, if not to the small, picked corps of Persian warriors, then certainly to the mass of their heterogeneous militia, we can with some degree of certainty attribute the retreat of the Persian forces to the apprehensions of the Persian generals that the militia, which in all probability constituted the bulk of their force, would not hold out in a battle with the Greeks. But we must not forget that this is only a surmise. The Persian generals may have had entirely different motives in retreating. Perhaps their force at the river was outnumbered by the Greeks. In that case, their motive for retreat was not their opinion that Greeks were superior in bravery, but their opinion that they were superior in number. Or perhaps the retreat was a ruse; perhaps the Persians wanted to lure the Greeks to a place where it would be easy to exterminate them; or perhaps the Persian generals retreated because they had received orders to hasten to defend some other province from another enemy—they may have had all sorts of other motives besides their opinion that the Greeks were brave. Nevertheless, our surmise is credible, and we cannot be censured for it in view of absence of data for a definite explanation of the incident.

But cases like the one we have assumed above occur rarely and, speaking generally, are of little importance. Usually, we either have such accounts of the facts that the course

of events is sufficiently explained by our definite knowledge
about the general qualities of human nature and by our information about the conditions of a nation at the given time, and
about the details of the case. Or else our information about
the particular qualities of a nation is so scanty and doubtful
that to use it as an explanation of the facts would be tantamount to converting history into pure fiction.

Our knowledge of the mental and moral qualities of nations of the past is not direct knowledge; it is derived from
our knowledge of facts in their lives. Obviously, therefore,
it is much scantier and much less exact and authentic
than our knowledge of the facts upon which it is based. In
relation to past nations, and to the past generations of present nations, this cannot be altered. We cannot learn about
their mental and moral qualities from anything but the
facts of their historical activities.

But can we in the case of present-day nations obtain
direct information about their mental and moral qualities
sufficiently full and exact to serve as a firm basis for explaining historical facts?

To ascertain whether this is possible, let us draw up a
list of the people we know well and note their qualities.
Let our list contain the names of a hundred persons. Will this
test be finished soon if we perform it with an accuracy satisfactory for scientific purposes?

Many qualities of a man can be very easily ascertained.
Such, for example, are his appearance and physical strength.
Under the circumstances in which we usually meet people it
is sufficient to glance at a man to get a fairly precise idea of
his appearance; and to obtain a fairly precise idea of his
strength it is sufficient to see him lift a heavy object. But it
is not easy to learn everything even about physical qualities.
For example, the effects of some diseases cannot be detect-
ed until they are very far advanced. A man may be brought
to death's door by the effects of such a disease, but he may
seem to be in good health. By way of example we can mention
certain forms of typhus and smallpox. A man already infect-
ed goes about looking perfectly well. Is physical health a
man's quality, or not? Should it be included in the conception
of a man's character? In answer to the first question, everybody will probably say yes; in answer to the second, numerous
scholars who are fond of explaining the history of nations
by their qualities will say no. Nevertheless, they usually

speak about the temperament of nations: "this nation is of a cheerful temperament, that nation is of a morose temperament." Temperament is greatly influenced by changes in health. As a rule, a sick man is less cheerful than a healthy man. A slight chronic ailment due to unsatisfactory conditions of life is not called illness, but it has a considerable effect upon a man's mood.

Let us leave the examination of questions concerning physical qualities. Should a man's knowledge be included in his mental qualities and his habits in his moral qualities? If the answer is no, we shall have no means of characterizing a man's mental and moral qualities. If, however, we include a man's knowledge and habits in the conception of his character, we shall rarely find a man about whom it would be possible to say, for example, that at forty he has retained the character he had at twenty.

However short our list of mental amd moral qualities may be, it will include some that are difficult to recognize. For example, we will certainly not forget to include prudence, strong will and honesty. If we include at least one of these qualities, we shall in many cases find it difficult to decide what remark to put against our acquaintance's name on this item. One can live with a man for years and not know for certain whether he is prudent or not, whether he is strong or weak-willed, or whether he is unshakeably honest? He himself may live to the age of thirty, or fifty, and not know what act of high nobility or low meanness, of courage or cowardice he is capable of performing. Who among us has not had occasion to hear a close acquaintance say: "However could I have done such a thing?" and with him express surprise at actions which completely contradict our conception of his character. A man who has lived to the age of fifty without committing an imprudent action finds himself in difficulties he never experienced before, loses his head and acts rashly—are there not numerous cases of this kind? But let us not be inconvenienced by the inadequacy of our knowledge about those of our acquaintances' mental and moral qualities that are difficult to recognize. Let us attribute to the people we are characterizing prudence, rashness, strong will or weak will, without troubling to ascertain whether there are any grounds for our opinion. If we were to set out in search of these grounds we would start on a quest so long and arduous that, in all probability,

15 — 3857

we would never reach the end. By refraining from this troublesome task we shall compile the characterization of our
acquaintances according to our list of qualities easily and
quickly. It goes without saying, that such a list will have
very little scientific value. In it, true knowledge will be so
mixed up with a multitude of errors that the best thing to do
with it would be to throw it into the fire. But let us do that
one minute after it is completed, and during this minute let
us see how varied are the characters that we have drawn.
We shall find that they are very diverse indeed.

But, in all probability, we all know this without going
to the trouble of putting our opinion of our acquaintances'
characters in writing. If that is the case, there is no need
for us to make the experiment we have spoken about. Let
us formulate the deductions that would have followed from
it had we made it.

Among the acquaintances of any one of us there are no
two persons whose characters do not differ in very important
respects. The combinations of qualities are extremely diverse. For example, prudence is sometimes combined with
high intellect and sometimes with a degree of mental ability that borders on stupidity. Many people described as
being of low mental ability are very prudent. Thus, we
already have four categories of people: gifted and prudent;
gifted and imprudent; dull-witted and prudent; dull-witted
and imprudent. If we add an appraisal of some third quality,
honesty, say, each category will break up into two. How
many categories will we have if we make appraisals of nine
qualities? If not all of the 1,024 categories resulting from the
formula of combinations are found in reality, hundreds of
these types certainly are.

The experiment we proposed produces results that lack
scientific value because it can be completed only if we record our opinions of our acquaintances' characters without
troubling to test the soundness of our opinions. But has even
such a superficial attempt been made to define the characters of people comprising not the circle of our personal acquaintances, but a whole nation? Who has ever made an attempt to ascertain what proportion of all the members of a giv-
en nation are, say, prudent or imprudent, strong-willed or
weak-willed, and so forth, and what proportion of the total
constitute one or other of the mental and moral types formed
by the combination of different qualities? Nothing of the

kind has ever been done with respect to any nation. And it must be added that the amount of work a good, direct investigation of the mental and moral qualities of any one of the civilized nations would entail would far exceed the capacities of the scientists of that nation.

We are therefore compelled to content ourselves with our subjective, casual and very limited observations of people's characters and with the deductions concerning moral qualities drawn from our knowledge of the mode of life and of the important events in the lives of nations. The sum of knowledge obtained from these sources is small and suffers from an admixture of hazy surmises. It would be a good thing, however, if we took the trouble to make use of at least this unsatisfactory material with care and attention. We are not doing even this. The current conceptions of the character of nations have been formed carelessly, or else under the overwhelming influence of our sympathies or antipathies. As an example of carelessness we shall quote the generally accepted definition of the national character of the ancient Greeks. We all remember the following characterization of the qualities of the ancient Greek people:

"The national qualities of the Greeks were love of art, a fine aesthetic sense, preference for refinement to luxury, restraint in pleasure, moderation in the drinking of wine and still more in eating. The feasts of the Greeks were merry, but there was no drunkenness or gluttony."

Let us confine ourselves to these features of the national character ascribed to the Greeks.

Let us take that period of the life of the Greek people which made them famous. It began about the time of the battle of Marathon and ended about the time of the battle of Chaeronea.[5] The most important Greek states in this period were Sparta, Athens, Thebes and Syracuse. Of great importance were also Corinth and Agrigentum. Nor must it be forgotten that the largest region of Greece proper was Thessaly.

According to the historians who defined the character of the entire Greek people by the features enumerated above, the Spartans sacrificed all cares and pleasures to the needs of military exercises and discipline. From the time about which we begin to obtain exact information concerning the Spartans we see that these warriors, who were compelled to lead a domestic life as stern and stringent as camp life, gave

15*

themselves up to orgies the moment they were free. Pausanias, the victor at Plataea, the first Spartan about whose life we have precise information, was exactly like that. Remaining free in Byzantium, he began to live like a Persian satrap and yielded to the lust for luxurious debauch to such a degree that he was willing to surrender Greece to the Persian crown in order to rule over her as a satrap in the capacity of Persian viceroy. Less famous, but sufficiently well-known, are Lysander's harmosts, who also behaved like Persian satraps. What artists, poets or scholars did Sparta produce? None; if there were any good musicians in Sparta, they came from abroad.

All historians assure us that the Thebans were drunkards, gluttons, and dullards. Taken up with their drinking and gluttony, they sank into dull mental and moral apathy. The Thessalians were rude, licentious drunkards and held all intellectual pursuits in contempt.

The Syracusans and Agrigentians knew no restraint in anything. The wise Greek moderation in pleasure was unknown to them. They shared the lot of the Sibarites, the historians tell us. About the Corinthians, they say that they were licentious, like the Asians.

To which of the Greeks is the characterization of the entire Greek people applicable? Only to the Athenians, and then only to the two generations that lived in the period between the battle of Marathon and the beginning of the Peloponnesian war. At the time of this war the Athenians had already deteriorated, the historians tell us, whereas before the battle of Marathon they had not yet displayed the qualities for which they were famous in Pericles' time. We see that instead of a characterization of the Greek people we are given a characterization of the Athenians in Pericles's time.

The characterization of the Greek people which is repeated by most historians was drawn up carelessly, but it at least possesses the merit of not having been prompted by vicious motives.

The current characterizations of existing nations lack even this merit. We shall mention only one of them.

The Italians, as all the civilized nations except the Italians themselves know, are cowardly and perfidious, and if they are not referred to as a "vile nation," it is only because it is regarded as bad form in our polite times to use rude epithets; but the meaning of the characterization of the Italian nation that is current on the other side of the Alps is what in plain language is called "vile."

We have chosen the characterization of the Italian nation for our example because, in analyzing it, censure for its dishonesty falls not upon any single nation, but upon three nations: the Spanish, French and German. The English took no part in drawing it up only because they had no occasion to undertake numerous expeditions for the purpose of subjugating Italy. Their scientists received the characterization ready-made, and they accepted it.

How did this characterization of the Italian nation arise? It was prompted chiefly by the vexation felt by the conquerors at the desire of the Italians to liberate themselves from their rule. Italy was invaded by the Germans, the Spaniards and the French; all of them conquered the country, or part of it; at the very first opportunity the conquered broke their pledges to the conquerors and tried to throw off their yoke. What conquered nation has not acted in exactly the same way? In political affairs onerous pledges are kept only as long as there is no hope of evading them. We see this in the history of all the European nations, or parts of nations; there are no examples of the opposite. One of two things: either the historians of every other European nation ought to say that their nation is perfidious, or they have no right to abuse the Italian nation for the very thing for which they glorify their own nation, viz., its love of independence.

But the Italians are not only perfidious, they are cowards. How else, we are asked, can the conquests of foreigners in Italy be explained if not by the superior courage of the conquerors, that is, by the relative lack of courage on the part of the Italians? If we recall the circumstances under which the Italians were vanquished we will see that the course of events was determined by an alignment of forces under which the Italians would have been vanquished even if their courage had been superior to that of their foreign foes. In the tenth century, all the territory that comprised the empire of Charlemagne broke up into a number of small states. The same process of disintegration took place in Germany, but it was slower than in France and Italy. The King of Germany still retained fairly considerable power over the regional princes at the time when the King of France had already become powerless beyond the borders of his own domain. What happened in France also happened in Italy. In this respect, nothing derogatory can be said about the Italians that would not equally apply to the French and to the Germans. On the contrary, there were circumstances which made the loss of national strength more pardonable for the Italians. The southern part of their country remained under Byzantian rule; their shores were more vulnerable than the French to attacks by African Moslems. Italy, like France, was broken up, but she was richer than France. The German kings rightly deemed it more profitable to loot and subjugate Italy than to do that to France, and they therefore invaded Italy. Can small states be accused of lacking courage because the king of a big state vanquishes them? It is said: the Italians themselves made it easy for foreigners to conquer them by engaging in internecine strife. But is there anything peculiar in that? Among which people that was split up into a number of states was there no internecine strife? When the eastern part of Spain united to form a powerful state, and when the French royal dynasty united the greater part of France under the direct rule of the king, and made Provence a dominion of the king's relatives, the Aragonians and the French began to attack Italy. Thus, the Italians were obliged to beat off the attacks of three powerful nations. Does the fact that they were vanquished testify to their lack of courage? This situation continued until recent times. If we examine the details of the struggle the small Italian states waged against the powerful alien forces, we shall find numerous examples showing that the Italians fought more bravely than their conquerors.

The historians who say that the Italians are cowards in general, adhere to the theory that the qualities of a nation comprise the immutable hereditary character of that nation, passed on from ancestors to descendants. How far this is in harmony with the facts we shall discuss later. At present we will observe that the scientists who adhere to this theory obviously ought to regard the Italians as a very brave nation. Indeed, who were the ancestors of the Italians? the Romans; or if we add the secondary elements, there were also the Greeks, the Langobards, the Normans and the Arabs. All these peoples are regarded as having been very brave. How, then, can the descendants of brave peoples be called cowards by writers who are constantly harping on the existence of an immutable hereditary character? Very easily. The theory of heredity is preached in those pages where the author deems it necessary to reiterate it, but in the intervening pages, where this theory is unsuitable, its place is taken by some other theory, more congenial to the author during these hours of his cogitation, most often, the theory of degeneration. If the historian who preaches the theory of the immutability of national qualities is writing a detailed story about the invasions of Italy in medieval times, in these pages of the story the Italians degenerate and regenerate again and again. For example, a large foreign force is approaching Rome. Just before that time Rome was torn by internal strife; the vanquished party hinders its hated opponents in defending the city, or else treacherously opens the gates to the foreign enemy. There is, however, nothing specifically Roman or Italian in this. This was done in all countries, and in all cities, when internecine strife raged. But did the ancient Romans do this when Hannibal was approaching the city?[6] No. They did not allow Hannibal to enter. But now, in such and such a year in the eleventh or twelfth century, the Romans surrendered to the German king.[7] Obviously, in relating this, it is very convenient to write melodramatic tirades embellished with exclamation marks, such as: "No, the Romans did not now behave as worthy descendants of those Romans who auctioned the leases of the land outside of Rome that was occupied by Hannibal and, firmly confident that the powerful enemy would be repulsed, bid the same high rents as had been paid in peacetime! There were no true Romans in Rome now! The wretched people who called themselves Romans were..." and then follows a string of epithets as strong as the author's respectability will allow. The German king enters Rome. He is crowned by the Pope. During the coronation festivities the German soldiers run amok. The inhabitants of Rome are driven to desperation and, forgetting that their chances of success are small, they take to arms against the Germans. The issue, of course, depended upon whether nearly all the Germans had become dead drunk by this time or whether most of them could still keep on their feet and had retained enough sense to line up in fighting formation. In the latter case, the well-disciplined and excellently armed troops would gain victory over the unorganized mob, among whom there were few experienced soldiers. If, however, the Germans were too drunk to fight, the people would drive them out of Rome.

In that case the historian would be faced with the problem of whether or not to include in his narrative a tirade about how the Romans had proved to be worthy descendants of their glorious ancestors. If he finds that the tirade about their cowardice is not separated by a sufficient number of pages from the one he is now writing to allow for their regeneration, then they remain unregenerated for the time being. But five or seven years later the German king, now Roman emperor, again marches on Rome. This time there is no internecine strife among the Romans, or else the victorious party has succeeded in establishing a strong government and the vanquished parties, conscious of their impotence, have made peace with the victors. There is no treachery; the government has put in a large stock of provisions; the city holds out against a long siege; the Germans are defeated by a successful sortie, or else most of them have been killed in battle or have died of disease; they retreat, the Romans pursue them. Here the historian feels a strong urge to regenerate the Romans and there is nothing to hinder him in this, because his tirade about their cowardice is at least ten pages away from the one he is now writing, and so, under his pen, the Romans are regenerated. If you are charitably inclined, do not hasten to rejoice; a sufficient number of pages later they will degenerate again, but know in advance that there is no need for you to grieve very much over this; several pages later on they will be regenerated for the twentieth, or twenty-first time.

The Italians performed numerous deeds of heroism during the long centuries during which they were divided, but from the time of the conquest of the Langobard Kingdom by Charlemagne[8] until very recent times they were unable to repel their numerous and powerful enemies. Every neighbour who could muster a large force marched or sailed to plunder this rich but divided country. If the Italians succeeded in repelling him, he resumed his attack after he had recovered. If he remained weak for a long time, a different neighbour marched to plunder the country. Thus, although they fought numerous successful battles, the Italians had no respite and their victories were useless. After repelling the Germans, they were attacked by the Spaniards, or by the French. Even the Hungarians marched many times to plunder Italy. After repelling one attack, the exhausted Italians fell victims to a second, or a third, and again proved to be cowards in the opinion of the victors, an opinion echoed to this day by most of the historians of other nations. Historians are, in general, prone to laud the victors and to decry the vanquished. This is not a professional ailment, but simply the result of the fact that their judgment is moulded by the public opinion of the nations to which they belong.

Today, we may presume that Italy will retain her independence. It looks as though the nations which sought to plunder and subjugate her are beginning to accustom themselves to the idea that the Italian nation will not submit to foreign rule without stubborn resistance, that the desire to subjugate it must be abandoned as unfeasible. When they grow accustomed to think this way, their historians will judge the past of the Italian nation more justly, they will admit that although, when split up, it lacked the strength successfully to resist foreign invasions, its separate and therefore feeble parts displayed as much courage in the first battles as their conquerors.

Then, one of the vulgar inventions that serve to prop up the theory that nations degenerate with the decline of their military might will disappear.

The Italians are the descendants of the people who conquered and civilized the Iberian Peninsula, Gaul, Britain and part of Germany, conquered all the lands around the Mediterranean Sea and many lands far removed from it. The Roman state had begun to lose strength; the eastern half, in which Greek civilization had predominated, became a separate state; the western half, which remained under Roman rule, grew feebler and was soon vanquished and plundered by barbarians. From this the conclusion is drawn that the Romans degenerated. But the matter is explained by facts which leave no room for such a verdict. When did this alleged degeneration of the Romans begin? It is usually considered that the first important manifestation of this was the defeat of Varus in the Teutoburg Forest.[9] But more than a hundred years before that the Cymbrians and Teutons annihilated several Roman armies no less numerous than Varus' army and burst into Italy. And a hundred years before that a still more characteristic event occurred. Hannibal invaded Italy, inflicted several defeats on Roman forces which outnumbered his own, remained in Italy for thirteen years, and left it only in obedience to the orders of the government of his country. Should not the degeneration of the Romans be counted from that time? Glimpses of such an assumption can be seen in the works of some historians. From the standpoint of those who judge the moral qualities of a nation by the number of successful battles it fought it is a correct one. But the war which for a long time brought ignominy to the Romans finally ended in their victory, and after it they made immense conquests. This precludes the assumption that they had degenerated at the time of Hannibal's invasion. But that creates no difficulty. Let us say that they had degenerated before the Second Punic War[10] and were regenerated during it; that will explain everything. It will explain the ignominious defeats at Trebia, at Lake Trasimeno, and at Cannes,[11] the Romans' still more disgraceful cowardice in allowing enfeebled Hannibal to remain in Italy for thirteen years after the battle of Cannes, and the Romans' victory over him and their subsequent conquests. After making enormous conquests, the Romans began to lose strength and were finally vanquished by barbarians. From this it is deduced that they had degenerated. But these very same historians relate facts which sufficiently explain the fall of the Roman Empire without this fantastic assumption. We have only to recall that change in circumstances which caused the change in the composition of the Roman army to make the fall of the Roman Empire understandable without resorting to sheer inventions. When, after subjugating the neighbouring Italian lands, the Romans began to cross the Alps and to send troops overseas, it became no longer possible for their warriors to combine the trade of war with domestic life. The nation split up into two classes. Since military service could no longer be combined with domestic life, the majority of the citizens gave up the former, while the minority, abandoning domestic life, became a professional military caste bereft of social ties. The mentality of the Roman soldiers became like that of the later medieval mercenaries; it was all the same to them whom they fought, as long as they got their pay and the chance to loot. The Roman generals became like the Italian condottieri. Such was Marius, and much earlier a similar position was already held by Scipio, who defeated Hannibal. The bulk of the troops with whom he sailed to Africa were men who did not serve the Senate, or the popular assembly, but the general himself, who promised them loot and gave them the first installment of their pay out of his own purse. Whether the majority of the Romans, who had grown unaccustomed to bear arms, remained brave or not makes no difference; they could not resist the armed forces. The situation was similar to that which existed all over Western Europe from the end of the Middle Ages until recent times. The French and Germans, the Spaniards and English of the sixteenth century, and of the two centuries following it, were equally incapable of resisting the armed forces of their respective countries. Would we say that all these nations were cowardly at that time? They were simply unacquainted with the art of war. Recall the situation in England at the time of the Wars of the Roses. One side mustered an army of professional soldiers who guarded the Welsh border, while the other side mustered an army of professional soldiers who guarded the Scottish border. They marched against each other. The victor entered London and became the ruler of England. The wars between Sulla and Marius, and Caesar and Pompey, were similar. At last, in Rome, the hereditary office of supreme commander is assumed by the family of Julius Caesar. All the generals submit to this commander-in-chief of the armed forces of the Roman state. The same thing begins in England after Henry Tudor has captured the throne. In the seventeenth century the masses of the German people were the defenceless victims of the armies of Tilly, Wallenstein, and Bernhard of Saxony. It was for Bernhard to determine whether he should establish a state for himself in Southwest Germany or surrender all his conquests to the King of France. Franconia and Swabia belonged to him in the same way as Italy had belonged to Marius in the absence of Sulla. Western Europe survived this ordeal and was able gradually to emerge from it towards the beginning of the present century because on the frontiers of Spain, France and Germany there were no barbarians whose chief thought was to plunder the neighbouring civilized countries, and who had learnt the art of war while in the service of the people of these countries. "But an essential sign of the degeneration of the Romans in the third and fourth centuries of our era is precisely the fact that they took masses of foreigners into their service," we are told. But what did the French do from the end of the fifteenth to the beginning of the eighteenth century? Did not the French government at that time keep in its service a numerous corps of Swiss mercenaries? And how many foreigners did

Friedrich II have in his army? As many as he could hire; the more the merrier!

Since historians have deemed it necessary to study political economy and to talk about division of labour, they themselves have been explaining in their books on the latter period of the Roman Republic and on the Roman Empire what economic forces caused the transformation of the army from one of citizen soldiers to one of professional soldiers, and later caused the replacement of Italian soldiers by natives of the less civilized regions and by foreign barbarians. Consequently, it is high time to abandon the fantastic idea about the degeneration of the Romans and to say merely that the bulk of the army that waged war on the remote frontiers and lived there in fortified camps no longer consisted of the ordinary Italian population. Thus, the fall of the Roman Empire and the conquest of Italy by barbarians, is sufficiently explained by this one fact of the change the enormous conquests of the Romans had caused in the composition of their armed forces. But other changes brought about by these conquests, besides the military change, had the same destructive effect. Particularly important among these was the change in the political structure of the state; it was more important than the military change. If we combine the effect of these changes, we will find that the fantastic invention about the degeneration of the Roman people is totally superfluous.

Let us leave our dispute against fantastic opinions and proceed to explain those conceptions of national character that correspond to the present state of knowledge about the life of nations. For the sake of simplicity, we shall speak only of those nations that belong to the Romance and Teuton branches of the Aryan family. It is doubtful whether a historian can be found today who would not admit that all branches of the Aryan family originally had the same mental and moral qualities. Still less will people who are familiar with researches into the primitive periods of the life of the Aryans oppose the idea that originally there was no difference in the mental and moral qualities of the people belonging to the two neighbouring branches of the Aryan family than now inhabit Western Europe, a large part of America, some parts of Australia and South Africa. Whoever disputes this opinion will only betray a desire to deny the results of philological and archeological research.

Thus, the ancestors of the Romance and Teutonic peoples had the same mental and moral qualities. At the present time these nations differ much from one another in their institutions and customs. How did these differences arise? There is an opinion which ascribes them to the influence of people of non-Aryan origin. It is said, for example, that the Iberians (the ancestors of the Basques), a people from a non-Aryan family, constituted a large proportion of the Roman (or Romance) speaking population of the West Goth state. It is said that the present-day Spaniards and Portuguese still have a considerable admixture of Arab and Berber blood. This admixture is not nearly as large as the scientists who talk about it believe, but we shall not argue about that. Granted that the influence of foreign elements on the formation of the present-day Spanish and Portuguese nations was considerable; nevertheless, it cannot be denied that among the French people, the admixture of the blood of any people except the Celts, Romans and Teutons is very small. Nearly all the people in Western Germany are descendants of the Teutons. Nearly all the people in England and Scotland are descendants of Celts, Italians and Teutons, or Scandinavians. The Celts are now regarded as having a nationality that is more akin to the Latin than the original German was. Thus, the principal elements of the French, English and West-German population must be regarded as being identical (insofar as the primitive Italians and Germans were identical). But what do we see today? We shall not speak of the differences between the English, French and West-Germans; we shall devote our attention to each of these nations separately. Let us take France. The French nation consists of several tribal branches. If we compare the commonly accepted characterizations of them we shall not find a single feature that is common to them all except that they belong to one philological nationality. According to current characterizations, the people of Normandy differ more in their mental and moral qualities from the Gascons than they do from the English. Great Britain is only one fourth the size of France, but she too is divided into several regions, each of which, judging by the characterizations given by ethnographers, is inhabited by a people who in their mental and moral qualities do not at all resemble the other sections of the British people. We shall quote one example. It is the common opinion of English and Scottish

ethnographers that the inhabitants of South Scotland differ
sharply in their mental and moral qualities from the bulk of
the English people. In the opinion of the English, these Scots
are far more shrewd and parsimonious (the Scots themselves
call it frugality) than they are. But the inhabitants of the
North of England speak the same dialect and have the same
habits as these Scots and differ in no way from them except
that they call themselves English and not Scottish. Needless
to say, in ethnographical characteristics the Swabians in
no way resemble the Westphalians. This is sufficient as
regards Western Germany, among the inhabitants of which
there is no foreign admixture.

True, the current characterizations of the French, English and German nations are fantastic, so much so that the
Frenchman is surprised and, depending on his mood, is
either amused or angry when he reads the absurdities which
among foreigners are regarded as characterizations of the
French people. The very same impression is made on the
Germans by the characterizations current among foreigners
of the German nation, and upon the English by the Continental characterizations of the English nation. For all that,
there is some difference in the habits of these nations. Absurd, also, are those current characterizations which depict
the different sections of the inhabitants of France, Great
Britain and Western Germany as differing entirely from one
another, although differences in regional habits do actually
exist. What is the origin of these regional and national differences between people who have descended from ancestors
who had the same qualities and habits, from ancestors of
the same branch, of the same linguistic family?

A nation is a group of people. The qualities of a nation
are the sum of the individual qualities of the people who
constitute this group. Hence, the qualities of a nation change
with the change in the qualities of the individual people,
and the causes of the change are the same in both cases.
How, for example, does a nation that speaks one language
begin to speak another? Individuals find it necessary to
learn a foreign language. If the same necessity arises for
all the adults of a family, the children in that family will
grow accustomed to speaking in a language that formerly
had been foreign to them. If this change takes place in the
majority of families, the bulk of the people will forget
their former language and make the new language their

own. The only difference between the change of language in the case of an individual and in that of a nation is the length of time required for this change to take place.

The same applies to the acquisition, or loss, of all kinds of knowledge or habits. A change in knowledge and habits causes a change in what is called the character of people.

Why does a man acquire new knowledge? Partly because of the inclination of every thinking being to study objects and to ponder over them, and partly because different kinds of knowledge are needed in the everyday affairs of life.

Desire for knowledge, the inclination to observe and reflect, is a natural quality not only of man, but of all beings that possess a mind. It is doubtful whether a naturalist will be found today who would not admit that all beings that possess a nervous system and eyes are thinking beings, that they study the circumstances of their lives and strive to improve them. Therefore, we must frankly say that the prejudice which induced scientists in the olden days to ascribe desire for knowledge only to some nations and to deny it in the case of others is not deserving of attention. There has never been, nor can there be, a single sound-minded man who has not had some desire for knowledge and some desire to improve his conditions of life.

Thus, the desire to acquire knowledge and the inclination to improve one's conditions of life are innate human qualities, like the functioning of the stomach. But the functioning of the stomach and the desire for food may be harmfully affected by unfavourable external circumstances, and in some cases the appetite vanishes entirely. When the external circumstances are unfavourable for the acquisition of knowledge and for success in the endeavour to improve the conditions of life, mental activity will be feebler than when circumstances are favourable. In some cases it may come to a standstill, as do many other promptings of human nature, without affecting the activity of the lungs, stomach or other so-called functions of man's vegetative life. If a man is deprived of food too long, he dies; but if his desire for knowledge ceases, or if he loses his aesthetic sense, he does not die, his mind merely becomes blunted in these respects. What can happen to an individual can happen to the overwhelming majority of a nation if they are subjected to the pressure of the same circumstances, and to a whole nation if all the people comprising it are subjected to it. Under favourable circumstances a man's innate inclination to acquire knowledge and to improve his conditions of life develops. The same undoubtedly applies to a nation, because all the changes in its physical or mental state are the sum of the changes that take place in the state of individuals.

In the old days people used to argue about whether man's innate inclinations were good or bad. Today, all doubts about whether they are good must be cast aside as outworn. This is again a particular case of a far wider law of life of organic beings which are endowed with a mind. There are genera, or species, of living beings which prefer a solitary life, which shun the society of their own kind. Among the mammals, the mole, they say, is of that kind. But the overwhelming majority of species of mammals find it pleasant to be friendly with their own kind. We know this for certain about all those classes of mammals which in physical structure are less remote from man than the mole. As long as it was considered possible to regard all living beings except man as beings bereft of a mind, there was some justification for asking whether man was naturally good or bad. Today, however, there is no sense in this question. Like all living beings which prefer life in the society of their kind to a solitary life, man has an innate inclination to goodwill towards the beings of his own species.

But the inclination to goodwill may also wane under the influence of unfavourable circumstances. Beings of the meekest nature quarrel among themselves when the circumstances that rouse enmity are more powerful than the inclination to goodwill. Even does and doves fight one another. It is doubtful whether exact investigation has been made to ascertain to what degree their temper deteriorates under the influence of circumstances that develop bad temper, but as regards those mammals which have long been the objects of constant and close observation, the horse, for example, everybody knows that when the course of their lives is one of continuous irritation their temper can deteriorate very much.

On the other hand, we know that mammals which by nature are cruel to beings of other species and are inclined to be quarrelsome among themselves whenever their inter-

ests clash in the slightest degree, acquire a rather mild
temper when man takes the trouble to cultivate their goodwill. In this connection the dog is usually referred to.
Still more remarkable, however, is the development of mild-
ness in the cat. In its natural inclinations, the cat is much
fiercer than the wolf. Nevertheless, we know that it is easy
to train a cat not to molest poultry. Many stories are told
of cats which meekly tolerate the torments that children
subject them to when playing with them.

One of the most important differences between mammals
as far as their moral qualities are concerned is that which
is determined by the structure of the stomach, as a consequence of which some families subsist exclusively on vegetable food and others exclusively on animal food. We
all know that the dog, which is related to the wolf and
the jackal, animals that subsist exclusively by devouring
other animals, easily gets accustomed to eating bread and
all the other kinds of vegetable food that humans eat.
The only thing that the dog cannot eat is hay, but nor can
man eat hay. It is doubtful whether any exact investigations have been made to ascertain whether dogs can dispense with flesh food altogether, but everybody knows that
certain breeds of hunting dogs are trained to loathe the
flesh of the animals in the hunting of which they are
employed. Such dogs, even when famished, cannot eat so-
called game. On the other hand, the horse and cow, or ox,
easily get accustomed to meat broth. Cases have been observed of chamois or antelopes in captivity eating pork fat.
When we recall these sharp changes in the qualities that
are determined by the structure of the stomach, then all
doubt about whether qualities less stable than those which
are determined by the structure of the stomach can change
very much under the influence of circumstances should
vanish.

Mental and moral qualities are less stable than physical qualities and therefore, it must be supposed that they
are less stable in respect to heredity. The degree to which
they are hereditary has not yet been ascertained by scientific investigation with the precision that is needed for
solving the problems connected with the resemblance, or
difference, between the mental and moral qualities of people
of the same physical type. We have to form an idea of this
only from the casual and fragmentary information we

obtain from everyday observation of the resemblance, or
difference, between children and parents, or between
brothers and sisters.

To determine what actually is the opinion sensible
people gain from the everyday observation of these resem-
blances or differences, let us employ a method of dealing
with clearly formulated hypotheses that the naturalists
employ when explaining conceptions of problems that are
difficult to solve by an analysis of concrete facts.

Let us set ourselves the following problem. In a remote
village in a country in Western Europe there live a husband
and wife of the same physical type and having the same
characters. All the men in this village are farmers, and the
women help the men in their farm work. The husband and
wife referred to lead the same kind of life; they are industrious, honest and kind. A son is born to them. A year
after he is born the parents die. The orphan's next of kin
is his mother's cousin, who is married, but childless. All
we know about him and his wife is that they are honest,
kind, industrious and not poor; that they live in the capital of a foreign country, where they were born and brought
up; that they speak the language spoken in that capital
and know no other, and that they have seen cornfields only,
perhaps, through a train window when on a railway journey.
This is all we know about them. We do not know to what
class of people in this capital they belong, or what kind
of life they lead; all we have been told about them is that
they are honest. On learning of the death of their kinswom-
an and her husband and of their having left an orphan,
they decide to adopt the child and bring it up. Twenty-nine
years pass. The adopted son is now a man of thirty. His
foster parents are still alive; they love him as if he were
their own son. He also loves them as if they were his own
parents. Like them, he is industrious. Nothing extraordinary happened in his life all the time he lived with them.
This is all we know about him. The question is: what are
his habits and qualities, apart from being industrious, and
what is his occupation? On some points we can make surmises that will possess a very considerable degree of probability. For example, it is very probable that this man has
adopted the nationality of the bulk of the inhabitants of
the capital. This is suggested by the information we have
that his foster parents did not know his native language

and spoke the language of the capital in which they were brought up. It is also very probable that he is a town dweller and not a farmer. This assumption is also based on what we know about his foster parents. Is he a farmer? This is very doubtful; well-to-do town dwellers in Western Europe do not consider farming profitable and do not bring up their children for this occupation. In all probability he is a town dweller. What urban occupation does he engage in? Is he an artisan, a schoolteacher, a lawyer or physician? We cannot give any confident answer to this question because we do not know what urban occupation his foster father was engaged in, or what the latter and his wife thought about this occupation, whether they thought that it was suitable for their adopted son, or whether they preferred some other.

It is now easy for us to ascertain the true nature of our opinion as to whether the influence of birth or the influence of life operates most strongly in the moulding of moral qualities. We have found that it is probable that the orphan grew up to be an honest man. He was brought up in an honest family; protected from poverty by the prosperity and the love of his foster parents, he easily acquired the habit of abhorring theft and other dishonest practices. To test whether we really ascribe the development of good qualities to the influence of life and not to the influence of birth, let us change the conditions of the hypothesis and assume that the people who adopted the orphan lived by dishonesty and deemed it foolish to be honest towards other people. Is there any great probability that the orphan they brought up became an honest man? We see that the moral qualities of his parents are not taken into consideration at all, because he became an orphan before he could learn anything bad or good from them.

We shall now proceed to elucidate those conceptions of the development of the characters of individuals that correspond to the present state of theoretical knowledge and to the deductions drawn from observations of everyday life. For the sake of simplicity, we shall speak only of the West-European branch of the Aryan family. When the people of advanced nations become accustomed to judge one another fairly they will be ready to judge the people of other linguistic or racial branches more fairly than they do now.

16*

Let us take a two-year-old child. It has already passed the period most dangerous for physical development. It is a sturdy, healthy child. Assuming that it had no exceptional troubles in the subsequent years of its development, we ask ourselves whether any favourable conditions of life are needed for it to grow up healthy. We know that for this are needed, among other things, satisfactory food and a satisfactory home life. Given these conditions, eighty or ninety out of every hundred healthy two-year-old children will remain healthy to the age of twenty. If, however, these children's parents sink into poverty at about the time the children reach the age of two and they grow up in damp and stuffy premises and receive bad and insufficient food, very many of them will die before reaching adult age, and many of those who survive will be suffering from some disease caused by bad food and damp living quarters.

The physical qualities of a two-year-old child are incomparably more stable than its moral qualities, or to be more exact, not qualities, but a disposition towards qualities. A two-year-old child already shows signs of all the specific physical qualities it will have in adult age if it remains healthy. We cannot, however, form any well-founded opinion about the future talents of a two-year-old child. When we say that children of this age are gifted or dull, we are only imagining things on the basis of our sympathies or antipathies. It is difficult to say whether eight-year-old, let alone two-year-old children, will be talented or stupid when they grow up. And moral qualities are even less stable than mental qualities.

It has now been proved that the children of tubercular parents are born free from this disease. It is usually the case, however, that tubercular parents are anaemic and weak-chested, and these defects are inherited by the children. But if the anaemic and weak-chested infant receives an upbringing that strengthens its health, its disposition for diseases that lead to tuberculosis will diminish, or disappear completely. Thus, children inherit from their parents only a disposition for tuberculosis, and whether this develops, diminishes, or disappears, depends upon the children's subsequent conditions of life. The children of healthy parents are, as a rule, born healthy, but they can very easily be robbed of this heritage by unfavourable conditions of life.

As regards moral qualities, it must be supposed that children inherit from their parents those inclinations which are directly determined by what is called temperament (in those cases where temperament is inherited). But even this, probably correct, view must be qualified to remain correct, if it is correct. For the sake of simplicity, let us divide all temperaments into two types: sanguine and phlegmatic. Let us assume that if a father and mother have the same temperament, all their children have that temperament too. From this, however, no deduction can yet be drawn about the heredity of good or bad moral qualities. Temperament determines only the degree of rapidity of movements and, probably, of changes of mood. It must be supposed that a man who walks with a quick step is inclined to a more rapid change of mood than one whose movements are slow. But this difference does not determine which of them is more industrious, and still less does it determine the degree of honesty or benevolence of one or the other; nor does it determine the degree of prudence. Rashness or irresolution are not temperamental qualities, but the result of habit or restrictive circumstances. People whose movements are slow can also be fussy, rash, imprudent; and people with a quick step can be irresolute. Every good observer of people is aware of this. But what deserves special attention is the fact that among whole classes and among whole nations, quick movements, rapid speech, vigorous gestures and the other qualities that are regarded as signs of a natural disposition, of what is called the sanguine temperament, and the opposite qualities, which are regarded as signs of the phlegmatic temperament, are nothing but the result of habit. Nearly all people whose elder relations and friends have taught them to behave with restraint are accustomed from very early age to speak and deport themselves with restraint; but among those classes in which peremptory speech and movements are deemed necessary, nearly everybody gets accustomed from his youth to vigorous and rapid movements and rapid and peremptory speech. Among those nations in which society is divided into sharply defined classes, these seeming signs of temperament are actually found to be only class habits.

Those mental and moral qualities that are less closely connected with the physical type than temperament are less stable in the individual than temperament. From this it is evident that the power of hereditary transmission of these qualities is less than that of temperament.

The concept of national character is a complex one. It embraces everything which distinguishes one nation from another that does not come within the concept of physical type. Examining this collection of numerous concepts, we can divide them into a number of categories, differing very much in degree of stability. One category includes those mental and moral qualities which are directly determined by differences in physical types. Another includes differences in language. Then come separate categories for differences of mode of life, customs, degree of education, and theoretical convictions. The most stable are those differences that are directly determined by differences in physical types and are called temperaments. But if we are to speak of the European branch of the Aryan family, it is impossible to find in it a single big nation that consists of people of all the same temperament. Moreover, although the physical type of an individual remains unchanged all his life and is usually transmitted from parents to children and, therefore, has firm hereditary stability, the mental and moral qualities which are the result of it are altered by conditions of life to such a degree that their dependence on physical type remains in force only if conditions of life operate in the same direction. If, however, the course of life develops other qualities, temperament yields to its influence, and that side of a man's actual character which comes under the term temperament is found to be entirely different from the qualities the man could be presumed to have according to our conceptions of the mental and moral results of the physical type. Every one of the big European nations consists, as we have said, of people of different physical types, and no calculation of the relative proportions of these types has been made. That is why we have not yet any well-grounded conceptions of what category of temperament the majority of the people of a given nation belong to. But perhaps justification can be found for one of the current opinions about the overwhelming predominance of a given physical type among the relatively small nations, such as, for example, the Dutch, the Danes and the Norwegians? Let us suppose that a given characterization of the physical type of one of these nations really applies to the vast majority of the people of this nation, and let us study the characters of these people by personal observation or, if we are unable to spend much time in that country, from the unprejudiced narratives of other people about the private lives of the people of this nation, about how they work, talk and amuse themselves. We will see that a very considerable section of the people of this nation possess mental and moral qualities different from those that correspond to the conception of temperament created by the nation's specific physical type. Let us suppose, for example, that the physical type of the people of this nation corresponds to what is regarded as the phlegmatic temperament; the predominant characteristics among them should therefore be slow movements and speech. Actually, however, we see that very many of them have the opposite qualities, which are regarded as belonging to the sanguine temperament. Nobody has calculated the relative proportions of the two categories among the people of this nation or of any other; but if we look closely we will find that slowness or rapidity of movements and speech among the people of this nation is closely connected with the habits of the classes or occupations to which they belong, with their conceptions of their personal, family importance, or with the lowness of their social, family, personal position, with their satisfaction or dissatisfaction with the course of their lives, with the state of their health, and with other circumstances that influence a person's mood. No matter what the natural build of a man's body may be, only very few people whose health has been undermined by depressing sickness retain vivacity of movement and speech. On the other hand, among those who suffer from diseases which have an irritating effect, very few can move and speak calmly and with restraint. All other circumstances that depress or irritate, grieve or cheer a man, operate in the same way. In those places where the bulk of the peasants live tolerably well, but have no large stocks of grain left over from past harvests and possess little money, the agricultural population, every ordinary harvest year, passes through two states: the sanguine and the phlegmatic. Before the harvest they begin to be cheerful and, notwithstanding the weariness they feel after a hard day's work in the fields, their mood in their leisure hours is sanguine. This mood rises until the new grain is threshed and begins to be used for food. For some time the cheerfulness continues, gestures are quick, conver-

sation is noisy and vivacious. Then begins the worry about
whether the grain will last until the autumn. It is found
necessary to economize in food, the cheerfulness subsides
and after a little while gives way to gloom. This lasts until
that season of the year when thoughts about the approaching
new harvest gain the upper hand over thoughts about the
exhaustion of food stocks. In general, natural temperament
is eclipsed by the influences of life, so that it is far more
difficult to discern it than is usually supposed. Carefully
examining the facts, we are forced to the conclusion that
innate disposition for rapidity or slowness of movement and
speech is feeble and flexible, that the chief factor is not
this disposition, but the influence exercised by conditions of
life on nations, tribes, and classes among nations.

On the question as to whether the natural differences
between nations as regards vivacity and vigour of mental
faculties are great or small, opinion is extremely divided.
If it is a question of nations of different races or linguistic
families, the answer is determined by our conception of
races and linguistic families. It is the bounden duty of people who hold a given opinion on this question carefully to
analyze the opposite opinion. When, however, it is a question, as it is in the present case, only of advanced nations,
of the West-European branch of the Aryan family, no theory
that there are mental differences between people according
to the origin of their ancestors can be regarded as being
applicable to the question. Granted that there is an admixture of non-Aryan blood among the people in the south
and northeastern regions of Western Europe, for example,
an admixture of Arab and Berber blood in Sicily and in
the southern half of the Iberian Peninsula, and an admixture of Finnish blood in the north of the Scandinavian Peninsula; but even in Sicily and Andalusia the admixture of
non-Aryan blood is small. We see this from the similarity
between the physical types that predominate there and
the ancient and present-day Greek types. The admixture
of Finnish blood among the inhabitants of the northern
parts of Norway and Sweden is even smaller. Thus, the entire
mass of the population of Western Europe originates from
people of the same branch of the Aryan family and must
be regarded as having the same hereditary mental qualities.
The assumption that the different nations of Western Europe
have different hereditary mental qualities is fantastic

and is refuted by philological research. Therefore, if there
are any differences in the mental qualities of the western
nations at the present time, they are not due to the nature
of the ancestors of these nations, but solely to their historical lives, and whether these differences will continue or
not will be determined by the future course of their lives.

When people talk about the differences in the mental
qualities of nations, they have in mind not mental vigour
as such, but the degree of education of the respective nations. This is the only reason why those definite opinions
that have become current could have arisen. To judge a
nation's mental qualities as such by any other criterion
than that of their brilliance or dullness due to high or low
degree of education is a very difficult matter. In the present state of science it cannot help us to draw any definite
conclusions even in those cases when nations of the yellow
race are compared with nations of the white race. When
different nations of the same branch of the same linguistic family are compared, it seems to be only a pretext for
self-praise or for calumny. Persistence in the old arguments
about innate differences between the nations of Western Europe as regards mental qualities reveals failure to understand
the results long ago achieved by linguistics, which proved
that all these nations are descendants of the same people.

Differences in language are of enormous importance
in practical life. People who speak the same language are
inclined to regard themselves as a single national entity.
When they grow accustomed to living in a single political
state they develop national patriotism and a dislike, more
or less marked, for people who speak languages other than
their own. This actual relation between languages is, perhaps, the most important feature of the differences between
nations. But very often a theoretical significance is attached
to differences in language; it is imagined that the specific
features of a nation's mental qualities can be determined
by the specific features of its grammar. This is sheer fantasy.
Morphology divorced from the rules of syntax is of no importance whatever; but in all languages, the rules of syntax
satisfactorily determine the logical relation between words
with or without the aid of morphology. The essential difference between languages consists solely in the richness
or paucity of their vocabulary; and their vocabulary corresponds to the degree of the respective nation's knowledge.

so that it serves only as a criterion of its knowledge, of its degree of education, of its everyday occupations, of its mode of life, and partly, of its intercourse with other nations.

As regards mode of life, there are very important differences between people. In Western Europe, however, all the essential differences in this sphere are not national, but class, or occupational. The peasant's mode of life is different from that of the artisan who works in a workshop, but there is not a single nation in Western Europe in which there are no peasants and artisans. The mode of life of the upper class differs from that of peasants and artisans; but again, there is an upper class among all the European nations, even among those, like the Norwegians, in which aristocratic titles have disappeared, or have almost disappeared. It is not a matter of titles, but of the habit of occupying a high social position.

The habits that are of real importance are different among the different classes or occupations due to the differences in mode of life. There are numerous other habits that are not of a class, but of a national character. But these are trivial, they serve only for amusement or for ostentation. Sensible people are indifferent towards them, and they persist only because these people ignore them as trivial and unworthy of their attention. These trivialities may be very important for the archeologist, in the same way as ancient coins found in the ground are important for the numismatist, but they are of very little importance in the serious life of a nation.

Every nation in Western Europe has a separate language and a separate national patriotism. These two features are the only ones that distinguish a nation as a whole from all the other nations of Western Europe. But a nation also has class and occupational divisions. In all aspects of mental and moral life except language and national sentiment, each of these divisions possesses a special mode of life in which they resemble the class divisions that exist among the other western nations. These specifically class or occupational features are so important that, except for language and patriotism, each class or occupational division in a given West-European nation differs far more in mental and moral respects from the other divisions in that nation than it does from its corresponding division among the other West-European nations. As regards mode of life and conceptions,

the peasant class throughout the whole of Western Europe
appears to constitute a single entity. The same must be said
about the artisan class, about the wealthy class among the
common people, and about the upper class. In respect to
mode of life and conceptions, a Portuguese grandee resembles the Swedish aristocrat more than he does the peasants
of his nation. The Portuguese peasant resembles the Scottish or Norwegian peasant in these respects more than he
does the rich Lisbon merchant. In international affairs,
a nation that constitutes a political entity, or is striving
to become one, does, indeed, represent a single whole, at
all events under ordinary circumstances. In domestic affairs,
however, it consists of class, or occupational divisions, the
relations between which are approximately the same as
those between nations. There have been cases in the history
of all West-European nations when the conflict between
the mutually antagonistic sections invaded even the sphere
of international affairs, when the weaker section called
in foreigners to help it against its internal enemies, or
gladly welcomed foreigners who came uninvited to subjugate
its country. Perhaps this readiness on the part of the weaker section of a nation to join foreigners in an armed struggle against its fellow countrymen has diminished nowadays. Probably it was never an easy matter for any part
of any European nation to betray its country; but in ancient
times internecine strife assumed such ferocious forms that
the losing side was driven to desperation. To save their
lives people will do things that are loathsome to themselves.
If it is true that class or political conflicts among the civilized nations of the present day can no longer assume
such ferocious forms as to drive the vanquished internal
opponents to desperation, then there will be no cases of
any section of any civilized nation joining foreigners against
its fellow countrymen.

Some publicists think that there are grounds for such
a hope. It is beyond dispute, however, that until recent
times this was not the case. Therefore, when describing
the life of a nation, the historian must always bear in
mind that a nation is a combination of diverse classes,
the ties between which, in the past, were not strong enough
to prevent outbursts of mutual hate.

All historians now appreciate the importance of class
strife, and if they frequently speak of a nation as a single

entity in relating matters on which the different classes
were not unanimous, their mistake in doing so is not due
to ignorance, but to temporary forgetfulness, or to some
other cause. The majority of educated people, however,
and, therefore, the majority of historians, still retain a
largely wrong conception of classes. There are two chief
reasons for this. The bulk of the public and, therefore, the
majority of the historians, are not closely acquainted with
the actual customs and conceptions of the classes which
are remote from them in social position and mode of life,
and, moreover, their judgment of them is influenced by political class bias. Let us take, for example, the prevailing
conception of the agricultural class. It is generally supposed that the morals of the peasants are purer than those
of artisans. In some cases, this, in all probability, is true.
For example, if the majority of the peasants live in plenty
and the majority of the artisans live in want, then, of course,
the bad qualities that are engendered by poverty will be
much more strongly developed among artisans than among
peasants. Scientists, as a rule, live in big cities and, therefore, often see the bad housing conditions and other signs
of the material distress suffered by artisans. They know
far less about how the peasants live, and the chances are
very great that the personal impressions they casually obtain of the life of the peasants will be wrong as far as the
majority of this class is concerned. The second cause of
the mistakes is political bias. The peasants are regarded as
a conservative class. Hence, scientists of a conservative
turn of mind praise the prudence and pure morals of the
peasant class. Those scientists who stand for social change
think and speak of the peasant class under the influence of
political hostility.

In addition to class and occupational divisions, every
civilized nation has extremely important divisions according to degree of education. In this respect, it is the custom
to divide a nation into three main classes, viz., the uneducated, the superficially educated, and the thoroughly educated. Whatever our opinions may be about the harmfulness or benefits of education, whether we praise ignorance
or regard it as harmful, everybody will agree that the conceptions of the vast majority of people who have not received an education and have been unable to educate themselves differ very much—for the good or bad is not the ques-

tion now—from those of the vast majority of educated people. And people's conceptions are one of the forces that control their lives.

Let us draw the conclusions from this survey of the actual situation as regards our knowledge of national character.

We have very little direct and exact information about the mental and moral qualities even of those modern nations with which we are most closely acquainted, and the current conceptions of their characters are based not only on inadequate, but on biassed and carelessly collected material. The most usual example of carelessness is that when chance information about the qualities of some small group of people is used to characterize a whole nation. To substitute true characterizations of nations for careless and biassed ones is a very troublesome business, and the majority of scientists have no serious desire that this should be done, for the usual object of characterizing a nation is not to present an unbiassed picture, but to express opinions which seem to be to our advantage, or flatter our vanity. People who wish to speak impartially about other nations refrain from resorting to this extremely arbitrary mode of forming an opinion and content themselves with information which is obtained much more easily and is more authentic. They study the modes of life and the big events in the life of a nation, and confine themselves to such opinions of the qualities of that nation that are easily deduced from these authentic and definite facts. Such opinions are less sweeping than the current characterizations. The essential difference between them is that the former, in dealing with every feature, indicate to what section of the nation and to what period the opinion relates. This is as it should be with serious conceptions of the character of large groups of people.

We do not know the qualities of a nation, we know only the state of these qualities in a given period. The state of mental and moral qualities changes very considerably under the influence of circumstances. When circumstances change, a corresponding change takes place in the state of these qualities.

Concerning every civilized nation of the present day we know that its earlier modes of life were different from the present one. Modes of life influence people's moral qualities. Changes in modes of life cause changes in these qualities. For this reason alone, every characterization of a civilized nation that ascribes to it some kind of immutable moral qualities must be regarded as false. Concerning all the nations that reached the state of civilization, except the Egyptian, we have definite information about the times when they were deeply steeped in crude ignorance. It is sufficient to recall that even in the *Iliad* and the *Odyssey* the Greeks are still unable to read and write. Examining the legends preserved among the Greeks in the form of myths, we see features of a totally savage mode of life. Many scholars even find in these legends vestiges of cannibalism. Irrespective of whether cannibalism existed among the people who spoke the Greek language, or whether the deduction that it did is mistaken, we know for certain that at one time the Greek people had no civilized conceptions or habits whatever. Can the moral qualities of a highly civilized people remain the same as those of their savage ancestors? Only the physical type and those features of temperament that are directly determined by it can, perhaps, remain the same, and even this will be true only if to the term "the same," are added such reservations as rob it of nearly all significance. For example: the colour of the eyes has remained the same; but formerly, the expression of the eyes was dull, almost senseless, but subsequently they assumed an expression that corresponds to high mental development. The contours of the face have remained the same, but formerly they were crude, now they are pleasing. Quick temper has remained, but it manifests itself less often and in different forms. Did the changes in circumstances that caused changes in the mode of life always affect all classes alike? This could have happened only in rare cases. Customs did not change equally among the different classes and, consequently, the resemblance between them grew less than it was before. A nation acquired knowledge and this caused a change in its conceptions; change in conceptions brought about a change in morals; but this series of changes did not affect all classes, or all the parts of the country inhabited by this nation, to an equal degree. Thus, the life of every present-day civilized nation represents a series of changes in mode of life and conceptions, which, however, did not equally affect all sections of the nation. Hence, exact characterizations can apply only to the particular groups of the people that constitute a nation, and only to particular periods of their history.

The consequence of the striving to explain the history of a nation by specific, immutable mental and moral qualities is that the laws of human nature are forgotten. When concentrating our attention on the real or apparent differences between objects we fall into the habit of ignoring the qualities that are common to them all. If these objects belong to extremely diverse categories, this may not harmfully affect our judgment of them. For example, if we are speaking of a plant and a stone, it is not always necessary to remember that these two objects have certain qualities in common. The difference between them is great, and in the circumstances under which the two are usually discussed, the stone displays qualities different from those of the plant. But this is not the case in history. All the beings about whose lives it tells us are organisms of the same species. The differences between them are not as great as the similarity of their qualities. The influences that cause changes in the lives of these beings are usually of a kind that have the same consequences for them all. Let us take food, for example. The food of different nations, and of the different classes of a nation, is not the same. There is also a difference in the quantity of the same kind of food needed by adults under different modes of life in order to feel satisfied and to keep in good health. But every man grows weak if he does not get enough food, and every man is in a bad mood when he is tormented by hunger.

Consideration for the qualities of the functioning of the stomach that are common to all adult people is incomparably more important than the true or imaginary differences that may be deduced from consideration for the different kinds of food different people are accustomed to eat. Habit enables people to tolerate conditions which people not habituated to them cannot tolerate; but strong as habit may be, the demands of the common qualities of human nature remain in force. A man can never lose the desire to improve his conditions of life, and if we fail to see this striving in some people, it is only because we are unable to perceive the thoughts they are concealing from us for some reason or other, most often because they think that it is of no use talking about what cannot be done.

When a man has grown accustomed to his conditions of life, the improvement he desires is usually only a little better than the conditions to which he is accustomed. For example, all a peasant wants is that his labour should be eased somewhat, or that it should bring him a somewhat bigger reward than it does at present. This does not mean that when this desire is satisfied a new one will not arise. He merely wants to be reasonable in his desires, for he thinks that it is unwise to wish for too much. If a nation has lived in great distress for a long time, its desires are usually moderate. This does not mean that it is incapable of wishing for much more when its present wishes are satisfied. If we bear this in mind we will abandon the fantastic idea of dividing nations according to capability or incapability of reaching a high state of civilization. Its place will be taken by the distinction between conditions which favour the development of the desire for progress and conditions which compel a nation not to think about what, in its opinion, cannot be achieved.

If circumstances for a long time remain such as to prevent a nation from increasing its stock of knowledge, it grows accustomed to the idea that it is useless to strive to increase it. But as soon as the opportunity occurs to learn something new that is beneficial for life, the desire, innate in all people, to gain more knowledge, is awakened in that nation. The same applies to all the blessings, the sum total of which is called civilization.

4

THE GENERAL CHARACTER OF THE ELEMENTS THAT PROMOTE PROGRESS

The most essential differences between people are the differences in their mental and moral development and in their degrees of material prosperity. It is said that in tribes at a very low stage of development all the members of a given tribal community have the same conceptions, knowledge and moral habits. This opinion is a rhetorical exaggeration of the fact that the differences in the habits and conceptions of people in a small tribe at a low stage of civilization are smaller than among the people of a big and highly civilized nation. The differences are smaller, but they exist, and they are big differences. Nor can it be otherwise. Big differences in the habits and occupations are observed even in a herd of animals. Thus, apart from the difference between males and females, the male who exercises the authority of leader of the herd displays far more intelligence, resourcefulness, caution and courage than the rest of the males who are accustomed to follow his guidance. The minds of savages at the lowest stage of development are, after all, more developed than those of even elephants and orang-outangs. The conclusion to be drawn from this is that the differences in the breadth of knowledge and in the character of the habits of the people of a given savage tribe must be much bigger than these differences among the members of a given animal herd.

Let us, however, leave this debatable question, which is of relatively little importance for history, and turn our attention only to those tribes and nations that are of some historical importance. Here we see that in each of them there are some people whose mental and moral qualities are above the average of their tribe or nation, while some are far below it. The difference is so great that in the most civilized nation there is a fairly large number of people who in mental and moral respects are inferior to the most developed members of tribes which, in general, have risen little above the state of savagery. Let us take, for example, that category of knowledge regarding which it is particularly easy to decide whether this or that man possesses it, viz., the ability to count. In England, France and Germany there are numerous physically and mentally sound adults who are unable to solve arithmetical problems that are easily solved by traders or tax collectors in the Negro states of Central Africa. A comparison of people according to their moral qualities is far more vague than a definition of their mental level. Here too, however, we may draw fairly definite conclusions if we compare not all the moral qualities, but some definite quality, for example, how a mother or a father treats his or her children. If we take this element of moral development we shall have to admit that in tribes which lead a very primitive mode of life there are many parents who treat their children less cruelly than many parents who belong to advanced nations.

Thus, every nation of historical importance is comprised of people who differ very much in degree of mental

and moral development. The ignorance and moral crudeness
of a section of each nation is on a par with that of the most
ignorant and cruellest savages. Other sections occupy various intermediary stages between these worst and the
best representatives of the nation.

Hence, when it is said that a given nation has reached
a high degree of education, it does not mean that all the
people of this nation have risen much above savages in their
habits and mental development; but the fact that this nation is called highly civilized expresses the opinion that
the majority of the people comprising it stand far higher
than savages in mental development and in the merits of
their moral habits.

All serious scientists are now agreed in recognizing
as true that all the specific features which elevate civilized
people above the rudest and most ignorant of savage tribes
have been historically acquired.

The question is: What elements brought about this
improvement in conceptions and habits?

To make it clear what the essence of the answer to this
question must necessarily be, let us put the question more
broadly: let us ask ourselves not what elements raised the
mental and moral qualities of some people above those of
others, but what, in general, raised human life above the
life of other living beings whose bodies are organized similarly to those of human beings? The answer has been
known since time immemorial to all people who have
reached the stage of mental development at which they are
conscious of the difference between man and the so-called
nonreasoning animals.

We all know that all the advantages that human life
enjoys over the life of those mammals which are not endowed
with the same mental faculties that man possesses are the
result of man's mental superiority.

This commonly known and commonly accepted answer
to the general question of the origin of all the advantages
that human life enjoys obviously includes the answer to
the particular question of the force that promotes progress
in the life of nations. The principal force that elevates
human life is man's mental development. It goes without
saying that a man can misuse his mental faculties, as he
can any other faculty, so that they do not benefit but harm
other people, and even himself. For example, the interests

of an ambitious man usually do not coincide with the interests of his nation, and he employs his mental superiority
to the general mass of the people to their detriment. If he
achieves success, he very often gets accustomed to such an
unrestrained satisfaction of his passions that it ruins his
own mental, and finally, physical health. What has happened
to ambitious individuals has also happened to whole nations. Thus, the Athenians, misusing their mental superiority to the majority of other Greeks, ruined them and themselves. Later, the Romans, misusing their mental superiority to the Spaniards, Gauls and other little educated peoples
of Europe and of the parts of Africa and Asia adjacent to
Europe, ruined all the civilized peoples and ruined themselves. Mental power can, and often does, produce harmful
results, but it does so only under the pressure of forces or
circumstances which distort its natural character. Under
the influence of passion, a very intelligent and educated
man may behave in a manner far worse than the vast majority of his fellow countrymen who lack his natural mental
gifts and his education. It is now recognized, however, that
all such behaviour is due to circumstances which hindered
the normal development of such a man's spiritual life. In
itself, mental development tends to improve a man's conceptions of his duties towards other people, to make him
more benevolent, to develop his conception of justice and
honesty.

Every change in the life of a nation is the sum of the
changes that have taken place in the lives of the individuals
comprising this nation. Hence, when we want to ascertain
what circumstances promote or hinder the improvement
of a nation's mental and moral life we must ascertain what
circumstances improve or mar the mental and moral qualities of the individual.

In the old days, questions of this kind were obscured
by the crude conceptions which the majority of scientists
have inherited from the ancient, barbarian period of their
nations' history. At the present time these questions present
no great difficulties from the theoretical aspect. The fundamental truths are now clear to the majority of educated
people in the advanced nations, and the minority who
regard these truths as being incompatible with their interests are ashamed to deny them openly and are compelled
to combat them by means of casuistry. They say that, on the

whole, they share the honest convictions of the majority, but are only trying to prove that these truths do not fully apply to the particular case in which they run counter to their interests. Numerous excuses of this kind can be met with, but their falsity is usually obvious to everybody who has no personal interest in arguing that they are sound.

In the darkest period of the Middle Ages the opinion prevailed among scholars that man is by nature inclined to do evil, and that he does good only under coercion. Applying this to the question of mental development, the pedagogues of those times asserted that the teaching of theoretical knowledge is successful only when cruel punishment is resorted to. Similarly, the scholars who wrote about the moral life of society said that the masses of the people are inclined to lead a vicious life, to commit all sorts of crimes, and that the only means of maintaining public order is oppression, that only force compels people to be industrious and honest. It is now recognized that all opinions of this kind are the result of ignorance and contradict human nature.

Of the sciences that deal with the laws of social life, the first to work out exact formulae of the conditions of progress was political economy. It established as an indefeasible principle of all theories about human well-being that only the voluntary actions of a man produce good results, that everything a man does under external compulsion turns out to be very bad, that he does successfully only what he wishes to do. Political economy employs this general idea to explain the laws that determine the success of material human labour and shows that all forms of forced labour are unproductive, and that material prosperity can be enjoyed only by that society in which the people till the land, make clothing and build houses, each being personally convinced that the work in which he is engaged is useful for him.

Applying this principle to the question of the acquisition and preservation of mental and moral wealth, the other branches of social science now recognize that only those people become enlightened and moral who themselves wish to become so, and that a man cannot keep on the level attained in these respects, let alone rise above it, unless he himself wishes to do so and voluntarily strives to do so. Indeed, we all know from our observations of everyday life

that if a learned man loses his love of learning he soon loses
the knowledge he has acquired and gradually becomes an
ignoramus. The same must be said about other aspects of
civilization. If, for example, a man loses love of honesty
he is quickly drawn into such a number of evil actions that
he grows accustomed to dishonest rules of life. No external
coercion can keep a man on a high mental or moral level
if he himself does not wish to keep there.

At the time when cruel pedagogical systems were prevalent it was said that people—in this case people who
had not yet reached adult age, children—learn reading,
writing, arithmetic, and so forth, only under coercion, only
out of fear of being punished for indolence. Everybody now
knows that this is not the case at all, that every healthy
child has a natural desire for knowledge, and that if unfortunate external circumstances do not kill this desire,
the child learns willingly and finds pleasure in acquiring
knowledge.

The people who take part in historical events are not
children, but adults, whose minds and will are stronger than
those of children. If a child's life was at all satisfactory in
material respects, and not too bad in mental respects, it
is found that it understands things better and behaves more
wisely on reaching adolescence than it did five years
before.

Speaking generally, a ten-year-old child knows more,
is more intelligent and has a stronger character than a child
of five; a fifteen-year-old adolescent is superior in all these
qualities to a child of ten, and if the next few years of his
life are not too bad, then at the age of twenty he will know
still more, will be still more intelligent, and have a still
stronger will. On reaching full physical development, a
man's mental and moral progress becomes less rapid, but
just as a man's physical strength continues to grow for many
years after he has reached adult age, so, in all probability,
his mental strength and ability to be firm in the pursuit
of his aims also grow. It may be supposed that growth of
strength usually ceases at the age of thirty, but if the course
of life is favourable, it continues for a few years more.
When it ceases, the man's physical, mental and moral
strength remains for a fairly long time at approximately
the highest level attained and, in all probability, the mental
and moral strength of a healthy man does not begin to wane

until his physical strength begins to wane. This is now the opinion of naturalists who study the human organism.

At what age does a man begin to regard himself as being equal in mental and moral strength to people who have reached full development? Vanity usually induces a man to think that he has reached this level earlier than he has grounds for thinking so; but the overwhelming majority of people whom adults regard as juveniles are nevertheless inclined to follow the example of adults, and fifteen-year-old youths, for example, are, in general, inclined to copy their older relations and friends. Thus, we all know definitely that the development of most people, even of those fairly near to adult age, is determined by the qualities of the older generation. Just as they did in infancy, so on attaining full physical height and fairly considerable physical strength, they strive to become like their elders, and hence, no coercion whatever is needed to make boys and girls develop exactly in the way their elders want them to develop; they themselves feel a strong urge to develop in this way. What is needed to encourage this is not coercion, but benevolent assistance to help them to achieve what they themselves desire. Do not hinder children in their striving to become wise and honest—such is the fundamental demand of present-day pedagogics. Help their development as much as you can, it adds, but know that inadequate assistance will be less harmful than coercion. If you are unable to influence children in any other way than by resorting to coercion, it would be better for them to do without your assistance than to receive it in the form of coercion.

We mention the fundamental principle of pedagogics because it is still very much the custom to compare foreign uneducated peoples and the lower classes of one's own nation with children, and from this to deduce the right of educated nations forcibly to bring about changes in the mode of life of subject uncivilized peoples, and the right of the educated ruling classes in the country to do the same with the mode of life of the uneducated masses of their own nation. This deduction is false if only for the reason that the comparison of uneducated adults with children is a mere rhetorical flourish which puts on a par two entirely different categories of beings. The rudest of savages are not children, but adults, exactly as we are. Still less do

the common people of civilized nations resemble children.
Even if we were to assume for a moment that this false deduction is not false, but correct, it would not give anybody,
even the most educated and benevolent people, the slightest right forcibly to change those aspects of the mode of
life of the common people, or even of savages, that are
brought up in justification of tyrannical orders concerning
their mode of life. Suppose they are little children (but
certainly not suckling babes, for they take their food with
their own hands and masticate it with their teeth, and do
not feed at the breasts of the wives of their educated guard-
ians). Suppose we are the most tender of fathers of these
certainly not two-month, but, at least, two-year-old infants. What of it? Does pedagogics permit a father to restrict a two-year-old child more than is necessary to protect
the infant's arms and legs, forehead and eyes? Does it permit
him to compel the infant to do nothing that he, the father,
does not do, and to do everything that he does? The father
eats with a knife and fork; must he whip the two-year-old
child if it takes a piece of food with its hand? "But the child
will burn its poor little fingers if it takes a piece of roast
meat." Let it; it will not be as bad as a whipping. Those
who are fond of comparing savages and the common people
with children will probably admit that the objects of their
tender care who plough the land, herd cattle, or at least
gather berries for their sustenance, are not less than ten
years of age. Very well, but what rights has a father, let
alone a tutor, over a ten-year-old child? Has he even the
right to force him to learn? Pedagogics says: "No, if a ten-
year-old child detests its lessons, it is not the child that is
to blame, but the teacher who killed its desire for knowledge by his bad teaching methods, or by the unsuitable content of what he taught." What is needed here is not coercion
of the pupil, but the retraining and re-education of the teacher. Instead of being a dry, fatuous, stern pedant, he must
become a kind and intelligent teacher; he must cast out of
his mind the wild conceptions that stifle his common sense
and acquire rational ones. When the teacher complies with
these demands of science, the boy will eagerly learn everything the now rational and kind teacher deems it necessary
to teach him. The coercive power adults exercise over a
ten-year-old boy is limited to restraining him from doing
harm to himself and others. But there are different kinds

of harm. In the case of coercive measures to avert harm, it is self-evident that it is no use averting minor harm by causing greater harm. By its very nature, coercion is harmful; it vexes the one who is restricted and punished, it spoils his character, rouses his resentment against those who restrict and punish him, and brings him into conflict with them. Therefore, reasonable parents, other adult relatives and teachers, deem it permissible to resort to forcible measures against a ten-year-old boy only in a few of the gravest cases of his behaving in a manner which in their opinion is harmful to himself. When the harm is not very great, they influence the boy only by means of good advice and by creating conditions under which he will get out of the habit of doing harm. They rightly believe that minor pranks which do no great harm to the boy, or to others, should not be matters for threats or punishment. Let life wean him from these pranks, they think, and they strive to help in this by means of advice, by providing the boy with better forms of recreation, and confine themselves to this. It is beyond dispute that cases occur when the harm caused by what is prohibited is greater than that done by prohibition. In such cases, coercive measures are justified by reason and are prescribed by conscience, with this reservation, of course, that they are not more severe or restrictive than is necessary for the good of the boys who are subjected to them. Let us suppose, for example, that the teacher has been put in charge of a gang of boys who are in the habit of fighting with sticks and stones. It is the teacher's duty to put a stop to this form of fighting, in which injuries, sometimes fatal, are inflicted. But is it matters of this kind that are meant when the employment of coercive measures against the allegedly childlike common people or against savages is justified on the ground that it is the teacher's duty to prevent children from harming themselves? No, such arguments cannot apply to facts of this kind. Firstly, if facts of this kind are meant, there is nothing to argue about, there is nothing to prove; nobody denies a government's right to prohibit brawling. Secondly, when speaking of the prohibition of brawling, this prohibition must not apply to any particular category of people, it must apply to all people who engage in brawling. It does not matter what their degree of education is, they are engaged in a brawl, and that is enough. No matter who they are, upper class or lower class, educated or ignorant, their brawling must be stopped. Has only a government the right to put a stop to a brawl? No, the conscience of every reasonable man dictates to him the duty to stop, if he can, any brawl he may witness, and the laws of every civilized country justify everybody who performs this duty dictated by his conscience. Is there any need to argue that a government also has the right to stop brawling? In every civilized country there is a law, approved by the people, which not only gives the government the right, but also makes it incumbent upon it to stop brawling. In every civilized country the people always demand that the government should enforce this law. And in every civilized country, this law applies equally to the entire population. Nc license or restriction in the matter of brawling exists for any class of people, be they high or low, educated or ignorant; no such license is or ought to be granted. In no civilized country is there any argument about this. What, then, was the purpose of talking about the common people being like children and the government being like a schoolteacher to these "pupils," who are sturdy men and grey-haired oldsters, if those who compare the common people with children only wanted to show that a government has the right to put a stop to brawling among the common people? Obviously, those who are fond of comparing the common people with children have in mind not the prohibition of brawling, but something entirely different. They want the common people to live in conformity with their whims, they want to remould the habits of the people as they think fit. Let us suppose that all the rules of life of the common people that they dislike are bad and all the rules of life that they want to substitute for them would really, in themselves, be good; but they are lovers of coercion, and although they speak in the language of civilized society, they are at heart people from barbarous times.

In all civilized countries the mass of the population have numerous bad habits; but to attempt to eradicate them forcibly would mean accustoming the people to even worse rules of life, to deception, hypocrisy and dishonesty. People give up bad habits only when they themselves wish to do so; and they acquire good habits only when they themselves learn that they are good and find it possible to assimilate them. These two conditions contain the whole essence of the matter: first, that a man should learn to know what is good; second, that he should find it possible to assimilate what is good. A man will never lack the desire to assimilate it. It is not in man's nature not to desire what is good, for that is not in the nature of any living being. It is needless to ask whether the beings which, like man, breathe through lungs and possess a highly developed nervous system desire good for themselves. Let us examine the movements of a worm: even a worm creeps away from what it feels is bad and towards what it feels is good. Attraction for what seems good is a fundamental quality of the nature of all living beings.

If we, the educated people of a given nation, wish to benefit the mass of our fellow countrymen who have habits that are harmful to them, our duty is to acquaint them with good habits and to strive to create for them the possibility of assimilating them. It is totally useless to resort to coercion. When the only obstacle to the substitution of good for bad is ignorance of what is good, we can easily achieve success in our desire to improve the lives of our fellow countrymen. The truths they have to learn are not brain-racking theorems of special sciences, but the common rules of rational life, which can be learnt by every adult person, however ignorant. The difficulty does not lie in explaining to the common people the harmfulness of what is bad and the usefulness of what is good; the major truths of this kind are well known to the vast majority of the common people of every nation in the state of our European civilization. They themselves wish to give up their bad habits and to adopt good ones. They do not put their desire into execution only because they lack the means to lead that mode of life which they regard as good, and which they would like to lead. They need not sermons, but the means with which to substitute good for bad. In every nation in the civilized world, the minority which wants to live according to rules that educated people rightly regard as bad is insignificant. It consists of people whom the bulk of the common people also regard as bad, just as the bulk of the educated people do. Except for these few morally sick people, all the common people, like all educated people, wish to behave well, and if they behave badly, it is only because the bad circumstances of their lives compel them to do so. They are all painfully aware of this, and all wish to change the circumstances of their lives in order to avoid being drawn into bad conduct. The duty of those who wish to benefit their nation is to help the overwhelming majority of people of all classes to accomplish this desire. What is needed here is not coercion against the common people, or any other class in the nation, but assistance in accomplishing the common desire.

Such ought to be the attitude of educated people towards the mass of their fellow countrymen. And it must be said that, for a fairly long time already, all governments of civilized states have adhered to these wise concepts. The governments of all the European states, all without exception, long ago abandoned the barbarous method of bringing about changes in national life by forcible measures. Even the Turkish government has abandoned attempts to force benefits upon its people; even that government knows now that, far from improving the life of the nation it governs, forcible measures only worsen it.

The scientists who want the government of any civilized country to take forcible measures in order to change the life of its nation are less enlightened than the Turkish rulers.

Whether we are Frenchmen, or Germans, Russians, Spaniards, Swedes, or Greeks, we have a right to think that our nation is less ignorant than the Turkish nation; hence, we have a right to demand that the scientists of our nationality should not deny our nation the respect that the Turkish Pashas accord their nation.

Some scientists who are ashamed to demand forcible intervention in the life of their own nation are not ashamed to say that it is the duty of a government of a civilized nation to take forcible measures to improve the customs of subject uncivilized alien tribes.

Power over foreign lands is acquired and maintained by military force. Thus, the question of the rights of governments of civilized nations over uncivilized tribes is a question of the cases in which reason and conscience can justify conquest. All these cases come within the concept of self-defence. Not a single settled nation follows such customs as would make it necessary for any other nation to attempt to conquer it as a measure of self-defence. Every settled nation pursues a peaceful mode of life and obtains its means of subsistence by honest, peaceful labour. Military conflicts arise between settled nations not because of the fundamental

rules of their lives, but solely because of misunderstanding,
or outbursts of passion. If one settled nation is so superior
in strength to another settled nation that it is able to
subjugate it, then it is obvious that it is more than strong
enough to repel attacks by that nation. Hence, the conquest
of a settled nation can never be regarded as a necessary
means of self-defence for the conquering nation. The interests of every settled nation demand peace. If the stronger
nation acts justly towards its weaker settled neighbour,
it will rarely be attacked by it. An attack by the weak side
must fail because of the superior strength of the defending
side. If, after repelling the attack of the weak side, the strong
side concludes peace with it on just terms, if it does not
take advantage of its victory, the vanquished side will
lose the desire to resume hostilities for a long time to come.
Thus, the stronger nation is always in a position to arrange
its relations with its weaker settled neighbour in such a
way that they will be of an essentially peaceful character. The conquest of a settled nation is always a violation
of justice, and violation of justice can never be beneficial
for the victim of such violation, it is always harmful. Thus,
never being a necessary measure of self-defence for the
conquering nation, the conquest of a settled nation can
never be justified. The relations between settled nations
and nomads is a different matter. They can be such that
the subjugation of a neighbouring nomad tribe is a necessary
measure of self-defence for a settled nation. Some nomads
are peaceful; their subjugation can never be necessary;
but among many nomads, their mode of life is to plunder
their neighbours. The subjugation of such nomads may
become a necessity, and would be justified by reason and
conscience. The question is, however, have the civilized
conquerors a right to compel the conquered nomads to
change their customs? Yes, it is necessary in order to achieve
the aim that justifies the conquest, i.e., to put a stop to
plunder. The conquered savages engaged in plunder. The
conqueror not only has a right to put a stop to this, it is
his duty to do so. But what is the purpose of putting a
stop to plunder? To improve the morals of the savages?
No. Their morals may be (and often are) improved as a
result of their ceasing to engage in plunder; but the motive
behind the suppression of plunder is the protection of the
civilized nation and not consideration for the welfare of

the predatory savages. The civilized conquerors must protect their peaceful labour; it is, therefore, the duty of their government to put a stop to the plunder perpetrated by the conquered savages. Whether this is beneficial for the savages or not makes no difference. It may be beneficial for them, but it is not done for their benefit; it is done for the benefit of the conquerors. The government of the civilized nation catches and punishes robbers and thieves of its own nationality in its own country. Why does it do this? For the benefit of the robbers and thieves? No, it is done to protect the peaceful and honest people in the country; the people deem it necessary that robbers and thieves be caught and punished, and they impose this duty upon the government. Until recent times, even among advanced nations, the function of governments in relation to robbers, and the wishes of society concerning them, were limited to catching and punishing them. Today, enlightened society deems it necessary to improve the rules of life of robbers and thieves who are caught and punished. The governments of civilized nations strive to carry out this wise and benevolent idea of the educated classes, and if this is done in the proper way many of the robbers and thieves undergoing punishment become honest and industrious. But how is this result achieved? The prison authorities ease the lot of the prisoners, provide them with profitable work and rational recreation during their prison life and, if they reform, their term of imprisonment is reduced. And so, how are these people reformed? Not by force and harsh punishment, but by gentleness and care, which mitigate their punishment and stimulate in them a disposition towards good rules of life. Deprivation of liberty in itself irritates people, corrupts them, develops in them base and evil inclinations; harsher punishment than mere detention in prison has a still worse effect. Similarly, when the government of the civilized nation deprives a predatory tribe of its independence in order to rid its own country of the predatory raids of this tribe, it can take measures to acquaint the subjugated savages with the good way of life and provide them with means of pursuing it; this will not be violence, but benevolence. If it is done in the proper way, the habits of the savages will improve, and as they improve, the conquerors can relax their power over the vanquished. This generous policy will greatly help to improve the lives of the subjugated people. Thus, when a conquered tribe is benefited by being conquered, the good results are obtained not by force, but by gentleness and relaxation of force.

As regards people of our times, it is definitely known that force corrupts, while gentle and benevolent treatment improves their moral qualities. Was this the case also in the past? Natural science tells us that this was always the case not only in the life of man, but also before that, in the life of man's ancestors. That branch of zoology which studies the mental and moral life of warm-blooded beings has proved that all their classes, families and species without exception are irritated and morally corrupted when force is exerted upon them, and that their moral qualities are improved when they are treated with benevolence, gentleness and care. When investigating the laws of human life there is no need to widen the scope of the question beyond the sphere of the warm-blooded beings. Moreover, I do not think that material has been collected for elucidating the forms and laws of moral life of some of the cold-blooded vertebrates or of the majority of invertebrate living beings. As regards warm-blooded beings, however, natural science has fully revealed that the general law of the moral life of all of these is deterioration of moral qualities as a result of any kind of cruelty or force, and improvement as a result of gentle treatment.

What, however, are we to think of the soundness of the numerous historical proofs that are brought forward to show that force has improved the habits of savages who have been conquered by civilized nations? Exactly what we think about the truth of other stories and arguments that contradict the laws of nature. The historian who is familiar with the laws of human nature can have no doubt that all stories of this kind are pure fiction. His task in relation to them is to explain how they arose, to find the source of the errors, or the motives for the deliberate lies that gave rise to them.

* * *

It is now recognized that all living beings that are able to feel impressions produced on them by external objects and to feel pain or pleasure, strive to adapt the circumstances of their lives to their needs, to occupy in them a position that is most pleasant for themselves, and with this aim strive to learn as much as they can about these circumstances. As regards all those beings whose organs of hearing and vision are constructed more or less like ours, that is, among others, as regards all mammals, it is now known that, in addition to the desire to learn as much as possible about the circumstances of their lives with the practical aim of improving the satisfaction of their needs, they also have a desire for theoretical knowledge. They enjoy looking at certain objects and listening to certain sounds. They have an inclination to look and listen solely because it gives them pleasure, quite apart from gain in the material sense of the term. Now that zoology has established these facts in relation to all mammals, it is impossible to deny that man has an innate desire to improve his conditions of life, and an innate desire for knowledge. These qualities, which a man cannot lose as long as his nervous system continues to function healthily, are the first two fundamental forces that promote progress.

There are living beings which are inimical to their own kind. This is what is said about spiders. But among those beings which, according to zoological classification, belong to the higher branches of the mammal class, there is not a single species that comes under the category of beings which are inimical to their own kind. On the contrary, all are benevolently disposed towards the beings of their own species. Some lead a solitary life, wolves, for example; but this is only a necessity imposed upon them by the difficulty of procuring food, just as hunters keep far apart in those places where game is scarce. It is common knowledge that, whenever possible, wolves combine in small communities; they like to be together. Those beings which in shape of teeth and structure of stomach are nearer to man than the wolf, and which feed exclusively, or chiefly, on vegetable food, live in communities.

There is no need to dilate on sexual affection. Everybody knows that in the higher branches of the mammals this is very strong; and since we all know that the lion and lioness tenderly love each other, that the tiger goes out to procure food for his mate who is nursing her young, it is absurd to doubt that sexual feeling among humans disposes male and female to mutual goodwill. Among mammals maternal love of children is strongly developed. If this feeling were absent, not one of their species could survive, for the young

of each of these species are for a long period dependent
for their existence upon their mothers who suckle them.
In every species of mammals the mother strongly loves
her young during the whole period they are dependent
upon her care. Therefore, there can be no room for doubt
that the human mother has a natural ardent love for her
children, and that this love lasts throughout all the years
the child is unable to procure its own food and defend itself
from enemies. In the human race this is a long period. It
is doubtful whether even in the most favourable places, as
far as procuring food and security from enemies is concerned, a
five-year-old human child could survive if it were left entirely
without the care of its parents. Speaking generally, the period
of maternal care for children in the human race lasts longer
than five years; but even if we take this obviously too short
period, it must be admitted that it is more than long enough
for mother and child to acquire the habit of living together.

It is now said that the family was not the original form
of the human mode of life, that at one time people lived
in large promiscuous groups in which there were no permanent ties between individual males and females. There is
no need for us here to go into the question as to whether this
theory in the form it is usually expounded is correct or not.
Even if we grant that, in the beginning, men and women
living together knew no other ties than those prevailing
in a herd of antelopes, it does not in the least affect our conception of what forces should be regarded as the promoters
of progress in human life. Granted that a woman who gave
birth to a child was not regarded as having closer ties with
it than all the other women in the same tribal community.
Let us make even such an assumption, although it contradicts a fact in the lives of all mammals—a cow knows her
calf and loves to feed it with her milk, and the same applies
to all mammals—but in spite of this, let us assume that
there was a time when a woman did not know which of the
children in the tribal group she had borne, or, at all events,
did not regard it as her duty, and had no desire, to suckle
the particular child she had borne. Nevertheless, the children of the people of those times could not have survived
had they not been suckled. And since the human race has
not disappeared, it shows that the infants of those times
were suckled by some women, their own mothers or not,
and that a group of children of a given tribal community

received the care of a group of women who were able to suckle them, and grew up only because they received the care of this group of women.

We concede to the advocates of this theory everything they can wish for; we are ready to concede that the beings which already had a human organism were lower in mental and moral respects than a sheep, if only they adduce facts which will make such an assumption probable. We must say, however, that for this it would be necessary to alter the physiology of the nervous system and to prove that a being with a shape of body similar to that of the human body of the present day had a brain that was less highly organized than that of a sheep. Until this is done, as long as physiology continues to say what it says today about the correlation between the manlike brain and the manlike shape of body, we must think, as physiology tells us to think, that those beings that were human were mentally superior to sheep. It must also be presumed that the children of those beings needed maternal care much longer than lambs need it, and it is beyond doubt that in those times, as at present, the existence of the human race was conditioned by the love of mothers for their children. Let us, despite comparative anatomy, even assume that the beings that had human-shaped bodies were at one time at a stage of mental and moral development that must be called lower not only than that of sheep, but of all other warm-blooded beings. Even if the people of those times had no benevolent feelings whatever, they, nevertheless, lived in some kind of groups, even if each consisted of one woman and her children of the age at which they could not yet procure food for themselves. Let us assume that the mother did not love her children, and that she suckled her new-born infant only because of an instinctive desire to relieve the inconvenience caused by the accumulation of milk in her breasts, and that when she ceased suckling her child she did not share her food with it, but drove it away and devoured all she could, and that the child ate only the leavings that she could not eat herself. For all that, her children lived with her for a fairly long period of time; they saw what she did, and even if she did not take the trouble to teach them — although not only the dog and the cat, but even the cow teaches its young—they nevertheless learned from her by following her example.

But, of course, it was not so. From the time beings with human-shaped bodies appeared on earth there was some inclination towards mutual goodwill among them. This inclination, which was independent of sexual or kinship relations, resulted in the adult males finding pleasure in talking to each other. If their language was not yet human, they were, nevertheless, able by the sounds of their voices to express at least those thoughts and feelings that wolves, horses or sheep express to one another; and they were able to explain the sounds of their voices by means of some kind of gestures as all mammals are able to do. But even if they were unable to express their feelings and exchange their thoughts in the way that all beings that breathe through lungs and have a windpipe and vocal chords are able to do, nevertheless, the males found pleasure in sitting together and gazing at one another. And the females found pleasure in this too. Sexual desire must have produced at least the same mutual sympathy between human males and females as it produces in the tiger and tigress. The ties between mother and infant were no less tender than they are between a tigress, or a ewe, and their young, and were of longer duration. It could not be that the mother did not teach her child, or that the men did not protect the women and children from danger. The feeling of mutual goodwill that has existed among humans ever since beings with human-shaped bodies appeared fostered the innate striving of each one of them to improve his conditions of life and to satisfy his desire for knowledge. By natural desire the young ones followed the example of their elders; children learned, the young men acquired experience by watching the actions of those who were more experienced, and strove to assimilate their practical knowledge. These desires exist among all mammals; hence, there can be no doubt that they have been among the chief attributes of human nature since the very beginning of man's existence.

Thus, we have two categories of forces that promote improvement in human life. One of them is a man's striving fully to satisfy the needs of his organism and his desire to acquire knowledge irrespective of its practical utility, solely because he finds pleasure in doing so; the other is the human relationships that arise from mutual goodwill. They are different forms of the pleasure and utility that people derive from living in the same group, and two stronger forms of mutual goodwill that are created not only by the requirements of the nervous system, such as the mutual goodwill between men or between women who are unrelated to each other, but belong to the so-called physiological functions of the organism. One of these forms of goodwill is sexual desire and the love between a man and a woman that arises from it. The other form is maternal love and the desire of a man to care for the woman with whom he is cohabiting and for the children he has with her.

These forces also operate among other mammals. If we examine the influence they exercise, we will have to admit that it was they that caused the improvement in those organisms which in their present forms we call mammals.

Owing to certain specific features of the history of his ancestors, man's brain developed to a degree not reached by any other beings with similarly shaped bodies. What were these specific features of history that caused a higher development of the mental faculties of man's ancestors? Their general character is clearly defined by our knowledge of physiology. Concerning requirements, we can make surmises that will be highly probable, but it is doubtful whether historical facts have been found that would give the authentic parts of the answer more clarity than is given by physiology. The latter shows that improvements in organisms are brought about by favourable conditions. On this basis we can definitely say that if the mental faculties of man's ancestors developed to a higher degree than those of the beings on whose level they had once stood, then their history must have been more favourable for their organic development than the history of those beings who did not rise so high above their former common level. This is physiological truth. But we can only surmise what circumstances favoured the physiological development of man's ancestors. It is quite probable that owing to some fortunate circumstance, man's ancestors obtained greater security against enemies than the other beings that resembled them, or were quite like them. They may have migrated to another region more suitable for peaceful life, having numerous places of refuge like caves, which neither poisonous snakes nor big beasts of prey could penetrate. They may have migrated to an extensive forest that was free from these foes, or where there were numerous trees on which it was convenient and safe to live. Or perhaps the advantage of the place was a greater

18*

N. G. CHERNYSHEVSKY

abundance of good food than in the place in which the beings, who after this began to lag behind the mental development of man's ancestors, had remained, or to which they had been forced to migrate. These and similar surmises are in accord with the laws of physiological development and are therefore probable; which of them is in accord with the actual facts, we are as yet unable to say owing to lack of information.

But by some means, owing to the influence of certain favourable circumstances of their lives, man's ancestors achieved such a high degree of mental development that they became human. It is only from this period that the history of their life commences which gives rise to questions not of a general physiological character, but such as relate specifically to human life.

These beings were mentally far superior to all the species of mammals which, because of their physical strength, were, like them, fairly safe from enemies. And it is superior mentality that explains the whole of the subsequent progress of human life. It goes without saying that beings whose mentality is incomparably superior to that of the buffalo, or the camel, must find it incomparably easier to surmount obstacles to the improvement of their lives. A buffalo cannot devise ways of making itself quite secure against big beasts of prey or poisonous snakes while it is sleeping. The savage at the lowest stage of human development we know of knows how to ensure his safety while asleep, and we see that the simplest of these precautions could easily have been taken by people of even a lower degree of mental development than that of the lowest of the present-day savages. It is said, and in all probability it is true, that the ability to pick up a piece of rock, or a club, and use these against an enemy enhanced people's security, made it possible for them to improve their material conditions of life, and, as a result of this improvement, to acquire more highly developed mental faculties. We see that the most intelligent of the other mammals have not acquired the art of skilfully using this mode of defence against powerful enemies. It is said that orang-outangs and gorillas fight well with stones or clubs, but in this appraisal the term "well" is not used in comparison with man's skill in this form of defence, but only in comparison with the very clumsy way in which a bear throws clumps of earth at an enemy. If orang-outangs and gorillas had been able to fight with clubs at all skilfully, let alone as skilfully as savages, they would have driven human beings out of those countries, the climate of which is suitable for them; there would not be a single human being in that zone of Africa where gorillas live, or in Borneo. The expulsion of the human beings would have inexorably taken place for the purpose of seizing the fruits of their agricultural labour.

Again we lack positive information of how, precisely, people at a lower stage of development than the rudest of present-day savages rose to their present relatively high level of mental development. All serious scientists have accepted as the fundamental rule of scientific explanation the law of logic that when no direct information about the origin of a certain fact is available and it is explained by the operation of forces that create analogous facts before our eyes, we have no right to assume that it was created by any other forces, that we must regard it as the result of the operation of the forces that are now creating the same facts. We know definitely that people's organisms are improved by their favourable conditions of life, that with an improvement in the organization of the brain there is an improvement in man's mental faculties, that moral and material progress is the result of an improvement in mental and moral faculties. This definite information about the course of progress in our times, and in previous epochs well known to us, is quite sufficient to explain the progress of human life in those epochs, of the history of which we have no direct information.

Let us take, for example, three immense improvements in human life: the acquisition of the art of using fire and of maintaining or kindling it; the domestication of animals; the discovery of the art of tilling the soil for the purpose of growing cereals. For these discoveries, so important for human life, there had to be certain fortunate circumstances that made them possible.

It is now believed that people who did not know the use of fire lived not only in places where the atmosphere is sufficiently warm for man all the year round, but also in countries that have cold seasons. If this was so, then the tribes or small groups who lived in climes that have cold seasons must have suffered from cold more than those who lived nearer to the equator. But can we assume that the art of protecting oneself from cold by lighting a fire was discovered by the people who suffered most from cold? No. This is rightly regarded as a totally uncalled for hypothesis. The people who lived near the equator also needed fire. Even near the equator the nights are colder than is pleasant for people accustomed to live in a very warm atmosphere. The need of the people in the equatorial zone to warm themselves was also so great that the art of kindling fire must have been a precious improvement in their lives. Hence, the matter is explained not by the difference in the benefits of fire for people living under different climates, but only by the country in which facts occurred which people utilized for discovering means of maintaining and kindling fire. A man who has eaten nothing for two days will gladly snatch and eat any food that comes his way; but a man who has not eaten for only one day will do the same; one is hungrier than the other, but the other is hungry enough to be glad to come across food. Therefore, it is absurd to say: "people who have starved for two days are glad of the opportunity to eat." Limiting the content of the idea by postulating the necessity of two days of starvation distorts the physiological truth. We shall express ourselves correctly only if we omit this superfluous postulate and say generally: "hungry people are glad of the opportunity to eat." The time a hungry man has not eaten—twelve, twenty-four or forty-eight hours—has nothing to do with the case. The difference in the time is important in connection with other physiological problems, but not with the question as to whether a hungry man is glad to eat. If a man often starves for two days at a stretch he becomes physically weak; ordinarily healthy people can go without food for intervals of twelve hours without being affected in this way. True, at the end of such an interval the man has lost considerable physical strength, but his organism is not disturbed; he can go without food for twelve hours every day for a whole year and remain as strong as he was before. But deprivation of food for regular periods of forty-eight hours during a whole year will weaken the strongest men. If we do apply the concept of difference between these two forms of hunger to the question of ability to find means of satisfying it, we must say: the longer the periods between the satisfaction of hunger, the less able is the hungry one to procure food. This is obvious, because he is physically weaker and is less able to work; or if food is not procured by work, but by hunting, or by gathering wild fruit, berries and roots, then he is less able to do this than a strong man. Let us apply the same argument to the question of the discovery of fire for protecting the body from cold. It is believed that the circumstances that led to this discovery were cases of fire produced by nature. A man saw a tree struck by lightning and catch fire. The tree continued to burn after the storm had passed and the man had recovered from his fright. He went up to the burning tree, and his body having been chilled by the storm, he felt the pleasant sensation of warmth. Looking round, he saw that the burning branches which had sunk to the ground had set fire to some drywood lying near, and so forth. This is the story that is related of a number of observations that end with the discovery of means for keeping the embers glowing under the ashes and of kindling new fire with them. The story is not absolutely authentic, the discovery may have been made in a different way, but it must be regarded as being highly probable. Very well, let us try to ascertain in which country there were most opportunities for making such observations. The savage near the equator lives in the open air all the year round. In a country where the savage suffers greatly from the cold a considerable part of the year he tries to spend that period in some refuge that is protected from the wind. During this part of the year he is unable to make the observations, which, according to the most probable story, led to the discovery of the art of kindling fire. The chances that the art of using fire was discovered in places remote from the equator are reduced in proportion to the number of days in the year that were unsuitable for these observations, and it is therefore more probable that the art of preserving and kindling fire was discovered by people who lived in the permanently high-temperature zone.

It is rightly said that the domestication of animals marked a very great improvement in the life of man. Let us, then, examine certain definite facts about this matter and try to ascertain under what circumstances these facts could have occurred. Let us begin with the domestication of the animal, whose descendants are our present European house dogs. Who the ancestors of these dogs were has not, I think, been quite definitely ascertained, but there can be no doubt that they were species of animals similar to the present-day wolf, jackal or dingo. The question is: what character must we presume this breed of wild animals possessed? Was it more or less hostile than that of the breed of wolf that is most hostile to man? Everybody will agree that it must have been less hostile and therefore must have allowed itself to be fed and yielded to kindness, and must have been easier to domesticate. Thus, we all agree that the relatively mild character of the animal that is able to help man in his hunting, to protect him from other wild animals and protect his property from other people, was the circumstance that facilitated this important step in the improvement of human life.

Let us pass to agriculture. Where did it begin, in a place where there were wild plants bearing grain suitable for human food, or in a place where there were no such plants? And what kind of soil did the first agriculturists till for the artificial reproduction of these plants, soil that seemed to them to be fertile or such as seemed to them to be unfertile? We all think it probable that agriculture began in a country where many of the cereals which, after being improved by cultivation, are now wheat, barley or rye, grew in a wild state, and that for the first experiments in cultivating them plots of land were chosen similar to that on which they grew in a wild state. Thus, we are all of the opinion that conveniences for making the first attempts artificially to reproduce cereals were the circumstances which raised man from the nomad to the settled, agricultural mode of life.

The opinions we have expressed will probably not seem to anybody to contain anything new. Every reader will probably say that he has known them a long time, and that he has held them ever since he became old enough to be interested in social questions and to read serious books. We have expounded the commonly known and commonly accepted solutions of the problems of the beginning of the use of fire, the domestication of animals and the cultivation of the soil precisely for the purpose of emphasizing what everybody thinks about the circumstances that promote progress. When we judge them in conformity with the rules of common sense and with the deductions of our everyday experience, we find that the successes of civilization are due to facts which are favourable for human life.

This opinion is dictated to us by reason and by everyday experience.

THE AESTHETIC RELATION
OF ART TO REALITY [1]

(A Dissertation)

THE PRESENT treatise is limited to general conclusions
drawn from facts, confirmed only by general references to
facts. This is the first point that must be explained. This
is the age of monographs, and the present work is liable
to the reproach of being out of date. The exclusion from it
of all special researches may be construed as neglect of
such, or be attributed to the author's opinion that general
conclusions do not have to be confirmed by facts. But such
a view would be based only on the external form of this
work and not on its intrinsic character. The realistic trend
of the ideas developed in it is itself sufficient evidence that
they arose on the basis of reality, and that the author, in
general, attaches little importance for our times to flights
of fancy even in the sphere of art, let alone the sphere of
science. The essence of the concepts enunciated by the author is proof that he would have liked, had he been able,
to quote in his work the numerous facts on which he has
based his opinions. But had he dared to yield to his wishes,
the dimensions of this work would have far exceeded the
limits set for it.[2] The author is of the opinion, however,
that the general references he makes are sufficient to recall
to the reader's mind tens and hundreds of facts in favour
of the opinions enunciated in this treatise, and he therefore
hopes that brevity of explanation will not be taken as
lack of proof.

But why did the author choose as the subject for research
such a general, such a wide question as the aesthetic relation
of art to reality? Why did he not choose some specific question, as is most often done nowadays?

Whether the author is capable of dealing with the problem he undertook to solve is not, of course, a matter for
him to decide. But the subject which attracted his attention

has every right to the attention of all students of aesthetic problems, that is to say, of all those who are interested in art, poetry and literature.

The author is of the opinion that it is useless to discuss fundamental problems of science only when nothing new and fundamental can be said about them, when it is not yet possible to see the new trends of thought in science and to show the direction these trends must in all probability take. But when material for a new view of the fundamental problems of our particular science is available, these fundamental ideas can and must be expressed.

Respect for real life, distrust of a priori[3] hypotheses, even though they tickle one's fancy, such is the character of the trend that now predominates in science. The author is of the opinion that our aesthetic convictions, if it is still worth our while to discuss aesthetics, should also be brought into line with this.[4]

The author recognizes the need for special researches no less than others do, but he is of the opinion that it is also necessary from time to time to review the content of science from the general viewpoint; he is of the opinion that if it is important to collect and investigate facts, it is no less important to try to penetrate their meaning. We all recognize the high importance of the history of art, especially of the history of poetry; that being the case, the questions: what is art? what is poetry? cannot but be of high importance.

* * *

[In Hegelian philosophy, the concept of the beautiful is developed in the following way:

The life of the universe is the process of the realization of the absolute idea. The absolute idea can find perfect realization only in the entire space and entire course of existence of the universe; the absolute idea can never find perfect realization in any one object, limited by space and time. While being realized, the absolute idea is divided into a chain of definite ideas; and each definite idea, in its turn, can find perfect realization only in the infinite number of objects, or beings, it embraces; it can never be perfectly realized in one separate being.

But][5] all spheres of spiritual activity are subject to the law of ascent from immediacy to mediacy. As a consequence

of this law, the absolute idea, which becomes fully comprehensible only by thinking (cognition in the form of mediacy), first appears to the spirit in the form of immediacy,
or in the form of an impression. Therefore, it seems to the
human spirit that a separate being, limited by space and
time, fully corresponds to its conception of it, that in it
the idea finds perfect realization, and that in this definite
idea the general idea finds perfect realization. Such a view
of an object is a phantom (ist ein Schein) in the sense that
the idea never *fully* manifests itself in a separate object;
but behind this phantom lies the truth, for the general idea
does find realization in a definite idea to *some degree*, and
to some degree the definite idea finds realization in the
separate object. This phantom of the perfect manifestation
of the idea in the separate being, behind which lies the truth,
is the beautiful (das Schöne).*

This is how the concept of the beautiful is developed
in the prevailing system of aesthetics. From this fundamental
view follow the next definitions: the beautiful is the idea
in the form of a finite manifestation; the beautiful is a separate sensuous object, perceived as the pure expression
of the idea, so that nothing remains in the idea that would
not manifest itself sensuously in that separate object, and
there is nothing in the separate sensuous object that would
not be the pure expression of the idea. In this respect, the
separate object is called the image (das Bild). Thus, the
beautiful is complete correspondence, complete identity
of the idea and the image.

Needless to say, these fundamental concepts from which
Hegel deduces his definition of the beautiful will not stand
criticism, as is now already admitted. It is also needless
to say that the beautiful according to Hegel is only a "phantom" that comes from a superficial view, unenlightened by
philosophical thinking, which obscures the seeming perfect
manifestation of the idea in the separate object, so that
the more thinking is developed the less remains of beauty
until, at last, with fully developed thinking, only truth is
left, beauty has vanished. Nor is it necessary for me to refute this with the fact that actually the development of

---

* This is a citation, or rather, a paraphrase of a passage in
Vischer's *Aesthetik oder Wissenschaft des Schönen*, Reutlingen und
Leipzig, Carl-Mäckens-Verlag, 1846-58.—*Ed.*

human thinking does not in the least destroy man's aesthetical sense; all this has been said many times. As a consequence of the fundamental idea in the Hegelian system and a part of the metaphysical system, the conception of the beautiful outlined above falls together with it. But perhaps, although a system may be false, an individual idea contained in it may be correct if taken by itself, resting on its own foundation? Therefore, it remains to be proved that the Hegelian definition of the beautiful does not stand criticism even when taken separately from his now fallen system of metaphysics.

"That being is beautiful in which the idea of this being is fully expressed"—translated into ordinary language this means: "that is beautiful which is excellent of its kind; that of which nothing better of its kind can be imagined." It is quite true that a thing must be excellent of its kind to be called beautiful. For example, a wood may be beautiful, but only a "fine" wood, one in which the trees are tall and straight, a thick wood, in short, an excellent wood; a wood in which the trees are short, crooked and sparse cannot be beautiful. The rose is beautiful, but only a "fine," fresh rose, with all its petals intact. In short, all beautiful things are excellent of their kind. But not everything that is excellent of its kind is beautiful. A mole may be an excellent specimen of its kind, but it will never seem "beautiful." The same must be said about most of the amphibians, about many kinds of fish, even of many birds. The better an animal of a given kind may be for the naturalist, i.e., the more its idea is expressed in it, the less beautiful it is from the standpoint of aesthetics. The better a swamp is of its kind, the worse it is in aesthetic respects. Not everything that is excellent of its kind is beautiful, because not all kinds of things are beautiful. The definition of beauty given by Hegel, viz., the complete correspondence of an object to the idea of it, is too broad. It merely says that among those categories of objects, or phenomena, that can achieve beauty, it is the best of them that seem beautiful; but it does not explain why these categories of objects and phenomena are divided into such in which beauty appears and others in which we see nothing beautiful.

At the same time, the definition is too narrow. "That seems to be beautiful which seems to be the perfect realization of the idea of the kind," also means: "a beautiful being must possess everything that can be good in beings of this kind; it must be impossible to find anything good in other beings of this kind that the beautiful object does not possess." This is actually what we demand of beautiful phenomena and objects in those kingdoms of nature in which there is not a diversity of types in the same kinds of objects. For example, an oak can have only one sort of beauty: it must be tall and leafy; these features are always found in a beautiful oak, and no other good feature can be found in other oaks. But in animals, a variety of types of the same species appear as soon as they are domesticated. This diversity of types of beauty is even greater in man, and we cannot even imagine that one man can possess all the shades of human beauty.

The expression: "beauty is the perfect manifestation of the idea in a single object" is not a definition of beauty at all. But it has a truthful side, viz., that "beauty" lies in an individual living object and not in an abstract idea. It also contains another truthful hint at the nature of truly artistic works of art, viz., that they always contain something of interest to man in general, and not solely to the artist (this hint is contained in the statement that the idea "is something general that operates always and everywhere"); why this is so we shall see in the proper place.

Another expression, which, it is claimed, is identical with the first, viz., "beauty is the unity of the idea and the image, the complete merging of the idea with the image," * has an entirely different meaning. This expression does, indeed, point to an essential characteristic, not, however, of the idea of beauty in general, but of what is called a work of art. A work of art will indeed be beautiful only when the artist has conveyed to his work all that he had intended to convey to it. Of course, a portrait is a good one only when the artist has succeeded in painting exactly the features he had intended to paint. But to "paint a face *beautifully*" and to "paint a *beautiful* face" are two entirely different

---

* Here, and in the foregoing, Chernyshevsky makes a critical analysis of the definition of beauty given in the idealistic aesthetics of the Hegelian Vischer (*cf.* F. Th. Vischer, *Aesthetik oder Wissenschaft des Schönen*, Bd. I, I. Teil, "Die Metaphysik des Schönen," § 13, S. 50, 54; § 74, S. 189; § 51, S. 141; § 44, S. 129).—*Ed.*

things. We shall have occasion to discuss this quality of a work of art when we define the essence of art. Here, I think that it is not superfluous to observe that the definition of beauty as the unity of the idea and the image—a definition which has in view not the beauty of living nature, but beautiful works of art—already contains the germ, or the result, of that trend in aesthetics which usually prefers beauty in art to beauty in living reality.

What, then, is beauty, if it cannot be defined as "the unity of the idea and the image," or as "the perfect manifestation of the idea in an individual object"?

The new is not built as easily as the old is destroyed, and it is not so easy to defend as it is to attack; therefore it is quite possible that the opinion concerning the essence of beauty which seems to me correct may not seem satisfactory to everybody; but if in my essay the aesthetic concepts deduced from the now prevailing views on the relation of human thought to living reality have remained incomplete, one-sided or shaky, this, I hope, is due not to the defects in the concepts, but to the way I have enunciated them.

The sensation that beauty rouses in man is serene joy, like that which fills us in the presence of someone we love. * We disinterestedly *love* beauty, we admire it, it fills us with joy, and the one we love fills us with joy. From this it follows that there is something in beauty that is near and dear to our hearts. But this "something" must be all-embracing, must be capable of assuming the most diverse forms, must be extremely general, because the most diverse things and beings, having no resemblance to one another whatever, seem beautiful to us.

The most general thing that is dear to a man, than which there is nothing dearer in the world, is *life*; first, the life a man would like to lead, the life he loves, and then, any life; for, after all, it is better to be alive than dead: by their very nature, all living things have a horror of death, of

---

* I am speaking of what is intrinsically beautiful and not of what is beautifully depicted by art; of beautiful objects and phenomena and not of the beautiful way they are depicted in works of art: the artistic merits of a work of art may give one aesthetic pleasure, but the essence of what is depicted in it may cause sadness and even rouse disgust. Such, for example, are many of Lermontov's poems, and nearly all the works of Gogol.

nonexistence; they love life. And it seems to us that the
definition:

"beauty is life";

"beautiful is that being in which we see life as it should
be according to our conceptions; beautiful is the object
which expresses life, or reminds us of life,"—
seems to be one that satisfactorily explains all cases
that rouse in us the sense of beauty. Let us trace the chief
manifestations of beauty in different spheres of reality in
order to test it.

Among the common people, the "good life," "life as it
should be," means having enough to eat, living in a good
house, having enough sleep; but at the same time, the peasant's conception of life always contains the concept—
work: it is impossible to live without work; indeed, life
would be dull without it. As a consequence of a life of
sufficiency, accompanied by hard but not exhausting work,
the peasant lad or maiden will have a very fresh complexion and rosy cheeks—the first attribute of beauty according to the conceptions of the common people. Working
hard, and therefore being sturdily built, the peasant girl,
if she gets enough to eat, will be buxom—this too is an
essential attribute of the village beauty: rural people regard
the "ethereal" society beauty as decidedly "plain," and are
even disgusted by her, because they are accustomed to
regard "skinniness" as the result of illness or of a "sad lot."
Work, however, does not allow one to get fat: if a peasant
girl is fat, it is regarded as a kind of malady, they say she
is "flabby," and the people regard obesity as a defect. The
village beauty cannot have small hands and feet, because
she works hard—and these attributes of beauty are not
mentioned in our songs. In short, in the descriptions of
feminine beauty in our folk songs you will not find a single
attribute of beauty that does not express robust health and
a balanced constitution, which are always the result of a
life of sufficiency and constant real hard, but not exhausting,
work. The society beauty is entirely different. For a number
of generations her ancestors have lived without performing
physical work; with a life of idleness, little blood flows to
the limbs; with every new generation the muscles of the
arms and legs grow feebler, the bones become thinner.
An inevitable consequence of all this are small hands and
feet—they are the symptoms of the only kind of life the

upper classes of society think is possible—life without physical work. If a society lady has big hands and feet, it is either regarded as a defect, or as a sign that she does not come from a good, ancient family. For the same reason, the society beauty must have small ears. Migraine, as is known, is an interesting malady, and not without reason; as a consequence of idleness, all the blood remains in the middle organs and runs to the brain. Even without that, the nervous system is strained as a result of the general weakening of the constitution; the inevitable consequence of this are prolonged headaches and various kinds of nervous disturbances. What is to be done? Even sickness is interesting, almost enviable, when it is a consequence of the mode of life that we like. True, good health can never lose its value for a man, for even in a life of sufficiency and luxury, bad health is a drawback; hence, rosy cheeks and the freshness of good health are still attractive also for society people; but sickliness, frailty, lassitude and languor also have the virtue of beauty in their eyes as long as it seems to be the consequence of a life of idleness and luxury. Pallid cheeks, languor and sickliness have still another significance for society people: peasants seek rest and tranquility, but those who belong to educated society, who do not suffer from material want and physical fatigue, but often suffer from ennui resulting from idleness and the absence of material cares, seek the "thrills, excitement and passions," which lend colour, diversity and attraction to an otherwise dull and colourless society life. But thrills and ardent passions soon wear a person out; how can one fail to be charmed by a beauty's languor and paleness when they are a sign that she has lived a "fast life."

> We like a fresh and heightened colour,
> The sign of youthful vigour;
> But far above it we prefer
> A melancholy pallor. *

But while attraction for pale, sickly beauty is a sign of artificially corrupted taste, every truly educated man feels that true life is the life of the heart and mind. It leaves its impress on the expression of one's face, most clearly in one's eyes, and therefore, facial expression, of which little

---

* A verse from the ballad "Alina and Alsim," translated into Russian by V. Zhukovsky (1814).—*Ed.*

mention is made in folk songs, acquires enormous significance in the conception of beauty that prevails among
educated people; and it often happens that a person looks
beautiful to us only because he has beautiful,expressive eyes.
    I have examined, as far as space permitted, the chief
attributes of human beauty, and it seems to me that they
all impress us as being beautiful because we see in them
the expression of life as we understand it. We must now
examine the opposite side of the subject; we must investigate why a man is ugly.
    In referring to a person's ungainly figure people usually
say he is "badly built." We know very well that deformity
is a consequence of illness, or of accidents, particularly
if they occur in the first period of the person's development.
If life and its manifestations constitute beauty, then, quite
naturally, illness and its consequences constitute ugliness.
A person with an "ungainly figure" is also deformed, but to
a lesser degree, and the causes of an "ungainly figure" are
the same as those of deformity, only not so potent. If a
man is born a hunchback, it is a consequence of the unfortunate circumstances that accompanied the first period of
his development; but round shoulders are also a hump,
only to a lesser degree, and must have been caused by the
same circumstances. In general, a man with an ungainly
figure is a man to some degree deformed; his figure tells us
not of life, not of a happy development, but of the hard
sides of his development, of unfavourable circumstances.
Let us pass from the man's general figure to his face. His
face may be ugly in itself, or because of its expression. We
dislike the "evil," "unpleasant" expression of his face because
evil is venom that poisons our lives. Much more often, however, it is not the expression, but the features of the face,
that are "ugly." The features of a face are ugly when the
facial bones are badly arranged, when the cartilage and
muscles bear, more or less, the impress of deformation in the
course of development, i.e., when the first period of a man's
development took place in unfavourable circumstances.
    It is quite unnecessary to go into details to substantiate
the idea that man regards as beautiful in the animal kingdom that which according to human conceptions expresses
life, fresh, and full of health and strength. Among the
mammals, the physical structure of which, in our eyes, is
nearer to the human body, man regards as beautiful round-

ness of form, fullness and freshness; graceful movements
seem beautiful because the movements of a "well-built"
being are graceful, i.e., the movements of a being that
reminds one of a well-built and not of a deformed man.
Everything that is "clumsy" is ugly, i.e., everything that is
in some degree deformed according to our conceptions, which
everywhere seek resemblance to man. The shapes of the
crocodile, lizard and tortoise remind one of the mammals,
but in a deformed, distorted and absurd form; that is why liz-
ards and tortoises are repulsive. As for the frog, in addition
to its ugly shape, this animal is cold and slimy to the touch,
like a corpse, and this makes the frog still more repulsive.

There is no need to dilate on the fact that what
pleases us in plants is their fresh colouring and their rich
diversity of forms, indicative of fresh and vigorous life.
A wilted plant is ugly; a plant with little vital sap is ugly.

Furthermore, the sounds and movements of animals
remind us of the sounds and movements of human life.
To some degree we are reminded of it by the rustle of plants,
by the waving of their branches, by their fluttering leaves. This
is another source of beauty for us in the vegetable and animal
kingdoms; a landscape is beautiful when it is animated.

I deem it unnecessary to trace in detail, in the different
kingdoms of nature, the idea that beauty is life, in particular, life that reminds us of man and of human life, because
both Hegel and Vischer repeatedly say that beauty in nature
is that which reminds us of man (or, to use the Hegelian
term, is the harbinger of personality); they assert that
beauty in nature is beauty only insofar as it hints at man.
A great, profound idea! Oh, how good Hegelian aesthetics
would be if this idea, beautifully developed in it, were the
basic one, instead of the fantastic search for the perfect
manifestation of the idea! Therefore, having proved that
beauty in man is life, there is no need to prove that beauty
in all other spheres of reality—which becomes beauty in
man's eyes only because it hints at beauty in man and
in his life—is also life.

But I cannot refrain from adding that, in general, man
looks at nature with the eyes of an owner, and the things
on earth that are connected with happiness, satisfaction
with human life, also seem beautiful to him. Sunshine and
daylight are charmingly beautiful because, among other
things, they are the source of all life in nature, and because

daylight has a direct beneficial effect upon man's vital functions, it raises his organic activity, and consequently, has a beneficial effect upon our humour.

One may even say, in general, that, reading in Hegel's aesthetics those passages' which tell us what is beautiful in reality, one comes to the conclusion that unconsciously he accepted as the beautiful that in nature which tells us of life, and consciously asserted that beauty is the perfect manifestation of the idea. Vischer, in the section "On Beauty in Nature," repeatedly says that beauty is only that which is alive, or seems to be alive. In developing the idea of beauty, Hegel very often uses the word "life" in such a way that one is at last constrained to ask whether there is a radical difference between our definition "beauty is life" and his definition: "the beautiful is the complete identity of the idea and the image." This question arises all the more naturally for the reason that "idea" is taken by Hegel to mean "the general conception as determined by all the details of its real existence," and there is, therefore, a direct connection between the concept idea and the concept life (or, to be more exact, life force). Is not the definition we offer merely a rendering into ordinary language of what, in the prevailing definition, is expressed in the terminology of speculative philosophy?

We shall see that there is a substantial difference between the two conceptions of beauty. By defining beauty as the perfect manifestation of the idea in an individual being, we necessarily arrive at the conclusion: "beauty in reality is only a phantom, which we attribute to reality by our imagination." From this it will follow that, "properly speaking, beauty is created by our imagination, but in reality (or according to Hegel in nature), there is no true beauty." From the postulate that there is no true beauty in nature it will follow that "art originates from man's striving to fill the gap of beauty in objective reality," and that "beauty created by art is higher than beauty in objective reality." All these ideas constitute the essence of Hegelian aesthetics and appear in it not fortuitously, but as the result of the strictly logical development of the fundamental conception of beauty. *

---

* *Cf.* F. Th. Vischer, *op. cit.*, Bd. II, § 79, S. 221, et seq. and also G. W. Hegel, *Vorlesungen über die Aesthetik*. (*Sämtl. Werke*, Stuttgart 1927, Bd. XII, S. 200, et seq.("Mangelhaftigkeit des Naturschönen").—*Ed.*

On the contrary, from the definition "beauty is life,"
it will follow that true, the highest, beauty, is the beauty
that man meets with in the world of reality and not the
beauty created by art. In conformity with this view of
beauty in reality, the origin of art must be attributed to
an entirely different source; after that, the essential purpose
of art will appear in an entirely new light.[6]

Thus, it must be said that, being a deduction from
general views concerning the relation between the real
and imaginary world that differ radically from the views
formerly prevailing in science, and leading to a system of
aesthetics which also differs radically from the lately prevailing systems, the new conception of the essence of beauty
differs radically from previous conceptions of it. At the
same time, however, it appears as their necessary further
development. As regards the radical difference between the
prevailing system of aesthetics and the one we are offering,
we shall be constantly seeing it; to indicate the point
at which they enter into close kinship we shall say that
the new view explains the major facts of aesthetics that
were demonstrated by the previous system. For example,
the definition "beauty is life" makes it clear why there
are no abstract ideas, but only individual beings in
the sphere of beauty—we see life only in real living
beings; abstract, general ideas do not enter the sphere
of life.

As regards the radical difference between the previous
conception of beauty and the one we are offering, it, as we
have said, reveals itself at every step; the first proof of this
presents itself to us in the conception of the relation to
the beautiful of the sublime and the ridiculous, which, in
the prevailing system of aesthetics, are regarded as sub-
varieties of the beautiful, originating from the different
relation between its two factors, the idea and the image.
According to the Hegelian system, the pure unity of the
idea and the image, is beauty proper; but the image and
the idea are not always in a state of equilibrium; sometimes the idea preponderates over the image and, appearing
to us in its universality, in its infinity, it carries us into
the sphere of the absolute idea, into the sphere of the infinite—this is called the sublime (das Erhabene); sometimes the image suppresses and distorts the idea—this is
called the ridiculous (das Komische).[7]

After criticizing a fundamental concept, we must also criticize the views that follow from it; we must investigate the essence of the sublime and the ridiculous and their relation to beauty.

The prevailing system of aesthetics gives us two definitions of the sublime, just as it gave us two definitions of the beautiful. "The sublime is preponderance of the idea over the form," and "the sublime is the manifestation of the absolute." In essence, these two definitions are entirely different, just as we found that the two definitions of beauty presented by the prevailing system are radically different. Indeed, preponderance of the idea over the form does not produce the concept of the sublime, but the concept "nebulous," "indefinite," and the concept "ugliness" (das Häßliche), as it is excellently developed by Vischer, one of the latest aestheticians, in his treatise on the sublime, and in the introduction to his treatise on the ridiculous; whereas the formula "the sublime is that which rouses in us (or to use the terminology of the Hegelian school manifests in itself) the idea of the infinite" remains the definition of the sublime. Therefore, each of them must be examined separately.

It is very easy to show that the definition "the sublime is preponderance of the idea over the image" is inapplicable to the sublime, now that Vischer himself, who has accepted it, has done this, explaining that preponderance of the idea over the image (to express this idea in ordinary language: predominance of the force that manifests itself in an object over all the forces that restrict it, or, in organic nature, over the laws of the organism which manifests it) produces ugliness or indefiniteness.[8] Both these concepts differ entirely from the concept sublime. True, ugliness may be sublime when it is horrible; true, nebulous indefiniteness enhances the impression of the sublime created by the horrible and the immense; but when ugliness is not horrible it is simply repulsive, or plain; nebulousness, indefiniteness, has no aesthetic effect if the object is not immense, or horrible. Not all sublime things are ugly or nebulously indefinite; ugliness, or indefiniteness, is not always sublime. Obviously, these concepts differ from the concept sublime. Strictly speaking, "preponderance of the idea over the form" applies to those kinds of events in the moral world, and of phenomena in the material world, when the object is shattered by its own excess of strength. It is indisputable that such phenomena often bear a highly sublime character, but only when the force that destroys the vessel that contained it already bears a sublime character, or when the object it destroys already seems to us to be sublime, irrespective of its destruction by its own strength. Otherwise there is nothing sublime about them. When the Niagara Falls destroys the rock which forms it and destroys itself by the onrush of its own strength; when Alexander of Macedon perishes as a result of his own excessive energy; when Rome falls by its own weight—these are sublime phenomena; but that is because Niagara Falls, the Roman Empire and the personality of Alexander of Macedon already belong to the sphere of the sublime. The death is like the life that preceded it, the fall is like the activity that preceded it. Here, the secret of sublimity lies not in "the preponderance of the idea over the phenomenon," but in the character of the phenomenon itself; only from the grandeur of the phenomenon that is destroyed does the destruction acquire sublimity. Annihilation resulting from the preponderance of inherent strength over its temporary manifestation is not in itself a criterion of sublimity. "Preponderance of the idea over the form" manifests itself most clearly in the phenomenon of the embryo of a leaf growing and bursting the integument of the bud that engendered it; but this phenomenon certainly does not come under the category of the sublime. "Preponderance of the idea over the form," the destruction of an object by the excess of strength developing within itself, is what distinguishes the so-called negative form of sublimity from the positive form. It is true that negative sublimity is higher than the positive; therefore, it must be granted that "preponderance of the idea over the form" enhances the effect of sublimity, just as it can be enhanced by many other circumstances, for example, by the solitude of the sublime phenomenon (a pyramid in an open plain is more magnificent than it would be among other huge structures; among high hills its grandeur would vanish). But the circumstances that enhance the effect are not the source of the effect, and moreover, preponderance of the idea over the image, of strength over a phenomenon, often does not occur in positive sublimity. Any number of examples of this can be found in every textbook on aesthetics.

Let us pass to the other definition of the sublime: "The sublime is the manifestation of the idea of the infinite" to express it in Hegelian language, or, expressing this philosophical formula in ordinary language: "the sublime is that which rouses in us the idea of the infinite." The most cursory glance at the treatment of the sublime in the latest books on aesthetics convinces us that this definition is the essence of the Hegelian conception of the sublime. Nay more, the idea that presentiment of the infinite is roused in a man by sublime phenomena also predominates in the conceptions of people who are alien to strict science; one rarely finds a work in which it is not expressed if the occasion for it, however remote, occurs. Such a digression, or application, will be found in nearly every description of a magnificent landscape, in every story about some horrible event. Therefore, it is necessary to pay more attention to the conception that the absolute idea is roused by the magnificent than to the preceding one that in it the idea predominates over the image, criticism of which could be limited to a few words.

Unfortunately, this is not the place to analyze the idea of the "absolute," or the infinite, or to show the real meaning of the absolute in the sphere of metaphysical concepts; only when we understand this meaning shall we be able to see the utter fallacy of identifying the sublime with the infinite. But even without entering into polemics about metaphysics, we are able to see from facts that the idea of the infinite, whichever way we interpret it, is not always, or it would be better to say, is hardly ever connected with the idea of the sublime. If we strictly and impartially examine what goes on within us when we contemplate something that is sublime, we will be convinced that, 1) it is the object itself and not the thoughts roused by this object that seem to us sublime. For example, Mt. Kazbek itself is magnificent; the sea in itself is magnificent; the personality of Caesar, or of Cato, is itself magnificent. Of course, when contemplating some sublime object, various kinds of thoughts may be roused in our minds which heighten the impression the object makes upon us; but whether such thoughts are roused or not is a matter of chance, and the object remains sublime independently of it: thoughts and reminiscences that heighten a sensation are roused by every sensation, but they are the effect, not the cause of the original sensation. If, when pondering over the feat performed by Mucius Scaevola, the thought springs up in my mind: "Yes, infinite is the power of patriotism," that thought is only the effect of the impression made upon me, independently of it, by the *feat itself* performed by Mucius Scaevola, it is not the cause of this impression. Similarly, the thought: "there is nothing on earth more beautiful than man" that may come to my mind when musing over a picture of a beautiful face is not the cause of my admiration of it, but the effect of it having seemed beautiful to me before that thought arose independently of it. Therefore, even if we were to grant that contemplation of the sublime always leads to the idea of the infinite, the cause of the impression made upon us by the sublime, which engenders such a thought, but is not engendered by it, must lie not in the thought, but in something else. But, in examining our conception of a sublime object, we discover, 2) that very often the object seems to be sublime to us, without, however, ceasing to seem to us to be far from limitless; it remains in definite contrast to the idea of boundlessness. Thus, Mont Blanc, or Kazbek, is a sublime, a magnificent object; but none of us thinks, in contradiction to his own eyes, of regarding it as boundless, or as immeasurably large. The sea seems to be boundless when the shore is not in sight; but all aestheticians assert (and quite rightly) that the sea looks far more magnificent when the shore is visible than when it is not. Here you have a fact which reveals that far from being engendered by the idea of the boundless, the idea of the sublime may even (and often does) contradict it, that the condition of boundlessness may adversely affect the impression that is made by the sublime. Let us go further and examine a number of magnificent phenomena in relation to the enhancing effect they have upon the sense of the sublime. A thunderstorm is one of the most magnificent phenomena of nature; but one must have an extremely rapturous imagination to see any connection whatever between a thunderstorm and infinity. During a thunderstorm we are enraptured, but our thoughts are taken up entirely by the storm. "But during a thunderstorm a man feels his own insignificance compared with the forces of nature; the forces of nature seem to him to be infinitely greater than his own." It is true that the strength of a thunderstorm seems to us to be far greater than our own;

but the fact that a phenomenon overwhelms a man does not mean that it seems to us to be immeasurably, infinitely powerful. On the contrary, when watching a thunderstorm, a man is conscious all the time that it is powerless over the earth, that the lowest hill will firmly resist the entire force of the hurricane and every stroke of lightning. True, a stroke of lightning may kill a man, but what of that? That thought is not the reason why a thunderstorm seems magnificent to me. When I see the revolving sails of a windmill I also know very well that if I were hit by a sail my body would be broken like a reed, I am "conscious of the insignificance of my strength compared with the strength" of a windmill sail; but it is scarcely likely that the sight of a revolving windmill would rouse in anyone a sensation of the sublime. "But here no fear is roused in me for my safety; I know that I will not be hit by a windmill sail; I am not filled with the dread that a thunderstorm rouses in me." This is true, but this is something entirely different from what was said above; this means: "the sublime is the awesome, the dreadful." Let us examine this definition of "the sublime forces of nature," which we actually find in books on aesthetics. The dreadful is very often sublime, this is true, but it is not always sublime: a rattlesnake is more dreadful than a lion, but it is disgustingly, not sublimely dreadful. Dread may enhance the sensation of the sublime, but dread and the sublime are two totally different concepts. But let us proceed further with our series of magnificent phenomena. In nature we have not seen anything which speaks directly of infinity. Against the conclusion deduced from this it may be said: "true sublimity lies not in nature but in man." Let us grant this, although in nature too there is much that is truly sublime. But why does "boundless" love, or an outburst of "overwhelming" wrath, seem "sublime" to us? Is it because the force of these emotions is "irresistible," because, "being irresistible, it gives rise to the idea of the infinite"? If that is so, then the desire for sleep is far more irresistible: it is doubtful whether the most passionate lover can do without sleep for four days and nights. The desire for food and drink is far more irresistible than the desire for "love";[9] these are truly boundless desires, for there is not a man on earth who does not recognize their potency, although there are many who have no idea of what love is. Far greater and far more difficult feats are performed for the sake of these desires, than are performed for the sake of the "almighty" power of love. Why, then, is the idea of eating and drinking not sublime, while the idea of love is? The fact that something is irresistible does not in itself make it sublime; boundlessness and infinity have no connection whatever with the idea of the magnificent.

It is scarcely possible, after this, to share the view that "the sublime is preponderance of the idea over the form," or that "the essence of the sublime lies in that it gives rise to the idea of the infinite." What, then, is the sublime? We think that a very simple definition of the sublime will fully embrace and sufficiently explain all the phenomena relating to this sphere.

"The sublime is that which is much bigger than anything with which we compare it." "A sublime object is one whose dimensions far exceed those of the objects with which we compare it. A sublime phenomenon is one that is more powerful than other phenomena with which we compare it."

Mont Blanc and Kazbek are magnificent mountains because they are far more immense than the ordinary hills and hillocks that we are accustomed to see. A "magnificent" tree is five times taller than our apple trees and acacias, and a "magnificent" forest is thousands of times larger than our orchards and groves. The Volga is much wider than the Tvertsa or the Klyazma. The smooth surface of the sea is much wider than that of the ponds and small lakes which the wayfarer constantly meets. Sea waves are much higher than those on lakes, and that is why a storm at sea is a sublime phenomenon even if it does not threaten danger to anybody. The fierce gale that blows during a storm is a hundred times sronger than an ordinary wind, its noise and roar are much louder than the noise and whistling of an ordinary fresh breeze. During a storm it is much darker than at ordinary times, sometimes reaching to pitch darkness. Lightning is more dazzling than any light. All this makes a storm a sublime phenomenon. Love is a much stronger emotion than our everyday petty concerns and motives; anger, jealousy, all passion in general, are also stronger—therefore passion is a sublime phenomenon. Julius Caesar, Othello, Desdemona, Ophelia, are sublime personalities; because as a soldier and statesman, Julius

Caesar was greater than all the soldiers and statesmen of his time; Othello's love and jealousy are much more intense than those of ordinary men; Desdemona and Ophelia love and suffer with a fullness of devotion of which not every woman is capable. "Much bigger, much stronger"—such are the distinguishing features of the sublime.

It must be added that it would be much simpler and better to use the term "great" (das Grosse) instead of the term "sublime" (das Erhabene), for it is much more characteristic. Julius Caesar and Marius are not "sublime," but "great" characters. Moral sublimity is only one particular kind of greatness in general.

A perusal of the best textbooks on aesthetics will easily convince one that in our brief survey we have included in our conception of the sublime, or great, all its major variations. It remains for us to show the relation of our view of the essence of the sublime to similar ideas expressed in textbooks on aesthetics that enjoy exceptional popularity nowadays.

That the "sublime" is a consequence of superiority to environment has been postulated by Kant, by Hegel, by Vischer. They say: "We compare the sublime in space with the objects surrounding it; for this purpose, the sublime object must have simple divisions which would make it possible, when comparing, to calculate how many times bigger it is than the objects which surround it, how many times a mountain, for example, is bigger than the trees growing on it. The calculation is so long that we lose count before reaching the end; we start counting again, and again unsuccessfully. Thus, it seems to us, at last, that the mountain is immeasurably great, infinitely great." The idea that "for an object to seem sublime it must be compared with surrounding objects" comes very close to our view of the chief characteristic of the sublime. But usually it is applied only to the sublime in space, whereas it should be applied to all classes of the sublime. Usually it is said: "The sublime is the preponderance of the idea over the form, and at the lower stages of the sublime this preponderance is recognized by comparing the size of the object with surrounding objects." We think it should be put this way: "the superiority of the great (or sublime) over the small and ordinary lies in its far greater dimensions (the sublime in space or in time), or in far greater strength (the sublime forces of nature and the sublime in man)." In defining the sublime, comparison and superior size should be elevated from a secondary and particular characteristic of the sublime to the chief and general idea.

Thus, the relation of our conception of the sublime to the ordinary definition of it is exactly the same as the relation of our conception of the essence of the beautiful is to the old view—in both cases, what was formerly regarded as a specific and secondary characteristic and was hidden from view by other concepts, which we cast away as accessory, is raised to the degree of a general and essential principle.

As a consequence of the change of point of view, the sublime, like the beautiful, also appears to us as a phenomenon more independent of man, but for all that, nearer to man than had seemed before. At the same time, our view of the essence of the sublime recognizes its actual reality, whereas it is usually[10] supposed that in reality the sublime only *seems* sublime because of the intervention of our imagination, which magnifies the size or strength of the sublime object or phenomenon to infinity. And indeed, if the sublime is in essence infinite, there is nothing sublime in the world that is accessible to our senses and our mind.[11]

But while our definitions of the beautiful and the sublime make both independent of the imagination, they, on the other hand, put in the foreground their relation to man in general, and to his conceptions of those objects and phenomena which he regards as beautiful and sublime: beautiful is that in which *we* see life as *we* understand it and want it, as it pleases *us*; great is that which surpasses the objects with which *we* compare it. On the contrary, from the ordinary Hegelian definitions, it follows by a strange contradiction that beauty and greatness are introduced into reality by man's conception of things, that they are created by man, but have no connection with man's conceptions, with his conception of things. It is also clear that the definitions of the beautiful and the sublime which we think are right destroy the direct connection between these concepts, which are subordinated one to the other by the definitions: "the beautiful is equilibrium between the idea and the image," and "the sublime is preponderance of the idea over the image." Indeed, if we accept the definitions "beauty is life," and "sublime is that which is much bigger than anything close or similar to it," then we must say that the beautiful and the sublime are two entirely different concepts, not subordinate one to the other, but both subordinate only to one common concept, very remote from so-called aesthetic concepts, viz., the "interesting."

Therefore, if aesthetics is the science of the beautiful in content, it has no right to speak of the sublime, any more than it has a right to speak of the good, the true, and so forth. If, however, by aesthetics is meant the science of art, then, of course, it must speak of the sublime, because the sphere of art includes the sublime.

But in speaking of the sublime we have up till now not touched upon the tragic, which is usually regarded as the highest, most profound kind of the sublime.

The conceptions of the tragic that prevail in science today play a very important role not only in aesthetics, but also in many other branches of learning (for example, in history), and even merge with the common conceptions of life. I, therefore, think it will not be superfluous to expound them in some detail in order to provide a basis for my criticism. In doing so I will strictly adhere to what is said by Vischer, whose book on aesthetics is today regarded as the best in Germany.

"The subject, by nature, is an active being. In his activities he transmits his will to the external world and thereby comes into conflict with the law of necessity which governs the external world. But the subject's activity necessarily bears the impress of individual limitation and therefore disturbs the absolute unity of the world's objective ties. The guilt (die Schuld) of this offence rests upon the subject, and the consequence of it for him is that, being bound by ties of unity, the whole external world, as a single entity, is thrown into agitation by the subject's action and, as a result, this individual action of the subject leads to a vast and unforeseen series of consequences in which the subject no longer recognizes his action and his will. Nevertheless, he must see the necessary connection between all these succeeding consequences and his action and hold himself responsible for them. For the subject, responsibility for what he did not intend to do, but what he did, leads to suffering, i.e., the expression of the counteraction of the disturbed course of things in the external world to the

action which disturbed it. The necessity of this counteraction and suffering is enhanced by the fact that the imperilled
subject foresees the consequences, foresees evil for himself,
but falls under it by the very means by which he wanted
to avert it. The suffering may increase until the subject
and his cause perish. But the death of the subject's cause
is only apparent, it does not die completely: an objective
series of consequences survives the subject and, gradually
merging with the general unity, it purges itself of the individual limitations it inherited from the subject. If, when
at the point of death, the subject becomes conscious of the
justice of his suffering and realizes that his cause is not
perishing but is purging itself and triumphs in his death,
the reconciliation is complete, and the subject will spirit-
ually survive himself in his purged and triumphant cause.
The whole of this process is called fate, or "tragic." The
tragic assumes different forms. The first form is that in which
the subject is not actually, but only potentially guilty, and
in which the forces that encompass his downfall are therefore the blind forces of nature, which, in the case of an individual subject distinguished more for the outward splendour of wealth, and so forth, than for intrinsic virtues, give
an example of how the individual must perish because he
is an individual. Here, the subject perishes not by the operation of moral law, but by the operation of chance, which,
however, finds explanation and justification in the reconciling thought that death is a universal necessity. In the
case of the tragedy of simple guilt (die einfache Schuld),
potential guilt grows into actual guilt. But the guilt does
not lie in a necessary objective contradiction, but in some
confusion connected with the subject's action. This guilt
in some way disturbs the moral integrity of the world. As
a result of it, other subjects suffer, and since the guilt here
is on one side, it seems, at first, that they are innocent
sufferers. But in such a case the subjects would be simply
objects for another subject, which contradicts the meaning
of subjectivity. Therefore, they must reveal a weak side
by committing some error connected with their strong side
and perish as a result of this weak side: the suffering of the
chief subject, being the reverse side of his action, originates,
by force of the offended moral order, from the guilt
itself. The instrument of punishment may be either the
offended subjects, or the criminal himself, who becomes

conscious of his guilt. Lastly, the highest form of the tragic, viz., the tragedy of moral conflict. The general moral
law is split up into particular demands which may often
contradict one another, so that in meeting one a man necessarily offends another. This conflict, which arises from
inherent necessity and is not due to chance, may remain
an internal conflict within the heart of one person. Such is
the struggle in the heart of Sophocles' Antigone. But since
art personifies everything in separate images, the conflict
between two demands of the moral law is usually depicted
in art as a conflict between two persons. One of the two contradictory strivings is more just and therefore stronger
than the other; at first it vanquishes everything that resists
it and thereby becomes unjust, for it suppresses the just
right of the opposite striving. Justice is now on the side
that was at first vanquished, and the striving that, in essence,
is more just, perishes under the weight of its own injustice from the blows of the opposite striving whose right was
encroached upon and which, therefore, has the entire backing
of truth and justice at the beginning of its resistance, but
on achieving victory itself sinks to injustice, which leads
to death or suffering. The entire course of this form of the
tragic is beautifully unfolded in Shakespeare's *Julius
Caesar*. Rome is striving towards a monarchical form of
government; this striving is represented by Julius Caesar;
it is more just and therefore stronger than the opposite trend,
which is striving to preserve the old-established political
structure of Rome; Julius Caesar vanquishes Pompey. But
the old-established also has a right to existence; it is destroyed by Julius Caesar, and the outraged law rises against
him in the person of Brutus. Caesar dies, but the conspira-
tors are tormented by the consciousness that Caesar, whose
death they had encompassed, was greater than they,[12]
and the force that he had represented is resurrected in the
persons of the triumvirs. Brutus and Cassius die, but over
the body of Brutus, Antony and Octavianus pay him high
tribute.[13] This, at last, brings about the reconciliation between the opposite strivings, each of which is both just and
unjust in its one-sidedness, which is gradually eliminated
by the fall of both; out of conflict and death arise unity and
a new life." *

* F. Th. Vischer, *op. sit.*, Bd. I, §§ 123-138, S. 285-314.—*Ed.*

It is evident from the foregoing that in German aesthetics the concept tragic is combined with the concept fate,
hence, the tragic lot of a man is usually presented as "a man's
conflict with fate," as the consequence of "the intervention
of fate." The concept fate is usually distorted in the latest
European books, which try to explain it with our scientific
concepts, and even to link it with them; it is therefore necessary to expose it in all its stark nakedness. This will
relieve it of its incongruous confusion with scientific concepts, which actually contradict it, and expose its utter
unsoundness, which is hidden by the latest presentations
of it, remodelled to suit our tastes. A vivid and genuine
conception of fate was held by the ancient Greeks (i.e.,
before philosophy appeared among them) and it is held to
this day by many Oriental peoples; it predominates in the
tales of Herodotus, in the Greek myths, in the Indian poems,
in the *Arabian Nights*, etc. As regards the latest transfor-
mations of this fundamental concept under the influence
of the conceptions of the world presented by science, we
think it is superfluous to enumerate them, and still less
necessary to subject them to any special criticism, for all
of them, like the conception of the tragic held by the latest
aestheticians, are the result of the striving to reconcile the
irreconcilable—the fantastic ideas of the semisavage man
with scientific conceptions—and are just as unsound as
the conception of the tragic held by the latest aestheticians.
The only difference is that the far-fetched combination of
opposite principles was more obvious in the preceding
attempts at conciliation than it is in the conception of the
tragic that is drawn with extraordinary dialectical profundity. For this reason we deem it unnecessary to expound all
these distorted conceptions of fate and think it is sufficient
to show how angular the original basis appears even beneath
the latest and most skilfully designed dialectical garb in
which it is clothed in the now prevailing aesthetic conception of the tragic.

This is how peoples who hold a genuine conception of
fate conceive of the course of human life: if I take no precautions against misfortune I may survive, and will nearly
always survive; but if I take precautions I will certainly
perish, and perish as a result of the very means in which
I had sought safety. On starting out on a journey I take all
precaution against accidents likely to occur on the way;

among other things, knowing that it is impossible to obtain medical assistance everywhere, I take with me several bottles of the most necessary medicines and put them in the sidepocket of the coach. What must necessarily happen as a consequence of this according to the conceptions of the ancient Greeks? The following: my coach will be overturned on the road; the bottles will be thrown out of the pocket; I will be thrown out myself and strike my temple on one of the bottles; the force of the impact will break the bottle, a fragment of broken glass will enter my temple and I will die. Had I not taken precautions, this would not have happened; but I wanted to take measures in case of accidents and perished from the very means in which I had sought safety. Such a view of human life differs so widely from our conceptions that it has only a fantastic interest for us. A tragedy based on the Oriental or ancient Greek idea of fate will have for us the significance of a fable spoilt by revision. And yet, all the above-mentioned conceptions of the tragic contained in German aesthetics are only an attempt to harmonize the concept fate with the concepts of modern science.[14] This introduction into science of the concept fate by means of an aesthetical view of the essence of the tragic was performed with extraordinary profundity, which testifies to the greatness of the mental capacity of those who had laboured to reconcile views of life that are alien to science with scientific concepts; but this profound attempt serves as emphatic proof that such strivings can never be successful; science can only explain the origin of the fantastic ideas of semisavage man, but it cannot reconcile them with truth.[15] The concept fate arose and developed in the following way.[16]

One of the effects of education upon a man is that it widens his outlook and enables him to understand the true meaning of phenomena that differ from those immediately around him, and which alone seem to be understandable to the uneducated mind, which fails to understand phenomena outside the immediate sphere of its vital functions. Science enables a man to understand that the activities of inorganic nature and plant life are entirely different from human life, and that even the life of animals is not quite the same as the latter. The savage or semisavage cannot conceive of life other than that of which he has direct knowledge as human life. It seems to him that trees speak, feel, know pleasure and suffering just as man does, that animals behave in all things as consciously as man does, that they are even able to speak in human language and do not do so only because they are cunning and hope to gain more by silence than by speech. He pictures the life of rivers and rocks in the same way: a rock is a petrified giant who has retained the power to feel and think; a river is a naiad, a mermaid, a water sprite. Earthquakes occur in Sicily because the giant who lies buried under that island tries to throw off the weight that presses on his limbs. In the whole of nature the savage sees humanlike life; all natural phenomena are due to the conscious action of humanlike beings. Thus, he personifies the wind, cold, heat (recall the Russian fable about the dispute between the wind, the frost and the sun as to which of them was the strongest), disease (the tales about cholera, about the twelve sister fevers, and about scurvy; the latter among the Spitzbergen hunters); similarly, he personifies the power of chance. It is even easier to ascribe its operation to the arbitrary will of a humanlike being than to explain other phenomena of nature and life in this way, because the operation of chance is more capable than the operation of other forces of prompting the ideas of caprice, arbitrary will and all the attributes of human personality. Let us, then, see how the conception of chance as the action of a humanlike being develops into the attributes that savage and semisavage peoples ascribe to fate. The more important an undertaking planned by a man the more numerous are the conditions needed for the execution of this undertaking exactly as it was planned. It hardly ever happens that all the conditions the man counted on should become available, and therefore, an important undertaking is hardly ever carried out *exactly* as one calculated. This chance, which upsets our plans, seems to the semisavage, as we have said, to be the action of a humanlike being, *fate*; from this fundamental character observed in chance, or fate, automatically follow all the other attributes ascribed to fate by present-day savage peoples, very many Oriental peoples, and by the ancient Greeks. Obviously, it is the most important undertakings that are the sports of fate (for, as we have said, the more important an undertaking the larger is the number of conditions upon which its success depends, and hence, the wider is the field for the play of chance). Let us proceed further. Chance upsets our calculations—hence, fate likes to upset our calculations, likes to sport with man and his calculations. It is impossible to foresee chance and it is impossible to say why a thing happened this way and not another—hence, fate is capricious, wilful. Chance is often fatal for a man—hence, fate likes to do a man harm, fate is cruel; and indeed, the Greeks regarded fate as a misanthrope. A cruel, powerful man likes to injure the best, the wisest and happiest people—hence, it is such people that fate also prefers to ruin. A cruel, capricious and very powerful man likes to display his power and says to the one whom he intends to destroy: "This is what I intend to do to you, try to stop me"—and in the same way fate announces its intentions beforehand in order to take malicious delight in demonstrating to us how impotent we are in its hands and to laugh at our feeble and unavailing efforts to combat or to escape it. Such opinions seem strange to us today, but let us see how they are reflected in the aesthetical theory of the tragic.

This theory says: the free actions of man offend against the normal course of nature; nature and her laws rise against the abuser of their rights; as a consequence of this, the acting person suffers, and if the action was so powerful that the counteraction is serious, he dies: "Therefore, all that is great meets with a tragic fate." Nature is here presented as a living being, very irritable, very jealous of its inviolability. But does nature really take offence? Is nature really vindicative? No; it continues eternally to operate in conformity with its laws, it knows nothing about man and his affairs, about his happiness or his death; the operation of its laws may, and often does, have a fatal effect upon man and his affairs, but all human action is based on these laws. Nature is neutral towards man, it is neither his enemy nor his friend: at one moment it is a favourable, at another moment, an unfavourable field for his activities. There is no doubt that every important human undertaking calls for a stern struggle against nature, or against other people; but why is this so? Only because, however important the matter may be, we are accustomed to regard it as unimportant if it is accomplished without a stern struggle. Thus, breathing is the most important thing in a man's life; but we pay no attention to it because, as a rule, there is no obstacle to it. Food is equally important for the savage who feeds on the fruit of the bread tree, which he obtains gratis,

20*

and for the European who obtains bread only as a result
of hard agricultural labour; but the gathering of the fruit
of the bread tree is an "unimportant" matter, because it
is easy, whereas agriculture is "important" because it is
hard. Thus, not every matter that is important in itself
calls for a struggle; but we are accustomed to regard as important only those important matters that are hard to
accomplish. There are many precious things that have no
value because they are obtained gratis, for example, water
and sunlight; and there are many important matters to
which no importance is attached only because they are
easy to attain. But let us accept the ordinary phraseology;
let us grant that only those matters are important which
call for a severe struggle. But is this always a tragic struggle? By no means; sometimes it is tragic, sometimes it is
not, depending on circumstances. The mariner struggles
against the sea, against storms, against submerged rocks;
it is a strenuous struggle, but is it necessarily a tragic one?
For every vessel that is dashed against rocks in a storm, a
hundred reach their havens safely. Let us grant that struggle is always needed, but struggle is not always unfortunate.
And a fortunate struggle, however hard it may be, is not
suffering but joy, not tragic, but only dramatic. And is
it not true that, if all the necessary precautions are taken,
things nearly always end happily? Where, then, is the necessity for the tragic in nature? The tragic in the struggle
against nature is fortuitous. This alone shatters the theory
that it is a "law of the universe." "But society? Other people? Must not every great man endure a severe struggle
against them?" Again it must be said that not all great events
in history are accompanied by severe struggle; but we,
by an abuse of language, are accustomed to call great only
those events that are accompanied by severe struggle. The
adoption of Christianity by the Franks was a great event,
but was that accompanied by a severe struggle? Nor was
there a severe struggle when the Russians adopted Christianity. Is the fate of great men tragic? Sometimes it is
tragic, sometimes it is not, just as is the fate of little people;
there is no necessity in this at all. And it must, in general,
be said that the fate of great men is usually easier than that
of obscure people, again, be it said, not because fate is
exceptionally favourably disposed towards distinguished
men, or not favourably disposed towards obscure people,

but simply because the former possess greater strength, wisdom and energy, so that people respect and sympathize with them more and are readier to assist them. Although people are inclined to envy greatness in others, they are still more inclined to respect greatness; society will stand in awe of a great man if it has no casual reasons to regard him as being harmful to itself. Whether the fate of a great man is tragic or not depends on circumstances. In history too one meets with fewer great men whose fate was tragic than with those in whose lives there was much dramatism, but no tragedy. The fate of Croesus, Pompey and Julius Caesar was tragic; but the careers of Numa Pompilius, Marius, Sulla and Augustus were very happy to the end. What was tragic in the fate of Charlemagne, Peter the Great, Friedrich II, in the lives of Luther, Voltaire or Hegel himself? There was much struggle in the lives of these men; but, speaking generally, it must be admitted that success and good fortune were on their side. True, Cervantes died in poverty, but is this not the lot of thousands of obscure people who, no less than Cervantes, could count on a happy climax in their lives and who, because of their obscurity, could not at all come under the law of tragedy? The vicissitudes of life impartially afflict the distinguished and the obscure, and favour them impartially. But let us continue our survey, and from the general conception of the tragic let us pass to the tragic "simple guilt."

The prevailing aesthetical theory says: "There is always a weak side to the character of a great man; there is always something wrong, or criminal, in the actions of a great man. This weakness, misdemeanour, crime, causes his downfall. But they necessarily lie deeply embedded in his character, so that the great man perishes from the very thing that is the source of his greatness." There is not the slightest doubt that this often happens: endless wars exalted Napoleon; they, too, were the cause of his downfall; almost the same thing was the case with Louis XIV. But this does not always happen. Often, great men perish through no fault of their own. That is how Henry IV perished, and with him Sully fell. To a certain degree we find this innocent downfall also in tragedies, in spite of the fact that their authors were bound by their conceptions: was Desdemona really the cause of her own doom? Everybody sees that Iago's despicable cunning alone was the cause of it. Were Romeo and Juliet really the cause of their own doom? Of course, if we are determined to regard everyone who perishes as a criminal, then we can accuse them all. Desdemona was guilty of being an innocent soul and therefore could not foresee slander; Romeo and Juliet are guilty of having loved each other.[17] The idea of regarding every one who perishes as the guilty one is far-fetched and cruel. Its connection with the Greek idea of fate and its diverse variations is very clear. It is possible here to point to one aspect of this connection: in the Greek conception of fate, a man always perishes through his own fault; had he acted differently from the way he did, death would not have overtaken him.

The other kind of the tragic—the tragic moral conflict—is deduced by aesthetics from the very same idea, only taken the other way round: in the case of tragic simple guilt, the basis taken for tragic fate is the seeming truth that every disaster, and especially the greatest of all disasters, death, is the result of a crime. In the case of tragic moral conflict the aestheticians of the Hegelian school base themselves on the idea that crime is always followed by the punishment of the criminal by his death, or by the torments of his own conscience. This idea, too, obviously originates from the legend about the furies who scourge the criminal. It goes without saying that this idea relates to crime not in the legal sense of the term, which is always punished by the laws of the state, but to moral crime, which can be punished only by a conjunction of circumstances, by public opinion, or by the conscience of the criminal himself.

As regards punishment by a conjunction of circumstances, we have long ridiculed the old-fashioned novels which "always end with the triumph of virtue and the punishment of vice."[18] Nevertheless, many novelists and all authors of treatises on aesthetics insist that vice and crime should be punished on earth. And so a theory has arisen to the effect that they are *always* punished by public opinion and by qualms of conscience. But this, too, does not happen always. As regards public opinion, it does not by any means punish all[19] moral crimes. And if the voice of society does not rouse our conscience every moment, in the majority of cases it is not roused in us, or, if it is, it soon falls asleep again. Every educated man understands how ridiculous it is to look at the world with the eyes of the Greeks of the period of Herodotus; everybody understands perfectly now-

adays that the suffering and doom of great men are not
inevitable; that not every man who dies does so for his
crimes, that not every criminal dies; that not every crime
is punished by the court of public opinion, and so forth.[20]
Therefore, one cannot help saying that the tragic does
not always rouse in our minds the idea of necessity, that the
basis of its effect on a man is by no means the idea of necessity, and that its essence does not lie in this. Wherein, then,
lies the essence of the tragic?

The tragic is a man's suffering or death—this is quite
enough to fill us with horror and sympathy, even though
this suffering or death is not a result of "an infinitely mighty
and irresistible force." Whether a man's suffering and death
are due to chance or necessity makes no difference, suffering
and death are horrible whatever the cause. We are told:
"purely accidental death is absurd in a tragedy"; this may
be so in tragedies written by authors, but not in real life.
In poetry, the author deems it his bounden duty to "make
the denouement follow from the plot"; in real life, the denouement is often quite accidental, and a tragic fate may
be quite accidental without ceasing to be tragic. We agree
that the tragic fate of Macbeth and Lady Macbeth follows
necessarily from their status and from their deeds. But
what about Gustavus Adolphus, who was quite accidentally
killed in the battle of Lützen, on the road of triumphs and
victories? Was not his fate tragic? The definition:
"the tragic is that which is horrible in a man's life"
seems to be a full and complete definition of the tragic in
life and in art. It is true that most works of art give us the
right to add: "the horrible that afflicts a man more or less
inevitably." In the first place, however, there is a doubt as
to the extent to which art is right in presenting the horrible
as being nearly always inevitable when, in the majority
of cases, it is actually by no means inevitable, but purely
accidental.[21] In the second place, I think that very often
it is only from the habit of searching in every great work of
art for a "necessary conjunction of circumstances," for a
"necessary development of the action from the essence of
the action itself" that we find, and then with great difficulty, "necessity in the course of events" even where it does
not exist, for example, in most of Shakespeare's tragedies.[22]

With the prevailing definition of the ridiculous—"the
ridiculous is preponderance of the image over the idea,"

in other words: internal vacuity and insignificance concealed by an exterior with claims to content and real significance—one cannot but agree; but at the same time it must be said that Vischer, the author of the best work on aesthetics in Germany, excessively restricted the concept ridiculous by contrasting it, in order to preserve the Hegelian dialectical method of developing concepts, only to the concept of the sublime. Petty ridiculousness, and stupid or dull ridiculousness, are, of course, the opposite of the sublime; but monstrous ridiculousness, ugly ridiculousness, is the opposite of beauty and not of the sublime. As defined by Vischer, the sublime may be ugly; how, then, can ugly ridiculousness be the opposite of the sublime when they differ from each other not in essence, but in degree, not in quality, but in quantity, when petty ugliness belongs to the ridiculous and enormous or horrible ugliness belongs to the sublime? That ugliness is the opposite of beauty is self-evident.

Having completed our analysis of conceptions of the essence of the beautiful and the sublime, we must now proceed to analyze the prevailing views on the different methods of realizing the idea of the beautiful.

Here, it seems to me, the importance of the fundamental conceptions, the analysis of which has taken up so many pages of this essay, stands out most vividly: departure from the prevailing view of the essence of that which is the main content of art necessarily leads to a change in the conceptions of the very essence of art. The now prevailing system of aesthetics rightly distinguishes three forms of existence of beauty, in which are included, as variations of it, the sublime and the ridiculous. (We shall speak only of beauty, for it would be wearying to repeat the same thing three times; all that is said in the now prevailing system of aesthetics about beauty fully applies to its variations. Similarly, our criticism of the prevailing conceptions of the different forms of beauty, and our own conception of the relation of beauty in art to beauty in reality fully apply to all the other elements that go into the content of art, including the sublime and the ridiculous.)

The three different forms in which beauty exists are the following: beauty in reality (or in nature) as the Hegelian school expresses it, beauty in imagination, and beauty in art (in the actual existence lent it by man's creative

imagination). The first fundamental question that arises
here is that of the relation of beauty in reality to beauty
in imagination and in art. Hegelian aesthetics answers
this question as follows: beauty in objective reality suffers
from flaws which mar it, and our imagination is therefore
obliged to alter beauty as it is found in objective reality
in order to rid it of the flaws that are inseparable from its
real existence, in order to make it true beauty. Vischer
analyzes the flaws in objective beauty more deeply and brings
them out more sharply than other aestheticians. Therefore,
it is his analysis that must be criticized. To avoid the reproach of having deliberately toned down the flaws in objective beauty pointed to by the German aestheticians, I must
quote Vischer's critique of beauty in reality (*Aesthetik*,
II Teil, Seite 299 und folg).

The intrinsic unsoundness of the entire objective form of existence
of beauty is revealed by the extremely precarious relation in which
beauty stands to the aims of historical movement even in the field
where one would suppose its position to be most secure (*i.e., in man;
historical events often destroy much that is beautiful; for example,
says Vischer, the Reformation destroyed the happy freedom and colour-
ful variety of German life of the XIII-XV centuries*). But in general
it is evident that the favour of chance assumed in § 234 rarely occurs
in reality (§ 234 *says*: the existence of beauty demands that there shall
be no intervention of disturbing chance in the realization of the beautiful (der störende Zufall). The essence of chance is that it may occur
or not occur, or occur in a different way; hence, there may not be a
disturbing chance in an object. Therefore it seems that side by side
with ugly individuals there must also be truly *beautiful ones*). Furthermore, precisely because of its animation (Lebendigkeit), which is
an inalienable advantage possessed by beauty in reality, its beauty
is transient; this transience is due to the fact that beauty in reality
does not spring from the striving towards beauty; it springs from and
exists by virtue of the general striving of nature towards life, in the
realization of which it appears only as a result of fortuitous circumstances and not as something premeditated (alles Naturschöne nicht
gewollt ist)... Flashes of beauty are rare in history; the fully beautiful is also rare in nature in general. In his well-known letter, Raffaello,
who lived in a land of beauty, complained about carestia di belle
donne;* and in Rome one does not often meet with models like Vittoria of Albano in Rumohr's time. "The latest creation of ever upward striving nature is beautiful man. True, she *rarely* creates him,
because there are too many conditions that counteract her ideas"
(Goethe). All living things have a multitude of foes. The struggle
against them may be sublime or ridiculous; but only in rare cases
does ugliness pass into the sublime, or into the ridiculous. We stand
amidst life and its infinite variety of relations. That is why beauty

* The rarity of beautiful women.

in nature is animated; but finding itself among an incalculable variety of relations, it is subjected on all sides to collisions and damage; because nature is concerned about the entire mass of objects and not about one individual object, she needs preservation and not beauty as such. That being the case, nature has no need to keep beautiful even the little of beauty it has accidentally created: life surges forward not caring whether the image is killed, or preserving it only in its distorted form. "Nature fights for life and existence, to preserve and reproduce its creations, not caring whether they are beautiful or ugly. A form which was intended to be beautiful by birth may be damaged in some part by chance; this at once affects other parts too, because nature sometimes needs strength to restore a damaged part and it takes this strength from other parts, and this is necessarily detrimental to their development. The being no longer becomes what it should have been, but what it can become" (Goethe in a comment on Diderot). Perceptibly or imperceptibly the damage is repeated and grows until the entire being is destroyed. Transience, frailty is the sad lot of all that is beautiful in nature. Not only the beautiful illumination of a landscape, but also the flowering period of organic life is a matter of an instant. "Strictly speaking, it may be said that a beautiful person is beautiful only for an instant." "The period in which the human body may be called beautiful is extremely short" (Goethe). True, out of the fading beauty of youth develops the higher beauty. beauty of character, which is seen in the features of the face and in behaviour. But even this beauty is transient; for character is concerned with moral aims and not with beauty of figure and deportment in the striving to achieve them... At a certain time an individual is conscious of his moral aims, is as he is, beautiful in the profoundest meaning of the term; but at another time a man is engaged with something that has only indirect connection with his object in life, and then the true content of his character is not reflected in his facial expression; sometimes a man is engaged in a matter imposed upon him only by mundane or vital necessity, and then all lofty expression is buried beneath indifference, boredom, reluctance. This happens in all spheres of nature, irrespective of whether they belong to the moral sphere or not... This group of warriors engaged in combat line up and move as if inflamed with the spirit of Mars; but a moment later they are scattered, their movements are no longer beautiful, the best of them lie wounded or dead: these warriors are not a tableau vivant, their thoughts are concentrated on the battle and they are not thinking about making their battle look beautiful. Nonpremeditation (das Nichtgewolltsein) is the essence of all beauty in nature; it lies in its essence to such a degree that we are conscious of an extremely unpleasant sensation if in the sphere of real beauty we see any deliberate striving whatsoever after beautiful effect. Beauty which is conscious of its beauty, which busies itself with it, trains itself in front of a mirror to be beautiful, is vanity, i.e., paltry. The affectation of beauty in the really existent is the very opposite of true grace... Chance, nonpremeditated, unconscious beauty is the seed of death, but it is also the charm of beauty in reality; so that, in the conscious sphere, beauty vanishes the moment it learns of its beauty, begins to admire itself. The simple man loses his naïveté as soon as he is touched by civilization; folk songs disappear when they attract attention, when people begin to collect them; the picturesque dress of semisavage peoples ceases to please them when they see the smart clothes of the painter who has come to study them; when civilization, charmed by picturesque dress, wants to preserve it, it is transformed into a masque, and the people abandon it.

But favourable chance is not only rare and transient; it should, in general, be regarded as relatively favourable; harmful, disturbing chance is never completely vanquished in nature, if we cast aside the bright mask that remoteness of place and time puts upon our perception (Wahrnehmung) of beauty in nature and examine the object more strictly; disturbing chance introduces into an apparently beautiful grouping of a number of objects much that mars its full beauty; nay more, disturbing chance also invades the individual object which at first seemed beautiful to us, and we see that nothing has escaped its rule. If we failed to see the flaws at first, it was because of another favour of chance, viz., the happy mood we were in at the time, which made the subject capable of seeing the object from the point of view of pure form. This happy mood is directly created in us by the object itself owing to its relative freedom from disturbing chance.

It is only necessary to examine beauty in reality more closely to become convinced that it is not true beauty; it will then be clear that up till now we had only concealed from ourselves the obvious truth. This truth is the necessary and universal realm of disturbing chance. It is not we who have to prove that it extends to absolutely everything; it is the opposite view that needs proof; the onus of proof lies on those who are of the opinion that with the infinitely diverse and close interconnection of everything in the world, it is possible for any individual object to preserve its integrity against all obstacles, hindrances and disturbing collisions. Our task is only to investigate the source of the illusion which tells our senses that some objects are an exception to the general law of subordination to disturbing chance; this we shall do later on; at present we shall merely show that the apparent exceptions to the general rule are indeed an illusion, a phantom (ein Schein). Some beautiful objects are a combination of many objects; in such a case, if we examine them more closely, we shall always find, first, that we see these objects in such a connection, in such a relation, only because we accidentally took up a certain position, because we are accidentally looking at them from a certain point of view. This applies particularly to landscapes: their plains, mountains and trees know nothing of one another; they cannot take it into their heads to combine in a picturesque whole; we see them in harmonious line and colour only because we are standing in a particular position and no other. But even from this favourable point of view we see a bush here, or a hill there, which disturbs the harmony; here there is a lack of elevation, there a lack of shade, and we shall have to admit that our mind's eye has altered, supplemented and improved the landscape. The same applies to a moving, acting group of living beings. Sometimes a scene may indeed be full of significance and expression, but in it are groups which, connected in essence, are separated in space; and again our mind's eye eliminates the space, brings together what is connected and casts out what is extraneous, superfluous. Other objects are beautiful individually. In that case we abandon beauty of surroundings, leave surroundings out of the view, we separate the object from its surroundings, in most cases unconsciously, unintentionally; when a beautiful woman enters a room our eyes are concentrated exclusively upon her, we forget about everybody else. But in either case, whether we see beauty in a separate object or in a group of objects, if we examine beauty more strictly the result will be the same. On the surface of the beautiful object we shall find the same as what we shall find in the beautiful group of objects: among the beautiful parts there will be ugly ones, and they will be found in every object no matter how much it may have been favoured by happy chance. It is a good thing that our eye is not a microscope and that the naked eye idealizes objects, otherwise the mud and infusoria in the purest water and the dirt on the tenderest skin would kill all beauty for us. We can see only from a certain distance; but distance itself idealizes. It not only conceals the dirt on the surface, but in general smooths out the details of the bodies that rivet them to the earth, removes vulgar clarity and precision which counts every grain, takes every trifle into account. Thus, the very process of seeing takes upon itself part of the labour of putting the object into its pure form. Distance in time operates in the same way as distance in space: history and memory do not transmit to us all the minor details about a great man, or a great event; they remain silent about the petty, secondary motives of a great personality, about his weaknesses; they do not tell us how much time in the lives of great men was spent in dressing and undressing, eating, drinking, treating colds, and so forth. But not only does this hide from us the petty things that mar beauty; on close examination of an apparently most beautiful object we clearly see very many important and unimportant flaws. Even if a human figure, for example, does not bear on the surface any impress of disturbing chance, we are sure to find some disproportion in its main form. This will become clear the moment we glance at a plaster cast of the features of a real person. Rumohr, in the preface to his *Italian Researches*, has utterly confused all the concepts relating to this: he wants to expose the falseness of pseudo-idealism in art which strives to improve nature in its pure and constant forms; he rightly says against such idealism that art cannot alter the invariable forms of nature which nature necessarily and invariably gives it. But the question is: are there in reality absolutely purely developed forms of nature that are inviolable for art? Rumohr's answer to this is that nature is not a separate object that presents itself under the rule of chance, but the sum total of all living forms, the sum total of all that nature has produced, or it would be better to say, the producing force itself" — to it must the artist devote himself and not content himself with individual models. This is quite true. But later Rumohr drops into naturalism, which he wants to castigate as he castigates pseudo-idealism: his postulate that "nature best expresses everything by its forms," becomes dangerous when he applies it to individual phenomena, and when, contradicting what he had said before, he asserts that in reality there are "perfect models," for example, Vittoria of Albano, who was "more beautiful than all the creations of art in Rome, and whose beauty was unattainable for artists." We are firmly convinced that not one of the artists who employed her as a model could transmit to his work all her forms as he found them, because Vittoria was an *individual* beauty, and the individual cannot be absolute; this settles the matter and we do not wish to say any more about the question that Rumohr raises. Even if we were to grant that Vittoria was perfect in all her main forms, the blood, the warmth, the

process of life with the details that disturb beauty, and the traces of
which are left on the skin, all these details would be sufficient to place
the living being, about which Rumohr speaks, much lower than those
high works of art which have only imaginary blood, warmth, process
of life on the skin, and so forth.

Thus, an object which belongs to the rare phenomena of beauty,
proves on closer examination to be not truly beautiful, but only nearer to beauty than others, freer from disturbing chance.[23]

Before proceeding to criticize some of the reproaches
hurled at beauty in reality, we can boldly assert that it is
truly beautiful and fully satisfies a man of healthy mind
in spite of all its flaws, great as they may be. Of course, idle
fantasy can say about everything: "this is not as it should
be; here something is lacking; this is superfluous"; but such
a fantasy, which is never satisfied with anything, should
be regarded as morbid. A man of healthy mind meets in
reality numerous objects and phenomena which do not
rouse any desire that they should be different from what
they are, or better than they are. The opinion that man
must always have "perfection" is a fantastic one, if by "perfection" is meant an object that possesses all the possible
virtues and is free from all the flaws which a man with a
cold or satiated heart, and with nothing better to do, may
try to find. For me, "perfection" is that which fully satisfies my requirements in a given object. And the man of
healthy mind finds very many objects of this kind in reality. When a man's heart is empty, he can give free rein to
his imagination; but when there is at least some satisfactory reality, the wings of fantasy are bound. In general,
fantasy gets the upper hand over us when our reality is
too stinting. Lying on bare boards, a man is sometimes
given to dreaming of a luxurious bed, a bed made of some
unheard-of precious wood, of an eiderdown quilt, of pillows
bordered with Brabant lace, of a canopy made of wonderful Lyons silk; but will such dreams occur to a healthy-
minded man who sleeps not on a luxurious, but on a sufficiently soft and comfortable bed? "When you have sufficient you don't seek more." If a man is obliged to live in
the tundras of Siberia, or in the salt lands across the Volga,
he may dream of magic gardens with unearthly trees with
coral branches, emerald leaves and ruby fruit; but on transferring his residence to, say, the Kursk Gubernia, and being
able to roam to his heart's content in a modest but tolerable
orchard with apple, cherry and pear trees and with a dense

lime tree avenue, the dreamer will forget not only about the gardens in the *Arabian Nights*, but also about the lemon groves of Spain. The imagination builds castles in the air when the dreamer lacks not only a good house, but even a tolerable hut. It takes free rein when the feelings are not engaged; poverty in real life is the source of life in fantasy. But as soon as reality becomes at all tolerable, all the dreams of the imagination become pale and dull. The opinion that "man's desires are limitless" is false in the sense in which it is usually understood, viz., that "no reality can satisfy them"; on the contrary, a man is satisfied not only "with the best that can exist in reality," but also with a rather modest reality. A distinction must be drawn between what is actually felt and what is only said. Dreaming whips up desire to fever heat only when wholesome, even though fairly simple, food is lacking. This is a fact, proved by the whole course of human history and experienced by every man who has seen life and has watched himself. It is a particular case of the general law of human life that passions assume abnormal development only as a consequence of the abnormal conditions of the one who gives way to them, and only when the natural and, in essence, fairly moderate needs from which a given passion arises have been too long denied normal, by no means titanic, satisfaction. It is beyond doubt that the human organism does not need and cannot stand titanic desires and satisfactions. It is also beyond doubt that the desires of a healthy man are commensurate with the powers of his organism. From this general point let us pass to the particular.

It is well known that our senses soon tire and become satiated, i.e., satisfied. This is true not only of the baser senses (touch, smell and taste), but also of the higher (sight and hearing). Inseparably connected with the senses of sight and hearing is the aesthetic sense, and it is inconceivable without them. When, as a result of weariness, a man loses the desire to see beauty, he cannot but lose the aesthetic desire to enjoy beauty. A man cannot look at a picture, even by Raffaello, every day for a month without wearying of it; and then, there can be no doubt that, not only his eyes, but also his aesthetic sense is satiated, satisfied for a time. What is true about duration of pleasure must also be said about its intensity. With normal satisfaction the power of aesthetic enjoyment has its limits. If they are sometimes exceeded, it is not due to inner and natural development, but to special circumstances, more or less fortuitous and abnormal (for example, we admire beauty with exceptional rapture when we know that we will soon have to part with it, that we will not be able to enjoy it as long as we would like to, etc.). In short, it is obviously impossible to doubt the fact that our aesthetic sense, like all our other senses, has its normal limits of duration and intensity, and in this sense it cannot be called insatiable or infinite.

Similarly, it has its limits—and rather narrow ones— as regards discrimination, fineness, fastidiousness, or so-called desire for perfection. Later on we shall have occasion to say how much of even that which is not of first-class beauty satisfies the aesthetic sense in reality. Here we wish to say that in the sphere of art too it is, in essence, not very fastidious. For the sake of one particular virtue we forgive a hundred flaws in a work of art; we even fail to notice them if they are not too glaring. It is sufficient to refer, by way of example, to most of the Latin poetry. Only those who lack aesthetic sense can fail to admire Horace, Virgil and Ovid; but how many flaws there are in their poetry! Strictly speaking, everything in their poetry is weak, except one thing, viz., beauty of language and the development of ideas. They are entirely, or almost entirely, lacking in content; they have no independence, no freshness, no simplicity; nearly all the poetry of Virgil and Horace lacks even sincerity and fervour. Let the critics point to all these flaws; they at the same time add that the form of this poetry reaches a high degree of perfection, and this one drop of good is enough to satisfy our aesthetic sense and enable us to enjoy this poetry. And yet even as regards finish there are flaws in it. That of Ovid and Virgil is nearly always long drawn out; many of Horace's odes are also long drawn out; the work of all three poets is too monotonous; often artificiality and affectation strike the eye unpleasantly. For all that, something good remains, and it gives us pleasure. As a total contrast to the external finish of this poetry we can point to folk poetry. Whatever the original form of folk songs may have been, they nearly always come down to us distorted, altered, or torn to pieces; they too are extremely monotonous; and lastly, all folk songs betray the mechanical methods, expose the common springs by which their themes are always developed; but there is very much freshness and simplicity in folk poetry, and this is enough for our aesthetic sense to enable us to admire it.

In short, like every healthy sense, like every true require-ment, the aesthetic sense strives more to be satisfied than to put forward fastidious demands; by its nature it finds pleasure in satisfaction, is discontented when it has no food, and is therefore ready to be satisfied with the first tolerable object that comes its way. That the aesthetic sense is not fastidious is also proved by the fact that, although having first-class works at its command, it does not turn up its nose at second-class works. Raffaello's paintings do not induce us to judge those of Greuze as bad; although we have Shakespeare, we find pleasure in rereading the works of second-rate and even of third-rate poets. The aesthetic sense seeks what is good and not fantastic perfection. There-fore, even if there were many grave flaws in real beauty, we would, nevertheless, find satisfaction in it.[24] But let us examine more closely the reproaches hurled at beauty in reality and the deductions drawn from them, and see how far they are correct.

I. "Beauty in nature is unpremeditated; for this reason alone it cannot be as good as beauty in art, which is created deliberately." Indeed, inanimate nature does not think about the beauty of its creations, any more than a tree thinks about making its fruit delicious. Nevertheless, it must be admitted that our art has been unable to this day to create anything like an orange or an apple, let alone the luxurious fruit of tropical lands. Of course, the merits of a premeditated work will be higher than those of an unpre-meditated one, but only when the forces of their producers are equal. But man's forces are much weaker than those of nature; his work is exceedingly rough, crude and clumsy compared with the work of nature. Therefore, the superiority of works of art due to premeditation is outweighed, and far outweighed, by weakness of execution. Moreover, unpre-meditated beauty is found only in insensible, inanimate nature: birds and animals are concerned about their appear-ance, they are constantly preening themselves; nearly all of them love neatness. Beauty in man is rarely quite unpre-meditated: we are all very much concerned about our ap-pearance. We are not, of course, speaking of artificial means of imitating beauty, but have in mind the constant concern to maintain a good appearance that forms part of the people's hygiene. But if beauty in nature in the strict sense of the term cannot be called premeditated, and this applies to all the operations of the forces of nature, then, on the other hand, it cannot be said that nature does not, in general, strive to create beauty. On the contrary, if we regard beauty as the fullness of life, then we must admit that the striving for life that permeates organic nature is at the same time a striving to create beauty. If, in general, we must see in nature not purpose, but only results, and, therefore, cannot call beauty the purpose of nature, then we cannot but call it an essential result for the creation of which all the forces of nature are exerted. The unpremeditatedness (das Nichtgewolltsein), the unconsciousness of this striving, does not in the least prevent it from being real, just as the unconsciousness of the geometrical striving of bees does not prevent the cells of a honeycomb from assuming hexagonal shape, just as the unconsciousness of the striving for symmetry of vegetative force does not prevent the two halves of a leaf from being symmetrical.[25]

II. "The result of beauty in nature being unpremeditated is that beauty is rarely met with in reality." But if that were really the case, the rarity of beauty would be a loss only to our aesthetic sense; it would not in the least diminish the beauty of this small number of phenomena and objects. Diamonds the size of pigeon eggs are very rare; lovers of jewels may sincerely regret this, but they agree that these very rare diamonds are beautiful. The complaint that beauty in reality is rare is not, however, altogether justified; beauty is by no means as rare in reality as the German aestheticians assert. There are very many beautiful and magnificent landscapes; in some countries they are met with at every turn, for example, Finland, the Crimea, the banks of the Dnieper, even the banks of the middle part of the Volga, not to speak of Switzerland, the Alps, Italy. A man does not constantly meet with the magnificent in the course of his life, but it is doubtful whether he would wish it to be more frequent; great moments in life cost a man too dear, they are too exhausting; but he who feels the urge to seek them and possesses the spiritual strength to bear their influence, can find occasion for exalted feelings at every step: the path of valour, self-negation and lofty struggle against the base and pernicious, against the misfortunes and vices of mankind, is never closed to anybody. And there have always been thousands of people whose whole lives have been a continuous series of exalted feelings and deeds. The same must be said about the fascinatingly beautiful moments in a man's life. In general, a man has no right to complain if they are rare, because the degree to which his life is filled with beauty and greatness depends upon himself.[26] Empty and colourless are the lives only of colourless people who talk about feelings and desires, but are incapable of having any particular feelings or desires except the desire to pose.[27] We ought, in conclusion, to discuss what in particular is called beauty, to investigate to what degree feminine beauty is a rare phenomenon. But perhaps this is not quite appropriate in our abstract treatise; we shall confine ourselves to the remark that [28] nearly every woman in the bloom of youth seems beautiful to most people. Therefore, the only thing that could be said here is that most people lack discriminate aesthetic sense and not that beauty is a rare phenomenon. People with beautiful faces are not rarer than kind, clever, etc., people.[29]

How, then, are we to explain Raffaello's complaint about the rarity of beautiful women in Italy, the classic land of beauty? Very simply: he sought the most beautiful woman and, of course, there is only one most beautiful woman in the world; where could he find her? Of the first-rate of their kind there are always very few, and for a very simple reason: if there were many, we would again divide them into classes and describe as first-rate those of which there were two or three specimens and we would call all the rest second-rate.[30] And in general, it must be said that the idea that "beauty is rarely met with in reality" is based on a confusion of the terms "quite" and "first": of quite magnificent rivers there are very many; of the first among the magnificent rivers there is, of course, only one. There have been many great soldiers, but only one of them can be called first among the great soldiers of the world. The authors of treatises on aesthetics, in line with the prevailing school, reason as follows: if there is, or can be, an object superior to the one in front of my eyes, then the object in front of my eyes is base. But people do not feel that way. We know that the Amazon is more magnificent than the Volga; nevertheless, we regard the Volga too as a magnificent river.

The philosophical school to which these authors belong says that if one object is greater than another, then the superiority of the first to the second is a defect in the second. This is not the case at all; in reality, a defect is something positive and not something deduced from the superiority of other objects. A river that is a foot deep in places is not regarded as shallow because there are much deeper rivers; it is shallow in itself, without any comparison; we say it is shallow because it is unfit for navigation. A channel which is thirty feet deep is not shallow in real life, for it is quite fit for navigation; nobody thinks of calling it shallow, although everybody knows that the Straits of Dover are much deeper. An abstract mathematical comparison is not a conception of real life.[31] Let us suppose that *Othello* is superior to *Macbeth*, or that *Macbeth* is superior to *Othello*; in spite of the superiority of one of these tragedies to the other, both are beautiful. The merits of *Othello* cannot be charged as flaws in *Macbeth*, or vice versa. That is how we regard works of art. If we regard beautiful phenomena in reality in the same way, we shall very often have to admit that the beauty of one phenomenon is flawless, although the beauty of another is superior to it. Does anybody deny the beauty of nature in Italy, although that in the Antilles, or the East Indies, is richer? But it is only from such a point of view, which finds no confirmation in man's real feelings or judgment, that aestheticians assert that beauty is a rare phenomenon in the world of reality.

III. "Beauty in reality is transient."—Granted; but is it less beautiful for that reason? Besides, this is not always the case. A flower, it is true, soon fades, but human beauty lasts a long time; it may even be said that human beauty lasts as long as it is needed by the person who finds pleasure in it.[32] Perhaps it would not be quite in keeping with the abstract character of our treatise to go into details to prove this thesis; therefore, we shall merely say that the beauty of each generation exists, and must exist, for that generation; and the harmony of that generation is not in the least disturbed, there is nothing contrary to its aesthetic requirements, if its beauty fades with it—the next generations will have a new beauty of their own, and nobody has anything to complain about. Perhaps it would also be inappropriate here to go into details to prove that the desire "not to grow old" is a fantastic desire, that

actually, an elderly man wants to be elderly if his life
has been a normal one, and if he is not one of the superficial kind. But this is obvious without detailed proof. We
all recall our childhood "with regret" and sometimes say
that we would "like to go back to those happy times," but
it is doubtful whether anybody would really wish to become
a child again. The same must be said about the regret expressed that "the beauty of our youth has passed"—these
words have no real meaning if our youth has been at all satisfactory. It would be dull to go through again what one had
gone through before, just as it is dull listening to the same
anecdote a second time, even though it had seemed extremely funny on the first occasion. A distinction must be drawn
between real desires and imaginary, fictitious desires, which
one does not really wish to have satisfied. The wish that
beauty in reality should not fade is such a fictitious desire.
"Life sweeps forward and carries beauty in reality in its
course," say Hegel and Vischer; this is true, but with life
our desires sweep forward too, i.e., their content changes;
consequently, regrets that a beautiful phenomenon is passing away are fantastic—it is passing, having done its
work, having provided today as much aesthetic pleasure
as the present day could hold; tomorrow there will be another day, with new requirements, and only a new beauty
will be able to satisfy them. If beauty were indeed immobile
and immutable, "immortal," as the aestheticians demand,
we would grow sick and tired of it. Living man dislikes
immobility in life; therefore, he never grows tired of looking
at animated beauty, but he soon gets tired of looking at
a tableau vivant, which exceptional admirers of art who
despise reality prefer to animated scenes. In their opinion
beauty must not only be eternal, but also monotonous in
its eternity; therefore, a new accusation is hurled at beauty
in reality.

IV. "Beauty in reality is inconstant." This accusation
must be answered by putting the same question that was
put above: does this prevent it from being beautiful at a
given time? Is a landscape less beautiful in the morning
because its beauty temporarily fades after sunset? Again
it must be said that, in the majority of cases,
this reproach is unjust;[33] granted that the beauty of
some landscapes vanishes with the passing of the purple
haze of dawn; but most beautiful landscapes are beautiful

in all lights; and it must be added that unenviable is the beauty of a landscape that is beautiful only at a given moment and not all the time it exists. "Sometimes a face expresses the entire fullness of life, sometimes it expresses nothing." No, this is not correct. What is correct is that sometimes a face is extremely expressive, and sometimes it is much less expressive; but extremely rare are the moments when a face that shines with intelligence, or kindness, *lacks* expression. An intelligent face retains the expression of intelligence even when the person is asleep; a kind face retains the expression of kindness even when the person is asleep, and a fleeting diversity of expression on an expressive face lends it new beauty. Similarly, diversity of posture also lends new beauty to a living being. It very often happens that the disappearance of a beautiful posture is the only thing that keeps it precious for us: "a group of gladiators engaged in combat is beautiful; but within a few minutes it is broken up"—but what would happen if it did not break up, if the combat lasted for a whole day and night? We would grow tired of looking at it and would turn away, as, incidentally, often happens in reality. What is usually the end of the aesthetic impression by which an immobile, "eternally beautiful" picture, "eternally constant in its beauty," holds us for half an hour or an hour? We go away before the evening shadows "tear us away from the pleasure."

V. "Beauty in reality is beautiful only because we look at it from a point of view from which it looks beautiful."— On the contrary, it much more often happens that beauty is beautiful from every point of view. For example, in most cases a beautiful landscape is beautiful no matter from what angle you look at it.—Of course, it looks most beautiful from only *one* angle, but what of that? Even a work of art must be looked at from a particular spot in order to see it in all its beauty. This is due to the laws of perspective, which must be obeyed in enjoying beauty both in reality and in art.

In general, I think it must be said that all the reproaches levelled at beauty in reality that we have examined are exaggerations, and some of them are quite unjust; that not one of them is applicable to all kinds of beauty. But we have not yet examined the chief and most important flaws that the prevailing views on aesthetics have

discovered in beauty in the real world. The reproaches examined so far have been that beauty in reality is not satisfactory for man; now come the direct proofs that, properly
speaking, beauty in reality cannot be called beauty. Three
proofs are advanced. Let us examine them, starting from the
weakest and less general.

VI. "Beauty in reality is either a group of objects (a
landscape, a group of people) or one separate object. In
reality, disturbing chance always spoils a seemingly beautiful group by introducing into it extraneous, superfluous
objects which disturb the beauty and unity of the whole;
it also spoils a seemingly beautiful single object by spoiling
some of its parts: a close examination will always show us
that some parts of the seemingly beautiful real object are
not beautiful at all." Here we have again the idea that
beauty is perfection. But this idea is only a particular application of the general idea that man is satisfied only by
mathematical perfection. This is not so. Man's practical
life convinces us that he seeks only approximate perfection, which, strictly speaking, should not be called perfection. Man seeks only that which is good, he does not
seek perfection. Only abstract mathematics demands perfection; even applied mathematics is satisfied with approximate calculations. The quest for perfection in any sphere
of life whatsoever is prompted by abstract, morbid, or idle
fantasy. We want to breathe pure air; but do we notice that
absolutely pure air never exists anywhere? We want to
drink pure water, but not absolutely pure water: absolutely
pure (distilled) water is even unpleasant to the taste. These
examples are too materialistic? Let us quote others: would
anybody think of saying that a man who does not know
everything is ignorant? No, we do not even look for a man
who knows *everything*; we expect a learned man to know
all that is essential and many other things. Are we dissatisfied with a history, for example, in which not absolutely all problems are explained, not absolutely all details
are given, in which not absolutely all the author's views and
statements are correct? No, we are satisfied, extremely satisfied, with a book in which the *chief* problems are
solved, in which the most essential details are given,
in which the author's *principal* opinions are correct,
and in which there are *very few* wrong or inadequate explanations. (Later on we shall see that we are satisfied with

approximate perfection also in the sphere of art.) After these remarks it is possible to say without fearing strong contradiction that in the sphere of beauty in reality we are satisfied when we find the very good, but we do not seek mathematical perfection, free from *all* minor flaws. Would anybody really think of saying that a landscape is not beautiful if at a certain spot there are three bushes where it would have been better had there been two, or four? It is doubtful whether it has ever occurred to anybody admiring the sea that it might be better than it is; but if you look at the sea with mathematical strictness you will really find defects in it, primarily the defect that its surface is not flat, but convex. True, this defect is not visible; it is revealed not by the eye, but by mathematical calculation; therefore it is possible to add that it is ridiculous to talk about this defect, which cannot be seen, which can only be *known*. Such are the majority of the flaws in beauty in reality: they cannot be seen, they cannot be felt; they are revealed only by research, not by sight. Let us not forget that sense of beauty is connected with sight, not with science: what cannot be felt does not exist for the aesthetic sense. But is it true that most of the flaws in beauty in reality are insensitive to sight? Experience convinces us that it is. There is not a man gifted with aesthetic sense who has not in reality met thousands of faces, phenomena and objects which seemed to him to be flawlessly beautiful. But does it matter very much if flaws in a beautiful object are visible to the eye? They must be exceedingly unimportant if the object continues to seem beautiful in spite of them,—if they are important, the object will be ugly, not beautiful. The unimportant is not worth talking about. And indeed, a man with a healthy aesthetic sense pays no attention to them.[34] To a man untrained by a special study of the latest aesthetics, the second proof advanced by it that so-called beauty in reality cannot be beauty in the full sense of the term will sound strange.

VII. "A real object cannot be beautiful for the very reason that it is a living object, in which the real process of life takes place with all its crudeness, with all its unaesthetic details." A higher degree of fantastic idealism can scarcely be imagined. What, is a painted or a daguerreotype portrait beautiful and a living face not? Why? Because the living face always bears the material traces of

the process of life; because, if we examine the living face
with a microscope we will always find it covered with per-
spiration, and so forth. What, a living tree cannot be beautiful because tiny insects which feed on its leaves always
nest in it? This is a strange view, which does not even require refutation. What does my aesthetic vision care about
what it does not see? Can my senses be influenced by a
flaw that they do not feel? To refute this opinion it is not
even necessary to quote the truism that it is strange to
seek people who do not drink, do not eat, do not find it
necessary to wash and to change their linen. It is quite
superfluous to dilate on such needs. It will be better if
we examine one of the ideas that gave rise to such a strange
reproach against beauty in reality, the idea that constitutes
one of the fundamental views of prevailing aesthetics. Here
it is: "Beauty is not the object itself, but the pure surface,
the pure form (die reine Oberfläche) of the object."* The
unsoundness of this view of beauty is revealed when we
examine the sources from which it arose. Most often we
perceive beauty with our eyes; but our eyes in very many
cases see only the shell, the contours, the exterior of an object, they do not see its internal construction. From this
it is easy to deduce that beauty is the surface of the object
and not the object itself. But firstly, in addition to beauty
to the eye, there is also beauty to the ear (singing and music),
which has no surface. Secondly, we do not always see only
the surface with our eyes: in transparent objects we see the
whole of the object, all its internal construction; it is precisely transparency that lends beauty to water and to precious stones. Lastly, the human body, the most beautiful
object on earth, is semitransparent, and in a man we see
not only the surface: the flesh looms through the skin, and
this lends human beauty very much charm. Thirdly, it is
strange to say that even in totally opaque objects we see
only the surface and not the object itself: vision is not
an attribute exclusively of the eyes, the prompting and
discerning mind always participates in it; imagination always fills with matter the empty form that presents itself
to the eye. Man sees the object in *motion*, although his eye
does not perceive the motion; man sees the object at a distance, although his eye does not see the distance; similarly,

---

* F. Th. Vischer, *op. cit.*, Bd. I, §§ 54-55, S. 146 et seq.—*Ed.*

man sees the material object whereas his eye sees only the surface of the object. Another basis for the idea that "beauty is pure surface" is the assumption that aesthetic pleasure is incompatible with the material interest taken in an object. We will not here examine how the relation of the material interest we take in an object to the aesthetic pleasure it gives us is to be understood, although such an investigation would lead us to the conviction that although there is a difference between aesthetic pleasure and material interest, or the practical view of an object, they do not contradict each other. It will be sufficient to point to the evidence of experience that a real object may seem beautiful without rousing material interest: what selfish thoughts are roused in our minds when we admire the stars, the sea, or a forest (when I look at a real forest, must I necessarily think of whether the trees would be suitable for timber for building a house, or for firewood to heat it?); what selfish thoughts are roused in our minds when we hear the rustle of leaves, or the song of the nightingale? We often love a person without any selfish motives, without in the least thinking of ourselves; all the more likely are we to find aesthetic pleasure in him without it rousing any material (stoffartig) reflections about our relation to him. Lastly, the idea that beauty is pure form springs directly from the conception of beauty as a pure phantom, and this conception is a necessary corollary of the definition of beauty as the perfect realization of the idea in an individual object, and falls together with this definition.

After this long series of reproaches against beauty in reality, each more general and severer than the preceding one, we come to the last, the weightiest and most general reason why it is said that beauty in reality cannot be regarded as real beauty.

VIII. "An individual object cannot be beautiful for the simple reason that it is not absolute, for beauty is absolute." This is indeed irrefutable proof for the Hegelian school, and also for many other philosophical schools which take the absolute as their criterion not only of theoretical truths, but also of man's active strivings. But these systems have already broken down and have given way to others, which have developed from them by virtue of the inherent dialectical process, but which have quite a different conception of life. Limiting ourselves to this reference to the

philosophical unsoundness of the view which prompted the
classification of all human strivings in the category of the
absolute, we shall, for the purpose of our criticism, take
a different point of view, one that is nearer to purely
aesthetical conceptions, and say that, in general, man's activities do not strive towards the absolute and know nothing
about it, for they pursue purely human aims. In this respect man's aesthetic feelings and activities are exactly the
same as his other feelings and activities. In reality we do
not meet with anything absolute, therefore, we cannot say
from experience what impression absolute beauty would
make upon us; but this, at least, we do know from experience, viz., that similis simili gaudet,* that, therefore,
we individual beings who cannot transcend the limits of
our individuality, are very fond of individual beauty which
cannot transcend the limits of its individuality.³⁵ After
this, further refutation is superfluous. It is only necessary
to add that the idea of the individuality of true beauty
has been developed by the very system of aesthetic views
which uses the absolute as the criterion of beauty. The idea
that individuality is the most important attribute of beauty automatically gives rise to the thesis that the criterion
absolute is alien to the sphere of beauty—a deduction
that contradicts this system's fundamental view of beauty.
The source of such contradictions, not always avoided by
the system we are discussing, is that it confuses the brilliant deductions from experience with equally brilliant but
inherently unsound attempts to subordinate them all to
its a priori view, which often contradicts them

We have now examined all the reproaches more or less
unjustly levelled at beauty in reality and we can proceed
to solve the problem of the essential purpose of art. According to prevailing aesthetic conceptions, "art has its origin
in man's striving to free beauty of the flaws (we have examined) that prevent beauty, to the degree that it actually
exists in reality, from being fully satisfactory for man.
Beauty created by art is free of the flaws inherent in beauty
in reality." ³⁶ Let us, then, see how far beauty as created
by art is really superior to beauty in reality as regards
freedom from the reproaches hurled at the latter; after that
it will be easier to decide whether the prevailing view cor-

---

* Like loves like.—*Ed.*

rectly defines the origin of art and its relation to living reality.

I. "Beauty in nature is unpremeditated." Beauty in art is premeditated,—this is true; but is it so in all cases, and in all details? It is needless to ask how often, and to what degree, the artist and poet clearly understand what their works express. That artistic work is unconscious has long been a commonplace that everybody is talking about; perhaps it is necessary today to stress more strongly the dependence of beauty in a work of art upon the conscious strivings of the artist rather than to dilate upon the work of true artistic talent being always largely unpremeditated and instinctive. Be that as it may, both points of view are known and it is useless to dwell on them here. But perhaps it will not be superfluous to say that even the premeditated strivings of the artist (particularly of the poet) do not always justify the claim that concern for beauty is the true source of his artistic works. It is true that the poet always tries "to do his best," but this does not mean that his entire will and imagination are directed exclusively, or even mainly, by concern for the artistic or aesthetic merits of his work. Just as there are in nature numerous conflicting strivings, which in their conflict kill or mar beauty, so the artist and poet are prompted by many strivings which, influencing their striving for beauty, mar the beauty of their work. These include, firstly, the various strivings and requirements of everyday life which prevent the artist from being an artist and nothing but an artist; secondly, his intellectual and moral opinions, which also prevent him from thinking exclusively of beauty during his work; thirdly, and lastly, the idea of artistic creation is usually not roused in the artist's mind exclusively by the striving to create beauty: the artist worthy of the name usually wants to convey to us through his work his thoughts, his opinions, his feelings, and not only the beauty he creates. In short, just as beauty in reality develops in conflict with other strivings of nature, so beauty in art also develops in conflict with the other strivings and requirements of the one who creates it. If this conflict mars or kills beauty in reality, then the chances that it will mar or kill beauty in works of art are scarcely less. Just as beauty in reality develops under influences that are alien to it and prevent it from being *only* beauty, so the work of the artist or poet develops under the influence of numerous diverse strivings, which lead to the same result. It is true that there is more deliberate intention to create beauty in beautiful works of art than there is in the beautiful productions of other of man's activities, and it is beyond dispute that there is no premeditation at all in the works of nature; therefore, it would be right to grant that, in this respect, art would be superior to nature if its premeditation were free from the drawbacks that nature is free of. But, while gaining by premeditation on one side, art loses by it on the other. The fact is that while conceiving something he thinks is beautiful, the artist very often conceives something that is far from being beautiful: it is not enough to strive for beauty; it is necessary to understand what true beauty is — but how often artists are mistaken in their conceptions of beauty! How often they are deceived even by artistic instinct and not only reflective conceptions, which are mostly one-sided! In art, all the drawbacks of individuality are inseparable from premeditation.

II. "Beauty is rarely met with in reality." But is it met with more often in art? How many truly tragic or dramatic events occur every day! But are there many truly beautiful tragedies and dramas? In the whole of western literature there are three or four dozen, and in Russian literature, if we are not mistaken, except for *Boris Godunov* and *Scenes From the Days of Chivalry*, there is not one that stands above the mediocre. How many love dramas occur in real life! But are there many truly beautiful love stories? A few score in English and French literature, perhaps, and five or six in the Russian. Where are we more likely to see a beautiful landscape—in nature or in art? Why is this so? Because there are very few great poets and artists, as is the case with geniuses in all fields. If absolutely favourable opportunities for creating beauty, or the sublime, rarely occur in reality, favourable opportunities for the birth and unhindered development of a great genius are still more rare, for here the conjunction of a far larger number of favourable circumstances is needed. This reproach against reality falls with still greater weight upon art.

III. "Beauty in nature is transient." In art it is often eternal, this is true; but not always, for works of art are also subject to destruction or damage by accident. The Greek lyrics have perished for us, and so have the paintings by Apelles and the statues by Lysippus. Let us not dwell on this, but pass on to the causes of the transience of very many works of art from which beauty in nature is free, viz., fashion and the deterioration of material. Nature does not age; in place of its faded works it creates new ones. Art lacks this eternal capacity of reproduction and renewal, and time leaves its traces on its works. In poetical works, language quickly becomes obsolete.[37] Still more important is the fact that in the course of time poetical works become largely unintelligible to us (ideas and expressions borrowed from contemporary circumstances, allusions to events and persons); many become colourless and uninteresting; learned commentaries cannot make everything in them as clear and vivid for posterity as everything was clear for their contemporaries. Moreover, learned commentaries and aesthetic pleasure are opposite things, quite apart from the fact that, as a consequence of such commentaries, poetical works lose their popular character. Still more important is the fact that the development of civilization, change of conceptions, sometimes divests poetical works of all their beauty and sometimes even transforms them into something unpleasant or disgusting. We do not wish to cite other examples than the eclogues of Virgil, the most modest of the Roman poets.[38]

From poetry we pass to the other arts. Works of music perish with the instruments for which they were composed. The entire music of antiquity is dead to us.[39] The beauty of old works of music wanes with the improvement of orchestration. The colours in paintings very quickly fade and grow dark; paintings of the sixteenth and seventeenth centuries have long lost their original beauty. Strong as the influence of all these circumstances may be, they are not, however, the chief cause of transience in art. The chief cause is the influence of the tastes of the period; nearly always it is the fashionable mood, one-sided and very often false. Fashion has made half of each of Shakespeare's plays unfit for aesthetical enjoyment in our times; fashion, which affected the tragedies of Racine and Corneille, compels us not to enjoy them so much as to laugh at them. In painting, music and architecture it is scarcely possible to find a single work produced a hundred or a hundred and fifty years ago which does not today seem either insipid or ridiculous, in spite of the imprint of genius it may bear. And in fifty years time modern art will often raise a smile.

IV. "Beauty in reality is inconstant." This is true; but beauty in art is lifelessly motionless. This is much worse. One can look at a living face for several hours; a portrait will tire one in a quarter of an hour, and the dilettante who can stand in front of a picture for an hour is rare. Poetical works are more animated than painting, architecture and sculpture, but even they tire one fairly quickly. Of course, no man will be found who could read a novel five times running; on the other hand, life, living persons and real events, are fascinating because of their diversity.

V. "Beauty is introduced into nature only by our looking at it from a particular point of view and from no other." This idea is hardly ever correct; but it is nearly always applicable to works of art. All works of art of an epoch and civilization other than our own, invariably demand that we should transport ourselves to the epoch and civilization which created them; otherwise they seem unintelligible and strange to us, but not beautiful. If we do not transport ourselves to ancient Greece, the songs of Sappho and Anacreon will seem to us to be the expression of unaesthetic pleasure, something like the works of our times that are shunned by the press. If we do not mentally transport ourselves to patriarchal society, the songs of Homer will offend us by their cynicism, crude gluttony and lack of moral feeling.[40] But the Greek world is too remote from us; let us take an epoch that is nearer to us. How much in the works of Shakespeare and of the Italian painters can be understood and appreciated only if we transport ourselves to the past, with its conception of things! Let us take an example from a period that is still nearer to ours: Goethe's *Faust* seems a strange work to a man who is unable to transport himself to the epoch of striving and doubt of which *Faust* is an expression.[41]

VI. "Beauty in reality contains many ugly parts or details." Does this not apply to art, and to a much larger degree? Point to a work of art in which no flaws are to be found. Walter Scott's novels are too long drawn out; nearly all Dickens' novels are sickly-sentimental, and many of them are too long drawn out; some of Thackeray's novels (it would be better to say, very many of them) weary one by their constant pretensions to artlessness and biting satire. But the geniuses of our times rarely serve as guides in aesthetics; the latter prefers Homer, the Greek tragedies and

Shakespeare. Homer's poems lack coherence, Aeschylus and Sophocles are too stern and dry, and the works of Aeschylus, in addition, lack dramatism; Euripides is lachrymose; Shakespeare is rhetorical and pompous, the artistic construction of his plays would be quite good *if* they were altered somewhat, as Goethe suggested. If we pass to painting we shall have to admit the same thing: Raffaello is the only one against whom voices are rarely raised; as for all the other painters, numerous weak spots have long been discovered in their works. And Raffaello himself is accused of being ignorant of anatomy. Of music it is needless to speak: Beethoven is too obscure and often wild; Mozart's orchestration is weak; the works of the modern composers are too full of noise and clatter. In the opinion of the experts there is only one flawless opera—*Don Giovanni*; but laymen find it dull. If there is no perfection in nature and in living man, still less can it be found in art and in the works of man: "the effect cannot contain what is not contained in the cause, man."[42] A wide, a boundless field is open for the one who wishes to point to the weaknesses of all works of art in general. It goes without saying that such an undertaking would be evidence of a caustic mind, but not of impartiality. A man who does not admire the great works of art is deserving a pity; but it is pardonable, when exaggerated praise forces one to do so, to remind people that since there are spots on the sun, there are bound to be spots in the works of "mortal man."

VII. "A living object cannot be beautiful if only for the reason that the hard, rough process of life takes place in it." A work of art is a lifeless object; it would therefore seem to be safe from this reproach. But such a conclusion would be superficial. Facts contradict it. A work of art is the creation of the process of life, the creation of a living man, who created it not without a hard struggle, and the work bears the hard, rough traces of the struggle in production. Are there many poets and artists who do their work offhand, as Shakespeare, it is said, wrote his plays, offhand, without revising them? But if a work has been created by hard effort it will bear stains of the "midnight oil" the artist burned while at work on it. Heaviness may be found in nearly all works of art, no matter how light they may have seemed at the first glance. If they were indeed created without much hard work they will be of rough finish. Thus, one of the two: either roughness, or hard work—this is the Scylla and Charybdis for works of art.

I do not want to say that all the flaws revealed by this analysis are always sharply impressed on works of art to the point of crudity.[43] I only want to show that the carping criticism that is levelled against beauty in reality is fatal for beauty created by art.

It is evident from our survey that if art were prompted by our spirit's dissatisfaction with the flaws in beauty in living reality and by the striving to create something better, all man's aesthetical activities would be useless, fruitless, and, seeing that art was not satisfying his purpose, man would soon abandon them. Speaking generally, works of art suffer from all the flaws that are to be found in beauty in living reality; but although art in general has no right whatever to preference over nature and life, perhaps some particular branches of art possess some special advantages which place them above the corresponding phenomena in living reality? Perhaps, one or other branch of art even produces things that have no counterpart in the real world? We have not dealt with these questions in our general criticism, and so we must[44] examine particular cases in order to see the relation of beauty in definite branches of art to beauty in reality produced by nature independently of man's striving for beauty. Only such a survey will give us a definite answer to the question as to whether the origin of art can be attributed to the unsatisfactory aesthetic state of living nature.[45]

The series of arts is usually commenced with architecture; of all man's diverse activities in the pursuit of more or less practical aims, only building activities are conceded the right to be elevated to an art. But it is wrong to limit the field of art in this way if by "works of art" is meant "objects made by man under the overwhelming influence of his striving for beauty." The aesthetic sense of the people, or it would be more correct to say, of high society, reaches a stage of development where nearly all objects of human production: articles that contribute to the comforts of domestic life (furniture, utensils, house decoration), clothing, gardens, etc., are designed and made under the overwhelming influence of this striving. Etruscan vases and the ornaments of the ancients are universally recognized as "works of art"; they are classified as "sculpture," which is not quite correct, of course, but must we classify the art of furniture making as architecture? In what department should we include gardens and parks, the original purpose of which — to serve as places for strolling or for repose—is subordinated to the purpose of serving as objects of aesthetic pleasure? In some textbooks on aesthetics gardening is called a branch of architecture, but this is obviously far-fetched. The classification of art as all activity in the production of articles under the overwhelming influence of the aesthetic sense should greatly enlarge the field of art, for the essential identity of architecture, furniture making, dressmaking, gardening, sculpture, and so forth, cannot be denied. We shall be told: "architecture creates something new that does not exist in nature, it completely alters its material; other branches of human production leave their material in its original form." But this is not so; there are many branches of human activity which do not yield to architecture in this respect. Let us quote the example of horticulture: wild flowers do not in the least resemble the gorgeous flowers that owe their existence to horticulture. What is there in common between a wild forest and an artificial garden, or park? Just as architecture hews stone, so gardening prunes and straightens trees, gives every tree an appearance totally different from that which it had in the virgin forest. Just as architecture arranges stones in regular groups, so gardening arranges trees in regular groups in a park. In short, horticulture, or gardening, alters, works up "rough material" no less than architecture does. The same must be said about industry, which creates objects under the overwhelming influence of the striving for beauty, for example, fabrics, the like of which nature does not produce at all, and the original material of which is still more altered than stone is in architecture. "But architecture, as an art," much more than any other branch of practical activity, is subordinated exclusively to the demands of the aesthetic sense, for it totally abandons the striving to satisfy practical aims." But what practical aims are satisfied by flowers and artificial parks? And did not the Parthenon and the Alhambra serve a practical purpose? The arts of gardening, furniture making, the jeweller's art and dressmaking are subordinated to practical considerations far less than architecture, but no special chapters are devoted to them in textbooks on aesthetics. We see that the reason why, of

all practical activities, building alone is usually dignified
with the name of fine art, lies not in its essence, but in
that other branches of activity that rise to the level of art
are forgotten because of the "unimportance" of their products, whereas the products of architecture cannot be lost
sight of because of their importance, costliness, and lastly,
simply because of their dimensions, which strike the eye
first of all, and more than all other things made by man.
We regard as "arts," on a par with architecture, all branches
of industry, all handicrafts, that have the object of satisfying "taste," or the aesthetic sense, when their products are
conceived and executed under the overwhelming influence
of the striving for beauty, and when other purposes (which
architecture also serves) are subordinated to this chief aim.
The question as to the degree of respect deserved by productions of practical activity conceived and executed under
the overwhelming influence of the striving to produce, not
something that is really needed and useful, but something
that is beautiful, is another matter. How this question
should be answered is a subject beyond the scope of our
essay; but whichever way it is answered, the question as
to the degree of respect deserved by the productions of architecture from the standpoint of pure art and not of practical activity, must be answered in the same way. The thinker must regard an elegant pavilion that cost 10,000 francs
in the same way as he regards a cashmere shawl that cost
10,000 francs, or a clock that cost 10,000 francs.[46] Perhaps
he will say that these things are not so much works of art
as articles of luxury; perhaps he will say that true art abhors luxury, because the most essential characteristic of
beauty is simplicity. In what relation do these products of
frivolous art stand to inartistic reality? The answer to this
question is that all the cases we have indicated deal with
human practical activity which, while digressing from its
true purpose, viz., to produce something needed or useful,
nevertheless, preserves its essential character, viz., to produce something that nature does not produce. Hence, in
these cases, the question of the relation in which the beauty
of works of art stands to the beauty of the works of nature
does not arise: there are no objects in nature with which
to compare knives, forks, cloth and clocks; nor are there in
it objects with which to compare buildings, bridges, columns,
and so forth.

Thus, even if we include in the sphere of the fine arts all the articles created under the overwhelming influence of the striving for beauty we shall still have to say that the productions of architecture either preserve their practical character, in which case they have no right to be regarded as works of art, or indeed become works of art, of which art has as much right to be proud as of the work of the jeweller. According to our conception of the essence of art, the striving to create beauty in the sense of graceful, elegant, beautiful, is not in itself art; as we shall see, something more is needed for art; therefore, we cannot under any circumstances resolve to call the productions of architecture works of art. Architecture is one of man's practical activities, all of which reveal a striving for beautiful form, and in this respect it differs from furniture making not in essential character, but in the size of its productions.

The general defect of the productions of sculpture and painting which places them below the productions of nature and of life is that they are lifeless, motionless; this is universally admitted, and it is therefore unnecessary to dilate on this point. We shall do better by examining the alleged superiority of these arts to nature.

Sculpture depicts the form of the human body; all the rest in it is only accessory; we shall therefore only discuss the way it depicts the human figure.[47] It has become an axiom that the beauty of the contours of Venus of Medici, Venus of Milo, Apollo Belvedere, etc., is of a much higher order than the beauty of living people.[48] In St. Petersburg there is no Venus of Medici, nor an Apollo Belvedere, but there are works by Canova; therefore, we inhabitants of St. Petersburg may take the liberty to express some judgment of the beauty of sculpture. We must say that there is not in St. Petersburg a single statue which in beauty of features is not far inferior to an incalculable number of living people, and that it is enough to walk down any thronged street to meet a number of such people. The majority of those who are in the habit of thinking independently will agree with this. But we will not take this personal impression as proof. There is other proof, much stronger than this. That a work of art cannot compare with a living human face in beauty of features can be proved mathematically. It is well known that in art, execution is always far below the ideal that exists in the artist's imagination;

but this ideal cannot possibly be superior in beauty to those
human beings the artist had the opportunity to see. The
power of "creative imagination" is very limited: it can
only combine impressions obtained from experience; imagination only diversifies an object and magnifies it in
extent, but we cannot imagine anything more intense than
what we have seen or experienced. I can imagine the sun
being much larger in size than it really is, but I cannot
imagine it being brighter than it appears to me in reality.
Similarly, I can imagine a man being taller, stouter,
etc., than those men I have seen, but I cannot picture
to myself faces more beautiful than those I have had the
opportunity to see in reality. This is beyond the power of
human imagination. One thing the artist could do: he could
combine in his ideal the forehead of one beautiful woman,
the nose of a second, the mouth and chin of a third; we do
not deny that artists do this sometimes; but it is doubtful,
firstly, whether this should be done, and secondly, whether
the imagination is capable of combining these features that
belong to different faces. This would have to be done only
if the artist has seen only such faces in which some feature is beautiful while the others are ugly. As a rule,
however, all the features of a face are almost equally beautiful, or almost equally ugly, so that if the artist is satisfied
with, say, the forehead, he ought to be almost equally satisfied with the shape of the nose and mouth. As a rule,
unless a face is mutilated, all the parts harmonize so well
that to disturb them would mean spoiling the beauty of
the face. This we know from comparative anatomy. True,
one very often hears the remark: "how beautiful that face
would be if the nose were slightly tipped, if the lips were
a little thinner," and so forth. I have not the least doubt
that sometimes all the features of a face may be beautiful
except one, but I think that usually, or it would be more
correct to say, nearly always, such dissatisfaction is due
either to inability to appreciate harmony, or to caprice
bordering on lack of true and effective ability and need to
enjoy beauty. The parts of the human body, like those of
every living organism which is constantly being regenerated
under the influence of its unity, are most closely interconnected, so that the shape of one member depends on the
shapes of all the others, and they, in their turn, are dependent on the one. This applies still more to the parts of a

single organ, to the different parts of the face. As we have said, the interdependence of features is proved by science, but it is evident without the aid of science to everyone gifted with a sense of harmony. The human body is a single whole; you cannot tear it into parts and say: this part is beautiful, this part is ugly. Here, too, as in many other cases, picking and choosing, mosaics, eclecticism, lead to incongruity: take all or nothing—only then will you be right, at least from your own point of view. Only in the case of deformed people, those eclectic beings, is eclecticism a suitable criterion. But not they, of course, were the originals from which the "great works of sculpture" were made. If an artist were to take for his model the forehead of one person, the nose of a second and the mouth of a third, he would thereby prove only one thing, viz., his own lack of taste or, at all events, his inability to find a truly beautiful face for his model. For all the reasons we have stated, we think that the beauty of a statue cannot be higher than the beauty of a living individual, because a copy cannot be more beautiful than the original. True, a statue is not always a true copy of the model; sometimes "the artist incorporates his ideal in the statue," but we shall have occasion later on to speak about the manner in which artist's ideal, which differs from his model, is composed. We are not forgetting that in addition to contours, a piece of sculpture also has grouping and expression; but we find both these elements of beauty more fully in a painting than in a statue; we shall therefore analyze them when discussing painting, to which we now pass.

According to our present point of view, we ought to divide painting into the painting of individual figures and groups, the painting of the external world, and the painting of figures and groups in a landscape, or to put it more generally, in a setting.

As regards depicting the contours of an individual human figure, it must be said that in this respect painting yields not only to nature, but also to sculpture; it cannot make them as complete and distinct. On the other hand, operating with colours, its portraiture of man is much closer to living nature and it can lend his face much more expression than sculpture can. We do not know what degree of perfection will, in time, be reached in the making of colours; but in the present state of this branch of technology, painting cannot properly convey the colour of the human body in general, or of the face in particular. Compared with the actual colour of the body and face, its colours are crude, wretched imitations; instead of the tender body, it paints something greenish or reddish; and apart from, leaving out of account, the fact that extraordinary "ability" is needed to obtain even this greenish or reddish picture, we must admit that the living body cannot be satisfactorily depicted with lifeless colours. Painting can fairly well convey only one of its shades, viz., the dry, lifeless colour of an aged or coarsened face.[49] Pock-marked or sickly faces also come out in paintings far more satisfactorily than fresh, young faces. The best is conveyed by painting the least satisfactorily; the worst is conveyed most satisfactorily.

The same must be said about facial expression. The shades of life that painting succeeds in depicting better than others are the convulsive distortions of the face during destructively powerful emotion, such as, for example, anger, horror, ferocity, wild revelry, physical pain or mental suffering bordering on physical suffering. The reason for this is that, in such cases, the features undergo sharp changes which can be adequately depicted with fairly rough sweeps of the brush, and minor flaws or unsatisfactory details vanish among the big strokes: the roughest hint is intelligible to the viewer. Lunacy, stupidity, or a blank mind, are also expressions that painting conveys better than others. The reaison for this is that here there is almost nothing to convey, or it is necessary to convey disharmony, and disharmony is not marred, but improved, by imperfect execution. But all the other variations of facial expression are very unsatisfactorily conveyed by painting; because it can never attain those tender strokes, that harmony of all the minute changes of the muscles upon which depend the expressions of tender joy, pensiveness, gaiety, and so forth.[50] The human hands are coarse and are capable of doing satisfactorily only what does not require very satisfactory finish; "hack work" is the real name of all the plastic arts as soon as we compare them with nature.[51] Painting, however (and sculpture), boasts even more of its superiority over nature in the matter of grouping than it does about the contours or expression of its figures. But *this* boast is even less understandable. True, art sometimes succeeds in grouping figures flawlessly, but it has no grounds for boasting of its extremely rare

success, because in real life failure *never* occurs in this respect: in every group of living people all deport themselves
in complete conformity with 1) the essence of the scene that
is taking place among them, 2) the essence of their own
characters, and 3) the circumstances. All this is automatically adhered to in real life, but is achieved with extreme
difficulty in art. "Always and automatically" in nature,
"very rarely and with great exertion of effort" in art—
this is the fact that characterizes nature and art in nearly
all respects.[52]

We pass to painting that depicts nature. Neither the
contours of objects drawn by hand, nor even those pictured
in imagination, can possibly be better than those met with
in reality. The reason for this we have given above. The
imagination cannot picture a rose better than the rose in
nature; and execution is always inferior to the imaginary
ideal. The colours of some objects the painter's art succeeds
in conveying very well; but there are many objects whose
colours it cannot convey. It is most successful in conveying
dark colours and coarse, hard shades; it is less successful
with light ones. Worst of all is the coloration of objects lit
up by the sun; the shades of the blue midday sky, and the
pink and gold shades of morning and evening also come out
poorly. "But it is precisely for surmounting these difficulties that the great artists are famed," i.e., for surmounting
them better than other painters. We are not discussing the
relative merits of paintings; we are comparing the best of
them with nature. To the degree that the best of them are
superior to the rest, to that degree are they inferior to
nature.[53] "But cannot painting group a landscape better?"
We doubt it; at all events, in nature we, at every step,
meet with scenes to which nothing need be added and from
which nothing need be taken away. This is not accepted
by very many people who have devoted their lives to the
study of art and have lost sight of nature. But every man
with plain, natural feelings who has not been drawn into
the bias of artistic or dilettante one-sidedness will agree
with us when we say that there are very many locations
and views which one can only admire, and in which there
is nothing to condemn. Go into any decent forest—we do
not mean the forests of equatorial America, but those
forests which have already suffered at the hand of man,
our European forests—what does this forest lack? Would

anybody who has seen a decent forest think of saying that
something must be changed in it, that something must be
added to it to enable it to give complete aesthetic pleasure?
Travel two or three hundred versts along the road—we
will not say in Italy or in Switzerland, or in the parts of
Germany contiguous to it—but in central Russia, which
is said to be poor in scenery—how many places you will
come across during this short journey which you will admire,
and while admiring them you will not say "if this were
added here and this taken away from there the scene would
be improved." A man whose aesthetic sense has not been
corrupted finds full pleasure in nature and sees no flaws
in its beauty. The opinion that a painted landscape can be
more magnificent, grander, or in some other way better than
real nature, partly originated from the prejudice that in
our times is complacently laughed at even by those who,
in essence, have not yet rid themselves of it, viz., that
nature is coarse, base, grimy, that it must be washed and
adorned to make it dignified. This is the principle of
trimmed gardens. We shall analyze another source of the
opinion that painted landscapes are superior to real ones
later on, when we examine the question of what precisely
is the pleasure afforded us by works of art.

It remains for us to glance at the relation to nature of
the third category of paintings—those in which a group
of people are depicted in a landscape. We have seen that
groups and landscapes depicted in painting cannot possibly
be higher in idea than those presented to us by reality, and
that in execution they are always ever so much lower than
reality. It is true, however, that in a painting a group may
be placed in a more striking setting and one even more suitable for it than may be the case in reality (joyful scenes
often take place in rather dull and even depressing surroundings; thrilling, magnificent scenes often, even in the majority of cases, take place in surroundings by no means magnificent; on the contrary, very often a landscape contains
a group, the character of which is out of harmony with its
own character). Art can easily rectify this, and we are ready
to grant that in this respect it has an advantage over nature.
But, while granting this advantage, we must inquire,
first, how important this advantage is and, second, whether it is always a true advantage. A painting depicts a landscape, and a group of people in this landscape. Usually, in

such cases, the landscape is only a frame for the group, or
the group is only a minor accessory, whereas the main thing
in the painting is the landscape. In the first case, the
advantage art enjoys over reality is limited to the fact
that it provided the painting with a gilt frame instead of
a common one; in the second case art added a beautiful, perhaps, but for all that a minor accessory—not a very great
gain it must be admitted.[54] But is the intrinsic significance
of a painting really enhanced when the artist tries to give
a group a setting corresponding to its character? In most
cases this is doubtful. Will it not be too monotonous always
to light up a scene of felicitous love with the joyous rays
of the sun and to place it in a smiling green meadow, invariably in the spring when "the whole of nature breathes
love," and to light up a scene of crime with lightning and
place it among wild cliffs? Furthermore, will not a setting
which does not quite harmonize with the scene, as usually
happens in reality, by its disharmony enhance the impression created by the scene itself? And does not the setting
nearly always influence the character of the scene, does it
not lend it new shades and, as a result, lend it more freshness and more life?

The final conclusion to be drawn from these observations on sculpture and painting: we see that in respect to
many extremely important elements (beauty of contour,
absolute perfection of execution, expression, etc.) the productions of both these arts stand ever so much lower than
nature and life; and except for one unimportant advantage
enjoyed by painting, which we have just discussed, we see
absolutely nothing in which sculpture or painting stands
higher than nature and real life.

It now remains for us to speak of music and poetry—
the supreme and most perfect of the arts, before which, as
the prevailing theory of aesthetics says, exaggerating in
this case an idea that is correct if presented in a moderate
form, both painting and sculpture pale into insignificance.

But first of all we must draw attention to the question:
in what relation does instrumental music stand to vocal
music, and in which cases can vocal music be called
an art?

Art is activity by means of which man realizes his striving for beauty—such is the common definition of art.

We disagree with it; but until we have expressed our criticism we have no right to depart from it, and by substituting later on the definition we think correct for the one we are employing here we shall not thereby alter our conclusions regarding the question: is singing always an art, and in which cases does it become an art? What is the first need that prompts a person to sing? Does the striving for beauty play any part in it? It seems to us that this need is entirely different from concern for beauty. A person in a calm mood may be reserved, may remain silent. A man under the influence of joy or sorrow becomes communicative; nay more: he cannot refrain from giving outward expression to his feelings: "feelings beg to be released." How do they enter the external world? In various ways, depending on their character. A sudden and shocking sensation expresses itself by a shriek or an exclamation; unpleasant sensations bordering on physical pain express themselves by various contortions of the face and by gestures; the feeling of extreme discontent also expresses itself by restless, destructive gestures; lastly, the feelings of joy and sorrow find expression by the person affected relating them, if there is somebody to relate them to, or by singing, if there is nobody to relate them to, or if the person does not wish to relate them. This idea is to be found in every discussion of folk songs. It is strange, however, that nobody has drawn attention to the fact that singing, being, in essence, an expression of joy or sorrow, does not by any means spring from our striving for beauty. Is it to be expected that a person under the overwhelming influence of emotion will think about attaining charm and grace, will concern himself with form? Emotion and form are opposites. This alone shows that singing, the product of emotion, and art, which is concerned with form, are entirely different things. Originally, and in essence, singing—like conversation—is a product of practical life and not of art; but like every other accomplishment, singing requires knack, training and practice to reach a high degree of perfection. Like all the organs, the voice, the organ of singing, needs training in order to become an obedient tool of the will. In this respect natural singing becomes an "art," but only in the sense in which the ability to write, to count, to plough the earth, and every practical occupation is called "art," and by no means in the sense that aesthetics attribute to the term "art."

In contrast to natural singing there is artificial singing, which tries to imitate natural singing. Emotion lends exceptionally great interest to everything that is created under its influence; it even lends it exceptional charm, exceptional beauty. A face inspired by grief or joy is a thousand times more beautiful than a cold one. Natural singing as the expression of emotion, although a product of nature and not of art, which concerns itself with beauty, nevertheless possesses great beauty; that is why a person is prompted by the desire to sing deliberately, to imitate natural singing. In what relation does this artificial singing stand to natural singing? It is more deliberate, calculated, embellished with everything with which human genius can embellish it: what comparison can there be between an aria of an Italian opera and the simple, pale, monotonous melody of a folk song! But all the training in harmony, all the artistry of development, all the wealth of embellishment of a brilliant aria, all the flexibility and incomparable richness of the voice of the one who sings it cannot make up for the absence of the sincere emotion that permeates the pale melody of a folk song and the ordinary, untrained voice of the one who sings it not from a desire to pose and to display his voice and art, but from the need to express his feelings. The difference between natural and artificial singing is the difference between an actor playing his part, merry or sad, and a person who really feels merry or sad over something—it is the difference between the original and the copy, between the genuine thing and the imitation. We hasten to add that a composer may indeed be imbued with the feelings his music is supposed to express. If he is, he may compose something much superior to a folk song not only in external beauty, but also in intrinsic merit; but in that case his music will be a work of art, or "ability," only from the technical aspect, only in the sense that everything man makes with the aid of deep study, intelligence and concern to "turn out the best" can be called works of art. In essence, however, the music of the composer who wrote it under the overwhelming influence of involuntary emotion will be a work of nature (of life) in general, and not of art. Similarly, a skilful and impressionable vocalist may thoroughly enter into the part he is acting and become imbued with the feelings his song is supposed to express, and in that case he will sing it on the stage to an audience

348   N. G. CHERNYSHEVSKY

better than an ordinary person—from sheer exuberance
and not to display his talent; but in that case the vocalist
will cease to be an actor, and his singing will be the singing
of nature and not a work of art. We have no intention of
confusing this yielding to emotion with inspiration: inspiration is an exceptionally favourable mood of creative
imagination; the only thing it has in common with yielding to emotion is that in people gifted with poetic talent,
and also with exceptional impressionableness, inspiration
may pass into yielding to emotion when the inspiring object
disposes one to emotion. There is the same difference between
inspiration and emotion as there is between imagination
and reality, between dreams and impressions.

The original and essential purpose of instrumental music
was to serve as an accompaniment to singing. True, later
on, when singing became for the upper classes of society
mainly an art, when listeners began to be very exacting
towards the technique of singing, satisfactory singing became rare, and instrumental music tried to fill the gap and
become an independent branch of music. True, it had every
right to claim independent significance with the improvement of musical instruments, the extraordinary development of technical execution and the predominating biassed
preference for execution rather than for content. Nevertheless, the true relation of instrumental music to singing
is preserved in opera, the completest form of music as an
art, and in some branches of concert music. And we cannot
but observe that in spite of the utter artificiality of our
taste and refined partiality for all the difficulties and devices of brilliant technique, everybody continues to prefer
singing to instrumental music: as soon as the singing starts,
we cease to pay attention to the orchestra. The violin is
held in higher esteem than all other instruments because
"it comes nearer to the human voice than all other instruments"; the highest praise that is expressed of a violinist
is: "in the sounds of his instrument you can hear the human
voice." Thus: instrumental music is imitation of singing,
its accompaniment, or substitute; and singing as a work
of art is only an imitation of and substitute for singing as
a work of nature. After this, we have a right to say that in
music, art is only a feeble reproduction of the phenomena of life, which are independent of our strivings
for art.

Let us pass to the highest and completest of the arts, poetry, the problems of which constitute the entire theory of art. Poetry stands ever so much higher than the other arts because of its content; none of the other arts is able to tell us a hundredth part of what poetry tells us. But this relation changes entirely when we turn our attention to the force and vividness of the subjective impression made upon us by poetry on the one hand, and by the other arts on the other. All the other arts, like living reality, directly affect the senses; poetry affects the imagination. The imagination of some people is much more impressionable and lively than that of others, but in general it must be said that in a healthy person its images are pale and feeble compared to the reactions of the senses; therefore, it must be said that in strength and clarity the subjective impression created by poetry is far below not only reality, but all the other arts. Let us then see what degree of objective perfection is attained by the content and form of poetry, and whether it can compete with nature at least in this respect.

Many people speak of the "completeness," the "individuality," the "vivid definiteness" of the personages and characters depicted by the great poets. But at the same time we are told that "these, however, are not individual persons, but general types." After such a statement it is unnecessary to prove that the most definite, the best portrayed personage in poetry remains only a general, vaguely sketched outline, which is given living, definite individuality only by the imagination (properly speaking, the memory) of the reader. The relation of the image in poetry to the real living image is exactly the same as the relation of the word to the real object it designates,—it is but a pale and general, an indefinite allusion to reality. Many people regard this "generality" of the poetic image as its superiority to the personages we see in real life. This opinion is based on an assumed antithesis between the general significance of the being and its living individuality; on the assumption that "the general individualizes itself and thereby loses its generality" in reality and "is elevated to it again only by the power of art, which divests the individual of his individuality." We shall not enter into a metaphysical discussion about the actual relation between the general and the particular (if we did, it would necessarily lead to the conclusion that for man the general is only a pale and

lifeless extract of the individual, and for that reason the
relation between them is the same as that between the word
and reality); we shall merely say that actually, individual
details do not in the least disturb the general significance
of an object, but on the contrary, animate and supplement
it; that, at all events, poetry admits the high superiority
of the individual by its striving to give its images living
individuality; that, nevertheless, it cannot attain individuality, and succeeds only in approaching it somewhat,
and that the degree to which it approaches it determines
the merits of the poetic image. It strives for, but can never
attain what is always met with in the typical personages
of real life; obviously, poetic images are feeble, incomplete
and indefinite, compared with the corresponding images in
reality. "But are truly typical persons met with in reality"?
It is as sufficient to ask such a question and not wait for a
reply as it would be in the case of questions like: do we
in real life actually meet with kind and unkind people,
wastrels and misers, and so forth. Is ice cold, is bread very
nutritious, and so forth? Some people have to have everything pointed out and proved to them. But they cannot be
convinced by general proof in general combination; they
can be influenced only by separate things, they can be convinced only by special examples taken from their circle of
acquaintances in which, however small it may be, a few
truly-typical individuals can always be found. It is no use
pointing to typical personages in history; there are people
who are ready to say: "historical personages have been poet-
ized by legend, by the admiration of their contemporaries,
by the genius of historians, or by their exceptional position."

How the opinion arose that typical characters are depicted
much more clearly and better in poetry than they present
themselves to us in real life is a question we shall deal with
later; at present we shall turn our attention to the process
by which characters are "created" in poetry. It is usually
put forth as a guarantee that these images are more typical
than living personages. It is usually said: "The poet watches
numerous living individual personages; not one of them can
fully serve as a type; but the poet notes what is general and
typical in each of them; casting aside all the particular
things, he combines the features scattered among the different people in one artistic whole and in this way creates

a character that might be called the quintessence of real characters." Let us suppose that all this is absolutely correct and that this is exactly what always happens; but the quintessence of things is usually different from the things themselves; theine is not tea, alcohol is not wine; the rule quoted above is actually followed by "authors" who instead of real people give us the quintessence of heroism and of malice in the shape of monsters of vice and stone heroes. All, or nearly all, the young people fall in love—this is the general feature, in everything else they are different— and so in all poetical works we admire maidens and youths who are always dreaming and talking about love, and throughout the whole story do nothing but suffer from, or enjoy the bliss of, love; all the elderly people are fond of moralizing, but in everything else they are different; all the grandmothers love their grandchildren, and so forth—and so stories and novels are populated by old folk who do nothing but moralize, with grandmothers who do nothing but fondle their grandchildren, and so forth.[55] In the majority of cases, however, this recipe is not quite adhered to; when a poet is "creating" his character the image of some real personage usually looms before his mind's eye; sometimes consciously, and sometimes unconsciously, he "reproduces" him in his typical personage. In proof of this we point to the innumerable works in which the protagonist is a more or less faithful portrait of the author himself (for example: Faust, Don Carlos and Marqués de Poza, Byron's heroes, George Sand's heroes and heroines, Lensky, Onegin, Pechorin). We shall mention also the accusation, very often levelled at novelists, that "in their novels they portray their acquaintances." This accusation is usually scornfully and indignantly denied; in most cases, however, it is merely an exaggeration and not properly expressed, but it is not unjust in essence. Propriety, on the one hand, and a man's ordinary striving to be independent, "to create and not merely copy," on the other, compel the poet to alter the characters of the copies he makes of people he has met in real life, to present them to some degree different from what they are. Moreover, in the novel, the copy of a real person acts in an environment totally different from that in which the original lived, and this obliterates the outward resemblance. But all these changes do not prevent the character from being a copy and not a creation; a portrait, but not an original. It may be objected: true, the original of a person in poetry may very often be a real person, but the poet "raises him to general significance." There is usually no need to do this, however, for the original, too, has general significance in his individuality; it is only necessary—and herein lies one of the qualities of poetic genius—to understand the essence of the real person's character, to look at him with penetrating eyes. Furthermore, it is necessary to understand, or sense, how this man would act and speak under the circumstances the poet creates for him—this is another aspect of poetic genius. Thirdly, it is necessary to be able to depict him, to portray him as the poet conceives him—which is, perhaps, the most characteristic feature of poetic genius. To understand, to be able to perceive or feel by instinct and to convey what is understood—such is the poet's task in depicting most of the personages he portrays. The question as to what is meant by "raising to the ideal significance," "the poetization of prose and not of the incongruities of life," will present itself later on. We have not the slightest doubt, however, that there are very many personages in poetical works who cannot be called portraits, who have been "created" by the poet. But this is by no means due to the fact that no worthy models could be found in reality, but to an entirely different reason, most often simply forgetfulness, or lack of sufficient knowledge: if the poet has forgotten the living details and has retained in his memory only a general, abstract conception of the character, or if the poet knows about the typical person much less than is needed to make him in his portrait a living person, then, willy-nilly, he must supplement the general sketch, fill in the details. But these imaginary persons hardly ever present themselves to us as living characters.[56] In general, the more we know about the life of a poet, about the people he was intimate with the more portraits of living people do we see in his works. It is difficult not to agree that there is, and always has been, much less "creation" in the personages depicted by poets and much more copying from reality than is usually supposed; it is difficult to escape the conviction that in relation to his personages, the poet is nearly always only a historian or a memoirist. Of course, we do not mean that every word uttered by Mephistopheles was heard by Goethe from Merck.[57] Not only a poetic genius, but even the least resourceful story writer is capable of sticking one sentence on to another of the same kind, to add introductions and links.

"Independent invention," or "devising,"—we take the liberty of using these terms for the ordinary, excessively proud term "creation,"—occurs much more often in the events depicted by the poet, in the plot, its knotting and unravelling, etc., although it can very easily be proved that the subjects of stories and novels are usually events that have actually taken place, or anecdotes, stories of all kinds, and so forth (we point, for example, to all cf Pushkin's prose stories: *The Captain's Daughter*, is an anecdote; *Dubrovsky*, is an anecdote; *The Queen of Spades*, is an anecdote; *The Shot*, is an anecdote, and so forth). But the general outline of a plot does not by itself lend a story or novel high poetical merit; the author must be able to make use of the plot. Therefore, leaving aside the question of the "independence" of the plot, let us turn our attention to the question as to whether the plot, in poetical works, when already fully developed, is more "poetical" than the actual events. As a means of reaching a definite conclusion we shall put several questions, most of which answer themselves: 1) Do poetical events occur in reality? Do dramas, love stories, comedies, tragedies and farces occur in reality? Every moment of the day. 2) Are the development and denouement of these events truly poetical? Do they really possess artistic completeness and finish? Often they do not; but often they do. Very many events occur in which the strict poetic eye can find no artistic flaws. This point can be decided by reading the first well-written history that comes to hand, by the first evening spent in conversation with a man who has seen much in life, by the court cases reported in the first English or French newspaper that comes to hand. 3) Are there among these complete poetical events such as could without any alteration be put under the heading: "drama," "tragedy," "love story," and so forth? Very many. True, many of these real events appear improbable, are based on exceedingly rare, exceptional situations, or chains of circumstances and, therefore, in their actual shape have the appearance of a fairy tale or of far-fetched fiction (which shows that real life is often too dramatic for drama and too poetical for poetry). But very many events occur, which, though remarkable, contain nothing eccentric, nothing improbable, in which the whole chain of circumstances, the

whole course and denouement of what in poetry is called
the plot, is simple. 4) Have events in reality a "general"
side, which is essential in poetical works? Of course,
every event worthy of the attention of a thinking
person possesses it; and very many events of this kind
occur.

After this it is difficult to escape the conclusion that
many events occur in reality, which[58] it is only necessary
to know, to understand and be able to relate, in order that
the plain narrative of a historian, memoirist, or collector
of anecdotes should differ from real "poetical works" only
by its smaller volume and lesser development of scenes,
descriptions and similar details. In this we see the essential
difference between poetical works and the exact, plain
narration of actual events. Fuller detail, or what in inferior
works is called "rhetorical dilation," is what constitutes,
in essence, the entire superiority of poetry to an exact narrative. We are no less ready than others to ridicule rhetoric,
but, recognizing the legitimacy of all the needs of the human heart as soon as we see that they are universal, we recognize the importance of this poetical dilation because we
always see the striving for it everywhere in poetry: these
details, unnecessary for the essence of the event itself, but
necessary for its development, always exist in life; they
must, therefore, also exist in poetry. The only difference
is that in reality these details can never be mere padding
to draw out the story, whereas in poetical works they often actually sound like rhetoric, the mechanical drawing
out of the story. What is Shakespeare lauded for if not for
the fact that in his decisive, his best scenes, he cast aside
all these dilations? But how many of them can be found in
his works, and in those of Goethe and Schiller! It seems to
us (perhaps this betrays patriotic bias), that Russian poetry
contains the germ of revulsion to drawing out a subject by
means of mechanically chosen details. The common features of Pushkin's, Lermontov's and Gogol's tales and stories are brevity and swift action. Thus, in general, in plot,
and in the typical and complete portrayal of personages,
poetical works are far inferior to reality; but there are two
aspects in which they may be superior to reality: the embellishment of events by the addition of striking accessories
and in the harmonization of the characters of personages with
the events in which they participate.

We have said that painting more often than reality
places a group in a setting that corresponds to the essential
character of the scene. Similarly, poetry too, more often
than reality, puts up as the protagonists of and participants
in events, people whose essential characters correspond to
the spirit of the events. In reality, people of petty character
are very often protagonists in tragic, dramatic, etc., events; an
insignificant rake, at bottom, perhaps, not really a bad man,
can do many horrible things; a man who cannot in the least
be called bad may wreck the happiness of many people and
cause far more unhappiness than Iago or Mephistopheles.[59]
In poetical works, on the contrary, atrocious things are
usually done by atrocious people; good is done by exceptionally good people. In real life, one often does not know
whom to blame and whom to praise; in poetical works, honour or disgrace is usually accorded to whomever it is due.
But is this an advantage or a drawback? Sometimes it is one,
sometimes it is the other; most often it is a drawback. We
shall not for the moment deal with the fact that the consequence of this practice is idealization in the good or in the
bad direction, or, to put it simply, exaggeration; for we
have not yet discussed the essence of art and it is yet too
early to decide whether this idealization is a merit or a demerit. We shall merely say that a consequence of the constant
adaptation, in poetry, of the personages' characters to the
significance of events is monotony, the personages and even
the events become uniform; for variety in the character
of the personages would lend essentially similar events
a diversity of shade, as happens in real life, which is
eternally diverse, eternally new, whereas, in poetical
works we very often read repetitions.[60] In our days, embel-
lishments that do not spring from the essence of the
subject and are not needed for achieving the principal
aim, rouse ridicule; but to this day an apt expression, a
brilliant metaphor, and the thousands of devices invented
for the purpose of lending a work external polish, still
greatly influence opinion concerning poetical works.[61] As
regards embellishment, external magnificence, ingenuity,
etc., we admit that fiction can always excel reality. But
it is sufficient to point to this seeming merit of a story
or play for it to lose value in the eyes of people of taste
and to drop from the sphere of "art" into the sphere of
"artificiality."

23*

Our analysis has shown that works of art may be superior to reality only in two or three insignificant respects and necessarily remain far lower than it in essential qualities. We may be reproached for having limited the analysis to the most general points of view, for not having gone into detail and not giving examples. Indeed, the brevity of our analysis does seem a defect when one remembers how deep-rooted is the opinion that works of art are more beautiful than real objects, events and people; but when we see how unsound this opinion is, when we remember how the people who advance it contradict themselves at every step,[62] one would think that after stating the opinion that art is superior to reality, it would be enough to add the words: "it is not true," because everybody feels that real life is more beautiful than the products of "creative imagination." That being the case, what is the basis, or it would be better to say, what are the subjective causes of the exaggerated opinion concerning the merits of works of art?

The first cause of this opinion is man's natural inclination to prize highly things that are difficult and rare. Nobody praises a Frenchman for his pure accent when speaking French, or a German when speaking German; "that cost him no effort, and it is by no means rare." But if a German speaks tolerable French, or if a Frenchman speaks tolerable German, it is a matter of surprise to us and gives such a man a right to a certain degree of our respect. Why? Because, firstly, it is rare; and secondly, because this was achieved by years of effort. Properly speaking, nearly every Frenchman having a fair amount of literary or even ordinary education speaks French excellently—but how exacting we are in this case!—the slightest, almost imperceptible provincialism in his accent, a single, not quite graceful sentence, is enough to make us say: "this gentleman speaks his own language very badly." When a Russian speaks French he, in every sound, betrays the fact that his organs cannot attain the full purity of the French accent; he constantly betrays his foreign origin by his choice of words, by the construction of his sentences, by his whole manner of speech. But we forgive all these defects, we even fail to notice them, and declare that he speaks French excellently, inimitably, and finally we say: "This Russian speaks French better than the French," although we do not think of comparing him with real French people, but compare him only with other Rus-

sians who try to speak French. He really does speak ever
so much better than they do, but ever so much worse than
French people. This is taken for granted by everybody who
knows anything about the matter, but many people may be
misled by a hyperbolic sentence. The same applies to the
judgment of aesthetics on the creations of nature and of
art: the slightest real or seeming flaw in a work of nature
is enough to set aestheticians talking about defects; it shocks
them and causes them to forget about all merits, about all
its beauty: indeed, do these works of nature deserve to be
prized considering that they appeared without any effort?
A work of art may have the same flaw magnified a hundred
times; it may be a more glaring flaw and be surrounded by
hundreds of other flaws, but we fail to see them, and if we
do see them we forgive them and say: "There are spots
even on the sun!" Properly speaking, works of art can be
compared only with one another when defining their relative merits; some prove to be superior to all the rest; enraptured by their beauty (only relative), we exclaim: "They
are more beautiful than nature and real life! The beauty
of reality is nothing compared with the beauty of art!"
But rapture is biassed; it gives more than justice can give: we
prize difficulty —that is excellent; but we must not forget
essential, intrinsic merit, which is independent of the degree of difficulty; we become positively unjust when we prefer difficulty of execution to the merits of it. Nature and life
create beauty without thinking about beauty; it appears
in reality without effort and, therefore, has no merit in our
eyes, has no right to our sympathy, no right to indulgence;
and why be indulgent when there is so much beauty in reality? "Everything in reality that is not perfectly beautiful
is ugly; everything in art that is at all tolerable is excellent"—
this is the rule that serves as the basis of our judgment.
To show how highly difficulty of execution is prized and
what little value is attached to what comes of itself, without
any effort on our part, we point to daguerreotype portraits;
among them we find very many that are not only true portraits, but convey the expression of the face to perfection—
do we prize them? It would be surprising to hear eulogies
of daguerreotype portraits. Another example: how highly
calligraphy used to be respected! And yet, a fairly well printed book is ever so much more beautiful than any manuscript; but who admires the art of the printer, and who will

not admire a beautiful manuscript a thousand times more
than a well printed book, which is a thousand times more
beautiful than a manuscript? What is easy has little interest
for us, even though its intrinsic merit is ever so much higher
than of what is difficult. It goes without saying that even
from this point of view we are only subjectively right:
"reality produces beauty without effort" means only that the
effort was not exercised by the will of man: actually, everything in reality—the beautiful and the ugly, the great and
the small—is the result of the utmost unrelaxing and
tireless effort. But what do we care for effort and struggle in which we take no part, either physical or mental?
We do not want to know anything about them; we prize only human effort, we prize only man. And here is another
cause of our biassed admiration of works of art: they are
made by men; therefore, we are all proud of them, we regard
them as being related to us personally; they are witnesses
to human intelligence and to human strength and are therefore precious to us. It is obvious to all nations except the
French that Corneille, or Racine, is far inferior to Shakespeare, but to this day the French keep on comparing them—it
is difficult for them to reach the point of realizing that "our
man is not quite up to the mark." There are very many among
us Russians who are ready to assert that Pushkin is one of
the great poets of the world; there are even people who think
that he stands higher than Byron: this shows how highly
a man appraises his own.[63] Just as a nation exaggerates
the merits of its own poets, so man in general exaggerates
the merits of poetry in general.

The two causes of bias towards art that we have given
deserve respect because they are natural: how can man fail
to respect human labour, how can man not love man, how
can he fail to prize works which testify to human intelligence and strength? But it is doubtful whether the third
cause of our preference for art is worthy of such respect. Art
flatters our artificial tastes. We know very well how artificial were the customs, habits and the whole mode of thought
in the time of Louis XIV. We stand closer to nature, we understand and appreciate it far better than it was understood
and appreciated in seventeenth century society; nevertheless,
we are still a long way away from nature; our habits, customs,
our whole mode of life and, as a consequence, our whole mode
of thought are still very artificial. It is difficult to see the

faults of one's own age, especially since these faults have become less marked than they were in the past. Instead of seeing how much refined artificiality there is still within us, we see only that the nineteenth century stands higher in this respect than the seventeenth, that we understand nature better; but we forget that the abatement of an illness is not yet sound health. Our artificiality is evident in everything, beginning with our clothes, which we all laugh at, but which we all continue to wear, our food, which is seasoned with all sorts of spices which totally change the natural taste of the dishes we eat; from our refined conversational language to our refined language of literature, which continue to be embellished with paradoxes, witticisms, dilations on *loci topici*,* profound argument about threadbare subjects and profound observations on the human heart *à la* Corneille and Racine in *belles lettres*, and *à la* Johann Miller in historical works. Works of art flatter all the petty needs that arise from our love of artificiality. We shall not dwell on the fact that we are to this day fond of "washing" nature as they were fond of adorning it in the seventeenth century —this would lead us into a lengthy discussion about what is meant by "smut," and to what extent it ought to appear in works of art. But to this day there prevails in works of art a petty finish of detail, the object of which is not to bring the details into harmony with the spirit of the whole, but only to make each one of them in itself more interesting or beautiful, nearly always to the detriment of the general impression of the work, its probability and sincerity. There prevails a petty striving after effect in individual words, individual sentences and individual episodes, in the colouring of personages and events with not quite natural, but striking colours. Works of art are pettier than what we see in real life and in nature, and at the same time they are more striking—how, then, can the opinion fail to establish itself, that art is more beautiful than real nature and life, in which there is so little artificiality, and which do not strive to awaken interest?

Nature and life stand higher than art; but art tries to pander to our inclinations; reality, however, cannot be subordinated to our desire to see everything in the light and order that please us, or conform to our often biassed

---

* Commonplaces.—*Ed.*

conceptions. Of the numerous cases of this pandering to the prevailing mode of thought we shall point to one: many people demand that in satirical works there should be personages "in whom the reader's heart could find delight and rest," — a very natural demand, but reality very often fails to satisfy it, for it provides a multitude of events in which there is not a single pleasing personage. Art, however, nearly always panders to it. We cannot say whether there is a single author in Russian literature, except Gogol, who does not yield to this demand; and even in Gogol's works, the scarcity of "pleasing" personages is compensated by "highly lyrical" digressions. Another example: man is inclined to be sentimental; nature and life do not share this inclination; works of art nearly always satisfy it more or less. Both demands are a consequence of man's limitations. Nature and real life stand above these limitations. Yielding to them, and thereby falling below reality and very often even running the risk of becoming vulgar or feeble, works of art come close to man's ordinary requirements and thereby gain favour in his eyes. "But in that case, you yourself admit that works of art satisfy man's nature better and more fully than objective reality; consequently, they are better for man than the works of reality." This conclusion is not quite correct; the point is that an artificially developed man has many artificial requirements, so perverted as to be false and fantastic, which cannot be fully satisfied because in essence they are not the requirements of his nature, but the desires prompted by a distorted imagination, which it is almost impossible to please without earning the ridicule and contempt of the very man whom we strive to please, for he himself feels instinctively that his requirements are not worth pleasing. Thus, the public, followed by aesthetics, demand "pleasing" personages, sentimentality—and this very same public laughs at works of art which please these desires. Pandering to a person's whims does not mean satisfying his requirements. The very first of these requirements is truth.

We have discussed the reasons why works of art are preferred to the phenomena of nature and life as regards content and execution, but the impression made upon us by art or reality is also important: its degree is also a measure of the merits of a thing.

We have seen that the impression created by works of art must be much feebler than that created by living reality and, therefore, we do not think it necessary to adduce proof of this. In this respect, however, a work of art is in much more favourable circumstances than the phenomena of nature; these circumstances may lead a man who is not accustomed to analyze the causes of his sensations to assume that art in itself creates a stronger impression than living reality. Reality presents itself to our eyes independently of our will, most often at inopportune times.[64] Very often we go into company, to a party, with no intention of admiring human beauty, of observing characters, or of watching the drama of life; we go with a troubled mind and with our hearts closed to impressions. But who goes to a picture gallery without the intention of enjoying the beauty of the pictures? Who starts reading a novel without the intention of studying the characters of the personages depicted in it and of following the development of the plot? Usually, we are almost forced ourselves to pay attention to the beauty, the grandeur, of reality. Let it, if it can, attract our eyes which are riveted on entirely different objects, let it force itself into our heart, which is engaged with other things. We treat reality as we do an importunate visitor who is trying to thrust himself upon us: we try to keep the door shut against it. But moments occur when our hearts feel empty from our own neglect of reality—and then we turn to art and beg it to fill the vacuum; then we play the part of the humble petitioner. Our path of life is bestrewn with golden coins, but we do not see them because our mind is taken up with the goal and we pay no attention to the road under our feet; even if we do notice the coins we cannot stoop to pick them up because the "chariot of life" is irresistibly carrying us onward—such is our attitude towards reality. But when we have arrived at a post station and are bored to death waiting for a change of horses, we eagerly examine every pewter platter, which, perhaps, is not even worthy of attention—such is our attitude towards art. This is apart from the fact that each one of us must form his own judgment of the phenomena of life, because life presents special phenomena for each individual which others do not see, and on which, therefore, judgment is not pronounced by society as a whole, whereas works of art are judged by the court of public opinion. The beauty and grandeur of real life rarely presents itself to us with a label on it, and few people can notice and appreciate a thing that is not

publicly talked about. The phenomena of reality are gold
ingots without a hall mark: for this reason alone many refuse
to take them, being unable to distinguish them from pieces
of copper. A work of art is a bank note which has little
intrinsic value, but the nominal value of which is guaranteed
by the whole of society, and it is therefore prized by everybody, although only a few are aware that its value is due to
the fact that it represents a piece of gold. When we look at
reality it engages our attention as something entirely independent of us, and it rarely leaves us the opportunity mentally to transport ourselves into our subjective world, into
our past. But when I look at a work of art I have a wide field
for my subjective reflections, and it usually serves me only
as an occasion for conscious or unconscious dreams and reminiscences. When a tragic scene is enacted in front of my
eyes in reality my mind is too taken up with it to think of
myself; but when, in a novel, I read about a man being
killed, a clear or vague recollection rises in my mind of all
the dangers I myself have gone through, of all the cases of
people I had known personally being killed. The power of
art particularly of poetry is usually the power to awaken
memory. Because of its very incompleteness, indefiniteness,
precisely because it is usually only a "generalization," and
not a living individual image or event, a work of art is particularly capable of awakening our memory. Give me a
finished portrait—it will not remind me any of my friends,
and I will coldly turn away and say: "Not bad"; but show me,
at a favourable moment, a rough, vague sketch in which no
man will recognize himself—and this poor, feeble sketch
will remind me of the features of somebody dear to me,
and although I had looked coldly at a living face full of beauty and expression, I will gaze enraptured at this insignificant sketch which reminds me of someone dear to me,
and recalling my relations with that person it reminds
me of myself.

The power of art is the power of generalization. There
is yet another aspect of works of art which sets them in
the eyes of the inexperienced or shortsighted higher than
the phenomena of life and reality, viz., in them everything is exhibited and explained by the author, whereas
we must solve the riddles of nature and life ourselves.
The power of art is the power of commentary; but this we
shall have to discuss later on.

We have found many reasons why art is preferred to·
reality; but all of them only explain, they do not justify this preference. Unwilling to agree that art stands even
on a par with, let alone higher than reality in the intrinsic
merit of content and execution, we, of course, cannot agree
with the now prevailing view concerning the needs from which
art arose and the purpose, the object, of its existence. The
prevailing opinion of the origin and purpose of art says the
following: "Man is prompted by an irresistible striving for
beauty, but, unable to find true beauty in objective reality,
he is obliged to create objects, or works, corresponding to
this need, objects and phenomena that are truly beautiful";
or, according to the special terminology of the prevailing
school: "The idea of the beautiful not realized in reality,
is realized in works of art." We must analyze this definition
in order to reveal the true meaning of the incomplete and
one-sided allusions it contains. "Man is prompted by a
striving for beauty." But if beauty means what is meant by
this word in this definition, viz., perfect harmony between
the idea and the form, then it is necessary to deduce from the
striving for beauty not art in particular, but all man's activities in general, the basic principle of which is—the
perfect realization of a certain idea. The striving for the
unity of the idea and the image is the formal basis of all
technique, of all work directed towards the object of creating and perfecting all the articles we need. By deducing
art from the striving for beauty we confuse the two meanings
of this word: 1) the fine arts (poetry, music, etc.), and 2) the
ability, or desire, to do things well. Only the latter is deduced from the striving for unity of the idea and the form.
If, however, beauty means (as we think it does) that in which
man sees life, it is evident that the striving for it leads to
joyous love for all that is alive, and that it is fully satisfied by living reality. "Man does not meet true and full
beauty in reality." We have tried to prove that this is wrong,
that our imagination is not stimulated by the flaws in beauty
in reality, but by its absence; that real beauty
is full beauty, but, unfortunately, it is not always in front
of our eyes. If works of art had arisen as a consequence of
our striving for perfection and of our disdain for all that is
imperfect,[65] man would long ago have had to abandon all
striving for art as a fruitless effort, because works of art are
not perfect; whoever is dissatisfied with real beauty can be

still less satisfied with the beauty created by art. Thus, it is impossible to agree with the explanation usually given of the purpose of art; but this explanation contains allusions which may be called correct if they are properly interpreted. "Man is not satisfied with beauty in reality, this beauty is not, enough for him,"—herein lies the essence and the truth of the usual explanation, which, when falsely interpreted, needs explanation itself.

The sea is beautiful; when looking at it we do not think of being dissatisfied with it in the aesthetic sense. But not all people live near the sea; many never have an opportunity to see it even once in their lives, but they would like very much to see and admire it, so seascapes are interesting and pleasing to them. Of course, it is much preferable to see the sea itself rather than pictures of it; but when a good thing is not available, man is satisfied with an inferior one, when the genuine article is not available a substitute will do. Those people who are able to see and admire the real sea cannot always do so when they want to, so they recall their vision of it. But the imagination is weak, it has to be fostered and prompted, so in order to revive their recollections of the sea, in order to see it more vividly in their imagination, they look at seascapes. This is the sole aim and object of very many (the majority) of works of art: to give those people who have not been able to enjoy beauty in reality the opportunity to acquaint themselves with it at least to some degree; to serve as a reminder, to prompt and revive recollections of beauty in reality in the minds of those people who are acquainted with it by experience and love to recall it. (We shall leave for the time being the expression: "beauty is the essential content of art"; later on we shall substitute for the term "beauty" another term which, in our opinion defines the content of art more exactly and fully.)[66] Thus, the first purpose of art is to reproduce nature and life, and this applies to all works of art without exception. Their relation to the corresponding aspects and phenomena of reality is the same as the relation of an engraving to the picture from which it was copied, as the relation of a portrait to the person it represents. An engraving is made of a picture not because the latter is a bad one, but because it is a good one. Similarly, reality is reproduced in art not in order to eliminate flaws, not because reality as such is not sufficiently beautiful, but precisely because it is beautiful. In artistic respects, an engraving is not better than the picture from which it is copied, but much inferior to it. Similarly, works of art never attain the beauty and grandeur of reality; but the picture is unique, it can be admired only by those who go to the picture gallery which it adorns. The engraving, however, is sold in hundreds of copies all over the world, everybody can admire it whenever he pleases without leaving his room, without getting up from his couch, without throwing off his dressing gown. Similarly, a beautiful object in reality is not always accessible to everybody; reproductions of it (feeble, crude, pale, it is true, but reproductions for all that) in works of art make it always accessible to everybody. A portrait is made of a person we love and cherish not in order to eliminate the flaws in his features (what do we care about these flaws? We do not notice them, or if we do, we like them), but in order to give us the opportunity to admire that face even when it is not actually in front of our eyes. Such also is the aim and object of works of art; they do not rectify reality, do not embellish it, but reproduce it, serve as a substitute for it.

Thus, the first object of art is to reproduce reality. While not claiming in the least that these words express something entirely new in the history of aesthetical opinion, we, nevertheless, think that the pseudo-classical "imitation of nature theory" that prevailed in the seventeenth and eighteenth centuries demanded from art something different from the formal principle implied by the definition: "art is the reproduction of reality." In support of our statement that there is an essential difference between our view of art and that contained in the imitation of nature theory, we shall quote here a criticism of this theory taken from the best textbook on the now prevailing system of aesthetics.[67] This criticism will, on the one hand, show the difference between the conceptions it refutes and our views, and, on the other, will reveal what is lacking in our first definition of art as reproducing activity, and will thus enable us to pass on to a most exact exposition of the conceptions of art.

The definition of art as imitation of nature reveals only its formal object; in conformity with this object it should strive as far as possible to repeat what already exists in the external world. Such a repetition must be regarded as superfluous, for nature and life already present us with what, according to this conception, art should present to us. This is not enough: the imitation of nature is a vain effort which fails to achieve its object by a long way because, when imitating nature, art, owing to its restricted means, instead of truth, gives only deception, and instead of a really living being, gives only a lifeless mask.*

Here [68] we shall observe, first of all, that the words: "art is the reproduction of reality," as well as the sentence: "art is the imitation of nature," define only the formal principle of art; to define the content of art, it is necessary to supplement the first conclusion we have drawn concerning its aim, and this we shall do later on. The other objection does not in the least apply to the view we have expounded; from the preceding exposition it is evident that the reproduction or the "repetition" of objects and phenomena of nature by art is by no means superfluous; on the contrary, it is necessary. Proceeding to discuss the observation that repetition is a vain effort which fails to achieve its object by a long way, it must be said that this argument is valid only when [69] it is assumed that art wants to compete with reality and not simply serve as a substitute for it. We, however, assert that art cannot stand comparison with living reality and completely lacks the virility that reality possesses; we regard this as being beyond doubt.

Thus, the expression "art is the reproduction of reality" must be supplemented in order that it may be an all-round definition. Although it does not in this shape fully express the entire content of the defined concept, it is, nevertheless, correct, and for the time being objections to it can be based only on the implicit demand that art should be defined as being higher, more perfect, than reality. We tried to prove the objective unsoundness of this assumption and then discovered its subjective basis. Let us see whether the further objections to the imitation theory apply to our view.

Since it is impossible to achieve complete success in imitating nature, the only thing that remains is to take smug pleasure in the relative success of the hocus-pocus; but the more the copy bears an external resemblance to the original, the colder this pleasure becomes, and it even grows into satiety or revulsion. There are portraits which, as the saying goes, are awfully like the originals. An excellent imitation of the song of the nightingale begins to bore and disgust us as soon as we learn that it is not a real nightingale singing, but some skilful imitator of the nightingale's trilling; this is because we have

---

* Abbreviated passage from G. W. Hegel, *Vorlesungen über die Aesthetik*. (*Sämtl. Werke*, Stuttgart 1927, Bd. XII, S. 71-72.)—*Ed.*

a right to demand different music from a human. Such tricks in the extremely skilful imitation of nature may be compared with the art of the conjurer who without missing threw lentil beans through an aperture no bigger than a lentil bean, and whom Alexander the Great rewarded with a medimnos of lentils.*

These observations are quite correct, but they apply to the useless and senseless copying of what is not deserving of attention, or to the drawing of mere externals bereft of content. (How many vaunted works of art earn this biting, but deserved, ridicule!) Content worthy of the attention of a thinking individual is alone able to shield art from the reproach that it is merely a pastime, which it very often is. Artistic form does not save a work of art from contempt or a pitiful smile if the importance of its idea cannot answer the question: "Was it worth the trouble to make?" A useless thing has no right to respect. "Man is an aim in himself"; but the aim of the things man makes must be to satisfy man's needs and must not be an aim in itself. That is precisely why the more perfectly a useless imitation bears external resemblance to the original the more disgust it rouses. "Why was so much time and labour spent on it" we ask ourselves when looking at it. "And what a pity that such absence of content can go hand in hand with such perfect workmanship!" The boredom and disgust roused by the conjurer who imitates the song of the nightingale are explained by the very remarks of the critics who point to him: a man who fails to understand that he ought to sing human songs and not utter the trills that have sense only in the song of the nightingale, and which is lost when repeated by a human is deserving of pity. As regards portraits which are awfully like the originals, this must be understood as follows: to be true, all copies must convey the essential features of the originals; a portrait that fails to carry the chief, the most expressive, features of a face is not a true portrait; and when, at the same time, the petty details of the face are distinctly given, the portrait of the face is rendered ugly, senseless, lifeless—how can it be anything else than awful? Objection is often raised to what is called the "daguerreotype copying" of reality; would it not be better to say that copying, like everything that man does, calls for understanding, for the ability to distinguish the

* *Ibid.*, S. 73-74.

essential from the unessential features? "Lifeless copying" —
such is the usual phrase; but a man cannot make a true copy
if the lifeless mechanism is not guided by living meaning.
It is even impossible to make a true facsimile of an ordinary
manuscript if the meaning of the letters that are being
copied is not understood.

Before proceeding to define the essential content of art,
which will supplement our definition of its formal principle, we deem it necessary to make a few direct observations
concerning the relation of the "reproduction" theory to the
so-called "imitation" theory. Our conception of art springs
from the views accepted by the latest German aesthetics
and arises from them through the dialectical process, the
trend of which is determined by the general ideas of modern
science. Thus, it is most closely connected with two systems
of ideas—with that of the beginning of the present century, on the one hand, and that of the last decades on the
other. Every other relation is simply resemblance which
has no genetic influence. But whereas the conceptions of the
thinkers of antiquity and those of ancient times cannot,
with the present development of science, influence the present-day mode of thought, one cannot help seeing that
in many cases modern conceptions are similar to those of
previous ages. Particularly often do they resemble the conceptions of the Greek thinkers. This is the situation in the
present case. Our definition of the formal principle of art
is similar to the view that prevailed in the Greek world;
it is found in the works of Plato and Aristotle, and in all
probability was expressed by Democritus. Their μίμησις corresponds to our term "reproduction."* Later, this word was
interpreted as "imitation" (Nachahmung), but this translation is not exact, for it restricts the scope of the concept and
suggests the idea of imitation of external form but not the
conveying of the inherent content.[70] The pseudo-classical
theory did, indeed, interpret art as the imitation of reality
with the object of deceiving the senses, but this was an abuse
that belonged only to the epochs of corrupted taste.[71]

We must now supplement the definition of art we presented above, and from the examination of the formal principle of art pass on to the definition of its content.[72]

---

* This is treated in greater detail in Chernyshevsky's essay "The
Poetics of Aristotle" in this volume, pp. 423-53.—*Ed.*

Usually it is said that the content of art is beauty; but this restricts the sphere of art too much. Even if we grant that the sublime and the ridiculous are elements of the beautiful, the content of many works of art will not come under the three headings: the beautiful, the sublime, the ridiculous. In painting, these subdivisions do not apply to pictures of domestic life in which there is not a single beautiful or ridiculous person, pictures of old men or old women not distinguished for the exceptional beauty of age, and so forth. In music it is still more difficult to introduce the usual subdivisions; if we put marches, pathetic pieces, and so forth, under the heading of magnificent, if we put pieces that breathe the spirit of love or mirth under the heading of the beautiful, and if we find numerous comic songs, there still remains an enormous number which in their content cannot without stretching the point be put under any of these headings. Under what heading are we to put sad melodies—under sublime as suffering, or under beautiful as tender dreams?[73] But of all arts, the one that is most difficult to squeeze into the tight compartments of beauty and its subdivisions as regards content is poetry. Its sphere is the entire sphere of life and nature.[74] The poet's views on life in its diverse manifestations are as diverse as the thinker's conceptions of these diverse phenomena; and the thinker finds in reality much more than the beautiful, the sublime and the ridiculous. Not all grief reaches the point of tragedy; not all joy is graceful or comical.[75] That the content of poetry consists of something more than the well-known three elements can easily be seen from the fact that poetical works no longer fit into the frame of the old subdivisions. That dramatic poetry depicts not only the tragic or the comical is proved by the fact that, in addition to comedies and tragedies, dramas also had to appear. The place of the epic, which is mostly sublime, has been taken by the novel with all its innumerable categories. For most of the present-day lyrical poems it is impossible to find among the old subdivisions any heading that would indicate the character of their content; hundreds of headings would not suffice, so three are certainly not enough to embrace them all (we are speaking of the character of the content, but not of form, which must always be beautiful).

The simplest way to solve this riddle would be to say that the sphere of art is not limited only to beauty and its so-called elements, but embraces everything in reality (in nature and in life) that is of interest to man not as a scholar, but as an ordinary man; that which is of common interest—such is the content of art. The beautiful, the tragic and the comical are only the three most definite elements of the thousands upon which interest in life depends, and to enumerate these would mean enumerating all the feelings, all the strivings that stir a man's heart. It is scarcely necessary to adduce more detailed proof of the correctness of our conception of the content of art; therefore, although another, a narrower, definition of content is usually offered in aesthetics, our view predominates in actual fact, i.e., among the artists and poets. It constantly finds expression in literature and in life.[76] If it is deemed necessary to define beauty as the main, or to be more exact, the sole essential content of art,[77] the real reason for it is that the distinction between beauty as the object of art, and beauty of form, which is indeed an essential quality of every work of art, is only vaguely seen.[78] But this formal beauty, or unity of the idea and the image, of content and form, is not the special feature that distinguishes art from all other branches of human activity. A man's actions always have an aim, which constitutes the essence of his actions. The merits of our work are judged according to the degree to which it conforms to the aim we had set ourselves; all the works of man are judged according to the degree of perfection attained in their execution. This is a general law for handicraft, for industry, for scientific activity, etc. It also applies to works of art: the artist (consciously or unconsciously, it makes no difference) tries to reproduce for us a certain aspect of life; it goes without saying that the merits of his work will depend upon the way he has done his work. "A work of art strives for harmony between the idea and the image" no more and no less than does the shoemaker's craft, the jeweller's craft, calligraphy, engineering, moral resolve. "All work must be done well"—such is the meaning of the phrase "harmony between the idea and the image." Thus, 1) beauty as the unity of the idea and the image is by no means a characteristic feature of art in the sense that aesthetics attaches to this term; 2) "unity of the idea and the image" defines only the formal aspect of art and does not in the least apply to its content; it tells us *how* a thing should be done, but not *what* is being done. We have already ob-

served that the important word in this phrase is "image" —
it tells us that art expresses an idea not by means of abstract
concepts, but by means of a living, individual fact. When we
say "art is the reproduction of nature and of life" we say
the same thing: in nature and in life there are no abstract
beings; everything in them is concrete. A reproduction must
as far as possible preserve the essence of the thing reproduced; therefore, a work of art must contain as little of the
abstract as possible; everything in it must be, as far as possible, expressed concretely in living scenes and in individual
images. (Whether art can fully achieve this is quite another question. Painting, sculpture and music do achieve it;
poetry cannot always, and should not always, concern itself
too much with the plasticity of detail: it is enough if a poetical work is plastic on the whole; excessive concern for the
plastic finish of detail may disturb the unity of the whole
by bringing out its parts in too sharp relief, and what is
more important, will divert the artist's attention from the
most essential aspects of his work.) Beauty of form, which
is unity of the idea and the image, is the common attribute
not only of art (in the aesthetic sense of the term), but of
all of man's work, quite distinct from the idea of beauty as
the object of art, as an object of our joyous love in the
real world.[79] Confusion of beauty of form as an essential
quality of a work of art and beauty as one of the numerous
objects of art was one of the causes of sad abuses in art.
"The object of art is beauty," beauty at all costs, art has no
other content. What is the most beautiful thing in the world?
In human life—beauty and love; in nature—it is difficult to decide—there is so much beauty in it. And so, it
is necessary, appropriately and inappropriately, to fill
poetical works with descriptions of nature: the more there
is of this, the more beauty is there in our work. But beauty
and love are still more beautiful—and so (in most cases
inappropriately) love is in the forefront in plays, stories,
novels, etc. Inappropriate dilation on the beauty of nature
is not so harmful in a work of art; it can be skipped, for it
is stuck on the surface; but what is to be done with a love
plot? It cannot be ignored, for it is the basis to which everything is tied with Gordian knots, without it everything loses
coherence and meaning. Apart from the fact that the loving
couple, whether suffering or triumphant, makes thousands
of works frightfully monotonous, apart from the fact that

24*

N. G. CHERNYSHEVSKY

the vicissitudes of their love and the descriptions of beauty leave no room for essential details, this habit of depicting love, love, and eternal love, makes poets forget that life has other aspects, much more interesting for man in general. All poetry, and all life depicted in it, assumes a sort of sentimental, rosy hue; instead of seriously depicting human life very many works of art represent a too youthful (to refrain from using more exact epithets) view of life, and the poet usually appears to be a young, very young, lad whose stories are interesting only for people of the same mental or physiological age as himself. Lastly, this degrades art in the eyes of people who have emerged from the blissful period of early youth. Art seems to be a pastime, too sickly sentimental for grown-up people, and not without its dangers for young people. We do not by any means think that the poet ought to be prohibited from describing love; but aesthetics must demand that the poet should describe love only when he actually wants to do so. Why put love in the forefront when, properly speaking, not love, but some other aspects of life are dealt with? Why, for example, put love in the forefront in novels which, properly speaking, depict the life of a certain nation in a given epoch, or the life of certain classes of a nation? In works on history, psychology or ethnography, love is also dealt with, but only in its proper place, as is everything else. Walter Scott's historical novels are based on love adventures—but why? Was love the chief occupation of society and the chief motive force of events in the epochs described? "Walter Scott's novels are out of date"; but are not Dickens' novels appropriately and inappropriately filled with love; and George Sand's stories of rural life, which have nothing to do with love? "Write about what you want to write about" is a rule that the poet rarely dares to follow.[80] Love, appropriately or inappropriately,—this is the first harm that is inflicted on art by the conception that "the content of art is beauty." The second, closely connected with the first, is artificiality.[81] In our times people laugh at Racine and Madame Deshoulières, but it is doubtful whether modern art has left them far behind as regards simplicity, naturalness of the springs of action and genuine naturalness of dialogue. The division of dramatis personae into heroes and villains may to this day be applied to works of art in the pathetic category; how coherently, smoothly and eloquently these people speak! Monologues and dialogue in modern novels are not much less stilted than the monologues in pseudo-classical tragedies: "everything in works of art must be clothed in beauty"; one of the conditions of beauty is that all the details must develop out of the plot: so we are given such profoundly thought-out plans of action of the personages in novels and plays as persons in real life scarcely ever draw up; and if one of the personages takes an instinctive, thoughtless step, the author deems it necessary to justify it on the grounds of the essence of the personage's character, and the critics are displeased with the fact that "no motive is given for the action," as if an action is always prompted by individual character and not by circumstances and by the general qualities of the human heart.[82] "Beauty demands finished characters," so instead of living persons, diverse for all their typicalness, the dramatist or novelist gives us motionless statues. "Beauty in works of art demands finished dialogue," so instead of ordinary conversation we get artificial talk, in which the speakers, willy-nilly, betray their characters.[83] The consequence of this is the monotony of poetical works: the personages are all of the same pattern, events develop according to known recipes, it is evident from the first pages what will happen further on, and not only what will happen, but how it will happen. Let us, however, return to the question of the essential purpose of art.

The first and general purpose of all works of art, we have said, is to reproduce phenomena of real life that are of interest to man. By real life we, of course, mean not only man's relation to the objects and beings of the objective world, but also his inner life. Sometimes a man lives in a dream—in that case the dream has for him (to a certain degree and for a certain time) the significance of something objective. Still more often a man lives in the world of his emotions. These states, if they become interesting, are also reproduced by art. We mention this in order to show that our definition also takes in the imaginative content of art.

But we said above that art has another purpose besides reproduction, viz., to explain life. This is attainable to some degree by all arts; often it is sufficient to call attention to an object (which art always does) to explain its significance, or to enable people to understand life better. In this sense, art differs in no way from a statement about an object; the only difference here is that art achieves its purpose much better than a statement, particularly a learned statement: it is much easier for us to acquaint ourselves with an object, we begin to take an interest in it much more quickly, when it is presented to us in living form than when we get a dry reference to it. Fenimore Cooper's stories have done more to acquaint society with the life of savages than ethnographic narratives and arguments on the importance of studying this subject. But while all arts are able to point to new and interesting objects, poetry must of necessity point sharply and clearly to the essential features of an object. Painting reproduces an object in all its details, so does sculpture; but poetry cannot take in an excessive amount of detail and, of necessity leaving a great deal out of the picture, concentrates our attention on the features retained. This is pointed to as an advantage that poetic scenes have over reality; but every single word does the same to the object it designates. In the word (notion) too, all the casual things are left out and only the essential features of the object are retained. For the inexperienced mind the word that designates the object may be clearer than the object itself, but this clarity is only a concession.[84] We do not deny the relative utility of compendiums, but we do not think that Tappe's *Russian History*, which is very useful for juveniles, is better than Karamzin's *History*, of which it is an epitome.[85] An object or event may be more intelligible in a poetical work than in reality, but the only merit we recognize in this is the clear and vivid allusion to reality; we do not attach independent significance to it as something that could compete with the fullness of real life. We cannot refrain from adding that every prose narrative does the same as poetry.[86] The concentration of attention upon the essential features of an object is not the specific characteristic feature of poetry, but the common feature of all rational speech.[87]

The essential purpose of art is to reproduce what is of interest to man in real life.[88] But, being interested in the phenomena of life, man cannot but, consciously or unconsciously, pronounce judgment on them. The poet, or artist, being unable to cease to be a man, cannot, even if he wanted to, refrain from pronouncing judgment on the phenomena he depicts. This judgment is expressed in his work—this is another purpose of art, which places it among the moral activities of man. There are people whose judgment on the phenomena of life consists almost exclusively in that they betray an inclination for some aspects of reality and avoid others—there are people whose mental activity is sluggish.[89] The work of such a man—poet or artist— has no other purpose than that of reproducing his favourite aspect of life.[90] But if a man, whose mental activity is powerfully stimulated by the problems that are roused in his mind by his observation of life, is gifted with artistic talent, he will, in his works, consciously or unconsciously, express the striving to pronounce judgment on the phenomena that interest him (and his contemporaries, for a man who thinks cannot ponder over insignificant problems that interest nobody but himself). His paintings, or novels, poems and plays will present, or solve, the problems that arise out of life for the man who thinks; his works will be, as it were, essays on subjects presented by life.[91] This trend may find expression in all the arts (in painting, for example, we can point to pictures of social life and historical scenes), but it is developing chiefly in poetry, which provides the fullest opportunity to express a definite thought. In such a case,[92] the artist becomes a thinker, and works of art, while remaining in the sphere of art, acquire a scientific significance. It goes without saying that, in this respect, a work of art finds nothing corresponding to it in reality— but this applies only to form.[93] As regards content, as regards the problems presented or solved by art, they are all to be found in real life, only without premeditation, without arrière-pensée.* Let us suppose that a work of art develops the idea: "a temporary digression from the true path will not doom a strong nature," or: "one extreme calls forth another"; or that it depicts a man in conflict with himself; or, if you will, the conflict between passions and lofty strivings (we are pointing to different fundamental ideas that we have discerned in *Faust*)—does not real life provide cases where the same situation develops? Is not high wisdom obtained from the observation of life? Is not science simply the abstraction of life, the placing of life within a formula? Everything that is expressed by science and art is to be found in life, and to be found in its fullest and most perfect form, with all its living details, which

---

* Ulterior motive.—*Ed.*

usually contain the true meaning of the subject, and which are often not understood by science and art, and still more often cannot be embraced by them. In the events of real life everything is true, nothing is overlooked, there is not that one-sided, narrow view from which all the works of man suffer. As instruction, as learning, life is fuller, truer and even more artistic than all the works of scholars and poets. But life does not think of explaining its phenomena to us, it is not concerned with deducing axioms. In the works of science and art this is done. True, the deductions are not complete, the ideas are one-sided compared with what life presents; but they have been drawn for us by geniuses; without their aid our deductions would be still more one-sided, still poorer. Science and art (poetry) are a Handbuch for those who are beginning to study life; their purpose is to prepare the student for reading the original sources and later to serve as reference books from time to time. Science does not attempt to conceal this; nor do poets attempt to conceal this in their running comments on the essence of their works; aesthetics alone persists in asserting that art is higher than life and reality.

Connecting all that has been said, we get the following view on art: the essential purpose of art is to reproduce everything in life that is of interest to man. Very often, especially in poetical works, the explanation of life, judgment of its phenomena, also comes to the forefront. The relation of art to life is the same as that of history; the only difference in content is that history, while speaking of the life of mankind, is concerned mainly with factual truth, whereas art gives us stories about the lives of men in which the place of factual truth is taken by faithfulness to psychological and moral truth. The first function of history is to reproduce life; the second, which is not performed by all historians, is to explain it. By failing to perform the second function, the historian remains a mere chronicler and his work serves merely as material for the genuine historian, or as reading matter to satisfy curiosity. When performing this second function, the historian becomes a thinker and, as a consequence, his work acquires scientific merit. Exactly the same must be said about art. History does not set out to compete with real historical life; it admits that the pictures it paints are pale, incomplete, more or less incorrect, or at all events, one-sided. Aesthetics must admit that art too, and for the same reasons, must not even think of comparing itself with reality, and still less of excelling it in beauty.

But what becomes of creative imagination in such a view on art? What role is it accorded? We shall not go into the question of where, in art, imagination acquires the right to alter what the poet has seen and heard. That is clear from the aim of poetic creation, from which is demanded a true reproduction of a given aspect of life and not of some single case. We shall merely investigate the causes that necessitate the intervention of imagination as the ability to alter (by means of combination) the impressions of the senses and to create something new in form. We shall assume that the poet takes from the experience of his own life an event that is quite familiar to him (this does not often happen; usually, many extremely important details remain almost unknown and for the sake of coherence the story must be supplemented by the imagination). We shall also assume that the event taken is quite complete in artistic respects, so that the plain relation of it is a complete work of art, i. e., we shall take a case in which the intervention of combining imagination seems least necessary. No matter how good a memory one may have, it cannot retain all the details, especially those that are unimportant for the essence of the event; but many of them are needed for the artistic completeness of the story and must be borrowed from other scenes the poet remembers (for example, dialogue, descriptions of places, etc.). True, the addition of these details does not alter the event and, so far, the difference between the artistic narrative and the event related in it is only one of form. But the intervention of the imagination is not limited to this. In reality, the event overlapped other events only outwardly connected with it, there was no inherent connection between them. When we separate the event we have chosen from the other events and from unnecessary episodes, we find that this operation leaves new gaps in the living fullness of the story, and these, too, the poet must fill. But this is not all. Separation not only robs many moments of the event of living fullness, but often changes their character, and the event appears in the story different from what it was in reality. Or else, in order to preserve its essence, the poet is forced to *change* many of the details which have true meaning in the event

only under the actual circumstances that have been eliminated by the isolating narration.[94] As we see, the scope
of activity for the poet's artistic powers is little restricted
by our conception of the essence of art.[95] But the subject
of our investigation is art as objective production and not
as the subjective activities of the poet. It would therefore
be out of place to enumerate the poet's different relations
to the materials of his work. We have indicated one of these
relations, the one that is least favourable for the poet's independence, and have found that, in this respect too, our
view on the essence of art does not deprive the artist of the
essential character that belongs not to the poet or artist
in particular, but to man in general in all his activities —
of that most essential human right and quality to regard
objective reality only as a field for his activity.[96] Still wider scope for the intervention of combining imagination is
provided by other circumstances: for example, when a poet
is not quite familiar with the details of an event, having
learned of it (and of the personages involved) from the narratives of other people, narratives that are always one-
sided, erroneous and incomplete from the artistic point of
view, at all events, in the poet's own opinion.[97] It is not
that real life does not provide the phenomena that the poet or
artist wants to depict or does not provide in a much fuller
form than they can attain in works of art that necessitates
combination and alteration, but the fact that a picture of
real life does not belong to the same sphere of existence
as that to which real life belongs; the difference arises from
the fact that the poet does not possess the means that real
life possesses. When an opera is arranged for the pianoforte,
the greater and best part of the details and effects is lost;
much of it simply cannot be translated from the human voice,
or from a full orchestra, to the poor, wretched, lifeless
instrument that is to reproduce the opera, as far as that is
possible. Therefore, in rearranging the music much has to
be altered, much has to be added, not in the hope that the
piece will turn out better than it is in the original form, but
in order, to some extent, to make good the inevitable damage caused in rearranging the piece. It is not that the one who
rearranges rectifies the mistakes made by the composer, but
simply that he does not possess the means the composer possesses. Still greater is the difference between the means possessed by real life and those possessed by the poet. The trans-

lator of a poetical work from one language into another is obliged to some degree to alter the work he is translating; how, then, is it possible to avoid alteration when translating events from the language of life into the meagre, pale and lifeless language of poetry?

* * *

Defence of reality as against fantasy, the endeavour to prove that works of art cannot possibly stand comparison with living reality—such is the essence of this essay. But does not what the author says degrade art? Yes, if showing that art stands *lower* than real life in the artistic perfection of its works means degrading art.[98] But protesting against panegyrics does not mean disparagement. Science does not claim to stand higher than reality, but it has nothing to be ashamed of in that. Art, too, must not claim to stand higher than reality; that would not be degrading for it. Science is not ashamed to say that its aim is to understand and explain reality and then to use its explanation for the benefit of man. Let not art be ashamed to admit that its aim is to compensate man in case of absence of opportunity to enjoy the full aesthetic pleasure afforded by reality by, as far as possible, reproducing this precious reality, and by explaining it for the benefit of man.

Let art be content with its lofty, splendid mission of being a substitute for reality in case of its absence, and of being a textbook of life for man.

Reality stands higher than dreams, and essential purpose stands higher than fantastic claims.

* * *

The author's task was to investigate the question of the aesthetic relation of works of art to the phenomena of life, to test the correctness of the prevailing opinion that true beauty, which is regarded as the essential content of works of art, does not exist in objective reality, but is attained only by art. Inseparably connected with this question are the questions of the essence of beauty and the content of art. Investigation of the question of the essence of beauty has led the author to the conviction that beauty is life. After arriving at this conclusion it became necessary to investigate the concepts sublime and tragic, which according to the usual definition of beauty are elements of the latter,[99] and. we were forced to the conclusion that the sublime and the beautiful are not subsumed in art. This proved an important aid to the solution of the question of the content of art. But if beauty is life,[100] the question of the aesthetic relation of beauty in art to beauty in reality solves itself. Having arrived at the conclusion that art cannot owe its origin to man's dissatisfaction with beauty in reality, we had to ascertain what needs gave rise to art and to investigate its true purpose. The following are the chief conclusions to which this investigation brought us:

1) The definition of beauty as "the perfect manifestation of the general idea in the individual phenomenon" does not stand criticism; it is too broad, for this is the definition of the formal striving of all human activity.

2) The true definition of beauty is: "beauty is life." To man, a beautiful being is that being in which he sees life as he understands it; a beautiful object is an object that reminds him of life.

3) This objective beauty, or beauty in essence, must be distinguished from perfection of form, which consists in the unity of the idea and the form, or in the object fully answering its purpose.[101]

4) The sublime does not affect man by awakening in him the idea of the absolute; it hardly ever awakens it.

5) To man, the sublime is that which seems to be much bigger than the objects, or much more powerful than the phenomena, with which he compares it.

6) The tragic has no essential connection with the idea of fate or necessity. In real life the tragic is most often adventitious, it does not spring from the essence of preceding events. The form of necessity in which it is clothed by art springs from the ordinary principle of works of art: "the denouement must follow from the plot," or else is due to the artist's misplaced surrender to the conception of fate.

7) The tragic, according to the conception of recent European learning, is "the horrible in a man's life."

8) The sublime (and its element, the tragic) is not a variety of the beautiful; the idea of the sublime and the idea of the beautiful are two entirely different things; between them there is neither inherent connection nor inherent contrast.

9) Reality is not only more animated, but is also more perfect than imagination. The images of the imagination are only pale and nearly always unsuccessful imitations of reality.

10) Beauty in objective reality is fully beautiful.

11) Beauty in objective reality fully satisfies man.

12) Art does not spring from man's desire to make up for the flaws in beauty in reality.

13) Works of art are inferior to beauty in reality not only because the impression created by reality is more vivid than that created by works of art: works of art are inferior to beauty (and also inferior to the sublime, the tragic and the ridiculous) in reality also from the aesthetic point of view.

14) The sphere of art is not limited to the sphere of the beautiful in the aesthetic sense of the term, of beauty in its essence and not only in perfection of form; art reproduces everything that is of interest to man.

15) Perfection of form (unity of the idea and the form) is not the characteristic feature of art in the aesthetic sense of the term (the fine arts). Beauty as the unity of the idea and the image, or as the perfect realization of the idea, is the object of the striving of art in the broadest sense of the term, or of "accomplishment," the object of all man's practical activities.

16) The need that engenders art in the aesthetic sense of the term (the fine arts) is the same as that which is very clearly expressed in portrait painting. Portraits are not painted because the features of the living person do not satisfy us; they are painted in order to help us to remember the living person when he is not in front of our eyes and to give those who have not had occasion to see him some idea of what he is like. By its reproductions, art merely reminds us of what in life is of interest to us and strives to acquaint us to some degree with those interesting aspects of life which we have not had occasion to experience or see in reality.

17) Reproduction of life is the general characteristic feature of art and constitutes its essence. Works of art often have another purpose, viz., to explain life; they often also have the purpose of pronouncing judgment on the phenomena of life.[102]

THE AESTHETIC RELATION
OF ART TO REALITY

BY N. CHERNYSHEVSKY.
ST. PETERSBURG 1855 [1]

(Reviewed by the Author)

THE SYSTEMS of conceptions, out of which the prevailing aesthetic ideas developed, have now given way to other
conceptions of the world and of human life, which, less
seductive to the imagination, perhaps, are more in conformity with the deductions[2] drawn from the strict, unprejudiced investigations of facts in the present state of development of the natural, historical and moral sciences.
The author of the book under review is of the opinion that,
in view of the close dependence of aesthetics upon our general conceptions of nature and of man, a change in these
conceptions should cause a change in the theory of art. We
do not undertake to decide to what degree his own theory,
which he offers in place of the old, is correct; time will
decide that, and Mr. Chernyshevsky himself admits that
"his exposition may be incomplete, inadequate and one-
sided." It must be conceded, however, that the prevailing
views on aesthetics, deprived by modern analysis of the
metaphysical foundation on which they had so self-confident-
ly towered at the end of the last and beginning of the present century, must either find new support or yield to other conceptions if they are not reconfirmed by a strict analysis. The author is firmly convinced that the theory of art
must acquire a new form — we are ready to assume that it will,
because it is difficult for a separate part of a general philosophical edifice to remain standing when the whole edifice
is being rebuilt. In what way must the theory of art change?
"Respect for real life, distrust of a priori hypotheses, even
though they tickle one's fancy, such is the character of the
trend that now predominates in science," he says, and he
thinks that "our aesthetic convictions should also be brought

into line with this." To achieve this aim, he first analyzes the former conceptions of the essence of beauty, the sublime and the tragic, the relation of imagination to reality, the superiority of art to reality, the content and essential purpose of art, or the need from which arises man's striving to create works of art. Discovering, as he thinks, that these conceptions do not stand criticism, he tries to deduce from an analysis of facts a new conception, which, in his opinion, is more in conformity with the general character of the ideas that are accepted by science in our times. We have already said that we do not undertake to decide how far the author's opinions are correct or not; we shall confine ourselves to an exposition of them and point to the flaws which appear to us to be most striking. Literature and poetry possess enormous importance for us Russians, far greater, it may be confidently stated, than they possess elsewhere, and for this reason we think that the problems the author deals with deserve the reader's attention.

But do they really deserve the reader's attention? It is quite permissible to doubt this, for the author himself is evidently not quite sure about it. He deems it necessary to justify his choice of subject for investigation:

"This is the age of monographs," he says in his preface, "and my work is liable to the reproach of being out of date. Why did the author choose as the subject for research such a general, such a wide question as the aesthetic relation of art to reality? Why did he not choose some specific question, as is most often done nowadays?" And he answers in justification. "The author is of the opinion that it is useless to discuss fundamental problems of science only when nothing new and fundamental can be said about them. But when material for a new view of the fundamental problems of our particular science is available, these fundamental ideas can and must be expressed, *if it is still worth our while to discuss aesthetics.*"

We, however, think that the author either does not quite clearly understand the state of affairs, or that he is dissembling. We think he should have followed the example of the author who wrote the following preface to his works:

"My works are old rubbish, for the subjects—the essence of which I reveal—are not worth discussing nowadays; but as many people cannot find a more lively occupation

N. G. CHERNYSHEVSKY

for their minds, the edition we have undertaken will be of
some use for them."*

Had Mr. Chernyshevsky dared to imitate this exemplary
candour, he might have said in his preface the following:
"I admit that there is no particular need to dilate on aesthetical problems in our times, when they stand in the background of science; but as many people are writing about subjects that have still less inner content, I have every right to
write about aesthetics, which is indisputably of some interest for the mind." He might also have said: "Of course,
there are sciences that are more interesting than aesthetics;
but I have not succeeded in writing anything about them;
nor are others writing about them; and since 'when a good
thing is not available, man is satisfied with an inferior
one' ("The Aesthetic Relation of Art to Reality," p. 86),**
you, dear reader, will have to be satisfied with 'The Aesthetic Relation of Art to Reality.'" Such a preface would have
been frank and excellent.

Aesthetics may indeed be of some interest for the mind
because the solution of its problems depends upon the
solution of other, more interesting, problems, and we hope
that everybody who is familiar with good works on this
science will agree with this. But Mr. Chernyshevsky deals
too fleetingly with the points at which aesthetics comes
into contact with the general system of conceptions of nature and of life. When setting forth the prevailing theory
of art, he scarcely says anything about the general principles on which it is based, but examines each leaf only of that
branch of the "tree of thought" (following the example of
some of our home-grown thinkers,[3] we use an expression
in "A Lay of Igor's Host") which interests him especially
without telling us what kind of a tree it is that grew this
branch, although it is known that such reticence is not in
the least conducive to clarity. Similarly, in expounding
his own aesthetic conceptions, he supports them only with
facts taken from the sphere of aesthetics without setting
forth the general principles which, applied to aesthetical
problems, serve as the basis for his theory of art, although
it, to use his own expression, only "brings aesthetical problems into line with the modern conceptions of science con-

---

* From Feuerbach's preface to his *Collected Works* (1845).—*Ed.*
** In this volume, p. 364.—*Ed.*

cerning life and the world." This, in our opinion, is a grave
defect and is the reason why the inner meaning of the author's theory may seem obscure to many, and why the ideas
he develops may seem to be the author's own, although, in
our opinion, to this he cannot have the slightest claim:
he himself says that although the old theory of art, which
he rejects, is to this day adhered to in textbooks on aesthetics, the view he accepts "constantly finds expression in literature and in life" (p. 92).* He himself says: "Our conception of art springs from the views accepted by the latest German aesthetics" (and rejected by the author) "and arises
from them through the dialectical process, the trend of
which is determined by the general ideas of modern science.
Thus, it is most closely connected with two systems of ideas—
with that of the beginning of the present century, on the
one hand, and that of the last" (*two—we will add*) "decades
on the other." (P. 90.)** How is it possible, after this, we
ask, to refrain from setting forth these two systems of the
general conception of the world, to the degree that this
is necessary? This is a blunder that is totally inexplicable
to anybody except the author, perhaps, and, at all events,
it is a very palpable one.

In undertaking the task of merely setting forth the
author's theory, the reviewer must do what the author should
have done, but did not do in order to make his meaning clear.

Lately, a distinction is being rather often drawn between a man's "real, earnest and true" wishes, strivings and
needs and his "fictitious, imaginary, idle ones, to which the
man who expresses, or imagines he possesses, attaches no real
significance." As an example of a man in whom fictitious,
imaginary strivings that are in fact totally alien to him are
very strongly developed, we can point to that excellent person Grushnitsky in *A Hero of Our Time*. This amusing
Grushnitsky tries with all his might to feel what he does
not feel at all, to achieve that which, in essence, he does
not need at all. He wants to be wounded, he wants to be a
common soldier, he wants to be unhappy in love, to fall
into despair, and so forth—he cannot live without these,
to him, seductive qualities and blessings. But what grief

---

* In this volume, p. 370.—*Ed.*
** In this volume, p. 368.—*Ed.*

fate would inflict on him if it were to take it into its head
to fulfil his wishes! He would renounce love for ever
if he thought that any young woman could fail to fall in
love with him. He, in his heart, is tormented by the fact
that he is not yet an officer, he goes into raptures when he
receives news of his desired promotion and contemptuously
casts off the uniform of which he had pretended to be so
proud. There is a bit of the Grushnitsky in every man. In
general, a man who lives in a false environment has many
false desires. Formerly, no attention was paid to this important circumstance, and as soon as it was observed that a
man was inclined to dream, no matter what of, the whim
of a morbid or idle fancy was at once proclaimed a fundamental and inalienable requirement of human nature, necessarily demanding satisfaction. And what inalienable requirements were not found in man! All man's desires and strivings
were proclaimed boundless and insatiable. Today this is
done with greater circumspection. Today, an examination
is made of the circumstances under which certain desires
develop and the circumstances under which they abate. As
a result, a very modest but very consoling fact has been revealed, viz., in essence, the requirements of human nature
are very moderate. They reach fantastically enormous dimensions only as a consequence of extremes, only when a man
is morbidly excited by unfavourable circumstances, when
anything like moderate satisfaction is completely lacking.
Even man's passions "seethe like a turbulent flood" only
when they encounter too many obstacles: but when a man is
in favourable circumstances his passions cease to seethe and,
while retaining their force, they lose their disorderliness,
their all-devouring greed and destructiveness. A healthy
man is not lustful. Mr. Chernyshevsky quotes, in passing,
and in different places, several examples illustrating this.
The opinion that "man's desires are limitless," he says, is
false in the sense in which it is usually understood, viz.,
that "no reality can satisfy them." On the contrary, a man
is satisfied not only "with the best that can exist in reality,"
but also with a rather modest reality. A distinction must
be drawn between what is actually felt and what is only
said. Dreaming whips up desire to fever heat only
when wholesome, even though fairly simple, food is lacking. This is a fact, proved by the whole course of human
history and experienced by every man who has seen life

and has watched himself. It is a particular case of the general law of human life that passions assume abnormal development only as a consequence of the abnormal conditions of the one who gives way to them, and only when the natural and, in essence, fairly moderate needs from which a given passion arises have been too long denied calm and by no means titanic satisfaction. It is beyond doubt that the human organism does not need and cannot stand excessively turbulent and excessively intense satisfactions. It is also beyond doubt that the desires of a healthy man are commensurate with the powers of his organism. It must be noted, however, that here "health" includes moral health. Fever and high temperature occur when a man has caught cold; passion, moral fever, is also a symptom of illness, and it also affects a man when he comes under the destructive influence of unfavourable circumstances. One need not go far in search of examples: passion, chiefly "love" as it is described in hundreds of trashy novels, loses its romantic turbulence as soon as the obstacles to it are removed and the loving couple is joined in matrimony. Does this mean that husband and wife love each other less than they loved in the turbulent period when obstacles prevented them from coming together? Not at all; everybody knows that if a husband and wife live in harmony and happily, their mutual attachment grows year after year and at last reaches the stage when they literally "cannot live without each other," and if it so happens that one of them dies, life for the other loses its charm forever, loses it in the literal and not only in the figurative sense of the word. And yet, there is nothing turbulent about this extremely intense love. Why? Only because there are no obstacles in its way. We have fantastic, immoderate dreams only when our reality is too stinting. Lying on bare boards, a man is sometimes given to dreaming of an eiderdown quilt (continues Mr. Chernyshevsky); a healthy man who sleeps not on a luxurious, but on a sufficiently soft and comfortable bed has no occasion and no inclination to dream of eiderdown quilts. If a man is obliged to live in the tundras of Siberia he may dream of magic gardens with trees, unseen on earth, with coral branches, emerald leaves and ruby fruit; but on transferring his residence to a place no more remote than, say, the Kursk, or Kiev, gubernia, and being able to roam to his heart's content in a modest but tolerable orchard with apple, cherry

25*

and pear trees, the dreamer will forget not only about the gardens in the *Arabian Nights*, but also about the lemon groves of Spain. The imagination builds castles in the air when the dreamer lacks not only a good house, but even a tolerable hut. It takes free rein when the feelings are not engaged; the absence of satisfactory conditions in real life is the source of life in imagination. But as soon as reality becomes at all tolerable, all the dreams of the imagination become pale and dull. The indisputable fact that we forget and abandon the seemingly most luxurious and gorgeous dreams as unsatisfactory as soon as the phenomena of real life surround us, serves as indubitable proof that the dreams of the imagination are far less beautiful and attractive than what we find in reality. This concept constitutes one of the fundamental differences between the obsolete world out-look, under whose influence the transcendental systems of science arose, and science's present-day conception of nature and of life. Science today recognizes that reality is far superior to dreams, for it has learned how pale and unsatisfactory is life that is engrossed in the dreams of the imagination. Formerly, it was accepted without strict investigation that the dreams of the imagination are su-perior to and more attractive than the phenomena of real life. In the sphere of literature, this former preference for the dreamy life gave rise to romanticism.[4]

But, as we have said, no attention was formerly paid to the difference between fantastic dreams and the true strivings of human nature, between the requirements, the satisfaction of which is really demanded by the mind and heart of man, and the airy castles which a man would not want to live in even if they existed, because he would find in them nothing but emptiness, hunger and cold. The dreams of idle fantasy look gorgeous; the desires of a healthy mind and a healthy heart are very moderate. Therefore, until analysis showed how pale and pitiful were the dreams of the imagination which revelled in empty space, thinkers were deceived by the artificial splendour of their fictitious colours and put them higher than the real objects and phe-nomena that man meets with in life. But are the powers of our imagination really so feeble that they cannot rise higher than the objects and phenomena that we know of from experience? One can easily convince oneself that this is so. Let any person try to picture to himself, for example,

a beautiful woman whose features are better than those of
the beautiful women he has seen in reality. Whoever does
this will see, if he carefully examines the images his imagination tries to create, that these images are not in the least
better than the faces he can see with his own eyes, that
he can only say to himself: "I want to picture to myself a
human face more beautiful than the living faces I have
seen," but he cannot picture to himself any face more beautiful than they are. The imagination, when it wants to
rise above reality, will picture only extremely vague, indistinct features in which we can discern nothing definite
or really attractive. The same thing happens in all other
cases. I cannot, for example, clearly and definitely picture
to myself food more delicious than the dishes I have had
occasion to eat in reality, or light brighter than that which
I have seen in reality (thus, we Northerners, according
to the common opinion of all travellers, cannot have the
slightest idea of the dazzling light that pervades the atmosphere in tropical countries); we cannot picture to ourselves
anything more beautiful than the beauty we have seen,
nor any pleasure higher than those we have enjoyed in real
life. Mr. Chernyshevsky expresses this idea, but only casually, in passing, without developing it adequately: the
power of creative imagination, he says, is very limited;
it can only build up objects out of heterogeneous parts
(for example, picture a horse with wings), or magnify the
size of an object (for example, an eagle the size of an elephant); but we cannot picture anything more intense (i.e.,
more beautiful, brighter, more animated, more charming,
etc.), than what we have seen or experienced in real life.
I can picture the sun being much bigger than it appears to
be in reality, but I cannot picture it being brighter than it
appears to me in reality. Similarly, I can picture a man being taller, stouter, etc., than the men I have seen, but I
cannot picture a face more beautiful than those I have had
occasion to see in reality. Nevertheless, one can say whatever
one pleases; one can say: iron gold, warm ice, sweet bit-
terness, and so forth. True, our imagination cannot picture
warm ice, or iron gold, and therefore these remain empty
phrases, meaningless to the mind; but if we pay no attention to the circumstance that such idle phrases remain inaccessible to the imagination which vainly tries to picture
the objects they refer to, then, by confusing words with

pictures that are accessible to the mind, one might think
that the "dreams of the imagination are much richer, fuller
and more gorgeous than reality."

It was this mistake that led to the opinion that fantastic (absurd and, therefore, obscure to the imagination
itself) dreams must be regarded as man's true requirements.
All have been high-flown, but, in essence, meaningless word-
combinations that were invented by the idle imagination
and proclaimed as being highly attractive for a man, although, actually, he simply amuses himself with them out
of sheer idleness and does not perceive any clear meaning
in them. It was even proclaimed that reality is empty and
insignificant compared with these dreams. Indeed, what
a wretched thing a real apple is compared with the diamond
and ruby fruits in Aladdin's gardens, what wretched things
real gold and real iron are compared with golden iron,
that wonderful metal that is as bright and free from rust
as gold, and as cheap and hard as iron! How wretched is
the beauty of living people, our kinfolk and friends, compared with the beauty of the wonderful beings that inhabit
the ethereal world, those inexpressibly, inconceivably beautiful sylphs, houris, peris, and the like! How can one refrain from saying that reality is insignificant compared with
the dreams of the imagination? But one thing is lost sight
of here: we simply cannot picture these houris, peris and
sylphs to ourselves otherwise than as possessing the ordinary
features of real people. However much we may command our
imagination: "show me something more beautiful than man,"
it shows us man and nothing but man, although it boasts
that it is not showing man, but a more beautiful being;
or, if it labours to create something independent, something that has nothing corresponding to it in reality, it
drops from complete exhaustion after showing us a nebulous,
pale and indefinite phantom in which absolutely nothing
can be discerned. This has been noted by science lately,
and it is recognized as a fundamental fact in science
and in all the other spheres of human activity, that a man
cannot imagine anything higher or better than what he
meets with in reality. And what you don't know of, what
you have not the slightest idea of, you cannot wish for.

Until this important fact was recognized, people believed in what fantastic dreams "told" in the literal sense
of the word, without investigating whether there was any

meaning in what they told, whether they presented anything resembling a definite image, or were just empty words. Their high-flown language was taken as a guarantee of the superiority of these empty phrases to reality, and all human requirements and strivings were attributed to the striving for nebulous and totally meaningless phantoms. That was the period of idealism in the broadest sense of the term.

Among the phantoms that were introduced into science in this way was the phantom of fantastic perfection: "man is satisfied only with the absolute, he demands the absolutely perfect." Again, in Mr. Chernyshevsky's work we find in a number of places brief and fleeting remarks on this. The opinion that man must always have "perfection," he says (p. 39)* is a fantastic one, if by "perfection" is meant (and it is so meant) an object that possesses all the possible virtues and is free from all the flaws which an idle man with a cold or satiated heart, and with nothing better to do, may try to find. No, he says, in another place (p. 48)** man's practical life convinces us that he seeks only approximate perfection, which, strictly speaking, should not be called perfection. Man seeks only that which is "good," he does not seek "perfection." Only abstract mathematics demands perfection; even applied mathematics is satisfied with approximate calculations. The quest for perfection in any sphere of life whatsoever is prompted by abstract, morbid, or idle fantasy. We want to breathe pure air; but do we notice that absolutely pure air never exists anywhere? It always contains poisonous carbon dioxide and other noxious gases, but in such small quantities that they do not affect our organism and therefore do not in the least inconvenience us. We want to drink pure water, but the water in rivers, brooks and springs always contains mineral admixtures—if they are there in small quantities (as is always the case in good water) they do not mar our pleasure when we quench our thirst with water. As for absolutely pure (distilled) water, it is even unpleasant to the taste. These examples are too materialistic? Let us quote others: would anybody think of saying that a man who does not know *everything* is ignorant? No, we do not even look for

---

* In this volume, p. 317.—*Ed.*
** In this volume, p. 326.—*Ed.*

a man who knows *everything*; we expect a learned man to know all that is *essential*, and that he should know *many* (although by no means *all*) details. Are we dissatisfied with a history, for example, in which not absolutely all problems are explained, not absolutely all details are given, in which not absolutely all the author's views and statements are correct? No, we are satisfied, extremely satisfied, with a book in which the *chief* problems are solved, in which the most essential details are given, in which the author's *principal* opinions are correct, and in which there are *very few* wrong or inadequate explanations. In short, the requirements of human nature are satisfied by the "tolerable"; fantastic perfection is sought only by idle fantasy. Our senses, our mind and heart know nothing about it; and even fantasy only utters empty phrases about it; it, too, has no living, definite conception of it.

Thus, science has lately recognized the necessity of drawing a strict distinction between the true requirements of human nature, which seek, and have a right to find, satisfaction in real life, and fictitious, imaginary requirements, which remain, and must remain, idle dreams. In Mr. Chernyshevsky's work we several times find fleeting references to this necessity, and in one place he even develops this idea somewhat. "An artificially developed man" (i.e., one who has been corrupted by his unnatural position among other men) "has many artificial requirements, so perverted as to be false and fantastic, which cannot be fully satisfied because in essence they are not the requirements of his nature, but the desires prompted by a distorted imagination, which it is almost impossible to please without earning the ridicule and contempt of the very man whom we strive to please, for he himself feels instinctively that his requirements are not worth pleasing." (p. 82.)*

But if it is so important to distinguish between the fictitious, imaginary strivings,—which are doomed to remain the vague dreams of idle or morbidly excited fantasy—and the real and legitimate requirements of human nature, which necessarily demand satisfaction, by what sign is it possible unerringly to draw this distinction? Who is to be the judge in this important case? Man himself, his life, pronounces judgment; "practice," that unfailing

---

* In this volume, p. 360.—*Ed*.

touchstone of all theory, must be our guide here too. We see that some of our desires joyously rush to meet satisfaction, make a man exert all his efforts to find realization for them in real life—these are the true requirements of human nature. Other desires, on the contrary, fear contact with real life, timidly try to hide from it in the abstract realm of dreams—these are the fictitious, false desires which do not need fulfilment, which are seductive only because they will not be satisfied, for if they were to appear in the "broad daylight" of life they would betray their hollowness and unfitness for actually answering the requirements of human nature and the conditions under which man can enjoy life. "Deeds are the truth of thought." Thus, for example, deeds show whether a man is right when he thinks and says that he is brave, noble and truthful. A man's life reveals his nature; it, too, reveals his strivings and desires. You say that you are very hungry? Very well, we shall see whether you will be finical at table. If you refuse the common dishes and wait until the turkey and truffles are ready, it will show that not your stomach but your tongue is hungry. You say that you love science, but that will be proved by whether you are studying it or not. You think that you love art? That will be proved by whether you read Pushkin often, or whether his works lie on your table only for show, by whether you visit your picture gallery often—whether you go there alone and not only with your guests—or whether you have collected the pictures only in order to boast to others, and to yourself, about your love for art. Practice is the great exposer of deception and self-deception not only in practical matters, but also in matters of feeling and thought. And that is why science accepts it today as an essential criterion of all controversial points. "What is a matter of controversy in theory is fully settled by the practice of real life."

But these concepts would remain indefinite for many people if we did not mention here what the words "reality" and "practice" mean in present-day science. Reality embraces not only inanimate nature, but also human life, not only the present, but also the past, insofar as it has expressed itself in deeds, and also the future, insofar as it is prepared by the present. The deeds of Peter the Great belong to reality; Lomonosov's odes belong to it no less than his mosaic pictures. Only the idle words of people who say: "I want to be a painter," but who do not study painting, who say: "I want to be a poet," but who do not study man and nature, do not belong to reality. Thought is not the antithesis of reality, because thought is engendered by reality and strives to realize it, and is therefore an integral part of reality. But idle dreaming, which is engendered by idleness and remains the pastime of people who are fond of sitting with their arms folded and their eyes shut, is the antithesis of reality. Similarly, "practical life" also embraces not only man's material, but also his intellectual and moral activities.

This, perhaps, has now made clear the difference between the old, transcendental systems, which, believing in fantastic dreams, said that man everywhere seeks the absolute and not finding it in real life rejects the latter as unsatisfactory, the systems which judge reality on the basis of the nebulous dreams of the imagination, and the new views, which, recognizing the impotence of imagination that abstracts itself from reality, are guided in their judgment of the intrinsic value for man of his various desires by the facts supplied by man's real life and activity.

Mr. Chernyshevsky fully accepts the present-day trend in science as correct, and seeing, on the one hand, the unsoundness of the former metaphysical systems, and on the other, their inseverable connection with the prevailing theory of aesthetics, he deduces from this that the prevailing theory of art must give way to another theory that is more in conformity with science's new conceptions of nature and human life. But before setting forth his conceptions, which are only the application of the general views of the new times to aesthetic problems, we must explain the relations that bind the new views with the old in science in general. We often see the continuators of a scientific work turning against their predecessors whose work had served as the starting point of their own work. Thus, Aristotle looked with hostile eyes upon Plato, and Socrates infinitely belittled the Sophists, whose work he continued. Many examples will also be found in modern times. But sometimes we meet with gratifying cases when the founders of a new system clearly perceive the connection between their opinions and the ideas which had been expressed by their predecessors, and modestly call themselves the latter's disciples. When exposing the inadequacy of their predecessors' con-

ceptions, they nevertheless clearly say how much these
conceptions had helped to develop their own ideas. Such,
for example, was Spinoza's attitude towards Descartes.
It must be said to the credit of the founders of present-
day science that they regard their predecessors with rever-
ence and almost with filial love; they fully recognize their
genius and the nobility of their doctrines, in which they
point to the germs of their own views. Mr. Chernyshevsky
is aware of this and follows the example of the people whose
ideas he applies to aesthetical problems. His attitude towards the system of aesthetics, the inadequacy of which
he tries to prove, is by no means hostile; he admits that it
contains the germ of the theory that he himself is trying
to build, that he is merely developing extremely important
elements that are also to be found in the old theory, but
in opposition to other conceptions to which that theory attached greater importance and which seem to him to be unable
to stand criticism. He constantly tries to show that there
is a close kinship between his system and the former one,
although he does not conceal the fact that there is an important difference between them. This he definitely states
in a number of passages, of which we shall quote one: "The
relation of my conception of the sublime to the old definition of it which I reject" (he says on p. 21)* "is exactly
the same as the relation of my definition of the beautiful
is to the old view which I refute—in both cases, what
was formerly regarded as a specific and secondary characteristic and was hidden from view by other concepts, which
I reject as accessory, is raised to the degree of a general
and essential principle."

        In expounding Mr. Chernyshevsky's theory of aesthet-
ics, the reviewer will not express a final judgment on the
correctness or incorrectness of the author's ideas from the
purely aesthetical aspect. The reviewer has studied aesthetics only as a part of philosophy and therefore leaves
Mr. Chernyshevsky's particular ideas to the judgment of
those who can thoroughly judge them from the particular
aesthetical point of view which the reviewer does not hold.
But it seems to him that the author's theory of aesthetics
is important chiefly as the application of general views to
the problems of a particular science, and he therefore thinks

---

* In this volume, p. 300.—*Ed.*

that he will be examining the essence of the subject if he
examines the degree to which the author has applied them
correctly. The reviewer also thinks that this criticism from
the general point of view will be of greater interest to the
reader because, for the layman, aesthetics, as such, is of
interest only as a part of a general system of views of nature
and of life. Some readers may think that this entire essay
is too abstract, but the reviewer begs them not to judge
only by the surface. Abstractness appears in different forms:
sometimes it is dry and barren, but sometimes, on the
contrary, it is sufficient to pay attention to the ideas that
are expounded in an abstract form to be able in many cases
to apply them in real life. The reviewer is firmly convinced
that the ideas he has set forth above belong to the latter
category. He says this frankly, because they are the ideas
of science and not his private ideas; he has merely assimilated them and can therefore extol them, just as the
follower of a certain school can extol the system he has accepted without allowing his own vanity to intervene in
the matter.

In expounding Mr. Chernyshevsky's theory, however,
we will have to change the order followed by the author;
he, like the textbooks on aesthetics of the school that he
refutes, first examines the idea of the beautiful, then the
ideas of the sublime and the tragic, then engages in a criticism of the relation of art to reality, then discusses the
essential content of art, and lastly, he discusses the needs
from which it arises, or, the aims the artist achieves in his
works. This order is perfectly natural in the prevailing
theory of aesthetics because the conception of the essence
of the beautiful is the fundamental conception of the entire
theory. But it is not so in Mr. Chernyshevsky's theory. The
fundamental conception in his theory is the relation of art
to reality, and therefore, the author should have started
with that. By following an order borrowed from another
system alien to his own, the author, in our opinion, committed a grave mistake and destroyed the logical sequence of
his exposition. He was obliged, first, to discuss several
particular elements of the numerous elements which in his
opinion make up the content of art, then the relation of
art to reality, then, again, the content of art in general,
and then the essential purpose of art as determined by its
relation to reality. Thus, kindred problems are separated

by others, extraneous to the solution of the former. We shall take the liberty to rectify this mistake and set forth the author's ideas in an order that better answers the requirements of systematic sequence.

Proclaiming the absolute as the aim of man's desires, and placing the human desires that cannot find satisfaction in reality higher than the modest desires that can be satisfied by the objects and phenomena of the real world, the prevailing theory applies this general view, by which it explains the origin of all man's intellectual and moral activities, also to the origin of art, the content of which, according to this theory, is "beauty." The beauty that man meets with in reality, it says, suffers from serious flaws which mar it. But our aesthetic sense seeks perfection; therefore, to satisfy the demand of the aesthetic sense which cannot find satisfaction in reality, our imagination is roused to create a new beauty that will be free from the flaws that mar beauty in nature and in life. These works of creative imagination find realization in works of art that are free from the flaws that mar beauty in reality and, therefore, properly speaking, only works of art are truly beautiful, whereas the phenomena of nature and real life possess only illusory beauty. Thus, beauty created by art stands much higher than what seems (only seems) to be beauty in reality.

The sharp criticism to which beauty represented by reality is subjected with the object of exposing the numerous flaws that mar it conforms this thesis.

Mr. Chernyshevsky places reality above the dreams of the imagination and, therefore, cannot share the opinion that beauty created by the imagination stands higher than the beauty of the phenomena of reality. In this, applying his fundamental convictions to this particular question, he will be supported by all those who share these convictions, and he will be opposed by all those who adhere to the old opinion that imagination can rise above reality. Agreeing with Mr. Chernyshevsky's general scientific convictions, the reviewer must also admit the correctness of his particular deduction that the beauty of reality stands higher than the creations of the imagination realized by art.

But this must be proved, and so, to perform this duty, Mr. Chernyshevsky first examines the reproaches levelled at beauty in living nature and strives to prove that the flaws which the prevailing theory blames it for are not always to be found in it, and when they are found, they are not of such marring enormity as this theory believes. Then he inquires whether works of art are free from these flaws and strives to prove that all the reproaches levelled at beauty in living reality also apply to works of art, and that nearly all these flaws are cruder and more glaring than those in the beauty which living reality provides. From criticism of art in general he passes to an analysis of the separate arts and also argues that not one of the arts— neither sculpture, painting, music nor poetry—can produce works of such beauty as cannot be found in corresponding beautiful phenomena in reality, and that not one of the arts can produce works equal to the beauty of corresponding phenomena in reality. But here too we must observe that the author is again guilty of a very grave oversight in enumerating and refuting only the reproaches levelled against beauty in reality by Vischer, and in failing to supplement them with those expressed by Hegel. True, Vischer's criticism of beauty in living reality is fuller and more detailed than Hegel's, but, notwithstanding its brevity, in Hegel's criticism we find two reproaches which are forgotten by Vischer, but which are extremely profound—the Ungeistigkeit and Unfreiheit (unspiritualness, unconsciousness, or senselessness, and unfreeness) of all beauty in nature.* It must be added, however, that this incompleteness of exposition, for which the author should be blamed, is not detrimental to the essence of the views he advocates, because the reproaches he forgot to mention can be easily deflected from beauty in reality and turned against beauty in art by the very same means, and almost by the very same facts, which Mr. Chernyshevsky employs to counter the reproach of unpremeditatedness. Equally grave is another oversight: in his survey of the arts, the author forgot pantomime, dancing and the scenic art—he should have examined them, even though, like other aestheticians, he regards them as a branch of the plastic art (die Bildnerkunst), for the productions of these arts are entirely different in character from statues.[5]

---

* Cf. G. W. Hegel, *Vorlesungen über die Aesthetik*. (*Sämtl. Werke*, Stuttgart 1927, Bd. XII, S. 200-12, "Mangelhaftigkeit des Naturschönen").—*Ed.*

But if works of art stand lower than reality, on what grounds did the opinion arise that art is much superior to the phenomena of nature and of life? The author finds these grounds in the fact that man appraises an object not only by its intrinsic merit, but also by its rarity and the difficulty of obtaining it. Beauty in nature and in life appears without special effort on our part, and there is plenty of it. There are very few beautiful works of art, and they are produced with effort, sometimes with very great effort. Moreover, man is proud of them as the work of his own kind—in the same way as a Frenchman regards French poetry (which is really very feeble) as the best in the world, so, for man, art in general, becomes a special object of love because it is the work of man; bias for one's own speaks in favour of it. Furthermore, pandering to man's petty whims, to which nature and life pay no attention, and thereby degrading and deforming itself, art, together with the artists, like every flatterer, wins the love of very many. Lastly, we enjoy works of art whenever we want to, that is, whenever we are in the mood to contemplate their beauty and find pleasure in it, whereas beautiful phenomena in nature and in life very often occur when our attention and sympathy are taken up with other things and we do not notice them. The author, in addition, enumerates several other grounds for the exaggerated opinion of the merits of art. These explanations are not quite complete; the author forgot a very important circumstance, viz., that the opinion concerning the superiority of art to reality is the opinion of scholars, the opinion of a philosophical school, and not the judgment of the ordinary man who has no systematic convictions. It is true that the mass of the people appraise art very highly, higher, perhaps, than its intrinsic merit gives it a right to, and this bias is satisfactorily explained by the author; but the mass of the people do not place art higher than reality. They do not think of comparing their respective merits, but if they are compelled to give a clear answer, they will say that nature and life are more beautiful than art. Only aestheticians, and even then not of all schools, place art higher than reality, and this opinion, formed on the basis of special views which they alone hold, must be explained by those views. The aestheticians of the pseudo-classical school in particular preferred art to reality because they, in general, suffered from the malady of their

time and circle, viz., the artificiality of all their habits
and conceptions: not in art alone, but in all spheres of life,
they feared and shunned nature as it is, and loved nature
only "washed" and adorned. And the thinkers of the now
prevailing school place art, as something ideal, higher than
nature and life, which are real, because they, in general,
have not yet managed to free themselves from idealism —
in spite of flashes of genius in the direction of realism —
and in general, place ideal life higher than real life.

Let us return to Mr. Chernyshevsky's theory. He says:
if art cannot compare with reality in the beauty of its works,
its origin cannot be due to our dissatisfaction with the beauty
of reality and to our striving to create something better,
for if that were so, man would have abandoned art long
ago as fruitless, as something that totally failed to achieve
its aim. Therefore, the need which calls art into being
must be a different one from that which the prevailing theory believes it is. Up to this point, all those who share
Mr. Chernyshevsky's fundamental conceptions of human life
and nature, will probably say that his deductions are consistent. But we do not wish to decide whether the explanation he has found of the need that gave rise to art is entirely
correct; we shall present this deduction in his own words
in order to give the reader full opportunity to judge whether
it is correct or not.

The sea is beautiful; when looking at it we do not think of being
dissatisfied with it in the aesthetic sense; but not all people live near
the sea; many never have an opportunity to see it even once in their
lives, but they would like very much to see and admire it and seascapes are painted for them. Of course, it is much preferable to see the
sea itself rather than pictures of it; but when a good thing is not available, man is satisfied with an inferior one, when the genuine article
is not available a substitute will do. Those people who are able to
see and admire the real sea cannot always do so when they want to—
and they recall their vision of it. But the imagination is weak, it has
to be fostered and prompted—and in order to revive their recollections of the sea, in order to see it more vividly in their imagination,
they look at seascapes. This is the sole aim and object of very many
(the majority of) works of art: to give those people who have not been
able to enjoy beauty in reality the opportunity to acquaint themselves
with it at least to some degree; to serve as a reminder, to prompt
and revive recollections of beauty in reality in the minds of those
people who are acquainted with it by experience and love to recall
it. (We shall leave for the time being the expression: "beauty is the
essential content of art"; later on we shall substitute for the term "beauty" another term which, in our opinion, defines the content of art
more exactly and fully.) Thus, the first purpose of art is to reproduce

nature and life, and this applies to all works of art without exception. Their relation to the corresponding aspects and phenomena of reality is the same as the relation of an engraving to the picture from which it was copied, as the relation of a portrait to the person it represents. An engraving is made of a picture not because the latter is a bad one, but because it is a good one. Similarly, reality is reproduced in art not in order to eliminate flaws, not because reality as such is not sufficiently beautiful, but precisely because it is beautiful. In artistic respects, an engraving is not better than the picture from which it is copied, but much inferior to it. Similarly, works of art never attain the beauty and grandeur of reality; but the picture is unique, it can be admired only by those who go to the picture gallery which it adorns. The engraving, however, is sold in hundreds of copies all over the world, everybody can admire it whenever he pleases without leaving his room, without getting up from his couch, without throwing off his dressing gown. Similarly, a beautiful object in reality is not always accessible to everybody; reproductions of it (feeble, crude, pale, it is true, but reproductions for all that) in works of art make it always accessible to everybody. A portrait is made of a person not in order to eliminate the flaws in his features (what do we care about these flaws? We do not notice them, or if we do, we like them), but in order to give us the opportunity to admire that face even when it is not actually in front of our eyes. Such also is the aim and object of works of art in general. They do not rectify reality, do not embellish it, but reproduce it, serve as a substitute for it.

The author admits that his theory of reproduction is not new; a similar conception of art prevailed in the Greek world. Nevertheless, he asserts that his theory differs radically from the pseudo-classical imitation of nature theory, and he demonstrates this difference by quoting Hegel's criticism of the pseudo-classical conceptions: not one of Hegel's arguments, which are quite correct when brought against the imitation of nature theory, is applicable to the reproduction theory; therefore, the spirit of these two conceptions is also radically different. Indeed, the object of reproduction is to assist the imagination and not to deceive the senses as imitation wants to do, and it is not a mere pastime, like imitation, but work with a real aim.

There is no doubt that the reproduction theory, if it attracts attention, will be strongly attacked by the supporters of the creation theory. They will say that it leads to the daguerreotype copying of reality, against which they so often rise in arms. Anticipating this idea of slavish imitation, Mr. Chernyshevsky shows that in art, too, man cannot abandon his—we shall not say right, that is inadequate—his duty to employ all his moral and intellectual powers, including his imagination, even if he wants to do no more than make a faithful copy of an object. Instead of protesting against "daguerreotype copying," he adds, would it not be better to say that copying, like everything that man does, calls for understanding, for the ability to distinguish the essential from the unessential features? "Lifeless copying"—such is the usual phrase; but a man cannot make a true copy if the mechanism of his hand is not guided by living reason; it is impossible to make even a true facsimile of an ordinary manuscript if the meaning of the letters that are being copied is not understood.

But the words: "art is the reproduction of the phenomena of nature and of life" define only the method by which works of art are created. There still remains the question as to what phenomena art reproduces. After defining the formal principle of art it is necessary, in order to make the conception complete, to define also the real principle, or content, of art. Usually it is said that only beauty and its subsumed concepts—the sublime and the ridiculous—serve as the content of art. The author is of the opinion that this conception is too narrow, and he asserts that the sphere of art embraces everything in life and nature that is of interest to man. The proof of this thesis is little developed and is the most unsatisfactory part of Mr. Chernyshevsky's exposition. Evidently he regarded this point as being sufficiently clear and requiring scarcely any proof. We do not challenge the author's deduction; we are dissatisfied only with his exposition. He should have quoted far more examples in support of his idea that "the content of art cannot be squeezed into the tight frame of the beautiful, the sublime and the ridiculous." It would have been easy to find thousands of facts to prove that this idea is correct, and this increases the blame that rests on the author for troubling too little about this.

While, however, very many works of art have only one purpose—to reproduce phenomena of life of interest to man—very many, in addition to this fundamental purpose, acquire another and higher one, viz., to explain the phenomena that are reproduced. This must be said particularly about poetry, which, unable to embrace all details, leaves out of the scenes it depicts many minor things, and thereby focuses our attention on the few features that are retained. If the essential features are retained, as they ought to be, it helps to reveal the essence of the subject

to the inexperienced eye. Some people regard this as evidence
of the superiority of poetical scenes to reality, but the omission of all unessential details and the depicting of only the
main features is not a specific quality of poetry, but the
common feature of all rational speech, and the same also
occurs in plain narrative.[6]

Lastly, if the artist is a thinking individual he cannot
but have his own judgment of the phenomena he reproduces
and, willy-nilly, tacitly or avowedly, consciously or unconsciously, this judgment will be reflected in his work, which
thus acquires a third significance, viz., that of the judgment of the mind on the phenomena reproduced. This significance we find in poetry more often than in other arts.

Connecting all that has been said, says Mr. Chernyshevsky in conclusion, we get the following view on art: the
essential purpose of art is to reproduce everything in life
that is of interest to man. Very often, especially in poetical
works, the explanation of life, judgment of its phenomena,
also comes to the forefront. The relation of art to life is the
same as that of history; the only difference in content is
that history speaks of social life, whereas art speaks of
individual life; history speaks of the life of mankind, whereas art speaks of the life of a man (pictures of nature serve
only as the setting for phenomena of human life, or as an
allusion, a presentiment of these phenomena. As regards
difference in form, the author defines it as follows: history,
like every science, is concerned only with the clarity, in-
telligibility, of its scenes; art is concerned with the living
fullness of detail). The first function of history is to portray
the past. The second, which is not performed by all historians, is to explain it, to pronounce judgment on it. By
failing to perform the second function, the historian remains
a mere chronicler, and his work serves merely as material for
the genuine historian, or as reading matter to satisfy curiosity. When performing this second function, the historian
becomes a thinker, and his work acquires scientific merit.
Exactly the same must be said about art. When confining
himself to the reproduction of the phenomena of life, the
artist satisfies our curiosity or stimulates our recollections
of life. But if at the same time he explains and pronounces
judgment on the phenomena reproduced, he becomes a thinker and, in addition to its artistic merit, his work acquires
a still higher significance, viz., scientific significance.[7]

26*

From the general definition of the content of art it is natural to pass to the particular elements that make up that content, and we shall here set forth the author's views on the beautiful and the sublime, on the definition of the essence of which he disagrees with the prevailing theory because, on these points, it is out of harmony with the present stage in the development of science. He was obliged to analyze these concepts because, in their ordinary definition, they are the direct source of the idea that art stands higher than reality. In the prevailing theory they serve as links between the general idealist principles and the particular aesthetical ideas. The author was obliged to purge these important concepts of transcendental admixtures in order to bring them into harmony with the spirit of his own theory.

The prevailing theory has two formulas with which to express its conception of beauty: "beauty is unity between the idea and the image," and "beauty is the perfect manifestation of the idea in an individual object." The author is of the opinion that the latter formula speaks of the essential feature not of the idea of beauty, but of what is called a masterly work of art, or of all human activity in general, and that the first formula is too wide: it says that those objects are beautiful which are better than the others of their kind. But there are many kinds of objects that do not achieve beauty. He therefore regards both these prevailing expressions as not being quite satisfactory and was obliged to seek a more exact definition which he thinks he has found in the formula: "beauty is life; beautiful is that being in which we see life as it should be according to our conceptions; beautiful is the object which expresses life, or reminds us of life." We shall quote here a substantial part of the analysis on which this deduction rests, the analysis of the attributes of human beauty as understood by different classes of the people.

Among the common people, the "good life," "life as it should be," means having enough to eat, living in a good house, having enough sleep. But at the same time, the peasant's conception of life always contains the concept—work: it is impossible to live without work; indeed, life would be dull without it. As a consequence of a life of sufficiency, accompanied by hard but not exhausting work, the peasant maiden will have a very fresh complexion and rosy cheeks—the first attribute of beauty according to the conceptions of the common people. Working hard, and therefore being sturdily built, the peasant girl, if she gets enough to eat, will be buxom—this too is an essential attribute of the village beauty: rural people regard the "ethereal" society beauty as decidedly "plain," and are even disgusted by her, because they are accustomed to regard "skinniness" as the result of illness or of a "sad lot." Work, however, does not allow one to get fat: if a peasant girl is fat, it is regarded as a kind of malady, they say she is "flabby," and the people regard obesity as a defect. The village beauty cannot have small hands and feet, because she works hard—and these attributes of beauty are not mentioned in our songs. In short, in the descriptions of feminine beauty in our folk songs you will not find a single attribute of beauty that does not express robust health and a balanced constitution, which are always the result of a life of sufficiency and constant real hard, but not exhausting, work. The society beauty is entirely different. For a number of generations her ancestors have lived without performing physical work. With a life of idleness, little blood flows to the limbs. With every new generation the muscles of the arms and legs grow feebler, the bones become thinner. An inevitable consequence of all this are small hands and feet—they are the symptoms of the only kind of life the upper classes of society think is possible—life without physical work. If a society lady has big hands and feet, it is either regarded as a defect, or as a sign that she does not come from a good, ancient family. For the same reason, the society beauty must have small ears. Migraine, as is known, is an interesting malady, and not without reason. As a consequence of idleness, all the blood remains in the middle organs and runs to the brain. Even without that, the nervous system is strained as a result of the general weakening of the constitution. The inevitable consequences of this are prolonged headaches and various kinds of nervous disturbances. What is to be done? Even sickness is interesting, almost enviable when it is a consequence of the mode of life that we like. True, good health can never lose its value for a man, for even in a life of sufficiency and luxury, bad health is a drawback. Hence, rosy cheeks and the freshness of good health are still attractive also for society people; but sickliness, frailty, lassitude and languor also have the virtue of beauty in their eyes as long as it seems to be the consequence of a life of idleness and luxury. Pallid cheeks, languor and sickliness have still another significance for society people: peasants seek rest and tranquility, but those who belong to educated society, who do not suffer from material want and physical fatigue, but often suffer from ennui resulting from idleness and the absence of material cares, seek the "thrills, excitement and passions," which lend colour, diversity and attraction to an otherwise dull and colourless society life. But thrills and ardent passions soon wear a person out. How can one fail to be charmed by a beauty's languor and paleness when they are a sign that she has lived a "fast life."

> We like a fresh and heightened colour,
> The sign of youthful vigour;
> But far above it we prefer
> A melancholy pallor.

But while attraction for pale, sickly beauty is a sign of artificially corrupted taste, every truly educated man feels that true life is the life of the heart and mind. It leaves its impress on the expression of one's face, most clearly in one's eyes, and therefore, facial expression, of which little mention is made in folk songs, acquires enormous significance in the conception of beauty that prevails among educated people; and it often happens that a person looks beautiful to us only because he has beautiful, expressive eyes.... We must now examine the opposite side of the subject, we must investigate why a man is ugly. In referring to a person's ungainly figure people usually say he is "badly built." Deformity is a consequence of illness, or of accidents, particularly if they occur in the first period of the person's development. If life and its manifestations constitute beauty, quite naturally, illness and its consequences constitute ugliness. A person with an "ungainly figure" is also deformed, but to a lesser degree, and the causes of an "ungainly figure" are the same as those of deformity, only not so potent. A hump is a consequence of the unfortunate circumstances that accompanied the person's development. But round shoulders are also a hump, only to a lesser degree, and must have been caused by the same circumstances. In general, a man with an ungainly figure is a man to some degree deformed; his figure tells us not of life, not of a happy development, but of the hard sides of his development, of unfavourable circumstances. Let us pass from the man's general figure to his face. His face may be ugly in itself, or because of its expression. We dislike the "evil," "unpleasant" expression of his face because evil is venom that poisons our lives. But much more often it is not the expression, but the features of the face, that are "ugly." The features of a face are ugly when the facial bones are badly arranged, when the cartilage and muscles bear, more or less, the impress of deformation in the course of development, i.e., when the first period of a man's development took place in unfavourable circumstances.

The prevailing theory admits that beauty in the realm of nature is that which reminds us of man and of his beauty; it is obvious, therefore, that if beauty in man is life, then the same must be said about beauty in nature. The objection we have to Mr. Chernyshevsky's analysis of the conception of the essence of beauty is that the terms he employs leave it unclear as to whether man sees the connection between beauty and life instinctively or consciously. It goes without saying that in most cases it is instinctive. It is to be regretted that the author did not trouble to point to this important circumstance.

The difference between the author's conception of beauty and that which he rejects is very important. If beauty is "the perfect manifestation of the idea in an individual being", then there is no beauty in real objects, for the idea fully manifests itself only in the whole universe and cannot find complete realization in an individual object. From this it follows that beauty is introduced into reality only by our imagination, that, therefore, the true sphere of beauty is the sphere of imagination, and therefore, art, which realizes the ideals of the imagination, stands higher than reality and springs from man's striving to create beauty which he does not find in reality. On the other hand, from the conception proposed by the author, viz., "beauty is life," it follows that true beauty is the beauty of reality, that art (as the author believes) cannot create anything equal in beauty to the phenomena of the real world, and therefore, the origin of art is easily explained by the author's theory as we have set it forth above.

Criticizing the terms in which the concept of the sublime is defined in the prevailing system of aesthetics, viz., "the sublime is preponderance of the idea over the form" and "the sublime is that which rouses in us the idea of the infinite," the author arrives at the conclusion that these definitions are wrong. He is of the opinion that an object may create the impression of the sublime without in the least rousing the idea of the infinite. Therefore, the author is again obliged to seek another definition, and he thinks that all phenomena in the sphere of the sublime are embraced and explained by the following formula: "The sublime is that which is much bigger than anything with which we compare it." For example, he says, Kazbek is a magnificent mountain (although it does not seem to us to be boundless and infinite) because it is much bigger than the hills that we are accustomed to see. The Volga is a magnificent river because it is much wider than small rivers. Love is a sublime passion because it is much more intense than daily, petty calculations and intrigues. Julius Caesar, Othello and Desdemona are sublime personages because Julius Caesar is a greater genius than ordinary people, Othello loves and is jealous, and Desdemona loves much more intensely than ordinary people do.

From the prevailing definitions, which Mr. Chernyshevsky rejects, it follows that beauty and the sublime in the strict sense of the terms are not met with in reality, but are introduced into it only by our imagination. From Mr. Chernyshevsky's definitions it follows, on the contrary, that the beautiful and the sublime do actually exist in nature and in human life. But it also follows from it that the enjoyment of objects that possess these qualities depends directly upon the conceptions of the person concerned. Beautiful is that in which we see life that corresponds to *our* conceptions of life; the sublime is that which is much bigger than the objects with which *we* compare it. Thus, the objective existence of the beautiful and the sublime in reality is reconciled with man's subjective views.

The author also presents a new definition of the concept tragic, an extremely important branch of the sublime, in order to purge it of the transcendental admixture in which the prevailing theory enmeshes it, and which links it with the concept of fate, the intrinsic hollowness of which has now been proved by science. In conformity with the dictates of science, the author eliminated from the definition of the tragic all thought of fate or necessity, of inevitability, and defines the tragic simply as "that which is horrible in a man's life."[8]

The concept comical (vacuity, senseless form lacking content, or claiming content out of proportion to its insignificance) is developed in the prevailing theory in a way that corresponds to the character of modern science, so that the author has no need to alter it. The form in which it is usually expressed fully harmonizes with the spirit of his own theory. Thus, the task the author set himself, viz., to bring the fundamental concepts of aesthetics into line with the present development of science, has been carried out to the best of the author's ability, and he concludes his investigation with the following words:

Defence of reality as against fantasy, the endeavour to prove that works of art cannot possibly stand comparison with living reality—such is the essence of this essay. But does not what the author says degrade art? Yes, if showing that art stands *lower* than real life in the artistic perfection of its works means degrading art. But protesting against panegyrics does not mean disparagement. Science does not claim to stand higher than reality, but it has nothing to be ashamed of in that. Art, too, must not claim to stand higher than reality; that would not be degrading for it. Science is not ashamed to say that its aim is to understand and explain reality and then to use its explanation for the benefit of man. Let not art be ashamed to admit that its aim is to compensate man in case of absence of opportunity to enjoy the full aesthetic pleasure afforded by reality by, as far as possible, reproducing this precious reality, and by explaining it for the benefit of man.

This conclusion, in our opinion, is insufficiently developed. It still leaves for many people grounds for assuming that the significance of art is actually belittled by the rejection of fulsome praise of the absolute merit of its works, and by the substitution of the needs of man as its origin and aims for immeasurably lofty transcendental origin and aims. On the contrary, this is precisely what enhances the real significance of art, for this explanation gives it an unchallengeable and honourable place among the activities that benefit man; and to be of benefit to man means having the right to the highest respect of man. Man venerates that which serves to benefit him. He calls bread "father bread" because it is his food; he calls the earth "mother earth" because it feeds him. Father and mother! All the panegyrics in the world are nothing compared with these sacred names; all high-flown praise is hollow and empty compared with the sentiment of filial love and gratitude. Science too is deserving of this sentiment because it serves to benefit man. Art is deserving of it when it serves to benefit man. And it brings him many, many benefits, for the work of the artist, particularly of the poet worthy of the name, is a "textbook of life," as the author rightly calls it, and a textbook that is studied with pleasure by everybody, even by those who do not know of, or dislike, other textbooks. And art should be proud of this lofty, beautiful and beneficial significance it has for man.

We think that Mr. Chernyshevsky committed a very sad mistake in failing to develop in greater detail the idea of the practical purpose of art, of its beneficial influence on life and education. True, had he done so, he would have stepped beyond the limits of his subject, but sometimes such a digression is necessary in order to explain the subject methodically. As it is, notwithstanding the fact that Mr. Chernyshevsky's whole essay breathes respect for art because of its great importance for life, some people may refuse to notice this sentiment because a few pages of the essay are not especially devoted to it. They may think that he does not appreciate the beneficial influence of art on life as it deserves to be appreciated, or that he worships everything that represents reality. What Mr. Chernyshevsky thinks about this, or what others may think about him in this connection, makes no difference: he has left his ideas incompletely expressed and must answer for this neglect. We, however, must explain what he forgot to explain in order to characterize the attitude of present-day science towards reality.

The reality that surrounds us is not something homogeneous; nor is the relation of its innumerable phenomena to man's needs uniform. We find this idea expressed in Mr. Chernyshevsky's essay. "Nature," he says, "knows nothing about man and his affairs, about his happiness or his death. It is neutral towards man, it is neither his enemy nor his friend" (p. 28);* "often a man suffers and perishes through no fault of his own" (p. 30);** nature does not always correspond to his needs; therefore, for his peace and happiness man must in many things alter objective reality in order to adapt it to the requirements of his practical life. Indeed, among the phenomena that surround man there are very many that are unpleasant or harmful to him. To some extent instinct, but still more science (knowledge, reflection, experience) provide him with the means of understanding which phenomena of reality are good and beneficial for him, and which he should, therefore, help to foster and develop, and which, on the contrary, are burdensome and harmful to him and should, therefore, be eliminated, or at least abated, for man's happiness. And science provides him with the means of achieving this object. In this science receives exceedingly powerful assistance from art, which is extraordinarily capable of spreading among a vast mass of people the concepts attained by science, for it is much easier and pleasanter for a man to make himself familiar with works of art than with the formulas and stern analysis of science. In this respect, the significance of art for man is immense. We shall not speak of the pleasure that works of art afford man because it is quite superfluous to talk about the high value aesthetic pleasure has for man. There is already too much talk about this aspect of art while the other, more important, aspect that we are now discussing is forgotten.

Lastly, it seems to us that Mr. Chernyshevsky also committed a very grave mistake in failing to explain the attitude of the present-day positive, or practical, world outlook towards man's so-called "ideal" strivings, for here, too, it is often necessary to protest against misunderstanding. The practicalness that is accepted by science has nothing in common with that vulgar practicalness which dominates

---

* In this volume, p. 307.—*Ed.*
** In this volume, p. 309.—*Ed.*

feelingless people, and which is the opposite of ideal but healthy strivings. We have seen that the present-day world outlook regards science and art as urgent human needs on a par with food and air. Similarly, it favours all the other lofty human strivings that spring from the head or the heart. The head and the heart are just as essential for true human life as the stomach. If the head cannot exist without the stomach, the stomach will die of starvation if the head does not provide food for it. This is not all. A man is not a snail; he cannot live exclusively for the purpose of filling his stomach. Intellectual and moral life (which develops properly when the body is healthy, that is, when the material side of a man's life is satisfactory)—such is the life that truly befits man and is most attractive for him. Present-day science does not tear man into parts, does not mutilate his beautiful body by surgical amputations, and it regards as equally absurd and fatal the obsolete strivings to restrict human life either solely to the head or solely to the stomach. Both these organs are equally essential attributes of man, and both are equally essential for human life. That is why science regards man's noble striving for everything that is lofty and beautiful as being as essential a need as eating and drinking. It also loves—for science is not abstract and not cold: it loves and hates, pursues and protects— it loves noble people who concern themselves with man's moral needs and grieve when they see how often those needs remain unsatisfied, as much as it loves those people who concern themselves with the material needs of their fellow men.

We have set forth the ideas expressed by the author and have pointed to and corrected those of his mistakes which we have caught. It now remains for us to express our opinion of his book. We must say that the author reveals some ability to understand these general principles and some ability to apply them to the problems he discusses. He also reveals ability to distinguish in the given concepts the elements that are in harmony with the general views of present-day science from the other elements that are not in harmony with them. Hence, his theory possesses inner unity. How far it is correct, time will show. But, while readily granting that the ideas the author enunciated deserve attention, we must, nevertheless, say that in nearly every case he has merely enunciated and applied these

ideas, which had already been given him by science. Let
us, then, proceed to appraise his enunciation. The numerous
mistakes and omissions to which we have pointed show
that Mr. Chernyshevsky wrote his essay at the time when
the ideas he enunciates were still in the process of development in his own mind, when they had not yet become a full,
all-round and firmly-established system. Had he delayed
the publication of his essay for some time, it might have
acquired more scientific merit, if not in essence, then at
least in exposition. Evidently, he himself was conscious
of this when he said: "if in my essay the aesthetic concepts
deduced from the now prevailing views on the relation of
human thought to living reality have remained incomplete,
one-sided or shaky, this, I hope, is due not to the defects
in the concepts, but to the way I have enunciated them."
(P. 8.*)[9] A few words must also be said about the form of
the essay. We are definitely displeased with it because it
seems to us that it does not correspond to the author's aim
to call attention to the ideas on which he is trying to build
his theory of art. He might have achieved this aim[10] by
lending his general ideas lively interest by applying them to
the current problems of our literature. He might have
shown by numerous examples the living connection between
the general principles of science and the interests of the
day, which are engaging the attention of so many people.[11]

In this volume, p. 296.—*Ed.*

THE AESTHETIC RELATION
OF ART TO REALITY

(Preface to the Third Edition)[1]

IN THE FORTIES, the majority of the educated people in Russia took a lively interest in German philosophy. Our best publicists conveyed to the Russian public, as far as this was possible, the ideas then prevailing in German philosophy. These were the ideas of Hegel and his disciples. At the present time few followers of Hegel[2] are left in Germany; still fewer are left in Russia. But at the end of the forties and beginning of the fifties his philosophy predominated in our literature. Nearly all people of enlightened mind sympathized with it, insofar as they were familiar with it from the incomplete exposition of it by our publicists. A few, being in the habit of reading books on philosophy in the German language, explained in their circles what had been left unsaid in the printed Russian expositions. These commentators were eagerly listened to and they enjoyed the profound respect of their knowledge-seeking friends. During Hegel's lifetime, unity of thought among his disciples was maintained by his personal authority, but even in his lifetime researches appeared in German philosophical literature containing deductions from his fundamental ideas which he either passed over in silence, or, when it was extremely necessary, even censured. The most important of these researches was an anonymous work entitled *Thoughts on Death and Immortality (Gedanken über Tod und Unsterblichkeit).** It was published in 1830, the year before Hegel died. When the authoritative teacher died, the unity of thought among the bulk of his disciples began to wane, and in 1835, with the publication of Strauss'

---

* This work, written by Feuerbach, was confiscated immediately on its appearance.—*Ed.*

Life of Jesus (*Das Leben Jesu*), the Hegel school broke up
into three sections: some remained faithful to their teacher's
system of cautious liberalism. The most important of these
were Michelet and Rosenkranz; they formed a section that
was named the centre. Quite a number began openly to
express definitely progressive opinions; the most vigorous
representative of this trend was Strauss. He, and the philosophers who followed him, formed the left wing of the
Hegel school. Very many of Hegel's disciples were shocked
by the radical opinions they expressed, particularly by the
deductions drawn from Strauss' exegetics, and in polemics
with the left wing they cast aside the progressive elements
which in Hegel's system were combined with the conservative elements. This large group comprised the right wing.
The centre party tried to assuage the acerbity of the polemics
between the right and left wings, but this proved to be impossible; each followed its own trend. The gulf between
them grew ever wider, and just before the time when the
political events of 1848 gave the mass of the German public interests in face of which philosophical disputes lost
their importance, the rupture between the right- and left-
wing Hegelians had resulted in that the majority of the
philosophers of the right wing adhered only to the Hegelian
terminology, by means of which they expounded the ideas
of the eighteenth century, while the majority of the thinkers
of the left wing put into the frame of Hegelian dialectics
a content that more or less resembled the so-called philosophy of the Encyclopaedists.

    Ludwig Feuerbach, the author of *Thoughts on Death
and Immortality*, had for a number of years engaged in
work on the history of modern philosophy.[3] Probably this
enabled his conceptions to acquire a breadth far exceeding
the ordinary scope of ideas of the German philosophy that
developed after Kant. The left wing of the Hegel school
regarded Feuerbach as one of themselves. He retained part
of the Hegelian terminology. But in 1845, in the preface
to his *Collected Works*, he already said that philosophy had
outlived its time and that its place should be taken by
natural science. Reviewing the phases through which his
ideas had passed, and showing why he had not halted at
any one of them, had regarded each as obsolete and had
passed on to the next, he, after expounding the fundamental
ideas of his last works, asks: "But is not this point of view

also obsolete?" And he answers: "Unfortunately, yes, yes!"
Leider, leider! His statement that he also regarded as obsolete such of his works as *The Essence of Religion* (*Das
Wesen der Religion*)* was based on the hope of the early
appearance of naturalists capable of taking the place of
the philosophers in the work of explaining those wide problems, the investigation of which until that time had been
the special occupation of thinkers who were called philosophers.

Whether Feuerbach's hope has been realized today,
although over forty years have passed since it was expressed, is a question that I will not examine. My answer
to it would be a sad one.

The author of the pamphlet, to the third edition of
which I am writing this preface, obtained the opportunity
to use a good library and to spend a little money on purchasing books in 1846.[4] Until then he had read only such
books as can be obtained in provincial towns where there
are no decent libraries. He was familiar with the Russian
expositions of Hegel's system, which are very incomplete.
When he obtained the opportunity to read Hegel in the
original he began to read these treatises. He liked Hegel
in the original far less than he had been led to expect by
the Russian expositions. The reason for this was that the
Russian followers of Hegel expounded his system from the
standpoint of the left wing of the Hegelian school. In the
original, Hegel proved to resemble[5] the philosophers of
the seventeenth century, and even the scholastics more than
Hegel as he appeared in the Russian expositions of his system. Reading him was wearisome simply because of its
obvious uselessness for forming a scientific mode of thought.
It was at that time that the youth who wanted to form such
a mode of thought for himself accidentally came across one
of the principal works of Feuerbach. He became a follower
of that thinker; and until mundane cares diverted him from
scientific studies, he zealously read and reread the works
of Feuerbach.

About six years after he had made the acquaintance of
Feuerbach, the mundane necessity arose for him to write
a scientific treatise. It seemed to him that he could apply
the fundamental ideas of Feuerbach to the solution of

---

* This work appeared in 1845.—*Ed.*

certain problems in branches of knowledge that had not come within the scope of his teacher's researches.

The subject of the treatise he was to write had to be something dealing with literature. It occurred to him to meet this condition by expounding conceptions of art, and of poetry in particular, which seemed to him to be deductions from Feuerbach's ideas. Thus, the pamphlet to which I am writing this preface is an attempt to apply Feuerbach's ideas to the solution of the fundamental problems of aesthetics.

The author made no claim whatever to saying anything new of his own. He wished merely to interpret Feuerbach's ideas in application to aesthetics.

A strange incongruity with this was the fact that throughout his treatise he did not mention Feuerbach once. The reason for this was that at that time it was impossible to mention that name in a Russian book. Nor did the author mention Hegel, although the whole treatise was a polemic against Hegel's theory of aesthetics, which still prevailed in Russian literature at that time, but was expounded without mentioning Hegel. That name, also, could not be conveniently used in the Russian language.

Of the treatises on aesthetics of that time, Vischer's comprehensive and very learned work *Aesthetics, or the Science of the Beautiful* (*Aesthetik, oder Wissenschaft der Schönen*) was considered the best. Vischer was a left-wing Hegelian, but his name was not yet among the inconvenient ones, so the author mentions him whenever he finds it necessary to say against whom he is arguing; and whenever it is necessary to quote the actual words of an advocate of the conceptions of aesthetics he refutes, he quotes excerpts from Vischer's *Aesthetics*. At that time Hegel's *Aesthetics* was out of date in factual detail; this explains the preference then given to Vischer's *Aesthetics*, a work which was still new and fresh. Vischer is a fairly vigorous thinker, but compared with Hegel he is a pigmy. All his digressions from the fundamental ideas of Hegel's *Aesthetics* spoil them. The passages quoted by the author, however, expound Hegel's ideas without modification.

Applying Feuerbach's fundamental ideas to the solution of problems of aesthetics, the author arrives at a system of conceptions which are in complete contradiction to the theory of aesthetics held by the left-wing Hegelian

Vischer. This corresponds to the relation of Feuerbach's philosophy to Hegel's philosophy even in the shape the latter assumed in the works of the thinkers of the left wing of the Hegelian school. Feuerbach's philosophy is something entirely different from the metaphysical systems, the best of which from the scientific standpoint was the Hegelian system. Kinship in content has vanished; there remains only the use of some of the terms common to all German systems of philosophy, from Kant to Hegel. The left-wing thinkers of the Hegelian school saw that Feuerbach, having reached independence, was pursuing the same aims concerning social life as those pursued by themselves and by the majority of the enlightened people of that time, and therefore regarded him as one of themselves. Until 1848 they saw no radical difference between his mode of thought and their own conceptions. It was revealed by the difference in their views on the events in Germany in the spring of 1848. The revolution that took place in France at the end of February encouraged the party of reform in Germany; it believed that the mass of the German people sympathized with its aims, and in the first days of March, with the approval of the mass of the citizens, it seized power in Baden, Württemberg, in the small states of Western Germany. Several days later a revolution took place in Austria: Hungary became independent of the Vienna government. A week after the revolution in Vienna, a revolution took place in Berlin. The party of reform was now confident that not only would the governments of the minor and small German states, consisting of its local leaders, help to carry out its aims, but also that the Austrian and the Prussian governments, which now consisted of men of more or less liberal convictions and patriotic sentiment, would either assist it or, at least, submit to its demands. At the end of March a congress of numerous representatives of the Liberal Party gathered in Frankfort, the capital of the former German empire. They proclaimed that their assembly (Vorparlament, Preliminary Parliament) had the power and the duty to order the convocation of the German Parliament ("National Assembly"), to control the actions of the German Diet that was sitting in Frankfort, consisting of representatives of the German governments in conformity with the old system, and to take the measures necessary to make all the German governments, including the Prussian and Austrian,

obey this Diet, which was to adopt decisions dictated by
the Vorparlament. Indeed, all the governments, even the
Prussian and Austrian, did obey the Vorparlament and the
German Diet which it dominated. Throughout the whole
federation of states known as the German Federation that
was formed in 1815, elections took place of deputies to the
German Parliament which was to meet in Frankfort and
establish a new state system for Germany, to transform it
from a federation of states, Staatenbund, into a "federal
state," Bundesstaat. The National Assembly (as this German
parliament was called) was opened in Frankfort on May
18; all the governments recognized its authority. On June
14 it elected as temporary ruler of Germany, Archduke
Johann, the uncle of the Emperor of Austria, who had transferred to him the temporary government of Austria. The
Archduke put Austrian affairs in order, went to Frankfort, and on July 12 took over the government of the
German Federation. Not only the Austrian, but also
the Prussian government, recognized his authority. The
German National Assembly set to work to draw up a
Constitution for the German Federal State. It looked as
though the hopes of the German party of reform had been
realized.

     The entire left wing of the Hegelian school took an active
part in the events that resulted in the convocation of the
German National Assembly, the submission of the German
governments to it, the institution of a provisional central
government and the submission to it of all the separate
German governments.

     Feuerbach took no part in the agitation that led to these
successes, or in the deliberations of the German National
Assembly. By this he drew censure upon himself. When
the whole thing ended in the collapse of all the hopes of
the party of reform, he said that from the very outset he
had foreseen utter failure and therefore could not espouse
a cause which he from the very outset considered had no
chance of success. In his opinion, the program of the party
of reform was inconsistent, its forces were inadequate to
reform Germany, the hopes of its success were fantastic.
At the time he expressed this opinion, the vast majority
of the enlightened people in Germany already regarded it
as correct. Had he attempted to justify himself earlier,
the unjust censure would have been supplemented by the

just one that by expressing such an opinion he was weakening the party of reform. He, therefore, silently bore the reproach of lack of courage and of indifference to the good of the nation. Now that the cause of the party of reform was definitely lost, his justification of his conduct could no longer do it any harm.

The difference between his view of the political events of the spring of 1848 and that of the left wing of the Hegelian school corresponded to the difference between his system of philosophical convictions and the ideas it held. The philosophical mode of thought of those disciples of Hegel who, after his death, formed the left wing of the Hegelian school was not sufficiently consistent, it retained too many of the fantastic conceptions belonging specifically to Hegel's system, or common to all the metaphysical systems of German philosophy beginning with Kant, who, while protesting against metaphysics, became more immersed in it than the German philosophers of the Wolff school who preceded him, and whom he refuted. Furthermore, the philosophers of the left wing of the Hegelian school were not sufficiently discriminate in accepting the views of specialists in natural science and in the social sciences which seemed to them to be progressive; together with scientific truth, they took over from these special treatises many fallacious theories. These weak sides of the mode of thought of the philosophers of the left wing of the Hegelian school revealed themselves most glaringly in the works of Bruno Bauer, the one who stood intellectually higher than all the rest except Strauss.[6] Several times he passed from one extreme to another and, for example, having begun by condemning Strauss' exegetic criticism for its destructiveness, he himself, a little later, wrote an exegetic treatise compared with which Strauss' exegetics seemed conservative (for Strauss' myth theory he substituted the theory of the author's arbitrariness).[7] Therefore, his works, which testify to very high intellectual attainment, did not influence the minds of discreet people as much as the works of Strauss, who always remained discreet.

Constantly working to improve his conceptions, Strauss, at last, moulded them into a system which he expounded in the treatise *The Old and the New Faith* (*Der alte und der neue Glaube*). This book appeared in 1872. Evidently, Strauss then believed that he had completely purged his.

27*

conceptions of metaphysical elements. And so it seemed to
the majority of educated people in Germany. Actually,
however, while accepting all the deductions of natural
science, he retained in his ideas a fairly large number of
metaphysical elements; and he accepted the theories of
the naturalists with too little discrimination, being unable
to distinguish the misconceptions from the scientific truth
they contained.

Feuerbach was different; his system bears a purely scientific character.

But soon after he had worked it out his activity waned
as a result of sickness. He was not yet old, but he already
felt that he would not have time to expound in conformity
with fundamental scientific ideas those special sciences
which then remained, and remain today, the scientific
monopoly of the so-called philosophers, because the specialists lack the training to work out the broad conceptions
upon which the solution of the fundamental problems of
these branches of knowledge is based. (To mention these
sciences by their old names, the chief of them are: logic,
aesthetics, moral philosophy, social philosophy and the
philosophy of history.) That is why, in the preface he wrote
for his collected works in 1845, he already said that his
works ought to be replaced by others, but that he no longer
possessed the strength to do this. This feeling explains the
sad answer he gave to the question he put to himself: "Is
not your present point of view also obsolete? Unfortunately,
yes, yes!" Leider, leider! Is it really obsolete? Yes, of course,
in the sense that the weight of investigation of the widest
problems of science must be transferred from the sphere
of investigation of the theoretical convictions of the masses
of the people, and of scientific systems based on these conceptions of the common people, to the sphere of natural
science. But this has not been done to this day. Those naturalists who imagine that they are builders of all-embracing
theories have actually remained pupils, and usually dull
pupils, of the ancient thinkers who created the metaphysical
systems, and usually of thinkers whose systems had already
been shattered, partly by Schelling and utterly by Hegel.
It is sufficient to mention that the majority of the naturalists who are trying to build broad theories of the laws
governing the activity of the human mind are repeating
Kant's metaphysical theory about the subjectivity of our

knowledge, are repeating after Kant that the forms of our sense perceptions have no resemblance to the forms of really existing objects; that, therefore, really existing objects, their real qualities, and their real relations to one another, are unknowable to us, and that even if they were knowable, they could not be the subject of our thought, which puts the entire material of knowledge into forms which are entirely different from the forms of real existence; that even the very laws of thought possess only subjective significance; that what seems to us to be the link between cause and effect does not exist in reality, because there is no preceding and no subsequent, no whole and no parts, and so on and so forth. When the naturalists stop talking such and similar metaphysical nonsense they will become capable of working out, and probably will work out, on the basis of natural science, a system of conceptions that will be more exact and fuller than those expounded by Feuerbach. Meanwhile, the exposition of the scientific conceptions of the so-called fundamental problems of human inquiry made by Feuerbach remains the best.[8]

The author of the pamphlet of which a new edition is to appear, indicated in it, as far as he was able, that he attached importance only to those ideas which he had borrowed from the teacher's treatises—that these pages of his pamphlet constitute whatever merit may be found in it. The conclusions he drew from Feuerbach's ideas for the solution of the problems of aesthetics seemed to him to be correct at the time, but even at that time he did not think that they were particularly important. He was pleased with his small work only insofar as he had succeeded in conveying in the Russian language some of Feuerbach's ideas in the forms in which it was then necessary to adapt oneself to the conditions of Russian literature.

When analyzing the concept of the beautiful, the author says that the definition of this concept, which seems to him correct, constitutes, in his opinion, "a deduction from those general views on the relation of the real to the imaginary world which differ entirely from those which formerly prevailed in science." This must be interpreted as follows: he draws a deduction from Feuerbach's idea that the imaginary world is only a recasting of our knowledge of the real world made by our imagination to please our desires; that this recasting is pale in intensity and poor in content compared with the impression made on our minds by the objects of the real world.[9]

In general, only the particular ideas relating to the special problems of aesthetics are the author's own. All the wider ideas in the pamphlet are Feuerbach's. The author conveyed them faithfully, and as far as the conditions of Russian literature would allow, closely to the way they are expounded by Feuerbach.[10]

In going over the pamphlet we made several alterations in the text. These are confined exclusively to minor points. We did not want to revise the pamphlet that is being reprinted. It is not good to revise in old age what one wrote in his youth.

1888

THE POETICS OF ARISTOTLE

TRANSLATED, EXPOUNDED AND EXPLAINED BY B. ORDYNSKY,
MOSCOW, 1854 [1]

Mr. ORDYNSKY deserves full approval and gratitude for having chosen for his dissertation Aristotle's *Poetics*, this first and most fundamental treatise on aesthetics that served as the basis of all aesthetical conceptions up to the very end of the last century. But was his choice really a happy one? Quite a large number of people will be found nowadays who, not regarding aesthetics as a science worthy of special attention, are even ready to assert that aesthetics leads nowhere and is good for nothing, and that only its obscurity prevents one from seeing its hollowness. On the other hand, it is doubtful whether out of this large number, even one will be found who would not with a smile of pity say about Laharpe that "this really wise and learned historian of literature has no firm and definite basis for judging authors," and who would not regretfully say about Merzlyakov that "this critic was really remarkable for refinement of taste, but, unfortunately, he was only a 'Russian Laharpe,' and, therefore, perhaps, did Russian criticism, more harm than good." Such opinions, which, probably, not one of the present-day deprecators of aesthetics will repudiate, almost relieve us of the necessity of defending this science from the people who are so ill-disposed towards it, but who, however, do not doubt the necessity of the literary critic or historian of literature having "clear and firm general principles." What, then, is meant by aesthetics if not a system of general principles of art in general and of poetry in particular? We very well understand that aesthetics deserved the strongest censure when, because of it, the history of literature was forgotten, when for the space of twenty-five pages authors would write about "excellent," "very good," "fair" and "bad" stanzas of some ode and, after finishing this sorting process, discuss on an equal number of pages the "vigorous" or "wrong" expressions in these "excellent," "fair," etc., stanzas. But when did this prevail in our literature, as it prevails to this day in French literature, to the undoubted delight of the French, who despise all aesthetics? It ceased in our literature in the 1830's, from the time we began to acquaint ourselves with aesthetics. It is to aesthetics that we are indebted for the fact that not in the worst Russian book will we read, for example, the following judgment of "the great merits of Bossuet" taken from the very respectable *History of French Literature* by M. Demogeot (Paris, 1852!!): "Bossuet alone constitutes a separate world in the great literary world of the seventeenth century. The other writers are the children of Rome; he carries the East to the West *by an incredibly bold and new combination of words, by gigantic figures* (par des alliances de mots d'une hardiesse et d'une nouveauté incroyables, par des figures gigantesques), which European taste would not have suggested to him, but which he is able to subject to the laws of proportion by introducing measure into immeasurability itself. Such is the fruit of his constant occupation," and so forth. This passage, a gem of narrow-mindedness, pleased M. Demogeot so much that he borrowed it from another writer, that very capable historian, Henri Martin. Probably, M. Demogeot thinks that the reflections on tropes and figures which ornament his book are an exemplary judgment on the activities of a great writer!

Let us, then, be grateful to aesthetics for having relieved us of the labour of reading and writing similar judgments on Derzhavin or Karamzin. We repeat: we could understand this hostility to aesthetics if it were itself hostile to the history of literature; but the contrary is the case, we have always proclaimed the necessity of the history of literature, and people who have especially engaged in aesthetical criticism have also done a great deal—more than any of our present-day writers—for the history of literature.[2] In our literature it has always been recognized that aesthetics must be based on an exact study of facts, and the reproach that it is abstract and groundless in content can apply to it as little as it applies, say, to Russian grammar. If it did not in the past deserve the hostility of the advocates of historical research in literature, it can do so still less today, when every theoretical science is based on the most exact and ullest possible investigation of facts. But we are ready to ssume that there are still many among us who are mistaken about present-day conceptions of what theory is and what philosophy is. There are still many among us who think that transcendental ideas about "a priori knowledge," the "development of science out of itself," ohne Voraussetzung, and so forth, prevail among present-day thinkers. We take the liberty to assure them that in the opinion of present-day thinkers, these conceptions were very good, and chiefly, were very much needed as stepping stones, in the past forty, thirty and, perhaps, even twenty years ago, but not now; now they are obsolete and are regarded as one-sided and inadequate. We take the liberty to assert that genuinely modern thinkers understand "theory" to mean exactly what it was understood to mean by Bacon, and after him, by astronomers, chemists, physicists, physicians and other adepts in positive science. True, as far as we know, no formal "textbook on aesthetics" has yet been written according to these new conceptions; but the conceptions upon which it will be based have already been sufficiently discerned and developed in short articles and in parts of big works. We even dare to assert that the propositions contained in the old and now obsolete textbooks on so-called transcendental aesthetics were based on a far larger number of facts than their opponents think. Remember that in the chief of these textbooks, consisting of *three* volumes, the historical part takes up almost *two*, and more than half of the third is also taken up by historical details.* But we do not wish to presume that the opponents of aesthetics in particular, or of theory in general, needed this reminder. Not wishing to picture them as lagging behind the present-day trend of thought, we would rather presume that the reason for their dislike for aesthetics is a different, extremely flattering one, viz., that its opponents regard it as an abstract and barren theory, and attack it because of their devotion to the "living" sciences which are of some importance for so-called vital problems. Plato did not, as we shall see later on, attack aesthetics from this standpoint (that would not have been so important, and, besides, aesthetics did not yet exist in Plato's time, except for the fragments scattered in his own works). No. He attacked art itself, and we only regret that to some degree art deserved

---

* This refers to Hegel's work in three volumes, *Vorlesungen über die Aesthetik.—Ed.*

his attacks, although we cannot help sympathizing with
Plato. If poetry, literature, art are deemed subjects of such
importance that the history, say, of literature, ought to
be the object of universal attention and study, then the
general problems of the essence, the purpose, the influence
of poetry, literature and art ought to be of enormous interest, because their solution will determine our view of the
subject; and to obtain a clear and correct view, facts are
needed. What is the use of knowing facts if not for the purpose of drawing deductions from them? In short, we think
that the whole dispute against aesthetics is based on a
misunderstanding, on a mistaken conception of the nature
of aesthetics and of theoretical science in general. The history of art serves as the basis of the theory of art, and the
theory of art facilitates a more thorough and fuller study
of its history; a better study of the history will facilitate
the further improvement of the theory, and so forth. This
interaction of history and theory to their mutual benefit will
continue ad infinitum as long as people study facts and draw
deductions from them, and not become walking chronological tables and bibliographical lists which need not and
cannot think. Without a history of a subject there can be
no theory of the subject; but without a theory of a subject
its history cannot even be conceived of, because there is
no conception of the subject, of its purpose and limits.
This is as plain as twice two is four, and one is one; but
we know of people who, on the basis of Newton's binomial
theorem, argue that one is two....

We have, however, much that is interesting because it
is new, much besides the few, usually insignificant, books
in different languages, mostly in French, like the works of
a Michel Chevalier and of other "great scholars" and "profound and yet clear thinkers" like him, and also the last
issues of *Revue des deux Mondes* and its great savants. These
books are neither mysterious nor novel to anyone; but they
serve as a code for certain thinkers, as the object of their
profound reflections. In all probability, they have caused
many people to turn away from aesthetics: among the numerous truths these books and articles have preached to us
is the one that aesthetics is an obscure, lifeless, abstract
science that cannot be applied to anything.

Aesthetics—a lifeless science! We do not say that there
are no sciences more alive than it is; but it would be a good

thing if we devoted our minds to these sciences. No, we praise other sciences that are of far less lively interest. Aesthetics—a barren science! In answer to this we ask: Do we still remember Lessing, Goethe and Schiller, or have they lost the right to be remembered by us since we became acquainted with Thackeray? Do we recognize the merits of German poetry of the latter half of the last century?...

But perhaps there are some who do not deny that theoretical deductions are useful and necessary, but protest against their being squeezed into the narrow frame of a system? This would be an excellent motive for hostility if it had some ground, if any one of our contemporaries regarded anybody's system of any science as the eternal repository of all truth. But today, nearly everybody says (and the builders of systems usually more sincerely than all) that every system is engendered and destroyed, or it would be better to say changes, together with the conceptions of the time that brought it into being. Today, nobody compels you "jurare in verba magistri":[3] a system is only a temporary framework for science; and if you have outgrown the conceptions of the system you will not reject science, but create a new system for it, and everybody will be grateful to you. System in science is not a hindrance to its development. Teach us, and the more there is new in your new system, the greater will be your fame. But truths not moulded in a single, harmonious whole are inconvenient for use; only he who builds a system of science makes science popular, and his conceptions will spread among the masses, even though the conceptions of others were much profounder than his own. What is not formulated remains ineffective.

The best example illustrating the importance of system as a condition for fruitful thought is provided by the *Poetics* or, as Mr. Ordynsky calls it, *The Poetics of Aristotle*. Aristotle was the first to expound aesthetic conceptions in an independent system, and his conceptions prevailed for over two thousand years. But more truly great thoughts on art are to be found in Plato's works than in Aristotle's. Plato's theory is, perhaps, not only more profound, but even fuller than Aristotle's, but it was not moulded into a system, and until recent times attracted scarcely any attention.

To show what interest the aesthetical conceptions of these men who lived 2,200 years before us still have for our times, we shall try briefly to set forth the most general, most abstract problems of their aesthetics, viz., "the origin and purpose of art." Of course, the solution of these problems in modern theory is of far livelier interest, but ... who, in your opinion, stands higher—Pushkin or Gogol? Yesterday I heard a dispute about this, and Plato and Aristotle are ready to answer it. Indeed, the answer depends on the conception of the essence and purpose of art. Let us, then, bear the opinion on this subject of our great teachers in the matter of aesthetical judgment. If the essence of art really lies in idealization, as is claimed nowadays, if its aim is "to create the sweet and sublime sensation of the beautiful," then there is no poet in Russian literature equal to the author of *Poltava, Boris Godunov, The Bronze Horseman,* the *Stone Guest* and of all those innumerable perfumed poems. If, however, something else besides is demanded of art, then ... but what else besides this can constitute the essence and purpose of art?

And so, what is the essence of art? What, precisely, does a painter do when he paints a landscape, or a group of people. What does the poet do when in lyrical verse he depicts the rapture or suffering of love? What does the author do when in a novel or play he depicts people with their passions and characters? "He idealizes nature and people. The essence of art lies in the creation of ideals," answers the now prevailing theory of aesthetics. "Man has a presentiment and need of something better and fuller than pale and meagre reality" (the "prose of life" as the commonplace novelists call it), "which fails to satisfy his immortal spirit. This something better and fuller" (the ideal) "is vividly grasped by the artist and is conveyed to thirsting mankind in works of art." The former theory of art said something different:* "Art is nothing more than the imitation of what we see in reality; paintings, statues, novels, plays are nothing more than copies of the originals with which

---

* We deem it almost superfluous to note, for it must be obvious to everybody familiar with the subject, that, almost throughout this exposition of the aesthetical conceptions of the Greeks we are utilizing E. Müller's excellent work, *Geschichte der Theorie der Kunst bei den Alten,* Bd. 2 (*History of the Theory of Art Among the Ancients,* Vol. 2), Breslau 1834-1837.

reality provides the artist." This theory, derided nowadays because it is known only from the distorted version presented by Boileau and Batteux, which indeed deserves derision, is known as Aristotle's theory. Indeed, Aristotle admitted its correctness in those sections of his treatise on *Poetics*, which contain his general observations on the origin and essence of art in general, and of poetry in particular; and its fundamental idea is, indeed, that "art is imitation." But it would be quite wrong to regard Aristotle as the creator of the "imitation" theory: in all probability it already prevailed long before Socrates and Plato, and it is developed in Plato's works far more deeply and comprehensively than in Aristotle's. Basing his conception of art on the idea that "it is imitation," Plato did not confine himself to the rather restricted application of the fundamental principle that Aristotle was content with. Poetry is imitation, says Aristotle, hence, tragedies are an imitation of the actions of great men, comedies are an imitation of the actions of base men; he draws no other deductions. Plato, on the contrary, deduces vivid, brilliant, profound conclusions from his conception of art. Basing himself on his axiom, he defines the purpose of art in human life, its relation to other spheres of activity. Armed with this axiom he flogs art for its paleness, feebleness, uselessness and insignificance. His sarcasm is biting and apt, biassed, perhaps, especially for our times, but in many things just and noble in spite of its bias. But in order to explain Plato's contempt for art, a few words must be said about the essential trend of his doctrine.

Many people regard Plato as a sort of Greek romanticist, sighing for an unknown and nebulous, wonderful and beautiful land, striving "thither, thither" (dahin, dahin), no matter where, as long as it is far from men and the world.... Plato was not in the least like this. He was, indeed, gifted with a lofty spirit, and he was rapturously drawn to everything that was noble and great, but he was not an idle dreamer, he did not dream of astral worlds, but of the earth, not of phantoms, but of man. And above all, Plato thought that man must be a citizen of the state, that he must not dream of things that are useless for the state, but *live* a noble and active life and contribute to the material and moral welfare of his fellow citizens. A noble, not a dreamy, not speculative (as it was for Aristotle), but an active, practical

life was his ideal of human life. He looked upon science and
art, as upon everything else, not from the scientific or artistic point of view, but from the social and moral point of
view. Man does not exist for art or science (as many of
the great philosophers, including Aristotle, thought); science and art must serve to benefit man. After this, it is clear
how Plato must have looked upon art, which for the most
part is (whether it should be is another question), and in
Plato's time almost exclusively was, a beautiful and at the
same time an extremely costly and, perhaps, a very noble
pastime, but a pastime for all that, for people who had nothing else to do than admire more or less voluptuous paintings and statues and intoxicate themselves with the melody of more or less voluptuous verses. "Art is a pastime":
this decides everything for Plato. And the best proof that
he did not malign art in regarding it as a pastime is provided by one of the most serious of the poets, Schiller,who,
of course, did not look upon his own art with hostility: in his
opinion, Kant was quite right in calling art a *game* (or pastime, das Spiel), because, "only when playing is a man
fully a man."* We shall now present Plato's opinion on the
purpose of art, leaving out, however, his exceedingly harsh
thrusts.

There are two kinds of arts, says Plato: productive
and imitative (in our terminology: practical, or technical, and the fine arts). The first produces things needed for
the maintenance of life, useful things. These include, for
example, agriculture, handicrafts, gymnastics, which gives
a man strength, and medicine, which gives him health.
They deserve all respect. As for the imitative arts (in conformity with present-day terminology we shall call them
the fine arts), which give man nothing but deceptive and
totally useless copies of real objects, what comparison can
they stand with the former? Their significance is negligi-
ble. What purpose do they serve? As a pleasant, but useless,
pastime. They are games, useless ones in the eyes of a serious person. Some games, gymnastics, for example, have
a useful purpose, but the fine arts serve no such purpose.
No. Their purpose is only to amuse; they only pander to the
rabble; they belong to the same category of occupations as

---

* *On the Aesthetical Education of Man (Über die aesthetische
Erziehung des Menschen)*, Letter 15.

rhetoric (the art of choosing fine words), sophistry (the art of saying not what is useful, but what pleases the listeners), the hairdressing and culinary arts. Painting, music, poetry, even lofty and lauded tragedy, are fawning and flattering arts, for they strive only to please and not to benefit the rabble (we shall note, in passing, that the author of *Emile* and *New Héloise* regards the fine arts in the same way, and Campe, the celebrated German educationalist, says: "it is more useful to spin a pound of wool than to compose a book of poems"). And yet, what a high opinion these paltry arts have of themselves! The painter, for example, claims that he creates trees, people, land and sea! And how quickly — in an instant! And then he sells you land and sea for gold. True, his creations are not worth a copper coin, for they are merely phantoms that can be used only for the purpose of deceiving children. And these tricksters will not even admit that they are imitators—no; they talk to you about creation! (This shows that the idea: "art and creation," which is the basis of the now prevailing theory of aesthetics, already existed in Plato's time.) Can they produce anything but bad, unfaithful copies? An artist is not concerned about inner content; he needs only externals. He is satisfied with a superficial knowledge of the surface of an object: this is what he copies; more he does not know (the latest system of aestetics, according to these artists, or rather, according to the scathing remarks of Plato who speaks for them, admits that "beauty, the essential content of art, is a phantom, a pure phantom," ein Schein, ein reiner Schein, and that art deals only with the surface, the externals of an object, die Oberfläche). A physician is familiar with the structure of the human body, the artist is not. Similarly, the poet is not thoroughly familiar with human life or with the human heart. Such knowledge is acquired by a deep study of philosophy (in present-day terminology, "only through science") and not by sporadic observations of one's own experience, which is too incomplete and superficial. Do these proud fine arts even deserve the name of art? No! If my activities are to deserve the name of art, I must have a clear idea of what I am doing; the artist lacks this. A joiner who makes a table knows what he is making, and why and how he is making it. The painter and poet, however, do not know the true nature of the objects they are copying. Their art is not art, but working in the dark, by instinct, haphazard:

they call it "inspiration"; actually, their inspiration is combined with the ignorance of the dilletante.* The fine arts are a useless game that does not deserve the name of art.

Plato's polemics against art are very harsh, this is true, but they are engendered by a lofty and noble conception of human activity. It would be easy to show that many of his stern strictures are still true today in respect to modern art. But it is much pleasanter to speak in favour of art than against it, and therefore, renouncing the arduous duty of pointing to the weak sides that modern art suffers from in common with Greek art, we shall endeavour only to show on what grounds some of Plato's absolute judgments concerning the insignificant purpose of the fine arts may be modified in our times.

Plato protests against art because it is useless to man. We shall not refute this horrible reproach with the obsolete idea that "art must exist only for art's sake," that "to make art serve human needs means degrading it," and so forth. This idea had some meaning when it was necessary to show that the poet must not write magnificent odes, must not distort reality for the sake of various arbitrary and sentimental maxims. Unfortunately, it appeared too late for this purpose, when the fight was over. At the present time it

---

* To explain these last words it must be observed that Plato does not attack "inspiration," but the fact that, to the extreme detriment of art, very many poets (not to speak of other artists), relying only on their power of "creative genius, which instinctively penetrates the secrets of nature and life," disdain learning, which "rids their content of hollowness and childish backwardness";

"Ich singe, wie der Vogel singt" (Goethe), they say; but their singing, like that of the nightingale, is useful only as an idle pastime and soon bores one, as does listening to the song of the nightingale. The splendid doctrine that the poet writes by inspiration bereft of all calculation, and that the works of a deliberating, calculating poet are cold, unpoetical, prevailed in Greece from the time of the genius Democritus. Aristotle puts inspiration in the background: he *teaches* how to write tragedies, to choose effective plots and denouements according to definite rules. Even this shows that as an aesthetician Aristotle belongs to the period of the decadence of art: instead of the living spirit, he teaches rules, cold formalism. The only difference between him and Horace and Boileau, and all the subsequent writers on "rhetoric" and "poetics," is the difference between the teacher of genius and his dull pupils: the difference here is not in the essence of the conceptions, but in the degree of the intellect that develops them.

is certainly useless; art has succeeded in upholding its independence and must now think of how to utilize it. The idea of "art for art's sake" is as strange in our times as "wealth for wealth's sake," "science for science's sake," and so forth. All human activity must serve mankind if it is not to remain a useless and idle occupation. Wealth exists in order that man may benefit by it; science exists in order to be man's guide; art, too, must serve some useful purpose and not fruitless pleasure. "But aesthetic pleasure in itself is of great benefit to man, for it softens his heart and elevates his soul...." We do not wish to deduce any serious purpose in art even from this idea,which is correct, but says little in favour of art for all that. Of course, the pleasure afforded by works of art, like all (except criminal) pleasure, puts a man in a bright, happy mood; and a cheerful and contented man is, of course, kinder and better than a discontented and gloomy one. And we agree that on leaving a picture gallery or a theatre, a man feels kinder and better (at least for half an hour, while the aesthetic pleasure still lasts); but in the same way a man gets up from a good dinner feeling more affable and kinder than he did when his stomach was empty. The beneficial influence of art as art (apart from the particular content of a work) lies almost exclusively in the fact that art is a pleasant thing; all other pleasant occupations, relations, and objects upon which a "good mood" depends, possess the same beneficial quality. A healthy man is much less selfish, is much more benevolent than a sick one, who is always more or less irritable and cross. A good house also inclines a man to benevolence more than a damp, dingy and bleak one does. A man of untroubled mind (i.e., who is not suffering from vexation) is much more affable than one whose mind is troubled, and so forth. It must be said that the plain, practical, everyday conditions conducive to contentment with one's position have a stronger and more lasting effect upon a man than the pleasant impressions created by art. For most people art is only a pastime, i.e.,a rather insignificant thing, which cannot afford real contentment. Carefully weighing the facts, we come to the conclusion that many of the plainest, ordinary pastimes fill the human heart with more contentment and benevolence than art does. If Plato were to appear among us he would probably say that sitting and chatting on the bench outside the house (among peasants) or around the samovar (among town people)

has done more to develop among our people good humour
and a kindly disposition towards people than all paintings,
from cheap oleographs to the *Last Day of Pompeii.** That
art is useful as a source of contentment, for the development
of all that is good in man, is beyond doubt, but this usefulness is insignificant compared with the benefit derived from
other favourable relations and conditions of life. That is
why we do not wish to point to that usefulness to indicate the
lofty purpose of art in life. True, the influence of art on moral development is not usually understood in the way we
have presented it. It is said that aesthetic pleasure does
not merely soften the heart as a source of good humour,
but directly exalts and ennobles the soul because of the exalt-
edness and nobility of the objects and sentiments which we
admire in works of art. Usually it is said that what seems
to us "beautiful" in art is by that very fact alone noble
and exalted. But, having no wish whatever to touch upon
the delicate question of the real purpose of the essential content of most works of art, we have even refrained from citing
Plato's formidable attacks on art because of its content;
still less are we ourselves inclined to indulge in such attacks.
We shall merely remind the reader that art is obliged to pander to the requirements of the public, and most people, regarding art as a pastime, of course, demand of a pastime
not an exalted or noble content, but gracefulness, interest,
amusement and even frivolity. One of the most serious
and noble poets of our times[4] says in the preface to his songs:
"I did not in the least want to sing in praise of love, but who
would have read my songs if their content had been grave?
Therefore, after writing several serious songs, the only kind
I would have liked to write, I had to submerge them in a
multitude of love songs, so that, together with this bait, the
public should swallow the wholesome food." Such is nearly
always the position of the artist who follows a serious and
noble trend (we do not wish to add that not all artists do so).
Whoever thinks that these brief hints are inadequate, let
him take the trouble to recall that the chief content of poetry (the most serious of the arts) is "love," i.e., being in love,
which is very far from true love, and has very little serious
significance. The usual concern of art is to rouse interest,
to attract—how and by what means does not matter.

---

* Painted by K. Bryullov (1834).—*Ed.*

But although, when striving to achieve this aim, art nearly always forgets about other, most important, aims, it must be admitted that it very successfully attracts an enormous mass of people, and thereby unintentionally helps to spread education, a clear conception of things—everything which is of intellectual, and therefore, of subsequent material benefit to the people. Art, or it would be better to say poetry (only poetry, for the other arts do very little in this respect), spreads among the mass of the reading public an enormous amount of knowledge and, what is still more important, familiarizes them with the concepts worked out by science—such is poetry's great purpose in life.

It is strange in our times—although, perhaps, still not altogether superfluous—to have to enter into a detailed explanation of what science is, what its purpose in life is, and how great that purpose is. Science is the repository of the experience and reflections of the human race; and it is chiefly on the basis of science that people's conceptions, and subsequently their morals and lives, are improved. But the discoveries and deductions of science are really beneficial only when they spread among the mass of the public. Science is stern and forbidding in its original shape; it does not attract the crowd. Science demands of its followers a vast amount of preliminary knowledge and, what is even more rarely met with among the majority, the habit of serious thinking. Therefore, to permeate the masses, science must divest itself of scientific form. Its hard kernel must be ground into flour and mixed with water so as to become tasty and digestible food. This is achieved by means of "popular" expositions of science. But even popular books do not do all that is needed to spread scientific conceptions among the majority of the public; they offer easy, but not palatable reading, and the majority of readers want books to be sweet dessert. This palatable reading is provided by novels, stories, etc. There cannot be the slightest doubt that very few fiction writers think, like Walter Scott, of employing their talent to spread education among the reading public. But, just as a person of little education always learns something new from conversation with an educated person, even if the conversation does not seem to touch upon a serious subject, so from the reading of novels and stories, at least historical ones, and even of poems, written by people who are at least more highly educated than most of their readers,

28*

the mass of the public learns a great deal even if it reads nothing else than these novels and stories. Nor can there be any doubt that not only *Yuri Miloslavsky*, but even *Leonid, or Some Features*, etc.,* have considerably widened the scope of their readers' knowledge. If popular books mint into current coin the heavy gold ingots smelted by science, poetry releases the small silver coins which circulate where gold rarely reaches, but which, nevertheless, have an intrinsic value. As a disseminator of knowledge and education, poetry is of great importance for life. It is a "pastime" that promotes the intellectual development of its devotees; therefore, while remaining a pastime for the mass of readers, poetry acquires serious importance in the eyes of the thinker.

And so, forced to admit the justice of many of Plato's attacks on art, we, nevertheless, have a right to say that poetry is of great importance for education and for the improvement in morals and material welfare that follows from it; it possesses this importance even when it does not pursue this purpose. But there have been numerous poets who consciously and seriously tried to serve morality and education, who realized that their talent imposed upon them the duty of being the mentors of their fellow citizens. There were such poets in Plato's time; we know definitely that Aristophanes was one of them. "The poet is the teacher of adults," he said, and all his comedies are written in the most serious strain. It is superfluous to speak of the important practical significance poetry acquires in their hands. But if Plato reveals bias in regarding poetry merely as a useless pastime, he has this to his credit that he regarded art in its connection with life; and justification of his censure is found in the conceptions of art held by the majority of artists, and even of philosophers, who believe that the significance of art does not depend upon its mundane uses, that "to serve any interests whatever other than its own is degrading and fatal for art," that "it is an aim in itself," that "the sole purpose of art is to afford aesthetic pleasure." These at present prevailing views do, indeed, rob art of all practical significance; they convert it into a mere game and fully deserve Plato's severe censure,

---

* *Vuri Miloslavsky*, a novel by M. Zagoskin; *Leonid, or Some Features of the Life of Napoleon*, a novel by R. Zotov.—*Ed.*

in which he showed that by renouncing a practical purpose in life, art, like everything else that lacks such a purpose, becomes a useless pastime in the eyes of the thinker.

Less exalted in his demands than Plato, Aristotle looks much more indulgently, even endearingly, at art, particularly at poetry and music. His conceptions of the purpose of music and poetry are not as edifying as Plato's, but they are much more comprehensive, although, it is true, sometimes petty.

In his opinion, the first use of art for man (for Aristotle also demands that art should be *useful*) is precisely what Plato regarded as the cause of the paleness and insignificance of works of art compared with living reality, viz., imitation. "The striving to imitate, which is the origin of art, is directly connected with thirst for knowledge. Thirst for knowledge, which compels one to compare a copy with the original, is the cause of the pleasure that works of art afford us. When copying an object and then comparing the copy with the original, we study the object, study it easily and quickly; herein lies the secret of the pleasure afforded by art." Thus, art is in close kinship with the most important and loftiest striving of the human spirit; for Aristotle places learning higher than life, and intellectual activity higher than practical activity. This is a line of thought that easily arises in the minds of men for whom learning is the chief aim in life. This explanation of its origin gives art a very honourable place among the loftiest strivings of the human spirit; but the argument that the desire to imitate springs from thirst for knowledge does not stand criticism. In general, we imitate because we wish to make, not to learn something; imitation is not a theoretical but a practical striving. What is true is that *sometimes* (rather rarely) we *read* a poetical work out of a desire to learn something of the habits of men, of the customs of nations remote from us, and so forth. As a rule, however, this is not the reason why we read poetical works, and they are certainly not written because the poet wants to clear up some problem for himself (as scientific treatises are written). The desire to *create* (by copying, or "reproduction" as it is called nowadays), to produce—such is the origin of poetical activity. Admiration of creative talent, the pleasure afforded by the consciousness of human genius—such is the source of the pleasure that works of art afford us. We shall not point to other origins of art and sources of the pleasure afforded by art, for this would carry us far away from Aristotle (just as in the foregoing, when supplementing Plato's opinions, we confined ourselves to pointing only to one aspect of the high significance of art in order not to go into superfluous details).

But while Aristotle gives a one-sided explanation of man's striving for imitation and of the origin of art, we cannot but give him full credit for trying to find for art a high purpose in the sphere of intellectual activity; and although we cannot agree with his opinion about the origin of art in general, we cannot but wonder at the correct way in which he defines the relation of poetry to philosophy. In Aristotle's opinion, poetry, which depicts human life from the general point of view, presenting not its casual and insignificant details, but what is essential and characteristic in life, has very much philosophical merit. He thinks that, in this respect, it stands higher than history, which must indiscriminately describe the important and unimportant, the essential and characteristic, as well as casual facts which have no intrinsic importance. Poetry stands much higher than history also because it presents everything in its inner connection, whereas history presents everything without any inner connection; it relates in chronological order diverse facts that have nothing in common with one another. In poetical scenes there is sense and coherence; a history contains numerous details that tell us nothing, and there is no coherence; it does not give us scenes, but snatches of scenes. Here is this profound and celebrated passage as translated into Russian by Mr. Ordynsky, which we quote in order to give the reader an idea of his style.

It is the function of the poet to relate not what has happened, but what may happen, i.e., what is possible according to the law of probability or necessity (*a thought which to this day serves as the basis of our idea of how a poet must handle the materials provided him by reality, of what he ought to take for his scenes and what he ought to reject*). The difference between the historian and the poet is not that one speaks in metre and the other does not. Herodotus' work could be put into metre, and in metre, as without any metre, it would still be history. The difference between them is that one relates what happened, whereas the other relates what may happen. Therefore, poetry is deeper and more significant than history. Poetry relates what is more general, history the particular. The general is: what a certain person will say or do according to the law of probability or necessity. This is achieved by poetry, which invents names. The particular is: what did Alcibiades do, or what happened to him? In comedies this is obvious: comedy writers who invent probable events, give arbitrary names and do not deal ... with particulars. As for tragedies ... in some, there are one or two well-known names; the rest are fictitious; in others, none is well known, as in Agathon's *The Flower*, in which the action and the names are alike fictitious, nevertheless it gives pleasure.*

The scientist does art justice to such a degree that he puts it above science (true, not his own branch of science). This is a remarkable thing.... But Aristotle's opinion of history requires explanation. It is applicable only to that form of history that was known in his time; it was not history in the proper sense, but the writing of chronicles. The works of Herodotus do, indeed, lack inherent connection: all the nine books of his *History* are full of episodes. He wants to write the history of the "War of the Persians and the Greeks," but manages to start the story only in the sixth book. He wants to talk about everything he knows of the history and customs of the peoples known to him. His method is as follows: The Persians waged war against the Egyptians: let us talk about the Egyptians—and then follows a whole book about Egypt. They also waged war against the Scythians: let us talk about the Scythians—and there follows a whole book about the Scythians and Scythia. Within every episode there are other episodes, interwoven almost as follows: the Egyptians' capital is Memphis—description of Memphis. I, too, have been to Memphis—description of what he saw in Memphis. Among other places, I visited a temple—description of the temple. In this temple I saw a priest—description of the priest and of his garments. The priest told me so-and-so—a relation of what the priest told him. But others have something different to say about this—a relation of what others say about it, and so on and so forth. Herodotus is a raconteur and has travelled much, and his history is like the genial, interesting, but incoherent narrative of all people who have travelled much. Thucydides is a pure chronicler, a learned and profound chronicler it is true, but he arranged his *History of the Peloponnesian War* as follows: In the sixth winter of the war the following happened in Attica. In the same winter the following happened in the Peloponnesus. At the same time, the following

* Cf. *The Poetics of Aristotle*, Leningrad 1927. IX, 1451 b., pp. 51-52.—*Ed.*

occurred in Corcyra and the following occurred in Thrace. This is what occurred in Lesbos, and so forth. In the ensuing summer, the following occurred in Attica, the following in the Peloponnesus, and so forth. Thucydides' narrative has still less inner connection than Herodotus'; not a single event is related at one stretch; the beginning, the middle and the end are scattered in different books according to "winters" and "summers." It is quite natural, that such histories should contain many petty details that are totally unnecessary for characterizing the chief events and personalities. History assumed the form of a science only in our times; strict unity prevails in all the works of our great modern historians; useless details will not be found in them; they contain only the facts and features "of general importance" that Aristotle demands, i.e., only those that are needed to characterize the age and the people.

The foregoing is enough to show how penetrating and comprehensive was Aristotle's mind; but in spite of his genius he often dropped into pettiness owing to his constant striving to find a profound philosophical explanation not only of the chief phenomena, but also of all their details. This striving, expressed in the axiom of a modern philosopher,[5] a rival of Aristotle's: "all that is real is rational, all that is rational is real," often compelled both thinkers to attach great importance to minor facts only because these facts fitted well into their system. An excellent example of this is the passage we have copied from Aristotle. Quite rightly observing that poetry depicts not petty details, but that which is general and characteristic, in what does he find justification of this conception? In the fact that the writers of comedies always, and of tragedies sometimes, give characteristic names to the personages in the play, i.e., the now obsolete custom of bringing on to the stage characters bearing the names Vorovatin (thievish), Pravdin (truthful), Pryamosudov (straightforward), Korshunov (hawk), Razlulyaev (merry fellow), Borodkin (old-fashioned), Starodumov (old-fashion minded),[6] and so forth.

We have devoted a number of pages to the opinions of Plato and Aristotle on the "imitative arts," and have scores of times used the word "imitate," but up till now the reader has not once come across the ordinary expression "imitating nature." Why? Does Plato, and particularly Aristotle, the teacher of all the Batteux, Boileau and Horaces, not regard art as the imitation of *nature*, the term we are all accustomed to use when speaking of the imitation theory? No, both Plato and Aristotle regard not nature, but *human* life as the true content of art, and of poetry in particular. To them belongs the honour of thinking about the chief content of art what since their time has been expressed only by Lessing, and what all their followers could not understand. In Aristotle's *Poetics* there is not a word about nature: he speaks of people, of their actions, of what happens to people, as of the things which poetry imitates. The word "nature" could have been adopted in poetics only in the heyday of flabby and false descriptive poetry (which almost threatens to come into fashion again) and, inseparable from it, didactic poetry—kinds which Aristotle banished from poetry. The imitation of *nature* is alien to true poetry, the chief subject of which is—man. "Nature" comes into the forefront only in landscape painting, and the phrase "imitating *nature*" was first heard from the lips of the painter; but even the painter did not utter it in the sense that it was given by the contemporaries of Deshoulières and Delille. Pliny relates that when Lysippus, then still a youth, asked Eupompus, the celebrated painter of that time, which of the former great artists ought to be imitated, Eupompus answered, pointing to the crowd of people among whom they were standing: "you must imitate not the artists, but nature." Clearly, he meant that living reality must serve as the artist's material and model and not the "gardens' that Delille extolled, and not the "lakes" described by Wordsworth, Wilson and that fraternity.[7]

This should convince one that many of the objections raised against the imitation theory apply not to that theory as such, but to the distorted form in which it has been presented by the theoreticians of the pseudo-classical school. This is not the place to express our own convictions, and therefore, we shall not attempt to prove our opinion that it would be more correct to call art the reproduction of reality (using a modern term for the word "imitation," which does not satisfactorily convey the meaning of the Greek word mimesis) than to think that art realizes in its works our idea of perfect beauty, which, it is alleged, does not exist in reality. But we cannot refrain from observing that it is wrong to think that by presenting the reproduction of reality as the supreme principle of art we compel it "to make

crude and vulgar copies and banish idealization from art."
To avoid entering into an exposition of opinions not generally accepted by present-day theory, we shall not discuss the point that the only idealization that is needed is
the exclusion from poetical works of details, no matter of
what kind, not essential for the purpose of obtaining a full
picture; that if by idealization is meant "ennobling" the
objects and characters depicted, it will be tantamount
to primness, pompousness, false dramatization. But here
is a passage from Aristotle's *Poetics* which shows that even
in the latter sense idealization fits very well into the system
of aesthetics which regards imitation, or reproduction, as
the fundamental principle of poetry:

"Since tragedy is the imitation of the best (*reproduces
the actions and adventures of people possessing great and
not petty characters, we would say now; but Aristotle is tak-
en up with Aeschylus and Sophocles and therefore says*:
people better than the ordinary), they, *the tragedy writers*, must imitate the good portrait painters: when por-
traying somebody in his true form they make the portrait
resemble the original, but they also make it more beautiful. So the poet, when imitating surliness, indolence, and
other defects in the character of persons, i.e., when *reproducing their characters*, should ennoble them.*

"Poetry has broken up into two kinds," says Aristotle
further, "according to the character of the poets: those of
serious mind described the lofty deeds of men of lofty character, and first wrote hymns and later tragedies; the trivial ones described "mean" people: first they composed
iambics" (satires) "and later comedies."** Again, what
one-sidedness! Plato can be pardoned for saying that works
of art have no serious moral significance and for not re-
minding us of a splendid exception, the comedies of Aristophanes—the latter's enmity towards Socrates excuses the
silence of Socrates' faithful disciple. But Aristotle, who
could not have felt any resentment towards Aristophanes,
also refuses to see the lofty significance of comedies.

The idea that "art is imitation" of living reality and
that it mainly reproduces human life was regarded as un-

---

* *Cf. The Poetics of Aristotle*, Leningrad 1927, II, 1448a.,
pp. 42-43.—*Ed.*

** *Ibid.*, IV, 1448 b., p. 44.—*Ed.*

questionably correct in ancient Greece. Both Plato and Aristotle used it as the basis of their aesthetical conceptions. They, like all their contemporaries, were so convinced of the indisputable truth of this principle that they expressed it everywhere as an axiom without taking the trouble to prove it. On what grounds, then, is the term "Platonic theory" applied to an entirely different theory of art, the very opposite of the one expounded by Plato, the theory that explains the origin of art as follows: "the idea of beauty inherent in the human spirit, finding no correspondence or satisfaction in the real world, compels man to create art in which it finds perfect realization"? And who was the first thinker to express the principle of this theory?

The "ideal principle" of art was first expressed by Plotinus, one of those hazy thinkers who are called Neo-Platonists. With them nothing is simple and clear; everything is mysterious and inexpressible. With them nothing is positive and real, everything is transcendental and dreamy. All their conceptions ... but we are wrong: they have no conceptions, for a conception is something definite that can be grasped by the ordinary mind; they have dreams, to which there are no corresponding objects anywhere, which one can grasp only when in a state of ecstasy, when, as a result of an artificial mode of life, of unnatural mental exertion, a man becomes submerged in a mysterious world inaccessible to all the senses. These dreams are magnificent, but magnificent only for an imagination that has liberated itself from the power of reason. The slightest contact with positive, clear thought destroys them. The Neo-Platonists were people who wanted to combine the ancient Greek philosophy with the mysterious Asian philosophies, to give the dreams of inflamed Egyptian and Indian imagination the form of science. The result of this combination was something stranger and more fantastic than these Indian and Egyptian philosophies. The ideas that arise on such a transcendental soil can scarcely hold for long the positive and enlightened minds of nations that possess experimental science, which subjects everything to analysis. But this is not the place to expound our conception of the "ideal principle" of art: what we have said about the strange source from which it was taken is sufficient. Nor shall we expound Plotinus' ideas of the essence of beauty, partly for the reason that to do so would be almost the same as expounding the now prevailing principles of aesthetics. Incidentally, it is doubtful whether we are right in calling these opinions about the ideal principle of art "modern." The system of conceptions to which they belong has now been abandoned by everybody; its importance was transient, and it is now forgotten, together with romanticism which it had begotten. And if the aesthetic conceptions disseminated throughout the world by the Schlegels and their companions, and later adopted by their opponents, have not yet been ousted from modern aesthetics by other conceptions, it is only because present-day science, being engaged with other problems, has scarcely touched aesthetics.

The Neo-Platonists altered Plato's philosophy according to the Egyptian pattern; but while differing entirely from Plato's philosophy in essence, their doctrine retained features that resembled it externally. This explains why much was ascribed to Plato that was not his, including the doctrine of the ideal principle of art. Under the influence of the Neo-Platonic system, his conception of beauty was confused with his conception of art. While he sees beauty in living reality, he sees higher beauty in the ideas and actions of the sage. From this it is evident that his "beauty" is, in general, what we call "beautiful" in ordinary conversation (virtue is beautiful; patriotism is a beautiful sentiment, a noble mind is beautiful; a garden in bloom is beautiful, and so forth), and not what aesthetics calls "the beautiful," i.e., the perfection of material form which fully manifests its inner content.

But let us return to Aristotle and his *Poetics*. In it, in addition to his theory of the origin of art in general which we have expounded, and from which he hurriedly passes to the special problem of tragedies, we find many opinions that are of interest for our times. We shall say a few words about them. The opinions which are applicable only to Greek poetry and are now only of historical interest do not come within the scope of this review, and so we shall not deal with them. Similarly, we must pass over in silence the numerous excellent ideas about the essence of dramatic poetry, because their correctness is now admitted by all; and if present-day dramatists do not always conform to them in their works, it is only because they lack the power, or the art, to do so. Such, for example, is the idea that the most essential thing in drama (Aristotle speaks of this in

connection with tragedy) is action, the insufficiency of which
inevitably makes a play feeble, however great its other
merits may be. The strictest unity of action must predominate in a play (we deem it superfluous to repeat the idea, expressed long ago by everybody, that except for unity of
action, Aristotle demands no other unities), etc.

We often hear the opinion that events in real life should
not be depicted in poetry exactly as they occurred; that in
a historical novel, for example, historical events must
without fail be modified to meet the requirements of art,
"because a bare historical fact never has sufficient inner
unity and concatenation of parts." Aristotle arrives at this
problem in connection with historical tragedies and
solves it in this way: Poetry demands that the details of
the action should necessarily flow one from the other, and
that their concatenation should seem probable. Nothing
prevents some actual events from satisfying this demand;
everything in them developed of necessity, and everything
is probable—why, then, should not the poet take them in
their true form? After this, what is the purpose of all the
fictitious heroes, who eclipse the real heroes and are introduced only in order, by their fictitious adventures, "to lend
poetic unity" to the epoch described, as if it were impossible to find truly poetical events in the lives of the real heroes
of the novel? But the fashion for historical novels has passed
away and, therefore, we shall turn our remarks to stories
and plays about present-day life. What is the purpose of
this unceremonious dramatization of actual events that we
meet with so often in novels and stories? Choose a connected
and probable event and relate it as it really happened:
if your choice is good (and that is so easy!) your story of
real life will be better than any one altered "to meet the
requirements of art," i.e., usually, the requirements of literary effect. In what, then, will your "creativeness" be manifested? In your ability to sift the essential from the unessential, the essence of the event from what is extraneous.

The false conception of the necessary connection between the plot and the denouement was the source of the
false conception of the essence of the tragic in present-day
aesthetics. A tragic event is usually presented as taking
place under the influence of some sort of a special "tragic
fate," which crushes everything that is great and beautiful.
Aristotle, to whom the concept "fate" was much nearer than

N. G. CHERNYSHEVSKY

it is to us, says nothing about the intervention of fate in the lot of heroes in tragedies. But do not the heroes in tragedies usually perish? Aristotle easily explains this by the fact that the object of a tragedy is to rouse feelings of horror and pity. But if the denouement is a happy one, it will obliterate this impression, even if it had been roused by the preceding scenes. To this you will answer that the personages who perish at the end of a tragedy are presented at the beginning as strong, happy, and so forth. Aristotle easily explains this too by the fact that contrast is more striking than uniformity: on seeing a healthy man dead, or a happy man ruined, the spectator is more strongly imbued with horror and pity than when this contrast is lacking. And Aristotle is quite right in not introducing "fate" in the concept of the tragic: this external, extraneous force only serves to weaken the inner connection of events and gives them a trend that does not flow from the essence of the action—such is the aesthetic harm "fate" does in tragedies. Poetry must depict human life—let it not distort its scenes with extraneous admixtures.

Lastly, our final remark: according to Aristotle, the chief difference between Homer's epics and the later tragedies lies in that the *Iliad* and the *Odyssey* are much longer than tragedies and lack that strict unity of action that is necessary for tragedies. In tragedies, episodes are out of place, but in an epic they do not mar the beauty of the whole. But Aristotle sees no difference whatever between tragedies and Homer's poems as regards trend, spirit, or character of content (the difference in the manner of relation he sees very well, of course). On the contrary, he seems to presume an essential identity of content in epics and tragedies when he says that the *Iliad* and the *Odyssey* could each make several tragedies. Can we regard as a slip on Aristotle's part his disagreement on this point with our latest aestheticians who hold that there is a radical difference between the content of the epic and that of the drama? Perhaps; but there are more reasons for thinking that our aestheticians assume too profound a difference in content between epic and dramatic poetry, which among the Greeks differed more in form than in content. Indeed, pondering dispassionately over the problem (and our aestheticians are obviously biassed in favour of the dramatic form, "the highest form of poetry"), one can scarcely escape the conclu-

sion that although many plots of stories and novels are
unfit for drama, there is scarcely a dramatic work, whose
plot could not just as well (or even better) be related in epic
form. And is not the fact that some stories and novels (very
good ones, but containing little action and many superfluous episodes and too much spouting, which, of course,
cannot be regarded as merits in an epic work) could not be
converted into tolerable plays due chiefly to the fact that
boredom—which is quite bearable and sometimes even
pleasant in solitude, and at an appropriate time for this—
becomes unbearable when it is magnified by the boredom of
a thousand people like yourself in the stifling atmosphere
of a theatre? If to this we add scores of other circumstances
of the same kind—for example, the unsatisfactory nature
of all adaptations for the stage, the fact that the narrator
ignored all the conditions of the stage, the limitations of
the dramatic form itself—we shall see that the unfitness
for the stage of many plays adapted from stories is sufficiently explained without the assumption of a radical difference
between epic and dramatic plots.

To this "final" remark we take the liberty of adding one
more, which will indeed be the last. Aristotle considers the
writers of tragedies superior to Homer and, while in every
case recognizing various merits in the latter's poems, he
is nevertheless of the opinion that the tragedies of Sophocles
and Euripides are incomparably more artistic in form (and
profounder in content, he could have added). Should we
not, following his excellent example, look at Shakespeare
without false obsequiousness? It was natural for Lessing
to place him above all the poets who have existed on earth
and to regard his tragedies as the Hercules' pillars of art.
But today, when we have Lessing himself, and Goethe,
Schiller and Byron, when the reasons for protesting against
the overzealous imitators of the French writers have passed
away, it has perhaps become not so natural to grant Shakespeare uncontrolled power over our aesthetic convictions,
in season and out of season to quote his tragedies as examples
of all that is beautiful, and to regard everything in them
as beautiful. Does not Goethe think that *Hamlet* needs
revision? And perhaps Schiller did not reveal indiscriminate
taste in revising Racine's *Phedre* on a par with Shakespeare's
Macbeth. We are impartial towards the distant past; why,
then, should we hesitate so long in recognizing the recent

past as the age of a higher development of poetry than the preceding one? Does not its development keep pace with the development of education and of life?

We have tried to show that in spite of the one-sidedness of some of his propositions, the pettiness of many of his facts and deductions, and his chief defect—the predominance of formalism over the living doctrine that beauty in poetry is a consequence of talent developed by learning and of nobility of thought (demands much more strongly expressed by Plato than by Aristotle)—that in spite of all these defects, Aristotle's work, *The Poetic Art,** still has much living significance for modern theory and was worthy of serving as a basis for all the succeeding aesthetical conceptions up to Wolff and Baumgarten, or even up to Lessing and Kant (the theories of Hogarth, Burke and Diderot did not have great significance, for they met with little sympathy). From this it is evident what a good thing Mr. Ordynsky did in deciding to contribute to Russian literature a work of such importance for science. Indeed, a happier choice could scarcely have been made. Just as true was the tact that guided Mr. Ordynsky in his choice of subjects for his previous works: *Theophrastus' "Characters,"* and *Aristophanes' Comedies.* Equally excellent was his intention to translate Homer in prose—a very correct idea at bottom, for the very best Russian hexameters are still garments too heavy and entangling for Homer's childishly simple soul. Mr. Ordynsky must also be given full credit for the conscientious way in which he has laboured on each of these works. So in his new essay one cannot fail to see work executed with extreme conscientiousness. Mr. Ordynsky studied the text of Aristotle's *Poetics* with exemplary accuracy; he utilized the works of all the best publishers and commentators and, with truly scientific modesty, always acknowledges his sources. The translation of the text has not been made hurriedly, it is not slipshod; Mr. Ordynsky weighed every word, pondered over every expression. In short, Mr. Ordynsky's translation and commentary meet most of the conditions that determine a work of merit. Nevertheless, one cannot help foreseeing that his translation of *Poet-*

---

* We are of the opinion that the translation of the title of Aristotle's book Περὶ ποιητικῆς—as *The Poetic Art*, having in mind τεχνης (*cf.* the title τέχνη ρητορική), is more correct than *Poetics* as given by Mr. Ordynsky.

ics will find rather little favour even among that small
section of the public that is particularly interested in classical literature; other readers it will certainly repel. And
it is doubtful whether Mr. Ordynsky's commentary, made
with great knowledge of the subject and care, will be of
much benefit to Russian readers. Mr. Ordynsky's translation is heavy and obscure, and the commentaries have been
written almost solely to prove the translator's own opinion
that Aristotle's book *The Poetic Art* has come down to us
in full and not in fragmentary abstracts as is usually thought,
and that the text of this work, or abstracts, has not been distorted and does not need correction. This is the question
that we must now discuss.

Does the text of Aristotle's *Poetics* need correction?
The degree to which the text of Aristotle's works is distorted is clearly evident, even to one who is not a philologist, from what had happened to them before they became
generally known, and they became known two and a half
centuries after Aristotle's death. This story is rather interesting and we shall therefore relate it in a few words. Aristotle's works were not published during his lifetime. On
his death they passed into the hands of his pupil Theophrastus, but he, too, refrained from publishing them, perhaps
because Aristotle, like Anaxagoras, towards the end of his
life had suffered severe persecution for repudiating poly-
theism; it is even believed that this persecution compelled
him to take poison. When on his deathbed, Theophrastus
transferred Aristotle's works, together with his library, to
Neleus of Scepsis. Neleus sold Aristotle's library to Ptolemy Philadelphus, King of Egypt, but he could not bear
to part with Aristotle's own works. Neleus' heirs were ignorant people who had no use for Aristotle's works, but they
had heard from Neleus that these books were very valuable.
Living within the domains of Pergamum, and, afraid
that the Kings of Pergamum—who were rivaling the Ptol-
emys in collecting a library as big and as complete as the
one at Alexandria, and were therefore searching for books
everywhere—would confiscate these treasures or buy them
at an insignificant price, they deemed it necessary to hide
them, and they did hide them in a cellar. There they remained for a long time. At last, Apellicon of Teos, a wealthy
Athenian book lover, accidentally heard where Aristotle's works were hidden and bought them at a high price.

This was already in the time of Mithridates the Great. Thus, they must have lain in the damp cellar for a hundred or a hundred and fifty years, if not more. Apellicon found them damaged by the dampness of the cellar and also eaten by worms. One can imagine how great the damage must have been, considering how long the manuscripts had been exposed to it. After bringing them to Athens, Apellicon had them copied, and the passages that had been obliterated by dampness or worms were *filled in* by guesswork. When Athens was conquered by Sulla, Apellicon's library was seized by the conqueror and transferred to Rome. In Rome there lived a learned Greek named Tyrannion, who received permission from Sulla to use the library. On discovering Aristotle's works there, he made a number of copies, which he gave, among others, to Cicero, Lucullus and Andronicus of Teos. Andronicus exerted all efforts to put the copy he received in order. He divided the books according to their contents, and corrected the text again. The works as revised by him circulated among the scholars. It must be supposed that, together with completed works, Apellicon must have received incomplete ones; in all probability, Aristotle had several copies of the same work, revised in different ways; there must also have been abstracts, rough drafts, and so forth. One of these abstracts, or rough sketches must, in all probability, have been the *Poetics* that has come down to us. Some scholars have tried to refute this story, but their arguments are feeble and the story remains authentic.[8] Thus, Aristotle's works, left in disorder, and half decayed and worm-eaten, were twice supplemented and corrected. Can there be any doubt after this that the text is very much in need of purging and critical correction?

Indeed, Aristotle's works have come down to us in a very disorderly state. Many of them perished; many of them have been badly compiled out of parts collected haphazard, intermixed with rough sketches, incomplete fragments, abstracts, and forged fragments. As a striking example we point to the character of the collection which bears the title *Aristotle's Metaphysics*, consisting of fourteen books. The 2nd and 3rd, in all probability, are not Aristotle's; if the 1st is his, it has nothing in common with the rest. The *Metaphysics* really starts only with the 4th book. The 5th must have been a separate work and was included in the *Metaphysics* by mistake. According to inner connec-

tion, the 4th book should have been immediately followed
by the 6th. The 10th is a repetition of the 4th and 5th;
it is either an abstract made by some reader, or a rough
manuscript out of which the 4th and 5th books were later
made. The 11th and 12th contain many abstracts from Aristotle supplemented by thoughts alien to him; they, too,
are a collection compiled by some reader. Thus, of the fourteen books of the *Metaphysics*, only books 4, 6, 7, 8, 9, 13
and 14 are Aristotle's and form a connected work. The rest
are composed either of rough drafts, or of abstracts and com-
pilations made up out of Aristotle's works by other scholars
and should not go in Aristotle's *Metaphysics*. Many of the
so-called "works of Aristotle" are definitely, from beginning
to end, only abstracts of his works made by other philosophers. For example, the *Big Ethics* is an abstract of his
Nicomachean Ethics; the *Opinions of Xenophanes, Zeno and
Gorgias* is a collection of fragments in which Xenophanes
is not discussed; the *Direction and Names of the Winds*
is a fragment of his *Signs of Storms*; the *Problems* is a later abstract of different works of his; the *History of Animals*, in nine or ten books (the genuineness of one is doubtful) is a fragment of a work of his consisting of at least fifty
books; in short, half, if not more, of the works of Aristotle
that have not perished, have come down to us incomplete
and not in their authentic form.

Therefore, it is not in the least surprising that we have
to regard Aristotle's *Poetics* also as a fragmentary abridg-
ment, or a rough sketch, the text of which is rather seriously
distorted. We shall not point to the minor proofs of the incompleteness of the text, they are met with at every step:
grammatical mistakes, omissions and incoherent sentences
are found in nearly every line. We constantly meet with
passages like: "here we must examine four cases," but only
two or three of the promised four are examined. Such criticism, while very convincing for the philologist, would be
unintelligible without lengthy grammatical explanations.
Let us glance only at the beginning and the end of the
Poetics as it has come down to us—they are sufficient to
enable us to judge of its completeness. At the very beginning
of his work Aristotle says that its contents will consist of
"epics, tragedy, comedy, dithyrambic poetry, auletics and
citharistics (different kinds of lyrical poetry with musical
accompaniment). But the text that has come down to us

29*

deals only with tragedy and very little with epics. Obviously, only part of the work has come down to us. Indeed, from excerpts of the *Poetics* quoted by other writers we know that it consisted of two (or even of three) books. Obviously, only part of the first book had come down to us, either in an abstract made by others, or in a rough sketch. The text that has come down to us ends with a sentence that contains the conjunction μέν, which necessarily calls for a corresponding succeeding sentence containing the conjunction δέ. To enable readers not familiar with the Greek language to understand why this addition is needed we will say that the correspondence of the conjunctions μέν and δέ may be compared with the correspondence of the phrases "on the one hand," "on the other hand," or the words "although— nevertheless." Let us suppose that the text of a book in our language ends with the words: "this, on the one hand, is what must be said about tragedies"... is it not obvious that the text of this book is unfinished and that the immediate continuation should be: "but on the other hand..."? The Greek text of Aristotle's *Poetics* ends in the same way.* Obviously, this is the end of only one section of the book, and then followed another section dealing with another form of poetry, probably comedy.

Thus, the underlying idea in Mr. Ordynsky's argument, viz., that "Aristotle's *Poetics* has come down to us complete and the text needs no correction," can scarcely be regarded as probable; yet the whole of his commentary is written with the object of proving it. It is, therefore, unsuitable for use.

Similarly, his translation of Aristotle's text would, probably, have been much more useful had it not been distinguished for the same striving for originality in language as his commentary is for originality in opinion. The reader must, of course, have noticed in the short excerpts we have quoted that Mr. Ordynsky has translated Aristotle in a language that is heavy and obscure. We do not claim that Aristotle's *Poetics* would be read by the entire Russian public however light and graceful the language of the translation would be; but it would find a fairly large number of readers if the translation were graceful. It is doubtful, however, whether Mr. Ordynsky's translation will attract many readers; it will share the fate of Martynov's very practical trans-

---

* Περὶ μὲν οὖν τῆς τραγῳδίας εἰρήσθω τοσαῦτα.

lations, which nobody reads, precisely because the language
is heavy and obscure. Why, then, did Mr. Ordynsky give
us such an unreadable translation when, in the same work,
the style of his commentary shows that he can write in very
lucid and fairly simple language? He says in his preface
that he tried to keep his translation as close to the original as possible—excellent! But, firstly, there is a limit
to everything, and to make a literal translation to the detriment of lucidity and correctness of language means not
making an exact translation, for what is clear in the original
ought to be clear in the translation; otherwise, what is the
use of a translation? Secondly, although Mr. Ordynsky's
translation is very close to the original, it cannot, however,
be called a word-for-word translation: in many cases, two
words in the original are translated with one, and one with
two words, even where a word-for-word translation could
have been made. It was possible to make a lucid and reada-
ble translation without departing from the original any more
than Mr. Ordynsky has done. The cause of the defects in
the translation is not the restricting closeness to the original, but Mr. Ordynsky's original conception of Russian
style. He strives after a sort of artificial popular language,
deliberately ignores the rules of literary language, tries
to avoid using literary words, and is fond of obsolete or
rarely used words. What is the purpose of this? Write as everybody does, and if you possess the living force of simplicity and popularity it will of itself lend your style simplicity and popularity, without deliberate effort. All deliberate striving for originality leads to pretentiousness; and
we think that Mr. Ordynsky's works, while retaining all their
undeniable merits, will be much more read and, therefore,
will be much more useful, if he abandons his striving for
originality in language, which is totally unnecessary for
a scientist.

It goes without saying, that we are uttering these remarks only because we respect Mr. Ordynsky's useful efforts
and would like to see his works acquire increasing popularity
among the Russian public. We, therefore, take our leave
of our young scholar—not for long, of course—hoping
that he will be a constant contributor to Russian literature
and remain as conscientious and diligent a student of Greek
philology as he has been up till now.

ESSAYS ON THE GOGOL PERIOD
OF RUSSIAN LITERATURE[1]

SIXTH ESSAY

BELINSKY

THE *Moskovsky Nablyudatel*[2] was placed at the disposal of Stankevich's friends when the funds for continuing publication had been completely exhausted, and it was only due to the unselfish energy of the new contributors that the magazine, which had been brought to ruin by their predecessors, could go on for another year. But this last, far too short, period in the life of the *Moskovsky Nablyudatel* had no parallel in the history of Russian journalism, except, perhaps, for the last issues of the *Teleskop*.[3] Even the *Telegraf*[4] in its best period was not so closely bound by unity of earnest thought, was not inspired by such an ardent striving to serve truth and art as the *Moskovsky Nablyudatel* was; and although we had had almanacs and magazines before that period with a much larger number of contributors who already enjoyed wide reputations, as, for example, the *Biblioteka Dlya Chteniya*[5] in 1834, and Pushkin's *Sovremennik* in 1836, never before had so much truly remarkable talent, so much true knowledge and genuine poetry, been united in a Russian magazine as there was in the *Moskovsky Nablyudatel* under the second editorship (Volumes XVI, XVII and XVIII of the first series, and Volumes I and II of the second). In 1838-39 the new contributors to the *Nablyudatel* were almost entirely unknown youths; but nearly all of them proved to be strong and gifted, nearly all of them were destined to win a firm, noble and unblemished reputation in our literature, and some of them to win illustrious fame. The future belonged to them, just as the present belongs to them and to those who joined them later.

The *Moskovsky Nablyudatel* is less well known than the *Telegraf* or the *Teleskop*. For this reason, before discussing

its views on science and literature, it will not be superfluous
to say two or three words about the general complexion
of the last volumes of the magazine, issued by the men
of the new generation whose activities now interest us.

Before the period in which Gogol's decisive influence
upon the young talents caused the majority of the gifted
writers to prefer the prose form of narration, poetry was the
brilliant side of our *belles lettres*. The *Moskovsky Nablyudatel* did not have Pushkin among its contributors as did the
almanacs of 1823-33, or the *Biblioteka* and (Pushkin's)
Sovremennik in their first years. But if we compare the
Nablyudatel's poetry section as a whole with the poetry
published in the almanacs that were formerly so famed for
it, and with Pushkin's own *Sovremennik* (not to speak
of the *Biblioteka*, which was far inferior in this respect to
the *Sovremennik*, *Severniye Tsvety*,[6] and others), we shall
have to admit that as regards its poetry section, the *Moskovsky Nablyudatel* was far superior to all our older magazines
and almanacs in which, apart from the works of Pushkin
and Zhukovsky's translations, only a few poems rose above
the level of colourless mediocrity. In the *Moskovsky Nablyudatel*, however, we scarcely find any poems that cannot be
read with pleasure even today, and, on the contrary, we do
find many which, in addition to the wonderful creations of
Koltsov, remain remarkable and beautiful to this day.*

---

* In addition to Koltsov's poems, the *Moskovsky Nablyudatel*
published the following:

Translations of Goethe and Schiller by Mr. K. S. Aksakov, who
deserves to be called one of our best poet translators. The opinion
sometimes expressed nowadays that the verse of his translations is
heavy is not altogether sound. On the contrary, we think that few
translations will be found as poetical and beautiful as, for example,
his translation of Goethe's "Auf dem See" (*Moskovsky Nablyudatel*, XVI, 92):

НА ОЗЕРЕ

Как освежается душа
И кровь течет быстрей!
О, как природа хороша!
Я на груди у ней!

Качает наш челнок волна,
В лад с нею весла бьют.
И горы в мшистых пеленах
Навстречу нам встают.

AUF DEM SEE

Und frische Nahrung, neues Blut
Sang' ich aus freier Welt;
Wie ist Natur so hold und gut,
Die mich am Busen hält!

Die Welle wieget unsern Kahn
Im Rudertakt hinauf,
Und Berge, wolkig himmelan;
Begegnen unserm Lauf.

It is not only that of the numerous poems published in the *Moskovsky Nablyudatel* under the second editorship, only a few could be called weak—a merit that none of our magazines before that time could boast of. These numerous poems possess another quality, still newer for those times, viz., positively, not a single one of them can be called vacuous verse. Every lyrical piece is permeated with feeling and meaning, so that the poetry section of the *Moskovsky Nablyudatel* cannot be compared with those found in the other magazines of that period.

Nor could the magazines of that time boast of their fiction. Very few good stories were written then, because only three or four writers could write prose in such a way that their works can now be read without a smile. But the fiction section of the *Moskovsky Nablyudatel* was, perhaps, superior to those in all the rest because it published stories by Nestroyev (Mr. Kudryavtsev), which should be placed in the very first rank in the history of the rise of our prose

Что же, мой взор, опускаешься ты? Вы ли опять, золотые мечты? О, прочь, мечтанье, хоть сладко оно ! Здесь все так любовью и жизнью полно	Aug', mein Aug', was sinkst du nieder? Goldne Träume, kommt ihr wieder? Weg, du Traum! So Gold du bist; Hier auch Lieb' und Leben ist.
Светлою толпою Звезды в волнах глядятся Туманы грядою На дальних высях ложатся;	Auf der Welle blinken Tausend schwebende Sterne, Weiche Nebel trinken Rings die türmende Ferne;
Ветер утра качает Деревья над зеркалом вод; Тихо отражает Озеро спеющий плод.	Morgenwind umflügelt Die beschattete Bucht, Und im See bespiegelt Sich die reifende Frucht.

Our object in quoting this poem is not only to prove that we are right in classing Mr. K. Aksakov's translations in the *Moskovsky Nablyudatel* among the works that have positive merit; for us, the poem serves as a poetical expression of the most characteristic feature of the world outlook that prevailed in the *Moskovsky Nablyudatel*.

Mr. Katkov's translations of Heine's poems and fragments of his excellent translation of Shakespeare's *Romeo and Juliet*.

Poems by Klyuchnikov (-Θ-) and by several other more or less remarkable talents.

Poems by Krasov, who was, perhaps, the best of our minor poets in the period when Koltsov and Lermontov wrote. They should have been collected and published long ago; they fully deserve it, and we do wrong in forgetting this splendid poet.

belles lettres. This essay is not the place in which to appraise Nestroyev's talent; we hope to do this on a later occasion; but there can be no doubt that for their artistic merit, his stories ought to occupy an honourable place in the history of Russian prose. Nestroyev was a writer of strong and independent talent equalled by very few in his time; it would be truer to say by scarcely anybody except such colossal talents as Pushkin, Gogol and Lermontov.

Thus, *belles lettres* in the *Moskovsky Nablyudatel* is remarkable for its artistic merit; but it is still more interesting for the reason that it is, in general, a true and full reflection of the principles that inspired the company of young men who were gathered around Stankevich. Before that time, only very few of our poets and fiction writers had been able to bring the meaning of their works into harmony with the ideas which seemed right to them. As a rule, stories and poems had very little relation to what is called the author's "world outlook," if, indeed, the author had a "world outlook." By way of example we point to Marlinsky, in whose works the most careful search will fail to reveal the slightest trace of the principles which the author no doubt held dear as a man.[7] As a rule, life and the convictions it aroused on the one hand, and poetry on the other, were each kept in separate compartments, as it were. The connection between the writer and the man was very feeble, and the living men themselves, when they took up the pen in the capacity of writers, were often concerned only with theories of fine style and not at all with the meaning of their works. They were not concerned about "introducing a living idea" into works of art (as the critics of the Gogol period were fond of expressing it). This defect—absence of connection between the author's fundamental convictions and his works— was one that the whole of our literature suffered from before things were changed by the influence of Gogol and Belinsky. The literary section of the *Moskovsky Nablyudatel* was, perhaps, the first germ of constant harmony between a man's convictions and the meaning of his artistic productions—of that harmony which now rules in our literature and gives it vigour and life. The young poets and novelists who contributed to this magazine wrote about what engaged their minds, and not about subjects suggested by other poets, the meaning of which was often unintelligible to the imitators who very zealously copied the external side of foreign productions. They understood what they wrote about— a quality very rarely observed among our earlier writers. There were very few exceptions to the rule of writing either works devoid of living meaning, or containing a meaning that remained a secret to the author; and the *Moskovsky Nablyudatel* was the first magazine in which meaning and poetry harmonized, and whose literary section always reflected conscious strivings. It was the first of the series of magazines, such as we have at the present time, in which poetry, fiction and literary criticism march in step towards a common goal, each supporting the other. A deep desire for truth and goodness on the one hand, and on the other, a fresh and healthy readiness to love all the joys provided by real life—preference for real life to abstract fantasy on the one hand, and on the other, extreme sympathy for what in the strivings of fantasy is a healthy reflection of the true need of the full enjoyment of real life—these fundamental features of the critical thought expressed by the *Moskovsky Nablyudatel* also constitute the essential character of that magazine's literary section. The strivings which inspire its poetry and fiction are obviously imbued with the philosophical idea that dominates over everything.

Indeed, a philosophical world outlook held undivided sway over the minds of the friendly circle, of which the last volumes of the *Moskovsky Nablyudatel* were the organ. These people positively lived only for philosophy, they talked about it day and night whenever they got together, they looked at everything and solved everything from the philosophical point of view. That was the time when we first made our acquaintance of Hegel, and the enthusiasm roused by the, for us, new, profound truths that were developed in that thinker's system with amazing dialectical force, naturally had to gain the upper hand for a time over all the other strivings of the men of the younger generation, who realized that it was their duty to be heralds of a truth as yet unknown among us, and which, in the first flush of their enthusiasm, seemed to them to light up and to reconcile everything, to give man both serene inner peace and robust strength for external activity. The chief significance of the *Moskovsky Nablyudatel* lies in that it was an organ of Hegelian philosophy.

Philosophical strivings have now been almost forgotten by our literature and literary criticism. We do not wish to decide how much literature and literary criticism have gained by this forgetfulness—we think they have gained absolutely nothing, but they have lost a great deal. But which-ever way one has decided for himself the question cf the significance of a philosophical world outlook for the present time, everyone must agree that the domination of philoso-phy over all our intellectual activities at the beginning of the present period of our literature is a remarkable histor-ical fact that deserves careful study. The *Moskovsky Nab-lyudatel* represents the first epoch of this rule of philosophy, when Hegel was regarded as its infallible interpreter, when every word of Hegel's was regarded as undoubted truth and every utterance of the great teacher was accepted by his new disciples in the literal sense; when there was, as yet, neither concern for testing these truths, nor any presenti-ment that Hegel was not consistent, that he contradicted himself at every step, that in accepting his principles the consistent thinker must arrive at conclusions entirely dif-ferent from those Hegel had arrived at. Later, when this was discovered, the false conclusions were refuted by the best of Hegel's former followers among us, and German philosophy appeared in an entirely new light. But that was already a different epoch, the epoch of the *Otechest-venniye Zapiski*, which we shall discuss in the next essay. At present we shall examine the Hegelian system of which the *Moskovsky Nablyudatel* was an ardent advocate.

The magazine's program was formulated in its first article—the preface to the translation of *Hegel's Gymna-sium Speeches* (*Moskovsky Nablyudatel*, XVI, pp. 5-20).[8] We quote in the footnote below the essential passages of this preface, adding explanations of the technical terms used in the Hegelian language, which readers unaccustomed to this terminology may find difficult to understand. They, we hope, will see that the matter was quite simple and lucid, and that all talk about the alleged obscurity of Hegelian philosophy is mere prejudice. It is only necessary to know the meaning of a few technical terms, and transcendental philoso-phy becomes clear and simple for the people of our times.*

_____

* To reason is only one of man's capabilities; knowledge is only one of his strivings. Therefore, reasoning about abstract prob-lems alone does not satisfy man. He also wants to love and live; not only to know, but also to enjoy; not only to think, but also to act. Nowadays, everybody understands this—such is the spirit of the age, such is the power of all-explaining time. But in the seventeenth

The content of Hegelian philosophy, in the way it
was expounded by Hegel himself and which was accepted
down to the minutest detail as indisputable truth by Stankevich's friends in 1838-39, seems to be the very opposite
of the mode of thought that was later expounded with such
ardour and success by the literary critics of the Gogol
period in the *Otechestvenniye Zapiski* (1840-46) and in
our magazine (1847-48). That is why the essays in the
Moskovsky Nablyudatel written by Belinsky and his like-
minded friends exclusively under the influence of Hegel's
works seem, at first sight, to utterly contradict the essays
the same Belinsky wrote several years later. This contradiction is due, as we have said, to the duality of Hegel's
system, to the contradiction between its principles and its
deductions, between its spirit and its content. Hegel's
principles were extremely powerful and broad; his deduc-

---

century science was in the hands of armchair philosophers who knew
only books, who thought only about scientific problems, shunned
life and did not understand mundane affairs. When, in the eighteenth
century, life demanded its rights with such vigour that it awoke
even the German scholars, they saw the inadequacy of their former
philosophical methods, which based everything on syllogisms, which
took abstract conceptions as the measure of all things. But they could
not pass from their musty studies into the forum of life at one step.
They were still too remote from the idea that *all* man's natural capabilities and strivings must help one another to solve the problems of
science and life. It seemed to them that it would be enough to change
the method of reasoning, while continuing to ignore man's heart and
body. They thought that the failure of the mind to embrace the whole
of living truth was not due to the fact that the head alone, without
a breast and hands, without a heart and sense of touch, was not enough
for a man. They tried to find out whether the head could dispense
with the assistance of the other members of the living organism if
the head alone would undertake the functions that belonged to the
heart, the stomach and the hands—and indeed, the head invented
"speculative thinking." The essence of this attempt was that the
mind, rejecting abstract concepts, tried to think in so-called "concrete" concepts—for example, in thinking of man, not to base its
conclusions on the old postulate: "man is a being endowed with reason," but on a real man, with hands and feet, a heart and a stomach.
This was a big step forward. Hegel was the last and most important
of the thinkers who had halted at this first phase of the conversion
of the armchair philosopher into a living man. The system that was
based on this substitution of more concrete concepts for the former
abstract ones was, of course, much fresher and fuller than the old totally abstract systems, which studied not people as they really are,
but phantoms created by the former method of thinking, which denied
that man had any capability and striving other than that of reasoning,
and which, of all the organs of the human being, regarded only the

tions were narrow and feeble. Despite all his colossal genius, the great thinker possessed only enough strength to express general ideas, but not enough strength undeviatingly to keep to these principles and logically to draw all the necessary deductions from them. He perceived the truth, but only in most general, abstract and altogether indefinite outlines. It was only the next generation that was able to see it face to face. Not only was Hegel unable to draw the deductions from his principles, but the principles themselves were not altogether clear to him, they were hazy to him. The next generation of thinkers took a step forward, and the principles that were vaguely, one-sidedly and abstractly expressed by Hegel appeared in all their fullness and clarity. Then, no room remained for vacillation, duality vanished, the false conclusions introduced into science by Hegel's inconsistency in developing fundamental propositions were eliminated, and content was brought into harmony with fundamental truths. Such was the course of affairs

---

brain as being worthy of its attention. That is why "transcendental" or "speculative" thinking (which strives to base its conclusions on conceptions of real objects) was justly proud of the fact that it was more concrete than the former scholastic method; and the ancient method of basing everything on abstract concepts was branded with the name of "phantom thinking" that belonged to the "abstract mind, or reason" (Verstand). All the concepts and deductions that were based on this "abstract, phantom thinking" were branded as "phantom concepts," "phantom deductions," and Hegel's disciples spoke with disdain of all the philosophers whose systems were not built on the foundation of "speculative thinking." In the opinion of Hegel and his followers, these people did not deserve to be called philosophers, and their systems were "phantom structures," in which "abstract phantoms" were given instead of living truth. Particular indignation was roused by French philosophy, which, having done its work, ceased to occupy vigorous minds and became the occupation of fantasts and windbags, and indeed, under Napoleon and during the Restoration became shallow and vulgar. At that time, everybody in France applied the term philosophy to every kind of nonsense that entered his head, and arbitrarily mixing this nonsense with the hastily borrowed ideas of other people, he proclaimed himself a genius and creator of a new philosophical system. It was against such fantasies devoid of scientific merit that the preface to Hegel's speeches, which served as the *Moskovsky Nablyudatel's* program, was directed. Here are the pertinent passages of this program:

"Who does not nowadays imagine that he is a philosopher, who does not make positive assertions about what truth is, and what it consists in? Everybody wants to have his own particular system. He who does not think in his own way, as he himself arbitrarily pleases,

in Germany, and so it was in our country. The development of consistent views from Hegel's ambiguous and totally unapplied hints took place in our country partly under the influence of the German thinkers who appeared after Hegel, and partly—we can proudly say this—as a result of our own efforts. Here, for the first time, the Russian mind proved that it was capable of taking part in the development of world science.[9]

Let us now examine those principles of Hegel's philosophy, the power and truth of which swept the men of the *Moskovsky Nablyudatel* into its current to such a degree that in the ardour of the enthusiasm roused by these lofty strivings they, for a time, forgot all the other demands of

---

lacks independent spirit, is a colourless individual; he who has not invented his own little idea is not a genius, is not a profound thinker; and no matter where you turn nowadays, you meet with geniuses. But what have these self-styled geniuses inented what is the fruit of their profound little ideas and views, what have they contributed to progress, what real thing have they done?

" 'We are making a lot of noise, brother, a lot of noise,' is the answer given for them by Repetilov in Griboyedov's comedy. Yes, a lot of noise, meaningless chatter—such is the only result of the horrible senseless anarchy of opinion that is the chief malady that has afflicted our abstract-minded, dreamy new generation, which shuns everything that is real. And all this noise, all this chatter, goes by the name of philosophy. Is it surprising, then, that the intelligent and practical Russian people do not allow themselves to be dazzled by this firework display of empty words and senseless thoughts? Is it surprising that they distrust philosophy when it is presented to them in such an unprepossessing and spectral guise? Up till now philosophy and abstraction, the spectral and unreal, have been synonymous. Whoever has taken up philosophy has necessarily bid farewell to reality and is roaming in this morbid estrangement from all natural and spiritual reality, in some fantastic, arbitrary, nonexistent world, or has armed himself against the real world and imagines that with his phantom weapons he can destroy its mighty existence, imagines that in the realization of the finite (*limited, one-sided*) postulates (*judgments*) of his finite (*limited, one-sided, abstract*) reasoning and the finite aims of his finite will lies the good of mankind. The poor fellow does not know that the real world stands higher than his wretched and impotent individuality (*personality*).... His life is a constant torment, a series of constant disappointments, of hopeless and endless struggle—and this inner collapse, this inner disintegration, is a necessary consequence of the abstract and phantom nature of finite reason, for which nothing is concrete, and which transforms all life into death. I repeat: the general distrust of philosophy is very well grounded because what has been presented to us as philosophy up till now destroys a man instead of reinvigorating him, instead of making him a useful and active member of society.

reason and life and accepted the whole content of the system that boasted of being based on these profound truths. We follow Hegel as little as we follow Descartes or Aristotle. Hegel now belongs to past history; the present has its own philosophy and clearly sees the flaws in the Hegelian system. It must be admitted, however, that the principles advanced by Hegel were indeed very near to the truth, and this thinker brought out some aspects of the truth with truly astonishing power. Of these truths, the discovery of some stands to Hegel's personal credit; others do not belong exclusively to his system, they belong to German philosophy as a whole from the time of Kant and Fichte; but nobody before Hegel had formulated them so clearly and had expressed them with such power as they were in his system.

First of all we shall point to the most fruitful principle underlying all progress which so sharply and brilliantly distinguishes German philosophy in general, and the Hegelian system in particular, from the hypocritical and

---

The source of this evil lies in the Reformation. When the mission of Papism—to substitute an external centre for the absent internal centre—ended ... the Reformation shook its authority ... the awakened mind, ridding itself of the swaddling clothes of authority, separating itself from the real world and becoming engrossed in itself, wanted to deduce everything from itself, to find the beginning and foundation of knowledge within itself.... But the human mind, just awakened from long slumber, could not cognize truth at one stroke, the real world of truth was more than it could cope with, it had not yet grown up for it, and it had to traverse a long road of trial, struggle and suffering before it could reach maturity. Truth is not obtained gratis. No! It is the fruit of severe suffering, of long and painful striving.... The result of the philosophy of reason (in Germany, with Fichte) was the destruction of all objectivity, of all reality and the submersion of the vacuous, abstract ego in self-loving, egoistical self-contemplation, the destruction of all love, and consequently, of all life and of all possibility of bliss.... But the German people were too strong, too realistic to fall victims to a phantom.... Hegel's system crowned the mind's long striving towards reality:

What is real is rational; *and*
What is rational is real,—

such is the basis of Hegel's philosophy.

Let us now turn to France and see how this separation of the ego from reality manifested itself there.... Man's mind, unable to penetrate the profound and sacred secret of life, repudiated everything that was inaccessible to it; but all truth and all reality are inaccessible to it. The whole life of France is nothing but the realization of its hollowness and the painful striving to fill it, no matter with what; and all craven views that predominated at that time (beginning of the nineteenth century) among the French and the English: "Truth is the supreme goal of thought; seek truth, for in truth lies good; whatever truth may be, it is better than falsehood; the first duty of the thinker is not to retreat from any results; he must be prepared to sacrifice his most cherished opinions to truth. Error is the source of all ruin; truth is the supreme good and the source of all other good." To be able to appraise the extreme importance of this demand, common to German philosophy as a whole since the time of Kant, but expressed with exceptional vigour by Hegel, one must remember what strange and narrow restrictions the thinkers of the other schools of that period imposed upon truth. They began to philosophize only in order to "justify their cherished convictions," i.e., they sought not truth, but support for their prejudices. Each took from truth only what pleased him and rejected every truth that was unpleasant to him, bluntly admitting that a pleasing error suited him much better than impartial truth. The German philosophers (especially Hegel) called this practice of seeking not truth but confirmation of pleasing prejudices "subjective thinking," philosophizing for personal pleasure, and not for the vital need of truth. Hegel fiercely denounced this idle and pernicious pastime. As a necessary precaution against inclinations to digress from truth in order to pander to personal desires and prejudices, Hegel advanced his cel-

---

the means it employs to fill itself are spectral and fruitless ... the French (*when they begin to philosophize*) transform all truth into hollow, meaningless phrases, into arbitrary and anarchical thinking, and into the concoction of new little ideas....

Unfortunately, this disease has also spread among us... The shallowness of our education is the chief cause of the phantom nature of our new generation. Instead of igniting the divine spark in a young man ... instead of imbuing him with deep aesthetic feeling which protects a man from all the sordid sides of life—instead of all this, his mind is filled with hollow, meaningless French phrases.... Instead of training the young mind for real work, instead of imbuing it with love of knowledge ... it is trained to disdain work ... this is the cause of our general malady, of our spectralness! Open any book of Russian verse you please and see what constitutes the food for the daily inspiration of our self-styled poets....

One proclaims that he does not believe in life, that he is disillusioned; another, that he does not believe in friendship; a third, that he does not believe in love...

Happiness does not lie in a phantom, not in an abstract dream, but in living reality. To rebel against reality is just the same as kill-

ebrated "dialectical method of thinking." The essence of this method lies in that the thinker must not rest content with any positive deduction, but must find out whether the object he is thinking about contains qualities and forces the opposite of those which the object had presented to him at first sight. Thus, the thinker was obliged to examine the object from all sides, and truth appeared to him only as a consequence of a conflict between all possible opposite opinions. Gradually, as a result of this method, the former one-sided conceptions of an object were supplanted by a full and all-sided investigation, and a living conception was obtained of all the real qualities of an object. To explain reality became the paramount duty of philosophical thought. As a result, extraordinary attention was paid to reality, which had been formerly ignored and unceremoniously distorted in order to pander to personal, one-sided prejudices. Thus, conscientious, tireless search for truth took the place of the former arbitrary interpretations. In reality, however, everything depends upon circumstances, upon the conditions of place and time, and therefore, Hegel found that the former general phrases by which good and evil were judged without an examination of the circumstances and causes that give rise to a given phenomenon, that these general, abstract aphorisms were unsatisfactory. Every object, every phenomenon, has its own significance, and it must be judged according to the circumstances, the environment, in which it exists. This rule was expressed by the formula: "There is no abstract truth; truth is concrete," i.e., a definite judgment can be pronounced only about a definite fact, after examining all the circumstances upon which it depends.*

---

ing every source of life within oneself. Reconciliation with reality in all respects, and in all spheres of life, is the chief task of our times, and Hegel and Goethe are the leaders of this reconciliation, of this return from death to life. Let us hope that our new generation will likewise abandon this phantom, will abandon empty and meaningless chatter, that it will realize that true knowledge and anarchic thought and arbitrary opinions are opposites; that strict discipline reigns in knowledge, and that without this discipline there is no knowledge. Let us hope that our new generation will, at last, enter into kinship with our beautiful Russian reality and that, abandoning all hollow claims to genius, will, at last, feel the legitimate need of being real Russian people.

* For example: "Is rain good or bad?" This is an abstract question; a definite answer cannot be given to it. Sometimes rain is beneficial, sometimes, although more rarely, it is harmful. One must

It goes without saying that this brief enumeration of some of the principles of Hegelian philosophy can give no idea of the amazing impression created by the works of the great philosopher who, in his time, carried with him even the most distrustful of his pupils by the extraordinary power and loftiness of his mind, which subjugated all spheres of existence, which in each sphere discovered laws of nature and history identical with its own law of dialectical development, which embraced all the facts of religion, art, the exact sciences, constitutional and private law, history and psychology in a net of systematic unity, so that everything is explained and reconciled. The period of this philosophy, of which Hegel was the last and greatest exponent, has passed for Germany. With the aid of the results it worked out, science, as we have said, took a step forward; but this new science was only a further development of the Hegelian system, which will forever retain historical importance as the bridge from abstract science to the science of life.

Such was the importance of Hegelian philosophy in our country. It served as the bridge from barren, scholastic philosophizing that bordered on apathy and ignorance to a simple and lucid conception of literature and life, because, as we have tried to explain, its principles contained the germ of this conception. Ardent and resolute minds

---

inquire specifically: "After the grain was sown it rained heavily for five hours—was the rain useful for the crop?"—only here is the answer: "that rain was very useful" clear and sensible. "But in that very same summer, just when harvest time arrived, it rained in torrents for a whole week—was that good for the crop?" The answer: "No. That rain was harmful," is equally clear and correct. That is how all questions are decided by Hegelian philosophy. "Is war disastrous or beneficial?" This cannot be answered definitely in general; one must know what kind of war is meant, everything depends upon circumstances, time and place. For savage peoples, the harmfulness of war is less palpable, the benefits of it are more tangible. For civilized peoples, war usually does more harm than good. But the war of 1812, for example, was a war of salvation for the Russian people. The battle of Marathon was a most beneficial event in the history of mankind. Such is the meaning of the axiom: "There is no abstract truth; truth is concrete"—a conception of an object is concrete when it presents itself with all the qualities and specific features and in the circumstances, environment, in which the object exists, and not abstracted from these circumstances and its living specific features (as it is presented by abstract thinking, the judgment of which has, therefore, no meaning for real life).

like Belinsky and several others could not long rest content with the narrow deductions to which the application of these principles in Hegel's system was limited. Soon they perceived the inadequacy of the very principles of this thinker. They, therefore, abandoned their absolute faith in his system and went forward; they did not, as Hegel did, stop halfway. But they, to the end, retained their respect for his philosophy, to which they were indeed much indebted.

We have already said, however, that the content of Hegel's system did not in the least correspond to the principles it proclaimed, and to which we have pointed. In the first flush of their enthusiasm, Belinsky and his friends did not perceive this inherent contradiction, and it would have been unnatural had they done so on their very first acquaintance with this system. This contradiction was extremely well concealed by the extraordinary power of Hegel's dialectics, so that even in Germany it was only the most mature and powerful minds who perceived, and then only after long study, the inherent contradiction between Hegel's fundamental ideas and the deductions he drew from them. The greatest of the present-day German thinkers, whose genius is in no way inferior to Hegel's, for a long time unreservedly accepted all his opinions. A long time passed before they recovered their independence and, disclosing Hegel's mistakes, laid the foundations of the new trend in science. This is always the case. Hegel himself was for a long time an unquestioning admirer of Schelling, Schelling was an admirer of Fichte, Fichte of Kant. Spinoza, whose genius was far higher than that of Descartes, for a very long time regarded himself as the latter's most faithful disciple.

We are saying all this in order to show how natural and inevitable it was for Belinsky and his friends to remain wholehearted followers of Hegel for a time. In this respect they shared the common lot of the greatest thinkers of our times. If, later on, Belinsky was angry with himself for his former unrestrained enthusiasm for Hegel, his fellows in this respect are men whose intellectual capacities are not inferior to his own, or to Hegel's.*[10]

---

* One of the present-day thinkers says about the essays he formerly wrote in the Hegelian spirit: "Now I cannot straighten out this confusion; only one alternative remains: either to strike it out entirely, or to leave it as it is—I prefer the latter. Many people still regard as wisdom what seemed wisdom to me when I wrote these essays—

All the German philosophers, from Kant to Hegel, suffer from the same defeet as that to which we pointed in Hegel's system. The deductions they drew from the principles they advanced did not in the least correspond to those principles. Their general ideas were profound, fruitful and magnificent; their deductions were petty, and partly, even vulgar. But with none of them was this contradiction of such colossal proportions as it was with Hegel, who, transcending all his predecessors in loftiness of principles, was, perhaps, weaker than all of them in his deductions. Both in Germany and in our country, narrow-minded and apathetic people were content with the deductions and forgot about the principles; but in our country, and in Germany, these disciples who were too faithful to the letter and, therefore, unfaithful to the spirit, were found only among second-rate people who lacked the strength for historical activity and were incapable of exercising any influence. On the other hand, in our country and in Germany, when the first flush of enthusiasm had passed off, all the truly gifted and strong people cast aside the false deductions, gladly sacrificed the teacher's errors to the demands of science and marched boldly forward. That is why Hegel's errors, like those of Kant, had no serious consequences, whereas the sound part of his doctrine had very fruitful effect.

We would be violating the law of historical perspective were we to speak about a subject of no historical importance, such as Hegel's errors, in as much detail as we would

----

let these people, when rereading them, see the road by which I reached my present convictions; following in my footsteps, it will be easier for them to reach truth." We must think the same about the essays written by Belinsky in the period of 1838-39. Those who are unable to share the mature and independent convictions Belinsky expressed later will benefit by reading his essays in chronological order, beginning with those with which Belinsky himself was later displeased. He who still stands too low needs a ladder in order to rise to the level of his times.

We shall observe, in passing, that in this essay we have used the reminiscences communicated to us by Mr. A., one of Belinsky's most intimate friends, and we can, therefore, vouch for the absolute authenticity of the facts we mention. We hope that Mr. A.'s interesting reminiscences will, in time, be made known to the public, and we hasten to warn the reader that, when that is done, it will be found that what we have said is no more than a development of his thoughts. For the assistance we have received from his reminiscences in writing this essay, our sincere gratitude is due to our highly esteemed Mr. A.[11]

about those of his ideas which have exercised great influence upon the course of intellectual development. But since these errors are, after all, a historical fact, although unimportant, we cannot remain silent about them. Later on the reader will see the essence of these errors in one of the excerpts we quote. Here we ought only to repeat that Stankevich's friends erred in the company of all the most remarkable German thinkers of their generation. For a time, Hegel's brilliant dialectics dazzled everybody, so that, for the sake of the principles, they all accepted the deductions that contradicted them as if they were necessary corollaries from them.

We cannot but admit that in Germany, and in our country, the people who accepted the entire content of the Hegelian system as pure truth were led by this authority into numerous and very grave errors. While not in the least defending what was really bad in those errors, it must be observed that not everything that would be unpardonable blindness today was a pernicious error twenty years ago. Many opinions which in our times would be definitely regarded as mistaken prejudices, still had reasonable grounds then—one-sided perhaps, and, perhaps, somewhat obsolete, but containing a considerable amount of truth for all that. Let us quote an example. The strict adherents of German philosophy from the time of Kant, and especially the strict Hegelians, despised and partly even hated everything French. Stankevich's friends shared this revulsion, and the *Moskovsky Nablyudatel* was permeated with "Francophobia," or "Franzosenfresserei," as the Germans called it. Franzosenfresserei colours many of the pages of the preface to Hegel's speeches, which, as we have seen, served as that magazine's program. We quote one of these pages in a footnote.* And it cannot but be said that in zealously carrying

* "The French never went beyond the sphere of arbitrary reasoning, and everything that is holy, great and noble in life fell under the blows of blind, lifeless reason. The result of French philosophism was materialism, the triumph of the corporeal flesh. The French people have lost the last spark of revelation. Christianity, that eternal and intransient proof of the creator's love for his creatures, has become the object of universal derision, universal contempt, and the poor human mind, incapable of penetrating the deep and sacred secret of life, has rejected everything it fails to grasp, and it fails to grasp everything that is true and everything that is real. It demanded clarity—but what clarity!—not that which lies in the depth of an

out all the points of its program, the *Moskovsky Nablyu-datel*, with equal zeal, carried out this one. It took every opportunity, took advantage of every pretext, to utter some stern philippic, or to make a derisive thrust at the French. If, for example, it reviewed Pushkin's essay on "Milton" in the *Sovremennik*, it paid most attention to those passages in which Pushkin derides the French, quoted his derisive remarks about Alfred de Vigny and Victor Hugo, his references to the flaws in Molière's comedies, etc., and added, on its own account, that Pushkin "had a true conception of art and an infinite aesthetic sense." If it reviewed another volume of the *Sovremennik* containing a fragment of *The Chronicles of a Russian In Paris*,[12] almost the entire review consisted of excerpts from those pages of the *Chronicles* which were particularly disparaging of the French. If it reviewed Mr. Weltman's *Virginia*, it turned out that the only thing that this novel could be praised for is that it "excellently portrays many of the features of French superficiality"; if it discussed the *Miscellany for 1838*, it turned out that it contained very many poems, some of

---

object. No,—that which lies on its surface. It tried to explain religion—and religion, inaccessible to its finite efforts, vanished, taking with it the happiness and peace of France. It tried to transform the shrine of learning into popular knowledge—and the mysterious meaning of true knowledge disappeared, and there remained only vulgar, barren and illusory reasoning—and Jean Jacques Rousseau proclaimed that an enlightened man is a depraved animal, and the revolution was a necessary consequence of this spiritual depravity. Where there is no religion there can be no state, and the revolution was the total negation of the state, of legal order; and the guillotine, performing its bloody levelling work, beheaded everything that to any degree stood higher than the senseless mob."

In his "The Last Housewarming" Lermontov literally put these words into verse:

Free rein I give my wrath and indignation
. . . .
I want to say to this great nation:
"You are a pitiful and foolish nation!
Pitiful, because faith, fame and genius,
All, all that on earth is great and holy,
With foolish ridicule and childish doubt
    Have you trampled in the dust.
Fame you have turned into hypocrisy's toy
Freedom—into a headsman's axe,
With which your fathers' cherished traditions
    You have slain...."

them even good ones, but the most interesting of the contents
was a translation of one of Schiller's epigrams in which
the French are called vandals. Reproducing this verse and
praising Schiller for it, the reviewer exultingly exclaimed,
addressing himself to the readers:

The French are vandals!!!—do you hear?

To make it more striking, this exclamation was even
printed in a separate line, as we do above. If the *Moskovsky Nablyudatel* referred to the return of our young professors from abroad, the most pleasant thing it found in that
event was that they had attended lectures in Berlin and
not in Paris. Needless to say, the *Moskovsky Nablyudatel* took
full advantage of the opportunity to denounce French
phrasemongering and frivolousness that was afforded by
the appearance of the translation of Michelet's *History of
France*.... Here the philippics became frightfully ruthless.
Some scientists who had written on special subjects were
just barely pardoned for being Frenchmen—but the French
writers, poets and thinkers were all ruthlessly beheaded,
from Mademoiselle Scudéry to Michelet, from Ronsard to
Lerminier. The only one who escaped the general verdict
was Béranger, the "idle reveller": idle revelry was just the
thing for the French, they were able to compose merry
songs about it, and you need not have to look for anything
better among them. In short, no matter what was under
discussion, the *Moskovsky Nablyudatel* would find a pretext
for taking a thrust or a dig at the French, and the general
deduction drawn from all these endless polemics was that,
whereas "the influence of the Germans upon us is beneficial
in many respects—in respect to science, art, and in the spi-
ritual-moral respect, our relation to the French is the
reverse of this: we are the hostile antithesis of them by
virtue of the essence of our national spirit". (*Moskovsky
Nablyudatel*, Vol. XVIII, p. 200).

Today, when the finest of the French people are
abandoning their arrogant claims, their contempt for other
nations, when the entire nation is abandoning its former
frivolousness and even the phrasemongering which has
been part of their lives for so long, when their national life
has turned to the solution of truly profound problems, such
enmity towards the French would be totally groundless.
But at that time, the trend of thought in France was en-

tirely different. The trends of thought that are now winning
France the sympathy of serious people were barely beginning
to reveal themselves, and then only in strange, still indefinite, fantastic, forms; they were not yet exercising any
influence upon the life of the nation. On the contrary, they
were ridiculed in literature and held in contempt in political life. All the brilliance of France of the period of the
first Empire and the Restoration was false and superficial,
or contradicted the true needs of moral and social life.
Everything was based on misunderstanding, or on deception and violence. In literature, for example, two schools,
equally false, prevailed: one, in the spirit of Châteaubriand
and Lamartine, donned the mask of pretentious admiration of doctrines which it did not understand, and about
which it really cared very little; the other donned the mask
of refined depravity and petty devilry (école satanique).*
Those who did not wear the hypocritical mask of idealism
or of cynicism, talked about trivialities. Béranger was the
only exception, but he was not understood, and was regarded a being no more than the bard of the grisettes. In
science, conceptions became frightfully shallow—the celebrated scientists of the time were charlatans and phrasemong-
ers, concerned with reconciling the irreconcilable, with justifying prejudices by science, with combining scientific truth
with arbitrary fantasies. Time has now shown what kind
of men Cousin, Guizot and Thiers were, and what they wanted; but they were the best of the celebrities of that day.
    Incidentally, let us recall what the celebrated "liberal-
ism," for which these celebrities were particularly famed,
really was. Events have revealed the hollowness and utter
uselessness of this liberalism, which was concerned only
with abstract rights and not with the welfare of the people,
the very conception of which was alien to it. Its best advocates were foolishly mistaken about the true needs of the
nation. Others used this so-called liberalism as a bait with
which to catch the nation on their hook, and the purpose
for which they wanted to catch the nation became apparent
when they succeeded in capturing power; they sought power
in order to fill their pockets.
    Such was the situation in France during the Restoration
and in the first years of the Orleanic dynasty. Phrases

---

* Satanic school.—Ed·

devoid of meaning rattled everywhere; frivolity and deceit reigned everywhere. But what was bound to rouse the indignation of people with earnest convictions and lofty principles most of all was the fact that the French celebrities of that time were utterly devoid of definite principles and of strict consistency in their mode of thought. Whatever they believed in they only half believed, timidly and pretentiously; whatever they denied they also half denied. They were all like the people whom our Pushkin portrayed in his works, like those in whose mouth Lermontov put the words:

> Rich are we almost from the cradle
> With the errors of our fathers, with their belated thoughts..
> To good and evil shamefully inert,
> Beginning our careers, we yield without a fight...
> Enviously concealing from neighbours and from friends
> Brighter hopes and passion's noble voice,
> By doubt and disbelief disdained.
> We scarcely touched the golden cup of pleasure,
> But did not thereby save our youthful vigour;
> From every joy, for fear of satiety,
> The best we plucked for all eternity.
> We do not hate, our love is adventitious,
> Sacrificing nothing to hatred or to love,
> A mysterious coldness reigns within our hearts...*

From these people, impotent in their narrow and satiated egoism, nothing good could, of course, be expected. These degenerates, who survived the great internal struggle which had absorbed all the noblest forces of the French people,[13] could not be expected to infuse new life into their nation; they could not serve as the ideal for us who were conscious of an exuberance of fresh and as yet untapped strength. Ardent youths, ready to love to the point of self-abnegation and to hate with a mortal hatred, thirsting for activity for the common weal, could not, of course, have any sympathy for people of that sort. Their enmity was aggravated particularly by the fact that these disillusioned, blasé people, eaten up with egoism, were regarded among us as oracles. Everybody here talked about the French, everybody admired the French—but Frenchmen of this sort were of no use whatever even for the French people, let alone for us. We needed enthusiasm. A wide field of activity lay open before

---

* Excerpt from Lermontov's poem *Meditation* (1848) ("Sadly I Gaze Upon Our Generation"). — *Ed.*

us. How could we help hating those who could communicate to us only their impotence, disillusionment and lassitude?

The dislike, which the French of the period of the first Empire and the Restoration deserved, was undeservedly extended to their forbears, and just as undeservedly the fresh trends of thought which arose among the young generation of thinkers who had nothing in common with the former celebrities, people with firm and lofty convictions and fresh strength, were also subjected to universal censure. The cause of this injustice was partly insufficient acquaintance with the new strivings that were arising in French literature, partly also the prejudice that had arisen against all Frenchmen in general, but most of all it was worship of the Hegelian system as the supreme and sole truth, outside of which nothing deserved attention.

As we have said, the worship of Hegel among Stankevich's friends reached an extreme which could not long be maintained by people of talent, endowed with independent minds and striving to go forward. Signs of unconscious dissatisfaction with the system they continued to admire were revealed by the most gifted members of this friendly circle in the fact that they talked in the Hegelian sense more emphatically and ruthlessly than Hegel himself; they, so to speak, became more Hegelian than Hegel. The most outstanding in this respect was Belinsky who, in general, was not the sort of man to give up logical convictions out of fear of deviating from the exact words of any authority. This testimony concerning him by people who knew him personally is confirmed by many pages written by him completely in the Hegelian spirit, but with an emphasis of which Hegel himself would not have approved. And in general, Hegel, who spoke of everything with the dispassion of the hoary sage, who looked at everything with the eyes of the armchair philosopher unperturbed by the commotion of life, could not long hold in absolute obedience the ardent, twenty-five-year-old man filled with virile strivings such as Belinsky was. The natures of the teacher and the disciple, the requirements of the two different societies in which they were active, were too much out of harmony. Soon, Belinsky cast aside everything in Hegel's doctrine that could restrict his thought, and shortly after he moved to St. Petersburg he became a completely independent thinker.

This change was inevitable because of Belinsky's very nature, but two circumstances helped it to take place quicker than
it would have done otherwise: the rapprochement between
Stankevich's friends and Mr. Ogaryov and his friends,[14] and
Belinsky's change of residence from Moscow to St. Petersburg.
    The first influences under which the evolution of Mr.
Ogaryov and his friends took place were entirely different
from those to which Stankevich's circle was subjected. They
were little interested in German philosophy because it was
too abstract. They devoted their attention to those sciences
that are directly related to the life of nations. At that time
new theories of national welfare were arising in France in
contrast to the soulless and deadening theory of the economists. The ideas that inspired the new science were still
expressed in fantastic forms, and it was easy for prejudiced
opponents, or those prompted by selfish motives, to ridicule
the systems they detested, ignoring the sound and lofty fundamental ideas of the new theoreticians and overemphasiz-
ing the visionary side which at the beginning no new science
can avoid. But beneath these quaint and fantastic dreams
these systems harboured profound and beneficial truths.[15]
The overwhelming majority of the scientists and of the
European public believed the biassed and superficial opinions expressed by the economists, and refused to understand the meaning of the new science. Everybody ridiculed
the impossible utopias, and hardly anybody deemed it
necessary to make a thorough and impartial study of them.
Appreciating their great importance for life, Mr. Ogaryov
and his friends took up these questions. At the same time
they devoted their attention to history, especially the history of our times, that is to say, the part that is most important for life. And since France had lately been the chief
theatre of historical development, they interested themselves
mainly with her history. In literature, too, they did not
show absolute preference for the Germans, for they were
acquainted with and valued the new French writers who,
although not yet predominating in literature, showed signs
that they would do so. Influenced by these studies, they
formed firm and consistent scientific and literary convictions.
    Thus, the leading figures of the young generation in
Moscow were divided into two circles having two different
trends. In one, Hegelian philosophy predominated; the
other studied the contemporary problems of historical life.

There were many points on which the two trends might have come into conflict; but beneath the apparent contradiction lay an essential identity of aims, differing only in those features which in both were one-sided defects. The aim of both was to conduct activities that would be fruitful for the development of Russian society; both regarded the revival of our literature and the stimulation of intellectual activity as the only means to this end; both saw their ideal in the future and not in the past, and they stood in relation to each other as theory stands to practice, which should supplement each other. The important question as to whether the sense of unity on essentials or antagonism on secondary but, for all that, very important questions would triumph, had to be settled one way or another by whether the people representing these different trends were really worthy of becoming leading figures in the history of the development of Russian society, and whether the principles that inspired them were really fertile. History tells us that as a rule, when a principle collapses, its adherents fall into uncompromising hostility with one another over secondary questions; but when a principle is developing, the people who are agreed on the main thing cooperate, no matter how important may be the secondary questions on which they disagree. Renunciation of narrow-minded pride, readiness to recognize a truth that had not been perceived before and to make this new truth discovered by another the cherished object of their strivings—such has been the essential quality of truly remarkable historical figures.

The people we are discussing were destined to play a truly important role in the development of our society; the principles that inspired them were indeed alive and fertile. Therefore, these principles necessarily had to merge and these people unite. Indeed, these people did unite with such noble earnestness and voluntary renunciation of their one-sidedness, and the principles merged in a single general trend with such perfect harmony, that this fact became one of those extremely rare and inspiring examples of the complete triumph of general truth over particular misunderstandings, triumph of the common striving to serve truth over personal conflicts.[16]

The first feelings were, naturally, unfriendly. The fact that their opinions mutually excluded each other roused mutual dislike. One side was displeased with the other,

and for a long time they refrained from intercourse with
each other. Stankevich's friends censured Mr. Ogaryov
and his friends for refusing to devote themselves to the study
of German philosophy and for refusing to admit that all
truth was contained in Hegel's system. Mr. Ogaryov's
friends censured Stankevich's circle for devoting all their
thoughts exclusively to extremely abstract problems while
devoting no attention to the problems of life, or else solving
them in the apathetic sense that Hegel prescribed. One
side said of the other: "They ignore true principles"; the other
side said of the first: "They preach apathy in life and, boasting that their system justifies everything in the world, they
are reconciled to all the defects in reality." Various external circumstances contributed to the fact that for a long
time no personal intercourse—which neither party at
first desired—existed between the people of the two trends.[17]

Stankevich was no longer in Moscow when Mr. Ogaryov
and his friends joined the circle of which Stankevich had
been the leading spirit.[18] Had that gentle and loving man
still been among his friends, the rapprochement, in all
probability, would have taken place at once. But Mr. Ogaryov was now the sole mediator and conciliator. Alone, having no one to help him, he was unable to reconcile the opponents in the heated controversy that took place at every
meeting. At one of these debates questions were put to
Belinsky with the object of forcing him to admit that not
everything in reality is rational. With his usual inexorable
consistency Belinsky answered that he regarded as rational
all the phenomena that had been indicated to him. This
proved that Belinsky's convictions could not be shaken,
and the attempts at conciliation ceased for a time, for a
very short time, as we shall see.[19]

Nevertheless, these attempts did not remain fruitless,
in spite of the fact that they seemed to have led to a complete
rupture. The people who debated with Belinsky and his
friends were amazed at the stubbornness with which the
followers of Hegel encountered the seemingly irrefutable
arguments against the Hegelian system, at the ease with
which the followers of Hegel found for themselves a fully
satisfactory answer for everything that apparently should
have embarrassed and perplexed them. The opponents of
the deductions drawn from Hegel's system realized that
Hegel could be vanquished only with his own weapons and,

therefore, they set to work to make a deep study of that thinker. They began this study with perfectly mature minds, with a power of penetration sharpened by the habit of independent thinking and by the rich experience of a life filled with all possible conflicts—with a stock of firm convictions obtained from life and strict science. And difficult as it was to stand up against the dialectics of the giant of German philosophy—the amazingly powerful dialectics which clothed his entire system with the armour of apparently iudestructible unity—these people found chinks and inconsistencies in Hegel's system, perceived the flaws in his deductions, the lack of harmony between principles and deductions, between fundamental ideas and their application. They also discerned the one-sidedness of the principles, and, at last, they were able to say: "Now we have grasped all that was grasped by Hegel, but we have grasped it more fully and clearly than he." Thus, Hegel's philosophy was, as German philosophy expresses it, overcome (überwunden), purged of the one-sidedness of the deductions from its own fundamental principles, subjected to criticism and elevated to supreme truth by the strongest followers of one of the two trends between which, until then, Hegel's system had been a barrier. But the profundity and harmony of the German philosophical systems created a strong impression on the minds of those who had undertaken the study of philosophy not so much from inclination for it as from the necessity of discovering its weak sides. The ablest of Mr. Ogaryov's friends themselves acquired a philosophical trend; without abandoning their former strivings, but, on the contrary, clinging to them more firmly than ever, they elevated their convictions to general philosophical principles, and perceiving that thereby their ideas gained much in firmness and harmony, they became zealous adherents of German philosophy, not of Hegel's system, of course, at which they could not halt, but of a new philosophy, to which Hegel's system was the last stepping stone.

On the other hand, a similar widening of mental horizon took place at about the same time among the ablest of Stankevich's friends. Until now, as we have said, they had been bound together by an absolute identity of conceptions and strivings, so that the specific features of each individual vanished in the unity of the common mood. When characterizing the *Moskovsky Nablyudatel*, of which Belinsky was director and most active contributor, we borrowed most of our excerpts from the preface to Hegel's speeches which was not written by Belinsky, but by one of his friends of that time.[20] We did so because at that time these people wrote in exactly the same strain. The only difference between them was that some could write better than others, but everything that Belinsky said was also said by all of Stankevich's friends and, vice versa, Belinsky always expressed convictions that were shared by all the rest. This went on until Belinsky arrived in St. Petersburg. Here he soon became an independent thinker, and from this point on we must speak not of the general activities of the group of which Belinsky was only a representative, but of the personal activities of Belinsky, who became the head of our literary movement and directed this movement in alliance with his new companions, who joined him not in the circle spirit, but because of their individual striving towards common aims, each of the allies retaining the specific features of his nature.

In Moscow, Belinsky, like his friends, had been engrossed in theoretical philosophizing and had paid little attention to what was going on in the real world. He had repeated over and over again that reality was more important than all dreaming, but, like his friends, he had looked at reality with the eyes of an idealist. He had not so much studied it as introduced his ideal into it, and had believed that the ideal had something corresponding to it in our reality, that at least the most important elements of reality resembled those ideals which had been found in Hegel's system. As everybody who has gone through the idealist period of thinking knows, St. Petersburg is not the place in which one can cling to such dreams. Real life there is so clamorous, restless and importunate that it is difficult to deceive oneself about its essence, it is difficult to escape the conviction that it does not move in conformity with the ideal plan of the Hegelian system, it is difficult to remain an idealist. With its customary readiness to provide a newcomer with every possible disillusionment, St. Petersburg did not delay in providing Belinsky with abundant material for testing the conclusions of the Hegelian system that were favourable for reality and in convincing him that the philistine German ideals had no resemblance whatever to Russian life.[21] He was obliged to abandon the conviction that the Hegelian

constructions correctly depicted real life; he was obliged
to look critically both at reality and at the Hegelian system.* The result of this test for theoretical convictions
was that Hegel's principles were purged of their one-sidedness, the false content that was stuck on to them was rejected and new deductions were drawn in keeping with the
spirit of strict modern science. The result for living strivings was that the former quietism, now wrecked by reality,
was rejected, the lofty conviction was retained that reason
and truth should, and would, rule in life, even though we
were still a long way from that time. Belinsky became convinced that reality contained very many false and pernicious elements and, devoting all his activities to the en-
thronement of reason and truth in life, he launched a tireless
and unrelenting struggle against everything that hindered
the achievement of this goal. For a virile nature like Belinsky's, the transition from abstract ideality, which had
reached the point of quietism and apathy, to a lively conception of reality, was natural and easy. For a time, Hegel's
system had carried him away by its grandeur, and we have
tried to show that this was justified by the novelty and
profundity of the truths contained in its fundamental
ideas. Its positive content, however, had never satisfied
Belinsky; he had always striven forward, fuming at Hegel's
restraining dispassion. He had always infused into this
cold contemplation the fervent heat of his own vivacious
nature. Such also had been the attitude towards Hegel of

---

* "A Moscovite soon gets accustomed to St. Petersburg if he comes
here to live. What becomes of the high-flown dreams, ideals, theories
and fantasies? In this respect, St. Petersburg is a touchstone for a
man: whoever, living here, has not allowed himself to be drawn into
the maelstrom of illusory life, has succeeded in retaining his soul
and heart without sacrificing common sense, in preserving human
dignity without becoming quixotic, may be boldly offered a hand as
a man. On some natures, St. Petersburg has a sobering effect. At
first it seems that its atmosphere causes one to shed one's most cherished convictions as a tree sheds its leaves; but soon one perceives
that these are not convictions, but dreams begotten of an idle life
and total ignorance of reality, and this, perhaps, leaves one very sad,
but there is so much that is sacred and human in that sadness.... What
are dreams? In the eyes of a *practical* (in the rational sense of the term)
man, the most seductive of them are of less value than the most bitter truth, for a fool's paradise is falsehood, whereas a practical man's
suffering is truth which, moreover, will be fruitful in the future...."
(Belinsky's essay "Moscow and St. Petersburg," in the Miscellany
The Physiology of St. Petersburg.)

the other able men among Stankevich's friends. It can be
seen from the excerpts we have quoted what had interested
them particularly in Hegel's system, why it had been so
precious to them. Every theoretical doctrine is a combination of two sides: abstract conception of truth, and the
relation of this conception to living reality. Hegel made
knowledge the chief, almost the sole aim of his system; the
consequences of this knowledge for life stand in the background in his system. From the very outset, the ablest of
Stankevich's friends changed this order. From the very
beginning they said: "Hegel's philosophy is beneficial for
life; therefore it is necessary to study the truths it reveals."
Clearly, for them, real life was in the foreground; abstract
knowledge was only of secondary importance.[22] People
with such natures could not have been satisfied with Hegel's
system for long; in one way or another, they had to cast off
their dependence upon it—and indeed, they did cast it
off, some in one way, some in another. Here we are interested in Belinsky, and we have seen that he was liberated
from unrestrained worship of Hegel by close acquaintance
with reality, of which he had always striven to be a driving
force, and which he was destined to become.

The preceding debates in Moscow with Mr. Ogaryov's
friends had also played a part in broadening Belinsky's
views. True, during these debates, no arguments could
in the least shake his belief in the absolute correctness of
the deductions drawn by Hegel's system. On the contrary,
as always happens with people who are strong and fearless
in their consistency,these debates had only served to strength-
en his mode of thought, had compelled him to be still
more consistent and strict in his conceptions, had imbued
him with an urgent desire to insist on them and to prove
the unsoundness of all doubts concerning what seemed to
him to be the truth. Some of the essays Belinsky published
immediately on his arrival in St. Petersburg were written
under the influence of this polemical inspiration, and in
them—they were published in the *Otechestvenniye Zapiski*—the opinions shared by all the contributors to the
Moskovsky Nablyudatel were carried to an amazing extreme
that can be attributed only to their polemical origin. The
important thing, however, is that the arguments raised
against him by his Moscow opponents had greatly interested
him, and he had not forgotten them. When the heat of the

first debates had cooled, when contact with real life had
begun to expose the one-sidedness of his former abstract
idealism, Belinsky had to examine more dispassionately
the opinions of his former opponents, which only recently
he had refuted from the lofty standpoint of idealism. He
found that these conceptions, which to the absolute follower
of Hegel's system had seemed narrow and superficial, stood
the test of facts much better than the deductions offered by
Hegel's philosophy, and that a thinking person could deduce
no other conceptions from life.Workers in the intellectual
world are divided into two classes. Some dislike truth if
it has been expressed by somebody else before them—they
are ready to claim a patent for their own ideas, probably
because they are conscious of the paucity of their produc-
tivity in this respect. Others are concerned only for truth,
not deeming it necessary to worry about patents—probably
because they are not afraid that their intellectual faculties
will diminish or that they will become poorer in ideas.
Some do not like to abandon mistakes—probably because
they are aware that all their claims are nothing but a conceited mistake. Others are not afflicted with this pride,
because their strivings are always based on truth. Belinsky
belonged to the latter category. At the very first opportunity he, with his habitual candour, admitted that St. Petersburg had taught him to value the views on reality that he
had formerly refused to accept, and that, on the questions
that had then been debated, truth had been on the side of
those who had rejected the deductions of the Hegelian
system as being out of harmony with the facts of real life.

Thus, the reasons for the division which only recently
had been an obstacle to friendly cooperation among the
best men of the young generation, disappeared. Some, who
had not formerly paid attention to German philosophy, became its zealous followers, finding in its principles a firm
basis for the convictions they had arrived at as a result
of their study of modern history and of present-day life.
Belinsky, the representative of the other trend in the literary movement, was taught by his observations of reality
to distinguish between the correct principles of Hegel's
philosophy and its one-sided deductions. He was aware of
the extreme importance of the problems to which the Stankevich circle had paid too little attention, and retained
from the Hegelian system only those convictions that stood

the test of the living phenomena of reality. All the most gifted men of the former Stankevich circle followed him, if they had not come out on the same road independently.* The one-sidedness of both trends was entirely eliminated.

This unity of conceptions and strivings was bound to draw the people closer together. At about this time, Granovsky returned from abroad. What Stankevich had been for his circle, Granovsky became equally for the friends of Stankevich and of Mr. Ogaryov. No man of noble mind could fail to love Granovsky with all his heart and soul. All the most noble minds of the young generation in Moscow united around him. Where Granovsky was there could be only one sentiment—brotherhood. In this he was assisted by Mr. Ogaryov. Soon, those who lived in St. Petersburg, as well as those in the provinces, submitted to their influence.

The influence of Granovsky, Belinsky and the others drew to their literary circle nearly all the gifted men of the younger generation who were already active in literature, or were entering this career.

Thus, out of the former friendly circles of Stankevich and Mr. Ogaryov, with the addition of the newcomers, there was formed a big literary society, whose chief organ, until the appearance of our magazine, was the *Otechestvenniye Zapiski* (from 1840, particularly 1841 to 1846). The chief worker on the *Otechestvenniye Zapiski* at that time was Belinsky. From the very outset, the honour of being the disseminators of new and sound ideas among the Russian public was worthily shared by other people, some of whom we have already mentioned, and some about whom we hope to speak later, namely—in addition to Granovsky— Mr. Galakhov, Mr. Katkov, Mr. Ketcher, Mr. Korsh, Mr. Kudryavtsev, Mr. Ogaryov and others. Stankevich died before the amalgamation; Klyuchnikov and Koltsov sur-

---

* The reader will understand that since we are here discussing only the literary movement, we have no right to mention people except in their relation to literature. There is no doubt that in Russian society of that time, there were many people in different fields of activity who were no less remarkable than Belinsky. We may assume that there were such people also in Stankevich's circle. But the reader will agree that the only one we can call the representative of this circle is Belinsky.[23] We have no wish whatever to elevate Belinsky above anybody—he does not in the least stand in need of that— we are merely giving an account of his literary activities.

vived Stankevich only by a few years, as did Lermontov, who, in his independent sympathies, belonged to this new trend and was prevented from taking part in the friendly discussions of Belinsky and his friends only by the fact that he spent the last period of his life in the Caucasus. These losses were compensated by the affiliation of new men who either joined Belinsky, Granovsky and Mr. Ogaryov, or were trained under their influence. Of these, mention must be made, among others, of Mr. Annenkov, Mr. Grigorovich, Mr. Kavelin, the late Kroneberg and V. Milyutin, Mr. Nekrasov, Mr. Panayev and Mr. Turgenev. All the talented men of the new generation, almost without exception, were more or less closely connected with this circle, or else were trained under the influence of Belinsky or Granovsky. Mr. Krayevsky, the editor of the magazine that served as the organ of the activities of Belinsky, Granovsky, Mr. Ogaryov and their friends, occupied a very honourable place in Russian literature, which, we are very glad to say, was much indebted to him at that time for giving Belinsky a place on his magazine which in literary respects was commensurate with that man's supreme importance for the magazine.

At about the same time one-sided trends in our country united in one, common, all-embracing system of views. A similar event occurred in Europe. The German scientists began to realize that life had rights not only over practice, but also over science. The French scientists and writers began to realize the necessity of making a deep study of general conceptions to which little attention had been paid hitherto. In both countries, the former one-sided theories began to give way to the new ideas, which no longer belonged exclusively to either of the nations, but belonged equally to all truly modern men, no matter where they were born, or what language they spoke. Such a trend of thought in all countries in the civilized world towards similar views on all important problems greatly strengthened the unity of the strivings of all truly modern men in each country. Thus, in our country, the study of the new phenomena which arose in the intellectual life of the principal nations of Western Europe, and which, in spite of their different origins and forms, were permeated with exactly the same spirit, strengthened the unity of the conceptions by which people with the modern outlook were bound together.

The unity of conceptions among our people, however, was only strengthened by foreign influences, it was not engendered by them. Of course, the people who took the lead of our intellectual movement at that time were encouraged by the fact that all the modern thinkers of Europe agreed with them and thus confirmed the correctness of their conceptions, but they were no longer dependent in their conceptions upon any outside authorities. We have already said that the progress in conceptions which eliminated the former disunity was made independently in our country. For the first time, the intellectual life of our country brought into being people who marched side by side with the thinkers of Europe and not in the train of their disciples, as had been the case in the past. In the past, each one of us had an oracle, or oracles, among the European writers. Some found them among the French, others among the German writers. But after the representatives of our intellectual movement had subjected the Hegelian system to independent criticism, that movement no longer submitted to any alien authority.

Belinsky and his chief companions became intellectually quite independent.

This fact—the independence Russian thought attained in Belinsky and his chief companions—is not only interesting because it pleases our national pride. It is important in the history of our literary thought because it accounts for some of the distinguishing qualities of the works of Belinsky and his allies, qualities which literary criticism in our country had not possessed before. It also partly accounts for the rapid spread of Belinsky's literary opinions among our public.

A man who has learnt to think independently is, by virtue of the definiteness of his concepts and their correct application, always superior to those who accept the concepts of others and are unable critically to examine the principles upon which they are based. Before Belinsky, our literary criticism was a reflection sometimes of French and sometimes of German theories and, therefore, its fundamental views lacked clarity and definiteness; and in appraising the essential meaning and merits of literary works, while expressing much that was true, it nearly always left much unsaid, or else interwove quaint misunderstandings with correct observations. In general, very soon, in a matter of five or six years, the opinions of the best critics who preceded Belinsky were found to be obsolete, groundless, or one-sided. Thus, the *Telegraf* was founded in 1825; but in 1829, anyone who read Nadezhdin's articles in the *Vestnik Yevropy*[24] could not think of Polevoi's "lofty views" without a smile, could not but be convinced that Polevoi's understanding of the significance of the most important phenomena in Russian literature in his time was far too unsatisfactory. The opinions of Nadezhdin himself represented a strange medley, a horrible mixture of true and sagacious observations and indefensible opinions, so that often one half of an article of his destroyed the other. Belinsky's opinions, on the contrary, retain their value to this day, and their correctness, in general, is such that those who opposed him were nearly always right only in what they borrowed from him. During the past few years many people among us have argued that Belinsky's conceptions are unsatisfactory. Among these epigones who imagined that they had gone beyond Belinsky there have been men of wisdom and talent; but it is enough to compare their writings with Belinsky's to be convinced that all these people's stock-in-trade consists of what they heard from Belinsky. They are eternally talking about the same things that Belinsky talked about, and if they talk about it differently, it is only because they become either one-sided or glaringly biassed. Since Belinsky's time, the materials for a history of literature are being thoroughly studied, but, in general, every new research only provides fresh confirmation of the correctness of his opinions.

His independence of mind was also one of the chief reasons of the sympathy with which his opinions were received. The weak side of people who repeat the thoughts of others is that in most cases they discuss subjects which rouse no interest among the public. Truth is always truth, but not all truth is always and everywhere equally important, or equally capable of rousing attention. Every age, every nation, has its own requirements. What interests a German is often of no interest to a Frenchman or a Russian, because it has no direct relation to the requirements of his life. We must deal with what our public needs in our times. Formerly, our literature often dealt with subjects of little interest for us, and served not so much to express our thoughts and to clear up our perplexities, as to echo the opinions of others on matters that did not concern us. Belinsky always spoke about what the public to whom he spoke needed and were interested to hear.

In our next essay we shall give an account of his activities in the mature period of his development. When characterizing Belinsky's literary views, we shall devote our attention mainly to his last essays, because that man went forward to the very end of his days, and the further he went the more fully and definitely he expressed his thoughts, and, of course, we shall have to base our judgment on the most mature expression of these thoughts. But before doing so we must trace the path of development of his views from the time his essays began to appear in the *Otechestvenniye Zapiski* to the pinnacle on which death overtook him. The most essential feature of the development of Belinsky's criticism from 1840 onwards may be briefly defined as follows:[25]

Belinsky's criticism became more and more permeated with the vital interests of our life; it grasped the phenomena of this life more and more clearly; and it more and more resolutely strove to explain to the public the significance of literature for life, and to explain to literature the relation in which it ought to stand to life as one of the main forces that direct its development.

With every passing year we find in Belinsky's essays less and less discussion of abstract subjects, or even of vital subjects from an abstract point of view; the predominance of the elements provided by life becomes more and more marked.

SEVENTH ESSAY

BELINSKY

The essential feature of the development of Belinsky's criticism in the *Otechestvenniye Zapiski* and in the *Sovremennik* is that it became more and more imbued with the living interests of our reality and, as a consequence, became more and more positive. In the footnote below we quote several passages from his last essays that express his most mature and exact conceptions of the paramount importance reality should have in intellectual and moral life, of which literature has been (and still is) the chief organ; here we shall say a few words about the way we should interpret "reality" and "positiveness," which, according to present-day conceptions, ought to acquire such important significance in all spheres of intellectual and moral activity.*

"The conception of 'reality' is quite new," says Belinsky

---

* "Were we asked what constitutes the distinguishing feature of present-day Russian literature we should answer: an increasing approach to life and reality, an ever-growing proximity to the mature and adult state." ("A View on Russian Literature in 1846," the *Sovremennik* 1847, No. 1. "Criticism," p. 1.) (*Cf.* Eng. ed., V. G. Belinsky, *Selected Philosophical Works*, Moscow 1948, p. 347.—*Ed.*)—Thus, maturity is measured by the degree of proximity to reality.

"...The entire movement of Russian literature (up to the time of Pushkin) consisted of a striving ... to come nearer to life, to reality" (*ibid.*, p. 4). (Eng. ed., p. 350.—*Ed.*)—Thus, the aim of the literary movement is reality.

"The artistic, poetical and creative merits of our literature ... bring it close to the mature and adult state which we mentioned at the beginning of our article. The so-called natural school cannot be accused of rhetoric, understanding this word to mean wilful or unintentional distortion of reality, false idealization of life.... But it is not in talents or in their numbers that we see real progress in literature; rather is it in their trend and their style of writing. Talents have always existed, but formerly they beautified nature, idealized reality, that is to say, depicted what did not exist, depicted the fantastic, whereas today they depict life and reality in their true light. This has given literature an important significance in the eyes of society," (*ibid.*, p. 10). (Eng. ed., pp. 356-57.)—Thus, positiveness abhors false idealization; art reaches maturity when it depicts life and reality in their true light.

"Instead of dreaming of the impossible, it were much better to accept the irresistible and invariable [i.e., *that which does not submit to fantasies*] reality of existence and act on its basis, guided by reason and common sense and not by Manilovian[26] fantasies" (*ibid.*, p. 14). (Eng. ed., pp. 360-61.—*Ed.*)

"The importance of theoretical problems depends upon the bearing which they have on reality.... We ourselves, in ourselves and around ourselves—that is where we should seek both the problems and their solution. That trend will be fruitful" (*ibid.*, p. 28). (Eng. ed., p. 375.—*Ed.*)

"It is to be regretted that this talent's (*a poet, whose poems were published in 1846*) fount of inspiration is not life, but dreams, and it therefore has no bearing on life and suffers from poetical paucity.... That there, at the altitudes he so yearns for, is a cold and breathless void.... No, give us the earth with its light and warmth, where everything is ours, simple and comprehensible, for here we live, here is the poetry of our life.... He who turns away from it without understanding it can never be a poet, and is but fit to chase cold and empty phrases in the cold heights" (*ibid.*, p. 31). (Eng. ed., pp. 378-79.—*Ed.*)

"Our literature ... from a rhetorical literature constantly strove to become a natural literature. It is this striving, attended as it is by noticeable and constant successes, that constitutes the sense and

(the *Sovremennik*, 1847, No· 1. "Criticism," p. 18),* and, indeed, it was defined and went into science only very recently, when our contemporary thinkers explained the obscure allusions of transcendental philosophy, which had recognized truth only in concrete realization. Like all the major truths of modern science, this view of reality is very simple, but very fruitful.

There was a time when the dreams of the imagination were regarded as being higher than reality, and when the power of the imagination was regarded as infinite. But our contemporary thinkers have examined this problem more carefully than did those of the past and have obtained results that are the very opposite of the old opinions, which proved to be totally untenable. The power of our imagination is extremely limited and its creations are very pale and feeble compared with reality. The most vivid imagination is overwhelmed by the thought of the millions of miles that separate the earth from the sun, and of the extreme rapidity of light and electric current. The most ideal figures painted by Raffaello proved to be portraits of living persons. The ugliest creations of mythology and popular superstition proved to be by no means so unlike the animals around us as the monsters discovered by the natural scientists. History and careful observation of present-day life have revealed that living people, even those who do not belong to the categories of arch scoundrels or of heroes of virtue, commit crimes far more horrible and feats far more exalted than those invented by poets. Imagination had to yield to reality; nay, more, it was forced to admit that its fictitious creations are only copies of what is provided by the phenomena of reality.

---

soul of the history of our literature. We shall assert without prevarication that in no other Russian writer was this striving so successful as it was in Gogol. This could be achieved only by making art base itself exclusively on real life, eschewing all ideals. Herein lies the great service rendered by Gogol. In this way he completely changed the prevailing view on art itself. The old and threadbare definition of poetry as "nature beautified" may be applied at a stretch to the works of any of the (former) Russian poets; but this cannot be done in regard to the works of Gogol. Another definition of art fits them— art as the representation of reality in all its fidelity." ("A View on Russian Literature in 1847," the *Sovremennik*, 1848, No. 1. "Criticism," p. 17.) (Eng. ed., pp. 412-13.—*Ed.*)

* V. G. Belinsky, *Selected Philosophical Works*, Moscow 1948, p. 365.—*Ed.*

But the phenomena of reality are extremely heterogeneous and diverse. They consist of many things that conform to man's desires and needs, and of many things that absolutely contradict these desires and needs. In the past, when reality was held in disdain and people were excessively proud of imaginary riches, it was believed that reality could very easily be altered in conformity with the dreams of the imagination. But when this pride waned, the scientists and poets could not but be convinced of that which in practical life had always been clear to people of common sense. Man by himself is very feeble; he obtains all his strength only from his knowledge of real life, and from his ability to utilize the forces of unreasoning nature and the innate qualities of human nature that are independent of man. By acting in conformity with the laws of nature and of human nature, and with the aid of these laws, man can gradually change those phenomena of reality that do not conform with his strivings, and thus gradually achieve very considerable success in improving his conditions of life and in satisfying his desires.

But not all desires find means of satisfaction in reality. Many of them contradict the laws of nature and of human nature. Neither a philosopher's stone that would turn all metals into gold, nor an elixir of life that would preserve our youth forever can be obtained from nature. And vain are all our demands that people should abandon egoism and passions; human nature does not submit to such apparently commendable demands.

This circumstance, which presupposes an obvious diversity in our desires, made it necessary to examine more closely those of them, whose satisfaction nature and people of common sense refuse to facilitate—to ascertain whether the satisfaction of these desires is indeed necessary for man. Evidently it is not, for, as we see, man lives and, under favourable circumstances, is even very happy without possessing either a philosopher's stone, or an elixir of life, or those charming boons and qualities by which he is lured by the magic of transcendental imagination. And if man can dispense with the boons that imagination says are essential for him, and life shows that he can, once it became revealed that imagination deceives man in respect to what is essential for him, it could not fail to come under suspicion from another aspect: would man really find pleasure in the realization of those dreams which contradict the laws of external nature and of his own nature? Careful observation showed that the realization of such desires would lead to nothing but disillusionment and pain. It was found that everything that is unnatural is harmful and painful for man, and that a morally healthy man, instinctively sensing this, does not in the least long for the realization of the dreams with which idle fantasy amuses itself.

Just as it was found that the dreams of imagination are of no value for life, so it was found that many of the hopes inspired by the imagination are of no value for life.

Man finds durable pleasure only in reality; only those desires that are based on reality are of real importance; only those hopes that are roused by reality can be realized, and only in such matters as are accomplished with the aid of the forces and circumstances provided by reality.

To reach such a conviction and to act in conformity with it means becoming a rational man.

But very often, people who regard themselves as rational are most cruelly and shamefully mistaken in this high opinion they hold of themselves, for they are indulging in imagination of a special kind precisely because of their narrow conception of reality.

For example, it would be wrong to regard a cold-hearted egoist as a rational man. Love and goodwill (the ability to rejoice in the happiness of the people around us and to grieve over their sufferings) are just as innate in man as egoism. Whoever in his actions is guided exclusively by egoism is acting contrary to human nature, is suppressing an innate and ineradicable human need. He, in his way, is as much a fantast as the one who dreams of idealistic self-abnegation; the only difference between them is that one is an inveterate fantast, the other is a dissembling one; but they resemble each other in that neither can achieve happiness, both are harmful to themselves and to others. A starving man cannot, of course, feel good; but nor can a well-fed man feel good when he hears the heart-rending groans of starving people around him. It is unnatural to seek happiness in egoism, and the lot of an egoist is not in the least enviable: he is a freak—and it is irksome and unpleasant to be a freak.

Similarly, it is quite wrong to describe as rational a man who, having realized that man acquires strength only from reality and that all other lasting pleasures are provided only by it, would take it into his head to proclaim that there are no phenomena in reality that man must and can change, that everything in reality is pleasant and good for man, and that he stands impotent before every fact. This, too, is imagination of a certain kind, as absurd as dreams about castles in the air. Equally mistaken is the man who wants to give up plain, wholesome food for ambrosia and nectar, and the one who asserts that all food is delicious and wholesome for man, that there are no poisonous plants in nature, that soup made of goosefoot* is nourishing, that it is impossible to clear fields of stones and weeds in order to sow wheat, that wheat should not and cannot be separated from tares.

All these people are fantasts to an equal degree, because they equally run to one-sided extremes, equally deny obvious facts, equally want to violate the laws of nature and of human life. Nero, Caligula and Tiberius were as near to insanity as Ritter Toggenburg and the Indian fakir Vitellius, who was such a glutton that he had to take an emetic every day, and suffered from stomach pains no less than a man who never gets a satisfying meal. A debauchee is as destitute of the best pleasures of life as a eunuch. All these people possess very little of what is practical in life. Only he is practical who wants to be a man in the full sense of the term: while concerning himself with his own welfare, he also loves others (because there is no happiness in isolation); while abandoning dreams that do not conform with the laws of nature, he does not abandon useful activity; while finding much that is beautiful in reality, he does not deny that there is much in it that is ugly, and strives with the aid of the forces and circumstances favourable for man to combat what is not favourable for human happiness. Only a loving and noble-hearted man can be a practical man in the true sense of the term. He whom nature has not endowed with love and nobility is a wretched monster, a Shakespearean Caliban, unworthy of the name of man, but of such there are very few, perhaps none at all. He in whom

---

* A weed used for food by starving peasants.—*Ed.*

circumstances have killed love and nobility is a wretched, unhappy, morally sick man. He who deliberately suppresses these sentiments in himself is an unpractical fantast living in contradiction to the laws of real life.

When fantasy is renounced, a man's needs and hopes become very moderate; he becomes forbearing and tolerant, for excessive fastidiousness and fanaticism are the products of a morbid fantasy. But this does not mean in the least that to be rational weakens one's power of feeling, or the vigour of one's demands. On the contrary, the feelings and demands that are prompted and fostered by reality are far more potent than all fantastic strivings and hopes. A man who dreams of castles in the air does not devote to his exceedingly radiant dreams a hundredth part of the thought that a man devotes to the building of a modest (as long as it is comfortable) house for himself. Needless to say, the dreamer spends his time lying on a couch, whereas a man who is animated by a rational desire labours tirelessly to satisfy it. The more real and practical a man's strivings, the more energetically he fights the circumstances that hinder their realization. Both love and hate are created and roused to the highest degree by objects that lie in the sphere of real life. In spite of all her inconceivable beauty, the Helen of fantasy fails to rouse in a healthy man even a faint shadow of the feeling that is roused in him by a real woman, even if she is not a dazzling beauty. On the other hand, the cruelty of cannibals, of which we, happily, know only from hearsay, does not rouse our indignation nearly as much as it is by the deeds committed in front of our eyes by the Skvoznik-Dmukhanovskies and the Chichikovs,[27] which are innocuous compared with cannibal cruelty.

Belinsky was a vigorous and resolute man; he spoke with great energy and extreme animation, but it would be an absurd mistake to call him, as some have done, a man of immoderate demands and hopes. His demands and hopes both sprang from the needs and circumstances of our activities; therefore, for all their vigour, they were extremely moderate. What interests us here is Russian literature, therefore, it is of literature that we shall speak. Belinsky admired the *Inspector General* and *Dead Souls*. Let us think well and ask: could a man of immoderate desires admire these works? Can it really be that Gogol's sarcasm knows no limits? On the contrary, it is sufficient to recall even

Dickens, not to speak of the French writers of the last century, to be forced to admit that Gogol's sarcasm is very modest and restrained. Belinsky wanted our literature to develop, but what were the limits of his demands and hopes? Did he demand that our literature should before our very eyes become as deep and as rich as, say, contemporary French or English literature (although both are far from perfect)? Not at all. He said plainly that at the present time this was impossible and it was no use thinking about it. It was already a good thing, in his opinion, that our literature was beginning to look something like literature. He thought that the progress it was making was very rapid and praiseworthy. This rapidity of our development was a constant source of joy to him, and yet, truth to tell, progress was rather slow: as in 1846, so in 1856, we are still far from the "maturity" towards which we are striving. Yes, Belinsky was a very patient and moderate man. Numerous examples of this can be quoted. They are to be found on every page of his essays. It would also be wrong to imagine that his criticism was too severe; on the contrary, he was very lenient. True, he was endowed with extremely fine and unerring taste, he could not fail to detect flaws, and he expressed his opinions about them without mincing his words; but if a work he was reviewing possessed the least bit of merit, he was ready for the sake of it to excuse all. the flaws for which some excuse could be found. It is doubtful whether any of our Russian critics was as tolerant towards other people's opinions as he was. If the convictions concerned were not absolutely absurd and harmful he always spoke of them with respect, no matter how much they differed from his own. Numerous examples of this can be quoted. We shall point to one, which we will have to discuss, viz., his controversy with the Slavophiles, in which he always displayed far more goodwill than his opponents did. He was even gratified by the increase in the number of adherents to this school. (Incidentally, Belinsky was mistaken in thinking so: it has now been revealed that Slavophilism is incapable of attracting followers.) Similarly, he was quite ready to recognize all the merits of literary works that were not written in the spirit which in his opinion most conformed to the requirements of our literature, if only these works possessed positive merits. By way of example we recall his review of Mr. Goncharov's *An Or-*

dinary Story. We give as an appendix to this essay* an excerpt from Belinsky's last review of Russian literature. It will remind the reader that Belinsky did not recognize "pure art" and deemed it the duty of art to serve the interests of life. And yet, in this review he speaks with equal good-will of Mr. Goncharov's novel, in which he perceives a striving for nothing but so-called pure art, and of another novel, which appeared at about the same time, written in the spirit which Belinsky liked most; [28] if anything, he was even more indulgent towards *An Ordinary Story*. We can also recall the extreme sympathy with which Belinsky always spoke about Pushkin, although he totally disagreed with his conceptions. It is superfluous, however, to quote more examples, for a multitude of them will occur to every-body who has retained a clear recollection of Belinsky's essays.

The opinion that Belinsky was not very moderate in his conceptions, or that he denounced every mode of thought that differed from his own, is totally unjust. Anybody can easily convince himself of this by perusing a few of his essays. There have been quite a considerable number of fanatics in our literature, but far from resembling them in any way, Belinsky always waged a most resolute struggle against them, irrespective of the colour of their fanaticism, or of the party they belonged to. He denounced the fanatics of the so-called "tendency" as sternly as he denounced the fanatics of the opposite school. As an example, it is suffi-cient to recall how emphatically he expressed his disapprov-al of the publication in book form of the works of two young poets of that day who sang about how "mankind, weeping tears of blood, will awaken," and about the necessity of "punishing the priests of falsehood." **

How could the opinion have arisen that Belinsky was not a man of very moderate opinions about our literature and the problems connected with it, when a perusal of his essays will absolutely convince everybody that his concep-tion of things was exactly the same as that of nearly all right-minded people in our times? Here, much must be

---

* Not included in this volume.—*Ed.*
** We are not speaking of Belinsky's moderation in order to praise or blame him, but simply because this moderation is a very important and indisputable fact, only too often lost sight of when judgment is passed on him.

attributed to the unfounded accusations levelled against him by his personal enemies whose pride had been hurt by his criticism. They called him an extremist on the same grounds, and with the same lack of justification, as they asserted that he attacked our old writers, when, as a matter of fact, he sought to restore their fame. But the causes that gave rise to the opinion which we regard as unjust cannot be limited to these personal and petty motives.

Belinsky's demands were very moderate, but they were firm and consistent, and were expressed with animation and vigour. Needless to say, the sternest judgment can be covered up with flowery phrases. Belinsky, a man of straightforward and resolute character, disdained such devices. He wrote what he thought, concerned only for truth, and employing precisely the words that most exactly expressed his thoughts. What was bad he bluntly called bad, disdaining to conceal his judgment with diplomatic reservations and ambiguous hints. That is why people to whom every word of truth seems harsh, no matter how moderate it may be, regarded Belinsky's opinions as harsh. This cannot be helped; many people always regard straightforwardness as harshness. But those who understand what they read know very well that Belinsky's desires and hopes were very modest. In general, he demanded nothing beyond what would seem to be absolutely necessary for every man with a developed mind. This explains the strong sympathy accorded him among our public, which, in general, is very moderate in its desires.

It was not Belinsky's habit to yield in debate with his opponents, and there was not a single case of a debate not ending in the utter defeat of his opponent on all points. Not a single literary debate ended without Belinsky's opponent losing the respect of the best part of the public. But it is only necessary to recall what opinions he combated to have to admit that these debates could not have ended otherwise. Belinsky combated only opinions that were positively harmful and utterly mistaken. It is impossible to point to a single case of his taking up the cudgels against opinions that were harmless, or not absurd. Consequently, it was not he but his opponents who were to blame if the debates (usually not started by Belinsky) ended in their utter defeat. Why did they defend opinions that could not and should not have been defended? Why did they protest against obvious truths? Why did they so often strive to carry literary problems into the sphere of law court accusations? All the cases in which Belinsky conducted vigorous debate come under the following definition: Belinsky said that $2 \times 2 = 4$; for this he was accused of being ignorant, of lacking taste, of being disloyal. It was hinted that the paradox he proclaimed—namely, that $2 \times 2 = 4$—that, for example, Pushkin's works are of higher artistic merit than Derzhavin's, and that *A Hero of Our Time* is superior to *Brynsky Forest* * or *Simeon Kirdyapa* **—that this terrible paradox would have the direst consequences for the Russian language, for our national literature, and that— who can tell!—the whole world was threatened with mortal danger by such unfounded and malicious invention. In repelling such attacks, it could not, of course, be admitted that the attackers had even a particle of truth on their side. Had they chosen something that was doubtful for the object of their indignation, had they observed any one-sidedness or oversight on the part of Belinsky, the debate might have been conducted differently. Whether he agreed or disagreed with his opponents' remarks, he would readily have admitted that what they said was not altogether devoid of common sense, that their opinions were worthy of respect. Whenever he found that he was mistaken, he was the first unhesitatingly to expose the mistake. But what could he do when, for example, one of his opponents expressed indignation at the complete absence of convictions in Belinsky's essays, when that same opponent asserted that Belinsky did not understand the meaning of the words he wrote—later he reiterated that Belinsky was borrowing his conceptions from him (when, in fact, the opposite was the case, as will be obvious to every one who compares the old *Moskvityanin* with the *Otechestvenniye Zapiski*)— when others objected to Belinsky's alleged disrespect towards Derzhavin and Karamzin (whose merits he was the first to appraise), and so forth? Here, with all his readiness to be compliant, he could not fail to see that his opponents' remarks contained not a spark of truth, and he could not possibly refrain from saying that they were utterly mistaken.

---

* One of the historical novels by Zagoskin.—*Ed.*
** A historical novel about fourteenth century Russia by Polevoi.—*Ed.*

Such also was the situation when Belinsky started a controversy. Could he refrain from saying that the opinions he challenged were totally devoid of foundation when those opinions were something like the following: Gogol is a writer destitute of talent. The best character in *Dead Souls* is Chichikov's coachman Selifan. Hegelian philosophy was borrowed from Vladimir Monomachus' *Precept*. Writers like Mr. Turgenev and Mr. Grigorovich deserve to be pitied for not taking Russian life for the content of their works. Lermontov was an imitator of Mr. Benediktov and was weak in versification. Dickens' novels are monstrous examples of mediocrity. Pushkin was a bad writer. The greatest poets of our age are Victor Hugo and Mr. Khomyakov. Mr. Solovyov knows nothing of Russian history. The Germans must be exterminated. Chapter VII of *Eugene Onegin* is a slavish imitation of one of the chapters of *Ivan Vyzhigin*.* Gogol's best work is his *Evenings on a Farm* (in the opinion of some) or his *Correspondence with Friends* (in the opinion of others), the rest are much feebler. England perished in 1827, or thereabouts, so that not a trace of her existence has remained, just as no trace has remained of Plato's Atlantis. England is the only virile state in Western Europe (the opinion of the same writer who discovered that she had perished). The wicked West is decaying and we must as quickly as possible regenerate it with the wisdom of Skovoroda. Byzantium must be our ideal. Education is harmful,[29] and so on and so forth. Can even a particle of truth be found in such opinions? Can any concessions be made to them? Does objecting to them mean displaying intolerance? When a person who imagined he was a scientist and who exercised great influence on a magazine which made a speciality of attacking Belinsky and the *Otechestvenniye Zapiski* took it into his head to assert that Galileo and Newton had turned astronomy on to a false road,[30] was it possible to argue against him in the following strain: "There is much truth in what you say. We must admit that there were errors in our former conceptions of astronomical laws. But while agreeing with you on the main thing, we must say that some of the details of your remarks are not quite clear to us"? To have spoken like that would have meant betraying the obvious truth and making one-

---

* A novel by F. Bulgarin.—*Ed.*

self a general laughingstock. Was it possible to speak in such a strain in respect to opinions, samples of which we quoted above, and which, in their way, are no better than the repudiation of Newton's theory? No, here it was impossible to combine denial with compliance, because it was impossible to discover anything resembling the truth in what the opponents had said. With respect to such opinions, no middle course can be taken: either say nothing about them, or say right out, without equivocation, that they totally lack foundation. The attacks on Galileo and Newton could, of course, have been ignored—there was no danger that anybody would be misled by them. The other opinions, however, were not so innocuous—it was necessary to expose their unsoundness. Does the fact that Belinsky could not agree that Gogol was a mediocre writer and that drunken Selifan must be regarded as being representative of the Russian people show that he was intolerant?

The people who took up the cudgels against Belinsky attacked truths that were only too obvious and important. Belinsky attacked only opinions that were positively absurd and pernicious. Being a man of firm convictions and of straightforward character, he expressed his opinions vigorously.

But whoever confuses these qualities with extreme opinions is totally mistaken. On the contrary, Belinsky expressed his opinions with exceptional force precisely because, in essence, they were very moderate.

Having made these necessary remarks concerning the character of Belinsky's general views, we ought now to deal with the question of how he regarded the relation of literature to society and to its interests. But in one of his last essays Belinsky himself expressed his opinion on this subject with such fullness and precision that the best thing would be to present it in his own words in the appendix. Here, it remains for us to make only a few remarks that will serve to explain the excerpt from Belinsky's essay that we give.

The opinions that Belinsky expresses with such force and conviction in this excerpt are the very opposite to the ideas of transcendental philosophy, and especially of the Hegelian system, which based its entire aesthetic doctrine on the principle that the sole object of art is to realize the idea of the beautiful. According to those idealist

32*

conceptions, art should keep completely independent of all human strivings, except the striving for beauty. Such art was called pure art.

In this case too, as almost in all others, the Hegelian system stopped halfway and, refraining from making a strictly logical deduction from its fundamental propositions, adopted obsolete ideas that contradicted these propositions. Thus, it said that truth exists only in concrete phenomena, and yet, in its aesthetics, it postulated the idea of the beautiful as the supreme truth, as if this idea existed independently and not in a real, living man. It was this inherent contradiction, which is repeated in nearly all the other parts of the Hegelian system, that made it unsatisfactory. What really exists is man, and the idea of the beautiful is only an abstract conception of one of his strivings. But a man is a living organic being, and all his parts and strivings are inseverably connected with one another. Consequently, to base the theory of art solely on the idea of the beautiful means becoming one-sided and building a theory that is out of harmony with reality. In every human action, all the strivings of human nature take part, even if only one of them is mainly interested in the given action. Therefore, art, too, is produced not by an abstract striving for beauty (the idea of the beautiful), but by the combined action of all the forces and capabilities of a living man. And as the need of, for example, truth, love and improvement of conditions is much stronger in human life than the striving for beauty, art not only always serves to some degree as the expression of these needs (and not only of the idea of the beautiful), but its productions (the productions of human life, this must not be forgotten) are nearly always created under the overwhelming influence of the need for truth (theoretical or practical), love and improvement of conditions; so that, in conformity with the natural law of human activity, the striving for beauty is the servant of these and the other strong needs of human nature. This is how all the creations of art that are remarkable for their merit were produced. Strivings that are abstracted from real life are impotent; therefore, if, and when, the striving for beauty did try to act in an abstract way (breaking its connection with the other strivings of human nature), it could not produce anything remarkable even in artistic respects. History does not know of works of art that were produced

solely by the idea of the beautiful. Even if there are, or
have been, such works, they fail to attract the attention
of contemporaries and are forgotten by history as being
very feeble—very feeble even in artistic respects.
    Such is the view of positive science, which obtains its
conceptions from reality. The excerpt that we give in the
appendix shows that this was exactly Belinsky's final
view of art and literature. His mind was now utterly free
of all that is fantastic and abstract.
    We have seen, however, that at first Belinsky was an
ardent follower of the Hegelian system, the strong side
of which is the striving for reality and rationality (it was
by this mainly that it had charmed Belinsky, as it had
charmed all the vigorous-minded men of the young generation of that time in Germany and, partly, also in our country), and the weak side of which is that this striving remains
unrealized, so that nearly the entire content of the system
remains abstract and ineffective. Soon after he moved to
St. Petersburg Belinsky freed himself of his unrestrained
worship of Hegel; but thought and execution, a principle
and the deduction from it, are two different phases that are
always separated from each other by a long period of
development. To say: "I understand that reality must be
the source and measuring rod of our conceptions," and to
readjust all our conceptions on the basis of reality, are two
totally different things. The second task, which is, perhaps,
more important than the first, is accomplished only by continuous effort.
    Belinsky worked for the St. Petersburg magazines for
about eight years. To trace his development during this
period in all its gradations and details would mean analyzing all his essays—or at least a hundred, or a hundred
and fifty of the most important ones. But even this would
not be sufficient. It would be necessary to resort to data
that can be supplied only by a detailed biography. As it
is our essays have assumed dimensions far exceeding those
which we had contemplated when we began to write them;
the collection of biographical data would have delayed
their completion for an indefinite time; a review of all that
Belinsky wrote would take up hundreds and hundreds of
pages. We shall, therefore, trace in general outline the two
chief periods of Belinsky's activities in St. Petersburg.
In the first half, the abstract element in his essays was still

fairly strong, but in the second half it almost completely, and towards the end of this half it completely, disappeared, and his system of positive views became quite consistent. We shall obtain material for a characterization of the first period from a perusal of the contents of a few of Belinsky's essays written in the first period after his arrival in St. Petersburg. A close perusal of his last essays will provide material for a very full review of his final views on Russian literature. His annual reviews of Russian literature which appeared regularly from 1841 onwards, and his essays on Pushkin, which he wrote in the course of three years (1843-46), will serve as the link between the first and the second survey. Thus, without losing sight of the most important points of view, we shall complete the first part of our "Essays" before the end of this year.

For the first issue of the *Otechestvenniye Zapiski* in 1840, Belinsky wrote a review of Griboyedov's comedy, a second edition of which had appeared at about that time. This is one of Belinsky's most successful and brilliant essays. It starts with an enunciation of the theory of art exclusively from the abstract, scientific point of view, although in it he strongly combats dreaminess and it is all permeated with the striving for reality and it strongly attacks fantasy, which holds reality in disdain. Here, for example, is an excerpt that follows after the explanation (still totally in the Hegelian spirit) that "poetical works are the highest reality":

There are people who are heart and soul convinced that poetry is a dream and not reality, and that in our *rational and industrial* age there can be no poetry. Exemplary ignorance! Absurdity of the first magnitude! What is a dream? A phantom, a form without content, engendered by a distorted imagination, an idle mind, a torpid heart! *Such* dreaminess found its poets in the Lamartines and its poetical works in idealist-sentimental novels like *Abbaddonna*.* But is Lamartine a poet or a dream—and is *Abbaddonna* a poetical work or a dream? And what is this wretched, obsolete idea about our *rational* and *industrial* age being inimical to art? Did not Byron, Walter Scott, Cooper, Thomas Moore, Wordsworth, Pushkin, Mickiewicz, Heine, Béranger, Oehlenschläger, Tegnér and others appear in our age? Did not Schiller and Goethe work in our age? Was it not our age that appraised and understood the creations of classical art and Shakespeare? Are these not facts? Industrialism is only one side of the many-sided nineteenth century, and it has not prevented either

---

* A novel by N. Polevoi.—*Ed.*

poetry, as represented by the poets we have mentioned, or music, represented by its Shakespeare—Beethoven, or philosophy, represented by Fichte, Schelling and Hegel, from reaching the highest peak of development. True, our age is inimical to dreams and dreaminess, but that is exactly why it is a great age! Dreaminess in the nineteenth century is just as ridiculous, vulgar and sickly sweet as sentimentality. *Reality*—this is the watchword and slogan of our age, reality in everything—in religion, in science, in art and in life. A great, courageous age, it cannot tolerate anything that is false, spurious, weak or diffuse, but it loves that which is mighty, strong and material. It bravely and unfalteringly listened to the joyless songs of Byron and, together with that gloomy bard, resolved that it was better to renounce all joy and all hope than rest content with the beggarly joys and hopes of the past century. It has stood the test of Kant's critique of reason and Fichte's postulate of reason; together with Schiller, it suffered all the maladies of the inner, subjective spirit which was striving towards reality through negation. But in Schelling it saw the dawn of infinite reality which, in Hegel's doctrine, lit up the world with luxurious, magnificent daylight, and which, even before these two great thinkers, appeared, not understood, directly in the works of Goethe—(*Otechestvenniye Zapiski*, Vol. VIII, "Criticism," pp. 11-12).

Although it is repeatedly stated in this essay that the poetry of our times is "the poetry of reality, the poetry of life," the chief function of modern art is, however, presented as one that is completely abstracted from life: "conciliation between the romantic and the classical," because our age is, in general, "an age of conciliation" in all spheres. Reality itself is still conceived in a one-sided way: it embraces only man's spiritual life, whereas the whole of the material side of life is regarded as "illusory": "a man eats, drinks, wears clothes—this is a world of phantoms, because the man's spirit takes no part whatever in this"; a man "feels, thinks, is aware of himself as an organ, a vessel, of the spirit, a finite part of the general and the infinite—this is the world of reality"—all this is pure Hegelianism. But in explaining the theory it is necessary to apply it to works of art. Belinsky chooses Gogol's stories as samples of truly epic poetry and then reviews the *Inspector General* as the best example of a work of art in dramatic form....

PREFACE TO AND COMMENTS
ON CARPENTER'S *ENERGY IN NATURE*[1]

TRANSLATOR'S PREFACE

THE AUTHOR intended to write in simple language. A good intention. The language of this translation is simpler than that of the original. In this respect, the author would probably be pleased with the translation if he knew Russian.

Perhaps he would also approve of the omission from the translation of his references to popular English books and essays by English scientists which are unavailable to the majority of Russian readers since they have not been translated into Russian. The omission of all these references is quite adequately compensated by one that we make here, viz., that all the details the author advises his readers to read in the books and essays he recommends can be found in any of the good new popular treatises on physics of which there are rather many in Russian.

In all cases where this was needed for clarity, calculations in English units of length and weight are given in the equivalent Russian units in footnotes indicated by numbers. It would not, of course, have been worth while mentioning such trifles were it not necessary to warn the reader that, except for those indicated by numbers, all the footnotes, indicated by asterisks, are the author's.

The two last pages of the book, in which the author launches into metaphysics, have been omitted, and comments in keeping with the fundamental truths of natural science have been substituted for them.

⟨POSTSCRIPT⟩[2]

... such an amusing thing should happen that the author took it into his head to seek in jurisprudence an explanation of the concept "laws of nature." We shall speak about this later on; at present, let us see how this concept is explained not by jurisprudence, but by natural science.

We see mountains and plains. On the mountains and in the plains we see rocks, clay and sand. We see woods and fields. In the woods we see trees, on the trees we see leaves. In the fields we see grass and flowers. In the woods and in the fields we see mammals and birds. All these, and objects and living beings similar to them, are objects and beings that are studied by natural science. The latter classes all these objects and beings under the common concept of material things, and in its technical language it refers to them as diverse combinations of matter.

What is there unintelligible in this? Absolutely nothing. Natural science says all this in a very clever and simple way. In natural science there are many problems that are so difficult that sometimes it is very difficult for the layman to understand the explanations of them given by the experts, and still more difficult to find out whether these explanations are correct or not. But those are problems of an entirely different kind. For example, is iron, or copper, a simple or a compound body? Have the sidereal periods of Jupiter any relation to the periods of growth and diminution of the spots on the sun? These problems are more or less difficult to solve. Many problems of this kind cannot be solved at all in the present state of natural science. Let us, for example, ask: how many planets revolve around that very remote sun that we call Halcyon? Astronomy answers: "in the present state of our knowledge about Halcyon, we cannot say how many planets revolve around it, because we do not even know whether Halcyon has any planets at all."

There are so many difficult problems in natural science, and so many that cannot be solved in the present state of our knowledge; but these problems are entirely different from such, for example, as to whether a diamond or flint, or any other stone, an oak, or a maple, or any other tree, and so on and so forth, is a material thing, and there is nothing unintelligible in the answer that natural science gives to the question as to whether a lime tree is a material thing. It says: a lime tree is a material thing. Is this answer unintelligible?

The next question is: in what are material things identical? Natural science answers: they are identical in that they are material. What is there unintelligible in this answer? There is nothing unintelligible in this answer either. It is quite clear.

The next question is: what do we call that in material things which makes them identical in that they are material? Natural science answers: that which makes material things identical is called matter. What is there unintelligible in this answer? There is nothing unintelligible in it; it too is very clear.

. In exactly the same way natural science arrives at the answers to the questions put to it about the properties, forces and laws of the objects it studies.

These objects have identical properties; the thing they consist of, matter, is identical; consequently, their identical properties are the properties of what is identical in them, the properties of matter.

The properties of matter produce action, and the properties of matter are matter itself; consequently, the action of the properties of matter is the action of matter.

Is this not clear?

Some of the actions of matter are identical, some are not. For example, an oak tree grows and a lime tree grows: these two facts are identical. Here are two more facts: an oak tree falls and a lime tree falls; these are also identical facts. But a lime tree grows and a lime tree falls—these are not identical facts. An oak tree grows and an oak tree falls—these are likewise not identical facts.

Natural science classes all identical facts in one group and says that these facts are identical; but every fact is an action, hence, that which acts in identical facts is identical. What shall we call that which acts in an identical way in identical facts? "Let's call it force," the naturalists agreed among themselves in the past. And that is the name they gave it. Whether the name was well-chosen or not made no difference; this well or not well-chosen term denoted facts, and everybody who was familiar with the facts designated by this term, and knew that this was the term by which these facts were designated, understood what it meant in the language of the naturalists. Force is that identical thing that produces identical actions. This is what this identical thing was called by common consent in the past. Today, naturalists have agreed among themselves to use the term "energy" instead of "force." Is this new term well-chosen? Is it better than the old one? Whether it is well or not well-chosen, better or worse than the old term, is only a question of terms; the essence of the matter remains unchanged, and the meaning of the new term is clear. Energy is that identical thing which produces identical actions.

But when a lime tree grows, what is it that grows? The lime tree. When an oak tree grows, what grows? The oak tree. And so, when an object acts, what is action? The acting object.

When we speak of the properties of an object we speak of the object, when we speak of the actions of an object we speak of the object.

An acting force is the acting object itself; and the energy of an object is the object itself.

Energy is that which is identical in identical actions as long as the actions are identical; how can that which is identical in these identical actions not be identical?

What term shall we use to denote that the action of an identical force (or identical energy, to use the new term) is identical? The naturalists agreed among themselves to use the term "law" to designate this.

And so, what are the laws of nature? Identical action due to an identical force (or to identical energy).

The actions of objects are the actions of the objects themselves; identity of actions is identity of the objects themselves, and the laws of nature are natural objects which we examine from the standpoint of their identical actions.

That is what natural science says about this.

Is what it says clear? Perfectly clear. What can there be unclear here when this is a very simple deduction from a very simple analysis of the perfectly obvious fact that "material objects are material"? Such deductions cannot but be clear; their clarity is on a par with that of the statements: "a lime tree is a lime tree," "a stone is a stone," etc., or of the general statement that embraces all particulars: "the objects of natural science are the objects of natural science."

The subject is repeated in the predicate; the entire analysis consists exclusively of such sentences. Every predicate repeats the subject. This is so clear that it is tedious to read this series of sentences, tedious because it is all nothing but a reiteration of one and the same obvious truth: "material objects are material." It is tedious because of its very clarity. Tedious? Yes. But it is absolutely clear.

No, say some naturalists: "It is not clear." Why not?
Well, people are supposed to obey the laws of the state,
but they do not always do so. Hence, nature also may not
obey the laws of nature, but she does. Therefore, we must
first find out why she obeys them; when we find this out,
everything will be clear.

But there is absolutely nothing to find out. The laws
of nature are nature herself, examined from the standpoint
of her actions. How can nature act contrary to her laws,
i.e., contrary to herself? Water is a compound of oxygen
and hydrogen. As long as water exists, it is water, i.e.,
as long as it exists it will invariably remain a compound of
hydrogen and oxygen. It cannot be anything else. Anything
else is something that is not water. The action of water is
the action of water, and if water acts in a certain way under certain circumstances, then, if these circumstances repeat
themselves, water cannot but act in exactly the same way.
It is the same water; the circumstances are the same; how
can the result not be the same? The factors in both cases
are the same; can the results be otherwise than the same in
both cases? Today, $2+3=5$. Can $2+3$ be anything else,
than$=5$ tomorrow? And if $2+3$ turns out to be$=5$ tomorrow, will this be an enigmatic, astonishing fact that calls
for explanation?

In the opinion of these naturalists it will. Very well,
let them explain this strange circumstance that $2+3$ is
always 5. We would like to hear them explain it. That
it will be an amusing explanation there can be no doubt,
because people who set out to explore the enigmatic cause
of the strange circumstance that $2+3$ always$=5$, cannot
but say amusing things.

And so they begin to explain that the laws of nature
must possess exactly the same quality as the laws of a state.
Our author is an Englishman and the pupil of Englishmen.
Hence, the state he has in mind is, of course, England. Very
well, let us take England. In England the laws are obeyed.
That is a good thing, of course. But why are they obeyed?
Because administrative officials and the courts see to it
that they are obeyed, and if anybody commits the slightest
breach of the law the officials haul him before a court, the
court examines the case, and if it finds the accused guilty
it punishes him. Seeing how badly this one fared, other
Englishmen refrain from breaking the law. That is why

the laws are obeyed in England. And this also explains why water, for example, obeys the laws of nature.

"So this is what they are after!" will be the astonished exclamation of those to whom this treatment of water as if it were a humanlike being is new. "So this is the aim of the naturalists who say that the fact that inanimate objects act in accordance with the laws of nature is unclear in itself and has to be attributed to other causes! It pleases them to imagine that water is a humanlike being." Do these men of learning, particularly those whose learning consists of expert knowledge of nature, seriously think of water as of a humanlike being? Do they really imagine that it is a humanlike being?

Yes.

That is to say, these naturalists think that all the things that we call inanimate are humanlike beings?

Yes, of course. Let us recall what we read in the very first pages of this booklet:

"The so-called forces of nature have been well and truly spoken of as the moods, or affections, of matter. The relations of an individual to the objects which surround him vary with the mood in which he is; in a similar way, the relations of any object in nature to other objects in its immediate neighbourhood vary with the mood of these objects."

Then begins a discourse on the passive mood of a leaden bullet, on its heated mood, and its destructive mood.

When you were reading these pages, you probably had no inkling of the serious significance the author attached to these arguments about the "moods" of a leaden bullet. Probably you supposed that the author employed the word "mood" in the same way as you yourself understood it, namely, in the figurative sense. But now you see that for him it is not a metaphor; he applies the term "mood" to the leaden bullet in the literal sense; he conceives of the leaden bullet as an animate object.

Is the translation correct? Has the English word which has been translated into the Russian word "nastroyeniye" the same psychological meaning as the word "nastroyeniye" has in the Russian language?

We have translated the word "mood" as "nastroyeniye," but we must say that this does not adequately express the meaning of the word. We did not want to divert the reader from the author's thoughts to our opinion of his thoughts.

But in order to translate the word "mood" in a way that would fully express the meaning it has in the English text, we would have had to make the comment that we shall make now. The Russian word "nastroyeniye" is much less definite than the English word "mood." There is no word in the Russian language that can fully convey the definiteness of the psychological meaning of the word "mood." To express the meaning as fully in Russian as it is expressed in English, the word "mood" must be translated not simply as "nastroyeniye," but as "dushevnoye nastroyeniye." The author does not speak of some indefinite "nastroyeniye"; no, he speaks positively, definitely and absolutely clearly of the mood — of what being? A leaden bullet.

If you do not trust your memory, turn to the book again and see. The author ascribes a "mood" not only to a leaden bullet, which, whatever its qualifications as an animate being may be, at least resembles animate beings in that it is a distinct, definite object; no, not only is a leaden bullet endowed with a soul; in the author's opinion all the objects of natural science, even those that are not distinct from their environment, that are only parts inseparable from the other parts of the formless environment that is diffused and dispersed in space, are so endowed? Water, ice, vapour, hydrogen, oxygen and nitrogen, are all animate beings. You remember that before discoursing on the mood of a leaden bullet, the author informed you that every object possesses "mood," every object, that is, hydrogen, nitrogen and so forth.

And let us recall what the author says about energy in a state of rest. Here it is:

"Energy may exist in two states, that of motion, and that of repose. It is obvious that any moving body possesses energy, or the power of doing work, but it is not quite so clear at first sight how there can be energy in repose. In order to understand it, let us recur again to the analogy of the energetic man; he may be very quiet, and yet be able to do a great deal of work when he chooses to set about it."

And here the explanation ends; he goes on to speak of energy at rest as of a state that has been completely elucidated. A fact that covers all substances — a heap of garbage, water and gas has been interpreted as being humanlike, and the problem is solved; it has become clear.

Rocks, lakes, rivers and clouds, hydrogen and oxygen, are all humanlike beings; the facts of their existence are psychological facts.

When a man reaches such a stage of clarity of conceptions that he can no longer remember the difference between inanimate objects and living beings, then, of course, he loses the ability to understand whether a thing is intelligible to him or not. He feels as though he were dazed, in delirium, and he cannot help crying out in anguish — appropriately or inappropriately, as the case may be: "I don't understand!" "It is impossible to understand!"

The author keeps on repeating, in and out of season, that he does not understand, that science does not explain — what? What is self-evident to everyone whose mind is not dazed and who, therefore, remembers the elementary truths of natural science, which the author himself has written, on this very same page, five lines above or five lines below his lamentation that science is unable to explain the riddle. He asserts that neither he nor anybody else in the world knows what, for example, "energy" is, that all scientists have given up all hope of ever learning what it is, so that "science does not undertake to solve it." But he himself has written what "energy" is. Energy is power of doing work, the author himself wrote. But this is not enough for him. He would like the term "energy" to have some other meaning besides the one it has in scientific language. Well, this wish can easily be fulfilled. Everyone of us is at liberty to use any term in any sense he pleases, but he must always make the reservation: "to this term I arbitrarily attach the following meaning."

What the author actually wants we already know: he wants everything in the world to be humanlike. Well, when a man is overcome by such a desire he may say: I want the term "energy" to mean human reason. Everything in the world will then become clear to him. There is one awkward thing about this, however: he will make himself ridiculous in his own eyes.

This is exactly the author's trouble. At the very beginning of his book he strives to make all inanimate things living beings, but this does not hang together with the contents of the book, and so, while writing it he laments over the inability of science to explain what energy is. Having written the book he is again ... free of the necessity of retaining respect for science and of obeying common sense. He again breaks loose from natural science and, casting aside the restrictive rules that common sense imposes upon the play of the mind, he rushes into the sphere of jurisprudence in order to rearrange everything in nature to suit his own taste. He does this and he is happy.

"But what should we think of him? Is he a fool, or is he crazy?" Oh no. True, he is not a genius, but he is not a fool, and as long as he keeps to his subject he is lucid, he writes in conformity with what is taught by the only branch of science he has studied seriously, namely, natural science. But he is ambitious, and this branch is too narrow for him. He wants to pose as a man who is able to overcome ... the barriers that divide natural science from the other branches of science, and he climbs to the top floor of the building where philosophers reside. From here one can survey the whole field of human knowledge, and the voice that comes from the top floor is heard all around, not like the voice that comes from the bottom floor, from the physics and chemistry laboratories. To philosophize is an alluring occupation! And so he philosophizes.

But if a man wants to philosophize he must first obtain some knowledge of philosophy. This the author did not take the trouble to do. The result was what it always is when a man starts orating on something he knows nothing about: he talked nonsense.

This book, the translation of which compelled the translator to write these comments, is not, of course, a phenomenal scientific work, and its author is not a particularly great authority in the scientific world. To tell the truth, the poor fellow is not to blame for the fact that his philosophy is absurd; he is only a pupil repeating, as best he can, the philosophical wisdom he has heard from the naturalists whom he regards as authorities.

Well, we have had enough of this wretched philosophy, of the confusion of conceptions that is called anthropomorphism.

It only remains for us to say a few words about the passages the author quotes from Stewart Balfour.

The theory of the conservation of energy has served as the basis for a formula, according to which, in the course of time, all motion in the universe will be converted into heat, motion will cease and the universe will forever become a lifeless mass.

If such a state were ever possible, it would have already come about in the infinite past. This is an axiom which cannot possibly be disputed.

If a series of facts which has no beginning has an end, then, no matter how long the series may be, that end must have been reached in the infinite past. A series of facts that has no beginning can exist until some definite point of time only if it cannot have an end. If it could have an end, it would have ended before any given point of time.

The formula which prophesies the end of motion in the universe contradicts the fact that motion exists in our times. This formula is false; when it was drawn up something was overlooked.

At present motion is converted into heat. The formula assumes that this process is never modified, that it has always gone on and will continue to go on until all motion has been converted into heat. But the fact that the process has not yet ended makes it obvious that it must have been interrupted an innumerable number of times by an opposite process, which converts heat into motion, so that the existence of the universe represents a series of countless periods, each consisting of two halves: in one, the sum of motion diminishes as it is converted into heat, and the sum of heat increases; in the other, the sum of heat diminishes as it is converted into motion, and the sum of motion increases. Taken on the whole, it is a continuous alternation of oscillations, which has no beginning, and cannot have an end.

LETTERS [1]

TO A. N. AND M. N. CHERNYSHEVSKY

⟨*March 8, 1878*⟩

My dear friends, Sasha and Misha,

Let us continue our talk about world history—we have examined the astronomical section of the preface to it. We have discussed Newton's hypothesis, that is, Newton's idea that the motion of celestial bodies in conformity with the natural law which he discovered, and which we call Newton's formula, is caused by the power of mutual attraction of matter. We stopped at the point where I said that to explain the fate of Newton's hypothesis in our times, it is necessary to see what fate has befallen the majority of specialists in natural science in general, including astronomers, that is, mathematicians, who have yielded to the little studied and still less understood theories of idealist philosophy.

And so, I continue:

* * *

My dear friends, every separate group of people has its own ambition. We shall discuss this very important, of course, unreasonable, and therefore harmful element in human life when, in due order, we come to analyze human desires. Here it suffices to say that in accordance with scientific conceptions, I firmly adhere to the following opinion: every illusion has a harmful effect upon the course of a man's affairs; and still more harmful are illusions, such as the exaltation of one's own group to the detriment of other people, which arise not from some innocent error, but from an evil motive.

We shall limit ourselves to these brief remarks about the harmfulness of all illusions and the exceptional harmfulness of evil illusions, and examine more closely only that category of evil illusions which includes the story of

Newton's hypothesis in our times, which are so replete with
the amazing feats performed by the majority of naturalists
who bubble with excessive zeal to make great discoveries
and so win fame for themselves.

In every trade or profession, the majority of specialists
are ignorant of everything except the narrow technique of
their particular occupation. For example, the majority of
shoemakers are ignorant of everything except shoemaking.
But an ignoramus must have something to boast about.
A man of broad views and sentiments finds sufficient pride
in the fact that he is a man. An ignorant shoemaker, however, is little interested in the fact that he is a man. He can
make shoes—within the scope of his views and sentiments,
this is the only thing he can understand, like, and take
pride in; and if you give him only half an hour for self-
praise, you will hear him teach you, and through you the
whole human race, that shoemaking is the most important
occupation in the world, and that shoemakers are the
greatest benefactors of the human race.

The same will be said about his trade by an ignorant
tailor, an ignorant hairdresser, an ignorant bricklayer,
an ignorant carpenter, and by ignorant men of every
other trade.

But the artisans of these and similar trades, shoemakers,
tailors, and so forth, very rarely find patient, respectful,
credulous and grateful listeners to their self-praise. If
we wanted to hear their wild outpourings about their being
our greatest benefactors, we would have to arrange a private interview with them with no one else present. Otherwise we would not hear anything truly remarkable, for at
the first word of the feeble and still hesitant opening of his
didactic speech the boaster would be interrupted by a burst
of laughter and would be crushed by the sarcasm of the
people whom we had carelessly invited to be present at the
experiment.

This is not the lot of those professional people who are
specialists in occupations that are held in higher esteem
than shoemaking, hairdressing or carpentry. The public
listens to these highly-respected people with awe. And
thanks to its professionally boastful intonation, their self-
praise is a constant source of instruction and pleasure to the
human race, which bows down to the ground in gratitude
to its benefactors.

33*

There are many kinds of these highly-esteemed pro-
fessions. For example, architecture, painting, sculpture,
and so forth; music, singing, dancing and so forth; jurisprudence, and so forth, history, and so forth.

You know that the celebrated dancer Vestris did, indeed,
regard himself as the benefactor of the whole of France, and
of the whole of the civilized world. He was a genial chatter-
box, and it was only his vain chatter that distinguished him
from the ordinary specialists. In essence, the ideas of all
ignorant experts in all occupations are on a par with Vestris' naive chatter.

My dear friends, please remember that I am speaking
of all those who boast about their particular occupations.
I am no more unjust to musicians than to lawyers, to dancers than to preachers of morals. I say that all sing the
same hymn of self-praise, except that the terminology of
one is different from that of another.

If I now speak about ignorant naturalists, and about
ignorant astronomer-mathematicians in particular, I shall
not be more unjust to them than to other esteemed ignorant
specialists. I do not think in the least that their ignorance
is more reprehensible than that of painters or lawyers, vo-
calists and dancers, or preachers. And their self-praise is
not more absurd, not worse or more harmful. I must speak
about them only because it is they and not the dancers and
musicians who set out to teach the human race what Newton's
hypothesis is. Had mankind turned to lawyers or dancers
and not to naturalists, and to the astronomer-mathematicians in particular, for an opinion on this question, I would
not in these pages have troubled the naturalists, and the
astronomer-mathematicians in particular, I would not
even have mentioned them, but would have censured the
lawyers and dancers for their ignorance.

But mankind has no inkling that it would hear from
lawyers and dancers an opinion on Newton's hypothesis
not less scientific and not less sound than the one they hear
from Messrs. astronomer-mathematicians and company,
namely: "Newton's hypothesis is a hypothesis." What could
be simpler than that? And what vocalist or dancer, or even
a washerwoman would find any difficulty in expressing it?

And I would censure even a washerwoman, or a peasant
woman, for expressing an opinion like that as severely as
I censure the astronomer-mathematicians, for the question

of Newton's hypothesis is so easy that it would be disgraceful even for a peasant woman not to be able to understand it if she were asked to express an opinion after she had been given an hour or two to hear the facts and to think about them.

But those gentlemen the naturalists, and those gentlemen the astronomer-mathematicians in particular, have assured the credulous majority of educated people that there is something in the "question"—question!—of Newton's hypothesis that cannot be grasped by anybody except specialists in natural science, especially mathematics; that there is something in this "question," to answer which no mathematics is required except the multiplication tables, for which an answer can be found even by an illiterate person unacquainted with figures, who counts with the aid of the words that designate figures in ordinary language; who adds instead of multiplying, and adds with the aid of his fingers. Those gentlemen the specialists have taken the matter out of the hands of the bulk of the educated people and have proclaimed themselves the sole judges of the "question" of Newton's hypothesis—the question!—which is as much a question as whether twice two is really four. It was their pleasure to present the matter in this way. And because it was their pleasure to make the matter entirely dependent upon themselves, I am compelled to speak about them.

I am not doing so of my own free will, they compel me to do so.

My dear children, it is hard and painful for your father to speak in this way about the majority of the naturalists, and in this case, mainly about the majority of mathematicians.

But what can he do? Those gentlemen compel him to do so. There is a limit to everything, so there must surely be a limit to the ignorance of the specialists. And there is a limit to every reasonable man's compliance and indulgence. And your father is compelled, against his will, to ask: how much do the majority of those gentlemen, the great mathematicians of our times, understand about the simplest and most fundamental of the special scientific truths of their special science, viz., mathematics?

My dear children, this necessity is painful to me. I appreciate the merits of the scientists about whom I am asking this humiliating question. It pains me to have to ask it, but I must.

The material that I have for answering it is Helmholtz's essay on "The Origin and Significance of Geometrical Axioms." Of course, I am familiar with it only in the Russian translation. It is published in *Znaniye* No. 8., 1876. I shall quote the translation word for word

¿. * *

The first lines of the essay:

"The object of the present essay is to discuss the philosophical significance of the latest researches in the sphere of geometrical axioms and to discuss the possibility of creating, by analytical means, new systems of geometry with axioms other than those of Euclid's."

This is said by Mr. Helmholtz, one of the greatest naturalists. I know he is one of the greatest naturalists, and I have read, willingly believe, and partly see for myself from his essay, that he is one of the best mathematicians of our times.

I understand perfectly everything that is written in this essay.

But I say that he, the author, does not understand what he is talking about, or what he is saying in it. He confuses mathematical terms, and in doing so, he muddles his own thoughts to such a degree that his head is filled with utter nonsense, and this he expounds in his essay.

I shall correct his mistakes in the use of terms and, as a result, the technical part of his essay will acquire the proper meaning. Without such correction it is utter nonsense.

Let us note a particular word in these first lines of the essay. Helmholtz wants to discuss the philosophical significance of the subject of the essay. "Philosophical." But he knows nothing about philosophy. This is exactly the reason why he wrote such nonsense.

Somewhere he read something he did not understand. We shall see where and what he read. We shall see, but he does not know. Pondering over ideas he failed to understand, he imagined that it is "possible to create by analytical means new systems of geometry," different from "Euclid's" geometry.

This is the wild fantasy of an ignoramus who does not know what he is talking about.

In essence, the matter is so simple that even I, in spite of my scanty knowledge of mathematics, fully understand it in all its technical details. The matter is as follows:

Every geometrical curve has its own specific features. The properties of an ellipse are different from those of a hyperbola, or a cycloid, or a sinusoid. Who does not know that? I know very little about the ellipse, and still less about the hyperbola, but even I know that they are different lines. And since they are different, I can quite understand that the equation of an ellipse is different from that of a hyperbola. I do not know either of the formulas, but I understand that they are different. I know next to nothing about the sinusoid, but I do know that it has its own special equation. I also know next to nothing about the cycloid, but I do know that it too has its own special equation.

And so? Not everything that is applicable to the ellipse is applicable to the other three lines. The same must be said about each of them; and also about every other geometrical line.

Now, would you like to use such expressions: "the geometry of the ellipse" instead of "chapter of conic sections examining the properties of the ellipse"; "the geometry of the hyperbola" instead of "another chapter of conic sections examining the properties of the hyperbola," and so forth? We can if we want to, but in that case we must say: "the geometry of equilateral rectilinear triangles on a plane"; "the geometry of isosceles, etc., triangles," etc. In the end, we shall have as many "geometries" as there are formulas in geometry in the ordinary sense of the term.

But in "creating" these thousands, perhaps millions, of "geometries," what do we "create"? New word combinations, nothing more. We must remember this. It is only a matter of words.

But this is exactly where poor Helmholtz went astray.

He and some other "latest" masters in the art of drawing up formulas—I don't remember who at the moment, but I shall recall them presently—succeeded in drawing up certain equations of certain lines and they imagine that their "discoveries" are very important. Are they? And are they discoveries? I think that they are trifles which Euler and Lagrange did not put into their treatises or essays only because they did not want to waste paper and time on writing about trivial things which are obvious even to me. You are better able to judge than I am whether this is so or not; but whichever way it is, my dear friends, it makes no difference to the essence of the matter. Let us say that these "discoveries" of Helmholtz and Co. are "discoveries," and "great" ones, but what damage have they inflicted on Euclid's axioms? None whatever, of course.

Every figure in higher geometry is only a special combination of the very same elementary combinations that Euclid speaks about. For example, if we stretch a circle we get an ellipse; if we cut an ellipse in half, bisecting the major axis and unbend the half we first get a parabola and then a hyperbola. Probably I am not expressing myself correctly, but you understand what I want to say: all the formulae of curvilinear geometry are only variations and combinations of the elementary solutions of "Euclid." Let geometry be perfected, that is splendid; but not only is there nothing in it now that contradicts "Euclid," but there never will be.

Thus, no development in mathematics in general will introduce anything in it that contradicts the rules of addition and subtraction and—descending the ladder of knowledge still lower—that contradicts even the arithmetic of savages able to count only up to three.

Is it possible that Helmholtz does not know this? The fact of the matter is that while philosophizing he got muddled; this is all his fault amounts to.

And so, he only got muddled. The amusing thing, however, is the nature of the muddle he got into.

He and his company made some discoveries, trifling in my opinion, but he thinks they are great ones. Let us assume that they are great. He made them and imagined he had discovered "new systems of geometry" that are not in accord with "Euclid." This is what "discussion of the philosophical significance" leads to when a man who does not know the first thing about philosophy begins to philosophize.

But one must be fair to these "new systems of geometry"; they contain such novelties that they are a pleasure to read. I shall quote some examples:

Page 4, line 9: "Let us picture to ourselves thinking beings of only two dimensions. These thinking beings 'live on a surface,' and beyond this 'surface' there is no 'space' for them. They are 'two-dimensional beings' and their 'space' is only 'two-dimensional.'"

This is sheer twaddle. One can expect such stuff from a juvenile who has only just begun to learn elementary geometry, and, having failed to learn his first lesson, he talks like this in answer to the teacher's question: "What is a geometrical body?" The poor child confused the term "surface" with the term "body" and speaks in conformity with Helmholtz's "new system of geometry." Helmholtz, however, speaks in conformity with this juvenile's "system of geometry" because of his excessive zeal in "philosophical research."

Further, on the same page, Helmholtz, in the most serious manner, discusses "four-dimensional space"; yes, four-dimensional space. What is it? That's easily explained. Let us write the letter a; at the top ⟨right hand⟩ corner let us add a small figure 4; what will we get? We will get a^4. What will that be? It will be number or quantity a in the fourth power. Let us put this into geometrical language. In the language of geometry power is called "dimension." So what will this a^4 be? It will be "four-dimensional space." But supposing we write not 4, but 999, what dimensional space will that be? It will be "nine hundred and ninety nine dimensional space." And if instead of 999 we write $1/10$, what will it be? "One tenth of one dimensional space." Very, very good "new systems of geometry," you must admit.

But Helmholtz imagines that the piffle that formed in his head about "two-dimensional space" and about "four-dimensional space" has some important significance, and he talks quite seriously about the "possibility" of such "spaces." For example, on this same page 4 he writes:

"Since we are unaware of any sense impression from such an unheard of event as the appearance of a fourth dimension, just as the hypothetical two-dimensional beings are unaware of any impression from the formation of our third dimension, we can no more have any conception of a fourth dimension than a person born blind can have of colour."

Thus, the nonexistence for us of a fourth dimension is due solely to the special arrangement of our senses! It is not a fact that space has three dimensions; it only seems so to us! It is not in the nature of things to have three dimensions, it is only an illusion created by the faulty arrangement of our senses! In this respect, we are only "born blind."

My dear friends, is it possible for a man of sound mind to have his head stuffed with such utter twaddle? It is not, as long as he refrains from "philosophizing." But if, lacking the training to understand and appraise Kant's philosophy, he begins to philosophize in, as he thinks, the Kantian style, then all sorts of nonsense can take shape in his poor little head out of the combinations that arise in it of words, the meaning of which is unclear to him. And not knowing what he is talking about, he imagines that this piffle is profound wisdom.

Let us imagine that a Russian country woman who does not know French wants to pose as a high-society lady who speaks French perfectly. She happens to hear a few French sentences. She cannot catch the foreign accent, and even if she caught a few sounds, she cannot repeat them properly. The construction of the sentences she does not understand at all. What will her high-society French conversation sound like? Like the jabbering of an idiot. But, except for the foolish ambition to pose as a high-society lady, she may be a very clever woman. This ambition is her only weakness. But what can this weakness lead to? There is no limit to the trouble and foolishness into which this vanity can land her. As a rule, such fools do not lose their reason in the medical sense of the term, although many of them do. As a rule, the trouble such fools land into is limited to their falling into the hands of male and female rascals, and they are robbed; and robbed, ridiculed and humiliated, they return to the backwoods from which they came.

We shall see that Helmholtz and his fellow natural scientists who like to pose as philosophers meet with the same little—comparatively speaking—little trouble; they do not lose their reason; they only fall into the hands of unscrupulous rascals. That is all.

Let us return to the essay written by that country bumpkin of the male sex who is very clever in his own village, but, who, alas, went off to the metropolis to astonish the inhabitants there with his high-society manners. Mathematics. What's mathematics? Who is interested in it, except mathematicians? It is a village in the backwoods about which nobody but its inhabitants is concerned. But philosophy is different. Philosophers are talked about in educated society all over the world. Philosophers are society people, the aristocracy who live in the capital. What will happen when this country bumpkin appears in the ballrooms of the high aristocracy? He will become famous throughout the world for his wit, talent and elegant manners.

And so we have seen this highly-esteemed—I don't deny it; on the contrary, I say that I greatly respect him for the good work he has done in his village—country bumpkin of the male sex, Mr. Helmholtz, set out on an excursion to the metropolis and we have admiringly contemplated his first successes in the aristocratic ballroom of Kant. The bumpkin posed as a "hypothetical two-dimensional being" and very amusingly twitted people with their ignorance of four-dimensional space due to their lack of a physiological organ with which to sense the fourth dimension.

The highly-esteemed person acquired aplomb and was very proud of his success. Later he very gracefully explains to us that "rational two-dimensional beings can exist in quite different 'spaces,' each of which has two dimensions."

My friends, this is literally what it says in this essay by that country bumpkin Mr. Helmholtz. You will find it on page 5 of his essay.

Of the different two-dimensional spaces, the first "space" is an "infinite plane" (page 5, line 8). In this "space," as in ours, there are "parallel lines." Who discovered that a "plane," that is, our conception of the boundaries of the geometrical part of space, the boundaries of a geometrical body, is "space," is not evident from Helmholtz's essay. Who the founder of the "new systems of geometry" is, I do not know. In our last talk I assumed that it was Gauss. Whether my assumption is correct or not, I do not know, of course; but for the sake of the honour of mathematics I hope that I am not mistaken, for if I am, the disgrace would spread to all, all the great mathematicians since Lagrange and Laplace. All these epigones will be to blame for this disgrace if only one of them, the greatest of them, Gauss, is not the sole culprit. I shall speak later about the inevitability of this "horn of a dilemma." If Gauss is not the sole culprit, then all the authoritative mathematicians who lived after Laplace, and who are living today, are to blame. I assumed it was Gauss only in order to avoid blaming the others. Gauss, in any case, is certainly to blame. And so, during our last talk, I decided to blame him alone. But later, after pondering over the matter, I began to doubt whether it would be just to acquit his fellow mathematicians. We shall speak about this later, however. At present, let us return to our examination of Helmholtz's piffle.

And so, the first sort of "two-dimensional space" is an infinite plane. Who invented this absurd word combination I do not know; I would like to think it was Gauss. But did he? Really, it makes no difference.

The second sort is a "spherical surface." In this space there are no "parallel lines." He says quite a lot of other original things that are not in accord with "Euclid's geometry." But I know all these original things, I have not yet forgotten "Euclid's" theorems for the surface of a sphere. They are quite different from those which "Euclid" applies to figures in a plane. To begin with, for example, the fact that a plane triangle is by no means a "spherical surface." All this, and everything like it, is not only given in "Euclid," but even I remember it, although I have forgotten nearly all my "Euclid."

There is also an "oval surface." This too I know. I do not know the theorems for it, but all that Helmholtz says about it I have known for about forty years, since the age of ten, when I was learning "Euclid." There is nothing in "Euclid" about this surface, but everybody who knows "Euclid's" theorems for the surface of a sphere, knows about all the differences between the oval surface and the spherical surface that Helmholtz talks about. And also since the age of ten have I known all the rest of what is dealt with in the technical, strictly geometrical section of Helmholtz's essay. All this newly-discovered wisdom has been known since the time of "Euclid" by everybody who has learnt even a little of "Euclid." The only new thing is that those "latest" sages, Messrs. Helmholtz and Co., having had their heads pummelled by Kant and unable to think because of their headache, imagine that these "surfaces," these boundaries of geometrical bodies, are "spaces." It is as new as the possibility of finding the square or cube of "a pair of boots," or finding the square root of "a pair of boots."

The "latest creators" of new "systems" of mathematics will, of course, have no difficulty in finding the square of "a pair of boots." It is enough for them to write the formula

$$N^2A^2$$

and they will at once begin to calculate: "Let a be 'boot'; a pair of boots will be $2a$; the square of $2a$ will be

$$4a^2$$

and they will read it as follows: "the square of a pair of boots will be equal to four boots square." But what is: "four boots square"? To us Russian-speaking people, the meaning of four boots square is obvious; it means: "boot on the wrong foot." Such, according to the "new system of mathematics," is the easy solution found for a problem which in the mistaken opinion of people who adhere to the old, universally-known "system of mathematics," is incompatible with human sense.

Here is another problem that Helmholtz and Cc. will also solve easily. "Given an assembly of 64 pedants who are obsessed with excessive vanity—find the square root." The answer is: "8 square roots of such pedants." Very well. And the cubic root? Answer: "4 cubic roots of such pedants."

Let us return to the essay of the poor fellow who got muddled while flaunting his knowledge of Kantian philosophy.

An oval two-dimensional space is uncomfortable for rational, two-dimensional beings. In moving about in it they would stretch and shrink unevenly in the same way as a piece of the pellicle of an egg is crumpled when moved about in the eggshell. That is correct, I know. And indeed, how could these "two-dimensional beings" be "rational" if their heads were constantly being crumpled by stretching and shrinking? But ... but ... suppose we assume that these "rational two-dimensional beings" are two-dimensional oysters? They are fastened to their places and they feel no discomfort; and besides, they have no heads. What inconvenience is caused them by the oval shape of their space? Ah, yes, we have forgotten: oysters have no hands and are, therefore, unable to write books; whereas for Helmholtz, the whole essence of "rational life" lies in writing books and essays on mathematics. It goes without saying that "oval two-dimensional space" is not worth talking about, and it is not worth while for rational two-dimensional beings to live in it.

But "spherical two-dimensional space" is a very good sort of space.

The third excellent sort is "pseudo-spherical two-dimensional space." What does it look like? The surface of a wire ring. The inventor of this surface is the celebrated, according to Helmholtz—celebrated! What for? Foolishness?—Italian mathematician Beltrami. I hope that this foolishness was—as I also hope it was in the case of Helmholtz—only a passing mental derangement and that he is celebrated not for this foolishness, but for some practical work done by him.

In one respect even this, though passing, foolishness is to be deplored! When he recovered his senses Beltrami should have repudiated it, but evidently he has not done this. And so, he has not fully recovered, and it continues to oppress his mind like a leaden dunce's cap. Yes, it is easy for a dunce who is obsessed with vanity to do foolish things, but it is difficult for him to heal himself of it. That is why the fundamental foolishness of vainglorious dunces, the stupidity of remaining dunces when they want to achieve fame as philosophers, is unpardonable. If they could learn something, perhaps their vanity would disappear together with their ignorance. As it is, they disgrace themselves and disgrace their special science by their wild fantasies.

According to Helmholtz, certain other figures besides wire rings have a "pseudo-spherical surface," and he enumerates its different forms. All these forms are very elementary. Whether each one of them had been given a special formula before Beltrami, I do not know, but even to me it is clear that all these formulas are very slight variations of the formulae for lines of the second degree. For example: the formulae for the surface of a wire ring are slight variations of the formulae for the cylindrical surface of a right cylinder; that is to say, the formulas of the surface of that ring are very easily and simply deduced from the formulae of a circle. And I believe that if in this piece of Beltrami's stupidity there are formulae not to be found in the treatises and essays of Euler and Lagrange, it is because they did not publish them, because they did not think it was worth while publishing corollaries of other formulae obvious to every decent mathematician.

Whether this is so or not makes no difference. Let us suppose that in this piece of stupidity Beltrami did give some new formulae that are not quite unimportant. For all that, the general character of the two works of his to which Helmholtz refers is stupid beyond measure. This is evident from their very titles: "An Essay on the Interpretation of Non-Euclidean Geometry," and "The Fundamental Theory of Spaces of Constant Curvature." I would be glad to throw all the blame for this stupidity on Helmholtz on the assumption that he put this wild fantasy into Beltrami's work, the practical and reasonable object of which was to find formulae for annular, bi-saddled and wineglass surfaces. Whether these formulae were important or unimportant, new or old in science, would not matter; the object of the work was a practical one; and if the author tried to find solutions already discovered by others, but unknown to him, his ignorance may have been accidental, and I would be glad to regard all such accidents as excusable. But, no! It was Beltrami who invented "non-Euclidean geometry," he himself. It was not Helmholtz who put this illiterate nonsense into his work; he himself boasts that he discovered a new geometry. And it was not Helmholtz who introduced the absurd confusion of the terms "line" and "surface" with the term "space." No. Beltrami himself speaks of "curved spaces." Oh, the monster!

Incidentally, Helmholtz found that Beltrami had a predecessor. This predecessor of the inventor of "curved spaces," a certain Lobachevsky, was formerly a professor at the Kazan University. As far back as 1829, says Helmholtz, "Lobachevsky drew up a system of geometry" which "excluded the axiom of parallel lines, and at that time it was already fully proved that this system is as sound as Euclid's." And Lobachevsky's system is "fully in accord" with Beltrami's new geometry....

What is "geometry without the axiom of parallel lines"? Children amuse themselves by hopping on one foot. Of course, they cannot move very fast in this fashion, nor can they go very far, a couple of versts, say. But by trying hard they can move with some speed for some distance. A few can keep up with a man who is walking slowly and accompany him for the whole of a quarter of a verst. This is a very difficult and praiseworthy feat, but only when it is the prank of a child. But if a grown-up man were to set out on a journey by hopping on one foot, and not out of fun, but seriously, on a serious errand, that journey would not be altogether unsuccessful, no, but it would be utterly foolish.

Is it possible to write Russian without verbs. Yes. Sometimes people write like that for fun. And sometimes it is rather amusing. But you know the lines:

> A rustle, a faint breeze,
> The warble of a nightingale,

is all I remember of the whole poem. It is composed entirely like these two lines, without verbs. It was written by a certain Fet, who was a celebrated poet in his day. And he wrote some very pretty poems. But considering their content, they could have been written by a horse if it learnt to write verse. They all deal with impressions and desires that horses share with human beings. I knew Fet. He was a perfect idiot; there are few like him in the world; but he was an idiot with poetic talent. And he wrote this pretty poem without verbs as a serious thing. As long as Fet was remembered, everybody knew this charming poem, and when anybody began to recite it, everybody, although they knew it by heart, laughed until their sides ached. It is such a clever thing that its effect was always astonishing, like a novelty.

You know that the most essential consonant in the French, Italian and Spanish languages is the letter L; it goes into the "article," without which it is difficult to say ten connected words. Well? At the time when vanquishing the laws of linguistics was the rage, many verses were written in these languages without the letter L. In the Spanish language there is even a whole epic poem, an enormous volume, without the letter L. I have forgotten the name of the fool, of an author. If you like, you can look up some treatise on seventeenth century Spanish poetry, the "time of decadent taste."

It is surprising what an amount of hocus-pocus can be got up to by those who like that sort of thing. As an amusement during leisure hours it is not bad fun. But whoever performs tricks not for fun, but labours to compose rebuses, charades and puns, thinking to "recreate" science with this tomfoolery, engages in a foolish occupation, and if he is not a born fool, he voluntarily makes a fool of himself.

* * *

Shall we continue to discuss Helmholtz's nonsense? No doubt you have long been thinking: "Enough!" No, my dear children, I think we ought to continue. I like to make everything transparently clear; and not feeling my own weariness from my lengthy explanations, I do not wish to note that of others. But it is time to finish, for the mail is going in a few hours time, and so I will leave all the further details of Helmholtz's piffle and proceed to reestablish the mathematical truths that have been mutilated by this piffle.

What is the real meaning of the formulas which Helmholtz and Co. foolishly apply to the concept of "space"? They are formulae of "the path of a ray of light."

In our immediate vicinity, at a distance of a few metres from our eyes, under ordinary conditions of atmospheric transparency and temperature, the path of a ray of light is a straight line. A sheaf of rays, spreading in straight lines, will form a simple cone, a right cone, "Euclid's" cone, the only cone of which I knew the formula. Am I right in calling this cone elementary geometry? It makes no difference. It is not a matter of whether I am an expert mathematician; I am not, and I do not wish to be. I have never had the time for it. The chief thing is that you should understand what I mean. I am speaking of that cone which for the purpose of our analysis we regard as a geometrical body produced by the rotation of a rectilinear, plane right-angled triangle around one of its sides; this side will be the "axis," the other will give the base of the cone; the hypotenuse will give the surface of the cone. Am I expressing this right? What do I care? It is not a matter of words. I only want you to see what kind of a cone I am speaking of.

This cone is Euclid's cone, the cone formed by a sheaf of rays in our immediate vicinity. It is the correct formulas of these rectilinear rays of light that have been most idiotically converted by an absurd fantasy—whose? I do not know; I would like to think that it was Gauss'—into the formula of "homaloid three-dimensional space," or "Euclid's space." Who invented the term "homaloid space"? Evidently it was not Gauss but Beltrami, the inventor of "curved spaces." At all events, the great teacher is to blame for all the absurdities uttered by the dull pupil. All these "spaces" have been fished out from Gauss' researches into the "measure of curvature of surfaces." Perhaps this work of Gauss' is very practical and very important. Whether this is so, I do not know, but I presume it is. I am willing to give Gauss his due for it. But evidently Gauss was confused by Kant's philosophy, and when he began to philosophize, he talked nonsense. In his research into the "measure of curvature of surfaces," or in some other work, he philosophized in the Kantian manner about the "forms of our sense perceptions," a subject entirely out of his sphere, and philosophizing, he got muddled. It seemed to him that Kant was partly right and partly wrong in his "theory of sense perceptions," so he set about correcting Kant, and being a simple-hearted, ignorant clodhopper on this "dialectical" and by no means mathematical question, the question of

the authenticity of our sense perceptions, he was fooled by
Kant. Fancy him, a backwood country bumpkin, setting
out to fight Kant! He did not even understand Kant, and
in his effort to refute him, repeated his ideas in a garbled
form. But of this anon. Suffice it for the present to say that
you will not find in Kant any incongruous, illiterate, clumsy,
clodhopper expressions like "two-dimensional space," or
"four-dimensional." Whether Gauss himself invented this
nonsense, or whether he merely talked a lot of nonsense
and Helmholtz, Beltrami and Co. thought it good material for their own nonsense, really makes no difference.

For the sake of the honour of mathematics, however,
it would have been better if all this nonsense had been
uttered by Gauss. In that case I would not blame the other
authoritative mathematicians for either repeating what
Gauss said, or for remaining silent, for not laughing when
reading the absurdities of Helmholtz, Beltrami, Riemann,
Liebmann and Co., quoted by Helmholtz as his companions.
The strength of Gauss' genius is the strength of a giant compared with all the mathematicians who came after Laplace,
including those of today. Pigmies in the grasp of a giant—
what can you expect of Helmholtz and Co.? How can one
blame them? They wriggle their puny arms and legs and
squeak as the giant orders them to. As for the rest of the pigmies—the bulk of the other great mathematicians, these
outsiders, these onlookers, pigmies, tremble and wonder,
and remain silent—how can one blame them?

That is how I would judge them if Gauss were the guilty
one; I would not scorn but pity them. Strictly speaking,
they would have been Gauss' innocent victims.

But I doubt whether this is the case. True, in studying
the tone of Helmholtz's essay, I am compelled to assume
that Helmholtz, Beltrami and Co. did directly take their
nonsense from Gauss; but Gauss' wild Kantian fantasies are
evidently the common fantasies of all the authoritative
mathematicians of our times. All of them find the square
of boots, and the cubic roots of boot uppers and blacking,
and, therefore, all of them have a hankering for two, four
and a million and four dimensional space, and for triangu-
lar and oval, tobacco, chocolate, tea, oak, blockhead, idiotic,
in short, for every kind of foolish and nonsensical space.

It is painful to write this, but the tone of Helmholtz's
essay leads to such an assumption.

Why does the situation in mathematics lead me to this assumption, which, I hope, is after all a mistaken one? You see, I am still only trying to reach the point of explaining the first reason, viz., the dependence of natural science in general, and mathematics in particular, upon the doctrines of idealist philosophy, and chiefly upon the Kantian system. We shall reach that point, but let us first finish with the essay of that poor, pitiful fellow Helmholtz, who revealed to me the disgrace of unhappy mathematics, which, left an orphan after the demise of grand old Laplace, fell into the clutches of men of the dark Middle Ages to be outraged and dishonoured.

Why did this ignorant clodhopper, this country bumpkin of the male sex, this great—I know—naturalist, and great—I willingly believe—mathematician Helmholtz, write his unfortunate essay?

Before quoting its idiotically boastful conclusion, let us recall the real truth that was distorted by the philosophical piffle of his wild imagination.

A ray of light in the immediate vicinity of our eyes, under ordinary atmospheric conditions, stretches for a distance of, let us say, several metres in a straight line. A sheaf of rays will, in that case, form a right cone. These cranks begin their fantasies, consciously or, apparently, unconsciously, with ideas appertaining to this fact, with correct ideas. But Kant knocked out of their poor heads the scientific truth that "three dimensions are a property of matter, the very nature of things." They want to pose as philosophers. They forget about the cone formed by the rays of light and think only about the base of the cone. This base is a surface formed by the rotation of one of the sides, that is, the rotation of a straight line. In other words, it is a plane. They expand this plane "to infinity" and imagine that they have invented "homaloidal two-dimensional space." How will rays of light go across this "space"? Oh, they have long forgotten about the cone of rays, and they decide that the rays will go across this plane in parallel lines. But they have also forgotten about the rays, and so they get "formulas of an analytical research" which creates a "geometry of homaloidal two-dimensional space."

Very nice. But is the cone of light rays absolutely right? Is a ray of light that reaches us from the sun, or from a candle under our noses, an absolutely straight line? No, never.

34*

This they forgot. Actually, this is impossible. Coming from the sun through the atmosphere, the ray bends. Coming from a candle it passes through hot air into cool and bends. This curve is insignificant under ordinary circumstances, but it is inevitable. In a mirage the curve is big; but a mirage is only a very high degree of what is a constant fact about all rays proceeding at an angle close to $=O$ from the horizontal line. All the lower strata of the air are a confusion of streaks and patches of air of different temperatures. Hence;—but who does not know all this, and all that follows from it?

These cranks know it too, but in their poor, sick heads, which have been pummelled by Kant, everything is mixed up and floats in a haze, and out of this haze emerge wild fantasies about spherical and pseudo-spherical spaces.

What is the simple scientific explanation of the matter? A ray of light is not an absolutely straight line; at a distance of several metres, under ordinary circumstances, the curve is insignificant, but sometimes it is big.

In short? These cranks have confused "dioptrics," a department of optics, with the formulas of abstract geometry. They have confused their rural geodesy, conducted "by eye," with the laws of the universe.

That is all. It does not do anybody any serious harm. Oh? Is that so? Very well, let us say that it does not. Let us say that they only made fools of themselves and flung their science, mathematics, into the clutches of men of the dark Middle Ages to be outraged by them. That's all. No great harm done. That's so. What harm would there have been if from the time of primitive savagery, counting on fingers, then arithmetic, and so forth, had been left only to fools. We would not have had Archimedes, Hipparchus, Copernicus, and all the rest up to Laplace, we would have remained half-savage nomads, that's all.

And so? The harm caused by the asinine wisdom of Helmholtz and Co. is not great. But we cannot say: "not very great." Instead of scientific truth, those fools are preaching the stupefying doctrine of wild, illiterate fantasy. That's all. No great harm done? Of course, compared with the plague, or a serious crop failure, it is not.

Enough of this. Let us pass to the finale of Helmholtz's essay, to the paeans of victory he sings in honour of himself and his companions.

To the astonished world there is revealed the aim of this nonsensical essay—an aim so vast that the mind fails to grasp it. It appears that the author is celebrating a victory and, it appears, a victory he achieved over Kant, whose garbled ideas comprised the entire material of his amazing philosophizings. He proclaims:

"To sum up:

"1. Geometrical axioms taken by themselves, apart from the principles of mechanics, do not express a relation between real things."

My dear little country bumpkin, you are all muddled up. You know nothing, absolutely nothing, about mechanics, or about geometry. Is not a triangle taken by itself a triangle? And has it not three angles? And axioms—the elements of which, combined in a certain way, produce a triangle—do they not, taken by themselves, express "a relation between real things"? Does a triangle become a triangle only when it has moved from one place to another? My dear little country bumpkin, "mechanics" deals with "equilibrium" and with "motion," whereas "geometry" deals with bodies and the elements of geometrical bodies, irrespective of whether they are motionless or in motion—this is the most elementary part of geometry; the "Theory of Functions" has a different point of view. But you, my dear fellow, don't see the difference between "Euclid" and the "Theory of Functions." True, in "Euclid" too it says: "let us draw a line," "let us rotate a line about one of its ends," and so forth; but, my dear fellow, these are only "teaching methods." They are not the "subject" of the axioms, but only "teaching methods" to help you to learn. In your ignorance, however, you got muddled over them and confused "Euclid" with mechanics. Continue, my dear country bumpkin.

"If we," continues the ignorant country bumpkin, "if we, having thus isolated them" (the axioms of geometry from mechanics) "look upon them together with Kant...."

Oh, take care, country bumpkin! Kant will squash you, you little ignoramus! ("look upon axioms together with Kant") ... "as upon the transcendentally given forms of intuition, we shall find...."

My dear fellow, a mathematician, or a naturalist in general, has no right to look upon anything "together with Kant." Kant repudiates all natural science, and he denies the reality of pure mathematics. My dear fellow, Kant doesn't care a hang about what you do, or about you. Kant is no companion for you. And he squashed you even before you thought of him. It was he who knocked into your wooden head that with which you started your hymn of victory. It was he who induced you to repudiate the intrinsic scientific truth of the axioms of geometry. It is not for you, you ignoramus, to talk about "the transcendentally given forms of intuition"; this idea cannot be grasped from your clodhopper point of view. Kant invented these "forms" in order to defend free will, the immortality of the soul, the existence of god, god's concern for men's welfare on earth and for their eternal bliss in future life. To defend these convictions so dear to his heart—from whom? From Diderot and his friends. This is what Kant was thinking about. For this purpose he broke up everything Diderot and his friends used for their support. Diderot used natural science, mathematics, as his support, and Kant, with unfaltering hand, shattered the whole of natural science, shattered all the formulas of mathematics; he did this with unfaltering hand although he himself was a much better naturalist than you are, my dear fellow, and a much better mathematician than your Gauss. That's just like the aristocrats in the metropolis: they are better than you are, little fool, little fool with a wooden soul. You are wooden, they are human; and to benefit mankind they do not hesitate to demolish the robbers' den. Robbers' den—that's your village in the backwoods. Kant was born in a village; he loved it, but since it was necessary for the benefit of mankind he demolished the village that served as a robbers' den. That's what Kant was like—he was a man filled with an ardent desire to benefit mankind. How dare you, little fool, to whom your backwood village is the most precious thing on earth, even think of "becoming a companion of Kant"? For the sake of men's welfare, eternal bliss and transcendental happiness he is leading them to demolish your backwood village. Is he right? It is not for you to judge, you ignoramus. But run, flee from him!

But these wooden-headed manikins to whom "men's welfare" is a trifle and only "resonators" and the "chords of upper harmony" are important, these wooden-headed manikins are incapable of understanding the great things Kant was concerned with. They imagine that Kant, like themselves, thought only about acoustics, or optics. Was Kant right? I expressed my opinion on this point sufficiently in the first of these talks. At all events, Kant knew what he was talking about.

Shall I continue to quote from the finale of this silly essay? No, I have no time; I have to post this letter. Therefore, I will only say:

The whole of this finale is a paraphrase in the clumsy, rural dialect of mathematics of the ideas of Kant, who repudiated natural science and mathematics. The result is that the ideas are garbled. But the fool, spurned by his teacher Kant, imagines that he has refuted him with his nonsense about "spherical two-dimensional space"—nonsense suggested to him by Kant who shattered the whole of mathematics in order, for the benefit of mankind, to save the rectified doctrines of Peter of Lombardy, Thomas Aquinas and Duns Scotus; in order, for the benefit of mankind, to save the rectified practical strivings of Pietro Damiani and Bernard of Clairvaux.

My point of view on this? The point of view of Lalande and Laplace—the point of view of Ludwig Feuerbach. And if you want to know not only what I think about it, but also what I feel about it, read, not Goethe's *Faust*, no, that is written from a point of view that is far too obsolete, but Goethe's *The Bride of Corinth*:

> Nach Korinthus von Athen gezogen
> Kam ein Jungling dort noch unbekannt,

that is all I remember, and I am ashamed that I do not know the whole of this wonderful poem by heart. Read it, my dear children.

And keep well.

I heartily grip your hand, my dear Sasha.

And yours, my dear Misha.

In our next talk we shall speak more about Newton and Laplace, and about a natural science that was not surrendered to Peter of Lombardy to be defiled by him, to Bernard of Clairvaux to be exterminated by him; about a natural science that enlightens the minds of men and gives them the strength to work successfully for the building of a life of prosperity, peace and honour.

I grip your hands, my dear children.

Your father, but more important than your father—also your friend. *N. Ch.*

I tore part of this page off to get the whole of this letter into a half-an-ounce envelope and not because I am short of paper and have to write on scraps. Don't think, my dear children, that I am short of paper, I have reams of it, and a heap of envelopes too. I don't need anything. I have plenty of everything. *N. Ch.*

* * *

TO A. N. AND M N. CHERNYSHEVSKY

April 6, 1878, Vilyuisk

My dear friends, Sasha and Misha,
Let us continue our talk on world history.
To understand the trend of my thoughts in this talk, it will be useful to recall the contents of the preceding ones.

* *

The preface to the history of mankind consists of:
The astronomical history of our planet;
The geological history of the globe;
The history of the development of the genealogical line of living beings to which man belongs.
This is scientific truth that has been known for ever so long.
The majority of naturalists have only recently deigned to recognize it as the truth.
And I said: until recent times, the majority of naturalists interested themselves in scientific truth less than they should have done. They know little about it even now; and this compels me to dispute with them a great deal.
To make clear what conceptions I regard as correct I gave a characterization of the scientific world outlook in relation to the subjects of natural science.
The main features of this characterization are:
That which exists is matter.
Our knowledge of the properties of matter is knowledge of matter as matter, which exists invariably. Any given property is invariably existing matter itself, regarded from one definite point of view.
Force is a property regarded from the aspect of its operation. Thus, force is matter itself.

The laws of nature are the mode of operation of force. Thus, the laws of nature are matter itself.

I said: no naturalist who has any respect for himself and is at all respected by other naturalists will dare to say that he does not hold these concepts to be true; every one of them will say that they are his own concepts.

And I added: yes, they will all say: "this is so," but very many—nearly all of them—will say—not having understood what they have read—that they know very little about these concepts; and in many things their trend of thought does not correspond to these concepts.

After making these general observations about the attitude of the majority of naturalists towards scientific truth, I reviewed the content of the astronomical section of the preface to the history of mankind.

The history of our solar system, and of our planet in particular, has been explained by Laplace. This work of his consists of a series of very simple and, from the scientific point of view, indisputable deductions from Newton's formula, accepted by all astronomers as a truth beyond all possibility of doubt, and of a few commonly known facts, the authenticity of which no astronomer denies.

This is so now, so it was at the time Laplace published his work, and so it remained in all subsequent times. No astronomer doubted, or deemed it possible to doubt in the slightest degree, either the correctness of Newton's formula, or any of the commonly known facts upon which Laplace's deductions rest.

The matter is so simple, and the validity of Laplace's deductions is so obvious, that from the time they were published they were accepted as undoubtedly true by all those familiar with them who earnestly loved truth and were aware that on matters intelligible to every educated man, every educated man can, and should, form his own judgment.

Of such people there were very many.

But the majority of the educated public had long been trained by the majority of astronomers to believe that nobody but astronomers can have an independent opinion about anything in astronomy.

The wisest men among the astronomers have always striven to explain to the public that this is not so. They

said that it is certainly necessary to possess special knowledge to be able to solve astronomical problems; but when
a solution has been found, it may prove to be based on
generally understood deductions from commonly known
facts. Laplace's deductions concerning the history of the
solar system are of this kind.

The majority of the educated public, however, yielded
to the authority of the majority of the astronomers. And it
was the pleasure of the majority of the astronomers to regard "Laplace's Hypothesis," as this series of deductions
was called, as "only a hypothesis."

And this was said for sixty years or more.

At last, the method was discovered of ascertaining the
chemical composition of bodies by examining their spectra.
This method was applied to the spectra of celestial bodies.

And everybody, specialist and layman, saw that the
planets and their satellites in our system, our sun, other
suns and the nebulous patches, contained some of the so-
called "simple chemical bodies" known on our planet.

The majority of astronomers then admitted that Laplace was right.

And yet, the facts discovered by the spectral analysis
of the composition of celestial bodies, taken by themselves,
did not testify to whether Laplace was right or wrong. The
only thing they showed was that the chemical composition
of celestial bodies more or less resembled the composition
of our planet. This idea is much older than "Laplace's
hypothesis," and compared with it is very indefinite.

But the bulk of the educated public became interested
in the results of the examination of the spectra of the celestial bodies, pondered over the dispute between the minority
and majority of the astronomers about Laplace's hypothesis,
resolved to settle the dispute by applying their own common
sense and decided that the minority of the astronomers
were right, namely, that Laplace's hypothesis was a hypothesis only in name, and that actually it consisted of an
indisputably valid series of deductions from indubitable facts.

The majority of the astronomers yielded to the decision
of the bulk of the educated public.

Such is the story of what is called "Laplace's hypothesis."

* * *

My dear friends,

I am writing nearly all this from memory.

The only reference book I have at hand is Brockhaus' *Encyclopedia*. How much can one find in that?

In view of these circumstances, if, in my talks, I say anything that you do not know definitely that it is correct, you must take the trouble to ascertain whether my memory has not betrayed me.

Let us, for example, investigate whether I have correctly told the story about Laplace's hypothesis.

The question can be reduced to two points:

Am I right in thinking that "sixty years or more" elapsed between the publication of Laplace's hypothesis and the application of spectral analysis to the spectra of celestial bodies? and

Have I correctly described the attitude of the majority of astronomers towards Laplace's hypothesis during this period?

All the rest is either an inevitable deduction from these two points, or trifles that cannot alter the essence of my story about Laplace's hypothesis, namely, that it was a disgrace to the majority of the astronomers of that period; and since the majority of the present-day authoritative astronomers were already working in the years that preceded the discovery of spectral analysis, it is also a disgrace to them. The correctness of my opinion of these gentlemen, the celebrated astronomers, is determined only by the degree of correctness of my first two postulates, namely, that "before the discovery of spectral analysis, these people and their predecessors claimed that Laplace's hypothesis was not proved, or erroneous, or likely to prove to be erroneous," and that "this lasted for sixty years or more."

Let us see how far these two ideas of mine may be wrong.

In what book, or pamphlet, or periodical, did Laplace publish his conclusions concerning the history of the solar system?

I do not know. If he did not publish them earlier, they were at all events given in his *Celestial Mechanics*. Is that not so?

I say that I do not know, I only assume. When did *Celestial Mechanics* appear? Without inquiring I assumed that it was in the very first years of our century. But this is given in Brockhaus. On consulting it, I found that it was published earlier, namely, in 1799. I also found that his popular edition of *Celestial Mechanics*, viz., *An Explanation of the System of the Universe*, Laplace managed to publish even earlier, in 1796.

And so, I begin my count from 1799, or 1796. Am I mistaken? Perhaps. I do not know. But ... I doubt whether there is any mistake here.

Let us assume it is a mistake. Let us assume that Laplace published his "Hypothesis" towards the very end of his life. When did he die? I thought it was about 1825. It is given in Brockhaus. I consulted it and found that Laplace died in 1827. After all, a fairly long time before the discovery of spectral analysis. Not "sixty years or more," but still, "thirty years or more." More than enough to justify the opinion that the duration of the stubbornness of the majority of the astronomers far exceeded the limit of what is excusable.

Yes, but do I correctly date the end of this period? When was spectral analysis first employed for studying celestial bodies? I do not know; I assume that it was about 1860, scarcely later than 1860. Is it so? I have no means of verifying this. My edition of Brockhaus is the tenth; the first volume appeared in 1851, the last in 1855. The only thing I can say is that there is nothing about spectral analysis in my edition. And so, let us assume that this was given in the first volume and that there was no occasion to make even a slight reference to it in the later volumes; assuming that the articles in the first volume, which appeared in 1851, were written a whole year earlier, that is, in 1850, I shall have an interval:

From 1827 to 1850—more than twenty years.

The duration of the stubborn opposition to obvious truth was more than long enough to be a disgrace to the majority of the astronomers—if it is indeed a fact that right up to the discovery of spectral analysis the majority of the astronomers stubbornly refused to admit that Laplace's hypothesis was correct.

Is it a fact? Did they really stubbornly oppose it?

As far as I remember, they did. Am I right? I have no means of verifying this.

Perhaps my memory is betraying me?

I again make every possible concession, not only in words, and not only now; I made them mentally when I

wrote the first of these talks; and I did so not only because
I think it is the duty of a scientist to be strict towards his
opinions, but because I was prompted to do so by my own
personal character, for whatever my faults may be, I am
not a vicious man. It is pleasant for me to excuse people
and painful to censure them, as is the case with every other
not particularly vicious person, that is, with the vast majority—if one is able to analyze the true feelings of people,
I say, it seems to me—the vast majority of people.

Thus, in this case I have made—and I have usually
been glad to make in all matters, and I hope in future to
be usually glad to make—every possible concession in
order to avoid the necessity of expressing censure.

But here is a circumstance which has often made me see
the facts of human life in a different light from that in which
they are seen by people who do not make a scientific analysis
of these matters:

I am accustomed, when analyzing facts, to eliminate
my personal wishes.

With many people this is a gift of nature. Such people
are called "perspicacious."

Perhaps I lack innate perspicacity, but I love truth;
and I have engaged a great deal in scientific analysis.
Therefore, whatever my judgment may be in the everyday
affairs of my personal life—and in these matters I do not
think I am at all perspicacious—in scientific matters I
am accustomed to examine facts not at all badly.

The majority of people who are not very perspicacious
by nature and are not accustomed to engage in the scientific analysis of the facts of human life, are strongly inclined
to substitute for facts their own thoughts, inclinations,
wishes, or, as is usually said about this, to look at life
through spectacles that are tinted with the colours that
please them.

We shall have much to say about this.

At present we shall note one feature of this habit.

One of our wishes is that others should think as we do,
particularly those whose opinions we regard as important.

And so, very many people, when reading something that
has been written by somebody whom they regard as an
authority, invest his words with a meaning that pleases
themselves.

I am free from this weakness.

Free from it for one thing because it affects me rarely, and not being habitual, it affects me very slightly. Among poets, scholars, writers in general, there are very few whom I regard as authorities; hence, the desire to interpret a book in my own way in spite of the truth is rare, not habitual with me; and it is easy to keep free from a weakness that is not habitual.

For example: I am inclined to subordinate my thoughts on subjects of natural science to the thoughts of Laplace. If I were to meet in Laplace an idea concerning some subject in natural science that interests me, but which I do not fully understand, the desire might arise to interpret this idea in conformity with my own opinion on this subject. Here I would have to exert some effort to prevent myself from investing Laplace's words with a meaning that I would like them to have; the desire might arise from a reluctance to have the opinion that pleases me shaken by Laplace's contradiction.

But of all the specialists in natural science who lived after Newton, he alone—Laplace—has such a significance for me.

Concerning all the others, I think to myself, quite indifferently: "He agrees with me, but this adds nothing to my judgment of the probability that the opinion which I believe is correct, actually is correct. His opinion contradicts mine, but this does not in the least diminish for me the probability that my opinion is correct."

What interest have I, then, in trying to interpret his words in a sense that pleases me and not in the sense they really have?

I hope you understand, my dear friends, that I am discussing here "opinions," not "knowledge"; theories, surmises, but not facts and the correct, necessary deductions drawn from facts.

Even if Laplace had renounced his history of the solar system, it would not in the least have affected my opinion about its validity. For me, its validity is a matter of "knowledge," not of "opinion."

In the matter of "knowledge," nobody's authority must have any significance; and it has no significance for a man who is able to distinguish between authentic knowledge, scientific truth, and "opinions"—theories or surmises.

The multiplication tables are something totally independent of anybody's "opinion." There is no authority superior or equal to them. All the authorities are nothing compared with them. The authority may come in only on such things for which they do not provide a solution; at the slightest disagreement with them, the authority is smashed to atoms.

Such is every other scientific truth. For example: on none of the things that rest on Newton's formula, or on Dalton's law of equivalents, or on the fact that the sun exists—on none of the things that rest on these truths has anybody's authority any significance whatever.

We shall have more to say about this when its turn comes.

I have mentioned it now merely in order to explain to you my attitude towards the "opinions" of the naturalists. For me Newton's "opinions" are authoritative; and of those who came after Newton, the "opinions" of Laplace are authoritative. Only these two. If there is something I do not "know," but I have an "opinion" about it, "my opinion" would be shaken if I happened to learn that the "opinion" of Newton, or of Laplace, was different. If the subject were sufficiently important, and if I had the opportunity, I would subject "my opinion" to a "scientific test," and it would cease to be an "opinion" and become "knowledge"; or it would turn out to contradict some "knowledge," in which case I would abandon my "opinion." If however, I thought that the subject was not worth the trouble of making a difficult analysis, or if, owing to my lack of special knowledge, I was unable to make such an analysis, I would reason as follows: "my opinion seems plausible to me for such and such reasons; why Newton (or Laplace) thought otherwise, I do not know and cannot guess; but he probably understood the matter better than I do; I cannot cast aside my reasons, but they may be mistaken." Although unable to cast my opinion entirely out of my mind I would, nevertheless, think (and say, of course) that, for all that, I prefer the opinion opposite to mine, the opinion of Newton (or Laplace).

As you see, I take an extreme case; my own reasons are not refuted in the least, while the reasons of Newton (or Laplace) remain entirely unknown to me; for all that, I prefer the unsupported word of Newton (or Laplace) to my own reasons.

It will be all the easier for me to give the opinion of Newton (or Laplace) decisive preponderance over my own if I notice the slightest error in my reasons, or if I manage to learn the reasons on which the surmise (an "opinion" is a surmise) of Newton (or Laplace) is based.

This is what recognizing somebody as an authority means.

In natural science I recognize only two authorities: Newton and Laplace. As far as I can judge there is nothing in my thoughts about natural science that has not been brought into harmony with their "opinions." (You will remember that for me "opinions" exist only in relation to subjects that have not yet been sufficiently elucidated, which have not yet been brought to a "scientific solution.")

In any case, natural science is not one of the subjects of my scientific studies or interests; and no "opinion" on any of the subjects of natural science is of any importance for me as a man who has his own interests, or for any subject of my own scientific studies.

Hence, it is easy for me to look "objectively," as they call it, even on the "opinions" of Newton and Laplace; it is easy for me to read them without any desire to substitute my own interpretation of their words for their actual meaning.

As for the words of all other naturalists, I am totally indifferent to them; let them say what they please, it is all the same to me. (I want you to remember, my friends, that we are discussing "opinions," surmises, not scientific solutions; "scientific truth" is sacred truth for me, no matter by whom discovered, expounded, or communicated to me.)

My dear friends, these are the good sides of my character:

Love of truth; the desire to exercise my abilities—be they great or small, it makes no difference—to utilize my abilities to ascertain independently what is true and what is not true; the consciousness that it is unworthy of a being endowed with reason, unworthy of a man, to renounce the right to employ his reason.

These are the good features of my character; but countless numbers of people possess these virtues. There is nothing exceptional in the fact that I possess them.

I possess other virtues besides these. I can read and write. That is very good. I know fairly well the grammar of my native language. That is very good. And I can say in all fairness that there is much more about me that is undoubtedly very good, only there is nothing exceptional about this.

Thus, I have nothing to boast about. Concerning many other people, however, I am forced to an opinion that I deplore very much.

Although there is nothing exceptional in my virtue of being "able to read and write," it is possessed only by a minority of people. The same applies to all my other virtues.

There are millions of people like me among the educated public in civilized countries.

But among the educated public in civilized countries there are tens of millions who renounce their right as rational beings to use their reason.

The vast majority of the educated public do not wish to take the trouble independently to judge scientific matters, which, in essence, can be understood by every educated person—and such are all, or nearly all, the scientific matters that are of great scientific importance. The vast majority of the educated public have not yet weaned themselves of that mental laziness that was at one time the natural quality of the barbarians who wrecked the civilization of Greece and Rome, and which remains today only an absurd habit of their descendants who have long been civilized.

It is merely a bad habit, totally out of harmony with the actual mental faculties of the people who are addicted to it. And every time these people wish to do so, they shake off this bad habit without the slightest effort and show that they are able to judge reasonably in scientific matters.

Yes, they can do so when they want to; but the times they have wanted to have been—at least in our century—but brief episodes, which arose as a result of special circumstances.

In the history of astronomy, such an episode was the assertion by the bulk of the educated public of the right to reason in connection with the results of spectral analysis. The bulk of the educated public pondered over Laplace's hypothesis and came to the conclusion that Laplace was right. And the majority of the astronomers forthwith discovered: "Yes, Laplace was right."

This was an extremely exceptional episode.

The usual state of affairs before this happened had been entirely different, and things reverted to that state after it.

The bulk of the educated public believes that it has no right to judge about anything in astronomy. This opinion of the bulk of the public flatters the conceit of the majority of the astronomers and they encourage the public to think that this is as it should be, for, they argue, everything in astronomy is so intricate that it cannot be understood without a knowledge of the theory of functions. Everything, absolutely everything in astronomy is just formulae, yard long formulae, bristling with Greek sigmas in enormous type and minute things from other alphabets in two, three and four storeys, one on top of the other—formulae that give splitting headaches even to the most expert mathematicians who, indeed, are extraordinarily clever people. They alone are competent to judge. It is the business of the public to listen to these geniuses with awe and wonder and to take what they say on trust.

And the majority of the public submits: it listens to them with awe and wonder and takes what they say on trust.

What is the result? Leaving aside the effect this has upon the mind of the bulk of the educated public, what is the result for these geniuses themselves?

Whoever escapes from the control of the public, escapes from the control of the public's common sense.

Some people's common sense is so sound that it does not need the backing of the public. But such people are very rare exceptions. Most people are like ourselves; not naturally stupid or lacking sense, but whose good qualities are all rather weak, and keep good only with the backing of public opinion.

What inevitably follows from this?

This is what generally happens to groups of people who escape, or try to escape, from the control of public opinion.

The vast majority of people in such groups steadily develop disdain for everything that is not peculiar to the given group, disdain for everything except that which distinguishes the group from the rest of the public.

Among other things, they develop disdain for ordinary, human common sense, and instead of reason prefer their own special wisdom, the wisdom of a special group.

The degree to which this special tendency to boast of special wisdom and to despise reason gains the upper hand at a given time in a given group depends on historical circumstances; but this tendency constantly operates in every such group, and constantly strives completely to subjugate every group of this kind; and it is always congenial to the majority of the people in every such group.

My explanations are rather long, are they not? Yes. I am aware of that myself. But, my dear friends, I must make one more remark.

Man's strength lies in reason. This is a universally accepted truth.

That being the case, what does contempt for reason lead to? To impotence.

And if specialists, of the scientific category, for example, despise reason and boast of their special wisdom, this special wisdom of theirs will be afflicted with impotence. They will become what is called

Great men in little things.

Perhaps they will be able skilfully to employ the technical tricks of their trade, but their skilful tricks will be meaningless.

As long as they have to deal with formalistic trifles they manage things skilfully; but as soon as they are faced with a serious and important matter they prove to be ignorant, incapable, hesitant; they fumble, talk nonsense, and do nonsensical things. This is because, to conduct serious matters reason, or in plain language, common sense is required.

My explanations have been lengthy, my dear friends. But for all their lengthiness, have they not been too short? I do not know. Most of the books you read, I mean the scientific books, are almost entirely filled with nonsense....

Therefore, I ask, have my lengthy explanations been sufficient for you, my dear friends? I do not know.

Or perhaps they have been superfluous? I do not know. I would like to think so.

Let us now employ the thoughts, the exposition of which I would like to think has been superfluous for you, to examine the question as to how far I may have been mistaken in saying that "the majority of astronomers stubbornly refused to regard Laplace's hypothesis as correct right up to the time when they were forced to do so by spectral analysis."

For me, personally, it is a matter of indifference. Whatever anybody said about Laplace's hypothesis is all the same to me, and has been so for thirty years.

For me, since early youth, Laplace's hypothesis has been "knowledge." Even if Laplace had himself renounced his deductions, it would not in the least have shaken my "knowledge" that these deductions of his are, from the scientific point of view, undisputable scientific truth.

Still less reason could there be for me to interpret in the way I pleased the opinions of the astronomers, or naturalists in general, who lived after Laplace, or who are alive today. I regard none of them as an authority. And their "opinion" has no weight with me even on subjects on which I myself have only an "opinion." As for their opinions about scientific truths, I think that all are inappropriate except one, the simple expression: "it is truth."

Now, it is precisely this one correct opinion that I have not met with, as far as I remember, in any book or essay written by any of the astronomers who lived after Laplace, or who are alive today; not in one of all those I have read until "recent times," when those gentlemen, the majority of astronomers, gained fame by discovering that Laplace was right.

All the opinions that I remember reading were merely variations of the theme: "Laplace's hypothesis is only a hypothesis." One argued that this "hypothesis" was unsound, another argued that it was probable, or even very probable, but nobody, as far as I remember, said that it was true.

The recollections of people of my age, or of those older than I am, of the times preceding the "recent time" when the great discovery that "Laplace was right" was made may be different from mine. Many may "remember" that the "majority" of the astronomers, or even "nearly all," or actually "all," "long ago," or "always," regarded Laplace's hypothesis as "true."

But I say: I think that such "recollections" are not "recollections," but the result of a misunderstanding, or illusion.

"Very probable" is something entirely different from a simple "yes."

"I have almost no doubt that Laplace's hypothesis is correct" is something entirely different from the simple: "Laplace's hypothesis is correct."

My friends, whoever would say: "it is highly probable that the multiplication tables are correct" would be a coward, a liar, or an ignoramus. To speak like that about scientific truths is indecent, vulgar and silly.

But whoever, because of lack of special knowledge, imagines that he has only an "opinion" about some special subject, and that only specialists are competent to decide such matters, such a one, in his helplessness, eagerly clutches at any support that he thinks the opinion of specialists he regards as authorities may give him, and he invests their words with the meaning he desires. He reads: "It is probable"—and he is delighted. Five minutes later he imagines that he read: "It seems to be beyond doubt." Another five minutes later he imagines he read: "it is beyond doubt."

The scientific rules I adhere to safeguard me against the desire to paint the books I read in the colours that please me.

It is all the same to me in what style it pleases any scientist to write. The few scientists whom I regard as authorities are such for me only because they do not play any hocus-pocus, do not boast, do not despise reason, and cherish scientific truth.

And I have no inclination to interpret their words to suit my taste because there is no need for me to do so; neither they nor I have any preference for any special "style"; for them, and for me, only the truth is good. No matter what the truth may be, for me, and for everybody else who loves truth, it is good.

Consider, my friends: why should my memory betray me on the question as to what the attitude of the majority of the astronomers towards Laplace's hypothesis was in that period—of certainly not less than sixty years—between the proclamation of this truth and the discovery of spectral analysis?

No special decision on anything relating especially to natural science has any influence on my personal scientific interests, or scientific desires, or on the subjects of my own scientific studies. Therefore, from the scientific point of view it is all the same to me who is right: Copernicus or

Ptolemy, Kepler or Cassini senior, Newton or Cassini senior and Cassini junior. Even if it were true that Ptolemy was right in saying that the sun, all the planets, and all the stars, revolve round the earth; or that Cassini senior, and the host of astronomers who fawned upon him, were right in saying that the orbits of the planets are not ellipses, but "lines of the fourth degree," Cassinoides, as they were called in honour of the victor over Kepler; or even if it were true that the earth is not flattened at the axis of its daily rotation, as that "ignoramus, fantast and fool" Newton claimed, but at the line of the equator, so that equatorial diameters are smaller than those between the poles, as was claimed by that genius Cassini senior, and by the no lesser genius Cassini junior. Even if all this were true, and also, even if it were true that every mammal has two or three heads and only one leg—it would all be a matter of indifference to the subjects of my own studies. All they demand from natural science is that truth should prevail in it; what the truth is in any problem of natural science makes no difference. Was Ptolemy right? Were the Cassinis right? Has every mammal three heads? This is a matter of indifference to me. All I demand is proof that it is true.

Why does all this disgust me? Only because it is falsehood. Am I speaking clearly? It is not the content of a particular falsehood in natural science that disgusts me; that is not the case. The only thing in this falsehood that disgusts me is that it is a falsehood; and vice versa, it is not the content of a particular truth in natural science that I need, or like; I do not need it for any of the subjects that come within the range of my own scientific interests or studies; I need and like truth in natural science only because it is truth.

Is that clear? I do not know, my dear friends, whether I have succeeded in explaining my attitude towards natural science so that it is clear to you. Taken by themselves, these things are easy to understand; but of the present-day scientists—naturalists, historians, or scientists in other branches of learning—only very few understand them as I do. I understand them as Laplace did.

All the astronomers are great adepts at copying and correcting (!) Laplace, but very few of them understand how Laplace regarded the relation between natural science and the other branches of science.

Why? Because, to understand these things, a scientist must be a thinker of that system of general conceptions, the only scientific one, a thinker, or the pupil of thinkers, of that system of conceptions to which Laplace adhered.

This is self-evident, but the majority of scientists obscure it with their fantasies.

Have I explained this simply enough for you? I do not know.

But whether these explanations of mine are clear to you or not, whether they are inadequate, or, perhaps, as I would like to think, superfluous for you, I will, at last, apply them to the matter in hand.

Whether Copernicus, or Newton, or Laplace was right does not interest me in the least. The only thing that is important for me is that Leucippus was right, or, to speak of science in Laplace's time, that Holbach was right. And Leucippus was right even if Archimedes were wrong. The truth that Leucippus explained is wider and deeper than the truths discovered by Archimedes, great and fundamental though they were. And Holbach was right apart from whether Copernicus, Galileo, Kepler, Newton and Laplace were right.

Shall I use an illustration from mathematics? For the sake of clarity, it would be as well.

I am like a man who wants to, and must, adhere to the four rules of arithmetic. The truth he adheres to is very elementary; but it is the most fundamental part of mathematical truth, and it is independent of geometry, algebra and of the higher analysis. On the other hand, all these departments of mathematics are based on this simple, very simple, truth. Everything that is not in harmony with it is not mathematics, nor science in general, and to put it even more generally, is not truth.

Is that clear?

And so, casting aside the comparison, which was made only for the sake of clarity, I say:

Everything that is out of harmony with the simple, very simple truth of which Leucippus was the first of the better-known exponents, is not true.

And I use this simple truth to test every theory, whether in natural science or in any other branch of science;—"theory," that is to say, surmise; not "truth," but only "surmise."

Will every special scientific truth in natural science, or in any other branch of science, be in harmony with this simple truth? I have no apprehensions, cares or "wishes" on this score; I know that it has always been so, and will always be so, in all things, everywhere. The multiplication tables were true in the eternal past, and will be true in the eternal future, everywhere: on Sirius, on Halcyon, everywhere, as on Earth. They are the true formulas of the very "nature of things," they are the "law of existence"; they are eternally and universally indefeasible. The scientific truth about the multiplication tables, as about every other truth, is: every truth is in harmony with every other truth. There is nothing here that calls for any effort at conciliation.

But you must be thinking, my friends, "how intolerably long and dull this is." Yes. So let us stop it. Let us sum up the matter that I have explained in this tedious fashion.

My recollections of the arguments advanced on Laplace's hypothesis by the astronomers whose books I read before the discovery of spectral analysis—are they correct?

I am indifferent towards the subject. If my recollections are clear and broad enough, they characterize it correctly— I think so.

But are my recollections clear and broad enough? That is another question. I had not read very much on astronomy. As for the books I did read, what interest had I to note the tone in which the authors wrote about Laplace's hypothesis? And even if I did note it, what interest had I to remember it?

Having read little, and noted still less, I have long forgotten nearly all of the little I knew about what the majority of astronomers thought about Laplace's hypothesis.

My recollections are correct, but not clear, and they are very few.

And so, perhaps I am mistaken in drawing deductions about the majority of astronomers from them?

I doubt it. Why? I will ask you to recall what I said about the great re-creator of geology, Lyell, for whom I have sincere respect. I said that he rejected Laplace's hypothesis. It is enough to ponder over this fact, which I distinctly remember, for the attitude of the vast majority of two generations of astronomers towards Laplace's hypothesis to be adequately characterized.

Lyell knew much less about mathematics than I. He went to astronomers for solutions of geometrical problems that were so simple that even I could easily solve them, and in footnotes he expressed ardent gratitude to the astronomers for the trouble they had gone to for his sake. This was ridiculously naive. But it was still more amusing when he himself embarked upon arithmetical exercises: to multiply two whole numbers, each of three figures, was a most intricate problem for him. In passing, I will say that this was no hindrance to him. What mathematics can be applied to geology in its present state? This heap of totally indefinite data is unfit, quite unfit, for mathematical analysis. Even the simplest arithmetical calculation here would be as much a waste of labour as counting the number of gnats or mosquitoes that are born in a given region, in a given spring, or a given summer. "A good many"—this is all we can know from the material available, with or without arithmetic.

Lyell, the man who was not well up even in arithmetic, was extremely modest and extraordinarily conscientious. An example of this is his renunciation of the theory of the immutability of species, which he had expounded at length for thirty years, in every new edition of his *Geology*. This voluntary renunciation of his favourite idea by a man of seventy, the teacher of all geologists, is a fact that does him great honour. We shall speak of this later.

For thirty years, the man who knew scarcely anything about mathematics, the man who on everything concerning astronomy consulted the astronomers, this extremely modest man kept reiterating in his *Geology* that Laplace's hypothesis was nonsense. I said thirty years. Is that right? I do not know. All I know is that I read Lyell in 1865, in the latest edition that was available at the time you bought the book for me. When was it bought? I do not know, but I think it was in the same year. What was the date of the edition? I do not know that either. How can I help myself to recall the date of that edition? Only by referring to Brockhaus. I consult Brockhaus and find that the first volume of the first edition of Lyell's *Principles of Geology* appeared in 1830. (He speaks of Laplace's hypothesis in the first volume, that is evident to me: I remember that it is in the first chapters of the treatise.) In 1853 the ninth edition appeared. The edition of Brockhaus that I have gives no information about Lyell later than this date. This volume of this edition of Brockhaus was printed in 1853. Thus, it may be assumed that the 1853 edition of the *Geology* was the last until 1865; and that was the edition, the ninth, that I had. If that is the case, I can vouch for only twenty-three years of Lyell's opposition to Laplace.

But is it likely that a book that had gone through nine editions in twenty-three years had no further editions for twelve whole years after that? Lyell was still alive, in good health, and was still working hard. I know this perfectly well. His book served as a reference book for all the geologists in the whole of the civilized world. How could there have been no new edition in the course of twelve years?

I therefore assume that the edition I read in 1865, the latest available at that time, was not the ninth, but the eleventh, or even the twelfth, and that it was printed not in 1853, but about 1860, probably later, about 1863. This is only a surmise on my part. It may be wrong. But, my friends, you see that it was not altogether without reason that I said that "the opposition lasted thirty years." But suppose I am mistaken, does it alter the essence of the matter? If not for thirty years, then certainly for not less than twenty-three years, Lyell reiterated that Laplace's hypothesis was nonsense.

Well, even twenty-three years of Lyell's mistaken opposition to Laplace is a fully sufficient attestation to the mentality of those gentlemen the astronomers—not the "majority" of them, no, nearly all; for the number of those who were right about Laplace was insignificant; that common sense minority was not seen or heard.

Otherwise, I cannot understand the following fact:

A man who is very modest, always ready to renounce any opinion if anybody notes that it is mistaken and explains it to him, a man who is ignorant of astronomy and makes not the slightest claim that he knows it, who on all matters concerning astronomy consults the astronomers, such a man—

reiterates, certainly for more than twenty years, and judging by all things, for thirty years and more, that Laplace's hypothesis is nonsense;

his book, in which this statement is printed and repeatedly reprinted, is one of the most important scientific books in the civilized world, a book well known to all naturalists, including all astronomers, in the whole of the civilized world;

and yet none of those gentlemen the astronomers takes the trouble to explain to the author of this book that it is wrong to dispute Laplace's hypothesis, that it is not a hypothesis, but authentic truth;

either none of the astronomers took the trouble to tell him this or, what was still worse, the voice of the astronomer who told the truth was drowned by the shouts of the majority: "Oh, no! It is only a hypothesis, it is quite permissible to dispute it."

I think the latter was the case.

Am I mistaken? Perhaps.

I think, however, that it is very improbable that I am mistaken.

It goes without saying, that a surmise can never fully coincide with the facts.

I am writing almost entirely from memory about subjects that have never been interesting to me. My knowledge about them—about everything in natural science—has always been scanty, and I have forgotten nearly everything I ever knew about them. With what can I fill the gaps in my extremely scanty knowledge? With Brockhaus' *Encyclopedia*. Is this a book for scientists? Can I find in it much of what I need for my talks with you, my friends? So I cannot help speaking from cogitation sometimes.

Memory is deceptive. Cogitating is only surmising.

If a single word of mine is unclear, or seems doubtful to you, you must verify it. But not a single error of mine relates, or can relate, to the essence of the matter. How can that be? Like this, for example.

Whatever the case may be, whether the majority of the astronomers behaved well or ill in the matter of Laplace's hypothesis during the sixty years between the appearance of *Celestial Mechanics* and the discovery of spectral analysis,

in general ... in general

the attitude of the majority of astronomers towards scientific truth is unworthy of people who are not by nature stupid or dishonest. Voluntarily to play the part of fool and liar is a reprehensible thing. But that is what they are doing. Why? For no reason except that it pleases them.

This is such a glaring fact that, unfortunately, there can be no mistake about its character. Of the books on astronomy that contain something besides formulas and figures, only one in ten, perhaps, is free from anti-scientific adulteration.

This is the essence of the matter that I am trying to put in the forefront in my talks with you, my friends.

Am I succeeding? I do not know. Not so well, I think. I am not skilful enough.

But I am trying.

For today, however, I have wearied you enough with my unbearably tedious explanations, consisting of only a repeatedly resumed and infinitely drawn out introduction to the subject. Let us try more quickly to go through our recapitulation of the contents of our preceding talks.

* * *

Everybody now admits that "Laplace was right."

The correctness of his conclusions concerning the history of our, and every other, solar system depends entirely upon whether what is called "Newton's formula" is correct — the formula by which Newton defined Kepler's laws of motion of the planets and their satellites in their orbits. The indubitable validity of Newton's formula is admitted by all.

But this formula is only an algebraic expression of what is called "Newton's hypothesis," that is, Newton's idea that the motion of the celestial bodies, algebraically expressed by his formula, is due to the universal power of mutual attraction of matter.

His formula has algebraic meaning without his hypothesis; but algebraic meaning is something that is fit only for technical work and not for real thinking about facts. For real thinking about facts, only such thoughts are satisfactory as have real meaning, and not such as have only the technical significance of symbols of unknown meaning, and which are used only for the purpose of facilitating the technical side of some special work.

For human common sense Newton's formula requires real interpretation. Newton's hypothesis provided this.

Whether Newton's hypothesis is correct or not makes no difference to the validity of Laplace's conclusions regarded from the point of view of technical mathematical verification. Human common sense, however, demands an answer to the question as to whether Newton's hypothesis is right.

I examined this question.

I do not want to repeat the details; you remember them.

The examination of the question of Newton's hypothesis compelled me to raise the question as to what the state of scientific truth is in the minds of those gentlemen, the experts in mathematics, who refuse to say, or to understand, that Newton's hypothesis is absolutely authentic knowledge.

And I saw something, the like of which is not to be found in the *Arabian Nights*; I saw this sort of thing being done in mathematics:

"Spaces" of different kinds, each of only two dimensions; "rational two-dimensional beings," and so forth in the same style—absolutely idiotic things invented by some, and approved and adopted in mathematics by other gentlemen, celebrated experts in mathematics.

While paying due tribute to the intellect of these gentlemen, I wanted to explain how they got this concussion of the brain that manifested itself in such absurd feats which raised them to fame and disgraced mathematics. To do that it was necessary to explain Kant's system, which had muddled them all up.

The exposition of Kant's system, however, would have taken up many pages, and that was not worth while. Kant's system is a lot of twaddle that was smashed to atoms long ago. And the illiterate revisions of this twaddle, composed by mathematicians, and naturalists in general, who have not been trained to understand any idealist philosophical system, and are still less capable of understanding the sophistry of the intricate idealist word-weaving so hopelessly entangled by Kant's genius—these illiterate products of these gentlemen's philosophizing were certainly not worth the expenditure of paper and ink for an examination of them.

And so I said that I would not enter into a long disquisition on these absurdities, but simply say that they are absurd. I think I have a perfect right to treat them in this unceremonious way. The mathematicians and astronomers who invent and approve "new systems of geometry," and their partners, the majority of the naturalists, are pleased to talk philosophical nonsense which they themselves do not understand. When talking this nonsense they are no

longer mathematicians or astronomers, they are no longer
naturalists, but ignoramuses talking philosophical nonsense.
Once upon a time I studied the history of philosophical
systems. They wandered into a sphere in which I am a specialist, but in which they are perfect ignoramuses. You,
my dear friends, know that I have studied philosophy a
great deal, and so you have a right to assume that my opinion about the philosophizing of these philosophical ignoramuses is not altogether groundless even if it is not backed
by argument. That being the case, I have a right to relieve
myself of the labour of writing, and you of the boredom of
reading, dry arguments about these gentlemen's philosophical twaddle, and so I relieve myself of this labour and you
of this boredom.

In this I am in all probability right, but being fond of
a joke, I have put it in a jocular way. As, however, I am
an awkward jester, my jokes are clumsy. This would not
be so important; what grieves me sorely is that my jokes
have been offensive to you, my dear friends. I realized this
when I recalled the content and tone of my jokes, but I
did so too late, after I had posted the letter. I regret that
I did not realize it before.

It cannot be helped now. I am to blame, and I ask
you to forgive me, my dear friends.

My recapitulation of our previous talks is finished and
I shall now continue.

* * *

The majority of naturalists say: "we do not know what
things are in themselves, what they are in reality; we know
only our perceptions of things, only our relation to them."
This is nonsense; nonsense that has no excuse for existence in
natural science. It is nonsense that has got into the heads of
the naturalist simpletons out of the idealist systems of philosophy, chiefly out of Plato's and Kant's systems. It is
not nonsense in Plato's system. Oh, no! It is very clever
sophistry. The aim of this clever sophistry was to refute all
truth that was not to Plato's taste and—I am not sure
now, I do not remember quite well, but I believe—not
to the taste of Plato's exalted teacher, Socrates. Socrates
was a man who by numerous actions showed that his was
a noble character. But he was an enemy of scientific truth,
and in his enmity he taught much that was absurd. And

remember, my dear friends, he was the teacher and friend of Alcibiades, that dishonest intriguer and enemy of his country. And Socrates was also the teacher and friend of Creteus, compared with whom Alcibiades was an honest patriot. And Plato wanted to win the friendship of Dionysius Syracuse. Naturally, not every scientific truth could be to the liking of people with such tendencies. So much for Plato's system.

As for Kant, he himself gave a sufficient commentary on his system by proclaiming that everything that was necessary for the purpose of firmly establishing the fantasies that seemed good to him must be regarded as actually existing. That is to say: science is nonsense; this nonsense must be composed according to what we think the people whom we like are fond of dreaming about.

Is this scientific thought? Is this love of truth?

And Kant's nonsense, which is senselessly repeated by the naturalist simpletons, had a very clever aim, as clever as Plato's; the very same, very clever and utterly anti-scientific aim, viz., to deny all truth that was not to the taste of Kant, or to the people he liked.

Plato and Kant denied everything in natural science that restricted their fantasies, or the fantasies of the people they liked.

Do the naturalists want to deny natural science? Do they want science to be a collection of compliments to their friends?

No. Then why do they talk this nonsense? Because they are simpletons; they want to pose as philosophers, that's all. An innocent motive, but a foolish one. And failing to understand what they are talking about, they prove to be only boastful ignoramuses, denying scientific truth, which they hold dear. Miserable pedants, poor, boastful ignoramuses.

I said that I will dispense with argument; but here is a little argument, by way of example.

We know objects. We know them exactly as they really are.

Let us take that sense concerning which the naturalists are fond of saying that the knowledge we obtain through it is not authentic, or not quite in conformity with an object's actual properties; let us take vision.

We see something, a tree, let us say. Somebody else is also looking at the same object. We look into his eyes.

There we see the reflection of the tree in exactly the same form as we see it. Well? Two pictures, absolutely alike: one we see directly, the other we see mirrored in the pupils of that man's eyes. That other picture is an exact copy of the first.

Well? The eyes add nothing and subtract nothing. We see that: there is no difference between the two pictures.

But our "inner sense," or the "cells of the centres of the organs of vision," or the "soul," or the "activity of our conscious life," do they not alter anything in this picture? We know that they do not. Let us ask that man what he sees. Let him describe what he sees when that picture is reflected in his eyes. We will find that he sees exactly the same picture that we see. What is the use of arguing?

$$A=B; \quad B=C;$$

Hence, $A=C$.

The original and the copy are the same; our perception is the same as the copy.

Our knowledge of our perception is the same as our knowledge of the object. (This is a popular exposition; in a strictly philosophical exposition we would speak of "one pair of pictures" in "two pairs of pupils"; but the meaning is the same, and the deduction is the same.)

We see things exactly as they actually exist.

"But at night we do not see well." Well, yes.

"But in the microscope we see details which we cannot see with the naked eye." Well, yes.

And it should be added: "The blind do not see at all." This is also true.

And let us add: "Empty chatterboxes talk nonsense." And that will also be true.

But these absolutely true observations have nothing whatever to do with the question as to whether we correctly see what we see when our eyes are sound.

We see only what we see. For example: we cannot see the atoms of carbon; we see only big heaps of these atoms. Or: at night we do not see the different colours of objects.

What we do not see, we do not see. That is so. But that is not what this nonsense says. It says that what we see is not what we see; or that we think we see what we do not see. This is utter nonsense when we are of sound mind and our eyes are sound. A man of sound mind with sound eyes sees the objects that he sees. Isn't that so? The simple analysis given above proves this as conclusively as $2 \times 2 = 4$. But the naturalist simpletons say: "No."

Well, let this be enough about the foolish, nonsensical, philosophical chatter of those gentlemen, the majority of the naturalists.

Think what you like, my dear friends, but it makes me feel sorry for natural science to think that I, who am not in the least concerned with natural science, should have to defend it from the vast majority of people who spend their lives in zealous work for the benefit of natural science! Clever workers! Zealous, yes. But are they clever?

I suppose you remember the story about the clever muzhik who was diligently sawing the bough he was sitting on. That muzhik, whose cleverness astonished passers-by, must have been the "common ancestor" of those naturalists who philosophize according to Plato and Kant. It would not be difficult to find an even more primitive prototype, namely, a parrot which had been taught by frolicsome children to call itself a fool. Alas! Such is the fate of all parrots which fall into the hands of practical jokers; they all learn to shout in ecstasy that they are fools.

Some people may think: poor innocent birds, how sad is their lot!

Not at all. They are delighted to be so clever. They are quite pleased with themselves.

But let us drop it, let us drop this parrot philosophy at last!

Let us return to Newton's hypothesis. We can now appraise at their true value the doubts of the majority of naturalists about whether Newton was right.

The people who have been muddled up by Kant do not know now whether the Sun actually exists, or whether they only "think" that it exists. It is quite conceivable, of course, that such people do not know whether Newton was right or wrong.

* * *

I ought to tell you the story about Newton's hypothesis. It goes without saying that this talk about it "not being known whether Newton is right," talk that is a disgrace to astronomy, to mathematics, and to natural science as

a whole, did not commence with the present-day astronomers.

But let it go. We will do without the story about this
clever talk.

It was, of course, disgracefully foolish talk even in the
olden days. But being merely empty, foolish talk bereft
of all real significance, at all events after the degree of the
meridian at the Arctic Circle had been measured, before
the middle of the last century, it has become utterly empty.
Pedants said: "Newton's hypothesis is only a hypothesis,"
and were delighted with having by this most wise utterance
expressed a profundity which no ordinary mortal could
grasp, and with this innocent and foolish boastfulness
the matter ended. The good simpletons of the olden days
had no real intention of using their chatter for the purpose
of altering astronomy to suit their own taste in order to
exalt themselves and to disgrace Newton.

Had things remained so, there would, of course, have
been no need for me to say anything about Newton's hypothesis. Why should I have defended it? Nobody attacked
it. Nobody had the slightest doubt about its validity and
irrefutability. These people simply talked nonsense, and
they themselves felt that they were talking nonsense.

But "in recent times," those gentlemen, the majority
of the naturalists, have been kind enough to make so many
great, truly amazing, discoveries that it has simply turned
their heads.

It is not surprising. They have discovered that "Laplace
was right"; they have discovered "the unity of forces";
they have discovered "molecular movement"; they have
discovered "the mechanical theory of nature."

All this has long been known to everybody who wished
to know it.

For example, even Russian magazines, over thirty years
ago, published comprehensive treatises on "the unity of
forces," and about all the other things I have enumerated.

But it was only recently that the bulk of the public
compelled the majority of those gentlemen the naturalists
to say without equivocation or reservation, to say straight-
forwardly, clearly and emphatically, that these truths are
really indisputable truths. This turned the heads of the
majority of the naturalists.

* * *

At this point I heard: "the post is going tomorrow," so I stopped and began to write to your mother, my friends.

I think that the torments my introductory remarks have caused you have come to an end; I shall rest content with the infinite boredom I have already inflicted upon you. I myself am glad that I have succeeded in finishing my comments on Kant and on the philosophy of the Kantian parrots—from John Herschel (Yes, my friends! John Herschel also, parrotlike, echoed Kant, or philosophers worse than Kant) and Tyndall (Yes, and Tyndall!) to Du Bois-Reymond (Yes, and Du Bois-Reymond) and Liebig (Yes, and Liebig, the great, truly great Liebig!)—I am glad that I managed to write my opinion about all this, and about them all, not in a whole book, but on two pages.

This is little, much too little; but it would have been tedious for you to read a long disquisition on the twaddle of Kant, which was put in the archives long ago, and on the worse twaddle of his parrots.

Let what I have written with such excessive brevity suffice.

If I can restrain myself from resuming my introductory remarks and from expounding the philosophy of those gentlemen the parrots, then, of course, we shall quickly, very quickly, go through the entire preface to history. It is important for me to see what really has a bearing on natural science! I do not know natural science, and I do not want to; I accept the whole content of natural science as I accept the "theory of functions," without knowing, without discrimination. I accept everything, everything—but I accept "natural science" and not the foolishness with which the parrots have adulterated it. I felt it my duty to defend natural science from these parrots, among whom, at times, are to be found—to the disgrace of natural science, and to their own disgrace in the eyes of the posterity, to my grief for science and for them—many great specialists in natural science, whom I hold in profound respect for the modest special work they have done; to defend natural science from these parrot philosophers of the anti-scientific trend.

Fear of boring you too much prevented me from defending it as I should have done.

But let what I have written in its defence suffice.

About natural science as such, about its special content, I know very little, and it interests me much less.

36*

I respect it more than it is respected by any of the naturalists who are today regarded as its best representatives;
but every scientist should use some "self-restraint" in choosing the subjects for his scientific work. I have always
considered that I have no right to spend time in studying
natural science; as it is, I have not managed to learn a
tenth of the facts and reasons that I was morally obliged
to learn on the subjects I have chosen for my scientific
work.

Therefore, we shall, of course, quickly go through the
whole of the preface to the history of mankind, if ... if I
do not resume my introductory remarks and return to the
defence of natural science from the foolishness of the philosophizing company of naturalists.

I think that I will restrain myself from boring you with
either of these two things, my dear friends. Keep well.
I grip your hands. Yours, *N. Ch.*

EXPLANATORY NOTES

THE ANTHROPOLOGICAL PRINCIPLE
IN PHILOSOPHY

[1] This essay was first published in the *Sovremennik*, No. 4, Vol. 80 and No. 5, Vol. 81, 1860. It is Chernyshevsky's most important essay dealing specifically with philosophical problems and it did much to spread the principles of materialism and to combat idealism and clericalism in Russia.

The essay is a review of a book by P. L. Lavrov entitled *Essays on Problems of Practical Philosophy*, in which the author made numerous references to Jules Simon, John Stuart Mill, Proudhon, Frauenstädt, Schopenhauer, and others, depicting them as representatives of the most advanced intellectual trend in Western Europe of that time. Chernyshevsky severely criticizes the author for his uncritical attitude towards these writers and defines the philosophical conceptions he expounds in his book as eclectical. In opposition to this kind of philosophy, Chernyshevsky, in this essay, develops the views of militant philosophical materialism. It was no accident that this essay roused the ire of all the representatives of the ruling classes in tsarist Russia, who hated revolution and its spiritual weapon, philosophical materialism. The tsar's censors were particularly alarmed by the appearance of this essay, as is evident from the letter sent by the Central Censorship Board to the chairman of the St. Petersburg Censorship Committee, calling attention to the publication in the *Sovremennik* of essays which "shake the principles of monarchical government, the significance of absolute law, the position of woman in the family and the spiritual side of man, and which rouse the hatred of one class against the other." Among the essays enumerated in this letter is "The Anthropological Principle in Philosophy," concerning which it says: "The Central Censorship Board having examined with special attention the last essay, which is characterized by materialism, and taking into consideration the general reprehensible trend of the *Sovremennik* during the present year, on July 9, this year, resolved: to reprimand censor Rakhmaninov for permitting the publication in the aforesaid magazine of a number of essays written against the fundamental principles of civil and public order."

In this volume the essay is given as it was published in the *Sovremennik*, but with the passages struck out by the censor restored.

p. 49

² This refers to John Stuart Mill's book *On Liberty*, published in England in 1859. **p. 55**

³ This refers to the French petty-bourgeois socialist P. J. Proudhon and his book *De la Justice dans la Révolution et dans l'Eglise* (*Justice in the Revolution and in the Church*). **p. 57**

⁴ Chernyshevsky here refers to the essay by A. I. Herzen entitled: "John Stuart Mill and His Book *On Liberty*," published in the *Kolokol* (*The Bell*), No. 40-41, April 15, 1859. **p. 62**

⁵ This evidently refers to M. A. Bakunin. **p. 67**

⁶ This refers to Austria's war, provoked by Napoleon III in April 1859, against the combined Franco-Sardinian armies in Italy. At that time Rechberg was the Austrian Minister for Foreign Affairs. **p. 72**

⁷ This refers to the crushing blow that was dealt religion by Copernicus' discovery that the earth revolves round the sun. **p. 84**

⁸ In the proofs, the first part of the essay ends as follows: "Thus, do not despair, reader: what you have not received now, you will receive in the not distant future. How I envy you your future, reader: the future will give you the realization of our idea of man, in addition to numerous equally precious gifts. But, no, the precious gifts of the future will not be quite gifts, for you are purchasing them at a heavy price: for example, was it easy, was it a pleasure for you to read this rather absurd essay, which is an earnest of, probably, a more interesting essay in the future? It is possible, however, to make a different assumption, more flattering to us: perhaps you read this essay with the same pleasure that we had in writing it. Oh, the things we Russian writers write! And with pleasure, too, and with pride, as if we were useful people! Oh, Russian public, the things you read, and with approval!" **p. 88**

⁹ In many of his works (in this essay, in his "An Essay on the Scientific Conception of Certain Problems of World History," and others), Chernyshevsky sharply criticizes the ostensibly "democratic" character of American institutions, which was actually a cover for the domination of the slaveholders. **p. 91**

¹⁰ In footnotes to his translation of John Stuart Mill's *Principles of Political Economy*, Chernyshevsky cites the ideas expressed here as an argument against the Malthusian "law" of diminishing returns. (*Cf.* Chernyshevsky, *Collected Works*, Vol. IX, Russ. ed., Goslitizdat, 1949, pp. 272-329.) **p. 102**

¹¹ In the magazine text the censor altered this to read: "It is debatable whether..." **p. 132**

¹² This is a collection of excerpts from ancient Russian documents chiefly of the fourteenth century, discovered by Shevyryov in the library of the Cyril-Byelozersky Monastery. **p. 133**

¹³ This refers to the publishers of the *Moskvityanin* (*The Moscovite*), Pogodin and Shevyryov. The magazine was founded in 1841 by Pogodin, an advocate of the reactionary theory of "official nationalism,"

i.e., the Orthodox Church and autocracy. From 1850 until it was closed in 1856, it was edited by the so-called "young editorial board," consisting of A. Grigoryev, A. Ostrovsky, A. Pisemsky, and others.

p. 133

POLEMICAL GEMS

1 These essays were first published in the *Sovremennik* in 1861; the "First Collection" in No. 6, Vol. 87, and the "Second Collection" in No. 7, Vol. 88. They are of enormous interest as an illustration of the political and ideological struggle that raged at that time between revolutionary democracy and the united reactionary camp of the big landlords, the liberals and the autocratic monarchy. In the period between the publication of Chernyshevsky's essay "The Anthropological Principle in Philosophy" (April-May, 1860) and of "Polemical Gems" (June-July, 1861), the "peasant reform" (as the emancipation of the serfs was called) was caried out. This "reform," as a result of which the peasants were robbed by the landlords and the bourgeoisie, still further intensified the political struggle in the country. These essays are striking evidence that far from laying down their arms, the revolutionary democrats continued the struggle against the united reaction with unabated vigour.

The "First Collection" called forth a response from the reactionary writer M. Katkov, who, in an article in the *Russky Vestnik*, June 1861, entitled "The 'Polemical Gems' in the *Sovremennik*" tried to discredit the social-political views of revolutionary democracy and did not hesitate openly to denounce Chernyshevsky as the leader of the "destruction gang." In another article in the *Russky Vestnik*, July 1861, entitled "Prospects of an Entente Cordiale with the *Sovremennik*," Katkov took up the cudgels on behalf of the liberal journalists (Albertini and others) and again denounced Chernyshevsky, this time for "mocking at Orthodox religion."

In the July issue of the liberal magazine *Otechestvenniye Zapiski*, the editor Dudyshkin published an article in reply to the first "collection" of "Polemical Gems," in which he defended the reactionary professor of the Kiev Theological Academy, Yurkevich, whom Chernyshevsky had ridiculed. As was to have been expected, "Polemical Gems" caused a flutter at the headquarters of the tsarist censorship. In a memorandum written in September 1861 on the trend followed by the *Sovremennik*, censor Berté wrote that the magazine persisted in its revolutionary democratic trend and that it vigorously advocated its "exceptionally destructive views in opposition to all other magazines in a newly introduced section 'Polemical Gems' (in the June and July issues)."

In this volume the essays are given as published in the *Sovremennik*, except that the passages which Chernyshevsky had deleted for reasons of the censorship have been reinserted. p. 136

2 *Russky Vestnik* (*Russian Messenger*), a monarchist magazine founded in 1856 by M. N. Katkov. p. 136

3 This refers to Ivan Yakovlevich Koreisha, a charlatan who gave himself out to be a prophet. The "story" about Koreisha was told in Katkov's article "Old Gods and New Gods." He was also

discussed in the *Sovremennik*, February 1861, in a scathing review of Pryzhov's book *The Life of Ivan Yakovlevich*.   p. 137

⁴ Antonovich's review of S. Gogotsky's *Philosophical Dictionary* was published in the *Sovremennik*, No. 2, 1861.   p. 138

⁵ *Sovremennik* (*The Contemporary*), a magazine founded in 1836 by A. S. Pushkin. After the latter's death it was published by P. A. Pletnyov, P. A. Vyazemsky, V. A. Zhukovsky and V. F. Odoyevsky. In 1847 the publication rights were acquired by I. I. Panayev and shared in the following year by N. Nekrasov. The heyday of the magazine's existence was the period (1854-62) in which Chernyshevsky and Dobrolyubov contributed to it. It was suppressed in 1866 by order of the tsar.   p. 138

⁶ By "the prevailing school of economics" Chernyshevsky means vulgar political economy.   p. 140

⁷ After this in the manuscript comes: "I despise the whole of Russian literature for the despicable position it occupies; I despise the society that is content with such a literature, and I also despise all those who are compelled to be Russian writers in such a state of society and literature. I sympathize with, but despise them. I entertain a due share of this feeling for myself."   p. 140

⁸ In the manuscript this passage reads as follows: "Unfortunately, very many, including the *Russky Vestnik*, do not regard the position of our literature with such indignation. Or no, I shall not be unjust; they feel as I do about it, but with them this feeling is assuaged by a certain amount of not altogether unjustified self-satisfaction. Their position is revolting."   p. 141

⁹ After this in the manuscript comes: "when Russian writers emerge from their despicable position, when it will be possible to be really useful to society and really to deserve a good reputation."   p. 142

¹⁰ P. A. Radishchev's article "Alexander Nikolayevich Radishchev," based on his reminiscences of his father, was published in the *Russky Vestnik*, Vol. 23, 1858.   p. 142

¹¹ Chernyshevsky wrote this article entitled "The Affair About Madame Svechina" and it was published in the *Sovremennik*, June, 1860. It was a comment on an article by Eugenie Tours (Countess Salias de Tournemir) entitled "Madame Svechina," published in the *Russky Vestnik* in 1860.   p. 143

¹² This refers to an article by P. P. Malinovsky entitled "Gunpowder Explosions," published in the *Russky Vestnik*, April and May 1860.   p. 143

¹³ Mme. Kokhanovskaya (the nom de plume of N. I. Sokhanskaya), a Slavophile writer who, in the stories she wrote for the *Otechestvenniye Zapiski* and the *Russky Vestnik*, idealized the life of the serfs.   p. 143

¹⁴ *Otechestvenniye Zapiski* (*Fatherland Notes*), a magazine founded in 1818 by P. Svinyin. Ceased publication in 1831 owing to lack of funds. It was revived two years later and appeared under different editors until 1884. As Chernyshevsky states, it acquired "definite predominance" in the 40's, when Belinsky's essays began to appear on its pages. In the later period of Chernyshevsky's activities it

adopted a hostile attitude towards him, forgetting the great traditions established by Belinsky. p. 145

[15] This refers to Antonovich's article "Two Types of Present-Day Philosophers" published in the *Sovremennik*, April 1861. p. 148

[16] The author of the "Letters on the Study of Nature" was Herzen. p. 149

[17] *Russkaya Beseda* (*Russian Conversation*), a Slavophile magazine published in Moscow from 1856 to 1860 by A. I. Koshelev. p. 149

[18] Aurore Dudevant, the real name of the authoress George Sand. p. 152

[19] Chernyshevsky here refers to Ludwig Feuerbach, whose name could not be mentioned in the censored press. p. 162

[20] Chernyshevsky wrote an unfavourable review of Rafail Zotov's novel *Leonid, or Sketches of the Life of Napoleon* for the *Sovremennik*, January 1856. p. 164

[21] Chernyshevsky wrote only the beginning of the third collection of "Polemical Gems." The *Russkaya Rech*, a magazine published in Moscow by the authoress Eugenie Tours from January 1861 to January 1862. p. 165

THE CHARACTER OF HUMAN KNOWLEDGE

[1] Chernyshevsky intended to have this article published in the *Vestnik Evropy* but on February 9, 1885, A. V. Zakharin informed Chernyshevsky, who was then living in Astrakhan, that the editors of that magazine "seem to be afraid to accept the article..." It was first published in the newspaper *Russkiye Vedomosti*, Nos. 63 and 64, 1885, signed "Andreyev," with the following editorial comment:
"The Naturphilosophie philosophizing which the esteemed author of this article derides and rejects, is very widespread among present-day naturalists; it is indulged in and preached even by such authorities in natural science as, for example, the celebrated Berlin professors Virchow and Du Bois-Reymond (cf. E. Du Bois-Reymond, *Ueber die Grenzen des Naturerkennens—Die sieben Welträtsel*, and Virchow, *Freiheit der Wissenschaft im modernen Staat*). Both loudly complain that the human mind has become conceited, that it has forgotten its limitations, and that it has the presumption to set out to solve great problems that are beyond its powers, problems that are insoluble and will remain unsolved forever. Du Bois-Reymond, in his pamphlet, puts these problems at the sacred number 7. In order to humble the pride of the human mind, the above-mentioned naturalists strive to prove that the human mind is limited, that its knowledge is extremely superficial, that it must bow in awe to the great problems and humbly abandon attempts to solve them. If any audacious mind does set out to solve them, it becomes entangled in incongruities and hopeless contradictions. Of course, the voices of scientists like those mentioned above have not remained unsupported. The Naturphilosophie ideas which they propound have been favourably received by many naturalists. It is these views, which, incidentally,

promote the spread of spiritualism, which the esteemed author of this article combats."

Chernyshevsky wrote this article twenty-five years after he wrote his essay "The Anthropological Principle in Philosophy"; nevertheless, it is thoroughly permeated with the spirit of the latter, and is an important supplement to it. In it Chernyshevsky turns the sharp weapon of criticism against neo-Kantianism and subjective idealism, to characterize which he uses the peculiar term "illusionism."

The article in this volume is reproduced from the manuscript.

p. 166

THE GRADUAL DEVELOPMENT OF ANCIENT PHILOSOPHICAL DOCTRINES IN CONNECTION WITH THE DEVELOPMENT OF PAGAN RELIGIONS

[1] This essay, first published in the *Sovremennik*, No. 6, Vol. 81, 1860, was written at the very height of the struggle Chernyshevsky waged against his ideological opponents in the camp of the reactionary landlords and liberals. It exposes the attempts of O. M. Novitsky, reactionary professor at the Kiev University, to link the development of human knowledge with religion. p. 185

AN ESSAY ON THE SCIENTIFIC CONCEPTION OF CERTAIN PROBLEMS OF WORLD HISTORY

[1] N. G. Chernyshevsky wrote this series of essays in 1887-88 as introductions to the last volumes of his Russian translation of Weber's *Weltgeschichte*, published by K. T. Soldatenkov. For reasons of the censorship it was stated on the title page that the translation was made by Andreyev. The essay on "Races" was first published in Volume 7 of the translation of the *Universal History*; the one on "The Classification of People According to Language" was published in Volume 8; the one on "Differences in National Character" was published in Volume 9; the one on "The General Character of the Elements That Promote Progress" was published in Volume 10; and the one on "Climate. The Astronomical Law of the Distribution of Solar Heat" was published in Volume 11. Of the five essays, the first, third and fourth are given in this volume.

On his return from Siberia, Chernyshevsky found all spheres of scientific activity closed to him. His intention to engage in important literary work was frustrated not only by the tsar's government, but also by the publishers of that time. The "wretchedly paid work" of a translator remained the only means of "earning a crust of bread." But Chernyshevsky undertook the task of translating Weber's work with the deliberate intention of doing what he subsequently explained in a letter to K. T. Soldatenkov: "When I asked you to meet the expenses of publishing Weber (the chief of which was my maintenance while working on it), my plan was to publish something entirely different from what I was obliged to do. The circumstances were as follows:

"I have not the right to put my name to my books. Weber's name was to have served merely as a screen for a treatise on world history of which I would be the actual author. Aware of my scientific abilities, I calculated that my treatise would be translated into German, French and English and would occupy an honourable place in the literature of every advanced nation.

"But to be able to revise Weber's book to such an extent that everything in it, except the name, would be mine, I had to have numerous books at hand: in the initial stages of the work this would have cost about a thousand rubles, and later the outlays would have amounted to another two or three thousand.

"And so I intended, when I had finished the small work on which (in my poverty) I was then living, to write to you as follows: send me the books and obtain credit for me at some Moscow bookseller who has connections with German and other booksellers. In the guise of a revision of Weber, I will write a book on world history entirely of my own; please be the publisher and provide for my maintenance while I am engaged in this work....

"But instead of that, what happened?

"I translate a book that I positively dislike; I waste time on translating work that is unbecoming for a man of my learning and—I will say without false modesty—my intellectual abilities...."
(N. G. Chernyshevsky, *Collected Works*, Vol. XV, Goslitizdat, 1950, pp. 769-770.)

Although obliged to confine himself to translating Weber's comprehensive work, Chernyshevsky did not, however, give up the idea of "purging" it of its "nonsense," "verbosity" and German nationalism. In addition to this "purge" he wrote introductory essays to several of the volumes. These essays possess independent value and are very important for characterizing Chernyshevsky's sociological views. In them he, particularly, severely criticizes the theory of racism and exposes its reactionary nature.

The essays given in this volume are reproduced from the respective volumes of George Weber's *Universal History*.　　　p. 199

[2] This refers to the war between the Northern and Southern (slaveholding) states of the U.S.A.　　　p. 200

[3] Chernyshevsky was, of course, mistaken in asserting that, after their emancipation, the Negroes in the U.S.A. enjoyed the rights of free citizens. Discrimination against Negroes, which is exceptionally glaring in the U.S.A. at the present time, has existed there all the time since slavery was abolished.　　　p. 215

[4] In the battle of Marathon in 490 B.C. the Athenians repelled the Persian invasion of Attica. In the battle of Salamis in 480 B.C., the Athenians repelled another Persian invasion. The battle of Plataea was fought in 479 B.C.

Under the command of Pausanias the Greeks achieved victory over the Persians. In 480 B.C. Plataea was destroyed by Xerxes.　　　p. 222

[5] At the battle of Chaeronea (338 B.C.) near the Boeotian city of Chaeronea Philip, King of Macedon, defeated the Athenians.　　　p. 227

[6] Crossing the Alps from the north, Hannibal reached Rome in 216 B.C. and inflicted a series of severe defeats upon the Romans.　　　p. 231

[7] This refers to the arrival in Rome, in 1155, of the German Emperor Friedrich Barbarossa, who was crowned by the Pope.

p. 231

[8] Charlemagne conquered the Langobard Kingdom in 773.

p. 232

[9] Varus was defeated in the Teutoburg Forest in the year 9. This defeat checked the Roman advance to the right bank of the Rhine.

p. 233

[10] The Second Punic War was fought in 218-201 B.C.

p. 234

[11] The Romans were defeated at Trebia in 218 B.C. and at Lake Trasimeno in 217 B.C. The defeat Hannibal inflicted on the Romans at Cannes in 216 B.C. was so severe that it brought Rome to the verge of collapse.

p. 234

THE AESTHETIC RELATION OF ART
TO REALITY
(A Dissertation)

[1] Chernyshevsky's works on aesthetic problems ("The Aesthetic Relation of Art to Reality," his own review of this essay, his preface to the third edition of it, and his review of a translation of Aristotle's *Poetics*), are of exceptional importance for an appraisal of his philosophical views. His aim was to apply the principles of his materialist philosophy to the concrete sphere of aesthetics. Consequently, all his works in this sphere, in addition to their special interest, are of enormous general philosophical importance. In working out the principles of scientific aesthetics from the standpoint of philosophical materialism and revolutionary democratism, he, in these works, wages an uncompromising struggle against Hegelian philosophy and aesthetics, against all the advocates of the idealist "pure art" theory.

Chernyshevsky's principal work on aesthetics is the dissertation he wrote for his Master of Arts degree, "The Aesthetic Relation of Art to Reality."

On September 21, 1853, he wrote to his father: "For my dissertation I am writing on aesthetics.... It can be said in confidence that the professors of literature here have not studied the subject I have chosen for my dissertation, and it is therefore doubtful whether they will see what relation my ideas have to the generally established conceptions of aesthetic problems. It would even seem to them that I am an adherent of those philosophers whose opinions I challenge if I did not speak of this clearly. Therefore, I do not think that the importance of the problems I discuss will be understood here unless I am obliged openly to explain it. In general, conceptions of philosophy have become very dim here since the people who understood philosophy and followed its development died, or have become silent" (N. G. Chernyshevsky, *Posthumous Works*, Vol. II, p. 199, Moscow-Leningrad, 1928).

Chernyshevsky's "Aesthetic Relation of Art to Reality" caused general attention to be rivetted again on philosophy. It was precisely the militant, materialist character of the dissertation that roused the ire of Prof. Nikitenko, to whom Chernyshevsky gave his work for preliminary review. On Nikitenko's insistence, Chernyshevsky was obliged to revise several passages of the dissertation in which his attack on the prevailing idealist aesthetics was exceptionally sharp. In particular, he was obliged to revise all those passages in which Hegel was mentioned and to confine himself to general allusions to his philosophy("the metaphysical system," etc.). Owing to the exceedingly strict censorship in Russia at that time, the open criticism of idealism and advocacy of materialism were impossible. The tremendous service Chernyshevsky rendered was that he succeeded, in spite of these obstacles, in creating one of the most remarkable monuments of materialist philosophy in Russia such as his work, "The Aesthetic Relation of Art to Reality."

On May 3, 1855, Chernyshevsky's dissertation "The Aesthetic Relation of Art to Reality" appeared in print. The appearance of such a book could not pass unnoticed among writers. The first opinions about it were extremely unfavourable. The conservative writers of that day realized that in Chernyshevsky they had a dangerous opponent.

The second edition of the book appeared in 1865, when Chernyshevsky was in exile. It roused tremendous interest and gave rise to a keen ideological conflict. In 1888, Chernyshevsky prepared a third edition for the press, but it was suppressed by the censor and it did not appear until 1906.

The text of "The Aesthetic Relation of Art to Reality" given in this volume is based on the first authorized edition of 1855, but it includes all the corrections the author made in 1888 for the third edition. Some of the passages of the dissertation which the author revised on Nikitenko's insistence have been restored according to the original manuscript and included in this text.   p. 281

2 In the manuscript the last part of this sentence, after the word "exceeded," reads: "the limits which I had to set for it." This passage was probably revised by Chernyshevsky on the insistence of Ustryalov, the Dean of the Faculty. After these words comes the following passage, which is struck out: "and—I do not wish to conceal another reason—the working up of the details would take several years. Therefore, regretfully renouncing factual fullness, I reserve the right and duty to present some time in the future, for the solution of the problem of the relation of art to reality, an analysis of all the most important phenomena of the most many-sided and fullest of the arts, poetry, in order to test the soundness of my deductions by the history of poetry. I regard the present essay only as the introduction to a future work."   p. 281

3 After the phrase "a priori" the following words come in the manuscript: "hypotheses, the development of science from metaphysical views—such is the character of the new trend that predominates in all the sciences."   p. 282

4 The ensuing passage was struck out of the manuscript: "Or has aesthetics already lost the right to our attention? Or are only bibliographical researches worthy of our attention? Or should we, for the sake of details, ignore the whole? It seems to me that such a view, which has many advocates nowadays, is one-sided, and that, if we recognize the importance of studying individual works of art,

or individual writers, we cannot but recognize the importance of studying the purpose of art. It would be strange to reject history and regard only questions concerning the details of individual events as being worthy of our attention, and it is strange to reject aesthetics for the sake of the details of the history of literature. However much (and rightly) the details of a subject may interest us, we cannot dispense with general conceptions of the subject, and we cannot but regard the striving to formulate such conceptions as correct and important.

"Or are these conceptions already so clear and generally accepted that they are not worth speaking about? No. They are vaguely sensed rather than definitely understood; therefore, to speak about them does not mean repeating what is already known."   p. 282

⁵ The passage in square brackets was struck out by Nikitenko. In the manuscript there are the following two marginal notes by him: "Cut out Hegel's philosophy!" and "This Hegelism must be revised, or cut out altogether."   p. 282

⁶ After this in the manuscript comes the following paragraph: "Thus, these two different definitions lead to two radically different views of the beautiful in objective reality, of the relation of imagination to reality, of the essence of art. They lead to two absolutely different systems of aesthetic conceptions. One of them, the one we accept, is based on an idea which, in the other, the generally accepted one, invades the system of aesthetics, it is true, but does so in spite of its essential trend; it is suppressed by the opposite views, and dies, leaving scarcely any fruit. The definition we offer makes the dignity and beauty of reality the fundamental idea of aesthetics."   p. 292

⁷ After this in the manuscript comes the following: "The sublime and the ridiculous thus constitute two one-sided manifestations of the beautiful."

Cf. V. Vischer, *op. cit.*, Vol. I, § 147, p. 334.   p. 292

⁸ After the word "indefiniteness" comes the following: "(I would say 'bezóbraznoye' [formless—*Tr.*] if I were not afraid of dropping into a play of words by placing bezóbraznoye in juxtaposition with bezobráznoye [ugly—*Tr.*])." Chernyshevsky deleted this when preparing the manuscript for the third edition.   p. 293

⁹ In the manuscript after the word "love" comes the following: "(i.e., to be madly in love, because it is this love that is usually depicted in sentimental novels and discussed in textbooks on aesthetics)."   p. 297

¹⁰ In the manuscript instead of the word "usually" comes: "the view, the unsoundness of which we have tried to prove, also accepts the sublime in reality, which is *only* a phantom introduced into objective things and phenomena *only* by human conceptions. The latest aesthetics assumes."   p. 300

¹¹ In the manuscript after the words "our mind" comes: "The definition 'great is much bigger' renders superfluous the intervention of imagination, the embellishment of reality with it. Whoever accepts it says that the truly sublime *exists* both in nature and in man."   p. 300

[12] In the manuscript after the words "greater than they" comes: "and finally, they are killed by the force against which they had rebelled and which is revived in the persons of the triumvirs."   p. 303

[13] In the manuscript after the word "tribute" comes: "and admit the justice of his cause."   p. 303

[14] In the manuscript this sentence is marked off in the margin by Nikitenko and after it comes the following: "We could even be reproached for having stopped to expose this attempt, the futility of which is evident to people who look at life simply, without learned prejudices. But if, on the one hand, it is necessary to explain the concepts worked out by science to people who have not made a special study of it, then, on the other hand, it is necessary scientifically to prove the unsoundness of conceptions that are alien to science, but which have managed to assume a scientific form even though their unsoundness is obvious to the layman, precisely because he is free from the prejudices to which specialists yield. If criticism is not conducted from the specialist point of view it will be unsatisfactory in scientific respects. In the present case, specialist criticism is all the more necessary for the reason that it is the introduction."   p. 305

[15] In the manuscript after the word "truth" comes: science can only indicate the origin of error, but it cannot share it."   p. 305

[16] In the manuscript it says: "In this way," then comes the following: "The semisavage cannot conceive of life that does not resemble his own. Therefore, all the forces of nature appear to him to be humanlike. Humanifying everything, the semisavage also conceives the force of *chance* as a humanlike being. This being he calls fate. Assuming that this brief allusion may need a very detailed explanation, we hasten to develop it further."   p. 305

[17] In the manuscript after the words "each other" comes the following: "Don Carlos and Marqués de Poza are guilty of having been men of noble character. And finally, the lamb in the fable which drinks at the same brook to which the wolf comes to drink is also guilty: why did it go to the brook where it was likely to meet the wolf? And chiefly: why did it not provide itself with such teeth as would enable it to devour the wolf?"   p. 310

[18] For the third edition the following was deleted: "True, we could have recalled that in our day too many novels like this are written (for example, most of Dickens'). But at all events, we are beginning to understand that the earth is not a courthouse, but a place to live in."   p. 310

[19] In the manuscript after the words "punish all" comes: "villainy, not all crimes. For example, society in our day regards the violation of moral purity as disgraceful only for women, not for men. In the opinion of most people it is not wrong for a young man to sow his wild oats, in fact, they think it would be wrong if he did not do so."   p. 310

[20] In the manuscript, instead of "and so forth," it says: "is not always punished even by qualms of conscience."   p. 311

[21] In the manuscript after "accidental" there is the following insertion: "(I shall have to touch upon this question when I deal with the relation of art to reality)."   p. 311

[22] In the manuscript after "Shakespeare's tragedies" comes the following: "This last idea needs extensive development, which the limits of the present essay do not permit, and I can, therefore, express it here merely as an opinion, reserving the right to prove it elsewhere. To explain why scenes of human suffering or death have a frightful or tragic effect upon a man seems to me to be quite superfluous. But to point to a special form of the tragic, the independence of which is, as far as I know, not yet admitted in aesthetics, is, I think, not altogether devoid of scientific interest.

"In addition to human suffering and death, we are tragically affected by a man's moral ruin—vice and heartless, strictly consistent egoism. *Evil*, when it is potent, has a tragic effect. The tragedy of pure evil could easily be forgotten by most of the people who have made a study of the tragic, because usually, the people who obviously suffer and perish as a result of evil are those who come into contact with a man of potent evil, and that is why it seems that the tragic effect is produced only by the suffering and death of the people who perish as a result of evil. But there are vices and crimes that are nice, jolly, endearing and mild, from which only morality obviously suffers, whereas individual people apparently suffer from them very little, and even gain by them. To explain what we mean, we shall quote the following example: Let us picture to ourselves an English lord who in epicurean style spends his enormous income on satisfying his passion for sensuous pleasure. This man loves comfort in all things, even in his conscience, and, therefore, never resorts to 'base' or 'criminal' means of satisfying his passion. Needless to say, he will not resort to violence or similar criminal measures, he will not even be a seducer. He is a very nice man, and fortunate are all those who enjoy his favours; nor are those unfortunate with whom he is already sated, for he does not send them away empty-handed. 'Have I caused anyone suffering?' he can proudly ask those around him. Indeed, he is not injurious to individuals; he is injurious only to society, which he contaminates and befouls; he is the enemy only of 'stern' morality. But actually, he is a criminal, worse than any other criminal, because he is a worse corrupter than all other corrupters. The example he sets says: 'Do not fear vice; vice need not harm anybody; vice can be kind and meek.' True, as far as we remember, art has not depicted such personalities from this point of view (it is possible, however, to point, in this respect, to Couture's well-known painting 'Roman Orgy'); but it has not depicted them because it is too difficult to restrain the feeling of indignation and disgust when depicting such a personality, and too difficult to restrain the desire to take vengeance on him for the terrible injury he has caused by depicting him not only as pernicious, but also pitiful, filthy and contemptible. Here, in spite of the author, tragedy is converted into irony, sarcasm. And this kind of tragedy comes under the definition given above.

"It naturally brings us to the ridiculous."   p. 311

[23] In the manuscript after the quotation from Vischer comes the following: "My excerpt is a long one, too long perhaps. But I had to present the critique of the beautiful in nature in full in order to avert the possibility of being reproached for having omitted, forgotten, or for not having brought out in sufficient relief, 'the most important flaws in beauty in reality'—I would always lay myself open to

such a reproach if I were myself to formulate ideas that seem wrong
to me, and the fallacy of which I want to expose."   p. 317

[24] The whole of this paragraph ending with the words "find satisfaction in it," the whole of the two preceding paragraphs and part of
the one before them, commencing with "Dreaming whips up desire,"
were written in place of another passage against which Nikitenko had
written this marginal note in the manuscript: "Too much about love."
The following is the full text of the deleted passage:

"Take, for example, the subject that is *most often* treated
in works of art—love and beauty. A man may dream about ideally
beautiful women, but he can do so only under two conditions: when
he has not yet, or no longer has, a real, earnest desire for love, but
has only a fantastic trend of thought towards the idea that 'love is
the supreme happiness in life,' and that 'he is an extraordinary person, superior to all these wretched people,' many of whom, however,
are actually wiser and more noble than he, and that, therefore, 'he
must love differently from the way they do,' that, therefore, he can
love only a woman whose extraordinary beauty is on a par with his
extraordinariness as a man.

"This is the first condition, but it is not enough; a second is needed,
viz., the man must be prevented from seeing beautiful women, prevented from seeing even ordinary good-looking women, for otherwise,
owing to his vacuity, he will forthwith fall head over heels in love
and tell himself and others how extraordinarily happy he is in having
met a 'celestial' being. But all this fantastic dreaming about 'celestial beauty,' all this fantastic falling in and falling out of love, is
pale, ridiculous and pitiful compared with real love.

"A man who is really in love—and there are far more of these
than there are of those who imagine they are, or want to be, in love—
does not worry about whether there are women in the world more beautiful than the one he loves. He does not care about others. He knows
very well that the woman he loves has her faults, but what is that to
him? He loves her nevertheless, for, after all, she is nice and sweet.
And if you begin 'to prove by analysis that she is not absolutely perfect,' he will say to you: 'I know that better than you do, and although
I see very many faults in her, I see far more in her that is worthy of
love. To put it short: I love her as she is:

'There are some who may shine o'er thee, Mary,
And many as frank and free,
And a few as fair,
But the summer air
Is not more sweet to me, Mary.'

"To avoid misunderstanding it may be added that we must regard
as real love that kind which in our society is usually developed within
the sphere of family life; occasionally it also occurs in the sphere of
old companionship, of close, friendly relations. 'Ardent' lovers will
laugh at this 'humdrum' sort of love, but what is to be done about
it when the prosaic feeling of parental, conjugal or even friendly love
is actually much stronger and, if the truth be told, much more ardent,
than the 'mad' love that so much is written about in 'poetical creations,' and is talked so much about in the company of young people?
I do not in the least wish to attack that kind of love, which chiefly

enjoys the title of love. I only want to say, firstly, that true love knows nothing about all these ideas concerning 'celestial' 'perfection'; secondly, that there are other kinds of love, much stronger and much more prosaic than the other kind, if by prosaic is meant everything that is free of fantastic illusions." p. 320

[25] After this in the manuscript comes the following: "Detailed proof that the essential result of the operation of the forces of nature is the production of beauty would carry us too far afield. But if we interpret beauty as life, such detailed proof is unnecessary, for there is a striving to produce life everywhere in nature. But even if our view of the essence of beauty is not accepted, the extremely intense efforts exerted by nature to produce beauty can be easily proved by the inexhaustible abundance of beauty in nature. At all events, it is evident that it is utterly wrong to regard the unpremeditatedness of beauty in reality as a defect. And so, let us pass to the next reproach deduced from this principle that we reject." p. 391

[26] In the manuscript after the words "depends upon himself" comes the following passage, struck out in pencil by Nikitenko: "The lives of people who are indeed filled with the need of greatness in life are nearly always replete with great deeds. By way of example, we point to people who are imbued with a striving for martial combat, for whom 'the whining of bullets is the only music that appeals to their hearts.' True, war is now more rare than it used to be, but, for all that, a man imbued with the truly martial spirit can find all the fighting his heart desires. Let the Russian go to the Caucasus, the Frenchman to Algiers, the Englishman to the East Indies; there they will find battles, marches, skirmishes and alarums galore. The German alone has nowhere to go to fight; but the existence of a martial spirit among the Germans at the present time is a matter of extreme doubt. In the epoch when that spirit prevailed among them, they had wars enough. But why insist on battles like those at Borodino and Leipzig? A true need is not so fastidious; and the man who waits for a battle of Borodino in order to rush into the fray is evidently not so very much tormented by the lust for battle. Furthermore, a true need is not so exclusive that a man filled with the desire for battle must necessarily fight against enemy troops to achieve happiness. Such a man is drawn to any kind of stubborn and hazardous struggle. If he has not the opportunity to spend all his life on the battlefield, he can find hazardous and arduous undertakings after his own heart in other fields. He will become an enterprising farmer who struggles with the soil; he will become a speculator who promotes extremely risky undertakings. In short, whatever his career may be, his life will be full of risk, alarm and conflict."

Then came the following sentence, which is absent in the printed text of the third edition: "Life is so broad and many-sided that a man can nearly always find his fill of everything a strong and true need compels him to seek." p. 322

[27] After the word "pose" comes the following sentence, which was deleted from the third edition: "This is because the spirit, the trend, the colour of a man's life are given it by the character of the man himself. A man does not determine the events of his life, but the spirit of these events is determined by his character. The skilful hunter attracts his quarry." p. 322

[28] In the manuscript this sentence was substituted for the following passage, which had been struck out and marked off in the margin by Nikitenko: "One usually hears in everyday life, and always reads in treatises on aesthetics, that there are very few beautiful women in the world, or strictly speaking, almost none at all. This is what people say, but it is doubtful whether they really mean it. It is very easy to test this. It is sufficient to take one of those people who complain about the scarcity of beautiful women for a walk along the Nevsky during the promenade hour. Every now and again he will jerk your arm and say: 'Look at that one, isn't she pretty!... Oh, here is another pretty one!... Oh, and here is another, look, look, she is a perfect beauty!' and so on and so forth, and within a quarter of an hour he will have pointed to no less than fifty or sixty beautiful women. It would be interesting to collect the following data: We may assume that in St. Petersburg there are about 150,000 women; of these, about 35,000 are between the ages of 16 and 25; how many of these thirty-five thousand enjoy the reputation of being beautiful in their respective circles? Several thousand without a doubt, and probably from eight to nine thousand. At all events, if one happens to be at an evening party where ten or twelve young women have gathered, one can always find among them three or four who enjoy the reputation of being beautiful. No. Instead of talking about the scarcity of beautiful women, it would be truer to say that there are too many." p. 322

[29] In the printed text the last two sentences were substituted for the following passage that was deleted from the manuscript: "No. Actually, people do not hold living human beauty in disdain. They can rather be reproached for not always being impartial and sufficiently discriminate in calling youth, just youth alone, beauty, and for admiring as beautiful women those whose entire beauty consists in that they are nineteen years of age." p. 322

[30] After this in the manuscript comes the following passage, struck out by Nikitenko: "There are different degrees of beauty in reality. But although the highest degree is more beautiful than the rest, it does not follow that true and full beauty cannot be found in the lower degrees. In Europe there is only one top-rank wealthy man— a person named Rothschild, and hardly anybody knows which one it is, the Parisian or the Italian. It does not follow, however, that because Rothschild is the richest man in Europe, everybody else in Europe is poor. And although we may agree with Rumohr that Vittoria of Albano was the most beautiful woman in Italy, we must nevertheless say that Italy is not populated with frights, and that, of course, there were in Rome at that time an incalculable number of women who were quite beautiful even beside Vittoria." p. 322

[31] In the manuscript after the words "real life" come two passages, one of which is struck out by Nikitenko and the other by Chernyshevsky. First passage: "The reproach levelled at philosophers that they adhere to an abstract point of view that is inapplicable to reality is a threadbare one, but it is very often true; and it may be justly applied to the aesthetic view which holds that beauty in reality is rare, only because first-class beauty is rare." Second passage: "In real life we regard a good object as good, irrespective of whether we have or have not found better objects. If it were possible to find in the world an object better than one which, having positive merits, had grave

defects, this comparison would not give us the right to regard as unsatisfactory (and we do not regard it so in real life) the less brilliant of the two objects compared. This rule is always adhered to in real life." Furthermore, the following passage was deleted from the third edition: "Therefore, while regarding object X as being more beautiful than object A, we, in real life, do not for a moment cease to regard object A as beautiful."   p. 323

[32] After this in the manuscript comes the following passage, struck out by Nikitenko: "It is common knowledge that people who are normally in love with each other, i.e., in love at a relatively equal age, for example, a woman of 18 and a man of 25, or a woman of 22 and a man of 30, age at the same time. Is it not ridiculous and foolish for a man of 60 to love a beautiful woman of 20? An elderly man whose morals are not corrupt can truly love only an elderly woman. Is not my complaint: 'My beautiful wife is ageing!' ridiculous, when I am ageing myself? It is ridiculous to grieve over the fact that an 8-year-old girl is not 18; and it is ridiculous to grieve over the fact that a 42-year-old woman is no longer twenty-two."   p. 323

[33] In the manuscript after the word "unjust" comes the following: "Of course, a society beauty is most beautiful in a ball dress, which, however, she cannot always wear; but it is a poor society beauty who is beautiful only in a ball dress. There are many beautiful women who are beautiful in any dress, and at all times." This passage was struck out by Nikitenko and revised by Chernyshevsky.
                                                             p. 324

[34] After this in the manuscript comes the following, struck out by Nikitenko: "To be irritated and offended by trifles is a sign of morbidity, or of ridiculous hypersensitiveness."   p. 327

[35] After this in the manuscript comes the following: "Philosophy must only explain experience, it has no right to reject it. It is an indisputable fact that a man likes individual beauty, it seems to him to be true beauty. This general, fundamental fact, which embraces all the phenomena of healthy aesthetic life, refutes the opinion that only absolute beauty is true beauty."   p. 330

[36] After this in the manuscript comes the following sentence, but it is struck out: "This is asserted by admirers of art who look down superciliously upon beauty in reality."   p. 330

[37] In the third edition the end of this sentence, after the words "becomes obsolete," was deleted. It continued as follows: "and if for no other reason, we cannot enjoy the works of Shakespeare, Dante and Wolfram as much as their contemporaries did."   p. 333

[38] After this in the manuscript comes the following, struck out by Nikitenko: "What the development of moral feeling does in relation to content, the development of aesthetic feeling does to form. Needless to say, the beauty of the works of the talented poets of the pseudo-classical epoch is dead to us—everybody agrees that even the language of Shakespeare is often awfully foppish and pompous."
                                                             p. 333

[39] After the words "is dead to us" in the manuscript comes: "because of the change in the system of musical notation," but these words were crossed out by Nikitenko. p. 333

[40] After this in the manuscript comes the following passage, which was omitted from this text: "It is needless for me to speak of the paintings and statues that depict Leda and Ganymede. Laymen are struck with horror by such myths, and it is strange that such paintings and statues are not kept in places accessible only to specialists. In general, it must be admitted that there is justification, and very considerable justification, for publications in usum Delphini, and for the fig leaf." p. 334

[41] In the manuscript after this sentence comes the following: "Proof of this is found in the opinion that is constantly expressed in our times, that Mephistopheles is a rather pitiful demon. Indeed, an educated person of the present day finds the doubts that convulsed Faust pitiful and ridiculous." The word "doubts" was followed by "and gibes," but this was struck out. p. 334

[42] This sentence is marked off in the margin by Nikitenko. In the manuscript the sentence ends as follows, after "in the cause." "this is an axiom known since the time of the scholastics; what there is not in man, there cannot be in art, the work of men." p. 335

[43] In the manuscript after these words comes the following: "I only want to say that if the flaws in works of art were examined through a microscope in the same way as aestheticians who prefer beauty in art to beauty in reality examine the flaws in beauty in reality, then very much could be said against works of art, much more than can be said against the beauty created by nature and life." p. 336

[44] In the manuscript the words "we must" are preceded by the following passage, which is struck out: "And so, we think that the opinion that the beauty created by art is, in general, superior to the beauty created by nature and life cannot be accepted by science as an axiom applicable to all particular cases. Now." p. 336

[45] After this sentence in the manuscript comes the following: "Only after we have reviewed the content, the essential merits and defects of the separate arts shall we be able to proceed to answer the question as to what is the purpose of art in general." p. 336

[46] After this sentence in the manuscript comes the following passage, which is struck out: "We think that all these things are equally insignificant; we think that the labour spent in making them was, in all cases, labour thrown to the winds." p. 338

[47] After this sentence in the manuscript comes the following: "We are constantly reading and hearing the remark: 'she (or he) is as beautiful as a Greek statue (or as the statue of Canova).' Equally often we read or hear the remark: 'the incomparable beauty of form, the incomparable beauty of profile, of the great works of sculpture,' and so forth." p. 339

[48] After this sentence in the manuscript comes the following: "'The beauty of some statues is superior to the beauty of real people'— it requires courage to protest against this pronouncement as it did at

one time to protest against the opinion that Virgil was the greatest
of all poets, or that every word of Aristotle's is indefeasible truth."
p. 339

⁴⁹ After this sentence in the manuscript comes the following:
"But painting is unable to convey the colour of a still fresh face, the
colour of a body that has not yet begun to grow numb. The faces of
aged people, faces coarsened by toil and privation, or sunburned faces,
come out much more satisfactorily than tender young faces, particularly feminine faces."   p. 342

⁵⁰ After this sentence in the manuscript comes the following:
"And the reason why painting is unable satisfactorily to portray anything that is serene, gentle, or exalted is very plain: the means at its
command are too coarse. Microscopic delicacy of finish is needed to
convey the microscopically-delicate, fine, harmonious tension and
relaxation of the muscles, the barely perceptible increase in pallor
or flush, the dullness, or fresh animation of colour in the face."
p. 342

⁵¹ After this in the manuscript comes: "It may be said that all
this has long been known and that I am only repeating commonplaces. On the one hand, such an observation would be correct. Everybody is convinced that art cannot compete with nature, that 'nature
is more artistic than all the artists.' But strange to say, nearly everybody continues to assert that the outline and expression of statues or
portraits of people are 'superior, more beautiful and fuller' than those
met with in living people. Speaking generally, there is no purpose in
arguing about the 'novelty' of one's ideas; if they are old and generally accepted, all the better. But, unfortunately, it is difficult to say
this in this case, because one usually reads and hears opinions that
are the very opposite of these."   p. 342

⁵² After this in the manuscript comes: "A man is scarcely ever
able to throw a stone in a perfectly perpendicular line. In reality, however, a stone always falls in a perfectly perpendicular line. If anybody did, at last, succeed in throwing a stone in a perpendicular line,
he could boast about it only to other people who are unable to do this,
but not to nature, which always does it without the slightest effort."
p. 343

⁵³ After this in the manuscript comes: "As a result, we get the
same as what we got above: painting cannot satisfactorily portray
objects in the shape they possess in reality."   p. 343

⁵⁴ After this in the manuscript comes: "Thus, if painting of this
kind is in any way superior to reality, the superiority is so slight that
it scarcely deserves attention."   p. 345

⁵⁵ After this in the manuscript comes: "and we see many 'typical characters' of this kind, who have long been called walking
puppets, with inscriptions on their foreheads: hero, villain, fool,
coward, etc."   p. 351

⁵⁶ After this in the manuscript comes: "Our review of the manner
in which the poet 'creates' typical characters is too general and brief
and therefore, of course, incomplete. To develop and prove the correctness of our view it would be necessary to write a lengthy monograph;
but it is doubtful whether a man who is not prejudiced by phrases

like 'the creation of types' will think that such a tangible view needs
extremely detailed development."   p. 352

57 The original manuscript read: "uttered by Marguerite and
Mephistopheles was heard by Goethe from Gretchen and Merck."
This was revised for the third edition.

Goethe met Merck in 1771. This was one of his most ardent friend-
ships. Many of Merck's features are reflected in the character of Mephistopheles. Goethe said: "Merck and I were like Mephistopheles and
Faust" (Eckermann, Johann Peter, *Gespräche mit Goethe in den let-
zten Jahren seines Lebens*).   p. 352

58 After this in the manuscript comes the following insertion:
"that deserve to be called dramas, love stories, etc., no less than the
dramas, love stories, etc., written by the greatest writers."   p. 398

59 Originally in the manuscript, this passage, after the words
"horrible things," read as follows: "a lady who cannot even be called
a scandalmonger can wreck the happiness of many people by a thoughtless word uttered, without any evil intent, only because she cannot,
like most people, hold her tongue." This is struck out and revised.
After the words "Iago and Mephistopheles" comes: "People who are
not particularly bad nor particularly good are prone to do things that
may be ascribed to 'villains' and 'heroes.' This is what usually happens in life."   p. 355

60 After the words "read repetitions" in the manuscript comes:
"In them nearly everything is nearly always done in the same way:
people fall in love, are jealous, are unfaithful, are perplexed, surprised, fall into despair—always in the same way, according to a common rule, for it is always an ardent young man who falls in love, a
mistrustful man who is jealous, a weak-willed woman who is unfaithful, and so forth. The same character always does the same thing in
keeping with the part ascribed to him."   p. 355

61 After this in the manuscript the following is struck out: "How
many people will be found who, when pronouncing judgment on a
novel or a story, will first of all, and most of all, talk about the style
in which it is written and, in essence, see nothing else."   p. 355

62 After this in the manuscript comes: "continually mentioning
that 'in nature there is true beauty,' when one remembers this." After
the words "one would think" the following is struck out: "that it is
scarcely worth while refuting such an unsound opinion, which is ready
to fall at a mere hint." At the end of the sentence, after the word "imagination" the following is struck out: "and then our too brief and too
general survey will appear to be too long and too detailed." After this
deleted passage comes: "We are definitely of the opinion that in respect to beauty of the whole, finish of detail, in short, in respect to
all the criteria on the basis of which the merits of an aesthetic work
are judged, the creations of reality and life are incomparably superior
to the creations of human art."   p. 356

63 The genius of the Russian poet Pushkin is universally
acknowledged.   p. 358

64 After this in the manuscript comes: "When I get the opportunity to see the sea my mind may be (and usually is) occupied with
quite other thoughts and I do not see the sea, and I am not disposed
to take aesthetic pleasure in it. But I can look at works of art when-

ever I please, whenever I am disposed to take pleasure in them, and I look at a seascape only when I am able to enjoy it."   p. 361

65 After this in the manuscript comes: "had they arisen as a consequence of the fact that 'there is no perfection on earth, and we need perfection.'"   p. 363

66 After this in the manuscript comes: "This is the predominating purpose of all the arts except poetry, which, in addition, has another purpose, viz., to explain life. Painting, sculpture, and particularly music, also strive, as far as their means will allow, to explain life sometimes, but their explanation is too indefinite, too vague, and therefore unintelligible; they must confine themselves mainly to reproduction, not to explanation."   p. 364

67 This refers to Hegel's *Lectures on Aesthetics*.   p. 365

68 In the manuscript this paragraph starts as follows: "It is obvious that of these absolutely correct objections to the theory which wants art to deceive the eyes with imitations of reality, not one is valid against our view; but."   p. 366

69 After "when" in the manuscript comes: "art rises higher than nature and real life, when."   p. 366

70 After this sentence in the manuscript comes: "The best proof that the Greek view was really distorted by the later so-called imitation of nature theory is provided by the criticism of that theory we quoted above. It is evident that in the opinion of the author of this criticism, art guided by the imitation theory strives to deceive by means of outward resemblance and to compel the viewer to take a lifeless imitation for the living object, a portrait for a real person, a stage setting for a real sea, or wood. If this were not so, the critic would not have said: 'When imitating nature, art, because of its restricted means, gives only deception instead of truth, and instead of a really living being, gives only a lifeless mask.'"   p. 368

71 In the manuscript this passage, after the word "senses," reads as follows: "We cannot be reproached for accusing the whole of art of this abuse which occurred only in the epochs of corrupted taste. In analyzing the defects of art, we did not take the point of view from which the author we have quoted regards the rules that are preached to art by the theory, against the false striving of which he quite justly protests. There are no grounds for accusing art in general of imitating nature."   p. 368

72 This sentence does not appear in the manuscript. Instead of it there is the following passage, which is struck out: "Thus, we regard the reproduction of reality as the formal principle of art." To this there is the following footnote, also struck out: "There is no need to explain that by 'reproduction of nature' we mean something entirely different from what was meant by words rather close to these in the eighteenth century."   p. 368

73 After this sentence in the manuscript comes: "It may be said that all melodies ought to be beautiful in form; but we are speaking of content, not of form (later on we shall discuss the point that beauty of form is an essential attribute of works of art, and then we shall

inquire whether it must be regarded as a characteristic feature
of art).”   p. 369

⁷⁴ After the word “nature” in the manuscript comes: “but reality
cannot entirely come under the headings: the beautiful, the sublime,
and the ridiculous.”   p. 369

⁷⁵ After the word “comical” in the manuscript comes: “not all
man’s intentions and actions are either ridiculous or sublime.” p. 369

⁷⁶ After this sentence in the manuscript comes: “Even those
aestheticians who want to limit the content of art to beauty protest
against setting wider boundaries for art only out of fear that if we
say: ‘the content of art is everything that is interesting for man in
life,’ we shall thereby set boundaries for it that are too indistinct,
too subjective. It is true that even in a single epoch the objects and
events that interest man are extremely diverse; and they will be even
more diverse if we take man at his various stages of development. But
it is equally true that all these diverse objects, events, problems and
aspects of life that interest man enter into the content of art, and if
our conception of the content of art set indistinct and unstable boundaries for it, it would still be correct; the indistinct borders of a fact
do not detract from its unity and truth. A strict investigation of the
relation of art to philosophy, history and the descriptive sciences
would, perhaps, show that even within our broad boundaries it is
possible fairly precisely to delimit the content of art from all the other
kindred trends of the human spirit, at all events, no less distinctly
than they have been delimited hitherto. But this would lead us into
a lengthy digression, which is scarcely necessary in the present case.”
                                                                  p. 370

⁷⁷ After the word “art” in the manuscript comes: “it is doubtful
whether this is due to the fear of depriving art of definite boundaries
and a special content. We think that.”   p. 370

⁷⁸ After this sentence in the manuscript comes: “Indeed, if by
the beautiful we mean the perfect realization of the idea, or the complete unity of content and form, as it is usually taken to mean, then we
are quite right in saying that the beautiful is an essential attribute
of every work of art. But in this, two circumstances must be kept in
view. The first circumstance is that.”   p. 370

⁷⁹ After this sentence in the manuscript comes: “Beauty as an
object, as a beautiful being, or beautiful thing, is not the sole content
of art. The joy, the fullness and the freshness of life are not the only
things that interest man; and beauty is not the only thing that art
reproduces.”   p. 371

⁸⁰ After the word “follow” in the manuscript comes: “who voluntarily ties his hands with love intrigues and spreads the haze of love
in front of his readers’ eyes.”   p. 372

⁸¹ Instead of “artificiality,” it says in the manuscript: “artificial
sentimentality, the primness, which permeate most of the works of
art of the last two centuries.”   p. 372

⁸² After this sentence in the manuscript comes: “And the critics
are right. Having presented an artificially finished character, the poet
no longer has a right to enlarge it by saying: ‘I will depict a mean egoist

who, however, when the opportunity occurs, is fond of flaunting his magnanimity,' or: 'I will depict a young man imbued with lofty sentiments and a desire to love passionately.' By saying that, the poet enumerates for us all the springs that prompt the man's actions and will be inconsistent in giving him an opportunity to reveal new sides of his character."
p. 373

[83] After "characters" in the manuscript comes: "whereas, actually, in conversation only a man's external character, his manner of speech is revealed, but not his heart."
p. 373

[84] After these words in the manuscript comes: "There was a time when 'abridgments' (epitomes) were preferred to the original works; why then should we not laud poetry for omitting unessentials and giving us the essence in a brief sketch, if the descendants of the great Romans found that Justin was better than Trogus Pompeius and that Eutropius was better than all the historians?"
p. 374

[85] This refers to August Tappe's *Epitome of N. M. Karamzin's Russian History*, "For Youths and Students of the Russian Language, with Accent Signs, Interpretations of Difficult Words and Phrases in German and in French, and with References to the Rules of Grammar," in two parts, St. Petersburg, 1819.
p. 374

[86] After this sentence in the manuscript comes: "Words always convey only the essential details, for a complete picture is presented only in a painting, not in words; the gradual course of events in all their details could be depicted only by a series of pictures, but not by a history or a novel."
p. 374

[87] This and the preceding sentence, including the insertion given in note 86, were substituted for the following passage that was struck out of the text: "In short, all the advantages art possesses over living reality can be defined as follows: 'inferior, much inferior, but cheaper; it does not require as much time, as much care, or as much penetration.'"
p. 374

[88] After the words "in real life" in the manuscript comes: "the reproduction of everything he thinks about, of everything that gives him joy or sorrow."
p. 374

[89] Instead of "sluggish" the manuscript says: "sluggish and indolent by nature or, because of fortuitous circumstances, little developed by learning and reflection. All they can say is: 'I like this, but I don't like that; this is good, but that is bad.'"
p. 375

[90] After these words in the manuscript comes: "His unsupported judgments have no obvious place in works of art; and even if he wanted to express them they would be of no value whatever, for they would be commonplace repetitions of threadbare phrases long familiar to everybody."
p. 375

[91] After these words in the manuscript comes: "In short, there are works of art which simply reproduce the phenomena of life that are of interest to man; and there are other works of art in which these phenomena are imbued with a definite idea."
p. 375

[92] In the manuscript this is followed by: "In such a case, a work of art in the strict sense of the term explains life"
p. 375

⁹³ Instead of "form," the manuscript says: "in this respect they are independent, as science is independent. But they are independent only in form: it is only in respect to form that they have nothing corresponding to themselves in the phenomena of real life, only in respect to premeditativeness."   p. 375

⁹⁴ After this sentence in the manuscript comes: "In short, a true reproduction of life by art is not a mere copy, particularly in poetry."   p. 378

⁹⁵ In the manuscript this sentence reads as follows: "In arguing that a poet (or an artist in general) can present nothing equal to a living event, to living people, to living nature in living fullness and artistic finish, we do not in the least wish to say that he must be an unimaginative copyist of individual events. As regards the scope of activity of the poet's artistic powers, it is not in the least restricted by our conception of the essence of art."   p. 378

⁹⁶ The end of this sentence was revised by the author for the third edition. In the first edition it read: "as material, only as a field for his activity, and, by utilizing it, to subjugate it."   p. 378

⁹⁷ After "in the poet's opinion" in the manuscript comes: "(or, placing the artist in general in such a position: when the artist who is reproducing reality has not got it in front of his eyes). The imagination needs even more scope when the artist is working under the influence of a definite trend, of a definite idea; in such cases he must alter and combine to a still greater extent."   p. 378

⁹⁸ After "degrading art" in the manuscript comes: "if protesting against exaggerated praise of it, proving that the panegyrists of art are attributing to it more than justice will allow."   p. 379

⁹⁹ After "elements of the latter" in the manuscript comes: "and only through it acquire the right to be the subject of art. The sublime and that element of it, the tragic, proved to be essentially different from the beautiful." After the words "subject of art" at the end of the sentence there is the following insertion: "entering art as elements of life in general."   p. 380

¹⁰⁰ After "life" in the manuscript comes: "or to put it more definitely, the fullness of life."   p. 380

¹⁰¹ After "purpose" in the manuscript comes: "and from beauty of form, which consists in perfection of finish." Then comes the following passage, which is struck out. "'The garden is beautiful' can be said in three different cases: 1) when everything in the garden is green, when everything is in bloom, when everything speaks of life (only in this sense should the aesthetician employ the term 'beautiful'); 2) when it yields a good income (the achievement of the aim, the unity of the idea and the individual object); the technical handbooks and the applied sciences speak of beauty in this sense; 3) when it is well-weeded and pruned, etc.; people with refined taste speak of beauty in this sense; concern for it is a matter of secondary importance, but such concern may spread throughout the world, and this kind of beauty is, indeed, not met with in nature or in serious life." After this deleted passage comes the following insertion: "Fulsome praise of beauty in works of art is in the majority of cases a survival of this refined striv-

ing after finish, a survival of the tastes that prevailed in France at
the beginning of the eighteenth century and is now rejected by everybody in principle, although it still exercises strong influence upon
the judgment of the majority of people."   p. 380

[102] In the manuscript there is another thesis, but it is struck out:
"18. Singing is an art only in certain cases, if by art we mean reproduction of the phenomena of life. In its original purpose singing is a
natural expression of a prolonged sensation, and in that case it is an
art only in the sense that one must learn to sing in order to be able
to do so very skilfully, it is an art only from the technical aspect."
Here the manuscript breaks off.   p. 381

THE AESTHETIC RELATION OF ART
TO REALITY
(Reviewed by the Author)

[1] Chernyshevsky's review of his own dissertation on "The Aesthetic Relation of Art to Reality" was first published in the *Sovremennik*, 1855, Vol. 51, No. 6. Signed: N. P.

This dissertation utterly refuted the principles of idealistic aesthetics, and when publishing it in 1855, Chernyshevsky was well aware
that his opinions would not be thoroughly reviewed or properly appraised by the critics of that day. It was this circumstance that induced him, soon after the appearance of his book, to write a review of
it himself and in the guise of a "critic" to explain to his readers what
he had not succeeded in developing in his book with sufficient fullness.

In writing this review of his own dissertation for the *Sovremennik*, Chernyshevsky felt less restricted than he had been at the time
he wrote the dissertation itself. In a magazine article he was able
to emphasize more distinctly and clearly the connection between his
aesthetics and the general system of materialist philosophical views,
whereas in the dissertation he was obliged carefully to veil this connection. It was on the pretext that in his dissertation "Mr. Chernyshevsky deals too fleetingly with the points at which aesthetics comes
into contact with the general system of conceptions of nature and life"
that the reviewer, disguised under the pseudonym of N. P., tried to
deal more comprehensively with this most important question of
principle. The sly digs at the "lack of fullness" that Chernyshevsky
pretends to level against himself were actually aimed against the
severe censorship that prevailed at that time, at the general ideological and political situation that reigned in the 1850's.

In this volume the article is published from the text as printed in
the *Sovremennik*. This text differs in many places from the original
manuscript. The most important of the revisions are given in the
following notes.   p. 382

[2] After the word "deductions" in the manuscript comes the following passage, which is struck out: "arrived at nowadays by strict
investigators of the phenomena of nature, of the history of the human
race, and are obtained by."   p. 382

³ This term "home-grown thinkers" probably applies to S. Shevy-ryov, A. Khomyakov and K. Aksakov. The reference to the "tree of thought" is taken from the opening lines of the twelfth century Russian poem: "A Lay of Igor's Host." p. 384

⁴ After this in the manuscript comes: "the deformity and inner paucity of which has long been recognized by everybody." p. 388

⁵ After this in the manuscript comes: "But for this mistake too, we add again, the author alone should be reproved; it does not harm the essence of the case he defends, because the same thing must be said, almost in the same words, about dancing and the scenic art, as what the author says in the section dealing with music." p. 398

⁶ After this in the manuscript it says: "the chapter headings of a book do the same to the text—it is easier, of course, to review the contents of a book by glancing at the chapter headings than by reading the whole text; but does it follow from this that the headings of Pushkin's poems are better than the poems themselves?" p. 403

⁷ After this in the manuscript comes: "The idea that the aesthetic merits of works of art cannot even reach the level of reality, let alone rise above it, is arrived at simply by the application of the general principles of the modern world outlook to the present problem, and the reviewer would claim the right to say that this idea can stand criticism. But Mr. Chernyshevsky's further, and more particular, ideas that art is reproduction of nature and that its content consists of all the phenomena of life that are of interest to man, while being in harmony with, and even in rather close dependence upon, the general conception of the relation of art to reality, are, nevertheless, fully determined not so much by this conception as by an analysis of the facts presented by art. Therefore, the reviewer must let the author take responsibility for these particular ideas, and if the reviewer takes the liberty to add that he too thinks that they are essentially right, he is only expressing his own opinion and not the final judgment of science. Justice demands, however, that it be said that in his analysis the author adduces a fairly large number of facts which confirm his theory." p. 403

⁸ After this in the manuscript comes the following passage which is struck out: "The reader has, of course, observed that the general result of the changes Mr. Chernyshevsky has introduced into the theory of art is that art is placed on the basis of purely human needs, instead of the former fantastic or transcendental foundations, the instability of which is now ⟨proved?⟩ by science. Art is brought nearer to real life and to the real requirements of the human heart. In this, the author is a faithful disciple of modern science, which bases all its views on man's needs, and all the theories of which aim at benefiting man." p. 408

⁹ After this in the manuscript comes: "Exactly. Most of the conceptions assimilated by the author must be said to be in harmony with modern views; the author's exposition of them, however, is very often unsatisfactory." p. 412

¹⁰ After this in the manuscript comes: "in two ways—either by giving his essay a forbidding but venerable exterior of unintelligible

language and numerous references to an incalculable number of scholars, and similar adjuncts which make a very deep impression upon people who imagine that they are scholars, or." p. 412

[11] After this in the manuscript comes: "What is to be done? A general principle attracts general attention only when it serves as the starting point for panegyrics, or for philippics. If it does not, it remains almost unnoticed, no matter how important it may be. But Mr. Chernyshevsky would not, or could not take advantage of his numerous opportunities for indulging in apologetics, and particularly in philippics. He did not mention a single name now prominent in literary circles. For this reason his essay will make a far feebler impression upon people who sympathize with literary problems than, of course, the author wanted to make with the ideas he has enunciated." p. 412

THE AESTHETIC RELATION OF ART TO REALITY
(Preface to the Third Edition)

[1] The second edition of "The Aesthetic Relation of Art to Reality" appeared anonymously in 1865, when Chernyshevsky was in exile in Siberia. In a letter to his son Alexander, dated November 2, 1887, he pointed to the desirability of publishing a new edition and wrote: "If any publisher thought it was necessary to issue a new edition of 'The Aesthetic Relation' I would ask you to inform me of this and to send me a copy of the book; I would revise it..." He received a copy of the book from his son and on December 12, 1887, he wrote to him: "When I find time I will write a preface to this book and write a few notes to it." Shortly after this, Alexander informed his father that L. F. Panteleyev had agreed to publish "The Aesthetic Relation." On April 17, 1888, Chernyshevsky wrote to his son Mikhail: "Thank you for the proposal to give 'The Aesthetic Relation' to Longin Fyodorovich; I have a copy of the book. On receiving your letter yesterday informing me that Longin Fyodorovich wishes to do me this service, I began to write a preface and to revise the text."

It took Chernyshevsky only a few days to prepare the book for the new edition. He started on April 16 and finished on April 20, 1888, when the revised text was sent to St. Petersburg. In a letter dated April 20, stating that he had sent the book off, Chernyshevsky wrote that for the new edition he had made "corrections on the margins of the book and on separate sheets of paper, and that he had added a preface."

On May 7, 1888 the censorship authorities informed A. V. Zakharin, who had undertaken the task of negotiating with the censors, that the publication of "The Aesthetic Relation" and the preface to it could not be permitted.

Nothing was done with the manuscript until 1906, when Chernyshevsky's "preface," written in 1888, was included in Part 2 of Vol. X of the Complete Works of Chernyshevsky.

V. I. Lenin, in his Materialism and Empirio-Criticism, Supplement to Chapter IV, Section I, "From What Angle Did N. G. Chernyshevsky Criticize Kantianism?" gives an exceptionally high appraisal of the general philosophical importance of Chernyshevsky's "Preface" to the proposed third edition of "The Aesthetic Relation of Art to Reality" (*cf.* V. I. Lenin, *Materialism and Empirio-Criticism*, Moscow 1952, p. 375-77). p. 413

[2] After "followers of Hegel" in the manuscript comes the following, which is struck out: "who remained faithful to Hegel; who would not have laughed at the hollow fantasy of the metaphysical systems, the last and strongest of which had been worked out by him." p. 413

[3] Feuerbach was the author of a number of works on historic-philosophical subjects: *A History of Modern Philosophy* (1833), *Pierre Bayle* (1836), *Leibnitz* (1836). p. 414

[4] Chernyshevsky is here referring to his transfer from Saratov to St. Petersburg to enter the university there. p. 415

[5] Here in the manuscript the name "Leibnitz" is struck out. p. 415

[6] In the manuscript the following words after "Strauss" are struck out: "and, perhaps, excelled even him in intellectual capacity." p. 419

[7] This refers to *A Criticism of the Synoptic Gospels* by Bruno Bauer (1841-42). p. 419

[8] V. I. Lenin analyzes this excellent argument of Chernyshevsky's, as he called it, in his *Materialism and Empirio-Criticism,* Supplement to Chapter IV, Section I, "From What Angle Did N. G. Chernyshevsky Criticize Kantianism?" p. 421

[9] The greater part of this passage, beginning from the words "our real knowledge of the real world," was struck out in the manuscript by the author, but was later restored by him. It is followed by the ensuing passage, also struck out, but not restored: "All the author's other references to the system of conceptions he employs to explain aesthetic conceptions must be interpreted in exactly the same way. This means that the conceptions on which he bases his analysis were acquired by him from Feuerbach; and the prevailing system of conceptions, the unsoundness of which he demonstrates, must always be understood to mean metaphysical philosophy, and Hegel's system in particular." p. 422

[10] After this sentence in the manuscript comes the following passage, which is struck out: "The changes he has made consist only in his substituting for terms that were inconvenient in the Russian language, broad terms, which removed the difficulties arising from the situation Russian literature is in. For example, for ontological terms signifying the play of chance, he substituted the term 'fate,' which has the same meaning, but indicates only one of the forms of the broader concept." p. 422

THE POETICS OF ARISTOTLE

[1] This review was first published in the *Otechestvenniye Zapiski*, 1854, Vol. 96, No. 9. The manuscript has not been preserved.

It was written on the appearance, in 1854, of a Russian translation by B. Ordynsky, of the *Poetics of Aristotle*.

In content, this review is closely related to "The Aesthetic Relation of Art to Reality," supplementing and explaining in a more popular style the main theses of the dissertation. p. 423

[2] It is perfectly evident that Chernyshevsky is here referring to Belinsky. p. 424

[3] Jurare in verba magistri—to swear by the authority of the teacher (Horace, *Epistolae*, 1, 1, 14). p. 427

[4] This refers to Heinrich Heine. p. 434

[5] This refers to Hegel. p. 440

[6] Pravdin and Starodum—characters in D. Fonvisin's *The Minor*. Korshunov and Razlyulayev—characters in Ostrovsky's comedy *Poverty Is No Crime*. Borodkin—a character in Ostrovsky's comedy *Don't Get Into Another's Sleigh*. p. 440

[7] This refers to a collection of poems, *Les Jardins (Gardens)* by the French poet Delille, whom Pushkin called "a Parnassian ant." "Wordsworth, Wilson, and that fraternity"—representatives of the so-called "lake school" of English poetry of the beginning of the nineteenth century. p. 441

[8] Subsequent research confirmed Chernyshevsky's statement that the *Poetics of Aristotle* in the form that work has come down to us is not complete. p. 450

ESSAYS ON THE GOGOL PERIOD OF RUSSIAN LITERATURE

[1] These essays were first published in the *Sovremennik*, the first essay in No. 12, 1855, and the rest in Nos. 1, 2, 4, 7, 9-12, 1856.
These essays are among Chernyshevsky's most important works, and their significance extends far beyond the scope of literary criticism. In them he gives what is practically a concise history of Russian public thought in the 30's-40's of the last century. The central figure in this period was Belinsky. Evading the severe obstacles of the censorship, Chernyshevsky restores and develops the revolutionary traditions of "the literary criticism of the Gogol period" (i.e., the period of Belinsky), contrasting it to the reactionary liberal-aristocratic "pure art" trend which, demagogically using the name of Pushkin, came out at that time under the flag of the "Pushkin principle." It must be borne in mind that the names of Gogol and Pushkin were merely symbols for two ideological trends championed by the representatives of two opposite class groupings. In these essays, Chernyshevsky came forward as the direct continuator of Belinsky's line. "We are all bound to it," he wrote (i.e., bound to the "literary criticism of the Gogol period" represented by Belinsky—*Ed.*), "with the ardent love of faithful and grateful disciples."
These essays are extremely important for a characterization of Chernyshevsky's philosophical views.
We give in this volume the whole of the Sixth essay and part of the Seventh, which contain an analysis of Belinsky's philosophi-

cal views and Chernyshevsky's splendid appraisal of Hegel's philosophy.   p. 454

² *Moskovsky Nablyudatel* (*The Moscow Observer*), a magazine directed from 1835 to 1837 by V. P. Androsov and S. P. Shevyryov. In 1838, the magazine passed into Belinsky's hands.   p. 454

³ *Teleskop* (*The Telescope*), "a journal of modern education," published in 1831-36 by N. I. Nadezhdin. Was suppressed in 1836 for publishing P. Y. Chaadayev's "Philosophical Letter." It was in this journal that Belinsky started on his career as a literary critic.
                                                                       p. 454

⁴ *Telegraf*, or *Moskovsky Telegraf* (*The Moscow Telegraph*), a journal of "literature, criticism, science and art," published from 1825 to 1834 by N. Polevoi. Later, Polevoi joined the reactionary camp in literature.   p. 454

⁵ *Biblioteka dlya Chteniya* (*Readers' Library*), a magazine founded in 1834 by A. F. Smirdin and O. I. Senkovsky. Was criticized by the *Otechestvenniye Zapiski* and the *Sovremennik* for its reactionary trend.   p. 454

⁶ *Severniye Tsvety* (*Northern Flowers*), a literary almanac published in 1825-31 by A. A. Delvig and O. M. Somov. Pushkin was a contributor.   p. 455

⁷ Chernyshevsky is here referring to the fact that the social ideals of the Decembrist A. Bestuzhev (Marlinsky) did not find expression in his works.   p. 457

⁸ This preface was written by M. Bakunin, who had also translated Hegel's "Gymnasium Speeches." At the time these essays were written Bakunin was a prisoner in the Schlüsselburg Fortress. Mention of his name was strictly forbidden by the censor.   p. 459

⁹ This refers to Herzen's *Letters on the Study of Nature* that were published in the *Otechestvenniye Zapiski* in 1845-46. Concerning them, Lenin wrote: "The first of his *Letters on the Study of Nature*, 'Empiricism and Idealism,' written in 1844, reveals to us a thinker who even now stands head and shoulders above the multitude of modern empiricist natural scientists and the swarms of present-day idealist and semi-idealist philosophers. Herzen stood on the threshold of dialectical materialism, and halted—before historical materialism." (V. I. Lenin, *Selected Works*, two-volume ed., Vol. I, Part 2, Moscow 1952, p. 274.)   p. 462

¹⁰ Here and in the preceding paragraph Chernyshevsky is referring to L. Feuerbach.   p. 467

¹¹ Mr. A.—Pavel Vasilyevich Annenkov.   p. 468

¹² *Moskovsky Nablyudatel*, 1838, parts 16 and 17. This refers to Belinsky's review of the *Sovremennik*, Nos. 1 and 2, 1838.
The Chronicles of a Russian in Paris were written by Alexander Ivanovich Turgenev (1785-1846), brother of the Decembrist N. I. Turgenev.   p. 470

¹³ This refers to the French bourgeois revolution at the end of the eighteenth century.   p. 473

[14] This was in 1840. Chernyshevsky could not mention Herzen by name for reasons of the censorship. p. 475

[15] This refers to the doctrines of the utopian socialist Fourier. p. 475

[16] *Cf.* the chapter "Young Moscow" in Herzen's *Biloye i Dumi* (*Reminiscences and Reflections*). p. 476

[17] By "external circumstances" Chernyshevsky means the arrest in 1834 and exile of Herzen and Ogaryov (Herzen was exiled to Perm and later to Vyatka, and Ogaryov to Penza). p. 477

[18] When Herzen returned from exile, Stankevich was ill in Italy, where he died on the night of June 24, 1840. p. 477

[19] For an account of these debates, *cf.* Herzen's *Reminiscences and Reflections*, Vol. I, Part IV. p. 477

[20] This refers to M. A. Bakunin, *cf.* note 8. p. 479

[21] In June 1840, Belinsky wrote to Botkin: "In St. Petersburg, from the uninhabited island" (this is what Belinsky called Stankevich's Moscow circle—*Ed.*), "I found myself in the capital, the magazine" (*Otechestvenniye Zapiski*—*Ed.*) "brought me face to face with society—and god knows how much I suffered!... I was crushed by this spectacle of a society in which rascals and mere mediocrities act and play a role, while all the noble and talented recline in shameful inaction on the uninhabited island." p. 479

[22] In the manuscript there is the following footnote to "secondary importance": "Recall what was said in the 'Preface to Hegel's Speeches': 'Happiness does not lie in abstract dreaming, but in living reality; reconciliation with reality' [i.e., *return from dreaming to reality*] 'in all spheres of life is the great task of our times, and Hegel and Goethe are the leaders of this return from death to life. Let us hope that the new generation will at last feel the legitimate need to be realistic Russians.'

"And Goethe, in the poem we quoted above, speaks of the return from abstract dreaming to nature and reality as the supreme source of all happiness:
"O, away with dreaming, sweet though it be!
Here love and life are so full and so free!"
(This refers to Goethe's poem "On the Lake," *cf.* pp. 499-500 in this volume.—*Ed.*) p. 481

[23] An allusion to the impossibility of speaking about Herzen and Bakunin. p. 483

[24] *Vestnik Yevropy* (*European Messenger*), one of the first Russian literary and political magazines. It was published in Moscow (1802-30) and first appeared under the editorship of N. M. Karamzin. In the 20's this magazine, then edited by M. T. Kachenovsky, held an extremely reactionary position. p. 486

[25] After this in the manuscript comes the following passage, which is struck out: "Belinsky's development as an independent thinker consisted in that he became more and more imbued with the living (needs) interests of Russian reality and became more and more

strongly convinced of the extremely close connection between literature and all the other strivings of the human spirit, and." p. 487

26 From the name of the landlord Manilov, a character in Go-. gol's *Dead Souls*, typifying the complacent, sentimental, idle dreamer. p. 488

27 Skvoznik-Dmukhanovsky—a character in Gogol's *Inspector General*.
Chichikov—the principal character in Gogol's *Dead Souls*. p. 493

28 In his essay "A View on Russian Literature of 1847," Belinsky reviews Goncharov's *An Ordinary Story* and also Iskander's (Herzen's) *Who Is To Blame?* p. 495

29 Chernyshevsky is here quoting the "judgment" of different opponents of Belinsky (Polevoi, Senkovsky, Shevyryov, Bulgarin, and others). p. 498

30 This refers to A. E. Studitsky. p. 498

PREFACE TO AND COMMENTS ON CARPENTER'S
ENERGY IN NATURE

1 Chernyshevsky translated this book in 1884 and it was published by L. F. Panteleyev without the preface and comment. The comment was written in place of the last two or three pages of the original, in which Carpenter attempted to link natural science with religion.
After completing the translation and sending it to St. Petersburg, Chernyshevsky, on February 25, 1884, wrote to Julia Pypina: "I threw out the last two or three pages of the original as they ran counter to my conceptions, and I substituted for them several pages of comments, in which I expound my own trend of thought. The first pages of these comments of mine are written in a serious tone, but in the last I deride the poor author for his anthropomorphic philosophy. I shall ask you, dear Julia, to tell Sasha" (A. Pypin—*Ed.*) "that I want him to tell the publisher of the Russian translation that, except for the correction of obvious slips of the pen, I will not permit any alteration of the manuscript I sent.... This demand applies all the more strongly to my 'Translator's Preface,' and to the fact that I threw out the last pages of the book, which must be kept out, and to the pages I wrote instead of them, which must go into the book exactly as I wrote them. If the publisher contravenes this demand of mine in the slightest degree, the manuscript must be thrown into the stove." (N. G. Chernyshevsky, *Collected Works*, Vol. XV, Goslitizdat, 1950, p. 450.) This demand was not carried out, and the preface and commentary, in which Chernyshevsky criticized Carpenter's anthropomorphism and his assertion that heat must inevitably die out, remained unpublished. p. 504

2 The beginning of the comments is missing in the manuscript. p. 504

38*

LETTERS

¹ These are two of a series of letters that Chernyshevsky wrote
to his sons from Vilyuisk, in Siberia, where he was in exile. This was
the only means the great revolutionary democrat had at that time of
expressing his views on theoretical problems. In the form of "talks"
to his sons he discussed problems of natural science, philosophy and
history, and the views he expressed were of great theoretical importance. Remaining true to philosophical materialism, he vigorously
championed the scientific materialist world outlook in opposition to
subjective idealism, neo-Kantianism and positivism, then becoming
the fashion in Western Europe and Russia.

It must be observed that in these letters Chernyshevsky gives a
mistaken appraisal of the distinguished Russian scientist N. I. Lobachevsky.   p. 514

NAME INDEX

A

Aeschylus (525-456 B.C.) — Greek tragic poet.— 335, 442.

Agassiz, Louis (1807-1873) — Swiss naturalist, author of *Recherches sur les poissons fossiles.*—200, 203.

Agathon (V cent. B.C.) — Athenian tragic poet.— 439.

Akhundov, Mirza Fatali (1812-1878)— prominent Azerbaijanian writer and materialist philosopher; founder of Azerbaijanian dramatic art and realistic literature.— 45.

Aksakov, Konstantin Sergeyevich (1817-1860)—one of the founders of the Slavophile movement, publicist, critic, poet and historian.— 10, 455, 456, 589.

Alcibiades (451-404 B.C.) — Athenian general and politician.—438, 559.

Alexander the Great (356-323 B.C.) — King of Macedon. — 93, 294, 367.

Anacreon (VI cent. B.C.) — Greek lyric poet.— 334.

Anaxagoras (V cent. B.C.) — Greek philosopher.—449.

Annenkov, Pavel Vasilyevich (1812-1877) — liberal, literary critic, translator, memoirist, editor and publisher of Pushkin's works.— 468, 484, 593.

Antonovich, Maxim Alexeyevich (1835-1918) — literary critic and publicist, materialist philosopher, one of N. G. Chernyshevsky's closest associates on the *Sovremennik.*— 45, 138, 142, 148, 149, 568.

Antony, Mark (82-30 B.C.) — Roman statesman, associate of Julius Caesar.— 303.

Apelles (IV cent. B.C.) — Greek painter.— 333.

Archimedes (287-212 B.C.) — Greek mathematician and inventor.— 532, 551.

Aristotle (384-322 B.C.) — Greek philosopher and scientist.— 134, 159, 185, 196, 201, 202, 394, 423, 427, 430, 432, 452, 463, 582.

Aristophanes (approx. 450-385 B.C.) — Greek dramatist. — 436, 442, 448.

Askochensky, Victor Ipatyevich (1820-1879) — reactionary publicist and man of letters. —151.

B

Babst, Ivan Kondratyevich (1824-1881) — bourgeois economist, publicist, professor at the Kazan and later at the Moscow universities.—44.

Bacon, Francis (1561-1626) — materialist philosopher.—159, 425.

600 NAME INDEX

Copernicus, Nikolaus (1473-1543) — 84, 211, 532, 549, 561, 576.

Corneille, Pierre (1606-1684)— French dramatic poet.—189, 333, 358, 359.

Cousin, Victor (1792-1867) — French eclectic philosopher. — 21, 67, 472.

Couture, Thomas (1815-1879)— French painter. — 576.

Croesus — a king of Lydia (560-546 B. C.) — renowned for his vast wealth.— 309.

Curtius, Marcus (IV cent. B. C.) — a Roman youth who according to legend sacrificed his life to save Rome.— 121.

Cuvier, Georges (1769-1832)— French naturalist.— 69.

D

Dalton, John (1766-1844) — chemist and physicist. — 543.

Damiani, Pietro (approx. 988-1072) — Italian cleric and writer.—535.

Dante, Alighieri (1265-1321).— 580.

Delille, Jacques (1738-1813) — French poet and translator. —441, 592.

Delvig, Anton Antonovich, Baron (1798-1831) — poet, Pushkin's friend at the Lyceum and one of his closest literary associates, publisher of the almanacs *Severniye Tsvety* and *Literaturnaya Gazeta.*—593.

Demogeot Jacques-Claude (1808-1894) — writer, author of *Histoire de la littérature française depuis son origine jusqu'à nos jours.*—424.

Democritus (460-370 B. C.)— Greek materialist philosopher.—368, 432.

Derzhavin, Gavriil Romanovich (1743-1816) — poet.—189, 191, 424, 497.

Descartes, René (1596-1650).— 160, 211, 394, 463, 467.

Deshoulières, Antoinette (1638-1694)— French poetess.—372, 441.

Dickens, Charles (1812-1870).— 334, 372, 494, 498.

Diderot, Denis (1713-1784).— 19, 314, 448, 534.

Dobrolyubov, Nikolai Alexandrovich (1836-1861) — distinguished Russian critic, revolutionary democrat, materialist, close friend and associate of N. G. Chernyshevsky. — 9, 31, 45, 568.

Druzhinin, Alexander Vasilyevich (1824-1864) — literary critic and fiction writer; from 1856 to 1861 editor of the magazine *Biblioteka dlya Chteniya.* — 11.

Du Bois-Reymond, Emil (1818-1896) — German physiologist. —563, 569.

Dudyshkin, Stepan Semyonovich (1820-1866) — journalist, literary critic, actual editor of the *Otechestvenniye Zapiski* in the period of its decline.— 11, 31, 145, 150, 165, 567.

Dumas, Alexandre the Elder (1803-1870)— French novelist and dramatist.— 52-53.

Dumas, Alexandre the Younger (1824-1895) — French writer. —53.

Duns Scotus, Joannes (died in 1308) — scholastic theologian. —535.

Dupont, Pierre (1821-1870) — French song-writer, follower of Béranger.— 189.

Printed in the Union of Soviet Socialist Republics

31

DATE DUE

MAR 1 3 '72			
MAR 1 3 '72			
GAYLORD			PRINTED IN U.S A.